THE READMISSION OF ASYLUM SEEKERS UNDER INTERNATIONAL LAW

This monograph could not be more timely, as discourses relating to refugees' access to territory, rescue at sea, push-back, and push-back by proxy dominate political debate. Looking at the questions which lie at the junction of migration control and refugee law standards, it explores the extent to which readmission can hamper refugees' access to protection. Though it draws mainly on European law, notably the European Convention on Human Rights, it also examines other international frameworks, including those employed by the United Nations and instruments such as the Refugee Convention. Therefore, this book is of importance to readers of international law, refugee law, human rights and migration studies at the global level. It offers an analysis of both the legal and policy questions at play, and engages fully with widely-disputed cases concerning readmission agreements, deportation with assurances and interception at sea. By so doing, this book seeks to clarify a complex field which has at times suffered from partiality in both its terminology and substance.

Volume 73 in the series Studies in International Law

Studies in International Law
Recent titles in this series

Human Rights Obligations of Non-State Armed Groups
Daragh Murray

Security and International Law
Edited by Mary E Footer, Julia Schmidt and Nigel D White

Complicity and its Limits in the Law of International Responsibility
Vladyslav Lanovoy

Complicity in International Criminal Law
Marina Aksenova

Arctic Law and Governance: The Role of China and Finland
Edited by Timo Koivurova, Qin Tianbao, Tapio Nykänen and Sébastien Duyck

States, the Law and Access to Refugee Protection: Fortresses and Fairness
Edited by Maria O'Sullivan and Dallal Stevens

Revisiting the Concept of Defence in the Jus ad Bellum: The Dual Face of Defence
Johanna Friman

The International Legal Protection of Persons in Humanitarian Crises
Dug Cubie

The International Committee of the Red Cross and its Mandate to Protect and Assist: Law and Practice
Christy Shucksmith

The Impact of Investment Treaty Law on Host States: Enabling Good Governance
Mavluda Sattorova

Allocating International Responsibility Between Member States and International Organisations
Nikolaos Voulgaris

Predictability and Flexibility in the Law of Maritime Delimitation, 2nd edition
Yoshifumi Tanaka

Feminist Engagement with International Criminal Law: Norm Transfer, Complementarity, Rape and Consent
Eithne Dowds

For a complete list of titles in this series, see www.bloomsburyprofessional.com/uk/series/studies-in-international-law

The Readmission of Asylum Seekers under International Law

Mariagiulia Giuffré

•HART•
OXFORD • LONDON • NEW YORK • NEW DELHI • SYDNEY

HART PUBLISHING

Bloomsbury Publishing Plc

Kemp House, Chawley Park, Cumnor Hill, Oxford, OX2 9PH, UK

1385 Broadway, New York, NY 10018, USA

HART PUBLISHING, the Hart/Stag logo, BLOOMSBURY and the Diana logo are trademarks of Bloomsbury Publishing Plc

First published in Great Britain 2020

A catalogue record for this book is available from the British Library.

Library of Congress Cataloging-in-Publication data

Names: Giuffré, Mariagiulia, author.

Title: The readmission of asylum seekers under international law / Mariagiulia Giuffré.

Description: Chicago : Hart Publishing, an imprint of Bloomsbury Publishing, 2020. | Series: Studies in international law; vol 73 | Includes bibliographical references and index.

Identifiers: LCCN 2019047059 (print) | LCCN 2019047060 (ebook) | ISBN 9781509902491 (hardback) | ISBN 9781509902521 (Epub)

Subjects: LCSH: Asylum, Right of. | Refugees—Legal status, laws, etc. | Forced migration. | Convention for the Protection of Human Rights and Fundamental Freedoms (1950 November 5) | International law and human rights. | Asylum, Right of—Europe.

Classification: LCC K3268.3 .G58 2020 (print) | LCC K3268.3 (ebook) | DDC 342.08/3—dc23

LC record available at https://lccn.loc.gov/2019047059

LC ebook record available at https://lccn.loc.gov/2019047060

ISBN: HB: 978-1-50990-249-1
ePDF: 978-1-50990-250-7
ePub: 978-1-50990-252-1

Typeset by Compuscript Ltd, Shannon
Printed and bound in Great Britain by CPI Group (UK) Ltd, Croydon CR0 4YY

FSC www.fsc.org MIX Paper from responsible sources FSC® C013604

A Tania

Foreword

THERE HAS BEEN a gap in the academic literature regarding the impact of states' bilateral and other agreements and arrangements intended to facilitate the readmission of people to their state of origin (or habitual residence) on the internationally recognised right to seek and enjoy asylum and in particular the right to *non-refoulement* (the right not to be sent to any place where there is a serious risk of persecution, torture, inhuman or degrading treatment or enforced disappearance). This book now fills that gap intelligently, elegantly and with impressive legal rigour. It is very timely, not least as its main geographical scope is Europe, a part of the world where ultra-patriotic politicians increasingly turn to scapegoating foreigners (including asylum seekers and even recognised refugees) for all the ills of their countries. This facile and false politics has led to an ever-increasing number of bilateral and multilateral agreements and arrangements which insufficiently protect the right to seek asylum and to *non-refoulement* in favour of expulsion. The issue is one on which the author has long reflected and which is at the core of her work.

By starting from the agreements and practices of readmission (as expulsion is termed) the author provides us with a clear and comprehensive understanding of the multiplicity of practices which European states are engaged in and which are designed to simplify expulsion of foreigners at all costs. These agreements and practices have the effect of undermining the right of refugees and others entitled to international protection to *non-refoulement* and the opportunity to seek asylum and to enjoy it. But the agreements and practices are all too often couched in neutral language with no reference to *non-refoulement* or the risk of persecution or torture in the destination country (or of onward expulsion to such a country). All too often, European states seek arrangements and agreements with countries with abysmal human rights records and which are source countries of refugees all over the world. The political purpose is that by promising their citizens more and faster expulsion of foreigners somehow the conditions at home will be better. This is a mendacious claim.

Asylum determination procedures are too often presented by such politicians as an obstacle to rapid expulsion. There is some truth in the argument that one of the obstacles to quick expulsion of foreigners is that they seek international protection. Yet, the duty on all European states to consider, in good faith, all applications for international protection and to ensure that those at risk of persecution or torture receive protection is both an old and a new obligation. It was codified in the Refugee Convention in 1951 but it has been included also in the Convention against Torture 1984 and more recently the Convention against Enforced Disappearance 2010. European states have duly ratified all these conventions recognising the paramount nature of the *non-refoulement* obligation. However, in recent years European states' expulsion practices have not always obviously incorporated the duty, and the arrangements which they make with other countries have clearly obstructed the exercise of the right to seek asylum.

This book is of great importance both in legal and political terms as it unpicks the ills of readmission arrangements and agreements. From a refugee and human rights protection perspective, the author takes to task both the political leaders and the jurists of European states which are implementing these policies and reminds them of their overarching duty to deliver *non-refoulement* to those in need of international protection. Taking a wide-lens approach to readmission arrangements, the author includes formal agreements, diplomatic assurances, pre-arrival maritime interception and agreements on technical and police cooperation which have the effect of preventing people from being able to travel to seek international protection. Correctly, the author classes these practices together, as their objective is the same. All too frequently academic jurists examining these practices are blinded by disingenuous arguments made by state jurists that these are utterly different and unrelated legal measures. However, by focusing on the impact on the duty of *non-refoulement* the author demonstrates clearly and decisively that in fact the objective of the legal measures is the same: to compromise the right to seek asylum and to enjoy it and states' obligation to respect their duty of *non-refoulement*. This book needs to be compulsory reading for all ministers of interior and their advisors when considering their international obligations to refugees.

Jean Monnet professor ad personam, Elspeth Guild
Queen Mary University of London and Radboud
University Netherlands
29 August 2019

Preface

This book reflects the overall relevant law and practice, to the best of my knowledge, as it stood on 30 June 2018. However, this does not preclude occasional reference to later developments. Earlier versions of the author's arguments in some Sections of Chapters three, four, and five have been published respectively as: 'Readmission Agreements and Refugee Rights: From a Critique to a Proposal' (2013) 32(3) *Refugee Survey Quarterly* 79; 'Deportation with Assurances and Human Rights: The Case of People Suspected or Convicted of Serious Crimes' (2017) 15(1) *Journal of International Criminal Justice* 75; 'State Responsibility beyond Borders: What Legal Basis for Italy's Push-Back to Libya?' (2012) 24(4) *International Journal of Refugee Law* 692; and (with Moreno-Lax) 'The Rise of Consensual Containment: From "Contactless Control" to "Contactless Responsibility" for Migratory Flows' in Satvinder Juss (ed), *The Research Handbook on International Refugee Law* (Edward Elgar Publishing, 2019).

Acknowledgements

THIS BOOK IS largely based on my doctoral thesis, but it also reflects many years of research and interest in international law, migration, and asylum in a time of crisis in refugee protection and attacks to the fundamental rights of migrants. I wish to thank all those who have accompanied me in one way or another on my PhD journey and in the drafting of this book. A host of people deserve to know the extent to which their help and closeness has contributed to make this period of intense work a more enjoyable one.

Foremost, I wish to hugely thank Antonino Alì, my doctoral supervisor from Trento University, for his expert academic guidance, readiness in discussing ideas, and encouragement. I am indebted to him and to the School of International Studies of Trento University for allowing me to conduct my research with freedom and originality, spending long periods of time abroad, especially in Sweden and the Netherlands.

My greatest debt of gratitude is owed to Gregor Noll who co-supervised my doctoral thesis during the years I spent as a Visiting Fellow at the Faculty of Law of Lund University, thanks to a Scholarship awarded by the Swedish Institute. It has been a privilege to work with a person who was so generous to me and so knowledgeable in international migration and refugee law. Without his encouragement and support, invaluable comments, critical reading, intense and inspiring discussions, reassurance and ever-challenging questions I would have never finalised my doctoral manuscript.

I am very grateful to Ulf Linderfalk and Alexandra Popovic for participating as discussants at my mid-seminar and to Jens Vedsted-Hansen for his constructive reading and invaluable commentary at my final doctoral seminar in Lund. Particular thanks must go also to my two final examiners, Maryellen Fullerton and Elspeth Guild, for their instructive feedback during the viva in Trento, and for their continuous encouragement. My appreciation goes to the Faculty of Law of Lund University for the unforgettable experience of living in Sweden, for offering me an excellent environment for brainstorming and research, for allowing me to teach at the LLM programme in International Human Rights Law, and for organising public seminars where I had the opportunity to showcase my research and the main findings of my work. At Lund University, I not only found an office space for the duration of my Visiting Fellowship, but more importantly, a group of ever-supportive colleagues and friends who helped me with their suggestions and insights on my research, and profoundly enriched my professional and personal life by sharing with me *fika*, after-work drinks, daily chats, and long weekends. My special thanks go to Sanja Bogogevic,

Olena Bokareva, Moa De Lucia Dahlbeck, Alejandro Fuentes, Eduardo Gil-Pedro, Xavier Groussot, Markus Gunneflo, Andrea Iossa, Sverker Jönsson, Ida Koch, Radu Mares, Amin Parsa, Niklas Selberg, Britta Sjöstedt, and Vladislava Stoyanova. Many other precious friends outside *Juridicum* also contributed in making my days in Sweden warmer and more memorable.

I am further indebted to the Centre for Migration Law of the Radboud University, Nijmegen, where I spent five months in the early stage of my PhD. At the Centre, I had the good fortune of meeting encouraging and inspiring colleagues, such as Elspeth Guild, Karin Zwaan, and Tineke Strik, who generously shared their time and thoughts, thus helping me frame my present work and choose the specific topics that deserved the most attention. I also wish to thank Edge Hill University, and in particular the support received by the Department of Law and Criminology and the Research Office.

I owe debts of gratitude to my PhD colleagues in Trento, all those who have read and commented on various chapters of my work, and the various anonymous journal and book referees, including the editors at Hart for their patience and assistance. My special thanks go to Mark de Barros, Mark Beittel, Carol Bohmer, David Cantor, Jean Pierre Cassarino, Bhupinder Singh Chimni, Alice Diver, Paula Garcia Andrade, Giulia Crescini, Jean-Pierre Gauci, Eleni Karageorgiou, Meltem İneli Ciğer, Violeta Moreno Lax, Akis Papastavridis, Marco Pertile, Claudia Pretto, Rosemary Rayfuse, Jessica Schultz, Lilian Tsourdi, and Eugenio Zaniboni. In the years after the end of my PhD, I have also benefited enormously from numerous inspiring conversations on international law, human rights and refugee law and policy with students and many people I have met at conferences, workshops, and lectures both within and outside Europe. As their insights and expertise have contributed to shape various aspects of my work, my thanks go, in particular, to Marcello de Filippo, Chiara Favilli, Pietro Fossati, Luca Guanziroli, Guy Goodwin-Gill, Carla Lacerda, Claudia Pellegrino, Paulo Pinto de Albuquerque, Seline Trevisanut, Françoise Tulkens, and Fulvio Vassallo Paleologo.

Although the collection of interviews is not formally part of my methodological approach, I wish to thank all those migrants and refugees who, having arrived in Italy by sea, with initial reticence and increasing trust, have agreed to tell me their stories, thus informing my research. In particular, I wish to thank Annalisa Pauciullo with whom I have visited the Greek islands of Lesvos and Chios during the influx of refugees in the aftermath of the EU–Turkey deal in 2016. The two organisations, ASGI and ARCI have also given me the opportunity to engage with practical issues concerning migrants and refugees' protection. I am also very grateful to the Refugee Law Initiative in London and the Refugee Studies Centre in Oxford, where I have been a Visiting Fellow both in 2015 and 2017. Here the supportive intellectual environment and the many opportunities for scholarly exchanges, especially with David Cantor, Cathryn Costello and Sarah Singer, have been particularly inspiring for my work.

I cannot forget to express my love to my cousins, my aunts, and many other amazing friends outside the PhD/work circuit who have always been part of my life and who will continue to be there to share with me hopes, thoughts, tango, yoga, laughter, our past, and our future. However, my most heartfelt thanks go to Triestino, for his never-ending love, his optimism, his sense of humour, his smile, and for keeping my spirits high, even when I felt weighed down by the burden of undertaking this seemingly insurmountable task.

Last but not least, all my love and gratitude to my island in the Mediterranean, and to my 'safe haven', my wonderful family who have constantly encouraged me with irreplaceable affection, care, patience, enthusiasm, and unconditional support. This book is, therefore, dedicated to my loves: my brother Giandomenico, my sister, Gloria, my dad, Gianni, and my mum, Tania, with the hope that she would have been proud of my work, and with the confidence that she would have been happy to share this part of life with me. Finally, my marvellous baby, just arrived in my life as the most beautiful gift. Tania, *Amore Mio … Grazie.* This work is for you.

Mariagiulia Giuffré

Contents

Part 3

List of Abbreviations

AIRE	Advice on Individual Rights in Europe
ATV	All-terrain vehicles
AJIL	American Journal of International Law
AI	Amnesty International
ACDI	Anuario Colombiano de Derecho Internacional
ATCSA	Anti-Terrorism, Crime and Security Act 2001
AC	Appeal Court
AFSJ	Area of Freedom, Security and Justice
AWR	Association for the Study of the World Refugee Problem
ASGI	Associazione per gli Studi Giuridici sull'Immigrazione
AIDA	Asylum Information Database
BYIL	British Yearbook of International Law
BVerfGE	Bundesverfassungsgericht
CUP	Cambridge University Press
CEPS	Centre for European Policy Studies
CEAR	Commission of Aid to Refugees (Spain)
LIBE	Committee on Civil Liberties, Justice and Home Affairs
CPT	Committee on the Prevention of Torture
CEAS	Common European Asylum System
CMLR	Common Market Law Review
CLR	Commonwealth Law Reports *(Australian's High Court law reporter)*
CAT	Convention against Torture
OAU Convention	Convention Governing Specific Aspects of Refugee Problems in Africa
CoE	Council of Europe

CFI	Court of First Instance
CJEU	Court of Justice of the European Union
DUDI	Diritti Umani e Diritto Internazionale
DCR	Dutch Council for Refugees
EWCA	England and Wales Court of Appeal
EWHC	England and Wales High Court
EUBAM	EU Border Assistance Mission to Libya
CFR	EU Charter of Fundamental Rights
MPF	EU Migration Partnership Framework
EBCG	European Border and Coast Guard
ECLI	European Case-Law Identifier
EC	European Community
ECL Rev	European Constitutional Law Review
ECHR	European Convention on Human Rights and Fundamental Freedoms
ECRE	European Council on Refugees and Exiles
ECtHR	European Court of Human Rights
ECJ	European Court of Justice
ECR	European Court Reports
EHRR	European Human Rights Reports
EJIL	European Journal of International Law
EJML	European Journal of Migration Law
EMN	European Migration Network
EU	European Union
EEAS	European Union External Action
EXCOM	Executive Committee of the High Commissioner's Programme
EWCA	England and Wales Court of Appeal
FCA	Federal Court of Australia
FCAFC	Federal Court of Australia Full Court

FCO	Foreign and Commonwealth Office
FROM	Former Republic of Macedonia
FOIA	Freedom of Information Act
EWHC	High Court of England and Wales
HRC	Human Rights Committee
HRW	Human Rights Watch
ICERD	International Convention on the Elimination of All Forms of Racial Discrimination
ILPA	Immigration Law Practitioners' Association
IACtHR	Inter-American Court of Human Rights
SOLAS	International Convention for the Safety of Life at Sea
SAR	International Convention on Maritime Search and Rescue
ICJ	International Court of Justice
ICCPR	International Covenant on Civil and Political Rights
ICESR	International Covenant on Economic and Social Rights
IJRL	International Journal of Refugee Law
ILC	International Law Commission
ILM	International Legal Materials
IMLI	International Maritime Law Institute
IMO	International Maritime Organization
IOM	International Organization for Migration
ITLOS	International Tribunal on the Law of the Sea
CILD	Italian Coalition for Civil Liberties and Rights
JHA	Justice and Home Affairs
NTC	Libyan National Transitional Council
MSC	Maritime Safety Committee
MSR	Maritime Surveillance Regulation
MOU	Memorandum of Understanding
MIMA	Minister for Immigration and Multicultural and Indigenous Affairs

MRT	Moldovan Republic of Transnistria
NKR	Nagorno Karabakh Republic
NGO	Non-Governmental Organization
NATO	North Atlantic Treaty Organization
OJ	Official Journal
OMDH	Organisation Marocaine des Droits Humains
OUP	Oxford University Press
PCIJ	Permanent Court of International Justice
QB	Queen's Bench
RSC	Refugee Studies Centre
RSAA	Refugee Status Appeals Authority (New Zealand)
RSD	Refugee Status Determination
RDP	Regional Disembarkation Platforms
SBC	Schengen Border Code
SAR	Search and Rescue
SSHD	Secretary of State of the Home Department
SIDI	Societa' Italiana di Diritto Internazionale
SRFC	Sub-Regional Fisheries Commission
ILC ASR	International Law Commission's Articles on Responsibility of States for Internationally Wrongful Acts
TEU	Treaty on the European Union
TFEU	Treaty on the Functioning of the European Union
SIAC	UK Special Immigration Appeals Commission
UNHCR	United Nations High Commissioner for Refugees
UK	United Kingdom
UKHL	United Kingdom House of Lords
UN	United Nations
UNCLOS	United Nations Convention on the Law of the Sea
UNGA	United Nations General Assembly

UNSC	United Nations Security Council
UNTS	United Nations Treaty Series
US	United States
UDHR	Universal Declaration of Human Rights
VCLT	Vienna Convention on the Law of Treaties
YBILC	Yearbook of the International Law Commission

Table of Cases

EUROPEAN COMMISSION/EUROPEAN COURT OF HUMAN RIGHTS

EUROPEAN COURT OF JUSTICE/COURT OF JUSTICE OF THE EUROPEAN UNION

EUROPEAN COURT OF FIRST INSTANCE/GENERAL COURT

COMMITTEE AGAINST TORTURE

HUMAN RIGHTS COMMITTEE

INTERNATIONAL COURT OF JUSTICE

INTERNATIONAL TRIBUNAL FOR THE LAW OF THE SEA

AWARDS

INTER-AMERICAN COMMISSION AND COURT OF HUMAN RIGHTS

AUSTRALIA

CANADA

FRANCE

GERMANY

HONG KONG SPECIAL ADMINISTRATIVE REGION

ITALY

NEW ZEALAND

THE NETHERLANDS

UK

US

1

Introduction

I. REFUGEE ENCOUNTERS WITH THE STATE

THIS BOOK LIES at the junction of migration control and refugee protection. As asylum is a migration-related matter, it can be difficult for some States to dissociate it from the struggle against irregular immigration. Asylum, as a measure for protecting refugees and other persons in need of international protection, may therefore easily come into conflict with policies and practices derived from strict border-control considerations.[1] This work explores the way that this conflict is managed, and investigates – primarily within the European geographical context – whether the implementation of *bilateral agreements linked to the readmission* of irregular migrants can hamper refugees' access to protection,[2] understood here as the combination of the right to *non-refoulement* and an individual's right to access asylum procedures and effective remedies prior to removal.

Fleeing persecution and gross human rights violations in their home country, refugees represent the most vulnerable category of people crossing international borders during the phases of both entry into and removal from the destination country. They frequently travel alongside economic migrants and are often unable to obtain identity and travel documents. As such, they are at a particularly high risk of being assimilated with those more commonly undocumented migrants who may be violating formal immigration control requirements.

As uninvited aliens, refugees are *in principio* 'outside the field of loyalty.'[3] Perceived as a menace to the peace and internal security of the host State, they

[1] See, eg, A Hurwitz, *The Collective Responsibility of States to Protect Refugees* (Oxford University Press 2009) ch 1; T Gammeltoft-Hansen, *Access to Asylum* (Cambridge University Press 2011) ch 2; GS Goodwin-Gill, 'The Right to Seek Asylum: Interception at Sea and the Principle of Non-Refoulement' (2011) 23(3) *International Journal of Refugee Law (IJRL)* 443; GS Goodwin Gill, 'Legal and practical issues raised by the movement of people across the Mediterranean' (2016) 51 *Forced Migration Review* 83.

[2] The expression 'agreements linked to readmission' was first coined by Cassarino in JP Cassarino, 'Informalizing Readmission Agreements in the EU Neighbourhood' (2007) 42(2) *The International Spectator* 179.

[3] E Guild, 'International Terrorism and EU Immigration, Asylum, and Borders Policy: The Unexpected Victims of 11 September 2011', in Carr, Fergus and Massey, Andrew (eds), *Public Policy and the New European Agendas* (Edward Elgar Publishing, 2006) 234 (Guild 2006).

have no community protecting them, and no linkage with their home country; as such, they are treated as outsiders whose claims must first be carefully assessed in order to decide whether they are legitimate. States' endeavours to impose ever more robust barriers against those who seek to enter their national territories continue to accelerate, and have therefore led to a 'tension between generosity towards those at home and wariness of those from abroad.'[4]

Whilst immigration to Europe from other continents and countries was modest during the first half of the twentieth century, more than 35 million people emigrated *from* Europe to extra-European destinations within the same period.[5] Only between 1950 and 1970 did European States begin to assume increased responsibilities with respect to the huge number of post-war refugees.[6] Moreover, since the early 1990s, a sharp increase in asylum applications has progressively been recorded across Western countries, in particular, Western Europe.[7] In terms of the present day, by the end of 2018, 70.8 million individuals were forcibly displaced worldwide because of persecution, conflict, or generalised violence, leading to 2.8 million new refugees and new asylum seekers.[8] As a result of the long-standing war in Syria, 362,000 refugees and migrants tried to reach Europe by sea in 2016, with this number significantly decreasing in 2018 due to the cooperation of European countries with third States of origin or transit to forestall departures and prevent arrivals by means of maritime interceptions.[9] The closure of Italian ports to NGO-operated ships carrying migrants has also caused humanitarian emergencies on board vessels left adrift for several days with no European State allowing them to dock. This will have

[4] M Fullerton, 'The International and National Protection of Refugees', in H Hannum (ed) *Guide to International Human Rights Practice* 4th edn (Transnational Publishers, 2004) 246.

[5] L Lucassen, J Lucassen, R de Jong, 'Cross-cultural migration in Western Europe 1901–2000: A preliminary estimate', IISH Research Paper, 28, 30, https://socialhistory.org/sites/default/files/docs/publications/researchpaper-52-lucassen-lucassen-et.al-versie_voor_web140801.pdf.

[6] Since the recognition of a person as a refugee is of a declaratory (and not constitutive) nature, asylum seekers may enjoy a *prima facie* refugee status until a determination of their status on the part of the State discredits their claim. Therefore, this work often uses the term 'refugee' to also refer to people seeking protection, although they have not been recognised as refugees yet. The declaratory value of refugee status recognition was also approved in *R v Secretary of State for the Home Department, ex parte Hoxha* [2002] EWCA Civ 1403 (14 Oct 2002). See also, UNHCR (the UN Refugee Agency), *Handbook on Procedures and Criteria for Determining Refugee Status* (1979, reedited 1992) para 28; UNHCR, *Note on International Protection*, UN doc A/AC.96/914, 7 July 1999, para 16; JC Hathaway, *The Rights of Refugees under International Law* (Cambridge University Press, 2005); A Zimmermann and C Mahler, 'Article 1A, para 2', in A Zimmermann (ed), *The 1951 Convention Relating to the Status of Refugees and its 1967 Protocol: A Commentary* (Oxford University Press, 2011) 73–74.

[7] See JT Hatton, 'Seeking Asylum in Europe' (April 2004) 19 *Economic Policy* 7.

[8] UNHCR, 'Global Trends 2018', https://www.unhcr.org/5d08d7ee7.pdf.

[9] By 23 November 2018, land arrivals in Europe were 102, 967 while sea arrivals were 109,073. Information is available at: https://data2.unhcr.org/en/situations/mediterranean. See also, V Chetail, 'Looking Beyond the Rhetoric of the Refugee Crisis: The Failed Reform of the Common European Asylum System' (2016) 5 *European Journal of Human Rights* 584.

severe consequences for the building of long-term solidarity in the management of such maritime migrations.[10] With many perishing *en route*, the Mediterranean has become the most dangerous sea in the world, and a deadly abyss for thousands of people, including children.[11] The question of '*who is responsible for refugees?*' has never been more pressing.

To find a cooperative approach aimed at enhancing the overall benefits of migration (while still addressing its risks and challenges for individuals and communities in countries of origin, transit and destination), UN Member States finalised the text for the Global Compact for Safe, Orderly and Regular Migration on 13 July 2018. Although not legally binding, the Global Compact for Migration is the first UN inter-governmental agreement on a common approach to international migration in terms of all of its aspects.[12] The Global Compact on Refugees aims instead to strengthen the international response to large movements of refugees and protracted refugee situations via four different objectives: 'eas[ing] the pressures on host countries; enhanc[ing] refugee self-reliance; expand[ing] access to third-country solutions; support[ing] conditions in countries of origin for return in safety and dignity.'[13]

Where European States have attempted to offer harmonised solutions to the migration challenge, (such as the progressive creation of the Common European Asylum System (CEAS)),[14] they have also employed a new logic of reinforcing

[10] Following an interim measure issued by the ECtHR on 29 January 2019, 47 people, who had been rescued by a vessels of the NGO SeaWatch, were eventually disembarked in Sicily after several days at sea. See *BG v Italy*, App no 5604/19 (29 January 2019). On ports' closure, see E Cusumano and Kristof Gombeer, 'In deep waters: The legal, humanitarian and political implications of closing Italian ports to migrant rescuers', *Mediterranean Politics*, 15 October 2018. See also, E Papastavridis, 'Recent "Non-Entrée" Policies in the Central Mediterranean and Their Legality: A New Form of "Refoulement"?' (2018/3) *Diritti Umani e Diritto Internazionale* 493–510.

[11] Over 2,075 people have believed to have died or gone missing at sea in 2018 only. See https://data2.unhcr.org/en/situations/mediterranean.

[12] The Intergovernmental Conference to Adopt the Global Compact for Safe, Orderly and Regular Migration was held on 10–11 December in Marrakech, Morocco. To read more on the Global Compact, see https://refugeesmigrants.un.org/migration-compact. See also C Carletti and M Borraccetti, 'Il Global Compact sulla migrazione tra scenari internazionali e realtà europea' (2018) 2 *Freedom, Security and Justice: European Legal Studies* 7; T Gammeltoft-Hansen, E Guild, V Moreno-Lax, M Panizzon, and I Roele, 'What is a Compact? Migrants' Rights and State Responsibilities Regarding the Design of the UN Global Compact for Safe, Orderly and Regular Migration' *Raoul Wallenberg Institute of Human Rights and Humanitarian Law* (October 2017).

[13] UNHCR, 'Global Compact on Refugees', https://www.unhcr.org/towards-a-global-compact-on-refugees.html; Report of the United Nations High Commissioner for Refugees, 'Global Compact on Refugees', General Assembly, Seventy-third Session, Supplement No. 12 (A/73/12 (Part II), https://www.unhcr.org/gcr/GCR_English.pdf. See also V Türk and M Garlick, 'From Burdens and Responsibilities to Opportunities: The Comprehensive Refugee Response Framework and a Global Compact on Refugees' (2016) 28(4) *IJRL* 656; A Betts, 'The Global Compact on Refugees: Towards a Theory of Change?' (2018) 30(4) *IJR L* 623–26.

[14] The aim of the CEAS is to establish common asylum procedures and equivalent conditions for persons in need of international protection valid throughout the EU. The four most important legislative measures adopted between 1999 and 2005 have undergone a recast process over the last years.

their territorial and maritime border controls, criminalising migrants,[15] and accelerating the procedures for removing unauthorised aliens to the countries they originated from, or transited through. Such a proactive management of irregular migratory flows – especially by both seeking readmission of unwanted foreigners and intercepting them on the high seas, far away from territorial borders – has been criticised at national, regional, and international levels, alerting, *inter alia*, legal scholars and human rights organisations.

With a view to stopping irregular migration – by both preventing the arrival of unauthorised flows of migrants and readmitting those individuals who do not have the status to stay within the territory of the host country – the cooperation of third countries outside Europe becomes necessary. And within such a 'globalization of migration control',[16] the opportunity to conduct research on the international human rights and refugee law obligations binding States in territorial and extraterritorial operative contexts is even more imperative. In Henkin's words, 'how [a State] behaves even in its own territory, [is] no longer … its own business: it has become a matter of international concern, of international politics, and of international law.'[17]

Likewise, readmission – whether performed before or after arrival at the border of the host, or would-be host country – lies at the intersection of distinct, often discrete disciplines, such as international law and international relations. In this respect, it has been argued that

> the readmission system is not only built on obligations which would be defined in international customary law. Nor is it only a system based on incentives, costs, and

See (i) Qualification Directive 2011/95/EU of 13 December 2011 on standards for the qualification of third-country nationals or stateless persons as beneficiaries of international protection, for a uniform status for refugees or for persons eligible for subsidiary protection, and for the content of the protection granted (Recast), OJ L 337/9, 20 December 2011 (*Recast Qualification Directive*); (ii) Directive 8260/2/13 of 7 June 2013 on common procedures for granting and withdrawing international protection status (Recast) (*Recast Procedures Directive*); (iii) Directive 14654/2/12 of 7 June 2013 on minimum standards for the reception of asylum seekers (Recast) (*Recast Reception Directive*); and (iv) Regulation of the European Parliament and of the Council 15605/3/12 of 7 June 2013 establishing the criteria and mechanisms for determining the Member State responsible for examining an application for international protection lodged in one of the Member States by a third-country national or a stateless person (*Recast Dublin Regulation*). The Recast Procedures Directive, the Recast Reception Directive, and the Recast Dublin Regulation have been adopted by European Parliament legislative resolution of 12 Jun 2013. For an overview of the historical development of asylum law, see R Byrne, G Noll and J Vedsted-Hansen, 'Understanding Refugee Law in an Enlarged European Union' (2004) 15 *European Journal of International Law (EJIL)* 355, 358–67.

[15] D Bigo, 'Criminalization of "Migrants": The Side Effect of the Will to Control the Frontiers and the Sovereign Illusion' in B Bogusz, R Cholewinski, A Cygan and E Szyszczak (eds), *Irregular Migration and Human Rights: Theoretical, European, and International Perspectives* (Martinus Nijoff Publishers, 2004) 61.

[16] See T Gammeltoft-Hansen, *Access to Asylum: International Refugee Law and the Globalization of Migration Control* (Cambridge University Press, 2011).

[17] L Henkin Lecture: The Robert L Levine Distinguished Lecture Series, 'That "S" Word: Sovereignty and Globalization, and Human Rights, et Cetera' (1999) 68 *Fordham Law Review* 1, 4.

> benefits. It is also a system contingent on predominant schemes of understanding, paradigms and a hegemonic lexicon shaping policy perceptions and hierarchies of priorities.[18]

This monograph does not, however, delve into international relations theory. Rather, it aims to provide a legal analysis of the implications of readmission schemes for the rights and safety of those seeking protection in Europe. Examining State practices on migration control against the backdrop of refugee rights assumed increasing relevance after 11 September 2001, when the new 'war on terror' exacerbated the tendency to perceive refugees as a threat to international peace and security.[19] In this interplay between human rights and State prerogatives, the refugee often ends up occupying

> a legal space characterised, on the one hand, by the principle of State sovereignty and the related principles of territorial supremacy and self-preservation; and, on the other hand, by competing humanitarian principles deriving from general international law ... and from treaty.[20]

Therefore, the debate on agreements linked to readmission and refugee rights reflects a political debate involving national identities and security concerns, further confirmed by the European trend of seeking to deflect responsibility for migrants and refugees as far as possible from European borders. As next section will show, this would entrench uncertain and fluid national security interests to the detriment of the protection of migrants and the fundamental rights of refugees.

II. OBJECTIVES AND STRUCTURE

In 2011, following the socio-political upheavals in North Africa, masses of undocumented migrants and refugees began landing in Italy in total disarray. A significant number of these individuals, especially Tunisians and Egyptians, were confined for long periods of time either in overcrowded detention centres or on-board ships, and subjected to summary identification procedures by their consular officials, or rapidly expelled back to their countries of origin, all in

[18] JP Cassarino, 'Inventory of the Agreements Linked to Readmission', http://www.jeanpierrecassarino.com/datasets/ra/.

[19] See, eg, para 3(f) and (g) of the UN Security Council Res. 1373, 28 September 2001, UN doc S/RES/1373 (2001). Addressing the issue of the relationship between terrorism and refugee law would be beyond the scope of this book. For literature in the field refer, *inter alia*, to: R Bruin and K Wouters, 'Terrorism and the Non-derogability of Non-refoulement' (2003)15(1) *IJRL* 5; Guild 2006, n 3 above; W Schabas, 'Non-refoulement', *Human Rights and International Cooperation in Counter-terrorism* (Liechtenstein, 2006); A Schmid, *Links between Terrorism and Migration: An Exploration* (The International Centre for Counter-Terrorism, 2016), http://dx.doi.org/10.19165/2016.1.04; M Paz, 'Asylum and Terrorism: The Death of Human Rights Law' (2016–17) 102 *Iowa Law Review Bulletin* 41.

[20] GS Goodwin-Gill and J McAdam, *The Refugee in International Law*, 3rd edn (OUP, 2007) 91.

the name of the efficiency required by the implementation of the *readmission agreements* between Italy and the two North-African countries.[21]

From 2005 to 2013, the UK government attempted to deport Mr Omar Othman (Abu Qatada) – a radical Muslim cleric who was granted refugee status in the UK – by seeking diplomatic assurances from Jordan as to his fair and humane treatment following removal. Abu Qatada is the first person to challenge, before the European Court of Human Rights (ECtHR), a deportation order issued on the basis of a *Memorandum of Understanding* (*MoU*), a framework agreement that can be used in cases of removal of an individual deemed to be a threat to public security.[22]

In May 2009, Italy embarked on a forcible and indiscriminate removal policy, deflecting hundreds of people to Libya before they could enter the territorial waters of a European State. This push-back campaign was carried out on the basis of bilateral *agreements for technical and police cooperation*. However, despite the dismal human rights conditions in Libya, deflections to this country continue to this day in differing forms, with Italy undertaking (or coordinating) overall search and rescue (SAR) at sea and delegating push-backs (pull-backs) to the Libyan authorities.[23]

The 'red thread' that runs through all these cases is that of *removal*; not least of the layered distances placed between the refugee and the State, and of the borders built and reinforced to sever, at the earliest point in time, the jurisdictional bridges between those-who-seek-protection and those-who-provide-protection. Under such logic, and in the wake of the pro-active management of European borders, diverse and bilateral cooperative strategies have been devised to firmly keep migrants and refugees well away from the doors of Europe.

This work primarily aims to investigate whether the implementation of bilateral agreements linked to readmission can hamper access to protection, meaning here the combination of refugees' right to *non-refoulement* and the right to access asylum procedures and effective remedies before removal. In answering this question, three sub-questions are addressed: firstly, what is the content and scope of the right to *non-refoulement*, as well as the right to access asylum procedures and effective remedies before removal?; secondly, what is the relationship between agreements linked to the readmission of unauthorised migrants and the decision to remove refugees to countries of origin or transit?; and, thirdly, to what extent is the text of bilateral agreements linked to readmission compatible with core refugee protection standards, as enshrined in the main international refugee and human rights law treaties?

[21] A more extended account of readmission agreements and informal practices of border control will be provided in Chapter 3 of this book.

[22] See Chapter 4 of this book for a description of the *Abu Qatada* case and the legal issues stemming from the use of MoUs setting diplomatic assurances on the fair and human treatment of deportees.

[23] See Chapter 5 of this book to read more on Italy–Libya cooperation resulting in push-backs and push-backs by proxy.

Chapter two explores the content and scope of the relevant international refugee and human rights protection standards, which are binding on European States when dealing with questions relating to the admission or readmission of refugees. Therefore, the legal content of the principle of *non-refoulement* as well as an individual's right to have access to asylum procedures and effective remedies before removal are examined, with a focus on the main international refugee and human rights treaties, *in primis* the 1951 Convention relating to the Status of Refugees (Geneva Convention),[24] the UN Convention against Torture (CAT),[25] the International Covenant on Civil and Political Rights (ICCPR),[26] and the 1950 European Convention on Human Rights and Fundamental Freedoms (ECHR).[27] This chapter provides a review of the jurisprudence of the relevant international human rights bodies. While each of these rights merits a book of their own, Chapter two is, however, principally designed to provide a backdrop of the relevant legal norms – as interpreted by international human rights courts and committees – against which the compatibility of bilateral agreements linked to readmission with refugee rights will be assessed in the subsequent chapters. Moreover, as these rights have already been the object of scholarly scrutiny,[28] this work will mainly offer further exploration of the issue of extraterritorial application of human rights treaties, especially when *refoulement* can result from 'contactless' migration controls. This is especially so where the element of 'effective control' and the relation between the right to an effective remedy and the right to access asylum procedures are more difficult to establish.

Chapters three, four, and five intend to separately peruse the main categories of agreements linked to readmission that have been identified as instruments of bilateral cooperation between European States and third countries. The expression 'agreements linked to readmission' is herein used as an overarching term encompassing the various patterns of bilateral cooperation designed to facilitate the removal and the readmission of unauthorised foreigners. This expression therefore includes: standard readmission agreements, examined in Chapter three; diplomatic assurances on the fair and human treatment of the deportees, with a focus on assurances contained within MOUs – analysed in Chapter four; and agreements providing for technical and police cooperation used to patrol

[24] Geneva Convention, 28 Jul 1951, in force 22 April 1954, 189 UNTS 150.

[25] CAT, New York, 10 December1984, in force 26 June 1987, 1465 UNTS 85.

[26] ICCPR, New York, 16 December 1966, in force 23 March 1976, 993 UNTS 171.

[27] ECHR, Rome, 4 November 1950, in force 3 September 1950, 213 UNTS 221.

[28] Recent books include: F De Weck, *Non-Refoulement under the European Convention on Human Rights and the UN Convention Against Torture: The Assessment of Individual Complaints* (Brill, 2014); M Reneman, *EU Asylum Procedures and the Right to an Effective Remedy* (Hart Publishing, 2014) 53–71; G Clayton, 'The right to have rights': The European convention on human rights and the procedural rights of asylum seekers' in A Abass and F Ippolito (eds), *Regional approaches to the protection of asylum seekers: An international legal perspective* (Ashgate, 2014) 191–211; E Hamdan, *The principle of non-refoulement under the ECHR and the UN Convention against Torture and Other Cruel, Inhuman or Degrading Treatment or Punishment* (Brill, 2016); V Moreno-Lax, *Accessing Asylum in Europe* (OUP, 2017) 247–460.

maritime borders and intercept/rescue undocumented migrants at sea, discussed in Chapter five.

A detailed reading of the text of these agreements along with the scrutiny of the readmission practices arising from their implementation demonstrates how their underlying object and purpose, even where not openly stated, is to facilitate the removal and readmission of unauthorised/unwanted foreigners. The element of 'effective control' over migrants and refugees is sufficient to trigger jurisdiction (and therefore potential responsibility) for a human rights violation, regardless of whether or not there is a legal basis for the actions of the State. However, this work intends to pinpoint the relationship between agreements linked to readmission and the removal order, thereby revealing the extent to which the latter is influenced by the former; the role that a given agreement may play in the actual decision of a State to jeopardise refugees' access to protection through formal or informal practices of containing migration and securing its borders, is also highlighted. Specific case studies for each category of agreement are used as units of analysis, while State practice, case law, and the technical and legal content of the bilateral agreements to hand will also be taken into account.

III. ON 'INFORMALISATION' AND 'DIVERSIFICATION' OF AGREEMENTS LINKED TO READMISSION

Readmission agreements are bilateral or multilateral treaties setting standards and procedures indicating how the removal of irregular migrants is to be conducted. However, this work is not limited to readmission agreements *strictu sensu*. Rather, it broadens the range of legal analysis applied to a multifaceted framework of bilateral cooperation arrangements connected to the readmission of irregular migrants from European States to third countries of origin or transit. It encompasses written agreements aimed at facilitating the removal of undocumented migrants (standard readmission agreements and diplomatic assurances on the fair and humane treatment of the deportee, especially if written within MoUs), and also those agreements for technical and police cooperation that are *de facto* utilised by European States to divert migrants back to the ports of departure before their physical arrival within the destination country. In this process of *diversification* (rather than 'informalisation')[29] of cooperative tools, the term *agreements linked to readmission* is better-suited for understanding the plethora of bilateral arrangements made by European States with third countries both to ease the removal of those irregular migrants with no status or right to stay any longer within their territory, and to prevent new arrivals by outsourcing migration controls and, indirectly, responsibilities relating to refugees.

The word 'informalisation' can give rise to different interpretations within the fields of law and international relations. Cassarino uses the expression

[29] I assume here that the term 'informalisation' has more to do with the law-making process.

'informalisation' to refer to alternative patterns of cooperation beyond standard readmission agreements to remove unauthorised migrants. Indeed, today, readmission is a network composed of differing institutional instruments – ranging from development aid, to visa facilitation, and from technical cooperation for the externalisation of migration controls, to labour exchanges[30] – tools which are all designed to make readmission more palatable for the requested State. In the analysis of the process of informalisation of agreements linked to readmission, this work relies on the findings of Pauwelyn, Wessel, and Wouters on 'informal international law-making'.[31] They regard as informal those international agreements which dispense with certain formalities (related to the output, process, or the actors involved) and which are traditionally associated with international law.[32] For instance, so-called 'informal agreements' might be recorded without all of the formalities required for the conclusion of treaties, and might be signed by officials whose treaty-making powers are in doubt.

In order to avoid misunderstandings related to terminology, this book will opt for the term 'diversification' of agreements designed to forcibly remove and readmit unauthorised migrants. In legal terms, so-called 'informal agreements' are international arrangements, which some consider to be 'outside the realm of law',[33] and whose binding character in international law is generally up for debate.[34] Rather than focusing only on the formal or informal nature of the agreements linked to readmission selected here, this work aims to emphasise their unifying theme, namely facilitating the removal and the readmission of unauthorised and unwanted third country nationals, regardless of their designation or their legal status under international law.

The concept of 'readmission' has often been fraught with a certain level of confusion and partiality from both a terminological and substantive point

[30] See Cassarino 2007, n 2 above, 185–87.

[31] J Pauwelyn, R Wessel and J Wouters, *Informal International Lawmaking* (OUP, 2014).

[32] J Pauwelyn, RA Wessel, and J Wouters, 'Informal International Lawmaking: An Assessment and Template to Keep It Both Effective and Accountable', in Pauwelyn, Wessel, and Wouters ibid, 500.

[33] While the highly disputed issue of the binary nature of law cannot be thoroughly expounded in this work, it should be observed that many scholars qualify soft law instruments as law as they still produce legal effects. For instance, they can play a role in the internationalisation of the subject-matter, offer guidelines for the interpretation of other legal acts, or pave the way for subsequent practice which can be taken into account for the emergence of customary international law. For a detailed analysis on the several types of softness in international law, see, Pauwelyn, Wessel, and Wouters, ibid, 1075 ff.

[34] See J Klabbers, *Developments in International Law: The Concept of Treaty in International Law* (Kluwer, 1996) 19. See also, K Widdows, 'What is an Agreement in International Law?' (1979) 50 *British Yearbook of International Law* 117; A Aust, 'The Theory and Practice of Informal International Instruments' (1986) 35 *International & Comparative Law Quarterly* 787; C Lipson, 'Why are Some International Agreements Informal?' (1991) 45(4) *International Organization* 495. See also AT Guzman, 'The Design of International Agreements' (2005) 16 *European Journal of International Law* 579; AE Boyle, 'Some Reflections on the Relationship of Treaties and Soft Law' (1999) 48 *International & Comparative Law Quarterly* 901.

of view. A frequent item of misunderstanding is the widespread use (in both literature and the popular press) of the 'readmission agreement' concept to interchangeably refer to diverse, non-overlapping legislative and administrative instruments.[35] What is important to underline is that these instruments authorise varied removal and readmission practices, ranging from post-arrival expulsions to pre-arrival interceptions. Thus, taking a first step toward the acceptance of a specific vocabulary, this work seeks to bring greater clarity to the readmission subject-matter, an issue that does not have a purely terminological purpose. This study will systematise this subject-matter in several distinct ways. Firstly, it will clarify the overall picture of various cooperative migration control instruments used by States to facilitate removal and readmission of unwanted foreigners. Secondly, it goes beyond a merely informative approach by interpreting State practices on removal and readmission through a three-dimensional systematisation of bilateral agreements linked to readmission in the light of their underlying *purpose*. Thirdly, identifying different types of agreements provides better understanding of their content, aims, and main functions, allowing for an assessment of the roles such agreements play in the decision to remove migrants and asylum seekers to countries of origin or transit, and not least in determining the extent to which they can influence such decisions. Finally, careful analysis of these diverse agreements linked to readmission reveals how impacts on refugees' rights can vary according to the different classes of agreements under examination.

Examining these bilateral arrangements as part of a wider, overarching concept of 'agreements linked to readmission' permits analysis of their similarities and common purpose, but also allows for exploration of the ways in which they differ. By influencing removal decisions to differing extents, the impact of their implementation on access to protection is subject to change: as a consequence of this, the follow up to the analysis varies from agreement to agreement. This is how a research journey that began with the intent to find uniformity, or at least commonalities between accords, ends up mapping out agreements linked to readmission much like a constellation of planets all orbiting around the same sun, but at different speeds and in different directions.

By specifically focusing on the standard readmission agreements concluded by Italy and the UK with non-European third countries on a bilateral basis,

[35] To give an example, the agreements for technical and police cooperation negotiated by Italy with Libya to prevent the arrival of unauthorized migratory flows at the EU border – through interceptions at sea – have frequently been labelled as 'readmission agreements.' See, *inter alia*, Parliamentary Assembly of the Council of Europe (CoE), *Report on Readmission Agreements: A Mechanism for Returning Irregular Migrants*, Doc 12168 (16 March 2010); Y Maccanico, *The EU's Self-Interested Response to Unrest in North Africa: the Meaning of Treaties and Readmission Agreements between Italy and North African States: the meaning of treaties and readmission agreements between Italy and north African states* (Statewatch, January 2012) 6, http://www.statewatch.org/analyses/no-165-eu-north-africa.pdf; M Panizzon, 'Readmission Agreements of EU Member States: A Case for EU Subsidiarity or Dualism?' (2012) 31(4) *Refugee Survey Quarterly* 101.

this work does not specifically cover EU readmission policy. However, since EU and State competencies on readmission are concurrent rather than exclusive, EU policies are relevant and frequently brought into the discussion. Coleman (2009) – the first legal book on migrants' readmission – focused on the policy of the EU on this subject-matter. It is therefore taken as a key benchmark and point of comparison when assessing interstate arrangements.[36] Coleman concluded that EU readmission agreements offer better guarantees against human rights violations and are not detrimental to refugee protection: he conceded however that more quantitative and qualitative studies in relation to informal border practices are needed.[37] In joining the debate, Chapter three of this work builds upon the similarities between EU and interstate readmission agreements and looks beyond EU-negotiated accords. It aims to assess whether the existence of readmission agreements could spark *de facto* informal practices on border control and removal of irregular migrants, including refugees. As readmission agreements do not generally include separate, detailed provisions on refugees, there is a real risk of removing asylum seekers, as unauthorised migrants, to allegedly 'safe third countries.' The chapter recommends, therefore, as added value, the insertion of both non-affection clauses and procedural human rights clauses creating extra safeguards for removable asylum seekers. To this end, this work makes a number of concrete proposals, such as draft provisions, as a platform for further discussion amongst legal scholars and policy-makers.

Chapter four challenges one of the most cutting-edge strategies European States are testing out to remove unwanted foreigners who are seen, or framed, as a threat to the safety of the host country. MoUs have been established with the intent of formalising, within a written standardised agreement, the human rights commitments of those third countries who might have a dismal human rights track record. It is herein argued that the format of a MoU cannot be used simply as a 'legal nicety'[38] to remove a person to a country that is, for example, notorious for its dubious interrogation techniques of detainees. As such, it is contended here that States should refrain from relying on diplomatic assurances – whether or not framed within standardised MoUs – with those countries that continue to employ torture tactics.

Chapter five deals with agreements concerning technical and police cooperation which are designed to intercept migrants and refugees at sea before arriving at the gates of Europe. Joint offshore migration controls operated through bilateral agreements between a European State and a third country have become increasingly popular because of the presumption that States can

[36] See N Coleman, *European Readmission Policy: Third Country Interests and Refugee Rights* (Martinus Nijhoff, 2009).

[37] ibid, 325.

[38] No claim is made here with respect to the legal status of MoUs and diplomatic assurances. This subject continues to be a divisive issue in scholarship and will be addressed in Chapter four.

be freed from their refugee and human rights law obligations when operating beyond their territorial borders. Therefore, this work also hopes to contribute to a more general understanding of the legal issues raised by the current trend toward externalisation of migration controls through bilateral agreements with migrants' countries of origin or transit – the rationale for which lies at the brink of both law and politics.

Moreover, this book combines areas of law and policy that are generally considered neatly discrete and distinct, even in a temporal sense. Removal and readmission are analysed in relation to refugees' access to the destination State's territory and to protection, in search of links that at face value appear overly remote. However, a deep scrutiny of practice reveals how, in certain operative scenarios (not least where extraterritorial migration controls are concerned), admission/non-admission and readmission do indeed overlap.

While there have been separate studies on standard readmission agreements, agreements for technical and police cooperation, as well as diplomatic assurances, these bilateral arrangements have not been conceptualised as falling within a broader category of *agreements linked to readmission* in light of their object and purpose, and subjected to a legal analysis.[39] The description of both legal texts and State practice is a stepping stone to ascertaining the relationship between bilateral agreements linked to readmission and the decision to remove refugees to countries of origin or transit, thereby handing them over to authorities of States where their life and liberty may be put at risk. Where the implementation of these bilateral arrangements hampers refugees' access to protection, individuals are entitled to seek a remedy before the treaty-monitoring bodies of the main international and European human rights conventions: these implicitly or explicitly embody the principle of *non-refoulement* and the right to access asylum procedures and effective remedies before removal.

This work will also explore the nebulous boundaries of State jurisdiction, particularly in extraterritorial contexts, and, consequently, the geographical reach of refugee and human rights obligations. Indeed, the activity of human rights courts and committees is, by and large, often openly or tacitly constrained by jurisdictional filters, which have traditionally been territorially limited. It follows that not all cases of alleged violations of rights can be considered admissible in court.

[39] Publications tackling agreements linked to readmission have so far addressed this topic from a non-legal perspective. See, eg, Cassarino 2007, n 2 above; JP Cassarino, 'Dealing with Unbalanced Reciprocities: Cooperation on Readmission and Implications' in JP Cassarino (ed), *Unbalanced Reciprocities: Cooperation on Readmission in the Euro-Mediterranean Area* (Middle East Institute, 2010). The PhD thesis by Emanuela Roman, *Cooperation on Readmission in the Mediterranean Area and its Human Rights Implications* (2017) deals more with informalisation of agreements linked to readmission, including mobility partnerships and EU readmission agreements, which are not, however, the focus of this book.

The rationale behind the decision to focus this research on human rights obligations (rather than on the general international rules on the responsibility of States for internationally wrongful acts) rests on the urgent need to determine, from the outset, the content of human rights standards and their normative potential. Indeed, State responsibility for an internationally wrongful act can be established only when two conditions are met: where the conduct at issue is attributable to the State, and where such conduct constitutes a violation of an international legal obligation.[40] It is this primary obligation, which must be interpreted and applied to the situation, to determine the substance of the required conduct, the standard to be observed, the result to be achieved, and so forth.[41] Delving into the substance of human rights law will also let us establish the efficacy of the legal guarantees to which every individual seeking protection in Europe is entitled, thereby serving to assist future research in the area of migration control and refugee rights.

Tracing the contours of ordinary obligations is, therefore, the foundation stone of any thorough analysis on State responsibility, in particular when States displace joint migration controls beyond borders to the high seas or the territorial waters of a third country, where the grounds for both exercising jurisdiction and engaging extraterritorial human rights obligations are arguably more tenuous. Whereas States seem to be committed to altering geographies and moving borders, it should be noted that clauses on common commitments are frequently inscribed within agreements linked to readmission with the objective of diluting or 'watering-down' the responsibilities of States. Therefore, once it is established that responsibility can be engaged, governments are called upon to forsake impermissible practices by adjusting their bilateral agreements and harmonising the activities they carry out on the interception and readmission of unauthorised migrants to international and European human rights standards. However, if the investigation of interstate responsibility enforcement mechanisms were any more broad or exhaustive, it would simply be beyond the overall objective of this work.

IV. DEFINING KEY CONCEPTS

Some preliminary terminological clarifications are needed with a view to agreeing on concepts whose meaning is always open to debate and interpretation. The title of this book refers to '*asylum seekers*'. The expression 'asylum seeker' does not exist in international refugee and human rights law treaties. It is, however, used by States to refer to a person seeking protection in a country other than

[40] Art 2 ILC of the 'Articles on the Responsibility of States for Internationally Wrongful Acts' (2001), UNGA A/56/10, corrected by A/56/49 vol I/Corr.4 (ILC Articles).

[41] Draft articles on Responsibility of States for Internationally Wrongful Acts, with commentaries, *Yearbook of the ILC 2001*, vol. II, Part Two, 54 (ILC Articles Commentary).

his/her own. The latter may be based on refugeehood according to the 1951 Convention, or on the need for complementary protection[42] – including subsidiary protection under EU law.[43]

Whilst individuals have a right to *seek asylum*,[44] they may not be able to claim a *right to asylum* in the sense of 'admission to residence and lasting protection against the jurisdiction of another State.'[45] According to the open definition adopted by the *Institut du Droit International* at its Bath Conference in 1950, 'the term *asylum* means the *protection* offered by a State on its territory or elsewhere to an individual who came to seek it (emphasis added).' More specifically, asylum – a word of Greek origin, which means 'what cannot be seized' – has been defined as an institution 'based on the principle of *non-refoulement* and internationally or nationally recognized refugee rights.'[46] It is offered only to foreigners who seek protection outside of their country of origin from some threat or danger, and can be granted either on the State territory or elsewhere, including at the border or abroad.

A further clarification concerns *the right of asylum*, which refers to '[t]he right of the State, by virtue of its territorial sovereignty and in the exercise of its discretion, to allow a non-national to enter and reside, and to resist the exercise of jurisdiction by any State over that individual.'[47] Chapter two is, however, dedicated to examining the content and scope of an individual's *right to access asylum procedures*, which, when mentioned here, refers to the right of an asylum seeker to obtain access to all those procedures both for the assessment

[42] In international law, 'the term "complementary protection" describes States' protection obligations arising from international legal instruments and customs that complement – or supplement – the 1951 Refugee Convention. It is, in effect, a shorthand term for the widened scope of *non-refoulement* under international law.' See Goodwin-Gill and McAdam 2007, n 20 above, 285. For a comprehensive analysis of the concept of protection and complementary protection, see J McAdam, *Complementary Protection in International Refugee Law* (Oxford University Press, 2007). See also, R Mandal, 'Protection Mechanisms Outside of the 1951 Convention ("Complementary Protection")' *UNHCR Legal and Protection Policy Research Series* (PPLA/2005/02, June 2005). For an overview of the regional systems of protection, see, DA Martin, TA Aleinkoff, H Motomura and M Fullerton, *Forced Migration: Law and Policy*, 2nd edn (West, 2013) 57–63.

[43] While the definition of refugee is entirely shaped on Article 1(a)(2) of the 1951 Geneva Convention (persecution for reasons of race, religion, nationality, membership of a particular social group or political opinion), the definition of subsidiary protection employed in the Recast Qualification Directive is based largely on international human rights instruments. Under Article 15 of the same Directive, an individual can obtain subsidiary protection if in her home country she would face a 'serious harm', defined as a 'serious and individual threat to a civilian's life or person by reason of indiscriminate violence in situations of international or internal armed conflict.' See Chapter 2 for further details.

[44] See, eg, Art 14 of the Universal Declaration on Human Rights (UDHR).

[45] Goodwin-Gill and McAdam 2007, n 20 above, 358.

[46] See European Migration Network (EMN) Glossary, 'Asylum', https://ec.europa.eu/home-affairs/content/asylum-0_en. The EMN's Glossary relies on authoritative sources of both universal and regional scope, such as the UNHCR and the EU Commission. For a thorough analysis of asylum in international law, see MT Gil Bazo, 'Asylum as a General Principle of International Law' (2015) 27(1) *IJRL* 3.

[47] EMN Glossary, 'Right of Asylum', https://ec.europa.eu/home-affairs/content/right-asylum-0_en.

of refugee status under the Geneva Convention, and other forms of complementary protection – including subsidiary protection.

One of this work's central goals is to investigate whether the implementation of bilateral agreements linked to readmission can hamper refugees' *access to protection*. In the absence of a uniform definition of 'protection',[48] this term is here meant as an overarching concept shaped by the combination of *non-refoulement* and the right to access asylum procedures and effective remedies before removal to the country where refugees originate from or have transited through before seeking asylum. There is, however, a need to pinpoint what the notion(s) of 'protection' stand for in international law. Under paragraph 1 of its Statute, the UNHCR (the UN Refugee Agency) 'shall assume the function of providing international protection ... to refugees which fall within the scope of the present Statute and of seeking permanent solutions for the problem of refugees.' However, the notion of 'protection' has undergone notable interpretative changes over time, ranging from pure diplomatic assistance to more procedural and material aid in the light of the various challenges created by new refugee situations. The shift in the meaning of the notion of 'international protection' can be summarised as follows:

> it has evolved from a surrogate for consular and diplomatic protection of refugees who can no longer enjoy such protection by their country of origin into a broader concept that includes protection not only of rights provided for by the 1951 Convention and the 1967 Protocol but also of refugees' human rights in general.[49]

While recognising that the meaning of 'protection' remains somewhat elusive because of the difficulty in determining the fundamental obligation at the core of protection,[50] the refugee rights regime seems to comprise not only the 1951 Geneva Convention, but also the ICCPR and the International Covenant on Economic, Social and Cultural Rights (ICESCR).[51]

At the EU level, the notion of 'international protection' has assumed its own legal significance, referring to 'refugee status and subsidiary protection status.'[52]

[48] Despite protection being the *raison d'être* of refugee policy, there is a neat definitional uncertainty. On this point, see GS Goodwin-Gill, 'The Language of Protection' (1989) 1(1) *IJRL* 6; and D Stevens, 'What do We Mean by Protection?' (2013) 20(1) *International Journal on Minority and Group Rights* 233.

[49] UNHCR, *Address by Ms Erika Feller, Director, Department of International Protection, UNHCR, to the XXVIII Round Table on Current Problems of International Humanitarian Law* (San Remo, 3 September 2004), http://www.unhcr.org/refworld/docid/42b7e2b92.html.

[50] Stevens 2013, n 48 above, 259.

[51] J Hathaway, *The Rights of Refugees under International Law* (Cambridge University Press, 2005) 8. In Stevens' words, 'the assurance of non-return facilitates the opportunity to access further rights, whether contained in the Refugee Convention or elsewhere. Though dependent on the approach of the asylum State, such access to rights is often deemed a form of protection that extends beyond pure territorial protection, and which might be described as "rights protection".' See Stevens 2013, n 48 above, 237.

[52] Art 2(a) of the Recast Qualification Directive.

What emerges from the foregoing is how the concept of '*protection*' has elicited several mutually reinforcing meanings from refugee law, human rights law, humanitarian law, and EU law by encompassing all of those 'activities aimed at obtaining full respect for the rights of the individual.'[53] In this regard, Chapter VII of the Recast Qualification Directive identifies as part of the content of 'international protection' many other rights which go beyond *non-refoulement* as the standard criterion of protection.

This work embraces all the above-mentioned facets of the notion of 'protection' outside the country of origin of the refugee and reconstructs it as an all-encompassing term that harmoniously embodies the principle of *non-refoulement* and the right to access asylum procedures and effective remedies before removal. The reasons for this are clear. The principle of *non-refoulement* is paramount to the protection regime and remains the cornerstone of international refugee law.[54] It is the primary obligation that States have to fulfil when dealing with a refugee, both at the border and beyond. Without it, protection would become meaningless. However, in order for *non-refoulement* to be satisfied, individuals need to be able to express their fear of return to their home country and have their claims fairly and thoroughly assessed on their merits. Therefore, the right to access asylum procedures and the right to an effective remedy against an unfavourable asylum determination or expulsion order amount to procedural entitlements and essential preconditions to *non-refoulement*. As such, these three rights, despite their differences, are addressed together as part of the notion of 'protection' in the host or would-be host State.

A. Terms Linked to Readmission

The International Organization for Migration (IOM) Glossary on Migration provides operational definitions to elucidate the use of partially overlapping terms in the field of irregular migration.[55] *Return* refers to 'the act or process of going back to the point of departure. This could be … between a host country (either transit or destination) and a country of origin.'[56] *Forced return*

[53] EMN Glossary, 'Protection', https://ec.europa.eu/home-affairs/content/protection-0_en.

[54] UNHCR, *Advisory Opinion on the Extraterritorial Application of Non-Refoulement Obligations under the 1951 Convention relating to the Status of Refugees and its 1967 Protocol* (26 January 2007) 2.

[55] IOM, Glossary on Migration, International Migration Law Series no 25, 2011 (IOM Glossary 2011). As we will observe throughout this Section, most of these definitions are similar in content to those proposed by the EU.

[56] ibid. In the definition provided by the Annex of the EU Commission Green paper on a Community Return Policy on Illegal Residents, return 'comprises comprehensively the preparation or implementation aiming at the way back to the country of origin or transit, irrespective of the question whether the return takes place voluntarily or forced.' COM(2002) 175 final, 10 April 2002, Annex I 'Proposed Definitions', http://eur-lex.europa.eu/LexUriServ/site/en/com/2002/com2002_0175en01.pdf.

comprises the 'compulsory return of an individual to the country of origin, transit or third country, on the basis of an administrative or judicial act.'[57] The notion of *readmission* refers instead to the 'act by a State accepting the re-entry of an individual (own national, third-country national or stateless person)' who has been found irregularly entering to, being present in, or residing in another State.[58] *Expulsion* concerns

> an [administrative or judicial] act by an authority of the State with the intention and with the effect of securing the removal of a person or persons (non-nationals or stateless persons) against his or her will from the territory of that State.[59]

Similarly, *deportation* refers to 'the act of a State in the exercise of its sovereignty in removing a non-national from its territory to his or her country of origin or third State after refusal of admission or termination of permission to remain.'[60] *Removal* is the 'enforcement of the obligation to return; physical transportation out of the country.'[61] While this work will use the terms removal/expulsion/deportation by and large interchangeably to refer to the transfer of migrants and refugees to third countries of origin or transit, these terms are deliberately distinguished from the word 'return', which can also have a voluntary dimension.[62] On the other hand, as 'return' is the expression mostly used by supranational and international organisations, this word will be utilized when citing, or referring to, texts and documents by relevant institutions, including international human rights bodies.

Extradition is instead a formal process concerning the 'surrender by one State to another of an individual accused or convicted of an offence outside its

[57] IOM Glossary 2011.

[58] ibid.

[59] ibid. Pursuant to Art 2(a) of the ILC Draft Articles on the Expulsion of Aliens, expulsion is 'a formal act, or conduct consisting of an action or omission, attributable to a State by which an alien is compelled to leave the territory of that State ...' See Draft Articles on the Expulsion of Aliens, in *Report of the International Law Commission on the Work of Its Sixty-Fourth Session*, UN GAOR, 64th Sess., Supp. no 10, 1–2, UN Doc A/67/10 (2006). Under Art 2, 'A State has the right to expel an alien from its territory. Expulsion shall be in accordance with the present draft articles, without prejudice to other applicable rules of international law, in particular those relating to human rights.'

[60] ibid. The IOM Glossary also defines a *deportation order* as 'an administrative or judicial decision or act ordering a removal'. In the Annex of the 2002 EU Commission Communication on 'Proposed Definitions', the term 'deportation' is used in the same context of 'removal.' See COM(2002) 175 final, Annex I 'Proposed Definitions.'

[61] IOM Glossary 2011.

[62] While a discussion on forced/voluntary return would be beyond the remit of this book, it should be observed that the 'voluntariness' of return has been critically questioned. For instance, referring to the Voluntary Repatriation Programme of the UNHCR, Chimni warns against 'the danger of coerced return'. BS Chimni, 'The Meaning of Words and the Role of UNHCR in Voluntary Repatriation' (1995) 5(3) *IJRL* 442. Similarly, Webber, finds that voluntary return programmes reflect policies aimed at swiftly removing irregular migrants and rejected asylum seekers without due regard for their safety and preparedness. F Webber, 'How voluntary are voluntary returns?' (2011) 52(4) *Race and Class* 98–107. See also, Cassarino 2010, n 39 above, 3; JP Cassarino, 'Return Migration and Development: The Significance of Migration Cycles' in A Triandafyllidou (ed), *Routledge Handbook of Immigration and Refugee Studies* (Routledge, 2016) 220.

territory and within the jurisdiction of the other, for the purpose of trial and punishment.'[63] It will be excluded from the ambit of this book for two reasons: first, extradition is not an instrument intended to combat or prevent irregular migration; second, there is an inverted relationship between the two involved parties. Indeed, the State requesting extradition is also the same one that will receive the surrender, while the requested State is the one that sends back the addressee.

In bilateral activities of migration control, by contrast, the two actors involved in the 'readmission' process are, on the one hand, the State that requests readmission (*requesting State*) and removes the unwanted migrant(s), and, on the other hand, the State that is requested to readmit (*requested State*). The third actor is the person to be readmitted, who is, in theory, either an irregular migrant or a rejected asylum seeker deemed to be a person who is not in need of international protection. However, as noted throughout the text, at times refugees are also involved in either formal or informal readmission procedures. For the purpose of this work, the terms *irregular* (with no regular status in the host country) and *undocumented/unauthorised* (without the required papers) migrant are synonymous and include foreigners without valid documents.[64]

To facilitate secondary movements from the host, or would-be host, country to another State, the notion of '*safe third country*' has been introduced. This concept – which will be discussed in more detail in Chapter two – has been described as 'a procedural mechanism for shuttling asylum seekers to other States said to have primary responsibility for them, thereby avoiding the necessity to make a decision on the merits because another country is deemed or imagined to be secure.'[65] As removal of refugees whose status has not yet been determined can also take place to a third country, at least three actors are involved in such transfers: the country of origin ('first' country), the European State where the asylum seeker makes, or wishes to make, her application ('second' country), and the country to which the individual is transferred (the 'third' country). This work moves across these States, following refugees on their way to Europe and through their eventual move away from Europe. The emphasis is, however, on the 'second country' whenever and wherever it encounters the refugee.

V. GEOGRAPHICAL SCOPE

Agreements linked to readmission are not a new phenomenon and have been adopted by several States worldwide. Although developing countries are home

[63] IOM Glossary 2011. See also, UNHCR, *Note on Extradition and International Refugee Protection* (April 2008) p 4, para 1.

[64] See E Guild, 'Who is an Irregular Migrant?' in B Bogusz, R Cholewinski, A Cygan and E Szyszczak (eds), *Irregular Migration and Human Rights: Theoretical, European and International Perspectives* (Martinus Nijhoff, 2004).

[65] Goodwin-Gill and McAdam 2007, n 20 above, 392.

to approximately 84 per cent of the world's refugees,[66] wealthy States have concluded a great number of readmission agreements to remove unwanted migrants, bilateral accords to carry out pre-emptive migration controls at sea, and, to a lesser extent, MoUs providing diplomatic assurances to facilitate the deportation of unwanted foreigners. In doing so, they use their political and economic clout to achieve cooperation with third countries, which often lack both the necessary resources and interest to tightly guard their land and sea borders.[67] Within this general picture, European States are those most frequently involved in bilateral readmission agreements with countries of origin and transit of immigrants, and rely upon such bilateral agreements as systematic and strategic tools to counter unauthorised entries.

With regard to the geographical scope of this work, Italy and the UK have been chosen as case studies for two interwoven reasons. Italy is one of the most involved European States in bilateral cooperation linked to readmission. The UK, on the other hand, has historically been less prone to conclude agreements with third countries of origin or transit of migrants. Nevertheless, these two States are experiencing a process of *diversification* of bilateral cooperation agreements designed to facilitate the removal and readmission of undesired immigrants and asylum seekers. Italy and the UK provide, indeed, some of the best examples of the typologies of arrangements falling under the 'agreements linked to readmission' definition.

It also bears pointing out that this work does not aim to conduct a comparative analysis of the readmission policies and national laws on migration in these two countries. Instead, it examines different case studies through a practical framework within the research's subject-matter.[68] The results drawn from this research's selective exercise are also relevant with regard to the same typologies of arrangements concluded by several other countries globally with the intent of removing or preventing the arrival of unwanted foreigners.

Within the European context, the EU has a well-developed readmission policy, which continues to be pursued together with its Member States. Given the system of shared competencies in the field of readmission,[69] a better understanding of how national systems carry out matters relating to readmission

[66] According to the UNHCR, over four out of five refugees flee to their neighbouring countries. See UNHCR Global Trends 2018, https://www.unhcr.org/5d08d7ee7.pdf.

[67] P Cuttitta, 'Readmission and Forcibly Return in the Relations between Italy and North African Mediterranean Countries' (Ninth Mediterranean Research Meeting, Florence, Montecatini Terme, 12–15 March 2008) 8, http://www.altrodiritto.unifi.it/frontier/storia/cuttitta.pdf.

[68] Further details surrounding the rationale behind these cases' selection will be provided in Chapters 3, 4, and 5).

[69] Since Art 4(2)(j) of the Treaty on the Functioning of the EU (TFEU) incorporates 'Freedom, Security and Justice' – which clearly encompasses also readmission – in the field of shared competence, the Union does not have the exclusive power to negotiate readmission agreements. The relationship between the EU and Member States is grounded on the principle of 'sincere cooperation' enshrined in Art 4(3) of the Treaty on the EU (TEU).

is essential, as States remain the primary actors in terms of the issuing and implementation of removal decisions.[70] It should also be noted that target third countries are selected with the aim of creating both a 'buffer zone' of States taking responsibility for transit migration around European borders, and establishing relations with States producing higher rates of migration.[71] In particular, the EU has employed the following criteria in selecting which countries it should enter into readmission agreements with:

> migration pressure from a third country concerned on a particular Member State or on the EU as a whole; the cooperation on return by the third country concerned; as well as the geographical position of the third country concerned situated at a migration route towards Europe.[72]

For example, the *readmission agreements* of Italy and the UK with Albania (Chapter three) are among the most sophisticated and detailed pieces of legislation within the varied category of existing standard readmission agreements.

In the framework of European States' counter-terrorism strategy and the strengthening of migration policies to avoid gaps in the asylum system (that could potentially be exploited by refuge seekers who are considered a threat to the security of the destination State), governments have elaborated new policy options for dealing with unwanted but not-removable aliens. In this sense, the UK has responded to the security dilemma somewhat oddly, by formalising *diplomatic assurances* for individuals to be deported pursuant to MoUs. The assurances exchanged between the UK with Ethiopia, Lebanon, Jordan, Libya, and Morocco are examples of such written agreements, through which a European State mediates and negotiates with third countries on issues related to how foreigners viewed as a threat to the safety of the sending State should be treated. The UK's MoUs are therefore part and parcel of this work (Chapter four).

It should also be noted that, by off-shoring or outsourcing migration controls to third countries (*in primis* Libya), Italy has carried out a practice of push-backs (and push-backs by proxy), which are clearly aimed at keeping migrants and refugees away from European borders. Diverse *agreements for technical and police cooperation* – which are among the main focuses of this analysis in Chapter five – have thus been concluded between Italy and Libya with the

[70] To date, only the EU readmission agreements concluded with Sri Lanka, Albania, Hong Kong, Macao, Russia, Bosnia and Herzegovina, Macedonia, Moldova, Montenegro, Pakistan, Serbia, Ukraine, Armenia, Azerbaijan, Turkey, and Cape Verde have entered into force.

[71] There are some exceptions, such as, for example, Hong Kong and Macao, which do not present any strategic interest for the EU and its Member States. Readmission agreements with these two countries were concluded only in conjunction with the lifting of visa requirements.

[72] Draft Council Conclusions defining the European Union strategy on readmission, 27 May 2011, para 4. Long before 2011, these criteria were already mentioned by the General Secretariat of the Council on 16 April 2002: 'Criteria for the identification of third countries with which new readmission agreements need to be negotiated' (Doc 7990/02), http://www.statewatch.org/news/2003/may/12i7990-02-c1.pdf.

ultimate goal of intercepting migrants and asylum seekers at sea well before they arrive at the shores of Europe.

VI. LAW AND PRACTICE OF READMISSION

In grasping divergences between the legal and practical aspects of the same institution, attention should be focused on the way in which rules (*in casu* bilateral agreements linked to readmission) are applied in practice. The acquisition of knowledge cannot be limited to the study of legal texts. Rather, it is necessary to separately scrutinise how legal rules are operationalised, especially when the content of bilateral arrangements of migration control is kept secret, or when a 'safe' deportation is based only upon diplomatic assurances, such as in the case of MoUs.

Readmission discourse has generally been accompanied by a sense of bewilderment and fragmentation because of the plethora of instruments used by European States both in removing undocumented migrants from their territory and in keeping them away from European borders. Cooperation with third countries on migration control is today conceivable as a network composed of different institutional instruments, ranging from development aid and labour exchanges to technical and police cooperation, and from standard readmission agreements to carrier sanctions, visa-policy, and liaison officers to monitor migration at a distance as well as directly within the countries of origin.[73]

Despite this multi-faceted apparatus of formal and informal measures of migration control, surveillance, and prevention, the scope of this work is limited to the main categories of bilateral agreements linked to readmission, which are examined against a backdrop of international refugee and human rights legal sources. As a first step, the terms of the selected accords are described comprehensively and separately, by means of an analytical approach. State practice – through a narrative of the facts concerning the implementation of the accords in specific situations and emblematic cases – is then examined to give more substance and shape to the theoretical discussion. Inevitably, any enquiry into State practice is fraught with an unavoidable degree of uncertainty due to the inaccessibility of relevant information, in particular with regards to communications between governments in the actual context of a maritime operation.

[73] For an overview, see A Meloni, 'The Development of a Common Visa Policy under the Treaty of Amsterdam' (2005) 42(5) *CML Rev* 1357–81; D Bigo and E Guild, 'Policing at a Distance: Schengen Visa Policies' in D Bigo and E Guild (eds), *Controlling Frontiers* (Ashgate, 2005) 233–63; S Peers and N Rogers, *EU Immigration and Asylum Law* (Martinus Nijhoff, 2006) 167–218; V Moreno-Lax, 'Carrier Sanctions' in S Peers, E Guild, D Acosta, K Groenendijk and V Moreno-Lax (eds), *EU Immigration and Asylum Law* Vol 2, 2nd edn (Martinus Nijhoff, 2012); J Hathaway and T Gammeltoft-Hansen, '*Non-Refoulement* in a World of Cooperative Deterrence' (2014) 53 *Columbia Journal of Transnational Law* 235–84; Moreno-Lax 2017, n 28 above.

States are not always required to make public their use of diplomatic assurances in the field of, for example, suspected terrorists' removal, so that State practice has commonly gone undocumented.[74]

To fully understand the real impact of bilateral agreements linked to readmission on refugee rights, it is necessary to acknowledge that the study of legal texts alone would not suffice in terms of achieving a fully comprehensive approach. Rather, equal attention must be given to the implementation of the law.[75] As in theatre, actors, both protagonists and extras, must stand on stage in performing their drama. They all follow the same plot. But, then, what makes the show either captivating or unpleasant is not simply down to a good or bad storyline, but how that storyline is acted out; the verve which actors bring to the words of their script; and how far they improvise their lines and steal the scene.

In this general landscape, there are not only texts, storylines, and scripts, but also scenes, (inter)actions, digressions, and detours. A theatrical production is usually the fruit of the intertwining of a given storyline – which aims to create a frame of certainty, and guidelines for actors – and the actual performance, which is much influenced by human inclination, sensibility, hitches, and contingencies. That is why theatre artwork is fundamentally irreproducible. Accordingly, the impact of bilateral agreements linked to readmission on refugees' access to protection is not only the upshot of a good or bad legal text, but also the result of mutable embraces between standardised written accords and their implementation by State authorities in increasingly and ever-diverse circumstances.

VII. TEXT, CONTEXT, AND *TELOS*

Dealing with formal and informal bilateral agreements as well as human rights conventions, this work looks to research in the field of treaty interpretation. The different actors involved in the process of interpretation – States parties, specified bodies and courts, or international bureaucracies – have the role of establishing the meaning of treaty texts and applying said interpretations to different situations.[76] Pursuant to Article 2(1)(a) of the Vienna Convention on the Law of Treaties (VCLT), treaties may be defined as 'international agreement[s] concluded between States in written form and governed by international law, whether embodied in a single instrument or in two or more related instruments

[74] See Human Rights Watch, *Still at Risk, Diplomatic Assurances, No Safeguard against Torture* (New York, April 2005) HRW Report Vol 17 no 4(d) 80.

[75] In the analysis of State practice, the following secondary sources will be used: policy papers; reports by international governmental and non-governmental organisations (NGOs) and European agencies; as well as newspaper articles and blogs. In assessing legal implementation, the decisions of judicial and quasi-judicial human rights bodies will also be particularly instructive.

[76] This list is not meant to be exhaustive. On actors engaged in the process of interpretation, see I Venzke, *How Interpretation Makes International Law: on Semantic Changes and Normative Twists* (OUP, 2012) 64–66.

and whatever its particular designation.'[77] The VCLT is the starting point for any study on the practice of treaties, as it establishes all of the procedures for making, bringing into force, amending, and terminating an international agreement (law of treaties).

The VCLT applies both to multilateral and bilateral treaties, but does not cover agreements falling under domestic jurisdiction and governed by national law.[78] Furthermore, international agreements that have been concluded in a simplified manner (or that are contained in a more informal instrument, such as a Memorandum or an Exchange of Letters) have the same legal effect as formal treaties, provided they meet all the criteria required by Article 2 of the VCLT.[79] Article 102 of the UN Charter requires the registration of 'every treaty and every international agreement.' However, since the concept of 'international agreements' is broader than the notion of 'treaties', 'all treaties are international agreements but not all international agreements are treaties.'[80] This is to say that if an agreement satisfies all the criteria of Article 2(a), the specific designation of an international instrument as an act, agreement, charter, covenant, convention, declaration, exchange of notes, memorandum of understanding, pact, or protocol, has no particular legal meaning and does not automatically indicate its status as legally binding or not.[81] Indeed, as the International Court of Justice (ICJ) held in the *South West Africa (Preliminary Objections)* case, 'there are many different types of acts to which the character of treaty stipulations has been attached.'[82]

Furthermore, even though Article 2 of the VCLT does not restrict the freedom of the parties to enter into a non-binding arrangement, the requirement that an agreement is governed by international law encompasses the *intention of the parties to create international legal obligations.*[83] The intention to create obligations under international law is a *conditio sine qua non* of treaties and it

[77] Although the VCLT refers only to international agreements in a written form, the legal force of oral agreements – which are, however, very rare – is not affected. See VCLT, 23 May 1969, in force 27 January 1988, 1155 UNTS 331, 8 ILM 679.

[78] Reference is to agreements between individuals or between private actors among themselves or with the State. See André Gros in the ILC, *Yearbook of the ILC 1962*, I, 173, 215, para 42; O Schachter, 'The Twilight Existence of Non-Binding International Agreements' (1997) 71(2) *American Journal of International Law* 296.

[79] See ILC Articles Commentary on Art 2 in *Yearbook of the ILC 1996*, II, 173, 188–89.

[80] Mark E Villiger, *Commentary on the 1969 Vienna Convention on the Law of Treaties* (Martinus Nijhoff, 2009) 77.

[81] See Villiger 2009, n 80 above, 80–81. In the *Customs Regime between Austria and Germany Advisory Opinion*, 5 September 1931, PCIJ Series A/B no 41, para 35, the Court affirmed that 'from the standpoint of the obligatory character of international engagements, it is well known that such engagements may be taken in the form of treaties, conventions, declarations, agreements, protocols, or exchange of notes.'

[82] *South West Africa (Ethiopia v South Africa; Liberia v South Africa)*; Preliminary Objections, 21 December 1962.

[83] ILC Report 1966, *Yearbook of the ILC 1966*, II 189, para 6. See also, Villiger 2009, n 80 above, 81.

must be inferred from the terms of the agreement and the context of its conclusion, rather than from subsequent statements of the parties that are solely concerned with their purpose.[84] This discussion will be particularly relevant to the second part of this book (Chapters three, four, and five) where the legal status of diverse agreements linked to readmission will be explored.

The VCLT does not require a treaty to be in a particular form or to use special wording, and it is up to the negotiating State to decide whether it will conclude a treaty, or something less.[85] Since international law places the principal emphasis on the intentions of the parties, 'the law prescribes no particular form [and] parties are free to choose what form they please provided their intention clearly results from it.'[86]

Treaties can be concluded between States and other subjects of international law as well as between international organisations.[87] Consent to be bound by a treaty may be expressed not only by heads of State but also by governments, ministries, and other State organs, provided they represent the State and are duly authorised to act on its behalf. Other public bodies that have a legal personality separate from that of the State cannot express consent. Furthermore, for a treaty to enter into force in a certain country, it is necessary that it becomes part of its domestic law. The fact that an agreement is 'concluded' implies that from that point in time the instrument binds the parties under international law; indeed, the purpose of treaties is to create legally binding relations between the parties, giving rise to rights and obligations, which may be invoked or enforced before national and international courts of law. This issue will be revisited in Chapter four, where the legally binding status of diplomatic assurances is questioned, because of the risks raised by those bilateral agreements that devolve human rights protection to the sphere of diplomacy and fluctuating foreign affairs interests.

With the aim of giving concrete meaning to individual refugee rights and State obligations, Chapter two will examine the principle of *non-refoulement* and the individual's right to have access to asylum procedures and effective remedies, as enshrined in international refugee and human rights treaties. Chapters three, four, and five will analyse, in contrast, the text of the different typologies of agreements linked to readmission and the impact of their implementation on

[84] *Qatar v Bahrain (Jurisdiction and Admissibility)*, 10 February 1992, ICJ Rep 112, paras 26–27. The intent to create obligations under international law also distinguishes treaties from agreements governed by domestic law where the law of the contract is that of one of the Contracting States. See FA Mann, 'Another Agreement between States under National Law?' (1974) 68 *American Journal of International Law* 490–96.

[85] This issue will be addressed more in depth in Chapter 4, which deals with the legal value, under international law, of diplomatic assurances.

[86] *Temple of Preah Vihear case (Cambodia v Thailand), Preliminary Objections*, 26 May 1961, ICJ Rep 17, 31.

[87] The conclusion of an agreement indicates that the treaty starts to produce legal effects and that the Parties consent to be bound by it as provided for in Arts 11–17 of the VCLT.

core refugee rights. In dealing with such a wide range of international agreements, this work relies on the general rules of treaty interpretation as enshrined in Articles 31–33 of the VCLT.[88] According to Article 31 of the VCLT, 'a treaty shall be interpreted in *good faith* in accordance with the *ordinary meaning* to be given to the terms of the treaty in their *context* and in light of its *object and purpose*' (emphasis added).[89] The single heading of Article 31 – 'General rule of interpretation' – indicates that Article 31 should be interpreted in a 'holistic manner',[90] concurrently encompassing an approach based on the text, the context, and the purpose of a treaty. Thus, starting from a literal reading of the text, this work will first take into account the meaning that would be attributed to the treaty at the time of its conclusion. As inferred from the reading of a great number of decisions of international courts and tribunals, the 'ordinary meaning' of a treaty is determined by reference to both every-day and technical language.[91]

At the same time, the reference to 'the object and purpose' of the agreement also implies a teleological argumentation. 'The object and purpose' of an agreement – as a single lexical unit[92] – refers to the reasons for which the treaty exists, to the *raison d'être* of a treaty,[93] as presumably conferred by the original

[88] Art 33 of the VCLT is about interpretation of treaties authenticated in two or more languages.

[89] Under Art 31(2) of the VCLT, 'The context for the purpose of the interpretation of a treaty shall comprise, in addition to the text, including its preamble and annexes: (*a*) any agreement relating to the treaty which was made between all the parties in connection with the conclusion of the treaty; (*b*) any instrument which was made by one or more parties in connection with the conclusion of the treaty and accepted by the other parties as an instrument related to the treaty.
(3) There shall be taken into account, together with the context: (*a*) any subsequent agreement between the parties regarding the interpretation of the treaty or the application of its provisions; (*b*) any subsequent practice in the application of the treaty which establishes the agreement of the parties regarding its interpretation; (*c*) any relevant rules of international law applicable in the relations between the parties.
(4) A special meaning shall be given to a term if it is established that the parties so intended.'

[90] See A Aust, *Modern Treaty Law and Practice* (CUP, 2000) 186. See also, A Watts, *The International Law Commission 1949–1998* Vol II (OUP, 1999) 685. With regard to refugees, more specifically, see *Refugee Appeal no 72668/01*, New Zealand RSAA, 5 April 2002, para 157; *A v Minister for Immigration & Ethnic Affairs*, High Court of Australia (1997) 190 CLR 225 (McHugh J). See also, *Refugee Appeal No 70366/96*, New Zealand RSAA, 5 April 2002, 24 speaking of treaty interpretation as a 'single combined operation'. For a broader discussion on this issue, see JC Hathaway, *The Rights of Refugees under International Law* (CUP, 2005) 49–51; M Foster, *International Refugee Law and Socio-Economic Rights: Refuge from Deprivation* (CUP, 2007) 40–42.

[91] See, eg, *Bankovic and Others v Belgium and Others*, App no 52207/99, Admissibility (12 December 2001) paras 59–62; *Application of the Convention on the Prevention and Punishment of the Crime of Genocide (Bosnia and Herzegovina v Serbia and Montenegro)*, 26 February 2007, ICJ Rep 43, paras 160–162 (Genocide Convention case *Dispute Concerning Filleting within the Gulf of St Lawrence (Canada v France) Arbitral Tribunal established by Agreement of 23 Oct 1985*, Award of 17 July 1986, 19 UNRIAA 225, 82 ILR 590; *James and Others v United Kingdom*, App no 8793/79 (21 February 1986) para 61; *Schiesser v Switzerland*, App no 7710/76 (4 December 1979) para 28. See also, U Linderfalk, *On the Interpretation of Treaties: The Modern International Law as Expressed in the 1969 Vienna Convention on the Law of Treaties* (Springer, 2007).

[92] Linderfalk 2007, n 91 above, 207–09.

[93] O Pessou, ILC's sixteenth session, 765th meeting, *Yearbook of the ILC 1964*, Vol 1, 278, para 45; Villiger 2009, n 80 above, 321.

lawmaker. The intentions of the parties are crucial to determining the 'object and purpose' of a treaty, which is always used in relation to the 'ordinary meaning' as a supplementary second step in the process of interpretation.[94] As 'object and purpose' can vary according to the circumstances,

> if it can be shown that the thing interpreted is a generic referring expression with a referent assumed by the parties to be alterable, then the *telos* of a treaty shall be determined based on the intentions held by the parties at the time when the treaty is interpreted. In all other cases, the *telos* shall be determined based on the intentions held at the time when the treaty was concluded.[95]

Moreover, as held by the International Law Commission (ILC),

> when a treaty is open to two interpretations one of which does and the other does not enable the treaty to have appropriate effects, good faith and the objects and purposes of the treaty demand that the former interpretation be adopted.[96]

Subsequent practice under Article 31(3) of the VCLT can be utilised, especially in its interaction with other means of interpretation, to clarify the meaning of a treaty.[97] As there is no exact number of parties that must actively engage in subsequent practice in order to establish an agreement under Article 31(3)(b), silence on the part of one or more parties can constitute acceptance of the subsequent practice.[98] The ECtHR has relied upon subsequent practice in several cases,[99] although it has always been very cautious in the application of this rule of the VCLT by requiring it to encompass only subsequent practice common to all Parties, and to take into account only that practice which is concordant, common and consistent.[100]

[94] This can be inferred from the *travaux preparatoires* of the VCLT. See Draft Articles with Commentaries, *Yearbook of the ILC 1966* vol II, 221, para 12. Relevant case law includes: *Hirsi Jamaa and Others v Italy*, App no 27765/09 (23 February 2012) paras 171–77; *Genocide Convention case*, paras 167–69; *Legal Consequences of the Construction of a Wall in the Occupied Palestinian Territory* (Advisory Opinion), 9 July 2004, ICJ Rep 136, para 109; *Loizidou v Turkey* App no 15318/89, Preliminary Objections (23 March 1995) para 62; *Legal Consequences for States of the Continued Presence of South Africa in Namibia (West Africa)*, 21 June 1971, ICJ Rep 16, paras 66–67 (*Namibia case*). See also, R Jennings and A Watts, *Oppenheim's International Law* vol 1, 9th edn (Oxford University Press, 1992) 1267; C McLachlan, 'The Principle of Systemic Integration and Article 31(3)(c) of the Vienna Convention' (2005) 54 *ICLQ* 287; Linderfalk 2007, n 91 above, 203.

[95] Linderfalk 2007, n 91 above, 211.

[96] ILC Report 1966, *Yearbook of the ILC 1966*, vol II, 239, para 6.

[97] International Law Commission, *Subsequent agreements and subsequent practice in relation to the interpretation of treaties*, Sixty-sixth session Geneva, 5 May–6 June and 7 July–8 August 2014, http://legal.un.org/docs/?symbol=A/CN.4/L.833.

[98] ibid. For a detailed examination of subsequent practice, see, generally, G Nolte (ed), *Treaties and Subsequent Practice* (OUP, 2013).

[99] See *Soering v United Kingdom*, App no 14038/88 (7 July 1989) paras 102–103; and *Al Saadoon and Mufdhi v United Kingdom*, App no 61498/08 (30 June 2009) para 120; *Hassan v United Kingdom*, App no 29750/09 (16 September 2014) para 100.

[100] See *Hassan v United Kingdom*, ibid, Partly Dissenting Opinion of Judge Spano Joined by Judges Nicolaou, Bianku and Kalaydjieva, para 13.

Pursuant to Article 32 of the VCLT,

> [r]ecourse may be had to supplementary means of interpretation, including the preparatory work of the treaty and the circumstances of its conclusion, in order to confirm the meaning resulting from the application of Article 31, or to determine the meaning when the interpretation according to Article 31: (*a*) leaves the meaning ambiguous or obscure; or (*b*) leads to a result which is manifestly absurd or unreasonable.

These interpretative rules apply to all treaties: each treaty has its own *telos*. Thus, whilst, for example, the purpose of a readmission agreement is to facilitate the arrangements for persons' movement and their readmission between both countries,[101] a different treaty, such as the Genocide Convention, 'was manifestly adopted for a purely humanitarian and civilizing purpose.'[102]

Furthermore, subject to dynamically evolving interpretations, a treaty should be conceived of as a living instrument, particularly in the light of socio-political changes in each era of its existence.[103] In support of this view, the ICJ, in its Advisory Opinion in the *Namibia* case, held that 'an international instrument has to be interpreted and applied within the entire legal system prevailing at the time of the interpretation.'[104] In conclusion, while the intentions of the parties do offer a supplementary means of interpretation, the main methods remain textual, contextual, and teleological.

VIII. THE INTERRELATION BETWEEN INTERNATIONAL REFUGEE LAW AND HUMAN RIGHTS LAW

This work rests on a premise. It is no longer possible to interpret and apply international refugee law (and, more specifically, the 1951 Geneva Convention) in isolation from the texts of international human rights treaties and their relevant case law.[105] As some authors argue, the protection of refugees is a cornerstone of

[101] See, eg, the Preambles to the readmission agreements concluded by the UK with Albania and Algeria.

[102] *Reservations to the Convention on the Prevention and Punishment of the Crime of Genocide (Advisory Opinion)* 28 May 1951, ICJ Rep 15, 23.

[103] R Bernhardt, 'Evolutive Treaty Interpretation, especially of the European Convention on Human Rights' (1999) 42 *German Yearbook of International Law* 12, 21.

[104] *Namibia case*, n 94 above, para 53.

[105] See, eg, T Clark and F Crépeau, 'Mainstreaming Refugee Rights. The 1951 Refugee Convention and International Human Rights Law' (1999) 17(4) *Netherlands Quarterly of Human Rights* 389, 389; V Chetail, 'Are Refugee Rights Human Rights? An Unorthodox Questioning on the Relations between Refugee Law and Human Rights Law' in R Rubio Marin (ed), *Human Rights and Immigration. Collected Courses of the Academy of European Law* (Oxford University Press, 2014) 19 ff. See also, the EXCOM Conclusion no 95 (LIV) on International Protection (10 October 2003) which underlines the 'complementary nature of international refugee and human rights law.'

international human rights law.[106] In this vein, the material and normative scope of the right to *non-refoulement*, the right to access asylum procedures, and the right to an effective remedy will likely be reconstructed through a *systemic interpretation* of the text of the relevant provisions of the Geneva Convention alongside international human rights treaties, and the case law of their monitoring bodies (ECtHR, Committee Against Torture, and Human Rights Committee (HRC)).[107] Such a comprehensive approach is particularly helpful in the context of maritime interceptions/rescue of migrants. As contended in Chapter five, States should indeed prioritise a systemic interpretation of their duties towards migrants and asylum seekers, thus making their border-control measures consistent and compliant with international human rights and refugee standards, as well as with the law of the sea and with their search and rescue obligations.

Despite decisions of international and regional courts and human rights bodies playing a subsidiary role as a source of international law,[108] they still amount to authoritative pronouncements on the law. Although the rules of precedent do not apply to them, international courts and human rights monitoring bodies strive (not always successfully) to both address disputed issues and maintain a certain degree of consistency within their decisions to preserve their credibility vis-à-vis States.[109] International courts and human rights bodies often refer to the practices of one another, thus bringing increasing uniformity in the interpretation of rights and State obligations.

In explaining why human rights law is handled here alongside refugee law (without overlapping), it should be kept in mind that the rights enshrined in the Geneva Convention are subject to a complex 'structure of entitlement', depending upon their relationship with the State in which they are present.[110] Thus, while all refugees falling under the *de jure* or *de facto* jurisdiction of a State party should benefit from a number of core rights, additional and different entitlements may accrue as follows: as soon as they enter a State party's territory; as soon as they are lawfully within that State's territory; when they are lawfully staying within that State's territory, or when they are permanently residing there.[111] Under Article 3, the Geneva Convention applies without discrimination only as to 'race, religion, or country of origin.' In contrast, international

[106] C Costello, 'The Asylum Procedures Directive and the Proliferation of Safe Country Practices: Deterrence, Deflection and the Dismantling of International Protection?' (2005) 7(1) *European Journal of Migration & Law* 35.

[107] Similar methods of parallel aggregate standards have also been adopted by other authors. See, eg, Moreno-Lax 2017, n 28 above, talking of 'integrative approach' in the interpretation of the EU CFR through a method of borrowing of international standards.

[108] See Art 38 of the ICJ Statute.

[109] R Higgins, *Problems and Process: International law and How We Use It* (Clarendon Press, 1995) 202–03.

[110] Hathaway 2005, n 90 above, 154. See also Goodwin-Gill and McAdam 2007, n 20 above, 154–92.

[111] Hathaway 2005, n 90 above, 154–55.

human rights law is not grounded in the concept of nationality or territory, but in the concept of jurisdiction, and as such it pertains to any individuals, without discrimination, by virtue of their *humanity*.[112]

It should also be observed that international human rights conventions have judicial or quasi-judicial treaty monitoring bodies, which can be used as redress mechanisms by both States and individuals whose rights have been violated. No such devices exist under the Geneva Convention, on the basis of which alleged victims may only lodge a complaint to the UNHCR or seek protection under domestic law. Human rights law would also embrace a wider number of potential victims of human rights abuses, since it applies to *all* persons in need of protection, regardless of their refugee status under Article 1(a)(2) of the Geneva Convention.

The concept of '*non-refoulement*' embodied in Article 33 of the Geneva Convention is less broad than the one found within the human rights treaties, which, therefore, stand as a bulwark against reliance on the regime of exceptions set forth in Article 33(2) of the Geneva Convention.[113] For those States parties to the Geneva Convention that have also ratified more expansive international human rights treaties, exclusion from refugee status – even when an individual is considered a threat to national security of the destination State – shall always be applied restrictively, bearing in mind that Article 33(2) exceptions can never be invoked when non-derogable human rights are concerned.[114]

The limitations of the Geneva Convention persuaded international human rights bodies to rely on relevant treaties to establish complementary forms of protection to be afforded to individuals falling outside the scope of the international refugee protection regime. By extending the basis of protection well beyond persecution to multiple situations in which serious harm is likely to be suffered, human rights law contributes to filling in the gaps created by the Geneva Convention, thus strengthening and reinforcing the overall safeguards afforded to individuals in need of protection outside their country of origin or habitual residence.[115]

[112] A Edwards, 'Human Security and the Rights of Refugees: Transcending Territorial and Disciplinary Borders' (2009) 30(3) *Michigan Journal of International Law* 763, 793. This work takes human rights as a bulwark and recognises the key role played by monitoring bodies, in particular the ECtHR, in advancing the protection of migrants and refugees in Europe. Notwithstanding this, it is aware of a vast body of literature which critically questions the nature and function of human rights law. While recognising the value of these arguments, an analysis of these theories will be beyond the remit of this book. See, *inter alia*, N Perugini and N Gordon, *The Human Right to Dominate* (OUP, 2015).

[113] Under Art 33(2) of the Geneva Convention, the principle of *non-refoulement* 'may not ... be claimed by a refugee whom there are reasonable grounds for regarding as a danger to the security of the country in which he is, or who, having been convicted by a final judgment of a particularly serious crime, constitutes a danger to the community of that country.'

[114] See Chapter 2 on the relevant jurisprudence of international human rights bodies. See also, *Hirsi v Italy*, above n 94, Concurring Opinion of Judge Pinto de Albuquerque 42.

[115] Edwards 2009, n 112 above, 795.

While offering crucial protections to migrants and refugees in the phases of both admission and readmission, the ECtHR might also be particularly deferential to State migration control prerogatives. As reiterated in Chapter two, particular attention will be placed here on the ECtHR due to its well-developed and abundant case law concerning migrants, refugees, and extraterritorial application of the relevant Convention. Lessons from the Court could also influence, *mutatis mutandis*, other international human rights regimes. The comprehensive approach of the international human rights bodies – especially the ECtHR – to the recognition of refugee rights and State obligations contributes to painting the content of '*protection*' as a mosaic composed of diverse but still-matching pieces. In order to be effective, protection must comprise not only guarantees of *non-refoulement*, but also the two procedural rights to access asylum procedures *and* effective remedies before removal.

IX. THE PROTECTION OF HUMAN RIGHTS IN EU LAW

The European paradigm of human rights protection constitutes a system whereby the coexistence of a plurality of domestic, international, and supranational regimes is engaged in promoting and safeguarding human rights and fundamental freedoms. Over past decades, we have witnessed more and more national courts seeking guidance from the judgments of international and supranational courts when ruling on substantive legal issues concerning human rights. At the same time, international and supranational courts have also, even more frequently, relied on domestic jurisprudence through a dialogic, interactive process.

Although EU law is not the focus of this work,[116] some considerations remain noteworthy. The autonomy and normative strength of EU law cannot be ignored considering that international human rights bodies do not have exclusive interpretive authority over human rights issues, and that the relevant legal regimes are not in any hierarchical relationship with each other. Beyond the salience of the Charter of Fundamental Rights (CFR) – which enshrines specific rights, such as the right to asylum – it should be stressed that the role of the Court of

[116] EU asylum law and the rights of protection seekers have already been thoroughly addressed in recent literature. See, eg, S Peers, E Guild and J Tomkin (eds), *EU Immigration and Asylum Law (Text and Commentary): Volume 1: Visas and Border Controls* (Brill, 2014); F Cherubini, *Asylum Law in the European Union* (Routledge, 2014); Reneman 2014, n 28 above; H O'Nions, *Asylum – A Right Denied. A Critical Analysis of European Asylum Policy* (Ashgate, 2014); C Bauloz, M Ineli-Ciger, S Singer and V Stoyanova, *Seeking Asylum in the European Union: Selected Protection Issues Raised by the Second Phase of the Common European Asylum System* (Brill, 2016); C Costello, *The Human Rights of Migrants and Refugees in European Law* (OUP, 2016); V Chetail, P De Bruycker and F Maiani, *Reforming the Common European Asylum System: The New European Refugee Law* (Brill, 2016); K Hailbronner and D Thym (ed), *EU Immigration and Asylum Law: A Commentary*. 2nd edn (CH Beck, 2016); Moreno-Lax 2017, n 28 above.

Justice of the EU (CJEU) is autonomous: the Court gives its own interpretation of refugee law and human rights law.[117] Moreover, when compared with international human rights monitoring bodies – which tend to accommodate States' migration control imperatives – the EU domain is characterised by a more balanced sharing of competencies in the field of migration, 'horizontally with other States and vertically with EU authorities.'[118]

While the relationship between the ECJ/CJEU and the ECtHR has not always been fully coherent, it seems to be governed by mutually cooperative interactions. On different occasions, the ECJ has tackled the same human rights as are set out in the ECHR.[119] It is also to be noted that the accession of the European Union to the ECHR has its legal basis in Article 59(2), as amended by Protocol 14 to the Convention, which entered into force on 1 June 2010. The accession became a legal obligation under Article 6 of the Treaty of the European Union (TEU), which provides that the EU will accede to the ECHR, recognises the rights and principles set out in the EU CFR, and affirms that 'fundamental rights, as guaranteed by the European Convention for the Protection of Human Rights and Fundamental Freedoms and as they result from the constitutional traditions common to the Member States, shall constitute general principles of the Union's law.'[120]

However, in its long-awaited *Opinion 2/13* (delivered on 18 December 2014),[121] the ECJ concluded that the Draft EU Accession Agreement – a treaty designed to take into consideration the shared human rights obligations of the

[117] See, eg, the *Elgafaji* case, where the CJEU holds that 'Article 15(c) of the [Qualification] Directive is a provision, the content of which is different from that of Article 3 of the ECHR, and the interpretation of which must, therefore, be carried out independently, although with due regard for fundamental rights, as they are guaranteed under the ECHR' (para 28). Moreover, the Court expand the scope of protection by submitting that a personal risk when the 'degree of indiscriminate violence [...] reaches such a high level that substantial grounds are shown for believing that a civilian [...] would solely on account of his presence on the territory of that country or region, face a real risk of being subject to the serious threat' (para 35). For further discussion on *Meki Elgafaji and Noor Elgafaji v Staatssecretaris van Justitie*, Case C-465/07 ECLI:EU:C:2009:94, see Chapter 2 of this book.

[118] Costello, for instance, speaks of the transformative potential of the EU, which has moved from mere 'passive receiver' of human rights to 'standard setter', particularly with regard to admission-seekers, See Costello 2016, n 116 above, 9–14.

[119] See, eg, *Parliament v Council*, Case C-540/03 [2006] ECR I-5769, para 104; *Mary Carpenter v Home Secretary*, Case C-60/00 [2002] ECR I-6279; *Home Secretary v Acene Akrich*, Case C-109/01 [2003] ECR I-9607; and *Georgios Orfanopoulos and Others v Land Baden-Württemberg* and *Raffaele Oliveri v Land Baden-Württemberg*, Joined Cases C-482 and 493/01 [2004] ECR I-5257.

[120] Pursuant to Art 2 of the TEU, '[the] Union is founded on the values of respect for human dignity, freedom, democracy, equality, the rule of law and respect for human rights, including the rights of persons belonging to minorities.' Additionally, Art 21(1) of the TEU reads that: '[the] Union's action on the international scene shall be guided by the principles which have inspired its own creation, development and enlargement, and which it seeks to advance in the wider world: democracy, the rule of law, the universality and indivisibility of human rights and fundamental freedoms, respect for human dignity, the principles of equality and solidarity, and respect for the principles of the United Nations Charter and international law.'

[121] *Opinion 2/13*, [2014] ECLI:EU:C:2014:2454.

EU and its Member States under the ECHR[122] – was not compatible with EU law. While discussing the relationship between EU and ECHR legal regimes is not the purpose of this work, it should be observed that this Opinion has immediately attracted much criticism[123] – and has brought accession to a standstill.

The EU CFR merits mention here, as it sets out a wide range of civil, juridical, economic and social rights, and has become legally binding via the Lisbon Treaty on 1 December 2009.[124] The incorporation of the CFR in the Treaty of Lisbon expands the power of the CJEU to interpret whether both the EU institutions and Member States are following human rights standards in making and implementing EU law, respectively.[125] Indeed, while the Charter will certainly apply to EU institutions, it only applies to the Member States when they implement EU law.

Additionally, the Lisbon Treaty also extends the CJEU's jurisdiction over asylum and immigration policy,[126] providing for the gradual introduction of an integrated management system for external borders,[127] and empowering the EU to develop common policies for asylum and immigration.[128] With regards to the legal effect of the Charter, it ranks now as primary Union Law and compliance with it has become a requirement for the validity and legality of the EU's secondary

[122] On accession, see generally, T Lock, 'End of an Epic? The Draft Accession Agreement on the EU's Accession to the ECHR' (2012) 31(1) *Yearbook of European Law* 162; V Kosta, N Skoutaris, and V Tzevelekos (eds), *The EU Accession to the ECHR* (Hart Publishing, 2014).

[123] See, eg, S Peers, 'The CJEU and the EU's Accession to the ECHR: A Clear and Present Danger to Human Rights Protection', *EU Law Analysis*, 18 December 2014; S Douglas Scott, 'The Relationship between the EU and the ECHR Five Years on from the Treaty of Lisbon' in S de Vries, U Bernitz, and S Weatherill (eds), *The EU Charter of Fundamental Rights as a Binding Instrument: Five Years Old and Growing* (Hart Publishing, 2015).

[124] Treaty of Lisbon amending the Treaty on European Union and the Treaty establishing the European Community, signed at Lisbon, 13 Dec 2007, entered into force, 1 December 2009.

[125] The incidence of human rights adjudication before the CJEU has significantly increased with the adoption of the Charter as a binding legal instrument. See G de Búrca, 'After the EU Charter of Fundamental Rights: The Court of Justice as a Human Rights Adjudicator?' (2013) 20(2) *Maastricht Journal of European and Comparative Law* 168–184. See also, Migration Watch UK, *The Lisbon European Reform Treaty Impact on Asylum and Immigration Policy*, http://www.migrationwatchuk.org/briefingPaper/document/82. The Protocol on the Application of the Charter of Fundamental Rights of the European Union to Poland and to the United Kingdom states that 'nothing in Title IV of the Charter creates justiciable rights applicable to Poland or the United Kingdom, except in so far as Poland or the United Kingdom has provided for such rights in its national law' (Art 1(2)). To read more on the contribution of the CJEU to the evolution of the CEAS, see E Tsourdi, 'What Role for the Court of Justice of the EU in the Development of a European Asylum Policy? The Case of Loss and Denial of International Protection in the EU' (2012) 2(3) *Tijdschrift voor Bestuurswetenschappen en Publiekrecht* 212.

[126] As, at the time of writing, the UK is still part of the EU, despite the result of the 2016 referendum on 'Brexit', it should be considered that ECJ's jurisdiction in immigration, asylum and civil law applies equally to all Member States, including the UK and Ireland, but only in so far as they have opted into the legislation. See S Peers, 'UK and Irish Opt-outs from EU Justice and Home Affairs (JHA) Law' *Statewatch Analysis* No 4, *EU Lisbon Treaty* (26 June 2009) 12, http://www.statewatch.org/news/2009/jun/uk-ireland-analysis-no-4-lisbon-opt-outs.pdf.

[127] See Art 62(1)(c), Chapter 2 under Title IV of the Lisbon Treaty.

[128] ibid, Art 63. The Lisbon Treaty brings Visas, Asylum and Immigration together with all matters on police cooperation and on civil and criminal law into a shared competence, now entitled 'Area of Freedom, Security and Justice' which constitutes the Title IV of Part III of the Lisbon Treaty.

legislation within the field of asylum. As established in Article 51 of the Charter, its scope of application is limited to the areas in which Member States are implementing Union Law and it 'does not establish any new power or task for the Community or the Union, or modify powers and tasks defined by the Treaties.'[129]

Pursuant to Article 52(4) of the Charter,

> insofar as this Charter contains rights, which correspond to rights guaranteed by the Convention for the Protection of Human Rights and Fundamental Freedoms, the meaning and scope of those rights shall be the same as those laid down by the said Convention. This provision shall not prevent Union law from providing more extensive protection.[130]

Therefore, the provisions of the Charter shall be interpreted and applied in accordance with ECHR principles as determined by the jurisprudence of the Courts of Strasbourg and Luxembourg. Other international human rights instruments can be considered sources of inspiration for provisions of the Charter. According to Article 53,

> Nothing in this Charter shall be interpreted as restricting or adversely affecting human rights and fundamental freedoms as recognized, in their respective fields of application, by Union law and international law and by international agreements to which the Union or all the Member States are party, including the European Convention for the Protection of Human Rights and Fundamental Freedoms, and by the Member States' constitutions.

Article 53 indicates how the Charter tends to expand rather than restrict human rights protection within the Union by recognising the relevance of international agreements to which Member States are a party, and interpreting and enhancing human rights principles as enshrined in the Charter itself. Moreover, human rights protection within the EU area is also enhanced by the EU's approach to jurisdiction. Being functional rather than territorial, Article 51 requires Member States to adhere to their EU fundamental rights obligations whenever they act within the scope of EU law,[131] even in extra-territorial contexts.[132]

It is also important to note that, on 12 June 2013, the European Parliament voted for the final adoption of the recast of the EU directives and regulations on asylum, with an obligation for States to transpose these new provisions into

[129] Art 6(1) TEU as amended by the Lisbon Treaty also states that the Charter 'does not extend in any way the competences of the Union as defined in the Treaties.'

[130] According to the 'Explanations' to Art 52, '[t]he reference to the ECHR covers both the Convention and the Protocols to it. The meaning and the scope of the guaranteed rights are determined not only by the text of those instruments, but also by the case law of the European Court of Human Rights and by the Court of Justice of the European Union. The last sentence of the paragraph is designed to allow the Union to guarantee more extensive protection. In any event, the level of protection afforded by the Charter may never be lower than that guaranteed by the ECHR.' See 'Explanations relating to the Charter of Fundamental Rights' (2007/C 303/02).

[131] See, Explanations to Art 51 EU CFR. 'Explanations relating to the Charter of Fundamental Rights' (2007/C 303/02) OJ C/303/17.

[132] C Costello, 'Courting Access to Asylum in Europe: Recent Supranational Jurisprudence Explored' (2012) 12(2) *Human Rights Law Review* 307.

their respective national legal frameworks within two years.[133] This work will occasionally refer to the text of the Asylum Directives, and will mainly rely on EU law when providing a background of the description of the legal instruments that apply to the rights of refugees in the European context. Although the reader could expect a more thorough analysis of the EU legal framework, this book is primarily about the standards of protection offered by international refugee and human rights law, in particular the ECHR. Nevertheless, EU law human rights principles are, in many cases, part and parcel of those standards and are discussed here where and when it is appropriate to do so. As stated above, EU law constitutes an additional regime of refugee protection, having the CJEU engaged in dialogue and interaction with international refugee and human rights law, of which it gives its own interpretation. However, attention is here shifted away from the CJEU and the EU legal regime, which – as stated above – has already received substantive scholarly attention in recent migration-related books, and is instead primarily focused on international refugee and human rights treaties and the case law of the relevant monitoring bodies.

X. CONCLUSION

Prompted by the disquieting discourses and current practices on maritime interception, port closure to vulnerable groups, criminalisation of migrants, and the swift removal of asylum seekers to allegedly 'safe third countries', this work primarily aims to investigate whether the implementation of bilateral agreements linked to readmission can hamper access to international protection. It will thus contribute to defining the contours of human rights and refugee law obligations binding States in territorial and extraterritorial operative contexts, engaging with issues that remain highly contested, not least the notion of jurisdiction and responsibility in cases of 'contactless' migration controls.

Speaking of *diversification* and *informalisation* of cooperative tools, this book aims to add clarity to the 'readmission' discourse, which has often been fraught with a certain level of confusion and partiality in both its terminology and substance. It broadens the legal analysis beyond standard readmission agreements to encompass a wider range of interstate accords whose unifying theme is both the facilitation of the removal of irregular migrants with no status or right to stay within European territory, and the prevention of arrivals by outsourcing migration controls, push-backs, and, indirectly, responsibilities relating to refugees. Concrete proposals are offered here to amend the texts of readmission agreements, and to contest both the use of diplomatic assurances with countries that resort to degrading treatments towards prisoners, and migrants' push-backs at sea, whether individually or by proxy.

[133] For an extensive analysis of the recasting process, see F Ippolito and S Velluti, 'The Recast Process of the EU Asylum System: A Balancing Act between Efficiency and Fairness' (2011) 30(3) *Refugee Survey Quarterly* 24.

2

Refugees' Admission and Readmission: International and European Protection Obligations

> Human rights law is important for asylum seekers because the focus on humanity transcends nationality in the construction of protection. The discourse of human rights envisages a community of entitlement based on notions of personhood rather than status.[1]

I. INTRODUCTION

In certain operative scenarios, especially in situations of extraterritorial migration controls, the practices of admission and readmission overlap. Through the lens of international human rights and refugee law, this chapter explores the scope of the relevant international refugee and human rights protection standards binding European States each time they deal with the admission or readmission of refugees. The relevant international human rights and refugee law instruments – found at two different levels and concurrently in force in every European State – encompass: at United Nations level, the 1951 Convention relating to the Status of Refugees (Geneva Convention) and its 1967 Protocol, the UN Convention against Torture (CAT), and the International Covenant on Civil and Political Rights (ICCPR); and, at the Council of Europe level, the 1950 European Convention on Human Rights and Fundamental Freedoms (ECHR).

The main question this work grapples with is whether the implementation of bilateral agreements linked to readmission may hamper refugees' access to protection, which is understood here as the combination of the foundational principle of *non-refoulement* (either direct or indirect) and two correlated procedural entitlements: the right to access asylum procedures and the right to an effective remedy before removal. This chapter will investigate whether these core international and European legal norms apply to individuals transferred

[1] C Harvey, *Seeking Asylum in the UK, Problems and Prospects* (Butterworths, 2000) 35.

(or about to be transferred) to countries of origin or transit whilst seeking protection within the territory of a European State, at its borders, or even on the high seas. Even though the above-mentioned spectrum of rights is not meant to be exhaustive, these legal principles can, however, be regarded as the primary international obligations applying to refugees (regardless of whether their status has been recognised or not) in the phase of arrival at, and expulsion from, the State of destination (or even at sea) to third countries.

A comprehensive analysis of the different interpretative approaches used to reconstruct the meaning, scope, and legal content of these international human rights principles would exceed the reach of this work. Rather, the primary aim is to draw a general overview of the above-mentioned international and European human rights law principles. The existence of a clear legal framework is particularly important when decisions are taken at the border, in transit zones, or beyond territorial borders with regard to an asylum seeker who is seeking to enter or has entered irregularly into a European State's territory.

These rights constitute the normative framework of this work, and are helpful in exploring how the international human rights legal regime both governs and restrains the unfolding State practices of formal and informal readmission, thereby linking Chapter two with the rest of the book. As they have already been the object of scholarly attention,[2] this work will mainly focus on the convoluted issue of extraterritorial application of human rights treaties and the element of 'effective control' in the exercise of jurisdiction, especially when *refoulement* occurs via 'contactless' migration controls beyond borders. It will also examine how the Strasbourg Court has construed and interpreted the right to an effective remedy, and the extent to which this might work towards filling the gaps in international law that stem from the absence of clear-cut provisions on the right to access asylum procedures. In portraying these two rights as complementary, it will also be shown how the right to access asylum procedures has become a fundamental procedural corollary to the principle of *non-refoulement*.

Additionally, the international jurisprudence on *non-refoulement* and the right to an effective remedy examined here also draws on cases of expulsion/extradition where the third-country national is not necessarily an asylum seeker – so long as they are functional in terms of defining the content of these rights. As stated in Chapter one, a thorough analysis of the EU legal regime of refugee protection is not the purpose of this work. However, this book recognises the

[2] See, inter alia, F De Weck, Non-Refoulement under the European Convention on Human Rights and the UN Convention Against Torture: The Assessment of Individual Complaints (Brill, 2014); M Reneman, *EU Asylum Procedures and the Right to an Effective Remedy* (Hart Publishing, 2014) 53–71; G Clayton, '"The right to have rights": The European convention on human rights and the procedural rights of asylum seekers', in A Abass and F Ippolito (eds), *Regional approaches to the protection of asylum seekers: An international legal perspective* (Ashgate, 2014) 191–211; E Hamdan, *The principle of non-refoulement under the ECHR and the UN Convention against Torture and Other Cruel, Inhuman or Degrading Treatment or Punishment* (Brill, 2016); V Moreno-Lax, *Accessing Asylum in Europe* (OUP, 2017) 247–460.

salience of EU law in the protection of fundamental rights and does not refrain from referring to the EU asylum directives and the EU Charter of Fundamental Rights (CFR), as well as select cases; it does not however, delve too far into the thriving jurisprudence of the ECJ and the CJEU.

Part 1
Refugee Rights before Removal

II. THE RIGHT TO *NON-REFOULEMENT*: INTRODUCTION

Non-refoulement is presented here as an overarching term: beyond its meaning in the 1951 Geneva Convention, this principle is constructed and understood through diverse international human rights treaties, which either explicitly or implicitly prohibit the removal of a person to a territory where she can suffer torture and other inhuman and degrading treatment, or where her life and liberty can be seriously threatened for reasons beyond the five grounds of persecution set out in Article 33(1) of the Geneva Convention.[3] Whereas the Geneva Convention constitutes the necessary entry point, the ICCPR, the CAT, and the ECHR contribute, as mutually reinforcing instruments, to the description of the content of *non-refoulement*. The EU CFR is also relevant. Bearing in mind that protection obligations towards refugees and asylum seekers generally flow from implicit or explicit prohibitions of *refoulement*, this book questions whether the aforementioned international instruments can be complementary to the construction of a regime of refugee protection, and whether they should be read consistently with one another.

Whilst the arguments supporting the peremptory nature of *non-refoulement* are less than compelling, State practice, since the adoption of the 1951 Geneva Convention, has provided persuasive evidence that the principle has achieved the status of customary international law.[4] Nevertheless, the customary status of

[3] According to Article 33(1) of the 1951 Geneva Convention, 'no contracting State shall expel or return a refugee in any manner whatsoever to the frontiers of territories where his life or freedom would be threatened on account of his race, religion, nationality, membership of a particular social group or political opinion.'

[4] The customary status of *non-refoulement* has also been endorsed by several scholars, including: E Lauterpacht and D Bethlehem, 'The Scope and Content of the Principle of *Non-refoulement*: Opinion' in E Feller, V Türk and F Nicholson (eds), *Refugee Protection in International Law: UNHCR's Global Consultations on International Protection* (Cambridge University Press, 2003); W Schabas, *Non-refoulement, Human Rights and International Cooperation in Counter-terrorism* (Liechtenstein, 2006) 7; A Duffy, 'Expulsion to Face Torture? *Non Refoulement* in International Law' (2008) 20(3) *International Journal of Refugee Law (IJRL)* 389; GS Goodwin-Gill and J McAdam, *The Refugee in International Law* (OUP, 2007); S Trevisanut, 'The Principle of *Non-Refoulement* at Sea' (2008) 12 *Max Planck UNYB* 218. See also the following cases: *Hirsi Jamaa and Others v Italy*, App no 27765/09 (23 February 2012); Inter-American Commission on Human Rights, *Haitian Centre for Human Rights* et al *v United States of America*, Decision of the Commission as to the merits of Case 10.675 United States, 13 March 1997.

this norm has been fiercely contested, not least by some of the scholarship that stresses how attention should be paid to, for example, those States in Asia and the Near East that have decided to not be formally bound by the *non-refoulement* obligation, and indeed to all of those countries that have opted to not accede to either the Geneva Convention or the 1967 Protocol.[5]

If the prohibition of *refoulement*, embodied in treaty law, is binding upon all EU Member States, it needs to be verified whether, as a matter of customary law, this principle is also binding on those few countries that have not ratified relevant international instruments on the protection of refugees. Indeed, all EU Member States are parties to the Geneva Convention and its Protocol, which are now regarded as part of the *acquis communautaire*. Outside the European framework, the 1969 Organization for African Unity Convention Governing Specific Aspects of Refugee Problems in Africa (OAU Convention) and the Cartagena Declaration on Refugees have contributed to enlarging the core meaning of the 'refugee' notion as a matter of customary international law.[6]

The existence of *non-refoulement* as a conventional principle, enshrined in different legal instruments, does not preclude the creation of a custom of similar content, and can also contribute to the formulation of such a customary principle. In the *North Sea Continental Shelf* case,[7] the ICJ identified three elements relevant to such a process of crystallising customary rules into the general *corpus* of international law.[8] Moreover, in the *Nicaragua* case, the ICJ held that 'it is not to be expected that in the practice of States, the application of the [rule] in question should have been perfect …'[9] The Court has not found that, for a principle to be established as customary, the corresponding practice must be in absolute and rigorous conformity with the rule. To deduce the existence of customary norms, the Court deems it sufficient that the conduct of States is generally consistent with such norms: it treats instances of State conduct inconsistent with a given rule as amounting to breaches of the existing principle, not as an indication of the recognition of a new rule.[10]

[5] K Hailbronner, 'Non-refoulement and 'Humanitarian' Refugees: Customary International Law or Wishful Legal Thinking?' in D Martin (ed), *The New Asylum Seekers: Refugee Law in the 1980s* (Martinus Nijhoff Publishers, 1988) 128–29; JC Hathaway, *The Rights of Refugees under International Law* (CUP, 2005) 363–70.

[6] GS Goodwin-Gill, '*Non-refoulement* and the New Asylum Seekers' (1986) 26 *Virginia Journal of International Law* 897, 902. Cartagena Declaration on Refugees, 22 November 1984.

[7] *North Sea Continental Shelf (Germany v Denmark)*, 20 February 1969, ICJ Rep 3.

[8] Firstly, the conventional norm 'should be of a fundamentally norm-creating character such as could be regarded as forming the basis of a general rule of law'; secondly, 'a very widespread and representative participation in the convention might suffice of itself, provided it included that of States whose interests are specially affected'; thirdly, 'State practice, including that of States whose interests are specially affected, should be both extensive and virtually uniform in the sense of the provision invoked – and should moreover have occurred in such a way as to show a general recognition that a rule of law or legal obligation is involved' (paras 72–74). For the purpose of this work, especially affected States are those nations which are most engaged in refugee-related issues, being either the States of refuge or the countries of origin or transit of migratory flows.

[9] *Military and Paramilitary Activities against Nicaragua (Merits)*, 26 June 1986, ICJ Rep 14, para 186.

[10] ibid.

With regard to the requirement of State support to the norm of *non-refoulement*, it should be observed that there exists a near universal acceptance of the principle, which goes further than a simple 'widespread and representative' participation in international conventions embodying the putative customary rule. At present, the majority of the 192 Members of the UN have ratified one or more binding international documents implicitly or explicitly incorporating the principle of *non-refoulement*.[11] Since these figures encompass those States whose interests are specifically affected by refugee-related issues, and *no State*, including the remaining UN members, has objected to the principle of *non-refoulement*, it can be concluded that around 90 per cent of UN membership has consented to the existence of such a norm.[12] Looking more specifically at the European context, all EU Member States are party to the Geneva Convention, the 1967 Protocol, the ICCPR, the CAT, the ECHR, and the CFR, which either directly or indirectly proscribe *refoulement*.

Over the last 70 years, no State has formally or informally opposed the principle, and even non-signatory States, such as Bangladesh, India, Pakistan and Thailand, have hosted large numbers of refugees, often in mass influx situations.[13] It is interesting to note how approached governments have generally reacted by indicating national acceptance of the principle of *non-refoulement* as guiding their actions. These States have frequently sought to provide additional explanations or justifications of their practices that have been inconsistent with the norm, by challenging, for instance, the refugee status of the individual concerned or by invoking issues of national security and public order. As held by the UNHCR itself, 'the fact that States have found it necessary to provide such explanations or justifications can reasonably be regarded as an implicit confirmation of their acceptance of the principle.'[14]

At the international law level, the practice of States on *non-refoulement* is fairly uniform: in a few cases, however, governments have shown their inability to manage mass influxes of refugees and have adopted restrictive measures toward asylum seekers.[15] Yet, in none of these cases have States publicly expressed an

[11] Reference is made only to conventions of a universal character: the 1951 Convention, the 1967 Protocol, the Convention Against Torture, and the ICCPR.

[12] These figures do not include States such as Switzerland and the Holy See, which are not members of the UN. However, while Switzerland has ratified the 1951 Geneva Convention, the 1967 Protocol, the ECHR and the ICCPR and the CAT, the Holy See is party to the 1951 Convention and the 1967 Protocol.

[13] Of the same view also the UNHCR, 'Advisory Opinion on the Extraterritorial Application of *Non-Refoulement* Obligations under the 1951 Convention relating to the Status of Refugees and its 1967 Protocol' (26 January 2007) 7, http://www.refworld.org/docid/45f17a1a4.html.

[14] UNHCR, *The Principle of Non-refoulement as a Norm of Customary International Law*, https://www.refworld.org/docid/437b6db64.html.

[15] For instance, in 1995 the government of Tanzania closed its borders to a group of more 50,000 Rwandan refugees, justifying such a measure on grounds of regional tensions, national security, and serious risks to the environment. The same fate was met by Liberian refugees who, fleeing a brutal civil war in 1996, were denied access by numerous West African ports, including Ghana, Ivory Coast, and Togo.

unwillingness to respect the principle or to abide by such a duty. On the contrary, they have only referred to their inability to shelter refugees for a number of domestic reasons. The fact that governments offer such justifications demonstrates that they recognise that the *non-refoulement* obligation exists, and that their actions were in breach of human rights law and international law more generally.

Recognising the customary status of *non-refoulement* is essential for acknowledging how even those States which are not formally bound by any specific convention, are still not free of their customary international legal obligations toward refugees. In other words, such States are obliged to not expel or extradite any person to a territory where her life or freedom would be seriously threatened. This principle is paramount in any case of readmission/deportation/interception (as discussed in the following chapters), and applies also when transfers are undertaken outside of a bilateral legal framework that explicitly refers to *non-refoulement*. Furthermore, customary international law can be useful either to complement or supplement national legislation on *non-refoulement*, and to enable national courts to apply norms of general international law on the treatment of refugees when there is no national legislation on the matter. All in all, the extensive participation of States in international human rights and refugee law instruments confirms the wide acceptance of *non-refoulement* as a customary international law principle, which has, therefore gradually moved beyond treaty law.

Non-refoulement has developed within two distinct contexts: international refugee law and human rights law. It is the intersection of these two contexts that shapes the content of this principle. In relation to refugee law, the meaning of *non-refoulement* concerns the interpretation of Article 33 of the 1951 Convention whereby, 'no Contracting State shall expel or return ('*refouler*') a refugee in any manner whatsoever to the frontiers of territories where his life or freedom would be threatened ....' State practice and international jurisprudence have both endorsed the meaning of *non-refoulement* as prohibiting expulsion and non-admittance at the border[16] resulting in the risk of persecution, threat to life, physical integrity, or liberty, or to a real risk of torture, cruel, inhuman, and degrading treatment or punishment. The prohibition of *refoulement* is valid even in those cases in which refugees are sent back to a country where they are exposed to the peril of being subsequently transferred to another territory in which they would face serious risks to their own life.[17]

[16] For example, the OAU Convention expressly excludes rejection at the frontier in Article 2(3). Pursuant to the UN Declaration on Territorial Asylum, no refugee 'shall be subjected to measures such as rejection at the frontier ....' See UN Declaration on Territorial Asylum (1967), GA Resolution 2312 (XXII); EXCOM Conclusion no 6 (XXVIII) on *Non-Refoulement* (12 October 1977) and EXCOM Conclusion no 85 (XLIX) on International Protection (9 October 1998). For a deeper analysis, see Goodwin-Gill 1986, n 6 above, 901.

[17] On the prohibition of indirect *refoulement*, see, *R v SSHD, ex parte Bugdaycay*, 19 February 1986, [1987] 1 AC 514, para 532 D, confirmed by *R v SSHD, ex parte Yogathas*, 18 October 2002, [2002] UKHL 36.

Although global State practice is not homogeneous, in some circumstances, States have offered protection from threats originating outside the five grounds of persecution recognised by Article 1(a) of the Geneva Convention.[18] It has therefore been argued that 'in keeping with the humanitarian objective of the Convention, the protective regime of Article 33(1) must be construed liberally in a manner that favours the widest possible scope of protection consistent with its terms.'[19]

III. THE LEGAL CONTENT OF *NON-REFOULEMENT* IN INTERNATIONAL HUMAN RIGHTS LAW

Whilst the 1951 Convention provides a set of exceptions on the grounds of overriding reasons of national security and public safety,[20] developments in the field of human rights law show a tendency to prohibit any derogation from the principle of *non-refoulement* where it results in the transfer of a person to a country where there is a risk of being subjected to serious human rights violations, particularly arbitrary loss of life,[21] torture, or other cruel, inhuman or degrading treatment or punishment.[22] Attention is here mainly on the absolute prohibition of torture as bar to *refoulement*, even in cases of exclusion from refugee status.[23]

[18] Guarantees of *non-refoulement* have been granted, for instance, to persons who have a well-founded fear of facing serious threats to their life or freedom as a result of an armed conflict or generalised violence if they were removed to their home country. JC Hathaway and CJ Harvey, 'Framing Refugee Protection in the New World Disorder' (2001) 34 *Cornell Journal of International Law* 289. For more recent literature, see, J-F Durieux, 'Of War, Flows, Laws and Flaws: A Reply to Hugo Storey' (2012) 31(3) *Refugee Survey Quarterly* 161; S Juss, 'Problematizing the Protection of "War Refugees": A Rejoinder to Hugo Storey and Jean-François Durieux' (2013) 32(1) *Refugee Survey Quarterly* 122.

Under Art 15 of the EU Recast Qualification Directive, 'serious harm' includes any 'serious and individual threat to a civilian's life or person by reason of indiscriminate violence in situations of international or internal armed conflict.' See H Lambert, 'The Next Frontier: Expanding Protection in Europe for Victims of Armed Conflict and Indiscriminate Violence' (2013) 24(2) *IJRL* 207; M Fullerton, 'A Tale of Two Decades: War Refugees and Asylum Policies in the European Union' (2011) 10 *Washington University Global Studies Law Review* 87, 121–31.

[19] Lauterpacht and Bethlehem 2003, n 4 above, 125. See also, EXCOM General Conclusion no 29 (XXXIV) on International Protection (1983) para (b); EXCOM General Conclusion on International Protection nos 79 (XLVII) 1996 and 81 (XLVIII) 1997, paras (j) and (i).

[20] See, eg, Art 33(2) whereby the benefits of *non-refoulement* 'may not … be claimed by a refugee whom there are reasonable grounds for regarding as a danger to the security of the country in which he is, or who, having been convicted by a final judgment of a particularly serious crime, constitutes a danger to the community of that country.'

[21] The right to life is enshrined, for example, in Art 6 of the ICCPR and Art 2 of the ECHR.

[22] The right to be free from torture is guaranteed under Art 1 of the CAT, which, in Art 16, also prohibits other cruel, inhuman or degrading treatment or punishment. A prohibition of torture and other cruel, inhuman or degrading treatment or punishment is provided by Art 7 of the ICCPR and Art 3 of the ECHR.

[23] FM Menendez, 'Recent Jurisprudence of the United Nations Committee Against Torture and the International Protection of Refugees' (2015) 34(1) *Refugee Survey Quarterly* 2015, 69.

Article 3(1) of the CAT explicitly provides that 'no State Party shall expel, return ('refouler') or extradite a person to another State where there are substantial grounds for believing that he would be in danger of being subjected to torture.' The present risk does not have to meet the test of being highly probable: it must however be 'foreseeable, real, and personal.'[24] According to the Committee, the prohibition on *refoulement* is non-derogable and applies in all circumstances,[25] including cases concerning terrorism.[26] Moreover, the Committee has asserted that the phrase 'another State' in Article 3 implies the extension of protection from expulsion to any country whence that individual may subsequently be 'expelled, returned, or extradited' onwards to another dangerous State.[27]

So far, the Committee Against Torture has received a huge number of communications (under Article 22 of the CAT) by asylum seekers falling outside of the scope of the Geneva Convention's persecution grounds. In many of these cases, it found that the forcible removal of the applicants would breach the prohibition of *refoulement*, enshrined in Article 3 of the Convention,[28] where the individual

On the finding of torture excluding removal in extradition cases, see, *Yousri Ktiti v Morocco*, Comm no 419/2010 (26 May 2011) UN Doc CAT/C/46/D/419/2010; and *Alexey Kalinichenko v Morocco*, Comm no 428/2010 (25 November 2011) UN Doc CAT/C/47/D/ 428/2010.

[24] In the following cases concerning asylum seekers challenging a deportation order, the Committee concluded that the existence of a 'foreseeable, real, and personal risk' could not be established. See eg *EA v Switzerland*, Comm no 28/1995 (10 November 1997) UN Doc Cat/C/19/D/28/1995, para 11.5; *X, Y, and Z v Sweden*, Comm no 61/1996 (6 May 1998) UN Doc CAT/C/20/61/1996, para 11.5; *IAO v Sweden*, Comm no 65/1997 (6 May 1998) UN Doc Cat/C/20/D/65/1997, para 14.5; *KN v Switzerland* Comm no 94/1997 (19 May 1998) UN Doc Cat/C/20/D/94/1997, para 10.5; *ALN v Switzerland* Comm no 90/1997 (19 May 1998) UN Doc Cat/C/20/D/90/1997, para 8.7; *JUA v Switzerland* Comm no 100/1997 (10 November 1998) UN Doc Cat/C/21/D/100/1997, para 6.5; *SMR and MMR v Sweden* Comm no 103/1998 (5 May 1999) UN Doc Cat/C/22/D/103/1998, para 9.7; *MBB v Sweden* Comm no 104/1998 (5 May 1999) UN Doc Cat/C/22/D/104/1998, para 6.8; *KT v Switzerland* Comm no 118/1998 (19 November 1999) UN Doc Cat/C/23/D/118/1998, para 6.5; *NM v Switzerland* Comm no 116/1998 (9 May 2000) UN Doc Cat/C/24/D/116/1998, para 6.7; *SC v Denmark* Comm no 143/1999 (10 May 2000) UN Doc Cat/C/24/D/143/1999, para 6.6; *HAD v Switzerland* Comm no 126/1999 (10 May 2000) UN Doc Cat/C/24/D/126/1999, para 4.10; *US v Finland* Comm no 197/2002 (1 May 2003) UN Doc Cat/C/30/D/197/2002, para 7.8; *MSH v Sweden* Comm no 235/2003 (14 December 2005) UN Doc Cat/C/35/D/235/2003, para 6.4.

[25] See, eg, *Gorki Ernesto Tapia Paez v Sweden*, Comm no 39/1996 (28 April 1997) UN Doc CAT/C/18/D/39/1996, para 14.5.

[26] See, eg, *Agiza v Sweden*, Comm no 233/2003 (20 May 2005) UN Doc CAT/C/34/D/233/2003. The same principle applies also in cases of extradition following exclusion of refugee. See, eg, *Toirjon Abdussamatov and 28 other complainants v Kazakhstan*, Comm no 444/2010 (1 June 2012) UN Doc CAT/C/48/D/444/2010, para 13.7.

[27] Committee Against Torture, *General Comment 1*, CAT/C/3/Rev.2, 21 November 1997, para 2. This principle was first recognized in the *Mutombo v Switzerland* Comm no 13/1993 (27 April 1994) UN Doc CAT/C/12/D/13/1993. See also, *A v The Netherlands*, Comm no 91/1997 (13 November 1998) UN Doc CAT/C/21/D/91/1997.

[28] See, eg, *Pauline Muzonzo Paku Kisoki v Sweden* Comm no 41/1996 (8 May 1996) UN Doc CAT/C/16/D/41/1996 (*Kisoki v Sweden*); *Ismail Alan v Switzerland* Comm no 21/1995 (8 May 1996) UN Doc CAT/C/16/D/21/1995; *CT and KM v Sweden* Comm 279/2005 (17 November 2006) CAT/C/37/D/279/2005; *Kaveh Yaragh Tala v Sweden* Comm no 43/1996 (15 November 1996) UN Doc CAT/C/17/D/43/1996; *Harminder Singh Khalsa* et al *v Switzerland* Comm no 336/2008

is *personally at risk*,[29] even if there are contradictions and inconsistencies within the author's story. Indeed, 'complete accuracy is seldom to be expected by victims of torture'.[30]

In the ICCPR, Article 7 provides that 'no one shall be subjected to torture or to cruel, inhuman or degrading treatment or punishment ….' In its interpretation of Article 7, the Human Rights Committee (HRC) has explained that 'States parties must not expose individuals to the danger of torture or cruel, inhuman or degrading treatment or punishment upon return to another country by way of their extradition, expulsion or refoulement.'[31] Like the Committee Against Torture, the HRC also considers that the prohibition of *refoulement* under the ICCPR applies in all circumstances,[32] with regard either to the country to which removal is sought, or any other country to which the person might subsequently be transferred.[33] The enjoyment of these Covenant rights extends to all individuals, 'regardless of nationality or statelessness, such as asylum seekers, refugees, migrant workers, and other persons who may find themselves in the territory or subject to the jurisdiction of the State Party.'[34]

In the *Ahani* case, concerning the deportation of an Iranian refugee (designated as a suspected terrorist by Canadian authorities), the Committee held that deportation to torture cannot be justified even in exceptional circumstances, such as removal of suspected terrorists.[35] Indeed, 'the prohibition on torture, including as expressed in article 7 of the Covenant, is an absolute one that is not subject to countervailing considerations.'[36]

(7 July 2011) UN Doc CAT/C/46/D/336/2008, para 11.8; *Mondal v Sweden* Comm 338/2008 (7 July 2011) UN Doc CAT/C/46/D/338/2008; *Nirmal Singh v Canada* Comm no 319/2007 (8 July 2011) UN Doc CAT/C/46/D/319/2007, para 9.

[29] In *Ismail Alan v Switzerland*, the Committee Against Torture argues that 'specific grounds must exist that indicate that the individual concerned would be *personally at risk*' (para 11.2). See also, *CT and KM v Sweden*, above n 28, para 7.2; *Tala v Sweden*, above n 28, para 10.1.

[30] *Ismail Alan v Switzerland*, n 28 above, para 11.3. See also, *CT and KM v Sweden*, above n 28, para 7.6; *Tala v Sweden*, above n 28, para 10.3.

[31] HRC, *General Comment no 20: Article 7 (Prohibition of torture, or other cruel, inhuman or degrading treatment or punishment)*, 10 March 1992, UN Doc HRI/ GEN/1/Rev.7, para 9. See also, *General Comment no 31 on the Nature of the General Legal Obligation on States Parties to the Covenant*, UN Doc CCPR/C/21/Rev.1/Add.13, 26 May 2004, para 12.

[32] See, eg, HRC, *General Comment no 29 on States of Emergency (Article 4)* UN Doc CCPR/C/21/ Rev.1/Add.11, 31 August 2001, para 11; *Concluding Observations/Comments* on Canada, UN Doc CCPR/C/CAN/CO/5, 20 April 2006, para 15. See also, *Alzery v Sweden*, Comm no 1416/2005 (3 November 2006) UN Doc CCPR/C/88/D/1416/2005.

[33] HRC, *General Comment no 31*, n 31 above, para 12.

[34] ibid, para 10.

[35] *Mansour Ahani v Canada*, Comm no 1051/2002 (29 March 2004) UN Doc CCPR/ C/80/D/1051/2002. See also *Zhakhongir Maksudov and Adil Rakhimov, Yakub Tashbaev and Rasuldzhon Pirmatov v Kyrgyzstan*, Comms nos 1461, 1462, 1476 and 1477/2006 (31 July 2008) UN Doc CCPR/C/93/D/, para 12.6; and *Alzery v Sweden*, above n 32. This case – which will be more thoroughly discussed in Chapter 4 of this book – concerns an Egyptian national deported for reasons of national security.

[36] *Ahani v Canada*, n 35 above, para 10.10. See also *C v Australia*, where the HRC stated that deporting the applicant to Iran, where it was unlikely that he would receive the treatment necessary for his mental illness, would amount to a violation of Article 7 of the Covenant. *C v Australia*, Comm no 900/1999, UN Doc CCPR/C/76/D/900/1999 (28 October 2002) para 8.5.

There is increasing consensus amongst human rights scholars that Article 3 of the ECHR offers more protection from *refoulement* than other international refugee and human rights instruments as it rules out, in absolute terms, any kind of ill-treatment,[37] regardless of the reasons behind it.[38] In addition to this, the judgments of the Court of Strasbourg can influence other jurisdictions beyond the regional area represented by Council of Europe States. Without forgetting that other provisions of the ECHR can also afford protection against *refoulement*, the Strasbourg jurisprudence on this point has so far been primarily based on Article 3,[39] which will be the main focus of this chapter.

As a general premise, a State is responsible under the ECHR if it commits a violation in respect of a person who is on its territory, and clearly within its jurisdiction.[40] Indeed, pursuant to Article 1 of the ECHR, 'the High Contracting Parties shall secure to everyone within their jurisdiction the rights and freedoms defined in Section I of this Convention.' In *Soering v UK*, the Court made clear that a State is responsible under the Convention if it renders a person to a country where there are substantial grounds for believing that she will face a real risk of being subjected to torture or to inhuman or degrading treatment or punishment, however heinous the crime allegedly committed.[41] However, as the mere possibility of inhuman treatment is not sufficient for a violation of Article 3 to be established,[42] an applicant must show that she would be exposed to a real risk of being subjected to inhuman or degrading treatment upon removal.[43] According to the Court, 'Article 3 does not refer exclusively to the infliction of physical

[37] See eg, H Lambert, 'Protection Against *Refoulement* from Europe: Human Rights Law Comes to the Rescue' (1999) 48 *International & Comparative Law Quarterly* 515.

[38] For a detailed investigation of the interrelation between the ECHR and UN human rights treaties, in particular the CAT, with regard to the principle of *non-refoulement*, see F De Weck, *Non-Refoulement under the European Convention on Human Rights and the UN Convention Against Torture: The Assessment of Individual Complaints* (Brill, 2014); E Hamdan, *The principle of non-refoulement under the ECHR and the UN Convention against Torture and Other Cruel, Inhuman or Degrading Treatment or Punishment* (Brill, 2016).

[39] The Court inferred *non-refoulement* from Art 2 of the ECHR in combination with Art 3 in *Bader v Sweden* App no 13284/04 (8 November 2005). In *Abu Qatada v UK* and *El Haski v Belgium*, the ECtHR held that deportation would breach Art 6 (right to a fair trial). See *Othman (Abu Qatada) v UK*, App no 8139/09 (17 January 2012); *El Haski v Belgium* App no 649/08 (25 September 2012). For an overview on literature, refer, inter alia, to H Lambert, 'The European Convention on Human Rights and the Protection of Refugees: Limits and Opportunities' (2005) 24(2) *Refugee Survey Quarterly* 39; See also M Den Heijer, 'Whose Rights and Which Rights? The Continuing Story of *Non-Refoulement* under the European Convention on Human Rights' (2008) 10(3) *European Journal of Migration and Law (EJML)* 277–314; C Michaelsen, 'The Reinassance of *Refoulement*? The *Othman (Abu Qatada)* Decision of the European Court of Human Rights' (2012) 61(3) *International & Comparative Law Quarterly* 750.

[40] *Bankovic and Others v Belgium and Others*, App no 52207/99, Admissibility (12 December 2001) para 68.

[41] *Soering v UK*, App no 14038/88 (7 July 1989) para 91.

[42] *Vilvarajah and Others v UK*, Apps no 13163/87, 13164/87, 13165/87, 13447/87, 13448/87 (30 October 1991) para 111; *Vijayanathan and Pusparajah v France*, Apps no 17550/90 and 17825/91, *Preliminary Objections* (26 June 1992).

[43] *Vilvarajah and Others v United Kingdom*, ibid, paras 114–115.

pain but also of mental suffering, which is caused by creating a state of anguish and stress by means other than bodily assault.'[44] Moreover, once the applicant has adduced evidence proving that there are substantial grounds for believing that deportation would expose her to a real risk of torture or inhuman treatment, it is then for the respondent State to dispel any doubts on this.[45]

A few years later, the European Court drew on the *Soering* principle in the *Chahal v UK* case by asserting that 'the prohibition provided by Article 3 against ill-treatment is equally *absolute in* expulsion cases ...' (emphasis added).[46] The landmark *Saadi v Italy* case contributes to the reaffirmation of *non-refoulement*, in cases dealing with expulsion of asylum seekers to unsafe third countries, as a principle having the value of an absolute right, particularly in an international climate calling on States to strike a balance between fundamental individual rights and the collective right to security that is threatened by terrorist violence.[47] Judge Zupancic asserted that the increased terrorist threat cannot call into question the absolute nature of Article 3 rights. Indeed, the Convention is conceived 'to protect the individual from the unbridled "interest" of the executive branch or sometimes even of the legislative branch of the State.'[48]

The implicit prohibition of *refoulement* under Article 3 of the ECHR was extended from the context of extradition in the *Soering* case to the field of asylum by the *Cruz Varas* judgment, which examined Sweden's expulsion of a Chilean protection-seeker back to Chile.[49] The ECtHR offers remarkable opportunities in terms of realising refugee rights because of the protections it ensures, *in exceptional circumstances*, against expulsion to countries where the applicants do not have access to adequate medical treatment[50] or an adequate

[44] *El-Masri v Former Republic of Macedonia* App no 39630/69 (13 December 2012) para 198 (*El-Masri v FROM*).

[45] *Saadi v Italy*, App no 37201/06 (29 January 2008) para 129. On this point, see, *inter alia*, S Borelli, 'Estradizione, espulsione e tutela dei diritti fondamentali', in L Pineschi (ed), *La tutela internazionale dei diritti umani* (Giuffré, 2006) 736–37.

[46] *Chahal v UK*, App no 22414/93 (25 October 1996/15 November 1996) para 80. The same principle has been extended also to other cases before the ECtHR concerning deportation, expulsion, and removal of asylum-seekers: *Cruz Varas and Others v Sweden*, Apps nos 46/1990/237/307 (20 March 1991); *Vilvarajah and Others v UK*, above n 42; and *Ahmed v Austria*, App no 25964/94 (17 December 1996).

[47] *Saadi v Italy*, above n 45, para 127. See, for example, the British Prime Minister's press conference, 5 August 2005, http://webarchive.nationalarchives.gov.uk/20040105034004/number10.gov.uk/page8041.

[48] *Saadi v Italy*, Concurring Opinion of Judge Zupancic, above n 45, para 2.

[49] *Cruz Varas v Sweden*, above n 46. See also, *NA v UK*, App no 25904/07 (17 July 2008); *Sufi and Elmi v UK*, Apps nos 8319/07 and 11449/07 (28 June 2011) para 218.

[50] See, eg, *D v UK*, App no 30240/96 (2 May 1997); *Nasri v France*, App no 19465/92 13 July 1995. Although space precludes a broader discussion, it should be observed that the ECHR provides tremendous opportunity for development of fundamental rights (other than the prohibition of torture) in cases concerning expulsion. This chapter will not investigate whether the obligation of *non-refoulement* is to be seen as a positive obligation, or means requiring a risk assessment to prevent a foreseeable violation. Stoyanova argues that framing the obligation not to *refoule* as a negative obligation – as the ECtHR does in the *Paposhvili* case concerning a migrant suffering from a life-threatening illness – is difficult to reconcile with the 'very exceptional' standard and its

standard of living.[51] Article 3 of the Convention also forbids direct and indirect *refoulement* to the country of origin via another State.[52] While the ECtHR elaborated upon this principle even in respect of a Contracting Party to the Convention,[53] the obligation of the transferring State of verifying – before the actual transfer – whether the intermediary country ensures adequate guarantees against the removal of the persons concerned to their countries of origin becomes even more compelling.[54]

The analysis of the jurisprudence of the Court also shows how the continuous shuttling of migrants between different States may result in a violation of Article 3 of the ECHR. Onward expulsions of asylum seekers to third countries inevitably carry with them a certain degree of uncertainty regarding the level of protection offered by the third States involved. Even if the latter are considered safe countries (ie, providing guarantees against *refoulement*), uncertainty remains and the fear of a certain dreaded event occurring, alongside an 'ever present and mounting anguish of anticipating' could well bring the treatment in question within the scope of Article 3 of the ECHR.

In sum, the cases examined so far demonstrate how international human rights bodies serve to counterbalance the leeway given to governments, when they are prioritising uncertain and potentially vague national security interests to the detriment of the protection of refugees' fundamental rights.

IV. INTRODUCING EXTRATERRITORIAL JURISDICTION

The attention here placed on jurisdiction will be functional to the analysis of State responsibility in Chapter five, especially in highly-debated cases of offshoring or outsourcing of migration controls. A reconstruction of the notion of jurisdiction is therefore needed. Public international law traditionally distinguishes between, on the one hand, 'prescriptive or legislative jurisdiction' – namely 'the power to make decisions or rules' – and on the other hand, 'enforcement or prerogative jurisdiction', which refers to 'the power to take executive action in

underlying distinction between 'natural' sources of harm and intentionally inflicted harm. *Paposhvili v Belgim*, App no 41738/10 (13 December 2016). See V Stoyanova, 'How Exceptional Must "Very Exceptional" Be? *Non-Refoulement*, Socio-Economic Deprivation, and *Paposhvili v Belgium*' (2017) 29(4) *IJRL* 580.

[51] See, eg, *MSS v Belgium and Greece*, App no 30696/09 (21 January 2011) para 253. For a critique of the ECtHR as a new European Asylum Court, see M Bossuyt, 'The Court of Strasbourg Acting as an Asylum Court' (2012) 8(2) *European Constitutional Law Review* 203.

[52] *Hirsi v Italy*, above n 4, para 114. The Court cites *Soering v UK*, above n 41, paras 90–91; *Vilvarajah v UK*, above n 42, para 103; *Jabari v Turkey*, App no 40035/ 98 (1 July 2000), para 38; *Ahmed v Austria*, above n 46, para 39; *HLR v France* (1997) 26 EHRR 29, para 34; and *Salah Sheekh v The Netherlands*, App no 1948/04 (11 January 2007) para 135. See also, *X and Others v Malta*, App no 43985/13 (31 July 2013).

[53] *TI v UK*, App no 43844/98 (7 March 2000).

[54] *Hirsi v Italy*, above n 4, para 147.

pursuance of or consequent on the making of decisions or rules.'[55] In both cases however, the legal basis for the exercise of jurisdiction lies in State sovereignty, and jurisdiction remains an expression of the power of the State.[56]

Whilst in public international law jurisdiction refers to the power and legal authority to affect people (and property),[57] extraterritorial jurisdiction in human rights law would be engaged also when a State exercises *de facto* authority, not necessarily *de jure*.[58] This means that the application of human rights treaties can be triggered even if a State acts abroad beyond its legal capacity.

Traditionally, the concept of jurisdiction referred to the exclusive authority of a State to regulate events occurring within its territory. Therefore, a claim of territorial jurisdiction could not overlap with a competing claim by another country, as it rested on conduct taking place within the regulating State.[59] Such a system – where States do not assume jurisdiction outside the limits of their own sovereignty, thus avoiding conflict with other States – seemed to create a satisfactory regime for all, with a clear division of competences. Indeed, sovereign States possess jurisdiction over all persons and things within their own territorial borders, as well as civil and criminal matters arising within those borders.[60] While States continue to consider territoriality as the most straightforward method to delimit competences between them, it is also true that over the course of the twentieth century, the notion of jurisdiction expanded to include authority over certain actions that occurred beyond borders, but the effects of which were felt within the territory of the regulating State.[61]

As examined below, in the field of human rights law, the concept of jurisdiction has acquired an obligatory dimension[62] requiring Contracting Parties to human rights treaties to secure fundamental rights to individuals falling within their jurisdiction, both within and outside State borders. Those supporting an extraterritorial reading of the human rights Conventions underline how nothing disallows such an interpretation within the text of the treaties. Accordingly, international bodies – *in primis* the ECtHR and the UN human rights committees – have interpreted jurisdiction as reflecting a *factual* notion, the exercise of State power or authority, regardless of the legality of the act

[55] I Brownlie, *Principles of Public International Law*, 6th edn (OUP, 2003) 297.

[56] M Gavouneli, *Functional Jurisdiction in the Law of the Sea* (Martinus Nijhoff, 2007) 6.

[57] For a detailed analysis on jurisdiction in international law, see A Mills, 'Rethinking Jurisdiction in International Law' (2014) 84 *British Yearbook of International Law* 187; C Ryngaert, *Jurisdiction in International Law* (OUP, 2015); L Raible, 'Title to Territory and Jurisdiction in International Human Rights Law: Three Models for a Fraught Relationship' (2018) 31(2) *Leiden Journal of International Law* 320–21.

[58] See below for case law of international human rights bodies.

[59] HL Buxbaum, 'Territory, Territoriality, and the Resolution of Jurisdictional Conflict' (2009) 57 *American Journal of Comparative Law* 631, 636.

[60] FA Mann, 'The Doctrine of Jurisdiction in International Law' (1964) 111 *Recueil des Cours* 1, 30.

[61] See, Ryngaert 2015, n 57 above.

[62] ibid.

under public international law.[63] Indeed, in public international law, jurisdiction presupposes legality and the power of a sovereign State to affect legal interests and the rights of persons.[64]

State jurisdiction is a *conditio sine qua non* for people to have human rights enforceable against the State and for the State to have duties toward those people. The relational nature of jurisdiction between a subject and the authorities is key to understanding the normative relationship that unites States parties to a human rights treaty with their subjects.[65] Part of the scholarship endorses a mere territorial application of human rights treaties by relying on a 'literal' interpretation of the jurisdictional clauses found in human rights treaties,[66] which is often supported by the relevant preparatory work.[67] According to the Permanent Court of International Justice in the *SS Lotus* case, jurisdiction is essentially territorial:

> Now the first and foremost restriction imposed by international law upon a State is that – failing the existence of a permissive rule to the contrary – it may not exercise its power in any form in the territory of another State. In this sense jurisdiction is certainly territorial; it cannot be exercised by a State outside its territory except by virtue of a permissive rule derived from international custom or from a convention.[68]

As analysed in the following Sections, substantive case law has been produced by international courts, and, in particular, by human rights monitoring bodies, on the extraterritorial applicability of the relevant conventions, thereby adopting a notion of jurisdiction which also applies beyond the territorial borders of the respondent State.[69] In Henkin's words, for instance:

> [i]ncreasingly … the categories [for the exercise of jurisdiction] have proved to be too fixed – and perhaps too few – to serve the interests of States … and the needs of the system (including new needs responding to new commitments to human values). Developments have blurred the traditional categories, suggesting that the assumption

[63] R Wilde, 'Triggering State Obligations Extraterritorially: The Spatial Test in Certain Human Rights Treaties' (2008) 40 *Israel Law Review* 142.

[64] On the concept of jurisdiction in public international law, see, *inter alia*, J Beale, 'The Jurisdiction of a Sovereign State' (1923) 36 *Harvard law Review* 241; C Ryngaert 2015, n 57 above.

[65] S Besson, 'The Extraterritoriality of the European Convention on Human Rights: Why Human Rights Depend on Jurisdiction and What Jurisdiction Amounts to' (2012) 25(4) *Leiden Journal of International Law* 857. See also, C Focarelli, *International Law as a Social Construct* (OUP, 2013) 397–98.

[66] See, eg, O'Boyle, 'The European Convention on Human Rights and Extraterritorial Jurisdiction: A Comment on "Life after Bankovic"' in F Coomans and M Kamminga (eds), *Extraterritorial Application of Human Rights Treaties* (Intersentia, 2004) 131; G Verdirame, 'Human Rights in Wartime: A Framework for Analysis' (2008) 6 *European Human Rights Law Review* 693–94.

[67] See the contributions in D Acosta Arcarazo and CC Murphy (eds), EU Security and Justice Law: After Lisbon and Stockholm (Hart Publishing, 2014) for an analysis of the preparatory work to the ICCPR, the CAT, and the ECtHR.

[68] *SS Lotus, France v Turkey*, 7 September 1927, PCIJ Ser A, no 10, para 45.

[69] For a thorough examination of the extraterritorial application of these three human rights treaties, see, Karen Da Costa, *The Extraterritorial Application of Selected Human Rights Treaties* (Martinus Nijhoff, 2013).

of rigid categories (territoriality, nationality) are no longer valid, and that a more flexible jurisprudence would better serve the purposes of the law and the needs of the system.[70]

A. Extraterritorial Applicability of the Principle of *Non-Refoulement*

The ensuing Sections are aimed at examining whether the prohibition of *refoulement* applies beyond the territory of the signatory States to the Geneva Convention, the ECHR, the CAT, the ICCPR, and the CFR in relation to persons who claim protection at the border of a State party (before access is allowed), or who are intercepted at sea. In the oft-quoted *Sale v Haitian Centres Council* case – grounded in a textual interpretation of the Treaty – the US Supreme Court construed Article 33(1) of the Geneva Convention as having no extraterritorial applicability and conclusively established that refugees claiming asylum outside the US borders were not entitled to procedural protection, or to escape repatriation, even in the face of persecution at the hands of their governments.[71] This judgment, however, has been sharply criticised, inter alia, by the Dissenting Opinion of Justice Blackmun,[72] several scholars,[73] domestic courts,[74] the Inter-American Commission,[75] as well as the UNHCR, according to whom Article 33(1) does not have any geographical limitation.[76] While specific territorial limitations have been set forth in other Articles of the Treaty, no such restriction is embodied in paragraph 1 of Article 33.[77]

Beyond the drafting history of the Geneva Convention,[78] it is notable how the issue of the applicability *ratione loci* of the prohibition of *refoulement* has

[70] L Henkin, *International Law: Politics, Values and Functions. General Course on Public International Law.* (1989) 280, 291.

[71] *Sale, Acting Commissioner, INS v Haitian Centres Council*, US Supreme Court, 509 US 155 (1993).

[72] Dissenting Opinion of Mr Justice Blackmun in *Sale*, ibid.

[73] GS Goodwin-Gill, 'The Haitian *Refoulement* Case: A Comment' (1994) 6 *IJRL* 103–10; HH Koh, 'Reflections on *Refoulement* and Haitian Centres Council' (1994) 35(1) *Harvard International Law Journal* 3; SH Legomsky, 'The USA and the Caribbean Interdiction Program' (2006) 18 *IJRL* 677, 679–83; JY Carlier, *Droit d'asile et des réfugiés: de la protection aux droits, Collected Courses of The Hague Academy of International Law*, Vol 332 (2007) 107.

[74] *Regina (European Roma Rights Centre) and Others v Immigration Officer at Prague Airport* [2003] EWCA Civ 666, paras 34–35.

[75] Inter-American Commission on Human Rights, *The Haitian Centre for Human Rights et al v US*, Case 10.675, Report no 51/96, para 157.

[76] UNHCR, *Gene McNary, Commissioner, Immigration and Naturalization Service*, et al *(Petitioners) v Haitian Centres Council, Inc et al (Respondents). Brief Amicus Curiae of the Office of the High Commissioner for Refugees in Support of Respondents*, October 1992, 85–102.

[77] See, R Bank, 'Refugees at Sea: Introduction to Art. 11 of the 1951 Convention', in Zimmermann 2011, n 78 below, 815, 833, 835.

[78] See, UN Ad Hoc Committee on Refugees and Stateless Persons, *Ad Hoc Committee on Statelessness and Related Problems, First Session: Summary Record of the Twenty-First Meeting Held at Lake Success*, New York, 2 February 1950, UN Doc E/AC.32/SR.21, paras 13–26. See also, A Grahl-Madsen, *The Status of Refugees in International Law*, vol 2 (AW Sijthoff, 1972) 100; Kälin, Caroni and Heim, 'Article 33 para 1 (Prohibition of Expulsion and Return (*Refoulement*)' in

fuelled a vivid doctrinal debate.[79] It follows, therefore, that extensive or restrictive readings of the Convention will depend on the interpretative methods used. One of the main points of discussion concerns the expression 'in any manner whatsoever' contained in Article 33(1).[80] Although the *language* of Article 33(1) does not concede any explicit indication of its extraterritorial applicability, scholars have not refrained from expanding the reach of this provision beyond situations at the territorial border.[81]

Some commentators have put the accent on where the refugee is sent *to* rather than where she is sent *from*. This reading would be supported by the inclusive wording of Article 33(1) whereby '[n]o Contracting State shall expel *or* return ("*refouler*") a refugee *in any manner whatsoever to the frontiers of territories* where his life or freedom would be threatened' (emphasis added).[82] One would expect that any action on migration control (wherever undertaken) resulting in *refoulement* to the borders of such territories would amount to a breach of Article 33(1).[83]

It has also been argued that the lack of emphasis on the extraterritorial scope of Article 33 can be due to the absence of any historical precedents, since the Convention was drafted mainly as a response to the plight of Jewish refugees in Europe during the Second World War.[84]

By stressing that the deciding criterion is whether a person is subject to that State's effective control and authority, the UNHCR itself is of the view that

> the purpose, intent, and meaning of Article 33(1) are unambiguous and establish an obligation not to return a refugee or asylum seeker to a country where he or she would be at risk of persecution or other serious harm, which applies *wherever a State exercises jurisdiction*, including at the frontier, on the high seas, or on the territory of another State (emphasis added).[85]

A Zimmermann (ed), *The 1951 Convention relating to the Status of Refugees and its 1967 Protocol: A Commentary* (OUP, 2011) 1367.

[79] For example, some suggest that the principle of *non-refoulement* does not apply to asylum-seekers intercepted on the high sea. See V Delicato, 'I traffici di migranti nel Mediterraneo e gli accordi internazionali per la cooperazione di polizia' (2010) *Gli Stranieri*.

[80] Lauterpacht and Bethlehem 2003, n 4 above, 122; Robinson, *Convention relating to the Status of Refugees: Its History, Contents, and Interpretation: A Commentary* (Institute of Jewish Affairs 1953) 162.

[81] For the purpose of this work, attention is drawn on measures of migration control carried out on the high seas, rather than on the territory of a third country. See, eg, Lauterpacht and Bethlehem 2003, n 4 above, 87, 110; Coleman 2009, n 244 below, 253; Kälin, Caroni and Heim 2011, n 78 above, 1361, 1367; UNHCR, Advisory Opinion on the Extraterritorial Application of *Non-refoulement*, 12, para 24. See also, Goodwin-Gill and McAdam 2007, n 4 above, 246; Hathaway 2005, n 5 above, 339.

[82] Weis 1995, n 369 below, 341; Hathaway 2005, n 5 above, 338; SH Legomsky, 'The USA and the Caribbean Interdiction Program' (2006) 18(3–4) *IJRL* 677; Goodwin-Gill and McAdam 2007, n 4 above, 246.

[83] T Gammeltoft-Hansen, *Access to Asylum* (CUP, 2011) 57–58; Lauterpacht and Bethlehem 2003, n 4 above, 122.

[84] Hathaway 2005, n 5 above, 337. See also, Justice Blackmun in *Sale*, above n 71, 7.

[85] UNHCR, 'Advisory Opinion on the Extraterritorial Application of *Non-refoulement*', para 24.

This extraterritorial reading of Article 33(1) of the Geneva Convention would also be in line with key developments within human rights law, which have placed particular emphasis upon the issue of where the refugee is sent to, rather than where the action is initiated.[86] The complementarity between international refugee law and human rights law can be grounded in Article 31(3)(c) of the VCLT, whereby, in interpreting a treaty, 'any relevant rules of international law applicable in the relations between the parties' shall be taken into account together with the context. Indeed, according to the International Law Commission (ILC), 'Article 31(3)(c) also requires the interpreter to consider other treaty-based rules so as to arrive at a consistent meaning.'[87]

Therefore, with regard to *non-refoulement*, what matters is whether a certain conduct giving rise to a breach of a primary obligation is attributable to the State, and not whether it takes place within or beyond its borders. A State will therefore be responsible for complying with the obligation of *non-refoulement* each time a person is subject to or is within its jurisdiction – ie that individual is within the territory of the State concerned, under its control, or affected by organs acting on behalf of that State.[88]

Additionally, given the lack of a clause explicitly restricting the geographical scope of Article 33 to the territory of the Contracting Parties, no reason exists to exclude its applicability anytime a State exercises jurisdiction over a refugee, even in extraterritorial contexts.[89] Jurisdiction is triggered 'wherever a person is under the effective control of, or is directly affected by those acting on behalf of, the State in question.'[90] Therefore, upholding a broader understanding of Article 33 would not only be in line with evolving State practices to carry out migration controls beyond territorial borders,[91] but would also prevent the establishment of a double system whereby refugees who are able to elude migration controls (thus claiming asylum within borders) would obtain greater protection than those intercepted before reaching the territory of the destination State where they expect to find refuge.[92]

B. Under the ICCPR and the CAT

The extraterritorial relevance of the prohibition of *refoulement* has been endorsed, in several instances, by the UN human rights treaty monitoring

[86] Goodwin-Gill and McAdam 2007, n 4 above, 250.

[87] ILC, Report of the 58th Session (2006), UN Doc A/61/10, 414–15.

[88] Lauterpacht and Bethlehem 2003, n 4 above, 87, 110. See also, Goodwin-Gill and McAdam 2007, n 4 above, 246. For a broader examination of the concept of jurisdiction, see Chapter 5 of this book.

[89] Kälin, Caroni and Heim 2011, n 78 above, 1361.

[90] ibid.

[91] Hathaway 2005, n 5 above, 67.

[92] See, e.g., A Fischer Lescano and T Lohr, *Border Control at Sea: Requirements under International Human Rights and Refugee Law* (European Centre for Constitutional and Human Rights, 2007).

bodies in relation to Article 7(1) of the ICCPR and Article 3(1) of the CAT. The ICCPR preparatory works show the intense debate behind the drafting of the jurisdictional clause under Article 2(1). Pursuant to Article 2(1) of the ICCPR, '[e]ach State Party to the present Covenant undertakes to respect and to ensure to all individuals *within its territory and subject to its jurisdiction* the rights recognised in the present Covenant' (emphasis added). A restrictive and cumulative interpretation whereby the ICCPR only applies to people who are at the same time physically in the territory *and* under the jurisdiction of the country is supported neither by doctrine nor by the HRC jurisprudence,[93] and would significantly curb human rights protection.

By contrast, a State party to the ICCPR is responsible for guaranteeing the rights of the Covenant to all individuals who are present either within or outside its territory provided they fall within its jurisdiction. From the case law of the HRC and its *General Comment no 31*, it emerges that what is decisive in establishing State responsibility is the *relationship* between the individual and the State – whether, then, a person is under the jurisdiction or the effective control of the Contracting State, regardless of her location, and in relation to a violation of any of the rights set forth in the Covenant.[94]

Tomuschat's opinion, attached to the *Lopez Burgos v Uruguay* and *Celiberti de Casariego v Uruguay* cases, can be instructive, in terms of better understanding the intentions of the drafters of the Covenant:

> To construe the words 'within its territory' pursuant to their strict literal meaning as excluding any responsibility for conduct occurring beyond the national boundaries would, however, lead to utterly absurd results. ... Never was it envisaged ... to grant States parties unfettered discretionary power to carry out wilful and deliberate attacks against the freedom and personal integrity of their citizens living abroad. Consequently, despite the wording of Article 2(1), the events, which took place outside Uruguay, come within the purview of the Covenant.[95]

[93] See, eg, *Delia Saldias de Lopez v Uruguay*, Comm no 52/1979 (29 July 1981) UN Doc CCPR/C/OP/1, paras 12.1–12.3 (*Lopez Burgos v Uruguay*); and *Lilian Celiberti de Casariego v Uruguay*, Comm no 56/1979 (29 July 1981) UN Doc CCPR/C/13/D/56/1979, para 10.3. See inter alia, L Condorelli and P De Sena, 'The Relevance of the Obligations Flowing from the UN Covenant on Civil and Political Rights to US Courts Dealing with Guantanamo Detainees' (2004) *Journal of International Criminal Justice* 111–12; M Nowak, *UN Covenant on Civil and Political Rights. CCPR Commentary*, 2nd revised edn (Kehl, NP Engel Publisher, 2005) 44; K Wouters, *International Legal Standards for the Protection from Refoulement: A Legal Analysis of the Prohibitions on Refoulement Contained in the Refugee Convention, the European Convention on Human Rights, the International Covenant on Civil and Political Rights and the Convention against Torture* (Intersentia, 2009) 370–71; Raible 2018, n 57 above, 317.

[94] HRC, *General Comment no 31*, para 10; *Lopez Burgos v Uruguay*, above n 93, paras 12.1–12.3. See also, *General Comment no 23: The Rights of Minorities* UN Doc CCPR/C/21/Rev.1/Add.5 (4 August 1994) para 4.

[95] Individual Opinion by Tomuschat appended to *Lopez Burgos v Uruguay* and *Celiberti de Casariego v Uruguay* cases, above n 93.

Indeed, in *Lopez Burgos v Uruguay* and in *Celiberti de Casariego v Uruguay*, the Committee held that

> it would be unconscionable to so interpret the responsibility under Article 2 of the Covenant as to permit a State party to perpetrate violations of the Covenant on the territory of another State, which violations it could not perpetrate on its own territory.[96]

What is interesting to note is that the view of the Committee seems to indicate that jurisdiction arises from a *factual* relationship of the State with the individual, rather than from a *legal* relationship, such as the nationality of the victim. Furthermore, in a number of Concluding Observations, the Committee has upheld the view that a State party is responsible toward anyone within the effective control and power of the State in question, regardless of the place where the violation occurred.[97] For example, the HRC has considered as beneficiaries of the ICCPR all those within the area of the Palestinian Occupied Territories. Indeed, it notes that:

> the provisions of the Covenant apply to the benefit of the population of the occupied territories, including in the Gaza Strip, for all actions by the State party's authorities or agents in those territories affecting the enjoyment of rights enshrined in the Covenant, and fall within the ambit of State responsibility of Israel under the principles of public international law (arts. 2 and 40).
>
> The State party should ensure the full application of the Covenant in Israel as well in the occupied territories .... In accordance with the Committee's general comment No. 31, the State party should ensure that all persons *under its jurisdiction and effective control* are afforded the full enjoyment of the rights enshrined in the Covenant (emphasis added).[98]

[96] *Lopez Burgos v Uruguay*, above n 93, paras 12.1–12.3; *Celiberti de Casariego v Uruguay*, above n 93, paras 10.1–10.3.

[97] HRC, *Concluding Observations on Israel*, 21 August 2003, UN Doc CCPR/CO/78/ISR, para 11; *Concluding Observations on Croatia*, 28 December 1992, UN Doc CCPR/C/79/Add.15, para 9; *Concluding Observations on Belgium*, 19 November 1998, UN Doc CCPR/C/79/Add.99, para 14; *Concluding Observations on Belgium*, 12 August 2004, UN Doc CCPR/CO/81/BEL, para 6; *Concluding Observations on the United States of America*, 18 December 2006, UN Doc CCPR/C/USA/CO/3Rev. 1, para 10.

[98] HRC, *Concluding observations on Israel*, UN Doc CCPR/C/ISR/CO/3 (2010), para 5. In a number of cases, the ICJ has cemented the approach whereby the ICCPR applies 'in respect of acts done by a State in the exercise of its jurisdiction outside its own territory'. See eg, *Armed Activities on the Territory of Congo (Democratic Republic of Congo v Uganda)*, 19 December 2005, ICJ Rep 168, paras 178–180, 216 and 219; and *Order on the Request for the Indication of Provisional Measures, Case Concerning the Application of the International Convention on the Elimination of All Forms of Racial Discrimination (Georgia v Russia)*, 15 October 2008, ICJ Gen List no 140, para 109. On the contrary, in the *Nicaragua* case, the ICJ did not consider that the assistance given by the United States to the contras amounted to 'effective control' of the military or paramilitary operations in the course of which the alleged violations were committed. See *Military and Paramilitary Activities against Nicaragua (Merits)*, 26 June 1986, ICJ Rep 1, paras 115–116.

This passage, in line with the ICJ's Advisory Opinion on the Legal Consequences of the Construction of a Wall in the Occupied Palestinian territory,[99] also shows that the HRC applies the general rules of international law on jurisdiction and responsibility. The Committee criticised the restrictive approach of the UK whereby the Covenant only applies to persons held in the custody of the armed forces, in British-run military detention facilities outside of the UK. It thus urged the UK to clearly state that 'the Covenant applies to all individuals who are subject to its jurisdiction or control.'[100] Moreover, the HRC recognises the prohibition on removing a person where reliable grounds exist to believe that she will suffer irreparable harm either in the readmitting country or in any other country to which she could subsequently be transferred.[101] In its *General Comment no 31*, it held that 'States Parties are required by Article 2, paragraph 1, to respect and to ensure the Covenant rights to *all persons who may be within their territory and to all persons subject to their jurisdiction*' (emphasis added).[102] The elements of Article 2(1) are interpreted disjunctively: for the Committee, reference either to territory or to jurisdiction suffices to consider the Covenant applicable. Although the Committee does not explain what exactly the threshold should be to deem State control exercised beyond borders as 'effective', it clearly indicates that the Covenant might apply abroad 'regardless of the circumstances in which such power or effective control was obtained.'[103] Therefore, in line with the position adopted in *Lopez Burgos*, Covenant rights apply even in the absence of a legal basis for State action abroad.[104] This reading suggests that the Committee both favours a factual rather than a legal notion of power and effective control, and endorses the extraterritorial applicability of the treaty, which will benefit all individuals, regardless of their nationality or status.

The case law of the HRC seems to confirm the extraterritorial scope of the Covenant to include the *non-refoulement* obligation where individuals are under the power or actual control of the State itself. For example, the HRC confirms the extraterritorial applicability of the prohibition on *refoulement* in the *Munaf v Romania* case, where it found, however, no breach of the Covenant's articles with regards to the handover of an Iraqi-American dual nationality criminal suspect from the Romanian Embassy in Baghdad to the custody of the multinational forces in Iraq.[105]

[99] Advisory Opinion, ICJ Reports 2004, 136.

[100] HRC *Concluding Observations on the Sixth Report of the United Kingdom of Great Britain and Northern Ireland*, 30 July 2008, CCPR/C/GBR/CO/6, para 14. See also, HRC *Concluding Observations on the Fifth Report of Italy*, 24 April 2006, CCPR/C/ITA/CO/5, para 3; HRC *Concluding Observations on the Fifth Report of Poland*, 2 December 2004, CCPR/CO/82/POL, para 3.

[101] HRC, *General Comment 31*, para 12. See also, HRC, *Concluding Observations on the United States of America*, 18 December 2006, UN Doc CCPR/C/USA/CO/3Rev. 1, para 16.

[102] HRC, *General Comment 31*, paras 3 and 10.

[103] HRC, *General Comment 31*, para 10.

[104] See, *Lopez Burgos v Uruguay*, above n 93, para 12.3.

[105] HRC, *Mohammad Munaf v Romania* Comm no 1539/2006, UN doc CCPR/C/96/D/1539/2006 (21 August 2009) paras 14.2 and 15.

The CAT does not contain a specific jurisdictional clause and the debate generally revolves around the application of certain provisions, which refer to 'any territory under its jurisdiction.' It is suggested that those articles containing such phrasing are meant to ensure a wider spatial reach of the treaty.[106] The Committee Against Torture maintains that the *non-refoulement* obligation contained in Article 3 of the CAT applies in any territory under a State party's jurisdiction – that is to say 'all areas under the *de facto* effective control of the State party, by whichever military or civil authorities such control is exercised.'[107]

The CAT offers a vast range of guarantees to people subjected to a removal decision: no restriction is made on the personal scope of Article 3. Moreover, the expression 'another State' not only encompasses the country of origin but shall be broadly interpreted as referring 'to any transfer of a person from one State jurisdiction to another.'[108] Although this Convention does not contain any general provision on the territorial scope of Article 3, the textual meanings of the terms 'expel' and 'return' imply both a territorial and extraterritorial application of the principle of *non-refoulement*. The decisive factor is the *de facto* causal relationship between the State and the individual and the capacity of the former to affect or protect the rights of the latter.

From case law and General Comments of the Committee Against Torture, it can be inferred that Article 3 of the CAT is also pertinent to situations in which the denial of access to the territory at the border has, as a direct consequence, the removal of a person to a territory where she risks being subjected to torture.[109] The Committee has determined the extraterritorial applicability of Article 3(1) of the Convention in situations of *non-refoulement* at sea. In the 2008 *JHA v Spain (Marine I)* case, the Committee emphasised how Spain exercised control over the intercepted people from the outset, by providing assistance in the context of search and rescue after receiving the distress call from the vessel, throughout their detention in Mauritania, and the process of repatriation.[110] In issuing its final views, the Committee Against Torture:

> Recalls its General Comment no 2, in which it states that the jurisdiction of a State party refers to any territory in which it exercises, *directly or indirectly, in whole or in part, de jure or de facto effective control*, in accordance with international law. ... It considers that such jurisdiction must also include situations where a State party exercises, directly or indirectly, *de facto* or *de jure* control over persons in

[106] To read more on this point, see, K da Costa, *The Extraterritorial Application of Selected Human Rights Treaties* (Brill, 2012) 264–65.

[107] *Conclusions and Recommendations of the Committee against Torture concerning the second report of the United States of America*, UN Doc CAT/C/USA/CO/2, 25 July 2006, paras 15, 20.

[108] M Nowak and E McArthur, *The United Nations Convention Against Torture: A Commentary* (OUP, 2008) 199.

[109] W Suntinger, 'The Principle of *Non-Refoulement*: Looking rather to Geneva than to Strasbourg?' (1995) 49 *Austrian Journal of Public and International Law* 203, 210.

[110] *JHA v Spain*, Comm no 323/2007 (21 November 2008) UN Doc CAT/C/41/D/323/2007. The case was declared inadmissible because the complainant was not properly authorised to represent the alleged victims.

> detention … In particular, the State party exercised, by virtue of a diplomatic agreement concluded with Mauritania, constant *de facto* control over the alleged victims during their detention in Nouadhibou. Consequently, the Committee considers that the alleged victims are subject to Spanish jurisdiction … (emphasis added).[111]

Similar reasoning was followed by the Committee Against Torture in the *Sonko v Spain* case[112] concerning the death of a migrant intercepted by the Spanish Civil Guard whilst swimming in an effort to enter the Autonomous City of Ceuta. The Committee held that the concept of jurisdiction as 'effective control and authority' is applicable in respect of all the provisions of the CAT. It concluded that the Civil Guard officers were exercising effective control over the persons onboard – even if the vessel was in Moroccan territorial waters – and were therefore responsible for the safety of the intercepted migrants.[113]

C. Under the ECHR

This Section will expound on the highly debated issue of State jurisdiction under the ECHR. The major focus and level of detail here – in comparison with previous Sections – is mainly due to the well-developed and abundant case law of the ECtHR on the extraterritorial application of the relevant Convention. However, lessons from the Court could be applied, *mutatis mutandis*, also to other international human rights regimes.[114]

The case law of the ECtHR shows how jurisdiction under Article 1 of the Convention does not stem from territorial sovereignty only, but – as will be observed later – also from lesser degrees of dominance, such as occupation or 'effective overall control.'[115] Today, jurisdiction is conceived of as being essentially 'functional' (ie, it pertains to the function of jurisdiction), as it solely concerns the normative relationship that unites States parties to a human rights treaty and their subjects, without restriction of its scope to a given territory or to nationals. Therefore, while jurisdiction has territorial and personal dimensions, these are to be considered as specific instances of a functional approach to jurisdiction.[116] As Besson puts it, 'jurisdiction is a function that is exercised through direct personal control, or through territorial control, and personal and territorial jurisdiction are merely types of jurisdiction as a result.'[117]

[111] ibid, para 8.2.
[112] *Sonko v Spain*, Comm no 368/2008 (20 February 2012) UN Doc CAT/C/47/D/368/2008.
[113] ibid, para 10.3.
[114] For similar arguments, see O De Schutter, 'Globalization and Jurisdiction: Lessons from the European Convention on Human Rights' (2006) 6 *Baltic Yearbook of International Law* 185, 192.
[115] *Loizidou v Turkey*, App no 15318/89, Preliminary Objections (23 February 1995); and App no 15318/89, Merits (18 December 1996); *Cyprus v Turkey*, App no 25781/94, Judgment – Just Satisfaction (10 May 2001). See also, L Caflish, 'Attribution, Responsibility and Jurisdiction in International Human Rights Law' (2017) *Anuario Colombiano de Derecho Internacional (ACDI)* 161.
[116] Besson 2012, n 65 above, 863.
[117] ibid, 876.

In human rights treaties, 'jurisdiction' generally refers to the 'actual exercise of control and authority' by a State over persons or territory.[118] Every time a State exercises this power, it must protect and ensure the rights of people under its control. In *Hirsi v Italy*, the ECtHR dealt with the question of the extraterritorial interpretation of 'jurisdiction' somewhat briefly; it did however develop its previous jurisprudence by affirming that the *ratione loci* scope of the Convention extends also to the high seas, provided that the State exercises effective control and authority through its organs over the individuals concerned.[119]

Pursuant to Article 1 of the ECHR, 'The High Contracting Parties shall secure to everyone [therefore even refugees, stateless persons, and undocumented migrants] within their jurisdiction the rights and freedoms defined in Section I of this Convention.' Since the phrasing of Article 1 'under its jurisdiction' is not geographically limited, it could be interpreted as exceeding the territorial borders of the State in question. Jurisdiction is therefore understood to be a threshold criterion that triggers human rights obligations of States towards certain people, within and outside the territory of a Contracting Party to the ECHR.[120]

A heated debate on the extraterritorial applicability of the ECHR has unfolded in the wake of the *Bankovic v Belgium* case, where the Court rejected the responsibility of the respondent States with regard to the NATO bombing of Serbia, a country that was considered as not falling within the legal space of the ECHR Contracting Parties.[121] Discarding the *Bankovic* paradigm and the

[118] T Meron, 'Extraterritoriality of Human Rights Treaties' (1995) 89 *American Journal of International Law* 78–83; P De Sena, *La nozione di Giurisdizione Statale nei Trattati sui Diritti dell'Uomo* (Giappichelli, 2002); G Ress, 'Problems of Extraterritorial Human Rights Violations. The Jurisdiction of the European Court of Human Rights' (2002) 12(1) *Italian Yearbook of International Law* 51–67; M Milanovic, *The Extraterritorial Application of Human Rights Treaties* (OUP, 2011) 8.

[119] *Hirsi v Italy*, above n 4, paras 76–82.

[120] See *Al-Skeini v UK*, App no 55721/07 (7 July 2011), para 140. M O'Boyle, 'The European Convention on Human Rights and Extraterritorial Jurisdiction: A Comment on "Life after Bankovic"' in Coomans and Kamminga 2004, n 66 above, 125, 130, 133. To read more on the concept of jurisdiction under Art 1 of the ECHR, see, GS Goodwin-Gill, 'The Extraterritorial Reach of Human Rights Obligations: a Brief Perspective on the Link to Jurisdiction' in L Boisson de Chazournes and MC Kohen (eds), *International Law and the Quest for its Implementation/Le Droit International et la Quête de sa Mise en Oeuvre: Liber Amicorum Vera Gowlland-Debbas* (Brill, 2010) 306; R Nigro, 'Giurisdizione e Obblighi Positivi degli Stati Parti della Convenzione Europea dei Diritti dell'Uomo: il Caso *Ilascu*' (2005) *Rivista di Diritto Internazionale* 413–40; M Gondek, 'Extraterritorial Application of the European Convention on Human Rights: Territorial Focus in the Age of Globalization' (2005) 52 *Netherlands International Law Review* 349–87; P De Sena, 'The Notion of 'Contracting Parties' Jurisdiction' under Article 1 of the ECHR: Some Marginal Remarks on Nigro's Paper' ('La nozione di 'giurisdizione degli Stati contraenti' nell'articolo 1 della Convenzione europea dei diritti dell'uomo: alcune osservazioni critiche in margine all'intervento di R Nigro') (2011) 20 *Italian Yearbook of International Law* 75–83; Besson 2012, n 65 above, 862–64.

[121] *Bankovic v Belgium*, above n 40. For an extended critical analysis of the *Bankovic* case, see R Lawson, 'Life after Bankovic – On the Extraterritorial Application of the European Convention on Human Rights' in F Coomans and M Kamminga 2004, n 66 above, 104; K Wouters, *International Legal Standards for the Protection from Refoulement* (Intersentia, 2009) 205–06.

requirement of *legal authority* to establish jurisdiction, the Court has accepted extraterritorial jurisdiction and, therefore, the consequent responsibility of governments for actions performed by their authorities outside of their borders, in several other cases concerning three different circumstances:[122] (i) cases 'where the acts of State authorities produced effects or were performed outside their own territory';[123] (ii) cases in which a contracting party 'exercised effective control of an area outside its national territory' as a consequence of military action;[124] (iii) cases involving the activities of a contracting party's 'diplomatic or consular agents abroad and on board craft and vessels registered in, or flying the flag of, that State.'[125]

In several other instances where States acted outside of the ECHR space, the Court found violations of Convention rights.[126] Beyond legal authority, a *factual* appraisal, determined 'with reference to the particular facts', can be sufficient to establish jurisdiction.[127] This would be in line, for example, with the ICJ's position that 'physical control of a territory, and not sovereignty or legitimacy of title, is the basis for State liability for acts affecting other States.'[128] The main approach of the ECtHR is that jurisdiction depends on whether a certain *de facto* power gives rise to human rights obligations with regard to a certain territory or individual.[129] Although, in *Hirsi v Italy*, the Court reaffirmed that the jurisdiction of a State is essentially territorial,[130] it upholds legal precedents by endorsing the view that for extraterritorial jurisdiction to be triggered, the applicants should be 'under the continuous and exclusive *de jure* and *de facto* control of the [respondent State's] authorities.'[131]

[122] The first three categories of exceptions were first set out by the ECtHR in *Loizidou v Turkey*, above n 115, para 62. *Bankovic v Belgium*, above n 40, essentially reaffirmed and refined these categories of exceptions (paras 68–70, 73).

[123] ibid, para 69; See *Drozd and Janousek v France and Spain*, App no 12747/87 (26 June 1992), para 91.

[124] *Bankovic v Belgium*, above n 40, para 70. See also, *Cyprus v Turkey*, above n 115, para 76.

[125] *Bankovic v Belgium*, above n 40, para 73. In this regard, the Court in *Hirsi v Italy* also cites *Al Saadoon and Mufdhi v United Kingdom*, App no 61498/08 (30 June 2009) para 85.

[126] See eg, *Medvedyev and Others v France*, App 3394/03 (29 March 2010). With regard to State security forces acting abroad, see eg, *Öcalan v Turkey*, App no 46221/99 (12 May 2005); and *Ilich Sanchez Ramirez v France*, App no 59450/00 (4 July 2006). On cases of military presence abroad, see *Al-Saadoon*, above n 169; *Al-Skeini v UK*, App no 55721/07 (7 July 2011); *Al-Jedda v UK*, App no 27021/08 (7 July 2011). With regard to military intervention exercising effective control, see *Markovic and Others v Italy*, App no 1398/03 (14 December 2006); *Mansur PAD and Others v Turkey*, App no 60167/00, Admissibility (28 June 2007).

[127] *Al-Skeini v UK*, above n 126, para 132.

[128] *Legal Consequences for States of the Continued Presence of South Africa in Namibia (West Africa)*, 21 June 1971, ICJ Rep 16, para 118.

[129] See, E Roxstrom, M Gibney and T Einarsen, 'The Nato Bombing Case (*Bankovic et al v Belgium et al*), and the Limits of Western Human Rights Protection' (2005) 23 *Boston University International Law Journal* 55, 112; see also Moreno-Lax 2017, n 2 above, 275.

[130] *Hirsi v Italy*, above n 4, para 71.

[131] ibid, paras 81, 73. The Court refers here to *Al-Skeini v UK*, above n 126, paras 132 and 136; and to *Medvedyev v France*, above n 126, para 67.

The next Section will discuss how the border materialises wherever a State exercises its functions of migration control, and how *non-refoulement* can be interpreted as a 'principle of non-rejection at the maritime frontier.'[132] In line with this 'functional' notion of jurisdiction, it can be argued that the ECtHR in *Hirsi* could have inferred Italy's jurisdiction even without referring to Article 4 of the Navigation Code whereby Italian vessels ought to be considered part of Italian territory.[133] The Court was eager to show that its decision was consistent with its previous jurisprudence. For instance, in 1992, the European Commission on Human Rights had already dealt with cases concerning extraterritorial *non-refoulement* from an embassy in the territory of a non-Contracting Party to the ECHR.[134]

The *Al-Jedda v UK* case concerned an Iraqi national who – for overarching reasons of security in Iraq – in October 2004 was arrested on suspicion of involvement in terrorism and subsequently detained for over three years at a detention facility in Basra (Iraq) run by British forces. When major military operations in Iraq were declared complete in May 2003, a United Nations Assistance Mission for Iraq (UNAMI) was established and the UK became an occupying power. According to the ECtHR, although UN Resolution 1511, adopted on 16 October 2003, authorised 'a multinational force under unified command to take all necessary measures to contribute to the maintenance of security and stability in Iraq', the acts of soldiers within the Multi-National Force continued to be attributable to the troop-contributing nations, and not to the UN.[135] Moreover, the US and the UK, through the establishment of the Coalition Provisional Authority, 'continued to exercise the powers of government in Iraq.'[136] Therefore, because the UK exercised continuous authority and control over Mr Al-Jedda throughout his internment (which took place within a detention facility controlled exclusively by British forces), the applicant clearly fell within the jurisdiction of the UK for the purpose of Article 1 of the Convention.[137]

In the *Al Saadoon and Mufdhi v UK* case,[138] the ECtHR held that the UK exercised jurisdiction when it handed over the applicants in its custody in Iraq to the authorities of the host country. Indeed, 'given the total and exclusive *de facto*, and subsequently also *de jure*, control exercised by the British authorities over the premises in question, the individuals detained there, including the applicants, were within the UK's jurisdiction',[139] despite the existence of a

[132] S Trevisanut, 'The Principle of *Non-Refoulement* and the De-Territorialization of Border Control at Sea' (2014) 27 *Leiden Journal of International Law* 661, 672–73.

[133] *Hirsi v Italy*, above n 4, para 7.

[134] *WM v Denmark*, App no 17392/90 (14 October 1992) para 1.

[135] *Al-Jedda v UK*, above n 126, para 80.

[136] ibid, para 80.

[137] ibid, paras 85–86.

[138] *Al Saadoon and Mufdhi v United Kingdom*, App no 61498/08 (30 June 2009).

[139] ibid para 88.

bilateral agreement with Iraq obliging the British authorities to hand over the detainees.[140] Considering the lack of a binding assurance that the death penalty would not be imposed (causing severe psychological suffering on the part of the applicants), the Court found a violation of Article 3 of the Convention.[141]

In *Al-Skeini v UK*, the ECtHR recognised that full and exclusive control over individuals was sufficient for triggering the extraterritorial jurisdiction of the acting State.[142] The six individuals killed in Iraq in the course of security operations fell under the jurisdiction of British authorities who had responsibility for maintaining security in South East Iraq. Indeed, by virtue of the relevant UN Security Council Resolution and Regulations of the Coalition Provisional Authority in Iraq,[143] the UK and the US took on the exercise of some *public powers* normally exercised by a sovereign government.[144]

Whilst *de jure* jurisdiction refers to the lawful exercise of authority extraterritorially,

> *De facto* jurisdiction can arise in at least three ways. The first is a territorial conception based on the occupying power-type scenario. The second scenario is personal and involves individuals subject to the State's physical power or control. The third reflects a combination of the territorial and personal elements of the first two, with an emphasis on the background exercise of governmental authority.[145]

To conclude, the recent jurisprudence of the Court suggests that extraterritorial applicability of the Convention can be established only on a casuistic basis every time either *de jure* or *de facto* jurisdiction arises. The inclusion of '*de facto* jurisdiction' implies that accountability under human rights law can also be established where there is no entitlement to act under general international law.

(i) Discussing the 'Effective Control' Criterion

Extraterritorial jurisdiction in human rights law would be engaged when a State exercises *de facto* authority and effective control over an area or persons beyond its borders. Particularly with human rights treaties, the effectiveness of human rights requires States to interpret relevant treaties in a way that does not make such rights illusory or theoretical, but rather renders them practical and effective,[146] in keeping with their object and purpose.

In order to qualify as jurisdiction, State control should be 'effective', 'overall', and 'normative'.[147] The normative dimension of authority in jurisdiction is

[140] ibid paras 126–28, 140–45.
[141] ibid paras 143–44.
[142] *Al-Skeini v UK*, above n 126, para 149.
[143] ibid, paras 143–48.
[144] ibid, para 149.
[145] C Costello, *The Human Rights of Migrants and Refugees in European Law* (OUP, 2016) 241.
[146] See ECtHR, *Artico v Italy*, App no 6694/74 (13 May 1980) para 33.
[147] To read more on this systematisation, see Besson 2012, n 65 above, 872–74.

understood to be the 'exercise of some or all of the public powers normally to be exercised by a sovereign government.'[148] The 'effective control' element – which should be assessed as a matter of fact – was introduced by the ECtHR in the 1995 *Loizidou* case.[149] The same case also refers to 'effective *overall* control' over a foreign territory.[150] Such phrasing was not used in *Al-Skeini* whose focus was more on personal control.[151] In *Al Skeini*, the Court found the UK responsible for exercising authority and control over individuals through its soldiers. It thus confirmed the dual approach of 'state agent's control and authority' (personal) and the 'control over an area abroad' (territorial).[152] Moreover, it specified that jurisdiction can also be established *de facto*, via 'the use of force'[153] and 'the exercise of physical power and control over the person in question'.[154] However, the responsibility of the UK was here justified as an *exceptional* circumstance, where the respondent State had exercised *public powers* in Iraq (powers which are normally exerted by a sovereign government). By focusing on the standard of public authority as the key element, the ECtHR preserved the logic of control, but made the criterion of effectiveness recede. As held by Tzevelekos,

> States exercising public authority (especially if they do so willingly, as a consequence of military invasion) are automatically presumed to exercise control leading to the expansion of their jurisdiction beyond their own territory, that is over the territory under their authority. Although the factual element of effectiveness recedes, the question of control remains intact. [155]

As mentioned above, the ECtHR introduced the concept of effective control in the *Loizidou* case, holding that what matters in cases of extraterritorial wrongdoing is not the attribution of certain conduct to a State party to the ECHR, but rather the effective control it exercises over a situation, which can then engage its extraterritorial jurisdiction:

> The responsibility of a Contracting Party may also arise when as a consequence of military action – whether lawful or unlawful – it exercises *effective control* of an area outside its national territory. The obligation to secure, in such an area, the rights and freedoms set out in the Convention derives from the fact of such control, whether it be exercised directly, through its armed forces, or through a subordinate local administration (emphasis added).[156]

[148] ibid.
[149] See *Loizidou v Turkey*, above n 115, para 62; *Al-Skeini v UK*, above n 126, para 133 and 138.
[150] *Loizidou v Turkey*, above n 115, para 62.
[151] *Al-Skeini v UK*, above n 126, para 138.
[152] *Al-Skeini v UK*, above n 126, paras 132–133 ff.
[153] ibid, para 136.
[154] ibid.
[155] VP Tzevelekos, 'Reconstructing the Effective Control Criterion in Extraterritorial Human Rights Breaches: Direct Attribution of Wrongfulness, Due Diligence, and Concurrent Responsibility' (2014) 36 *Michigan Journal of International Law* 129, 150.
[156] *Loizidou v Turkey*, above n 115, para 62.

The inclusion of the 'effective control' criterion represents a departure from earlier (pre-1995) Strasbourg reasoning. For instance, in *Drozd v France*, the ECtHR affirmed that jurisdiction is not exclusively territorial, and that in a case of extraterritorial wrongful conduct, the question is 'whether the acts complained of … can be attributed to [the respondent State], even though they were not performed on the territory of those States.'[157] Responsibility is therefore linked here only to attribution. State jurisdiction is not one of the criteria that ILC norms require for holding a State responsible for extraterritorial wrongdoing. What counts is causality, namely a nexus between the person affected and the perpetrator of an alleged violation, which will thus engage the responsibility of the State in question.[158] To give another example, in *Stocké v Federal Republic of Germany*,[159] the European Commission on Human Rights did not mention effective control as a precondition for jurisdiction, and argued that jurisdiction

> is not limited to the national territory of the High Contracting Party concerned, but extends to all persons under its *actual authority and responsibility*, whether this authority is exercised on its own territory or abroad. … *Insofar as the State's acts or omissions affect such persons*, the responsibility of that State is engaged (emphasis added).[160]

The ECtHR has also followed an approach similar to its earlier jurisprudence in the more recent *Ilascu* case concerning the actions of the Moldovan Republic of Transnistria (MRT), a non-state entity under the effective authority of Russia, which is found responsible for the MRT's conduct. Moreover, in disregarding the effective control test as a precondition to jurisdiction, the Court upholds – as an exception – the responsibility of Moldova, even though it does not exercise control over the territory of the MRT. Therefore, in a key passage, the Court affirms that:

> *Even in the absence of effective control* over the Transdniestrian region, Moldova still has a positive obligation under Article 1 of the Convention to take the diplomatic, economic, judicial or other measures that it is in its power to take and are in accordance with international law to secure to the applicants the rights guaranteed by the Convention. … Responsibility for the acts complained of, committed in the territory of the MRT, over which [Moldova] exercises no effective authority, is to be assessed in the light of its *positive obligations* under the Convention (emphasis added).[161]

What is essential here is that the respondent State would exercise jurisdiction (regarding the actions of a third party) over the territory and the victims

157 *Drozd and Janousek v France and Spain*, above n 123, para 91.

158 FJ Hampson, 'Using International Human Rights Machinery to Enforce the International Law of Armed Conflicts' (1992) 31 *Revue de Droit Militaire et de Droit de la Guerre* 119, 122.

159 *Stocké v Federal Republic of Germany*, App no 11755/85 (12 October 1989).

160 ibid, para 166.

161 *Ilascu v Moldova and Russia*, App no 48787/99 (8 July 2004) paras 331 and 335.

despite the lack of effective control.[162] This would represent a case of concurrent responsibility deriving from the same factual situation: Russia is liable for direct violation of the right to liberty, while Moldova is responsible for indirect violation of the same rule for its failure to comply with its positive obligation to fight – to the best of its (limited) *effective* means – the wrong in question, which is attributed to Russia. In similar cases, such as *Catan* and *Ivantoc*, both against Moldova and Russia, the Court was instead satisfied that Moldova had made substantial efforts to assist people suffering from the wrongful conduct of a third party. Although it exercised no control over the area in question, it sufficiently fulfilled its positive obligations according to its available, limited capabilities and capacity.[163]

Alongside cases such as *Ilascu* and *Catan*, where the ECtHR applied the attribution test in order to establish jurisdiction of Russia because of its 'decisive influence' and control over the actions of the MRT, in the 2014 *Jaloud v Netherlands*, the Court even more neatly conflated the concepts of jurisdiction and attribution. An attribution test aims to identify *who* should be held accountable rather than asking *whether* the ECHR is applicable outside territorial borders of the respondent State through 'physical force'[164] or 'custody'[165] over an individual, or military presence over a territory.[166] What counts is indeed the degree of control that the State has over the entities perpetrating rights' violations, rather than the control of the State over a certain territory.[167] In *Jaloud*, the Netherlands was found responsible despite the fact it was not one of the Occupying Powers (UK and US) in Iraq. What was decisive in the establishment of jurisdiction (by means of attributing acts to the respondent State) was that it was in 'full command'.[168] The fact that the Netherlands asserted 'authority and control over persons passing through the checkpoint', within the limits of its Stabilization Force in Iraq mission (SFIR),[169] is deemed by Rooney to be a 'rhetorical flourish rather that an assertion that the Court based its findings of jurisdiction on a "State agent authority and control" test.'[170]

The case concerned the death of an individual shot to death at a checkpoint in Iraq which was nominally manned by the Iraqi Civil Defence Corps (ICDC), subordinated to the Coalition Forces. However, what mattered was that the Netherlands 'assumed responsibility for providing security in that area, to

[162] ibid, para 335.

[163] *Catan v Moldova and Russia*, Apps nos 43370/04, 8252/05 and 18454/06 (19 October 2012) paras 147–148; *Ivantoc and Others v Republic of Moldova and Russia*, App no 23687/05 (15 November 2011) para 108.

[164] See *Ocalan v Turkey*, App no 46221/99 (12 May 2005) para 93.

[165] *Al-Skeini v UK*, above n 126, para 136.

[166] *Issa v Turkey*, App no 31821/96 (16 November 2004) para 75.

[167] JM Rooney, 'The Relationship between Jurisdiction and Attribution after *Jaloud v the Netherlands*' (2015) 62 *Netherlands International Law Review* 408–09.

[168] *Jaloud v the Netherlands*, App no 47708/08 (20 November 2014) paras 143, 147, 149.

[169] ibid, para 152.

[170] Rooney 2015, n 167 above, 414.

the exclusion of other participating States, and retained full command over its contingent there.'[171] Therefore, the Court found that the Netherlands engaged jurisdiction as it exercised control over the checkpoint where the shooting occurred, and was responsible for violation of the procedural duty under Article 2's right to life, to carry out an effective investigation of the death of the applicant's son.[172]

Referring to the *Al-Skeini* judgment, in *Hassan v UK*,[173] the Court argued that from 1 May 2003 until 28 June 2005, British troops were mandated to maintain security in Southern Iraq. Therefore, it was unnecessary to assess whether a certain person was under their sovereignty and jurisdiction, as the UK was exercising effective military control.[174] In the *Hassan* case, the Grand Chamber held that, under the agreement on the administration of the detention camp, the applicant's brother was under the authority and control of the UK. Although Camp Bucca was under the operational command of the US, and the respondent State contended that jurisdiction had passed from the UK to the US upon the arrival of the applicant's brother at the camp, and that certain aspects of detention in this camp were dealt by the US troops, the individual in question remained a British prisoner: the UK 'retained authority and control over all aspects of the detention relevant to the applicant's complaints under Article 5'.[175] Therefore, the notion of extraterritorial jurisdiction is here expanded, as it no longer rests upon the concept of 'effective military control' over a certain area, or on 'overall control', but rather on the more vague notion of 'specific powers of decision and control, and on the power to release the detainee.'[176]

'Overall control' refers to a situation of continuous dominion over a foreign area so as to establish a form of extended (*de facto*) jurisdiction. In these circumstances, 'the controlling State has responsibility under Article 1 to secure within the area under its control, the entire range of substantive rights set out in the Convention and in those additional Protocols which it has ratified.'[177] Instead in situations of specific control of a certain area, the State in question has a duty to comply only with the rights that are relevant in those particular circumstances.[178] *Hassan* and *Jaloud* prove that jurisdiction under Article 1 of the Convention is engaged as long as the respondent States are in control of the *specific* event or situation (either a checkpoint or the detention of a prisoner),

[171] *Jaloud v the Netherlands*, above n 168, para 149.
[172] ibid, para 227.
[173] *Hassan v UK*, App no 29750/09 (16 September 2014).
[174] ibid, para 75.
[175] ibid, paras 77–78. For an analysis of the case, see, C De Koker, '*Hassan v United Kingdom*: The Interaction of Human Rights Law and International Humanitarian Law with regard to the Deprivation of Liberty in Armed Conflicts' (2015) 31(81) *Utrecht Journal of International and European Law* 90–96.
[176] Caflish 2017, n 115 above, 192.
[177] *Al -Skeini v UK*, above n 126, para 138 referring to *Cyprus v Turkey*, above n 115, paras 76–77.
[178] *Al-Skeini v UK*, above n 126, para 137.

regardless of whether they are occupants or exercising exclusive control of a certain area.[179]

Another case to be mentioned is *Pisari v Republic of Moldova and Russia* concerning the shooting of a young Moldovan by a Russian soldier in the 'security zone' separating Moldova from Transnistria, and manned by military personnel from Moldova, Russia and Transnistria.[180] In finding Russia responsible for a procedural violation of Article 2 of the Convention, the ECtHR held that extraterritorial jurisdiction can be engaged, on the basis of an *international agreement*, when the agents of a Contracting State

> carry out executive functions on the territory of another State … In the present case, the checkpoint in question, situated in the security zone, was manned and commanded by Russian soldiers in accordance with the agreement putting an end to the military conflict in the Transnistrian region of Moldova ….[181]

To conclude, while restricting its regional sphere of competence by delimiting extraterritorial jurisdiction to cases of effective control might be a legitimate goal for the ECtHR – which strives not to become a 'universal court – it could have better explained the reasons why it departed from its previous case law and from general international law. States should not be allowed to violate human rights outside borders, regardless of the degree of effective control they exercise over a person, land, ship, or a situation.[182] Indeed, as held by the Court in the *Issa* case, 'Article 1 of the Convention cannot be interpreted so as to allow a State party to perpetrate violations of the Convention on the territory of another State which it could not perpetrate on its own territory.'[183] In this regard, Clapham radically invites us to consider as the starting point the fact that individuals have inherent human rights under international law. Therefore, treaty law or constitutional law limitations can be deemed jurisdictional barriers to accessing a particular court, but they do not alter the fact that human rights violations have been committed outside territorial borders. 'We should not fall into the trap' – he argues – 'of equating the limits to the jurisdiction of a Court in Strasbourg or Ottawa or Washington, or the Strand, with the scope of international human rights law.'[184] Although compelling, such a discussion would flow however, into moral philosophy, thereby opening up a new chapter, which would go beyond the remit of this work.

[179] For a reconstruction of the ECtHR's recent practice on extraterritorial jurisdiction, see Caflish 2017, n 115 above, 189–97.

[180] *Pisari v Republic of Moldova and Russia*, App no 42139712 (21 April 2015).

[181] ibid, para 33.

[182] VP Tzevelekos and K Proukaki, 'Migrants at Sea: A Duty of Plural States to Protect (Extraterritorially)?' (2017) 86(4) *Nordic Journal of International Law* 427.

[183] *Issa and Others v Turkey* App no 31821/96 (16 November 2004) para 69.

[184] A Clapham, 'The Changing Character of Human Rights', *European Lecture delivered at Nissan Lecture Theatre St. Antony's College*, Oxford, 12 November 2015.

(ii) Non-refoulement *in Migration Control Activities Beyond Borders: The ECtHR's Take*

As a preliminary note, the emphasis of this Sub-section will primarily lie on jurisdiction and State responsibility regarding the treatment of refugees arriving by sea, as this analysis is preparatory to the assessment of bilateral interception practices addressed in Chapter five of this work. Nonetheless, conclusions drawn from this investigation would also be relevant for other forms of extraterritorial immigration controls. Despite the notion of jurisdiction being primarily territorial, international human rights bodies have applied the relevant treaties beyond the borders of Contracting States every time they exercise authority or control abroad, in relation to persons or areas, and regardless of the legality of the act. In the previous Sub-section, the notion of extraterritorial jurisdiction was seen to no longer rest only on the concept of effective military control over a certain area, physical force over an individual or overall control, but also on the freer notion of *specific* powers of decision and control. Recent cases show indeed that what counts is the degree of control by the State over the entities perpetrating rights' violation, rather than the control by the State over territory.

The arguments made above in favour of the extraterritorial applicability of the ECHR to territories outside the geographic area of the Council of Europe imply that even protection claims made at the border of the destination State fall under its jurisdiction. Therefore, under the Convention, a State shall be responsible for any act or omission concerning the protection-claimant and the entry request.[185] In these circumstances, no difference exists between removal and denial of entry, given that both situations would potentially expose the individual to proscribed ill-treatment.[186] Hence, the prohibition of *refoulement*, implicit in Article 3 of the Convention, shall be applied to people claiming protection within the territory of a Contracting State, as well as to those intercepted at the border, without distinction.[187]

Whereas the applicability of the principle of *non-refoulement* to protection seekers claiming asylum at the border is quite evident, the applicability of this principle to people intercepted at sea during offshore migration controls is less conclusive. As Gavouneli explains with regard to the law of the sea and the maritime context,

> the extent of the territorial jurisdiction does not coincide with the territory of the State. Typically, it acquires a functional nature when it extends to the contiguous zone [Article 33 UNCLOS], where the coastal State can exercise jurisdiction in relation to customs, fiscal, sanitary, and immigration matters.[188]

Following this thread, Trevisanut emphasises how the functional nature of State jurisdiction at sea distinguishes maritime frontiers from land borders.

[185] Noll 2000, n 286 below, 441–42.
[186] ibid, 442.
[187] ibid, 441–45.
[188] Gavouneli 2007, n 56 above, 10.

The fluidity of maritime frontiers is due to the absence of fixed checkpoints for migration control. Therefore, on the one hand, there are maritime borders drawn on maps, which delineate a physical area in which a State exercises its diverse degrees of sovereignty according to the legal regimes of the differing maritime zones. Here, the powers that the State exercises are functional, for the protection of certain interests that international law deems fundamental within that particular maritime zone.

On the other hand, there is a 'functional maritime frontier',[189] which materialises wherever the State performs its functions of border control, including on the high seas – that is to say beyond the physical space delimited by the 'map maritime frontier'.[190] While engaged in such extraterritorial activities, States exercise powers pertaining to border control prerogatives, which find their legal basis in national policies or bilateral/multilateral cooperation mechanisms. Such legal bases (legislative jurisdiction) limit and shape the content of the acting State's enforcement jurisdiction, namely its power 'to take executive action in pursuance of or consequent upon the making of decisions or rules'.[191] When States 'offshore' their migration controls, they move only part of the border's legal regime, as not all the elements linked with the territory can apply outside the territory. Nevertheless, all the elements concerning the persons under control do apply. This means that the principle of *non-refoulement* – related to the removal of a person to a country where her life and liberty can be threatened – is binding also when States de-territorialise their migration controls. Within this picture, *non-refoulement* – which has been interpreted as also including non-rejection at the physical border – translates into a 'principle of non-rejection at the maritime frontier' (in its broader functional meaning).[192]

To shed light on the extraterritorial applicability of the ECHR, it may help to go back to the views adopted by the Court in previous cases. In *Xhavara and Others v Italy and Albania*, the Court held that Italy had a responsibility toward intercepted individuals during the performance of border surveillance measures on the high seas – and *a fortiori* for the protection of the principle of *non-refoulement*.[193] The case was declared inadmissible due to a failure to exhaust domestic remedies. Nonetheless, the Court clarified that the sinking of a boat carrying Albanian migrants following a collision with an Italian warship – deployed in the framework of an agreement authorising the Italian Navy to board and search Albanian vessels – could not exclude the international responsibility of Italy.[194]

[189] Trevisanut 2014, n 132 above, 672.

[190] Ibid.

[191] Brownlie 2003, n 55 above, 297. See also, *inter alia*, V Lowe and C Staker, 'Jurisdiction', in M Evans (ed), *International Law* (OUP, 2010) 313; B Simma and AT Muller, 'Exercise and Limits of Jurisdiction', in J Crawford and M Koskenniemi (eds), *The Cambridge Companion to International Law* (CUP, 2012) 134.

[192] Trevisanut 2014, n 132 above, 673.

[193] *Xhavara v Italy*, App no 39473/98, Admissibility Decision (11 January 2001).

[194] See R Weinzierl and U Lisson, *Border Management and Human Rights* (German Institute for Human Rights, 2007) 63, 70.

Hirsi extends the decision in *Xhavara* insofar as it is the first case in which the Court was called upon to deal with persons claiming refuge against *refoulement* on the high seas, further away from the territory of a Contracting Party. In *Xhavara*, Albanians did not seek such protection, and as a consequence, the Court did not investigate what obligations Italy might have had in this respect. But, as recognised by the ECtHR, in the 2009 push-backs, individuals in distress on the high seas were entitled to protection and to have their claims assessed. Indeed, they were, *de facto*, under the actual control of Italian authorities, who were therefore in a position to either protect or violate their rights.

The *Hirsi* reasoning on jurisdiction is grounded in the ECtHR's jurisprudence concerning interdiction of vessels on the high seas.[195] In the 2010 *Medvedyev and Others v France* decision, the Grand Chamber stated that

> the special nature of the maritime environment ... cannot justify an area outside the law where ships' crews are covered by no legal system capable of affording them enjoyment of the rights and guarantees protected by the Convention which the States have undertaken to secure to everyone within their jurisdiction, any more than it can provide offenders with a 'safe haven'.[196]

In the *Hirsi v Italy* case, despite the fact that the interception occurred in international waters, the Italian government never disputed the jurisdiction of the Court under Article 1 of the Convention. The applicants were, indeed, put on-board ships whose crews were composed of Italian military personnel and who exercised a 'continuous and exclusive *de jure* and *de facto* control' over the intercepted people.[197] And, in line with the *Medvedyev* principle, this deduction would be valid even in circumstances where the passengers were simply escorted to Tripoli. In *Hirsi*, the Court found it decisive that Italy was the flag State, and therefore the applicants were within the exclusive jurisdiction of the State of the flag the vessel was flying. While here *de jure* and *de facto* jurisdiction accumulated, it seems that in the presence of *de jure* jurisdiction, triggered by either actions or omissions, minimal *de facto* control can also be sufficient to trigger Article 1 and thus engage extraterritorial responsibility under the Convention.[198]

By stressing that the issue of extraterritorial jurisdiction must be resolved with reference to the particular facts of the case,[199] and the acts or omissions imputable to the State,[200] the Grand Chamber held that intercepted individuals were

[195] See, eg, *Mevedyev v France*, above n 170; *Women on Waves and Others v Portugal*, App no 31276/05 (3 May 2009).

[196] *Medvedyev and Others v France*, above n 126, para 81. See, E Papastavridis, 'European Court of Human Rights: *Medvedyev et al v France*' (2010) 59(3) *International & Comparative Law Quarterly* 867–82.

[197] *Hirsi v Italy*, above n 4, para 81.

[198] On this point, see also Moreno-Lax 2017, n 2 above, 280.

[199] *Hirsi v Italy*, above n 4, para 73.

[200] ibid, para 70.

under the complete, effective, and exclusive control of Italian organs. Therefore, it rejected the Italian government's argument that it 'was not responsible for the fate of the applicants on account of the allegedly minimal control exercised by the authorities over the parties concerned at the material time.'[201] It concluded that *Hirsi* constituted 'a case of extra-territorial exercise of jurisdiction by Italy capable of engaging that State's responsibility under the Convention.'[202]

A possible interpretation of the 'effective control' element would link it to the establishment of physical contact between intercepting authorities and intercepted people.[203] However, shifting emphasis from State action *per se* to the *consequences* of such action, it seems fitting to argue that jurisdiction (and, potentially, responsibility) under international human rights law can also be engaged in those operations of looser-control at sea. Examples include causing a boat to modify its course by screaming (ordering to change course) or steaming nearby until it leaves the territorial waters or the contiguous zone, prohibiting rescued migrants from accessing ports, as well as either conducting or escorting the ship to a third country, all of which result in the push-back of migrants and refugees to frontiers of territories where their life and liberty can be seriously threatened.

The 'minimal control threshold' – requiring no more than 'authority over' or 'control of' a specific situation – was also applied in the *Al-Skeini* case in respect of one of the six persons killed in Iraq by British authorities. According to the applicant, he and his family were sitting around the dinner table when there was a sudden burst of machine-gunfire from outside the building and bullets struck his wife in the head.[204] The Court here attributed much significance to the 'functional' connection between the deceased and the British soldiers, thereby framing jurisdiction within the 'cause-and-effect' notion. Indeed, it held that:

> The third applicant's wife was killed during an exchange of fire between a patrol of British soldiers and unidentified gunmen and *it is not known which side fired the fatal bullet*. The Court considers that, since the death occurred in the course of a United Kingdom security operation, when British soldiers carried out a patrol in the vicinity of the applicant's home and joined in the fatal exchange of fire, there was a *jurisdictional link* between the United Kingdom and this deceased also (emphasis added).[205]

Reliance on such a 'functional test' to establish instantaneous jurisdiction also occurred in the *Andreou* case, which concerned the shooting of a demonstrator

[201] ibid, para 79.
[202] ibid, para 78.
[203] *Mutatis Mutandis*, this approach would be in line with the ECtHR's decision in *Bankovic v Belgium and Others*, above n 40; or the House of Lord's judgment in *Al-Skeini and Others (Respondents) v Secretary of State for Defence (Appellant); Al-Skeini and Others (Appellants) v Secretary of State for Defence (Respondent) (Consolidated Appeals)*, 13 June 2007, [2007] UKHL 26.
[204] *Al-Skeini v UK*, above n 126 para 44.
[205] ibid, para 149.

by the Turkish authorities within the buffer zone in Cyprus.[206] According to the Court,

> even though the applicant sustained her injuries in the territory over which Turkey exercised no control, opening fire on the crowd from close range, which was the immediate and direct cause of those injuries, was such that the applicant must be regarded as within the jurisdiction of Turkey.[207]

Likewise, the Court found Turkish jurisdiction in the *Isaak* case concerning an individual who was beaten to death by Turkish and Cypriot demonstrators and Turkish Republic of Northern Cyprus authorities inside the UN-controlled area, thereby implicitly corroborating the 'cause-and-effect' approach.[208] From a joint reading of these cases, it emerges that the concept of 'effective control' engaging Article 1 of the ECHR also involves those State actions that may fall short of arresting, detaining, or extraditing the individuals concerned.[209] 'Effective control' implies any coercive conduct imposed on a person through the use of direct force (ie, by shooting or bombing), 'but also less intrusive measures like forcing a boat off of its course',[210] or killing someone in an exchange of fire where it is not known which side fired the fatal bullet.[211]

Turning back to the context of migration controls at sea, if preventing entry into territorial waters does not automatically amount to *refoulement*, violations of this principle still may arise if refugees are removed to the borders of a dangerous and unsafe country. Therefore, interdicting authorities must always determine whether a specific third State is 'safe, accessible, and reachable for the boat in question.'[212] By referring to its previous case law in the context of expulsions in *Hirsi*, the Court confirmed that the prohibition of torture implies an obligation to not remove the individual in question where substantial grounds have been shown for believing that the removed person would face a real risk of treatment banned by Article 3.[213] Additionally, the Court had the chance to comment on those positive human rights obligations that are incumbent upon States during and after naval interdiction. By stating that the removal by Italy of interdicted migrants and refugees to Libya, in the absence of any procedural safeguards, was impermissible, the Court built on an emerging trend in international human rights law.

[206] *Andreou v Turkey*, App no 45653/99 (3 June 2008).

[207] ibid, 11.

[208] *Isaak v Turkey*, App no 44587/98 (28 September 2006) 16.

[209] See, eg, *Ocalan v Turkey*, above n 164; *Al-Saadoon and Mufdhi v UK*, above n 138; and *Medvedyev v France*, above n 126. See also, R Bank, 'Refugees at Sea; Introduction to Article 11 of the 1951 Convention' in Zimmermann 2011, n 77 above, 841.

[210] ibid.

[211] *Al-Saadoon v UK*, above n 138.

[212] Bank 2011, n 77 above, 849.

[213] *Hirsi v Italy*, above n 4, para 114. The Court cites *Soering v UK*, above n 41, paras 90–91; *Vilvarajah v UK*, above n 42, para 103; *Jabari v Turkey*, above n 52, para 38; *Ahmed v Austria*, above n 46, para 39; *HLR v France*, App no 24573/94 (29 April 1997) para 34; and *Salah Sheekh v The Netherlands*, App no 1948/04 (11 January 2007) para 135.

The extraterritorial applicability of *non-refoulement* can also be invoked in more recent cases of 'contactless' controls at sea where interceptions and rescue operations are conducted by third countries with the clear, profound support of European States.[214] On a number of occasions involving pull-backs of migrants by Libyan vessels, Italian authorities were operatively present, especially in the localisation of migrants' boats, not least in preventing them from continuing their journey towards a safe port in Europe, and in facilitating the diversion of migrants to the country of departure through cooperation and coordination with Libyan search and rescue services.

For instance, on 27 September 2017, a journalist shot a video directly on board a Libyan Coast Guard vessel engaged in a rescue operation on the high seas. This video shows the captain of the Libyan vessel saying that he received a call from an Italian warship informing him of a distress call and the position of migrants' boats. When Libyans reached the location, an Italian warship had already been there for a few hours to provide migrants with life vests and wait for Libyan intervention in the rescue and deflection of these migrants back to their port of departure.[215] Chapter five will assess in more detail whether these practices of push-back by proxy and externalisation of border controls, designed to avoid physical contact with migrants at sea, can engage the responsibility of European States. Indeed, their significant political, technical, logistical and economic support is clearly intended to delegate the rescue/interception and disembarkation of unwanted migrants and refugees to an unsafe third country.

V. EU LAW AND *NON-REFOULEMENT*

The EU prohibition of *refoulement* applies to everyone and is absolute.[216] Pursuant to Article 78(1) of the Treaty on the Functioning of the EU (TFEU),

> The Union shall develop a common policy on asylum, subsidiary protection and temporary protection with a view to offering appropriate status to any third-country national requiring international protection and ensuring compliance with the principle of *non-refoulement*. This policy must be in accordance with the Geneva Convention of 28 July 1951 and the Protocol of 31 January 1967 relating to the status of refugees, and other relevant treaties.

[214] M Giuffré and V Moreno-Lax, 'The Raise of Consensual Containment: From "Contactless Control" to 'Contactless Responsibility' for Migratory Flows' in S Juss (eds), *The Research Handbook on International Refugee Law* (Edward Elgar Publishing, 2019).

[215] See, P Biondi, 'Italy Strikes Back Again: A Push-Back Firsthand Account', *Border Criminologies*, 15 December 2017, https://www.law.ox.ac.uk/research-subject-groups/centre-criminology/centreborder-criminologies/blog/2017/12/italy-strikes.

[216] See, eg, Art 4 and 19(2) of the CFR using the expression 'no one'; Art 3(b) of the SBC referring to 'any person'; Article 34(2) of the EBCG Reg and Art 4(1) of the MSR relying on the formula 'no person'. *Non-refoulement* under EU law has already been substantively addressed in much of the recent literature. See eg, the following books: Moreno-Lax 2017, n 2 above; Costello 2016, n 145 above, 249–77, and Hamdan 2016, n 2 above.

Therefore, the 'right to asylum' (as enshrined in Article 18 of the CFR) should also be in conformity with the principle of *non-refoulement*. This interpretation is confirmed by the UNHCR[217] and the CJEU.[218] While Article 4 of the EU CFR provides that 'no one shall be subjected to torture or to inhuman or degrading treatment or punishment', the prohibition on *refoulement* is explicitly recognised by Article 19(2) of the EU CFR whereby 'no one may be removed, expelled or extradited to a State where there is a serious risk that he or she would be subjected to the death penalty, torture or other inhuman or degrading treatment or punishment.'[219] The 'Explanations' to the CFR – which apply as long as States are implementing EU law, whether or not their actions take place within, at, or beyond the territorial borders – further affirm that Article 19 incorporates the case law of the ECtHR on Article 3 of the relevant Convention and the content of Article 33 of the Geneva Convention.[220]

Instruments of secondary law can also give expression to general principles;[221] it is worth mentioning that Articles 9 and 15 of the Recast Qualification Directive define 'persecution' and 'serious harm' respectively, and serve the purpose of establishing when removal of a protection seeker is prohibited under the principle of *non-refoulement*.[222] According to Article 9, 'acts of persecution … must be sufficiently serious by their nature or repetition as to constitute a severe violation of basic human rights, in particular the rights from which derogation cannot be made under Article 15(2) [of the ECHR]'. 'Serious harm' comprises the death penalty or execution, torture, inhuman and degrading treatment as well as 'serious and individual threat to a civilian's life or person by reason of indiscriminate violence in situations of international or internal armed conflict.'[223]

The EU Schengen Border Code (SBC) refers, in its Preamble, to the rights and principles recognised by the EU CFR.[224] Whilst Article 3 sets forth that the

[217] EXCOM Conclusion no 82 (XLVIII) – 1997 – Safeguarding Asylum, para d. See also, UNHCR views on the interpretation of CEAS in *Zuheyr Frayeh Halaf v Darzhavna agentsia za bezhantsite pri Ministerskia savet*, Case C-528/11, ECLI:EU:C:2013:342, para 44.

[218] See, *HT*, Case C-373/13, ECLI:EU:C:2015:413, paras 65–68; see also, *Mohamed M'Bodj v État belge*, Case C-542/13, ECLI:EU:C:2014:2452, para 38; *NS v UK and ME v Ireland*, Joined Cases C-411/10 and C-493/10, [2011] ECR I-13095, para 75.

[219] See *Hirsi v Italy*, above n 4, paras 28, 135.

[220] According to the Presidium of the Convention that drafted the Charter, the Explanations 'have no legal value and are simply intended to clarify the provisions of the Charter.'

[221] See *Werner Mangold v Rüdiger Helm*, Case C-144/04 [2005] ECR I-9981; and *Viamex Agrar Handels GmbH v Hauptzol-lamt Hamburg-Jonas*, Case C-37/06 [2008] ECR-I-69.

[222] See also, proposal for a Regulation of the European Parliament and of the Council on standards for the qualification of third-country nationals or stateless persons as beneficiaries of international protection, for a uniform status for refugees or for persons eligible for subsidiary protection and for the content of the protection granted and amending Council Directive 2003/109/EC of 25 November 2003 concerning the status of third-country nationals who are long-term residents. COM/2016/0466 final – 2016/0223 (COD).

[223] Art 15(c)(d).

[224] Regulation of the European Parliament and of the Council (EC) 562/2006 15 March 2006 establishing a Community Code on the rules governing the movement of persons across borders [2006] OJ L105/1 (SBC).

Code is to be applied without prejudice to 'the rights of refugees and persons requesting international protection, in particular as regards *non-refoulement*', Article 5(4)(c) allows for derogation from normal entry criteria on humanitarian grounds or other international obligations. The Schengen Border Code is an EU migration law instrument of special significance by virtue of its application in extraterritorial immigration control scenarios.[225] It describes the border in geographical terms (Article 2(2)) and defines 'border guards' as public officials performing their surveillance functions 'along the border or the immediate vicinity of that border.' At the same time, when outlining the different control mechanisms, the *ratione loci* of the Code exceeds the territorial perimeter of EU Member States: extraterritorial controls, whether in airports which do not hold the status of international airports, or within the territory of a third country, are seen as possible solutions.[226]

The new European Border Coast Guard Regulation and the Maritime Surveillance Regulation in relation to maritime border operations coordinated by Frontex also provide that:

> in accordance with Union and international law, no person shall be disembarked in, or otherwise handed over to the authorities of a country in contravention of the principle of *non-refoulement*, or from which there is a risk of expulsion or return to another country in contravention of that principle.[227]

In the *Hirsi* case, the ECtHR attached particular weight to the content of a letter written on 15 May 2009 by Mr Jacques Barrot, Vice-President of the European Commission, which called for elaboration on the material scope of application of the Schengen Border Code.[228] He argued that Italy–Libya pushbacks amounted to border surveillance operations falling within the purview of the Code by virtue of Article 12 where border surveillance measures are aimed at preventing unauthorised border crossings. Therefore, in the wake of the Commission's reasoning, when engaging in interception activities, EU Member States shall always comply with international obligations on *non-refoulement* as required by the ECHR and the Schengen Border Code, whether such activities are conducted in its territorial waters or on the high seas.[229]

[225] *Hirsi v Italy*, above n 4, para 31.

[226] SBC, paras 2.1.3. and 2.2.1, Annex VI. While at sea, controls can be performed 'in the territory of a third country' (para 3.1.1, Annex VI), checks can be carried out also 'in [railway] stations in a third country where persons board the train' (para 1.2.2, Annex VI). For an analysis of the scope of application of the SBC, see, *inter alia*, M Den Heijer, 'Europe Beyond its Borders: Refugee and Human Rights Protection in Extraterritorial Immigration Control' in B Ryan and V Mitsilegas (eds), *Extraterritorial Immigration Control: Legal Challenges* (Martinus Nijhoff, 2010) 176–80.

[227] Art 34(2)(3) of the EBCG Reg; and Art 4(1) of the MSR.

[228] Letter from ex-Commissioner Barrot to the President of the LIBE Committee, 15 July 2009, as cited by the ECtHR in *Hirsi v Italy*, above n 4, paras 34, 135.

[229] ibid. See also B Nascimbene, 'Il Respingimento degli Immigrati e i Rapporti tra Italia e Unione Europea' (2009) *Affari Internazionali* 4; V Moreno-Lax, 'Seeking Asylum in the Mediterranean: Against a Fragmentary Reading of EU Member States' Obligations Accruing at Sea' (2011) 23 *IJRL* 174.

It is also worth adding that Article 21(1) of the Recast Qualification Directive clearly confirms the extraterritorial scope of *non-refoulement*, since it obliges Member States to respect this principle 'in accordance with their international obligations.' By contrast, Recital 21 and Article 3(1) of the Recast Procedures Directive limit its scope to territory, border, territorial waters, and transit zones. Article 51 of the CFR governs the field of application of the Charter and establishes that it applies whenever the institutions, bodies and agencies of the Union exercise their powers. It also operates whenever Member States 'are implementing EU law', an expression that has been interpreted widely so as to indicate that the Charter applies whenever Member States 'act within the scope of EU law.'[230] Also, when they operate in the framework of their national procedural autonomy, States are obliged to comply with Charter standards.[231] The fact that no reference to jurisdiction (and especially territorial constraints) exists within the text of the Charter points to its extraterritorial applicability, as also suggested by the case law of the CJEU.[232] Therefore, jurisdiction thresholds and 'effective control' notions, which define and restrict the scope of application of human rights treaties, do not hold for the definition of the geographical remit of EU fundamental rights, including the principle of *non-refoulement*.[233]

VI. THE RIGHT TO ACCESS ASYLUM PROCEDURES BEFORE REMOVAL: INTRODUCTION

This chapter discusses the right to access asylum procedures and effective remedies as procedural guarantees to impede *refoulement* of a protection seeker to a territory where her life and liberty can be put in danger.

Asylum is an expression of State sovereignty. According to the *Institut du Droit International*, 'the term *asylum* means the *protection* offered by a State

[230] Explanations to Art 51 of the CFR, at 32 referring to *Wachauf v Bundesamt für Ernährung und Forstwirtschaft*, Case 5/88 [1989] ECR 2609; *Elliniki Radiophonia Tileorassi AE (ERT) v Pliroforissis and Kouvelas*, Case C-260/89 [1991] ECR I-2925; *Annibaldi v Sindaco del Comune di Guidonia, Presidente Regione Lazio*, Case C-309/96 [1997] ECR I-7493.

[231] *Deutsche Energiehandels- und Beratungsgesellschaft mbH (DEB) v Bundesrepublik Deutschland*, Case C-279/09 [2010] ECR I-13849.

[232] See, eg. *Bank Saderat Iran v Council*, Case T-594/10 ECLI:EU:T:2013:59 (appeal dismissed in *P*, Case C-200/13 ECLI:EU:C:2016:284, paras 39–50). On the irrelevance of territory in treaty freedoms within the internal market, see, *Erny v Daimler AG – Werk Wörth*, Case C-172/11 ECLI:EU:C:2012:399; *Union Cycliste Internationale*, Case 36/74 [1974] ECR 1405, para 28; *SARL Prodest v Caisse Primaire d'Assurance Maladie de Paris*, Case 237/83 [1984] ECR 3153, paras 6 and 10; *Lopes de Veiga v Staatssecretaris van Justitie*, Case 9/88 [1989] ECR 2989, paras 16 and 19.

[233] Moreno-Lax 2017, n 2 above, 296. On the extraterritorial scope of the CFR, see, K Lenaerts, 'Exploring the Limits of the EU Charter of Fundamental Rights' (2012) 8 *ECL Rev* 375; S Peers, 'Immigration, Asylum and the EU Charter of Fundamental Rights', in E Guild and P Minderhoud (eds), *The First Decade of EU Migration and Asylum Law* (Brill, 2012) 437, 449; V Moreno-Lax and C Costello, 'The extraterritorial application of the EU Charter of Fundamental Rights: from territoriality to facticity, the effectiveness model', in Peers et al (eds), *The EU Charter of Fundamental Rights* (Hart, 2014) 1657.

on its territory or elsewhere to an individual who came to seek it (emphasis added).'[234] It consists of the protection that a State grants to an individual within its territory (territorial asylum) or in some other place, which is variously under the control of certain of its organs, such as diplomatic premises (diplomatic asylum) and warships.[235] The long historical tradition of asylum is grounded in the assumption that no individual right to receive asylum exists, but rather, that there is only a right to apply for it, and a right on the part of States to grant it. Asylum has thus been conceived of as a privilege that certain individuals can ask for, rather than as an absolute legal entitlement.[236] Its content remains in dispute, and a thorough analysis of the existence of a right to asylum under international law would be far beyond the remit of this chapter. However, is worth noting how the practices of a large number of States suggest the existence of a right of individuals to be granted asylum – a right recognised in domestic law, often of constitutional ranking, which is also acknowledged in international human rights instruments having a regional scope.[237]

At an international level, the scope of the right to asylum remains controversial, as no universal treaty exists which explicitly defines its content. Bearing in mind the separate, distinct natures of asylum and refugee status,[238] it should be noted that refugee protection has, in contrast, found expression in a number of instruments of both universal and regional scope. The Executive Committee of the UNHCR has often emphasised 'the need to admit refugees into the territories of States, which includes no rejection at frontiers without fair and effective procedures for determining status and protection needs.'[239] As the right to asylum has been recognised by a number of international instruments,[240] it has been argued that it can now be considered 'a right of individuals, which coexists with the already established right of States to grant it.'[241]

This chapter analyses the *right to access asylum procedures* as a principle corollary to that of *non-refoulement*, which can only be assured if an individual has access to a fair procedure that thoroughly assesses her protection claim. Hence, States shall grant access to their territory and to asylum procedures to individuals invoking international protection, since preventing a refugee from

[234] *Institut du Droit International*, Bath Conference, 1950.

[235] MT Gil Bazo, 'Asylum as a General Principle of International Law' (2015) 27(1) *IJRL* 7.

[236] See, eg, JH Simpson, *The Refugee Problem* (OUP, 1939) 230; A Grahal-Madsen, *The Status of Refugees in International Law*, vol II (Sijthoff, 1972) 22 ff; P Weis, *The present state of International Law on Territorial Asylum* (1974) 31 *Schweizerisiches Jahrbuch fur Internationales Recht* 71.

[237] For an extended account, see Gil Bazo 2015, n 235 above.

[238] While asylum constitutes the institution for protection, refugee status refers only to one category of people (refugees) who – among others – benefit from such protection. See, Gil Bazo 2015, n 235 above.

[239] EXCOM Conclusions no 82 *Safeguarding Asylum* (1997) para d(3).

[240] See, eg, Art 14 of the UDHR, Art 18 of the CFR, Art 22(7) of the American Convention on Human Rights, and Art 12(3) of the African Charter.

[241] MT Gil-Bazo, 'The Charter of Fundamental Rights of the European Union and the Right to be Granted Asylum in the Union's Law' (2008) 27(3) *Refugee Survey Quarterly* 33, 39.

accessing such procedures can have the equivalent effect of *refoulement*.[242] As Costello argues, 'access to asylum depends practically on access to a place of refuge. And securing *access to territory* means overcoming both physical and legal barriers (emphasis added).'[243]

In examining the right to access asylum procedures as a pre-removal procedural entitlement, this book refers to the assessment of refugee status under the Geneva Convention, but also to other forms of complementary protection – including subsidiary protection – afforded by international human rights law and EU law to persons under threat for reasons falling outside of the five grounds of persecution within the international refugee protection regime. The right to access asylum procedures before removal, as a precondition to *non-refoulement*, is however still subject to debate. Because undertaking status determination is not an express obligation of the Geneva Convention, some claim that 'expulsion may take place without a prior substantive examination of the protection claims.'[244] Indeed, the drafting history of the Convention reveals a deliberate omission of any duty on States to undertake status determination.[245] Nonetheless, 'fair and efficient procedures are a necessary component of protection, to ensure that those entitled to it are accurately identified, and those who are not are screened out.'[246]

Owing to the declaratory (and non-constitutive) nature of refugee status, the principle of *non-refoulement* – enshrined in Article 33(1) of the Geneva Convention not only covers recognised refugees but also asylum seekers whose status as refugees has not yet been determined. It means they enjoy a *prima facie* refugee status, pursuant to Article 1(a) of the Geneva Convention, until a full examination of their status by the State discredits their claims.[247] Including asylum claimants within the personal scope of Article 33(1) is the only way to ensure that the principle of *non-refoulement* is respected in practice.

The Geneva Convention sets up no procedural rules on how the examination of asylum claims should take place. However, as the UNHCR states in its intervention in the *IM v France* case before the ECtHR,

> while [the Geneva Convention] does not specifically regulate the asylum procedure, the enjoyment of the rights it provides for requires that the States Parties establish

[242] G Gilbert, 'Is Europe Living Up to Its Obligations to Refugees?' (2004) 15 *European Journal of International Law* 963, 966.

[243] C Costello, 'Courting Access to Asylum in Europe: Recent Supranational Jurisprudence Explored' (2012) 12(2) *Human Rights Law Review* 307, 338.

[244] N Coleman, *European Readmission Policy: Third Country Interests and Refugee Rights* (Martinus Nijhoff, 2009) 238.

[245] J McAdam, 'The Enduring Relevance of the 1951 Refugee Convention' (2017) 29(1) *IJRL* 1.

[246] ibid, 3. See also, J Vedsted-Hansen, 'The asylum procedures and the assessment of asylum requests' in Chetail and Bauloz (eds), *Research Handbook on International Law and Migration* (Edward Elgar Publishing, 2016) 439.

[247] Thus, once an individual fulfils the requirements of Art 1 of the Geneva Convention, she is entitled to some Convention benefits, regardless of her status having been determined or not. H Battjes, *European Asylum and International Law* (Martinus Niijhoff, 2006) 465.

> *fair and efficient asylum procedures*, which allow them to identify the persons in need of international protection (emphasis added).[248]

To avoid unfair asylum procedures that cause an unjustifiably high number of refugees to be removed to their persecutors in breach of Article 33(1), the Geneva Convention 'shall be interpreted in *good faith* in accordance with the *ordinary meaning* to be given to the terms of the treaty in their *context* and in light of its *object and purpose*', as provided by Article 31 of the VCLT. At a national level, domestic courts have confirmed the same principle.[249]

Thus, in the absence of procedures established by international law for the granting of protection, States may apply domestic procedural rules giving, however, 'full effect' to international asylum law both at first instance and in appeal procedures.[250] The duty to disembark refugees in a place of safety and examine their protection claims shall also apply as an obligation implicit in the principle of *non-refoulement*, in cases of extraterritorial migration controls and rescue operations on the high seas. In three experts' Roundtables convened by the UNHCR since 2002, the participants agreed that '*asylum must effectively be made available*' as part of the broader response to irregular maritime migration.[251] Accordingly, they concluded that

> persons claiming asylum should be allowed to enter the national asylum procedure without delay; in countries where no asylum procedure exists, they should be referred to UNHCR. The State providing for disembarkation will generally be the State whose refugee protection responsibilities are first engaged.[252]

Therefore, without facing rejection at the border, refugees should be provided with 'fair and effective procedures for determining status and protection needs'.[253]

In particular, a fair refugee determination procedure is based on two underlying aspects: firstly, privacy, and, secondly, safeguards for refugees with

[248] UNHCR's oral intervention at the ECtHR Hearing of the case of *IM v France*, App no 9152/09 (17 May 2011) (English translation of the French version as delivered), 1, http://www.unhcr.org/cgi-bin/texis/vtx/refworld/rwmain/opendocpdf.pdf?reldoc=y&docid=4dde1a882.

[249] See, eg, *VAJN and NJCM v The Netherlands*, Appeals Court of The Hague, 31 October 2002, RV 2002, para 5.2. Translation made by Hemme Battjes 2006.

[250] Battjes 2006, n 247 above, 293.

[251] UNHCR, *The treatment of persons rescued at sea: conclusions and recommendations from recent meetings and expert round tables convened by the Office of the United Nations High Commissioner for Refugees: Report of the Office of the United Nations High Commissioner for Refugees*, 11 April 2008, A/AC.259/17, para 6: http://www.unhcr.org/refworld/docid/49997aeb27.html; UNHCR, *Desperate Journeys: Refugees and migrants arriving in Europe and Europe's borders (January – August 2018)*, 15–17, December 2018, https://data2.unhcr.org/en/documents/download/65373#_ga=2.138122995.253764426.1550604132-1861362090.1547930043. For a wider debate on the State responsible for disembarkation in a place of safety, see Chapter 5 of this book.

[252] ibid. See also, K Wouters K and M Den Heijer, 'The Marine I Case: A Comment' (2010) 22(1) *IJRL* 1, 7–8.

[253] EXCOM *Conclusions No 82, Safeguarding Asylum* (1997) para d(iii), https://www.unhcr.org/excom/exconc/3ae68c958/safeguarding-asylum.html.

special vulnerabilities.[254] It has also been argued that the Geneva Convention may implicitly require States to carry out status determinations. In particular, this obligation may flow from the duty of States to perform treaty obligations 'in good faith' in light of the object and purpose of the Convention, as laid down in the Preamble.[255] For it to be effective, *non-refoulement* must also involve an obligation of assessing whether the removal of a person would endanger life and freedom.[256] It follows that States have to put in place appropriate procedural safeguards – according to their constitutional and administrative structures – to ensure that a refugee is not sent to an unsafe country.[257]

As suggested by the *UNHCR Handbook on RSD*, the principle of *non-refoulement* would entail a positive obligation to grant refugees a right to enter the territory of the State, at least on a temporary basis, in order to submit the protection claim to a competent authority in charge of ascertaining whether any risk upon removal can be excluded.[258] Additionally,

> States Parties [to the Geneva Convention] are required to make independent inquiries as to the need for international protection of persons seeking asylum, a duty recognized by a wide range of national and regional Courts, and provide them access to fair and efficient refugee determination procedures.[259]

Refugees should also be informed that their irregular position will not affect the outcome of their protection claims.[260] Moreover, in accordance with

[254] See, UNHCR, *Global Consultations in Budapest Conclusions*, para 15, http://www.unhcr.org/3b83b7314.html.

[255] H Meijers, 'Refugees in Western Europe, "Schengen" Affects the Entire Refugee Law' (1990) 2(3) *IJRL* 428, 433.

[256] K Wouters, *International Legal Standards for the Protection from Refoulement: A Legal Analysis of the Prohibitions on Refoulement Contained in the Refugee Convention, the European Convention on Human Rights, the International Covenant on Civil and Political Rights and the Convention against Torture* (Intersentia, 2009) 164.

[257] ibid, 571. See also, W Kälin, M Caroni and L Heim, 'Article 33 para 1 (Prohibition of Expulsion and Return (Refoulement)' in Zimmermann A (ed), *The 1951 Convention relating to the Status of Refugees and its 1967 Protocol: A Commentary* (Oxford University Press, 2011) 1375; UNHCR, *Handbook on procedures and criteria for determining refugee status under the 1951 Convention and the 1967 Protocol relating to the Status of Refugees*, HCR/1P/4/ENG/REV. 3, issued in 1979, and last re-edited in December 2011, http://www.unhcr.org/refworld/pdfid/4f33c8d92.pdf (*UNHCR Handbook on RSD*) para 189. *Non-refoulement* is respected automatically when States confer refugee status or temporary protection on the basis of *prima facie* recognition in situations of mass influxes.

[258] UNHCR, *Refugees without an Asylum Country*, 16 October 1979, Conclusion no 15 (1979), para c. See also, E Lauterpacht and D Bethlehem, 'The Scope and Content of the Principle of *Non-refoulement*: Opinion' in E Feller, V Türk and F Nicholson (eds), *Refugee Protection in International Law: UNHCR's Global Consultations on International Protection* (Cambridge University Press, 2003) 114; V Moreno-Lax, 'Seeking Asylum in the Mediterranean: Against a Fragmentary Reading of EU Member States' Obligations Accruing at Sea' (2011) 23(2) *IJRL* 174, 218.

[259] UNHCR, *B010 v Canada (Citizenship and Immigration)*, 2015 SCC 58, 3 SCR 704, 27 November 2015, Factum of the Intervener, 2 February 2015, para 13, https://www.refworld.org/docid/54d09bb44.html. See also, UNHCR, 'Intervention before the Court of Final Appeal of the Hong Kong Special Administrative Region in the case between *C, KMF, BF (Applicants) and Director of Immigration, Secretary for Security (Respondents)*', 31 January 2013, Civil Appeals nos 18, 19 and 20 of 2011.

[260] S Da Lomba, *The Right to Seek Refugee Status in the European Union* (Intersentia, 2004) 110.

Article 31(1) of the Geneva Convention, asylum seekers' procedural guarantees cannot be diminished because of their unauthorised entry, as the 'irregularity' of their presence is irrelevant for the purposes of qualification as a refugee under Article 1 of the Geneva Convention.

Although Article 33(1) does not confer any right to be granted asylum, States are required 'to adopt a course that does not amount to *refoulement*. This may amount to removal to a "safe third country" [quite a questionable alternative, in my view] or some other solution, such as temporary protection of refugees.'[261] In order to avoid the risk of *refoulement*, refugees cannot be removed without ascertaining whether their claim to protection is well-founded.[262] Whether, however, they are entitled to choose the country in which they will then claim refugee status is still a contested issue. Although some scholars advocate such an option on the grounds of the existence of family ties, language, or cultural linkages, no claim is made that this stance reflects binding principles of international law.[263] An exception might be represented, in the EU context, by the principle of family unity (whose salience is emphasised by Article 9 of the 2013 Recast Dublin Regulation).[264] None of the provisions of the Geneva Convention requires individuals to seek asylum in any particular State or lodge an application at any specific place.[265] Therefore, even in the absence of an explicit right to choose the country of the asylum claim, it should be noted that a certain 'element of choice is indeed open to refugees as to where they may properly claim asylum.'[266]

To conclude, the right to *non-refoulement* and the right to seek asylum are closely connected within or alongside the right to have one's protection claim examined, regardless of the place where the refugee is first found. It can thus be argued that the principle of *non-refoulement* 'provides a basis for procedural

[261] Lauterpacht and Bethlehem 2003, n 4 above, 87, 113.

[262] Kälin, Caroni, and Heim 2011, n 257 above, 1369.

[263] On the issue of whether the intentions of the asylum seeker should be taken into consideration in determining the responsible country, see generally, EW Vierdag, 'The Country of First Asylum: Some European Aspects' in David Martin (ed), *The New Asylum Seekers: Refugee Law in the 1980s*, (Martinus Nijhoff Publishers, 1988) 80–81; J Hathaway, *The Law of Refugee Status* (Butterworths, 1991) 46–50; UNHCR *Position on Readmission Agreements, 'Protection Elsewhere' and Asylum Policy* (1 August 1994), para 5, https://www.refworld.org/docid/3ae6b31cb8.html.

[264] For a definition of 'family member', see Article 2(g) of the Recast Dublin Regulation. The essential right of family unity for refugees was also confirmed by the Final Act of the Conference of Plenipotentiaries that adopted the 1951 Refugee Convention. See also, K Jastram and K Newland, 'Family Unity and Refugee Protection' in E Feller, F Nicholson, and V Turk (eds), *UNHCR Refugee Protection in International Law* (CUP, 2003).

[265] V Moreno-Lax, 'The "Safe Third Country" Notion Revisited: An Appraisal in light of General International Rules on the Law of Treaties', in Goodwin-Gill GS (ed), *International Migrations, 2010 Centre for Studies and Research in International Law and International Relations of The Hague Academy of International Law* (Martinus Nijhoff, 2013) 20. See also, MT Gil Bazo, 'The Practice of Mediterranean States in the Context of the European Union's Justice and Home Affairs External Dimension. The Safe Third Country Concept Revisited' (2006) 18(3–4) *IJRL* 571, 598.

[266] *R v Uxbridge Magistrates Court and Another, ex parte Adimi*, 12 August 1999, [1999] EWHC Admin 765, [2001] QB 667 (per S Brown LJ).

rights to refugee status determination insofar as it obliges States to determine whether a person they want to send back to the country of origin is a refugee.'[267]

As we will observe in the following Sections, the gaps in the Geneva Convention (ie on the existence of an express right to access refugee status determination procedures) can be filled by the synergic contribution of human rights law, in terms of refining the meaning and scope of the *non-refoulement* obligation.

VII. ACCESS TO ASYLUM PROCEDURES UNDER HUMAN RIGHTS LAW

Neither the ICCPR nor the CAT contains stand-alone obligations on the right to asylum. However, the views expressed in some cases by their monitoring bodies seem to contain an implied positive obligation to ensure access to asylum procedures, if it is relevant to providing effective protection from *refoulement*.

The recent case law of the HRC has firmly rejected the applicability of Article 14(1) of the ICCPR in those cases where asylum seekers challenge the fairness of national determination of asylum procedures.[268] However, it has also submitted that certain procedural standards do apply to refugee status determination by virtue of Article 7 (prohibition of torture) or 6 (right to life) of the ICCPR if such a procedure involves an assessment of the risk of serious harm. The HRC has pointed out that State parties to the ICCPR must always ensure that each claim for protection is subjected to a particularised assessment, irrespective of an individual's country of origin.[269]

A number of Concluding Observations seem also to suggest that the right to an effective remedy under Article 2(3) of the ICCPR entitles asylum seekers to appeal first instance decisions to an independent body.[270] Moreover the HRC has in some cases relied upon Article 13 of the ICCPR as a general source of procedural protection in the determination of refugee status, thus implying that a refugee seeking asylum has acquired a 'lawful' status within

[267] Kälin, Caroni and Heim 2011, n 257 above, 1395.

[268] Under Art 14(1) of the ICCPR, 'In the determination of any criminal charge against him, or of his rights and obligations in a suit at law, everyone shall be entitled to a fair and public hearing by a competent, independent and impartial tribunal established by law.' See, for example, HRC, *PK v Canada*, Comm no 1234/2003 (3 April 2007) UN Doc CCPR/C/89/D/1234/2003, paras 7.4 and 7.5; *AC and Others v The Netherlands*, Comm no 1494/2006 (22 July 2008) UN Doc CCPR/C/93/D/1494/2006, para 8.4; *X v Denmark*, Comm no 2007/2010 (12 May 2014) UN Doc CCPR/C/110/D/2007/2010, para 8.5. For an extensive analysis on this issue, see D Cantor, 'Reframing Relationships: Revisiting the Procedural Standards for Refugee Status Determination in Light of Recent Human Rights Treaty Body Jurisprudence' (2015) 34(1) *Refugee Survey Quarterly* 79, 86–87.

[269] See, eg, *XHL v The Netherlands*, Comm no 1564/2007 (22 July 2011) UN Doc CCPR/C/97/D/1564/2007, para 10.3.

[270] Under Art 2(3): Each State Party to the present Covenant undertakes: (a) To ensure that any person whose rights or freedoms as herein recognized are violated shall have an effective remedy ....' See, HRC, *Concluding Observations on Latvia*, UN Doc CCPR/CO/79/LVA, 1 December 2003, para 9; and *Concluding Observations on Lithuania*, UN Doc CCPR/CO/80/LTU, 4 May 2004, para 7.

the host country.[271] Article 13 has thus been used in relation to the right of a refugee to access the procedure,[272] enjoy a pending appeal against a negative first-instance decision,[273] and receiving free legal assistance in both ordinary and accelerated asylum procedures.[274]

Concerns over the realities of refugees substantiating claims in the context of speedy asylum procedures have also been expressed by the Committee Against Torture, in its *Concluding Observations on the Netherlands*.[275] In *X v Spain*, the Committee held that its authority 'does not extend to a determination of whether or not the claimant is entitled to asylum under national laws of a country, or can invoke the protection of the Geneva Convention ....'[276] Despite the lack of such a right in the text of the CAT, investigating a need for protection assumes special relevance in the context of alleged violations of Article 3 upon removal, including situations of mass influxes.[277]

The CAT does not indicate any specific procedural safeguards concerning the determination procedure, but the Committee has frequently urged States parties to adopt such safeguards in their national legislation, allowing, for instance, the individual to have a formal hearing, due process, and transparent and impartial proceedings.[278] In its Recommendations to Italy, the Committee was concerned that some asylum seekers might have been denied the right to apply for asylum and to have their asylum claims assessed individually by means of a fair and satisfactory procedure. It held, accordingly, that

> the State party should adopt appropriate measures to *ensure that all asylum seekers have access to a fair and prompt asylum procedure*. In this respect, the Committee recalls the obligation of the State party to ensure that the situation of each migrant is processed individually (emphasis added).[279]

[271] See, for example, HRC, *Concluding Observations on Lithuania*, n 270 above, para 15, and HRC, *Concluding Observations on Switzerland*, UN Doc CCPR/C/CHE/CO/3, 29 October 2009, para 18. See also HRC, Concluding Observations on Bulgaria, UN Doc CCPR/C/BGR/CO/3, 19 August 2011, para 16, where the HRC makes reference to Arts 6, 7, and 13. Under Art 13, 'An alien lawfully in the territory of a State Party to the present Covenant may be expelled therefrom only in pursuance of a decision reached in accordance with law ....'

[272] HRC, *Concluding Observations on Lithuania*, n 270 above, para 15.

[273] HRC, *Concluding Observations on Estonia*, UN Doc CCPR/C/EST/CO/3 (4 August 2010) para 13.

[274] HRC, *Concluding Observations on Switzerland*, n 271 above, para 18.

[275] *Concluding Observations on the Netherlands* UN Doc CAT/C/NET/CO/4 (3 August 2007) para 7(a) and (b).

[276] *X v Spain*, Comm no 23/1995 (15 November 1995), UN Doc CAT/C/15/D/23/, para 7.3. See also, *Seid Mortesa Aemei v Switzerland*, Comm no 34/1995 (29 May 1997) UN Doc CAT/C/18/D/34/1995, para 11.

[277] *Concluding Observations on the Former Yugoslav Republic of Macedonia*, UN Doc A/54/44 (1999) para 116; *Concluding Observations on France* UN Doc CAT/C/FRA/CO/3 (2006) para 6.

[278] *Concluding Observations on Venezuela*, UN Doc A/54/44 (1999) para 147; *Concluding Observations on Canada* UN Doc A/56/44 (2000) paras 54–59; *Concluding Observations on Bolivia* UN Doc A/56/44 (2001) paras 89–98.

[279] *Conclusions and Recommendations of the Committee against Torture, Italy*, UN Doc CAT/C/ITA/CO/4 (16 July 2007).

It has also added that

> individuals under the State party's jurisdiction *receive appropriate consideration by its competent authorities and guaranteed fair treatment at all stages of the proceedings*, including an opportunity for effective, independent and impartial review of decisions on expulsion, return or extradition (emphasis added).[280]

Finally, in its Observations to Greece in June 2012, the Committee expressed its concern regarding the widespread reluctance by asylum seekers to lodge applications because of the 'absence of a safe complaints mechanism, insufficient number of interpreters, and a lack of trust in authorities.'[281] In addition, it was critical of how '*asylum seekers face serious obstacles in accessing the asylum procedure* due to structural deficiencies and non-functioning screening mechanisms'(emphasis added).[282] Therefore, this lack of access to effective procedural guarantees, legal remedies and asylum procedures has been seen as creating a substantial risk of *refoulement*.[283]

Moving more specifically to the European context, the European Commission of Human Rights in 1959 affirmed that:

> Under general international law, a State has the right, in virtue of its sovereignty, to control the entry and exit of foreigners into and out of its territory. It is true that a right or freedom to enter the territory of States, Members of the Council of Europe, is not, as such, included among the rights and freedoms guaranteed in ... the Convention. However, a State ... must be understood as agreeing to restrict the free exercise of ... its right to control the entry and exit of foreigners to the extent and within the limits of the obligations which it has accepted under that Convention.[284]

This principle, confirmed by the ECtHR in other cases,[285] leads to the following question: Does Article 3 of the ECHR require States to undertake asylum procedures before expelling/pushing-back an asylum seeker to his or her country of origin? If so, what are the requirements for the examination of a protection claim that flow from this provision? Although the ECHR does not contain a general obligation to provide a substantive examination of asylum applications, the analysis of the jurisprudence of the Court proves the insistence of the Court on a positive obligation to provide a status determination in order to assess the consequences of the expulsion of an individual to the country of origin. The ECHR has indeed been identified as providing 'a rather impressive inherent right to access.'[286]

[280] *Conclusions and Recommendations of the Committee against Torture, Hungary*, UN Doc CAT/C/HUN/CO/4, para 10 (6 February 2007).

[281] *Concluding Observations of the Committee against Torture, Greece*, UN Doc CAT/C/GRC/CO/5-6 (27 June 2012) para 12.

[282] ibid, para 18.

[283] ibid, para 19.

[284] *X v Government of Sweden*, App no 434/58 (30 June 1959) 28 ILR 242.

[285] *Amuur v France*, App no 19776/92 (25 June 1996); *ZA v Russia*, App no 61411/15 (28 March 2017).

[286] G Noll, *Negotiating Asylum: The EU Acquis, Extraterritorial Protection and the Common Market of Deflection* (Martinus Nijhoff, 2000) 454.

In particular, Article 3 itself has been used to support a right of access to asylum procedures in order to prevent applicants' transfer to territories where they can suffer torture and other inhuman and degrading treatment. The Court has interpreted Article 3 as requiring 'rigorous scrutiny' of a protection claim.[287] The ruling in the *TI v UK* case – delivered four months before the *Jabari v Turkey* judgment – also raises the issue of the relationship between the Dublin Convention and the ECHR. Indeed, 'while the Dublin Convention may pursue laudable objectives, its effectiveness may be undermined in practice by the differing approaches adopted by Contracting States to the scope of protection offered.'[288]

The automatic application of a short time limit for submitting an asylum application without the possibility of undertaking a substantive examination of the claim would be at variance with the protection of the fundamental value of democratic societies embodied in Article 3 of the Convention.[289] In *Diallo v Czech Republic*, the Court found a violation of the right to an effective remedy in conjunction with Article 3 as the two asylum seekers' claims that there was a real risk of ill-treatment in their country of origin 'were not subjected to close and rigorous scrutiny.'[290] Likewise, in *Gebremedhin v France*, the Court highlighted the importance of having access to asylum procedures as a means toward *non-refoulement*. It noted, indeed, that 'a decision to refuse leave to enter the country acts as a bar to lodging an asylum application',[291] and results in having the person immediately removed to the country from which she claims to have fled.[292] In *Abdolkhani*, the Court held that

> by failing to consider the applicants' requests for temporary asylum, to notify them of the reasons for not taking their asylum requests into consideration and to authorize them to have access to legal assistance … the national authorities prevented the applicants from raising their allegations under Article 3 …[293]

In *Sharifi v Italy*, concerning the implementation of a readmission agreement between Italy and Greece and a summary rejection at the border, the Court affirmed that readmission 'deprived the persons concerned of any effective opportunity to submit an application for international protection and, eventually, of any other procedural and material guarantee.'[294] The Court found therefore a

[287] *TI v UK*, above n 53; *Mamadaliyev v Russia*, App no 5614/13 (24 July 2014) paras 64–65.

[288] ibid, 15–16.

[289] *Jabari v Turkey*, above n 52, paras 39–40. See also, *D and Others v Turkey*, App no 24245/03 (22 June 2006) para 51.

[290] *Diallo v Czech Republic*, App no 20493/07 (23 June 2011) paras 77, 85. See also, *ZNS v Turkey*, App no 21896/08 (19 January 2010) paras 47–49. For an extended analysis of the right to asylum in relation to the ECHR, see, N Mole and C Meredith, *Asylum and the European Convention of Human Rights* (Council of Europe Publishing, 2010) 103–07.

[291] *Gebremedhin v France*, App no 25389/05 (26 April 2007) paras 54, 60.

[292] ibid.

[293] *Abdolkhani and Karimnia v Turkey*, App no 30471/08 (22 September 2009) paras 113, 115.

[294] *Sharifi v Italy and Greece*, App no 16643/09 (21 October 2014) para 215.

violation of Article 3 (combined with Article 13 and Article 4 of Protocol 4) as a consequence of the immediate removal to the ports of departure (with the risk of *refoulement* to Afghanistan from which the applicant originated) without 'an examination of the personal circumstances of the applicant, including his protection needs.' Moreover, the Court submitted that expulsions *en masse* cannot be excused because of migratory pressure. Along the same line, *MSS v Belgium and Greece* confirms that migration controls are 'acceptable only in order to enable States to prevent unlawful immigration while complying with their international obligations, in particular under the 1951 Geneva Convention … and the ECHR.'[295] Accordingly, 'States' legitimate concerns to foil the increasingly frequent attempts to circumvent immigration restrictions must not deprive asylum seekers of the protection afforded by these conventions.'[296] As held in *Hirsi*, 'problems with managing migratory flows cannot justify having recourse to practices which are not compatible with the State's obligations.'[297]

Strasbourg judges explicitly emphasised the existence of a right to lodge asylum applications in *MA v Lithuania*.[298] According to the Court, preventing applicants from lodging asylum claims amounted to a violation of Article 3 of the Convention.[299] It also argued that a wish to apply for asylum can be expressed in different ways, and governments should guarantee the presence of border guards trained to be able to detect and understand asylum requests even where asylum seekers are not in a position to clearly communicate their intention to seek asylum.[300]

A. The Extraterritorial Applicability of the Right to Access Asylum Procedures under the ECHR

Over the last two decades, the ECtHR has heard several cases concerning extraterritorial State activities, thus letting the Convention emerge as a reliable instrument for securing access to protection in Europe.[301] For instance, it has generally interpreted the prohibition of *refoulement* as requiring access to an effective and rigorous examination of protection claims, even beyond borders. In the *Amuur v France* decision, the ECtHR asserted that effective access to asylum procedures must also be guaranteed with respect to asylum seekers retained in the international zone of an airport.[302] However, it also clarified that,

[295] *MSS v Belgium and Greece*, above n 51, para 216.
[296] ibid, para 216.
[297] *Hirsi*, above n 4, para 179.
[298] *MA v Lithuania*, App no 59793/17 (11 December 2018).
[299] ibid, para 115.
[300] ibid, para 109.
[301] Costello 2012, n 243 above, 306.
[302] *Amuur v France*, above n 285, para 43.

despite its name, the 'international zone' of an airport does not have extraterritorial status.[303]

Hirsi v Italy was the first case where the ECtHR ruled on the possibility of guaranteeing access to status determination when refugees are intercepted on the high seas. Greater attention will be, therefore, placed on this decision, where the Court was keen to stress that preventing people from lodging their protection claims would both heighten the risk of *refoulement* and indirectly lead to a violation of Article 3 of the Convention. Thus, by delivering its views on asylum, the impression is that the Grand Chamber intended to contribute to strengthening and refining the content of States' extraterritorial obligations toward protection seekers.[304]

In 2009, migrants and refugees were pre-emptively pushed back after interception in international waters and handed over to Libya without having any chance of being transported to safe European ports for identification and examination of their asylum claims. Any attempt to seek protection or to receive information was thus rendered futile. The *Hirsi* case set a critical precedent for those European States that try to shift the burden of responsibility for examining asylum applications to third countries, also with the help of bilateral agreements used to intercept migrants and refugees before their physical arrival at Europe's borders, as discussed in Chapter five.

Confusingly, in *Hirsi*, the Court seems to suggest the possibility of accessing asylum procedures on the high seas.[305] However, for a number of reasons, this reading is problematic. First of all, it is unrealistic that lawyers and translators may be made readily available for all of the different nationalities of migrants and refugees on the high seas. But even if this were the case, does the lack of an explicit recognition by the Court of a free-standing obligation to disembark passengers imply that asylum procedures can be effectively performed at sea?

In September 2018, the Italian and Austrian Ministries of the Interior proposed shipboard assessment of asylum claims by transferring those who manage to enter the territorial waters of a European State onto State vessels.[306] Therefore, after 'appropriate checks' those who are found to have satisfied the asylum determination procedure are allowed to disembark to claim asylum.[307]

[303] ibid para 52.

[304] See *Hirsi Jamaa and Others v Italy*, App no 27765/09 (23 February 2012), paras 185, 201–05.

[305] ibid, para 202.

[306] REUTERS, 'Austria, Italy propose holding migrants on ships for days' (14 September), https://www.reuters.com/article/us-europe-migrants-austria-italy/austria-italy-propose-holding-migrants-on-ships-for-days-idUSKCN1LU2C7; InfoMigrants, 'Austria, Italy propose processing refugees on ships' (17 September 2018), https://www.infomigrants.net/en/post/12031/austria-italy-propose-processing-refugees-on-ships.

[307] Italy had already made a similar proposal to the European Commission in 2016, but it was not adopted because of the concerns regarding the legality of this solution. See, JC Juncker, 'Remarks by President Jean-Claude Juncker at the Joint Press Briefing with Slovak Prime Minister Robert Fico',

Despite the lack of any explicit hints by the Grand Chamber in the *Hirsi* case, with regard to the possibility of applying for asylum either on the vessels or on the mainland, boats should not be considered an appropriate environment for processing asylum claims. Refugees cannot be fairly interviewed in the intimidating atmosphere of a warship with no respect for the privacy of individuals being assessed. After an exhausting journey, they should have time to recover, collect evidence, and be ready to disclose the reasons for their escape, and any possible ill-treatment they suffered in their country of origin. Given that most migrants do not have passports with them, collecting asylum applications on-board and transmitting them to inland border police would be particularly difficult.

Another question arises: If, hypothetically, intercepting vessels (not necessarily military crafts) were fully-equipped with all the facilities necessary for carrying out assessments of asylum applications, would they become appropriate places for rigorous scrutiny of protection claims? It would not be hard to imagine that passengers would be detained for long periods of time far away from any courts where they might seek to challenge a negative decision on asylum or an expulsion order. Despite video recording or other types of communication that could be entertained between at-sea and in-shore State authorities, 'the personnel, temporal and infrastructure preconditions to carry out proceedings [would not be] fulfilled in a way that would be possible for domestic official proceedings.'[308] Since refugees would essentially end up being detained against their will in on-board floating detention camps,[309] ships should be unreservedly dismissed as suitable *loci* for examining individual situations and assessing protection claims. Such a solution engenders a further question. If massive capital spending were to be employed to endow vessels with all the necessary facilities to guarantee access to asylum procedures and effective remedies, would one not expect governments to provide more than a basic explanation – in terms of real economy and policy efficiency – to justify their decision to create or preserve two parallel systems with duplicated roles, personnel, resources, and functions in order to simply accomplish identical objectives?

Advising refugees on their legal position and on the procedures to be followed to claim asylum is necessary if a State wishes to identify those genuinely in need of protection among interdicted persons. Refugees intercepted/rescued at sea, for instance, normally do not possess any knowledge of local legislation or language, making access to an interpreter or independent legal assistance

(Joint Press Briefing, Brussels, 1 June 2016), http://europa.eu/rapid/press-release_SPEECH-16-2033_en.htm; N Nielsen, 'Italy's "floating hotspot" idea to sink in legal waters', *EUObserver* (2 June 2016), https://euobserver.com/migration/133659.

308 A Fischer-Lescano, T Lohr and T Tohidipur, 'Border Controls at Sea: Requirements under International Human Rights and Refugee Law' (2009) 21 *IJRL* 256, 285.

309 In the *Medvedyev v France* case (above n 126), the ECtHR held that detention on the high seas amounted to a violation of Art 5 of the Convention.

a fundamental requirement for obtaining effective protection.[310] As lawyers and interpreters cannot always be available on-board, it would be very difficult for asylum seekers to build up trust with legal counsel over the telephone. The case of the United States reveals that the number of people processed at sea who are found to have protection needs, is much lower than the number of those processed on land. For instance, while between 1982 and 2014, 244,488 people have been intercepted at sea by US authorities, only 425 were transferred to Guantanamo Bay for further assessment of their protection claims between 1996 and 2014.[311]

It has also been suggested that people intercepted/rescued at sea should always be asked to explain why they fear their removal to the country from which they embarked *and* whether they want to apply for asylum. States should do this driven by awareness that the life of migrants and refugees could be in danger, and that, as States, they possess capacity to save people from harm.[312] *Mutatis mutandis*, such a contention would be in line with the doctrine of 'positive obligations' adopted by the Court in *Osman v UK*. Although the *Osman* case dealt with very different issues, and no asylum seeker was involved, the Court ruled that Article 2(1) of the ECHR embodies both the duty of States to refrain from the intentional and unlawful taking of life, and the duty to actively *take measures* to protect the lives of people under their jurisdiction, if State authorities knew (or ought to have known at the time) of the existence of a real and immediate risk to the life of an identified individual or individuals.[313]

It is thus auspicable that the Grand Chamber could recognise a violation of Article 3 in the pending *MN and Others v Belgium* case with regard to the refusal by Belgian authorities to issue a humanitarian visa to the members of a Syrian family whose life was seriously threatened in their home country.[314] Indeed, any measures of territorial or extraterritorial migration control 'the effect of which is to prevent migrants from reaching the borders of the [destination] State' may amount to *refoulement*, in particular if the respondent State has (or ought to have) knowledge of the risks in question.[315] Therefore, preventing access to safety abroad by refusing a visa could impinge on Article 3 of the Convention, in particular if, in the absence of available alternative legal routes to seek international protection, the applicants are exposed to a foreseeable real risk of ill-treatment.

[310] See International Law Association, 'Resolution 6/2002 on Refugee Procedures (Declaration on International Minimum Standards for Refugee Protection)' (2002) para 8. See also, Inter-American Commission on Human Rights, *Haitian Centre for Human Rights* et al *v US*, Case 10.675, para 163.

[311] A Dastyari, *United States, Migrant Interdiction and the Detention of Refugees in Guantánamo Bay* (Cambridge University Press, 2015) 5.

[312] T Spijkerboer, 'Subsidiarity and "Arguability": the European Court of Human Rights' Case Law on Judicial Review in Asylum Cases' (2009) 21 (1) I *JRL* 1, 13. T Spijkerboer, 'The Human Costs of Border Control' (2007) 9 *EJML* 137, 138.

[313] *Osman v UK*, App no 23452/94 (28 October 1998) para 116.

[314] *MN and Others v Belgium* App no 3599/18.

[315] *See, Hirsi*, above n 4, para 180; and *Sharifi*, above n 294, paras 112 and 115.

Such a discussion on access to territory to avoid irremediable risks would assume greater relevance in the context of the new policy of the Italian government directed at the 'closure of ports' to NGOs' vessels engaged in the rescue of migrants in the Mediterranean – a policy which has worsened in humanitarian terms the conditions of thousands of people (especially vulnerable groups) left at sea for several days before a European State might authorise disembarkation.[316] On 29 January 2019, the ECtHR decided to indicate to the Italian government, under Rule 39, to take all necessary measures, as soon as possible, in order to provide migrants on-board a vessel of the NGO SeaWatch with adequate medical care, food, water and basic supplies as necessary. The Government was also requested to provide adequate legal assistance (eg legal guardianship) to the 15 unaccompanied minors. Following the Court's decision, the vessel – which had been unable to reach a European port for 10 days due to the Italian government's refusal to grant permission to dock – could finally disembark those on board at Sicily.[317]

In the *Al Saadoon v UK* case, the Court stressed that

> a Contracting Party is responsible under Article 1 of the Convention for all acts and omissions of its organs. … Article 1 makes no distinction as to the type of rule or measure concerned and does not exclude any part of a Contracting Party's "jurisdiction" from scrutiny under the Convention.[318]

In light of the foregoing, must States ensure, under the ECHR, access to asylum procedures with regards to those refugees who have not managed to enter their territory, but are considered to be within their 'jurisdiction?' This critical question seems to be answered in the affirmative. It is important to note that, in *Hirsi*, the respondent State did not actually challenge the existence of a right to seek asylum on the high seas, and the duty of Italian authorities to handle asylum applications. But, as claimed by the Italian government, since no migrant, once on the intercepting ships, expressed an intention to apply for asylum,[319] there was no need to check, during search and rescue operations, the identity and nationality of passengers. Had migrants manifested their willingness to apply for asylum, they would have been taken to the mainland to examine their protection claims.[320]

On this point, the ECtHR replied that Italy could not circumvent 'jurisdiction' and human rights obligations under the Convention by labelling activities

[316] See eg, the cases concerning the Diciotti, Aquarius, OpenArms, SeaWatch and SeaEye rescue vessels (2018). See E Papastavridis, 'The Aquarius Incident and the Law of the Sea: Is Italy in Violation of the Relevant Rules?' *EJIL Talk* (27 June 2018).

[317] See, *BG v Italy*, App no 5604/19 (29 January 2019).

[318] *Al-Saadoon v UK*, above n 138, para 128.

[319] Response of the Italian Government to the Committee on the Prevention of Torture (CPT) Report, Appendix I, para d http://www.cpt.coe.int/documents/ita/2010-inf-15-eng.htm.

[320] ibid.

at sea as search and rescue operations.[321] Such a distinction is immaterial under international human rights law. Describing these maritime operations as 'salvage' rather than 'law enforcement' would also misleadingly introduce a subjective element into the notion of *de facto* jurisdiction, whose character is instead intrinsically objective. The establishment of *de facto* jurisdiction implies the duty to respect human rights, regardless of the existence of a permissive rule of international law (*de jure* jurisdiction) that makes lawful such exercises of power.[322] Additionally, a 'rescue' mission can only be considered fully successful when the stowaways are disembarked in a 'place of safety', meaning also a place where the lives and freedoms of those alleging a well-founded fear of persecution, torture, and ill-treatment would not be threatened.[323]

According to the Italian government, the fact that intercepted migrants explicitly voiced their desire not to be transferred to Libyan guardianship was not considered by Italian authorities as an international protection request. However – as the Court does in *Hirsi* – European States have a duty to verify, before removal, that the receiving country is actually safe for those refugees. Considering the significant amount of information provided by human rights organisations, Italy knew or should have known that as irregular migrants and refugees, the applicants would be exposed to treatments contrary to the ECHR, in Libya,[324] and would not be given any form of protection against arbitrary repatriation to Somalia and Eritrea.[325] Thus, earlier ratification by Libya of international human rights instruments would not be sufficient, *per se*, to justify a presumption of safety.[326] It is exactly on this point that the radical nature of the Court's ruling on the asylum policies of European States becomes most striking. The Grand Chamber affirmed that:

> Italy is not exempt from complying with its obligations under Article 3 of the Convention because the applicants failed to ask for asylum or to describe the risks faced as a result of the lack of an asylum system in Libya. It reiterates that the Italian authorities should have ascertained how the Libyan authorities fulfilled their international obligations in relation to the protection of refugees.[327]

A virtual distinction between people actively *seeking* international protection and people *in need of* international protection would be in line with the Court's

[321] *Hirsi v Italy*, above n 304, para 79.

[322] I Papanicolopulu, 'Human Rights and the Law of the Sea' in DJ Attard, M Fitzmaurice, NA Martínez Gutiérrez (eds), *The IMLI Manual on International Maritime Law: Volume I: The Law of the Sea* (OUP, 2014).

[323] On the definition of the expression 'place of safety', see *Guidelines on the treatment of persons rescued at sea of the International Maritime Organization* (IMO), Resolution MSC.167(78), 20 May 2004, para 6.17, subsequently endorsed by the UN General Assembly in UN Doc A/RES/61/222, 16 March 2007. A broader discussion on search and rescue, interception, and disembarkation in a place of safety, will be carried out in Chapter 5 of this book.

[324] *Hirsi v Italy*, above n 4, para 131.

[325] ibid, para 152.

[326] ibid, para 128.

[327] ibid, para 157.

contention that no automatic negative conclusion should be drawn from the absence of either an explicit asylum claim or the substantiation of an asylum application.[328] It could be the case that individuals fleeing generalised violence or persecution in their home country are traumatised and have no knowledge of their own rights or of the procedures that need to be fulfilled to claim asylum abroad. The positive obligation to act proactively by informing refugees of the possibility of requesting asylum overtly emerges from the jurisprudence of the ECtHR.[329] States shall also take all necessary measures to ensure *de facto* compliance with the principle of *non-refoulement* – the overarching goal of the asylum regime – thereby avoiding the delivery of refugees back to their persecutors as a consequence of States' omissions to act.[330] In demonstrating the close link between *non-refoulement* and the procedural right to access fair status determination mechanisms, in 2010 the UNHCR stated that:

> A fair refugee status determination procedure, *wherever undertaken*, requires submission of international protection claims to a specialized and professional first instance body, and an individual interview in the early stages of the procedure. Recognized international standards further include providing a reasoned decision in writing to all applicants, and ensuring that they have the opportunity to seek an independent review of any negative decision, with any appeal in principle having a suspensive effect (emphasis added).[331]

According to the ECtHR, the *non-refoulement* obligation attaches to any person in need of international protection who suffers a real risk of exposure to ill-treatment if removed (therefore regardless of whether they have sought asylum or are yet to have expressed their desire to be protected). More specifically, 'compliance with *non-refoulement* is only ensured if its prerequisite, refugee status … is adequately examined.'[332] Therefore, in order to avoid an unsafe removal, 'anyone should be entitled to obtain sufficient information enabling them to gain effective access to the relevant procedures and to substantiate their complaints.'[333]

VIII. EU LAW AND THE RIGHT TO ACCESS ASYLUM PROCEDURES

An instrument of great significance for the rights of people seeking protection in Europe is the CFR. Conceiving the right to asylum as a right belonging

[328] ibid Concurring Opinion 41.

[329] *Hirsi v Italy*, above n 4, para 204.

[330] See eg, *UNHCR Handbook on RSD*, n 257 above, para 192; GS Goodwin-Gill, 'The Right to Seek Asylum: Interception at Sea and the Principle of *Non-refoulement*' (2011) 23 *IJRL* 449. See also, UNHCR Protection Policy Paper, *Maritime Interception Operations and the Processing of International Protection Claims: Legal Standards and Policy Considerations with Respect to Extraterritorial Processing* (November 2010) 2:http://www.unhcr.org/refworld/pdfid/4cd12d3a2.pdf.

[331] UNHCR Report 2010, 6.

[332] Fischer-Lescano, Löhr and Tohidipur 2009, n 308 above, 285.

[333] *Hirsi v Italy*, above n 4, para 204. See also, *MSS v Belgium and Greece*, above n 51.

to individuals, rather than one belonging to States, Article 18 of the CFR establishes that

> *the right to asylum* shall be guaranteed with due respect for the rules of the Geneva Convention [...] and in accordance with the Treaty on European Union and the Treaty on the Functioning of the European Union (emphasis added).

Thus, for the first time, a European supranational instrument recognises not only the right to seek asylum, but also the right *to be granted asylum*, which becomes legally binding primary law in the Union. This interpretation emerges also from the *travaux préparatoires*, where the drafters of the Charter expressly avoided limiting the scope of Article 18 to the right *to seek* asylum. Since the right to asylum has not been recognised in any international treaty to which EU Member States are parties, its content must be inferred from the constitutional traditions common to the Member States, which inspired the drafting of the Charter. Many of these countries, for instance, have interpreted the right to asylum as an entitlement to both seek and receive protection.[334]

The 'Explanations' to Article 18 of the CFR affirm that the text of the Article has been based on Article 78 of the TFEU, according to which 'the Union shall develop a common policy on asylum, subsidiary protection and temporary protection ... in accordance with the Geneva Convention ... and other relevant treaties.' Article 18 seems to recognise the right to be granted asylum in respect of all those refugees who meet the criteria for refugee status embodied in Article 1(a) of the Geneva Convention or are entitled to subsidiary protection. Gil Bazo notes that:

> asylum in the Charter is to be construed as the protection to which all individuals with an international protection need are entitled, provided that their protection grounds are established by international law, irrespective of whether they are found in the Refugee Convention or in any other international human rights instrument.[335]

With the entry into force of the Lisbon Treaty, the right to asylum has become a 'subjective and enforceable right of individuals under the Union's legal order'[336] and is directly applicable in national legal orders without further incorporation and transposition. Moreover, since Article 51 of the CFR does not expressly provide for any territorial limitation, Member States shall comply with it every time they are implementing Union law, regardless of the place where the activity is carried out.[337]

[334] Examples are the constitutional traditions of France, Germany, Italy, Bulgaria, Hungary and Spain. See MT Gil-Bazo, 'The Charter of Fundamental Rights of the European Union and the Right to be Granted Asylum in the Union's Law' (2008) 27(3) *Refugee Survey Quarterly* 33, 47.

[335] ibid, 50.

[336] ibid, 33.

[337] See, Explanations to Art 51 of the CFR in: *Explanations relating to the Charter of Fundamental Rights* (2007/C 303/02). See also, Directorate General for Internal Policies, *Implementation of the EU Charter of Fundamental Rights and its Impact on EU Home Affairs Agencies: Frontex, Europol and the European Asylum Support Office* (European Parliament, 2011) 48–49.

This chapter focuses on the assessment of whether a right to access asylum procedures can be inferred from international human rights and refugee law treaties, thus casting aside a more detailed and comprehensive analysis of EU asylum procedures, which have been substantively examined elsewhere.[338] Nevertheless, it is worth noting that procedural safeguards established within the EU Recast Qualification and Procedures Directives are considered determinative for fair and effective asylum procedures in line with international human rights and refugee law standards.

Article 13 of the 2011 Recast Qualification Directive, by reasserting its compliance with the CFR, establishes that 'Member States shall grant refugee status to a third country national or stateless person who qualifies as a refugee.' In addition, Article 18 of the same Directive provides that 'Member States shall grant subsidiary protection status to a third country national or a stateless person eligible for subsidiary protection.'[339] It has therefore been argued that the Qualification Directive confers 'a subjective right to be granted asylum',[340] as recognised also by Advocate General Maduro in *Elgafaji*.[341] No margin of appreciation is allowed as long as the qualification criteria are met, as recognised both in *Abdulla*[342] and *M'Bodj*,[343] with regard to Articles 13 and 18, respectively. As a consequence, a residence permit – meaning the 'authorization issued by the authorities of a Member State … allowing a [third-country national] to reside in its territory'[344] – shall be issued in accordance with Article 24 of the Qualification Directive.[345] Although residence permits can be refused for a 'compelling reason of security or public order', the EU right to asylum entails a subjective claim to territorial protection.[346] Therefore, Article 18 of the CFR entails a procedural dimension as well as an obligation to grant asylum if all the requirements are met by the applicant. The CJEU considers fair and effective access

[338] See, *inter alia*, Battjes 2006, n 247 above; Costello 2012, n 243 above; M Reneman, *EU Asylum Procedures and the Right to an Effective Remedy* (Hart, 2014); A Del Guercio, *La protezione dei richiedenti asilo nel diritto internazionale ed europeo* (Editoriale Scientifica, 2016); V Moreno-Lax, *Accessing Asylum in Europe. Extraterritorial Border Controls and Refugee Rights under EU Law* (OUP, 2017).

[339] For an analysis of the Qualification Directive 2004/83/EC and the right to asylum, see Gil-Bazo, 'Refugee Status and Subsidiary Protection under EC Law: The Qualification Directive and the Right to be Granted Asylum' in H Toner, E Guild and A Baldaccini (eds), *Whose Freedom, Security and Justice? EU Immigration and Asylum Law and Policy* (Hart, 2007) 237.

[340] Gil-Bazo 2008, n 334 above, 48.

[341] *Elgafaji and Elgafaji v Staatssecretaris van Justitie*, Case C-465/07, ECLI:EU:C:2009:94, para 30.

[342] Joined Cases C-175/08; C-176/08; C-178/08 and C-179/08 *Salahadin Abdulla and Others*, [2010] ECR I-1493, para 62.

[343] *Mohamed M'Bodj v État Belge*, Case C-542/13 ECLI:EU:C:2014:2452, para 29.

[344] Art 2(m) of the Qualification Directive.

[345] The obligation to issue a residence permit has also been confirmed in *HT*, Case C-373/13 ECLI:EU:C:2015:413, para 53.

[346] ibid, para 63. See also, V Moreno-Lax and M Garlick, 'Qualification: Refugee Status and Subsidiary Protection', in Peers et al, *EU Immigration and Asylum Law*, Vol 3, 2nd edn (Brill, 2015) 65, 115–16.

to asylum procedures to be the main objective of the Procedures Directive.[347] Likewise, the Dublin Regulation recognises 'effective access to the procedures for granting international protection' as one of its main goals.[348] As corroborated by the Court of Luxembourg in the *NS and ME* case, any Dublin transfers should be carried out only if a real possibility exists in the readmitting country to seek out and enjoy international protection.[349]

In order to ensure access to asylum procedures, entry to the territory of the Member State should be granted. Rather than being an autonomous entitlement, it should however be conceived of as an 'ancillary' guarantee to ensure the exercise of Article 18 of the CFR and its *effet utile*.[350] The right to reside under EU law becomes an essential part of the institution of asylum, as already indicated by the early writers on international law.[351] According to Grahl-Madsen,

> [t]o say that an individual has a right to be granted asylum is to say that the requested State is … duty bound to admit him to its territory, to allow him to remain there, or to abstain from extraditing him.[352]

Asylum applications must be submitted to competent authorities bearing in mind that the authorities that receive the claims and those in charge of examining the application should not be the same. Lamentably, asylum applications are often submitted to immigration or border police officers who do not have adequate training in human rights and asylum procedures, and who are not competent to examine the merits of an asylum claim. Article 4(4) of the Recast Procedures Directive provides that 'Member States shall ensure that the personnel of that authority have the appropriate knowledge or receive the necessary training to fulfil their obligations when implementing this Directive.'[353] Additionally, first-instance decision-makers should be fully trained with respect to relevant standards applicable in the field of asylum and refugee law, should be independent from Member States' governments, and clearly identified, to ensure that decisions are taken individually, objectively, and impartially.[354]

Another example could concern language. Since communication is a critical aspect of fair and effective access to international protection, refugees shall always be entitled to the services of a competent interpreter in all phases of the asylum procedure and not only when the initial interview takes place.[355] In the

[347] *Diouf v Ministre du Travail, de l'Emploi et de l'Immigration*, Case C-69/10, ECLI:EU:C:2011:524, para 33.

[348] Art 3 of Dublin Regulation III.

[349] *NS and ME*, above n 218, paras 88–89.

[350] Moreno-Lax 2017, 390.

[351] See, eg, H Grotius *De iure belli ac pacis, libri duo* (translated by AC Campbell) (Batoche Books, 2001 [1625]) ch 2, no XVI, 84; E De Vattel, *The Law of Nations* (Carnegie Institute, 1916 [1758]), book I, ch 21, para 231.

[352] A Grahl-Madsen, *The Status of Refugees in International Law*, Vol II (Sijthoff, 1972) 79.

[353] This Article replaces Art 4(3) of the 2005 Procedures Directive.

[354] See, Arts 4 and 10 of the Recast Procedures Directive.

[355] On this issue see, *UNHCR Handbook on RSD*, n 257 above, para 192 (IV). See also, Art 12(1)(b) of the Recast Procedures Directive replacing Art 10(1)(b) of the 2005 Procedures Directive.

Sharifi case, the ECtHR affirmed that the lack of information in a language comprehensible to the applicants who had arrived at the Italian Adriatic ports deprived them of the possibility of seeking asylum.[356] Nonetheless, while the right to free legal assistance to appeal procedures against an unfavourable decision is guaranteed by Article 20(1) of the Recast Procedures Directive, effective access to legal advice is often hampered by financial problems and cuts in public funding.[357]

Moreover, applicants should be informed as early as possible of their right to submit their protection claim. They also need guidance on the procedure to be followed before the proceedings are initiated. It is also paramount that first instance proceedings have a suspensive effect to avoid a violation of the principle of *non-refoulement* as a consequence of the removal of asylum seekers to third countries while their claim is being examined. Under the Recast Procedures Directive, applicants are allowed to remain in the Member State only pending a decision in the first instance, and few exceptions exist in respect of cases of subsequent applications.[358] The right to appeal against unfavourable decisions with a suspensive effect is central to fair and effective asylum procedures, but it is frequently called into question by the application of accelerated mechanisms of identification, examination of asylum claims, and expulsion. These procedural guarantees are key before any readmission practice takes place, and as such they will be investigated in the following Sections concerning the right to an effective remedy.

IX. THE RIGHT TO AN EFFECTIVE REMEDY BEFORE REMOVAL: INTRODUCTION

The following Sections will investigate how the right to an effective remedy is governed by international refugee and human rights treaties, and how the relevant monitoring bodies ensure its availability and accessibility. As already explained in relation to the right to access asylum procedures, the right to an effective remedy is here understood as a procedural entitlement, a pre-condition to *non-refoulement*, that remains the cornerstone of refugee law. An effective remedy can imply the right to appeal against a decision to refuse asylum in the first instance, as well as the right to challenge an expulsion order with a view to either repealing the decision to expel or suspend the removal if there is a serious risk of ill-treatment for the person concerned.

The Geneva Convention does not contain an express provision on the right to an effective remedy against breaches of the rights provided therein. However,

[356] *Sharifi v Italy and Greece*, above n 293, para 217.

[357] See also, Art 22(1) of the Recast Procedures Directive replacing Art 15(2) of the 2005 Procedures Directive.

[358] Art 9(1) of the Recast Procedures Directive replacing Art 7(1) of the 2005 Procedures Directive. Exceptions are laid down in Art 9(2).

pursuant to Article 16(1) '[a] refugee shall have *free access to the courts of law* on the territory of all Contracting States' (emphasis added). This right – which applies to any type of legal proceedings, as confirmed by the lack of any restriction in the text of the Convention[359] – does not seem to have raised much debate since its entry into force. Additionally, part of the literature has rejected the applicability of Article 16 to the determination of refugee status under first instance procedures, as the Geneva Convention generally leaves procedural issues to the States.[360] Nevertheless, it can impact the right of a refugee to access fair status determination procedures by providing a remedy, in principle, against an unfavourable decision, thereby preventing States from excluding refugees from their territories.[361] This subjective right – as testified by the wording 'shall have' in Article 16(1) – does not require physical presence in the country the refugee intends to access and no reference to recognised refugees is made in its text.[362] Therefore, the right can be enjoyed even if the refugee is kept in 'international' or 'transit' zones or is brought to a third country.[363] Article 16(1) requires States to ensure 'free access' to courts, thus precluding any limitation based on refugee status, as recognition is purely declaratory and not constitutive of refugee status.[364] As 'free access' is also meant to be effective, any measures such as excessively strict time frames and formal requirements would deny the substance of this right.[365] An asylum seeker must have time to prepare her claim, collect evidence, appeal against a negative decision, and if detained, to challenge that detention in court. 'Free access' does not mean, however, free from payment, and States can ask refugees to pay court fees as with any other national in the same circumstances.

Although the Convention does not specify how access to courts can be ensured in practical terms, it seems, however, that the right to *access* a court of law, even before admission to a status determination procedure, shall not be undermined by acts or omissions of the host State, such as the failure to

[359] *Contra: Colafic and Others* Cour d'Appeal de Paris, JDI 90 (1963) 723, 29 November 1961, according to which the Geneva Convention 'merely intended that the refugee should have the opportunity of bringing or defending civil proceedings' as cited in B Elberling, 'Article 16. Access to Courts' in Zimmermann 2011, n 78 above, 939.

[360] For some examples, see P Boeles, 'Effective Legal Remedies for Asylum Seekers according to the Convention of Geneva of 1951' (1996) 43 *NILR* 291, 302. See also, *UNHCR Handbook on RSD*, para 12(ii).

[361] T Spijkerboer, 'Higher Judicial Remedies' in G Care and H Storey (eds), *Asylum Law: First International Judicial Conference on Asylum Law* (London, 1–2 December 1995) 217 ff; Boeles 1996, n 360 above, 302.

[362] On the territorial applicability of the Convention in general, see, MT Gil-Bazo, 'Article 40. Territorial Application Clause' in Zimmermann 2011, n 78 above, 1567 ff.

[363] A Francis, 'Bringing Protection Home: Healing the Schism between International Obligations and National Safeguards Created by Extraterritorial Processing' (2008) 20 *IJRL* 273; Elberling 2011, n 359 above, 945.

[364] In relation to Art 16, see, *R v SSHD, ex parte Jahangeer et al*, 11 June 1993, [1993] Imm AR 564.

[365] See on this point, Elberling 2011, n 359 above, 939; Boeles 1996, n 360 above, 291, 301.

provide legal aid services to refugees, according to Article 16(2).[366] This obligation belongs to Contracting Parties. The UNHCR cannot offer legal aid services, but can use its good offices to ensure that States comply with their obligations toward refugees, or assist refugees in paying their lawyers' bills.[367] Moreover, as Hathaway observes, 'to the extent that the State is willing, UNHCR may, of course, provide direct assistance to refugees to enforce their rights in the asylum country.'[368]

It is also to be observed that the wording of Article 16(1) concerns only 'courts of law' as opposed to administrative agencies,[369] which, instead, are included in Article 32(2), providing for access to a competent authority, and regulating access to remedies for refugees subjected to an *expulsion* decision. Article 32(2) requires that the decision to expel a refugee on grounds of national security or public order be taken 'in accordance with due process of law' and that,

> except where compelling reasons of national security otherwise require, the refugee shall be allowed to submit evidence to clear himself, and to appeal to and be represented for the purpose before a competent authority or person or persons specially designated by the competent authorities.[370]

Any reader would notice the margins both of overlap and divergence between Article 33 on *non-refoulement* and Article 32 on expulsion. First, whereas Article 32 applies only to refugees who are lawfully on the territory of one of the Contracting Parties, Article 33 encompasses all refugees within the jurisdiction of this State, regardless of their regular or irregular status. Secondly, Article 32 refers to expulsion enforced on the basis of an order to leave the country, while Article 33 pertains to a factual removal of refugees to the frontiers of territories where their life or freedom would be threatened on one of the five grounds of Article 1(a). Thirdly, State authorities have to comply with both Articles 32 and 33 when expelling a refugee. In other words, they may issue an expulsion order only for reasons of national security and public order (as required by Article 32(1)), must act in accordance with the procedural guarantees of Article 32(2) on due process and must also ensure that the actual removal does not result in *refoulement*, prohibited by Article 33. Finally, Article 32 does not pertain to those refugees falling under the cessation clause in Article 1(c) of the

[366] JC Hathaway, *The Rights of Refugees under International Law* (Cambridge University Press, 2005) 906. Art 16(2) provides that '[a] refugee shall enjoy in the Contracting State in which he has habitual residence the same treatment as a national in matters pertaining to access to the Courts, including legal assistance and exemption from *cautio judicatum solvi*.'

[367] ibid, 906–07.

[368] ibid, 992.

[369] On the distinction between courts of law and administrative authorities, see UNHCR EXCOM Conclusion no 8 (1977). See also UNHCR EXCOM Conclusion no 22 (1981); A Grahl-Madsen, 'Article 16' in UNHCR (ed), *Commentary on the Refugee Convention (Articles 2–11, 13–37)* (UNHCR 1963, republished 1997); P Weis, *The Refugee Convention, 1951: The Travaux Préparatoires Analysed with a Commentary by the Late Dr Paul Weis* (Cambridge University Press, 1995) 134.

[370] Art 32(2) of the Geneva Convention.

Geneva Convention, or those persons deemed unworthy of refugee status and excluded from the benefits of the Convention under Article 1(f).[371] However, the fact that Article 32 applies to refugees who are lawfully in the territory of one of the Contracting Parties does not have to lead States to assume that it is confined only to refugees with a permanent residence. Rather, its scope of application extends also to 'refugees whose stay is, at the material time, perceived as temporary and precarious',[372] and potentially also to asylum seekers who are scheduled to be removed to 'safe third countries'.[373]

The first element of the procedural safeguards contained in Article 32(2) is 'due process of law', which has been defined as a standard for national legislation, which must always be accessible and foreseeable and able to protect against arbitrary actions, as required by international human rights law.[374] Moreover, deportation 'must be reasonable, not arbitrary and must rest upon some ground … having a fair and substantial relation to the object of the legislation, so that all persons similarly circumstanced shall be treated alike.'[375]

As the 'due process' standard varies according to the nature of the endangered individual right, the list of rights included in the second sentence of paragraph 2 – the right to submit evidence to clear oneself, right to appeal and to be represented before a competent authority – is not meant to be exhaustive.[376] In light of the development of human rights law and refugee law as two interrelated disciplines, the scope of Article 32(2) cannot today be limited to a mere opportunity '*à présenter un recours*' before a court of law,[377] which conducts a formal examination of the case. The requirement of due process of law is satisfied only if an individual is informed of the possibility of lodging an appeal and her complaint is examined by an independent and impartial body that can determine both questions of law and fact.[378] Moreover, it is satisfied only if the refugee has the benefit of adversarial proceedings, that is to say the chance to present her point of view and contest the arguments put forward by the State authorities that have ordered her expulsion.[379] Finally, once domestic remedies have been exhausted and the expulsion order is issued – the refugee is entitled to have her deportation order delayed for a 'reasonable period' in order to seek admission into another country (paragraph 3). Another aspect that cannot be

[371] On the intertwining between Arts 32 and 33, see U Davy, 'Article 32: Expulsion' in Zimmermann 2011, n 78 above, 1294–95.

[372] ibid, 1324.

[373] ibid.

[374] *Lupsa v Romania*, App no 10337/04 (8 June 2006) para 55. See also, Hathaway 2005, n 5 above, 673.

[375] *Francis v Immigration and Naturalization Service* 532 F.2d 268 (2d Cir. 1976).

[376] On the procedural guarantees of Art 16(2), see Davy 2011, n 371 above, 1316.

[377] Hathaway 2005, n 5 above, 672.

[378] *Lupsa v Romania*, above n 374, para 38; *Al-Nashif v Bulgaria*, App no 50963/99 (20 September 2002) paras 123–124.

[379] ibid. See also, Davy 2011, n 371 above, 1318.

neglected is that the rights of Article 32(2) can be withdrawn on 'compelling reasons of national security.'

The following Sections will review the guarantees international human rights treaties put at the disposal of refugees to allow them to challenge an unfavourable decision on their status or an expulsion decision.

X. THE RIGHT TO AN EFFECTIVE REMEDY UNDER HUMAN RIGHTS LAW

The right to an effective remedy is explicitly recognised by Article 2(3) of the ICCPR whereby:

> Each State Party to the present Covenant undertakes: (a) To ensure that any person whose rights or freedoms as herein recognized are violated shall have an *effective remedy* ...; (b) To ensure that any person claiming such a remedy shall have his right thereto determined by competent judicial, administrative or legislative authorities, or by any other competent authority provided for by the legal system of the State, and to develop the possibilities of judicial remedy; (c) To ensure that the competent authorities shall enforce such remedies when granted (emphasis added).

The HRC has made clear that the prohibition of *refoulement*, implicit in Article 7 of the Covenant, entails the right to have a review or appeal of a negative decision that is available in law and practice, and imposes upon competent national authorities the duty to assess the substance of a claim and grant appropriate relief.[380] A remedy can be 'effectively assured by the judiciary, administrative mechanisms, and national human rights institutions.'[381] However, the HRC maintains that priority shall be placed on judicial remedies, as 'decisions made solely by political or subordinate administrative organs do not constitute an effective remedy within the meaning of paragraph 3(b).'[382]

It has also stressed that Article 7, read in conjunction with Article 2 of the Covenant, requires an effective review prior to expulsion in order to avoid both irremediable damage to the individual deported to the territory of a third State where she might be subjected to torture, and the risk of rendering 'the review otiose and devoid of meaning.'[383] For instance, in the *Judge v Canada* case, the Committee stated that:

> By preventing the author from exercising an appeal available to him under domestic law, the State party failed to demonstrate that the author's contention that his

[380] HRC, *General Comment no 31* (2004) para 12.

[381] ibid para. 15.

[382] See, eg, *RT v France*, Comm no 262/87 (30 March 1989) UN Doc CCPR/C/35/D/262/1987 (1989) para 74. See also, *Vicente and Others v Colombia* where the HRC stated that 'in case of violations of basic human rights, in particular, the right to life, purely administrative and disciplinary measures cannot be considered adequate and effective.' *Vicente and Others v Colombia*, Comm 612/1995 (14 March 1996) UN Doc CCPR/C/60/D/612/1995, para 5.2.

[383] *Alzery v Sweden*, above n 32, para 11.8.

> deportation to a country where he faces execution would violate his right to life, was sufficiently considered. … The decision to deport the author to a State where he is under sentence of death without affording him the *opportunity to avail himself of an available appeal*, was taken arbitrarily and in violation of article 6, together with article 2, paragraph 3, of the Covenant (emphasis added).[384]

If we read the *Judge v Canada* case in light of the case law of the HRC on the right to an effective remedy, it can be argued that the right to appeal under domestic law shall be guaranteed by the sending State to any applicants whose rights risk being violated upon deportation. The HRC requires, indeed, that 'the State party makes available an appellate system designed to safeguard any petitioner's, including the author's, *rights*, and *in particular* … – the right to life' (emphasis added). Therefore, the language used by the HRC is not exclusive with regards to the right to life, but it is implicitly open to an interpretation conferring a broader protection, including against torture or instances of persecution.

In the *XHL v The Netherlands* case, the HRC considered that

> the State party is under an obligation to provide the author with an effective remedy by reconsidering his claim in light of the evolution of the circumstances of the case, including the possibility of granting him a residence permit. The State party is also under an obligation to take steps to prevent similar violations occurring in the future.[385]

Therefore, a full reconsideration of the asylum seekers' claim before removal is required to avoid *refoulement*.[386]

With regard to the CAT, the right to an effective remedy can also be implicitly derived from Article 3 on the prohibition of *refoulement*. The requirements of effective, independent and impartial administrative or judicial review must always be respected even if national security concerns entail no possibility for review of the decision to expel.[387] In the *Agiza v Sweden* case, the Committee Against Torture affirmed that:

> [t]he right to an effective remedy for a breach of the Convention underpins the entire Convention, for otherwise the protection afforded by the Convention would be rendered largely illusory. … In the Committee's view, in order to reinforce the protection of the norm in question and understanding the Convention consistently, *the prohibition on refoulement contained in Article 3 should be interpreted the same way to encompass a remedy for its breach*, even though it may not contain on its face such a right to remedy for a breach thereof. … The nature of refoulement is such, however, that an allegation of breach of that article relates to a future expulsion or removal; accordingly, the right to an effective remedy contained in article 3 requires,

[384] *Judge v Canada*, Comm no 829/1998 (20 October 2003) UN Doc CCPR/C/78/D/829/1998, para 10.9. Art 6 of the ICCPR enshrines the right to life.

[385] *XHL v Netherlands*, above n 274, para 12.

[386] See, eg, *Pillai* et al *v Canada*, Comm no 1763/2008 (25 March 2011) UN Doc CCPR/C/101/D/1763/2008 para 13.

[387] *Agiza v Sweden*, Comm no 233/2003 (20 May 2005) UN Doc CAT/C/34/D/233/2003, para 13.8.

> in this context, an opportunity for *effective, independent and impartial review of the decision to expel or remove*, once that decision is made, when there is a plausible allegation that article 3 issues arise (emphasis added).[388]

A remedy that is effective in law and practice also warrants that the State will ensure adequate time to appeal.[389] In *Josu Arkauz Arana v France*, the Committee Against Torture first declared the communication admissible because the applicant was not granted sufficient time to appeal against a deportation order, which was enforced immediately after his notification thereof.[390] In its decision, it then held that 'a direct handover from police to police, without the intervention of a judicial authority and without any possibility for the author to contact his family or his lawyer' exposed the applicant to possible abuse in breach of Article 3.[391]

With regard to the ECHR, Article 13 provides that 'everyone whose rights and freedoms as set forth in [the] Convention are violated shall have an effective remedy before a national authority notwithstanding that the violation has been committed by persons acting in an official capacity.' Moreover, administrative 'decisions regarding the entry, stay and deportation of aliens do not concern the determination of an applicant civil rights or obligations.'[392] As Article 6 (right to a fair trial) does not apply in migration cases, Article 13 is the applicable provision. An 'effective remedy' is meant as a tool 'available and sufficient to afford redress in respect of the breaches alleged'[393] and is apt to allow the competent authority 'both to deal with the substance of the relevant Convention complaint and to grant appropriate relief.'[394] It must be able to quash the decision to expel and to suspend the enforcement of the deportation order.[395] To be effective, it is not necessary that the authority offering the remedy is a judicial authority in the strict sense, but its independence and impartiality are necessary for the remedy to be effective.[396] Considering that, in the *MSS* case, the Court recalled 'the rights of the defence' in the context of Dublin removal, it could be argued that the case law on Article 13 *de facto* introduces through the backdoor due process safeguards.

[388] ibid, paras 13.6–13.7.

[389] See, eg, *Iratxe Sorzábal Díaz v France*, Comm no 194/2001 (3 May 2005) UN Doc CAT/C/34/D/194/, para 6.1.

[390] *Josu Arkauz Arana v France*, Comm no 63/1997 (5 June 2000) UN Doc CAT/C/23/D/63/1997, para 6.1.

[391] ibid, para 11(4).

[392] *Maaouia v France*, App 39652/98 (10 October 2000) para 40.

[393] *Akdivar and Others v Turkey*, App no 21893/93 (16 September 1996) para 66.

[394] *Jabari v Turkey*, above n 52, para 48.

[395] See eg, *Soering v UK*, above n 41, para 121; *Vilvarajah and Others v UK*, Apps no 13163/87, 13164/87, 13165/87, 13447/87, 13448/87 (30 October 1991) para 123. See also, *Jabari v Turkey*, above n 52, para 50; *Conka v Belgium*, App no 51564/99 (5 February 2002) para 79.

[396] *Gebremedhin v France*, above n 291, para 53; *Silver v UK*, App no 5947/72 (25 March 1983) para 116; *Khan v UK*, App no 35394/97 (12 May 2000) paras 41–47 See also, P Van Dijk, F Van Hoof, A Van Rijn, L Zwaak, *Theory and Practice of the European Convention on Human Rights* (Intersentia, 2006) 1006.

Furthermore, the ECtHR's surveillance of State compliance with the Convention must always be subsidiary to the surveillance carried out by domestic courts.[397] As stated in *Gebremedhin v France*, 'the effect of Article 13 is … to require the provision of a domestic remedy to deal with the substance of an 'arguable complaint' under the Convention and to grant appropriate relief.'[398] The ECtHR has spoken up for the need to extend the requirement of 'independent and rigorous scrutiny' to legal remedies at the national level against expulsion in violation of Article 3 in order to ensure a more thorough assessment of the claim made by the applicant and the reasons for her fear of being deported.[399] It emerges, therefore, that the procedural guarantees offered by Article 13 are functional to protection under Article 3, given that the principle of *non-refoulement* and the right to an effective remedy are tightly interdependent. The latter is not, indeed, a free-standing right, but rather an accessory right to be read in conjunction with Article 3 of the ECHR.[400]

The term 'independent' is used in relation to the scrutiny by a decision-maker,[401] which becomes essential when considering the irreversible nature of the harm that might occur if the asylum seeker is physically sent back to a country where she risks ill-treatment. While attaching importance to the knowledge and experience of national authorities in examining asylum claims in a thorough manner,[402] the ECtHR has also explicitly indicated that its own role is to provide a rigorous examination of a risk of ill-treatment in breach of Article 3.[403] Such an evaluation implies the option of assessing the credibility of an asylum seeker whose claims seem implausible.[404]

Beyond Article 3 claims, the ECtHR has recognised violations of the right to an effective remedy in many cases where a State's failure to allow an individual to challenge a refusal of entry or an order of expulsion jeopardised the applicant's right to respect for family life.[405] In the *Conka v Belgium* case concerning

[397] M Verdussen, *L'Europe de la subsidiarité* (Bruylant, 2000) 45–50; Battjes, 2006, n 247 above, 321.

[398] *Gebremedhin v France*, above n 291, para 53.

[399] *Jabari v Turkey*, above n 52, paras 39, 50; *Shamaiev and Others v Georgia and Russia*, App 36378/02 (12 Apr 2005) paras 448, 460;

[400] H Lambert, 'The European Convention on Human Rights and the Protection of Refugees: Limits and Opportunities' (2005) 24(2) *Refugee Survey Quarterly* 39, 47; Fischer-Lescano, Lohr and Tohidipur 2009, n 308 above, 286. G Noll, 'Visions of the Exceptional: Legal and Theoretical Issues Raised by Transit Processing Centres and Protection Zones' (2003) 5 *EJML* 303, 332; A Edwards, 'Tampering with Refugee Protection: The Case of Australia' (2003) 15 *IJRL* 192, 210; Hathaway 2005, n 5 above, 279; R Weinzierl and U Lisson, *Border Management and Human Rights* (German Institute for Human Rights, 2007) 50.

[401] *Chahal v UK*, above n 46, para 151.

[402] *Cruz Varas v Sweden*, above n 46, para 81; *Vilvarajah v UK*, above n 42, para 114.

[403] See, eg, *Vilvarajah v UK*, above n 42, para 108; *Chahal v UK*, above n 46, para 96; *TI v UK*, above n 53, 14.

[404] *Said v The Netherlands*, App 2345/02 (5 July 2005) para 50; *N v Finland*, App no 38885/02 (26 July 2005) para 152; *Nasimi v Sweden*, App no 38865/02 (16 March 2004) 7.

[405] *Abdulaziz, Cabales and Balkandali v UK*, App nos 9214/80, 9473/81, and 9474/81 (24 April 1985). See also, *Al-Nashif v Bulgaria*, above n 378.

the detention and deportation of a Roma family that requested political asylum in Belgium, the Court singled out certain elements which significantly affected the accessibility of remedies. The factors considered by the Court included the lack of proper communication of the reasons for detention, the absence of an interpreter, and the lack of understandable information on the available remedies.[406] Although the Court declared that no violation existed of Article 13 in connection with Article 3, it found a violation of the right to an effective remedy in conjunction with Article 4 of Protocol 4 (prohibition of collective expulsions). According to the Court, 'the notion of an effective remedy under Article 13 requires that the remedy may prevent the execution of measures that are contrary to the Convention and whose effects are potentially irreversible.'[407]

This means that national courts or authorities must be able to suspend measures that might produce irremediable results entailing egregious infringements of Article 3. In the *Conka* judgment, the Court also significantly expanded the right to an effective remedy to include the duty to provide for an appeal with suspensive effect for a minimum reasonable period. If, in the *Jabari* case, the Court cautiously considered the suspension of the physical expulsion as a possibility rather than as an obligation of governments,[408] in *Gebremedhin v France*, the Court stressed State obligations to provide for suspensive effect '*de plein droit*' for a remedy to be effective.[409] The applicant alleged a violation of Article 13 of the Convention in conjunction with Article 3, as under French law there was no remedy with suspensive effect against decisions refusing leave to enter or ordering removal. The Court also added that Article 13 of the ECHR requires an effective remedy in the waiting zone before expulsion – even when removal takes place at the border after refusal of leave to enter – unless the claim is 'manifestly unfounded' with no *prima facie* risk that the expulsion would imply a breach of Article 3.[410] Likewise, in the 2018 *MA v Lithuania* case, the Court held that there was a breach of Article 13 despite the fact that the applicants had not appealed against the decisions refusing them entry into Lithuania. Since lodging such an appeal would have not automatically suspended their transfer to Belarus (and from there most probably to Chechnya) it could not be considered an effective domestic remedy.[411]

[406] E Brouwer, Effective Remedies in Immigration and Asylum Law Procedures: A Matter of General Principles of EU Law, in Toner, Guild and Baldaccini 2007, n 339 above, 73.

[407] *Conka v Belgium*, above n 395, para 79.

[408] A Skordas, 'Human Rights and Effective Migration Policies: An Uneasy Coexistence. The *Conka* Judgment of the European Court of Human Rights' in C Dias Urbano de Sousa and P de Bruycker (eds), *The Emergence of a European Asylum Policy* (Bruylant, 2004).

[409] *Gebremedhin v France*, above n 291, paras 66–67. See also *Shamayev v Georgia and Russia*, App no 36378/02 (12 Apr 2005) para 460; *Baysakov and Others v Ukraine*, App no 54131/08 (18 February 2010) paras 74–75.

[410] On the grounds to determine whether an application for asylum is 'manifestly unfounded', see *Gebremedhin v France*, above n 291, paras 61, 66–67.

[411] *MA v Lithuania*, above n 298, para 119, 83–84. See also, *Diallo v Czech Republic*, above n 290, para 85.

From the case law of the ECtHR, it seems that the right to an effective remedy can be invoked not only when a serious violation has taken place, but also where the asylum seeker makes an 'arguable' claim of such a violation.[412] A claim is 'arguable' when it is 'sufficiently credible for the Court to consider that it raises an issue of substance under Article 3. It follows that … the applicant is entitled in principle to rely on that provision in conjunction with Article 13.'[413] If an asylum seeker has an arguable claim, then she has a prima facie case, meaning that her application cannot be dismissed on formal grounds, even if procedural errors are made.[414] An infringement of Article 13 can, therefore, be invoked not only when a serious violation has already taken place, but also when an individual (including an asylum seeker), makes an 'arguable' claim that such a violation may occur upon removal to a third country.

In *Conka*, the Court explained what exactly it considered to be an 'effective' remedy. After asserting that a remedy 'must be *effective* in practice as well as in law', it clarified that such a factor:

> [d]oes not depend on the certainty of a favourable outcome for the applicant. Nor does the 'authority' referred to in that provision necessarily have to be a judicial authority; but if it is not, its powers and the guarantees which it affords are relevant in determining whether the remedy before it is effective. Also, even if a single remedy does not by itself entirely satisfy the requirements of Article 13, the aggregate of remedies provided for under domestic law may do so.[415]

According to the Court, the effectiveness of a remedy can be assessed also in light of the obligation to exhaust domestic remedies as set forth in Article 35 of the ECHR. Indeed, national authorities must guarantee 'the availability at national level of a remedy to enforce the substance of the Convention rights and freedoms in whatever form they might happen to be secured in the domestic legal order.'[416] National authorities must also be able to afford applicants 'a realistic possibility of using the remedy'.[417] In the *Bahaddar v The Netherlands* case, the Court reasoned that short time limits for lodging asylum claims can hamper access to an effective remedy if they are too short or applied too inflexibly to allow the applicant to supply evidence proving her claim.[418]

Rejecting an asylum application (including repeated applications) on formal grounds might lead to a violation of Article 3 if deportation is enforced to the

[412] See, eg, *Ilias and Ahmed v Hungary*, App no 47287/15 (14 March 2017), para 99.

[413] ibid para 55. See also, *Rotaru v Romania*, App no 28341/95 (4 May 2000) para 67; *Conka v Belgium*, above n 395, paras 75–76; *Shamayev and Others v Georgia and Russia*, above n 409, paras 444–45.

[414] See, eg, *Bahaddar v The Netherlands*, App no 25894/94 (19 February 1998) para 44; *Jabari v Turkey*, above n 52, para 40. On the meaning of 'arguability', see Spijkerboer 2009, n 312 above, 73, 74.

[415] *Conka v Belgium*, above n 395, para. 75. See also, *Kudła v Poland*, App no 30210/96 (26 October 2000).

[416] *Jabari v Turkey*, above n 52, para 48.

[417] *Conka v Belgium*, above n 395, para 46. See also, *Jabari v Turkey*, above n 52, para 40.

[418] *Bahaddar v The Netherlands*, above n 414.

borders of territory where the life or freedom of the claimant can be put at risk. While asylum seekers, like anyone else, should, in principle, comply with procedural rules, scrutiny of an arguable claim under Article 3 must always be ensured, and procedural mistakes should not automatically prevent applicants from obtaining access to an effective remedy. The Court does not disapprove, for instance, of a time frame requiring that an asylum application be submitted within five days. Rather, the Court's reasoning suggests that:

> The problem is not primarily in the rules themselves (procedural rules are formal by their very nature), but in their application. … Making the application of procedural rules in some way conditional on the merits of the case itself is the only way to reach a compromise between the procedural autonomy of States parties on the one hand, and the subsidiary role of the Court in examining applications based on Article 3 on the other.[419]

In several other cases, the ECtHR ruled that the fact that an applicant did not have the chance to appeal the decision of expulsion or extradition led to a violation of Article 13. In the *Shamayev and Others v Georgia and Russia* case, for instance, the Court underlined that the fact that applicants' lawyers were not granted sufficient information in time prevented them from challenging the extradition order. It therefore found a violation of Article 13 as national authorities had unjustifiably hindered the exercise of the right to appeal.[420]

Similarly, in *Gorabayev v Russia*, the Court held that

> it is inconsistent with Article 13 for [measures whose effects are potentially irreversible] to be executed before the national authorities have examined whether they are compatible with the Convention, although Contracting States are afforded some discretion as to the manner in which they conform to their obligations under this provision.[421]

The same line of reasoning was followed by the Court in *Baysakov and Others v Ukraine*, which confirmed how Article 13 embodies both the requirement of an independent and rigorous scrutiny of the claim that expulsion could result in ill-treatment contrary to Article 3, and the need for a remedy with automatic suspensive effect.[422]

Indeed, a remedy will be effective in preventing removal from the country only if it has an automatic suspensive effect.[423] In the *Olaechea Chuas v Spain*

[419] Spijkerboer 2009, n 312 above, 57–58. In *Bahaddar v The Netherlands* (above n 414) the Court did not examine the case in the merits as domestic remedies had not been exhausted. However, it emphasised how procedural rules must make due allowance for the fact that they are applied 'in the context of machinery for the protection of human rights.' Therefore, procedural rules 'must be applied with some degree of flexibility and without excessive formalism …' (para 44).

[420] *Shamayev and Others v Georgia and Russia*, above n 409, para 460.

[421] *Garabayev v Russia* App no 38411/02 (7 June 2007) para 105.

[422] *Baysakov and Others v Ukraine*, above n 409, para 71. See also, *Muminov v Russia*, App no 42502/06 (11 December 2008) para 101.

[423] ibid, para 75.

case, the applicant's transfer was scheduled for the day after the decision of the ECtHR to issue an interim measure pursuant to Rule 39.[424] The Court considered as unacceptable the justification that the Spanish government had not had enough time to suspend the extradition after receiving notification of the decision to apply interim measures, since this behaviour would risk hindering the effective exercise of the right of individual application.[425]

In *IM v France*, the ECtHR found that Articles 13 and 3 of the Convention had been violated because of France's failure to provide satisfactory legal and interpreting assistance.[426] It also added that for a detained asylum seeker, the use of accelerated procedures (five days to claim asylum and 48 hours to appeal the deportation order), the lack of suspensive effect of the removal decision, and the difficulty of gathering evidence, severely hindered his access to domestic effective remedies.[427] Likewise, in *Singh and Others v Belgium*, a violation of Article 13 in connection with Article 3 was due to the fact that the applicants were not given the chance to explain their fears of indirect *refoulement* through Russia, nor to defend their allegations of the ill-treatment they would face in Afghanistan as members of the Sikh minority.[428] Depriving the applicants' documents of any probative value without verifying their authenticity was inconsistent with the obligation to guarantee a rigorous scrutiny of the merits of the applicants' arguable complaints under Article 3, thereby violating their right to an effective remedy.[429]

Like the *Conka* case, the Court found a violation of Article 13 taken together with Article 4 of Protocol 4 in *ND and NT v Spain*.[430] The two African applicants, apprehended while trying to cross the border fence between Morocco and the Spanish enclave of Melilla, had no access to interpreters or legal assistance for the purpose of informing them of the procedures to claim asylum or challenge their expulsion. Therefore, in view of their immediate removal, the Court held that the applicants had been deprived of access to a domestic effective remedy.[431]

In the case of *Ilias and Ahmed v Hungary*, the Court found a violation of Article 13 taken together with Article 3, as the applicants did not have remedies enabling them to complain about the conditions in which they were held in the

[424] *Olaechea Chuas v Spain*, App no 24668/03 (10 August 2006).

[425] ibid, para 81.

[426] *IM v France*, above n 248, paras 155, 145.

[427] ibid, paras 159–60, 154, 156.

[428] *Singh and Others v Belgium*, App no 33210/11 (2 January 2013) para 101, 103. See also, *VM and Others v Belgium*, App no 60125/11 (7 July 2015). However, on 14 December 2015, the case was referred to the Grand Chamber at the request of the Government, and struck out of the list as the applicants had failed to maintain contact with their lawyer. *VM and Others v Belgium*, App no 60125/11 (17 November 2016).

[429] ibid, para 104.

[430] *ND and NT v Spain*, App 8675/15 and 8697/15 (3 October 2017). The case is now pending before the Grand Chamber.

[431] ibid, para 66.

transit zone in Hungary awaiting their removal to Serbia.[432] One of the key aspects of this judgment is the Court's contention that inclusion in a list of safe third countries is not per se a sufficient condition to deem that country safe for removal. States should work with the applicants, to satisfy themselves that there is no risk of violations of Article 3 on the basis of facts and relevant reports.

Such dynamic, evolving jurisprudence of the Court on the right to an effective remedy stands in contrast with the more restrictive approach of the Grand Chamber with regard to the procedural guarantees stemming from Article 4 of Protocol 4 in the *Khlaifia* case.[433] While affirming that an increasing influx of migrants cannot, per se, absolve a State of its obligations under Article 3,[434] the ECtHR also held that 'it would certainly be artificial' to disregard the difficult situation suffered by Italy, placed under migratory pressure in the aftermath of the Arab Spring.[435]

It went on to find a violation of Article 13 taken together with Article 3, but rejected a violation of Article 13 taken together with Article 4 of Protocol 4. In the Court's view, as long as the applicant is given the 'opportunity to put arguments against his expulsion … on an individual basis', there would be no reason to consider the expulsion collective.[436] Moreover, it overturned the Chamber's conclusion by holding that Article 4 of Protocol 4 does not warrant an unfettered right to an individual interview, but only the chance to challenge 'expulsion', including 'refusal of entry with removal' (under the bilateral agreements between Italy and Tunisia), as in the case at hand.[437] In *Khalifia*, however, the migrants did not submit any arguments to contest their expulsion, although they had the opportunity to do so during the two identification procedures with the Italian authorities and the Tunisian consul,[438] and did not show any fear of being removed or any other legal obstacle.[439] The procedural guarantees of Article 4 of Protocol 4 include – as shown in the cases examined above – a full and effective examination of each individual case, regardless of the regular or irregular status of the applicant.[440] Excluding the right to an individual

[432] *Ilias and Ahmed v Hungary*, above n 412, paras 100–101.

[433] *Khlaifia v Italy*, App no 16483/12 (GC, 15 December 2016).

For commentaries, see A Matonti, 'Garanzie procedurali derivanti dall'Art. 4 del Protocollo n 4 CEDU: il caso *Khlaifia*' (2017) 11(2) *Diritti Umani e Diritto Internazionale*, 523–31; MR Mauro, 'Detention and Expulsion of Migrants: the *Khlaifia v Italy* case' (2016) 25 *The Italian Yearbook of International Law* 85 ff; AR Gil, 'Collective expulsions in times of migratory crisis: Comments on the *Khlaifia* case of the ECHR' in *EU Immigration and Asylum Law and Policy* (11 February 2016), http://eumigrationlawblog.eu/collective-expulsions-in-times-of-migratory-crisis-comments-on-the-khlaifia-case-of-the-echr/.

[434] ibid, paras 184 and 185.

[435] ibid, paras 178–183, 185.

[436] ibid, para 239.

[437] ibid, para 248.

[438] ibid, paras 247 and 250.

[439] ibid, para 251.

[440] On this aspect, see the dissenting Opinion of Judge Serghides. See also, D Venturi, 'The Grand Chamber's ruling in *Khlaifia and Others v Italy:* one step forward, one step back?' in *Strasbourg Observers* (10 January 2017), https://strasbourgobservers.com/2017/01/10/the-grand-chambers-ruling-in-khlaifia-and-others-v-italy-one-step-forward-one-step-back/.

interview from the scope of Article 4 of Protocol 4, the General Chamber would indeed give a wider margin for manoeuvre to governments in the management of migratory movements. Such a singular departure from the Court's previously established case law would also reveal a potential lowering of the standards of protection, which might be particularly alarming in an era where attacks against migrants are in constant increase the world over.

A. The Extraterritorial Applicability of the Right to an Effective Remedy under the ECHR

Over the years, the Court has developed the requirement of providing effective remedies at national level against the potential effects of a decision of expulsion in the light of Article 3.[441] Strengthening its previous stance in *MSS v Belgium and Greece*, the Court in *Hirsi* reiterated the importance of providing anyone subject to a removal decision, in an extraterritorial context, with adequate information to enable him/her both to gain access to asylum procedures and to substantiate their complaints under Article 3 of the Convention and Article 4 of Protocol 4.[442] No effective remedy with a suspensive effect of the deportation order was in fact provided to prevent collective expulsions. The Court thus found a violation of Article 13 in combination with Article 4 of Protocol 4 (prohibition of collective expulsion).[443]

In *Hirsi*, the Grand Chamber did not review its previous case law on the issue. However, its decision complements and supplements established jurisprudence, analysed earlier in this chapter. If the Court recognises that States enjoy a certain leeway with respect to the manner in which they comply with the obligations stemming from Article 13, it also upholds the principle that obstacles to the right to an effective remedy because of accelerated procedures of expulsion or denial of effective status determination measures (including appeal) are unjustifiable. As examined above, the right to seek asylum on the high seas, and the prohibition of torture and ill-treatment imply an obligation for State authorities to ascertain the identity or the nationality of intercepted persons, and guarantee them access to the mainland to assess their protection claims.[444] If refugees are entitled to an in-country right to access asylum procedures, it follows that they also have a right to judicial review of an unfavourable decision with suspensive effect of the removal order, and within reasonable time limits. National authorities must always afford applicants 'a realistic possibility of using the remedy.'[445]

[441] See, eg, *Abdolkhani and Karimnia v Turkey*, above n 293, paras 111–114.
[442] ibid, para 204. See also *MSS v Belgium and Greece*, above n 51, para 304.
[443] *Hirsi v Italy*, above n 4, para 207.
[444] ibid.
[445] *Conka v Belgium*, above n 395, para 46.

The violation of Article 13 in the case of interception on the high seas and diversion to the country of embarkation results from a lack of mechanisms through which intercepted migrants can seek review, before an independent national authority, of the 'expulsion' decision, and through which they can substantiate their claims on the risk of torture and inhuman treatment if diverted to the country of departure. The infringement of Article 13 in *Hirsi* is the result of the lack of an accessible remedy granted to boat-migrants, who were not allowed to seek review of the push-back order informally issued by the Italian authorities on the high seas. Since such a remedy is due to any third-country nationals subjected to a decision of expulsion *from* the territory of the host country, a double system of protection would otherwise be created, which differentiates between those who have crossed the borders and those who are intercepted before entering the territorial jurisdiction of a European State.

As examined above, in *Gebremedhin v France* and *Abdolkhani and Karimnia v Turkey*, the Court held that Article 13 requires access to appeals 'with automatic suspensive effect', especially considering the irreversible nature of the damage if the risk of torture or inhumane treatment materialises in the receiving country.[446] Appeals submitted from abroad make the system of protection overly complex: first, because the possibility for the asylum seeker to lodge recourse from the third country is not secured; and second, because a successful appeal would render futile the attempts of the government to remove the applicant to a third country.

In the *Al Saadoon v UK* case, the ECtHR considered that 'any appeal to the House of Lords was unjustifiably nullified as a result of the Government's transfer of the applicants to the Iraqi authorities [in Iraq].'[447] By transferring the detainees out of the UK's jurisdiction, the applicants were exposed to a serious risk of irreparable harm, not least the lack of a binding assurance against the use of the death penalty. Therefore, in the Court's view, the UK did not take all steps that could reasonably have been taken in order to comply with the interim measure issued by the Court, thereby breaching Articles 13 and 34 of the Convention.[448]

In line with its previous jurisprudence, the decision in *Hirsi* corroborates the view that States can be held responsible under the Convention even for actions carried out by or on their behalf outside the space of the Convention.[449]

[446] *Gebremedhin v France*, above n 291, para 66; *Abdolkhani and Karimnia v Turkey*, above n 293, para 58.

[447] *Al Saadoon v UK*, above n 138, para 166.

[448] ibid, paras 164–66.

[449] *Al-Saadoonv v UK* (above n 138) addresses Art 13 in the context of State actions taking place in a territory outside of the Convention space. However, to read on further cases concerning extra-territorial jurisdiction, see, inter alia, *Medvedyev v France*, above n 126; *Al-Skeini v UK*, App no 55721/07 (7 July 2011); *Al-Jedda v UK*, above n 126; *Markovic and Others v Italy*, App no 1398/03 (14 December 2006); *Mansur PAD and Others v Turkey* App no 60167/00, Admissibility Decision (28 June 2007).

Therefore, if States set in motion offshore mechanisms of non-admission or removal after interdiction at sea, which limit the possibility of individuals to challenge State decisions, a violation of the right to an effective remedy under Article 13 of the ECHR could occur. The Court also asserted that the option of applicants applying to the Italian criminal courts upon their arrival in Libya was not feasible. Indeed, even if such a remedy was accessible in practice, criminal proceedings against military personnel who were on-board the warship would not meet the criterion of suspensive effect of the deportation order, which has a primary, not subsidiary, nature.[450] Violations of the right to an effective remedy have also been invoked in a number of cases against Italy brought before the ECtHR in 2018 in the context of migrants' interception by the Libyan Coastguard (financially, logistically and technically supported by Italy) which ended in their push-back to Libya,[451] and (in some other cases) from Libya onward to their country of origin, Gambia.[452]

Once removed to third countries, it would be overly complex for the applicants to claim asylum, bring proceedings against an offending State, and collect sufficient evidence and adequate information to support any such legal challenge. In a poignant illustration of the difficulties of bringing proceedings from third countries, the *Hussun v Italy* case – concerning the expulsion of a group of migrants, in 2005, from the Italian territory to Libya – is very telling.[453] The applicants complained before the Court of Strasbourg of the risk to which expulsion to Libya exposed them, the lack of an effective remedy against the deportation orders, their collective expulsion as foreigners, and also of having been deprived of their right to apply to the Court. In any event, the Court struck the case from the list because of a lack of authentic powers of attorney. The legal representatives had lost contact with all of the applicants, so the Court was unable to know exactly where in Libya the group concerned had been expelled to, or what kind of reception the Libyan authorities had given them. Such a distressing outcome is unlikely to be an isolated occurrence, and might become a dangerous precedent, especially when migrants are removed from transit zones or at sea without having the possibility to enter into contact with a lawyer.

XI. LEGAL REMEDIES IN EU IMMIGRATION AND ASYLUM LAW

The Tampere Conclusions adopted in October 1999 by the Heads of EU governments stated that common policies on asylum and immigration 'must be based

[450] See, *Hirsi v Italy*, above n 4, paras 206–207. The Court refers here to *Conka v Belgium*, above n 395; and to *MSS v Belgium and Greece*, above n 51, para 388.

[451] See, eg, the application submitted to the ECtHR in June 2018, *SS and Others v Italy*, App no 21660/18 (pending).

[452] See, eg, the case brought before the ECtHR in May 2018 (App no 31312/18).

[453] *Hussun and Others v Italy*, App nos 10171/05, 10601/05, 11593/05 and 17165/05 (19 January 2010).

on principles which are both clear to our own citizens and also offer guarantees to those who seek protection in, or access to, the European Union.'[454] This means procedural guarantees shall be provided not only to those lawfully residing in the EU but also to those third country nationals seeking protection in one of the EU Member States.

As argued in Chapter one, the provisions of the EU CFR shall be interpreted and applied in accordance with the ECHR principles as determined by the jurisprudence of the Courts of Strasbourg and Luxembourg.[455] However, as stated in Article 52(4) of the CFR, the similarities between rights guaranteed by both the ECHR and the CFR shall not prevent Union law from providing more extensive protection. While the 'Explanations' to Article 47 of the CFR confirm that the right to an effective remedy shall be interpreted in accordance with the criteria developed by the jurisprudence of the ECtHR with regard to Article 13, they also specify that the interpretation of this right under the Charter departs from the interpretation of the ECtHR according to which the right to a fair trial (Article 6 of the Convention) is not applicable to asylum cases.[456] Therefore, Article 47 of the CFR expands upon the procedural guarantees applicable to asylum seekers under the ECHR. Indeed, the right to access courts will apply to any claim concerning a Union right,[457] including administrative proceedings, such as asylum procedures.[458]

The need to comply with the ECHR has also been stated by the CJEU and the EU amended treaties according to which the Union is based on the rule of law and respect for human rights as defined and enshrined within the ECHR.[459] Additionally, the criteria developed by the ECtHR on the basis of Article 13 and incorporated in Article 47 of the CFR, can be equally invoked in national procedures in which domestic authorities apply EU law. This does not exclude

[454] Presidency Conclusions, Tampere European Council, 15–16 October 1999, para 3.

[455] See, Arts 52(4) and 53 of the EU CFR.

[456] *Maaouia v France*, above n 392. As the Explanations to Art 47 of the CFR read: 'In Union law, the right to a fair hearing is not confined to disputes relating to civil law rights and obligations.' See also, Case C-294/83 *Les Verts v European Parliament* [1986].

[457] See eg, *Benthem v The Netherlands*, App no 8848/80 (23 October 1985) para 32.

[458] On Art 6 of the ECHR as part of Art 47 CFR, see Opinion A-G Alber, *Evans v The Secretary of State for the Environment, Transport and the Regions and The Motor Insurers' Bureau*, Case C-63/01, ECLI:EU:C:2003:650, para 85. For an examination of Art 47 of the CFR, see A Prechal, 'The Court of Justice and Effective Judicial Protection: What Has the Charter Changed?' in C Paulussen, T Takacs, V Lazic and B van Rompuy (eds), *Fundamental Rights in International and European Law* (Springer, 2015) 143.

[459] The Court of First Instance (CFI) referred to the right to an effective remedy as a general principle of Community law, based on the constitutional traditions common to the Member States, on Arts 6 and 13 of the ECHR, and on Art 47 of the CFR. See the CFI in *Jégo-Quéré v Commission*, Case T-177/01 [2002] ECR II-23, paras 41–42. According to the ECJ, in order to ensure effective judicial protection, the appeal body must be a court or tribunal as defined by Community law. The appellate body shall satisfy the following criteria: being established by law, being permanent, independent, and impartial, exercising a compulsory jurisdiction, and holding an *inter partes* procedure. See Case C-506/04, *Graham Wilson* [2006] paras 47–48.

the possibility that European courts might reach different results in similar cases. For instance, in *Samba Diouf*, the CJEU affirmed that accelerated procedures to examine asylum applications were proportionate to the legitimate aim pursued.[460] Also, in the *HID* case, the CJEU found that the nationality of the applicant for asylum is an element which may be taken into account to justify an accelerated processing of his application, as long as such a procedure does not deprive applicants of their due rights guarantees, in accordance with Article 23 of the Procedures Directive.[461]

A number of EU instruments on immigration and asylum law, adopted on the basis of the former Title IV of the TEC, tackle the issue of effective remedy for asylum seekers subjected to a decision of expulsion or removal. The Schengen Borders Code[462] – adopted by a decision of the European Council in 2006 and replacing the Schengen Common Manual on Border Controls – needs to be mentioned before going into the details of specific legislative provisions on asylum. Article 13(2) of the final text of the Schengen Borders Code Regulation (SBC) establishes that States may refuse entry to a third-country national only with a substantiated decision indicating the procedures for appeal. Hence, the person refused entry shall have a right to appeal in accordance with national laws. While 'lodging such an appeal shall not have suspensive effect on a decision to refuse entry',[463] States' discretion to refuse entry into the territory are without prejudice to the application of special provisions concerning the right to asylum and to international protection.[464] If, therefore, Article 13(3) of the SBC is read in accordance with the case law of the ECtHR and the CJEU concerning Article 13 of the ECHR and Article 47 of the CFR, one would conclude that automatic suspensive effect is required for a remedy to be effective in precluding *refoulement* and ensuring the right to asylum.[465] In particular, the Schengen Borders Code – which applies extraterritorially (as explained above) – contains a standard refusal form that assumes relevance for third-country nationals denied entry at the borders. Indeed, border guards must provide such individuals with a refusal form that, on the one hand, explicitly states that the third-country national 'may appeal against the refusal of entry as provided for in national law,'[466] and on the other hand, requires that Member States make the decision of

[460] *Diouf v Ministre du Travail, de l'Emploi et de l'Immigration*, Case C-69/10, ECLI:EU:C:2011:524, para 67.

[461] *HID, BA v Refugee Applications Commissioner and others*, Case C-175/11, ECLI:EU:C:2013:45, para 73.

[462] Schengen Borders Code, Regulation 562/2006 of 15 March 2006 OJ L 105/1, which came into force on 13 October 2006.

[463] ibid, Art 13(3) second indent.

[464] Art 14(1) of the SBC.

[465] See, eg, CJEU, *Centre public d'action sociale d'Ottignies-Louvain-La-Neuve v Abdida*, Case C-562/13, ECLI:EU:C:2014:2453, paras 52–53; *Abdoulaye Amadou Tall v Centre public d'action sociale de Huy*, Case C-239/14, ECLI:EU:C:2015:824, para 54; *Gnandi v État belge*, Case C-181/16, ECLI:EU:C:2018:465.

[466] Detailed rules governing refusal of entry are now given in Part A of Annex V to the SBC.

refusal and indicate which national legal remedies individuals may rely upon.[467] The standard refusal form also draws upon an exhaustive list of all the grounds for prohibiting access to the EU territory so that people involved are able to know the reasons for refusal as well as being able to appeal against refusal of entry.

Of relevance also is Article 46(1) of the Recast Procedures Directive, which embodies an explicit right to access an effective remedy before a court or tribunal.[468] It also provides that the guarantees it offers shall be claimed before the national courts of EU Member States. As indicated in Chapter two, although the Recast Procedures Directive does not have an extraterritorial reach, it can nonetheless be applied at the border, including the territorial sea of the Member States. This right may be exercised not only against decisions to consider an application inadmissible or unfounded, but also with regards to decisions to withdraw international protection status, or against refusals to reopen an examination. The Directive contains a number of procedural guarantees for the asylum seeker, such as the right to be informed of the procedure, to receive legal aid and the services of an interpreter,[469] and the right to a personal interview.[470] It leaves, however, the issue of suspensive effect unsatisfactorily 'resolved' as it does not strictly require States to allow applicants to remain in the territory pending the outcome of their remedy.[471] Under Article 46(4) and (5),

> Member States shall provide for reasonable time limits and other necessary rules for the applicant to exercise his/her right to an effective remedy pursuant to paragraph 1. The time-limits shall not render such exercise impossible or excessively difficult …
>
> Member States shall allow applicants to remain in the territory until the time limit within which to exercise their right to an effective remedy has expired or, when this right has been exercised within the time limit, pending the outcome of the remedy.[472]

[467] A standard refusal form was included in the former Common Manual on Border Control by a Council Decision of 2004, Council Dec 2004/574/EC [2004] OJ L261/36.

[468] Ex Article 39(1) of the 2005 Procedures Directive. For an analysis of the Procedures Directive, see M Reneman, 'Access to an Effective Remedy before a Court or Tribunal in Asylum Cases' in E Guild and P Minderhoud (eds), *The First Decade of EU Migration and Asylum Law* (Martinus Nijhoff, 2011) 402–03.

[469] Art 12 of the Recast Procedures Directive.

[470] Art 14 of the Recast Procedures Directive. See also, *Moussa Sacko v Commissione Territoriale per il riconoscimento della Protezione internazionale di Milano*, Case C-348/16, ECLI:EU:C:2017:591.

[471] For a critique of the Recast Procedures Directive, see European Council on Refugees and Exiles (ECRE), *Comments from the European Council on Refugees and Exiles on the Amended Commission Proposal to Recast the Asylum Procedures Directive*, COM(2011) 319 final, September 2011; ILPA, *Comments on the Revised Commission Proposal of 1 June 2011 on Common Procedures for Granting and Withdrawing International Protection Status (Recast)* COM(2011) 319 final, 5 December 2011; and G Cornelisse, 'Territory, Procedures and Rights: Border Procedures in European Asylum Law' (2016) 35(1) *Refugee Survey Quarterly* 74.

[472] Ex Article 39(3) of the 2005 Procedures Directive. For a detailed analysis on the right to an effective remedy under EU law, see Reneman 2014, n 338 above.

In the context of Dublin transfers, the Court has also expanded the scope of the right to an effective remedy under the Dublin III Regulation by finding, for instance, that an applicant for international protection can challenge a Dublin transfer before a national court by invoking the expiry of the prescribed six-month time limit.[473] Without going into the details of the Court's approach, it is to be noted that the case law of the CJEU further reveals a substantial change concerning the right to an effective remedy as compared to the situation under the Dublin II Regulation. Indeed, in *Abdullahi* (2013) the CJEU had concluded that an asylum seeker could appeal against a Dublin transfer decision only if 'systemic deficiencies' existed in the asylum procedure or the reception conditions of the responsible Member State.[474] *Ghezelbash* (and *Karim* later) mark the change in the approach of the CJEU on the right to an effective remedy from the Dublin II to the Dublin III Regulation.[475] Indeed, the Court concludes that its reasoning in *Abdullahi* is no longer valid, as the scope of the effective remedy against a Dublin transfer decision also comprises of the correct application of the responsibility criteria and the cessation provisions under the Recast Regulation. According to the Court, the new provisions guarantee 'the involvement of asylum seekers in the process for determining the Member State responsible'.[476]

Beyond the right to be heard, which is also recognised by Article 4 of the Qualification Directive and case law of the CJEU, States have a duty to provide reasons, as enshrined in Article 296 of the TFEU (for both legal and administrative decisions). In the asylum context, the Court has clarified that submitted reasons must be 'sufficiently specific and concrete to allow the person to understand why his application is being rejected.'[477]

To sum up, recognition of the right to an effective remedy encompasses the right of every person to be defended, represented, and advised. For these reasons, this right assumes notable relevance in the case of refugees whose applications have been refused, who have been subjected to an exclusion order, or who have received a removal decision at the border (or beyond the border) without the opportunity to seek international protection.

[473] CJEU, Case C 201/16, *Madzhdi Shiri*, 25 October 2017.

[474] *Abdullahi v Bundesasylamt*, Case C-394/12 (10 December 2013) ECLI:EU:C:2013:813, para 60.

[475] *Ghezelbash v Staatssecretaris van Veiligheid en Justitie*, C-63/15, ECLI:EU:C:2016:409; *Karim v Migrationsverket*, C-155/15, ECLI:EU:C:2016:410.

[476] *Ghezelbash*, ibid, para 46. For an analysis of the relevant cases, see C Hruschka, 'Strengthening effective remedies for asylum seekers in the Dublin procedure: from *Abdullahi* to *Ghezelbash* and Karim', *European Database of Asylum Law (EDAL)* (23 June 2016), http://www.asylumlawdatabase.eu/en/journal/strengthening-effective-remedies-asylum-seekers-dublin-procedure-abdullahi-ghezelbash-and. See also, S Morgades-Gil, 'The Right to Benefit from an Effective Remedy against Decisions Implying the Return of Asylum-seekers to European *Safe* Countries' (2017) 19(3) *EJML* 255.

[477] *MM v Minister for Justice, Equality and Law Reform and others*, Case C-277/11, ECLI:EU:C:2012:744, para 88.

Part 2
The Safe Third Country in Context

XII. DEFINING THE CONCEPT OF A 'SAFE THIRD COUNTRY'

Over the last three decades, European States have developed various mechanisms to shift responsibility for asylum seekers to other countries either within or outside Europe. Whilst internal transfers of responsibility within the EU are governed by the Dublin Regulation,[478] external transfers to non-EU third countries are performed through the concepts of 'safe third country' and 'first country of asylum'.[479] Yet, most of the time, no formal agreement on attribution of State responsibility for refugees exists between a European State and a third country, thus giving an ample margin of discretion to governments to discern when a State is safe enough to assume responsibility for refugees. The analysis of *non-refoulement*, as well the right to access asylum procedures and effective remedies before removal, opens the way to an examination of the 'safe third country' notion, which links this chapter with the following ones. Indeed, readmission agreements, agreements for technical and police cooperation, and diplomatic assurances for removing people whose presence is considered to be not conducive to the public good, are some of the bilateral arrangements European States have traditionally relied upon to implement 'safe third country' policies.

The concept of 'safe country' has been described as 'a procedural mechanism for shuttling asylum seekers to other States said to have primary responsibility for them, thereby avoiding the necessity to make a decision on the merits because another country is deemed or imagined to be secure.'[480] Article 31(1) of the Geneva Convention has frequently been cited as a possible legal basis for 'safe third country' practices. It reads as follows:

> The Contracting States shall not impose penalties, on account of their illegal entry or presence, on refugees, who, coming directly from a territory where their life or freedom was threatened, enter or are present in the territory without authorization …

[478] The Dublin Regulation No 343/2003 establishes the principle that only one EU Member State is responsible for examining an asylum application, on the basis of a number of hierarchical criteria. The 2003 Dublin Regulation has now been replaced by the 2013 Recast Dublin Regulation. To read more on these two Regulations, see, inter alia, U Brandl, 'Distribution of Asylum Seekers in Europe?: Dublin II Regulation Determining the Responsibility for Examining an Asylum Application' in CD Urbano De Sousa and P De Bruycker (eds), *The Emergence of a European Asylum Policy/L'émergence d'une politique européenne d'asile* (Bruylant, 2004); R Roßkopf, 'Dublin III Beyond *MSS and NS:* Amending the Recast Proposal for the Dublin II Regulation No 343/2003' (2012) 50(2) *AWR Bulletin* 60–79.

[479] An analysis of the 'internal protection alternative' (IPA) is outside the scope of this book. On this issue, see J Schultz, 'The European Court of Human Rights and Internal Relocation: an Unduly Harsh Standard?' in JP Gauci, M Giuffré and L Tsourdi, *Forced Migration(s): Critical Perspectives on Refugee Law* (Martinus Nijhoff Publishers, 2014); J Schultz, *The Internal Protection Alternative in Refugee Law: Treaty Basis and Scope of Application under the 1951 Convention Relating to the Status of Refugees and Its 1967 Protocol* (Brill, 2018).

[480] Goodwin-Gill and McAdam 2007, n 4 above, 392.

However, Article 31(1) solely aims to regulate the benefit of non-penalisation, without creating any rule obligating the asylum seeker to file a protection claim in a 'first country of asylum' or 'safe third country.'[481]

The notion of 'safe third country', which has been integrated into the EU Recast Procedures Directive, the 2016 proposal for an Asylum Procedures Regulation,[482] and the asylum legislation of almost all EU Member States,[483] continues to be very controversial.[484] In outlining the contours of the term 'safe', Article 38 of the Recast Procedures Directive allows Member States to apply the 'safe third country' concept only where the competent authorities are satisfied that a person seeking asylum will be treated in accordance with the following principles in the third country concerned:

(a) Life and liberty are not threatened on account of race, religion, nationality, membership of a particular social group or political opinion;
(b) there is no risk of serious harm as defined in Directive 2011/95/EU;
(c) the principle of *non-refoulement* in accordance with the Geneva Convention is respected;
(d) the prohibition of removal, in violation of the right to freedom from torture and cruel, inhuman or degrading treatment as laid down in international law, is respected; and
(e) the possibility exists to request refugee status and if found to be a refugee, to receive protection in accordance with the Geneva Convention.

Article 38(2)(a) requires the existence of a reasonable connection with the third country that could justify transfer to that State. However, it fails to specify what exactly a 'reasonable' connection means, thereby leaving it up to Member States to determine whether even mere transit could per se be sufficient reason for that person to be removed to that specific country.[485] Moreover, under Article 38(2)(b), Member States may decide either to adopt a case-by-case method

[481] G Noll, 'Article 31 1951 Convention' in Zimmermann 2011, n 78 above, 1254.

[482] See Art 45 of the Proposal for a Regulation of the European Parliament and of the Council establishing a common procedure for international protection in the Union and repealing Directive 2013/32/EU https://ec.europa.eu/transparency/regdoc/rep/1/2016/EN/1-2016-467-EN-F1-1.PDF.

[483] S Waidlich, 'First Instance Asylum Proceedings in Europe: Do Bona Fide Refugees Find Protection?' (2000) 14 *Georgetown Immigration Law Journal* 643. On this practice, see also C Costello, 'The asylum procedures directive and the proliferation of safe country practices: deterrence, deflection and the dismantling of international protection' (2005) 7(1) *EJML* 35.

K Hailbronner, 'The Concept of "Safe Third Country" and Expeditious Asylum Procedures: A Western European Perspective' (1993) 5 *IJRL* 36–48; R Byrne and A Shacknove, 'The "Safe Third Country" Notion in European Asylum Law' (1996) 9 *Harvard Human Rights Journal* 185.

[484] See generally, G Bartolini, 'Osservazioni in Margine alla "Direttiva Procedure" 2005/85/EC' in P Benvenuti (ed), *Flussi Migratori e Fruizione dei Diritti Fondamentali* (Il Sirente, 2008); K Zwaan (ed), *The Procedures Directive. Central Themes, Problem Issues, and Implementation in Selected Member States* (Wolf Legal Publishers, 2008).

[485] Art 38 of the Recast Procedures Directive replaces Art 27 of the 2005 Procedures Directive. On the Recast Procedures Directive, see J Vedsted-Hansen, 'Asylum Procedures Directive 2013/32/EU' in K Hailbronner and D Thym (eds), *EU Immigration and Asylum Law: A Commentary* (CH Beck/Hart/Nomos, 2016) 1285.

to determine the safety of a country or to apply a more perfunctory approach based on national designation of countries generally considered to be safe.[486]

With regards to the concept of 'effective protection', Article 7(2) of the 2011 Recast Qualification Directive provides that: 'protection against persecution or serious harm must be effective and of a non-temporary nature.'[487]

Literature and jurisprudence generally accept 'safe third country' practices as long as a refugee can be transferred to a third country that guarantees protection either 'comparable' or 'equivalent' to that available within the sending State.[488] It has also been argued that an adequate country of first asylum 'has to provide refugee protection of a *quality, and at a level, in conformity with* the protection scheme laid down in the [Geneva] Convention (emphasis added).'[489] However, the principle of *non-refoulement*, as enshrined in Article 33 of the Geneva Convention, 'is a necessary, but not of itself a sufficient, criterion to establish a State as a genuine country of first asylum.'[490]

Destination States do not examine the substance of the protection claim if an asylum seeker has transited – either with or without authorisation – through a 'safe third country' that is willing to readmit her. A readmitting country can be considered safe only if the individual will have access to effective protection, 'will be treated in accordance with international standards',[491] and will have the opportunity to seek and enjoy asylum.[492] Thus, the literature has so far focused on the following questions: whether it is *de facto* possible for the sending State to determine the safety of the third country without carrying out a particularised assessment of the claim; and whether the mere ratification of international refugee and human rights instruments by the latter is sufficient for the former to infer safety.

Taking the example of readmission agreements, Chapter three will ask to what extent bilateral accords can be used to obtain a number of guarantees necessary to prevent the sending State from violating its international human rights obligations toward asylum seekers. The full gamut of these obligations

[486] The same phrasing was adopted by Art 27(2)(b) of the 2005 Procedures Directive.

[487] See also, *Abdulla*, n 342 above, ECLI:EU:C:2010:105.

[488] Australian case law on 'effective protection' is particularly profuse. See, eg, the Opinion of Judge Lee in *WAGH v Minister for Immigration and Multicultural and Indigenous Affairs* (MIMA) [2003] FCAFC 194, 27 August 2003, para 34. In his dissenting Opinion in the *Al-Rahal v MIMA* case, Judge Lee affirms that 'as far as the operation of the Treaty is concerned under international law, *equivalent protection to that required of a contracting State* under the Treaty must be secured to an applicant in a third country before it can be said that person is not a refugee requiring consideration under the Treaty' (*Al-Rahal v Minister for Immigration and Multicultural Affairs* [2001] FCAFC 1141, 20 August 2001, para 50). See Hathaway 2005, n 5 above, 332–33.

[489] J Vedsted-Hansen, 'Non-admission Policies and the Right to Protection: Refugees' Choice versus State's Exclusion' in F Nicholson and PM Twomey (eds), *Refugee Rights and Realities – Evolving International Concepts and Regimes* (CUP, 1999) 279.

[490] ibid.

[491] UNHCR Excom, UN Doc A/AC.96/914 (1999) para 19.

[492] ibid. See also, Goodwin-Gill and McAdam 2007, n 4 above, 394; H Battjes, *European Asylum and International Law* (Martinus Nijhoff Publishers, 2006) 398.

would arise from the mere fact that the sending State has encountered the asylum seeker at some point in time and space. While deciding not to take responsibility in that particular case, it shall nonetheless ensure, before removal is effectively executed, that another State is willing and able to take on responsibility in a way that is, if not equivalent, at least comparable to the protections that would be offered within its own territory.

Burgeoning literature has addressed the shortcomings of such 'safe third country' policies. For instance, it has been pointed out how removal to a 'safe third country' is 'a misguided approach to asylum which creates new problems and avoidable instances of *refoulement*.'[493] Moreover, these transfers are time-consuming and imply a waste of resources for both States and asylum seekers.[494] For example, in most instances, third countries make clear that they are only able to grant temporary stays to refugees without expectations of permanent integration.[495] As a consequence, asylum seekers may be shunted from one State to another, each of which must somehow examine individual protection claims before removing them to another 'responsible' third country. There is inevitable risk in increasing the number of refugees 'in orbit', ie repeatedly sent from country to country without receiving a determination on the merits of their claims.[496]

Other pitfalls of the 'safe third country' policy derive from the difficulty in determining the 'safety' of a third State and in finding a remedy for the problem of chain deportations, which can result in *refoulement*. This policy represents States' efforts, for reasons of 'procedural economy',[497] to expeditiously transfer asylum seekers on the basis of general assessments of 'safety.' Such a risk increases as long as European States enforce removal by means of bilateral readmission agreements without examining the merits of asylum applications. If requested States have concluded readmission arrangements with other countries further back in the transit chain, then conditions would be created whereby asylum seekers are ultimately sent back to the region of origin with serious risks to their life or liberty.[498]

Without denying their protection obligations toward refugees, sending States argue that they fulfil their protection duties by transferring asylum seekers to a

[493] G Borchelt, 'The Safe Third Country Practice in the European Union: A Misguided Approach to Asylum Law and a Violation of International Human Rights Standards' (2002) 33 *Columbia Human Rights Law Review* 522.

[494] ibid, 500.

[495] SH Legomsky, 'Secondary Refugee Movements and the Return of Asylum Seekers to Third Countries: The Meaning of Effective Protection' (2003) 15(4) *IJRL* 567, 597.

[496] European Council on Refugees and Exiles (ECRE), 'Safe Third Countries: Myths and Realities' (February1995) paras 27–33.

[497] G Noll, *Negotiating Asylum: The EU Acquis, Extraterritorial Protection and the Common Market of Deflection* (Kluwer International Law, 2000) 200.

[498] MJ Gibney and RA Hansen, *Immigration and Asylum: from 1900 to the Present* (ABC-CLIO, 2005) 495.

responsible third country.[499] Oblivious to the consequences, this approach could entail the refusal of asylum seekers' access to the sending country's legal system for both a determination of their protection claims and a review of any negative decision on their status. Therefore, the assessment of a third country's safety is a *conditio sine qua non* for European States to avoid triggering international responsibility for violations of the fundamental rights of the individuals in question.

The jurisprudence of the ECtHR has recognised, on several occasions, that 'safe third country' transfers must always comply with *non-refoulement*.[500] However, the risk of infringements of fundamental rights cannot a priori be excluded when they are transferred to countries where torture of detainees and migrants is a systematic practice or where a national regulatory framework for asylum is either totally absent or unduly rudimentary. In addition, if these States have concluded readmission agreements with notoriously unsafe countries, refugees would run the risk of being divested of their entitlement to remain in the territory because of the possibility of being removed to the borders of those countries from which they were originally fleeing.

Some jurists have emphasised how the rights acquired by refugees through their presence in the territory of the sending State cannot be 'removed' by means of 'safe third country' transfers.[501] In the *Amuur v France* case (concerning a group of Somalis applying for asylum in France and forced to stay at the Paris airport waiting for their deportation to Syria), the ECtHR held that

> [the] possibility [for asylum seekers to leave voluntarily the country] becomes theoretical if no other country offering *protection comparable* to the protection they expect to find in the country where they are seeking asylum is inclined or prepared to take them in.[502]

The assessment of whether the readmitting third country is actually safe not only includes a verification of whether efficient asylum procedures are in place, or whether international human rights and refugee law instruments have been ratified, but also seeks to ascertain whether no peril exists for people in need of international protection to be sent onward back into the arms of their persecutors. For example, in the *Hirsi v Italy* case, the ECtHR held that Italy had a duty to verify, before removal, that in the receiving country, refugees would be able to find protection from direct and indirect *refoulement*.[503]

'Protection elsewhere' policies become particularly problematic when States decide to engage in the negotiation of agreements linked to readmission with

[499] See M Foster, 'Protection Elsewhere: The Legal Implications of Requiring Refugees to Seek Protection in another State' (2006–07) 28 *Michigan Journal of International Law* 223, 234.

[500] See, eg, *TI v UK*, above n 53; *KRS v UK*, App no 32733/08 (2 December 2008); *Abdolkhani and Karimnia v Turkey*, above n 293; *MSS v Belgium and Greece*, above n 51.

[501] See, eg, Foster 2006–07, n 500 above.

[502] *Amuur v France*, above n 285, para 48.

[503] See, *Hirsi v Italy*, above n 4, paras 128, 131, 152, 157.

countries that have a doubtful track record in human rights or who are not bound by the same international human rights instruments. Some of these countries are, indeed, either among the largest 'producers' of refugees and protection claims, do not have adequate facilities to process applications and grant asylum, or have concluded further readmission agreements with countries of origin of refugees.[504] For example, although North African countries, such as Algeria, Morocco, Libya, and Tunisia – with whom Italy and the EU have plunged into bilateral cooperation on readmission – are signatories of the main international and regional instruments of refugee protection, they have not yet adopted national refugee legislation or established comprehensive asylum procedures that conform to international standards. However, even if a State is considered generally safe because of the presence of adequate asylum procedures and judicial oversight, every individual is entitled to rebut the presumption of safety of that country for him or her in that particular case.[505]

A. Rebutting Presumption of Safety?

Despite widespread criticism, the 'safe third country' rule continues to be included within both the Dublin Regulation and the Recast Procedures Directive.[506] On 4 May 2016, a legislative proposal for reform of the Dublin system was presented to replace the Dublin III Regulation, and provide for a corrective allocation mechanism for refugees, in compliance with the principle of solidarity.[507] However, several Eastern European countries have already

[504] R Dunstan, 'Playing Human Pinball, The Amnesty International United Kingdom Section Report on UK Home Office *"Safe Third Country"* Practice' (1995) 7(4) *IJRL* 606, 611.

[505] See, eg, *MSS v Belgium and Greece*, above n 51; *Hirsi v Italy*, above n 4. See also, T Spijkerboer, 'Stretching the Limits. European Maritime Border Control Policies and International Law' in MC Foblets et al (eds), *The External Dimension of the Immigration & Asylum Policy of the EU* (Bruylant, 2011).

[506] Art 3(3) of the Recast Dublin Regulation (Dublin III) retains the 'safe third country' principle. However, following the jurisprudence of the CJEU in *NS and ME*, Art 3(2) of the Regulation will explicitly oblige Member States to take responsibility for asylum seekers in two new situations: when there is no State which can be identified as responsible according to the hierarchy of criteria; and where the transfer would risk to expose the asylum seeker to inhuman or degrading treatment, within the meaning of Art 4 of the EU CFR, in the readmitting country that is primarily responsible. See, CJEU, *NS v UK and ME v Ireland*, above n 218.

[507] Proposal for a Regulation of the European parliament and of the Council establishing the criteria and mechanisms for determining the Member State responsible for examining an application for international protection lodged in one of the Member States by a third-country national or a stateless person (recast), Brussels, 4 May 2016 COM(2016) 270 final, https://ec.europa.eu/home-affairs/sites/homeaffairs/files/what-we-do/policies/european-agenda-migration/proposal-implementation-package/docs/20160504/dublin_reform_proposal_en.pdf. See also, European Parliament, *EU asylum policy: Reforming the Dublin rules to create a fairer system*, 19 October 2017, http://www.europarl.europa.eu/pdfs/news/expert/background/20171019BKG86403/20171019BKG86403_en.pdf. On the reform of the Dublin regulation, see M Di Filippo, 'The Reform of the Dublin System and the First (Half) Move of the Commission', *SIDIBlog* (2016), http://www.sidiblog.org/2016/05/12/the-reform-of-the-dublin-system-and-the-first-half-move-of-the-commission/.

opposed the system of quotas for a more equitable distribution of asylum seekers between Member States.[508]

Scholars have generally criticised an absolute presumption of safety, not open to rebuttal, instead requiring not only *de jure*, but also *de facto* compliance with international refugee and human rights law in the readmitting country for a safe transfer of responsibility to take place.[509] Nevertheless, in practice, presumption of safety might not always be rebuttable, especially with regard to those States that have created lists of countries considered irrefutably safe.[510] The safety of EU Member States, such as France, Germany, and Greece has been challenged more than once.[511]

In a number of cases, the ECtHR issued interim measures to halt the transfer of individuals to other European countries, and also found European States responsible for unsafe removals under the Dublin system.[512] For instance, in *MSS v Belgium and Greece*, the Court held the view that Belgian authorities should not have automatically relied on the presumption of safety contained in the Dublin Regulation, and that it was for them 'not merely to assume that the applicant would be treated in conformity with the Convention standards but … to first verify how the Greek authorities applied their legislation on asylum *in practice*.'[513] The mere 'existence of domestic laws and accession to

[508] H Gavin, '"We will decide who enters our countries!" Hungary and Poland reject EU refugee quotas', *Express*, 15 May 2018, https://www.express.co.uk/news/world/960125/eu-news-hungary-poland-oppose-european-union-refugee-quota-Viktor-Orban-Morawiecki.

[509] G Noll, 'Formalism v Empiricism: Some Reflections on the Dublin Convention on the Occasion of Recent European Case Law' (2001) 70 *Nordic Journal of International Law* 161–82.

[510] See, eg, Art 16 of the German Constitution. A proposal has also been made for a Regulation of the European Parliament and of the Council establishing an EU common list of safe countries of origin, and amending Directive 2013/32/EU. In the EU, at least 14 countries have a list of safe countries of origin. See EMN, 'Safe Countries of Origin', 4–5, https://ec.europa.eu/home-affairs/sites/homeaffairs/files/00_inform_safe_country_of_origin_final_en_1.pdf.

[511] See, eg, *R v SSHD, ex parte Adan; R v SSHD, ex parte Aitsegeur*, 23 July 1999, [1999] 3 WLR 1274. See also, *TI v UK*, above n 53. Furthermore, in its judgment of 19 May 2010, the French *Conseil d'État* for the first time overrode a decision to remove a Palestinian family to Greece under the Dublin Regulation on the ground that Greek authorities currently do not adequately safeguard the right to asylum. See Conseil d'état, Ordonnance no 339478.

Italy has also been labelled unsafe by German administrative tribunals. See eg, *Verwaltungsgericht (VG) Köln*, Decision of 10 October 2011, 20 L 1920/10.A, http://www.asyl.net/index.php?id=185&tx_ttnews[tt_news]=41626&cHash=6843dd2173; *Verwaltungsgericht Minden*, Decision of 22 June 2010, 12 L 284/10.A, http://www.asyl.net/index.php?id=185&tx_ttnews[tt_news]=39703&cHash=c1c307812e; *VG Köln*, Decision of 11 January 2011, 16 L 1913/10.A, http://www.asyl.net/index.php?id=185&tx_ttnews[tt_news]=41624&cHash=95aeea7956; *VG Darmstadt*, Decision of 11 January 2011, 4 L 1889/10.DA.A, http://www.asyl.net/index.php?id=185&tx_ttnews[tt_news]=41633&cHash=af5fb2319e. Details on these cases have been retrived from: F Vassallo Paleologo, 'Respingimento ed Accordi di Riammissione – Sotto Accusa l'Italia che non è un Paese Sicuro per Richiedenti Asilo' (Meltingpot, 31 January 2011), http://www.meltingpot.org/articolo16259.html.

[512] *MSS v Belgium and Greece*, above n 51, paras 88, 342. See also, *SD v Greece*, App no 53541/07 (20 June 2009) para 41; *Mohammed v Austria*, App no 2283/12 (6 June 2013); *Sharifi and Others v Italy and Greece*, above n 294; *Tarakhel v Switzerland*, App no 29217/12 (4 November 2014).

[513] *MSS v Belgium and Greece*, above n 51, para 359.

international treaties ... are not in themselves sufficient to ensure adequate protection against the risk of ill-treatment ...'[514] When the reality in the readmitting country is well-known, the sending State has an obligation to take positive measures to avoid infringements of Article 3 and to disprove the risk of an Article 3 violation.

On 21 December 2011, the ECJ delivered its judgment in the joint cases of *NS v UK* and *ME v Ireland* under the preliminary ruling procedure.[515] It held that in transferring an asylum seeker to another EU Member State under the Dublin Regulation, national courts must always follow the rebuttable presumption that in the readmitting country that individual will be treated in accordance with fundamental rights, and will not be exposed to the risk of onward expulsions to a persecuting State, in line with the Geneva Convention, the ECHR, and the CFR.[516] It means that asylum seekers should always be given the procedural possibility to rebut that presumption.[517] However, unlike the ECtHR, the EU Court particularly relied on the principles of 'mutual confidence' among Member States and 'presumption of compliance' with fundamental rights.[518] It also asserted that 'minor infringements' of EU asylum law and violations of rights other than the prohibition of torture do not suffice to suspend a transfer under the Dublin Regulation.[519]

A number of scholars have criticised the implementation of 'safe third country' policies – whether carried out through readmission agreements, push-backs, or bilateral or regional arrangements on the distribution of refugees.[520] The crucial issue is not whether the individual has a right to choose the country of asylum, but whether the State under whose jurisdiction the asylum seeker stands has any international obligations towards her.[521] As with other international human right treaties, the fact that refugees have transited through other countries before reaching the State where they claim asylum is immaterial from

[514] ibid 353, 367.
[515] ECJ, *NS and ME*, above n 218.
[516] ibid, para 80.
[517] ibid, paras 103–104.
[518] ibid, paras 78–80, 83. See also, G Vicini, 'The Dublin Regulation between Strasbourg and Luxembourg: reshaping *non-refoulement* in the name of mutual trust?' (2015) 8(2) *European Journal of Legal Studies* 50.
[519] ibid, paras 82, 86, 94, 106.
[520] See, eg, E Kjaergaard, 'The Concept of "Safe Third Country" in Contemporary European Refugee Law' (1994) 6 *IJRL* 649; Byrne and Shacknove 1996, n 484 above; Vedsted-Hansen 1999, n 490 above; S Taylor, 'Protection Elsewhere/Nowhere' (2006) 18 *IJRL* 283; MT Gil-Bazo, 'The Practice of Mediterranean States in the Context of the European Union's Justice and Home Affairs External Dimension. The Safe Third Country Concept Revisited' (2006) 18 *IJRL* 571; Goodwin-Gill and McAdam 2007, n 4 above, 390; V Moreno-Lax, 'The "Safe Third Country" Notion Revisited: An Appraisal in light of General International Rules on the Law of Treaties' in GS Goodwin-Gill (ed), *International Migrations, 2010 Centre for Studies and Research in International Law and International Relations of The Hague Academy of International Law* (Martinus Nijhoff, 2013).
[521] J-F Durieux, 'Protection Where? Or When?' (2009) 21 *IJRL* 75, 76.

the perspective of the responsibility of that State.[522] Therefore, a State cannot be absolved from its obligations *ex nunc* toward refugees who are under its jurisdiction on the ground that a transit country in the past may have become responsible and has failed to act.[523]

B. Access to Asylum Procedures in the Third Country as a Safety Condition

Despite the vast range of arguments contesting 'safe third country' policies, it is unlikely that this practice will disappear anytime soon from the migration containment and removal policies of Western States, and EU Member States in particular. For this reason and with a view to eliminating the baleful impact of 'safe third country' mechanisms on refugee rights, removing States must take a number of concrete measures. As already highlighted above, sending States have a duty to both verify that the asylum seeker will have access to effective protection in the readmitting country, and that readmitting countries offer effective protection from indirect *refoulement* either by granting permission to stay, or via access to an examination procedure.[524] According to Goodwin-Gill and McAdam, 'substantive evidence of admissibility' in the readmitting State is a key requirement for permitting removal under international refugee law.[525]

If there is no prospect of a durable solution in the third country because of the foreseeable risk of expulsion to a fourth State, the second State would fail to provide effective protection from *refoulement*.[526] This entitlement to a durable solution would not amount to a right to asylum by itself, but would be, rather, a 'side-effect' of the principle of *non-refoulement*, as applicable also to refugees who fall under the jurisdiction of a European State, whether they apply at the border or beyond the border.[527]

With regard to pre-removal procedures, although the ECHR does not recognise a right to asylum, the Court of Strasbourg holds the view that access to status determination is a fundamental element in avoiding 'immediate or summary removal' to an unsafe country. An individual determination of the safety of a readmitting country for the asylum seeker concerned (including the assurances by the readmitting State that the protection claim will be examined

[522] See, eg, *MSS v Belgium and Greece*, above n 51, para 218; *Chahal v UK*, above n 46, para 79; and *Saadi v Italy*, above n 45, paras 127 and 138–139.

[523] See, *NAGV and NAGW of 2002 v Minister of Immigration and Multicultural and Indigenous Affairs* [2005] HCA 6, 2 March 2005, para 84. *Contra: Bugdaycay v Secretary of State for the Home Department* [1987] 1 AC 514.

[524] Battjes 2006, n 247 above, 398.

[525] GS Goodwin-Gill and J McAdam, *The Refugee in International Law* (Oxford University Press, 2010) 395; see also H Lambert, 'Safe Third Country' in the European Union: An Evolving Concept in International Law and Implications for the UK' (2012) 26(4) *Journal of Immigration, Asylum and Nationality Law* 318.

[526] EXCOM Conclusion no 85 (XLIX), para (aa).

[527] Battjes 2006, n 247 above, 401.

before issuing a new deportation order) is deemed necessary to minimise the risk of irremediable damage to the person subject to a removal decision, and thus to exclude the responsibility of the sending State.[528]

It could also be argued that an effective application of Article 3 of the Convention would entail a 'meaningful assessment' of both the claim for protection and the offer of an effective remedy against an unfavourable decision.[529] While, the *TI v UK* case confirms that the presumption of safety among the States of the Dublin system is not absolute,[530] in *KRS v UK*, the Court relied on an absolute presumption of safety.[531] The Luxembourg Court in the *NS and ME* cases affirmed that the State within which the asylum application has been submitted must take responsibility in those circumstances in which the presumption of safety in the requested country is displaced.[532] Such a procedural guarantee will be taken into account in Chapter three when exploring possible amendments to readmission clauses.

The elements the UNHCR has focused upon to infer safety before removal are the express consent of the third State to readmit, protection against direct and indirect *refoulement*, respect for fundamental human rights, and access to a fair refugee status determination procedure.[533] Therefore, sending States must verify, on an individual basis, whether the readmitting country effectively respects these safety criteria. Moreover, sending States must also receive formal assurances in advance of the third country expressly consenting to the transfer by accepting admittance of the asylum seeker into its territory and agreeing to examine her protection claim.[534] It is thus not enough that European States provide the claimant with a notification informing the third country that the application of the individual it is being asked to take back has not been examined on its merits. The readmitting State should also expressly consent to assess the merits of the protection claim made by the individual.[535] In order to reduce the risk of irremediable mistakes in the overall procedure, the asylum seeker should also be entitled to challenge the transfer decision, with a suspensive effect, by contesting the safety of the readmitting country. Although these safeguards can be inferred from the EU Recast Procedures Directive and the jurisprudence of the ECtHR, they do not always find application in practice.[536]

[528] See, eg, *TI v UK*, above n 53, 17.

[529] Battjes 2006, n 247 above, 402.

[530] *TI v UK*, above n 53, 20.

[531] *KRS v UK*, above n 501, 16 citing *Waite and Kennedy v Germany*, App no 26083/94 (18 February 1999) paras 18, 67. For a comprehensive analysis of *TI v UK* and *KRS v UK* in relation also to *MSS v Belgium and Greece*, see V Moreno-Lax, 'Dismantling the Dublin System: *MSS v Belgium and Greece*' (2012) 14(1) *EJML* 1.

[532] *NS and ME*, above n 131, paras 98 and 108.

[533] See UNHCR *Global Consultations in Budapest Conclusions*, para 15, http://www.unhcr.org/3b83b7314.html.

[534] ibid.

[535] On the issue of express consent by the readmitting State, see Chapter 3 of this book.

[536] See, eg, *Ilias and Ahmed v Hungary*, above n 412, paras 121–22.

The analysis, in Chapters three, four, and five, of readmission practices (starting from the agreements of Italy and the UK with third countries) will ask whether sending States ensure access to protection before removal, and will scrupulously assess whether readmitting countries are required to effectively guarantee safety criteria and procedural safeguards for removed asylum seekers.

XIII. CONCLUSION

This chapter described the principle of *non-refoulement* as an overarching term whose full meaning can be reconstructed only through the use of different international refugee and human rights instruments. This principle entails that expulsion, removal, or extradition to a country where an individual can be subjected to the death penalty, torture or other inhuman or degrading treatment or punishment should be outlawed, regardless of the irregular status or dangerousness of the individual concerned.

It clearly matters whether the prohibition of *refoulement* applies beyond the territory of the States that are signatories of the Geneva Convention, the CAT, the ICCPR, the ECHR, and the CFR in relation to persons who claim protection at the border of a State party, or who are intercepted at sea. In respect of the Geneva Convention (silent on the issue of its extraterritorial application), there is much room for debate. The extraterritorial applicability of the principle of *non-refoulement* – including in contexts of interception on the high seas – is instead increasingly gaining recognition in the case law of the Committee Against Torture, the HRC, and the ECtHR. Jurisdiction under Article 1 of the ECHR is mainly, but not exclusively, territorial. States' extraterritorial human rights obligations are triggered, therefore, wherever they exercise jurisdiction (effective control and authority), which includes the high seas. The ECtHR has indeed found violations of direct and indirect *refoulement*. The logic of cross-fertilisation between human rights and refugee law has led the UNHCR and an even greater number of scholars and domestic courts to uphold that the principle of *non-refoulement*, as enshrined in Article 33(1) of the Geneva Convention, applies in extraterritorial contexts as well. From the text of this provision it emerges that the 'essential purpose' of *non-refoulement* is to ban refugees' removal, extradition, or expulsion, *in any manner whatsoever*, to countries where their life and liberty may be endangered. A wider interpretation of Article 33(1), attempting to ensure the widest possible exercise of the rights therein enshrined and also keeping abreast of the evolution of both migratory phenomena and border control techniques, would also find cogency in the Preamble of the Geneva Convention recognising 'the social and humanitarian character of the problem of refugees.' Although the Geneva Convention does not expressly require States to guarantee access to fair refugee status determination procedures, it is true that depriving refugees of an individual examination of their claims would be tantamount to accepting the risk that these individuals could be erroneously *refouled* either directly or indirectly through onward expulsions that could jeopardise their fundamental rights.

There is no uniformity in the literature on the issue of whether undertaking status determination is an implied obligation under the Geneva Convention. However, the right to access asylum procedures can also be inferred from the principle of *non-refoulement* (Article 33(1)) whose content and scope needs to be shaped through the accrual of international human rights law instruments. Therefore, not only should refugees be entitled to substantiate their protection claims before competent authorities at the border, they should also be permitted to disembark in a safe place and receive access to fair and effective asylum procedures.[537]

While the ECHR does not contain a general obligation to provide access to a substantive examination of asylum applications, the analysis of the jurisprudence of the Court of Strasbourg proves that 'a rigorous scrutiny must necessarily be conducted of an individual's claim to exclude the risk that this person could be subjected to treatments contrary to Article 3 of the ECHR once returned in his home country.'[538] This implies also a duty to scrutinise the substance of an asylum application before expelling a person to a third State different from the country of origin, if the situation in the home country gives rise to concerns for her life and liberty.[539] All in all, what we can note from the case law of the ECtHR (as well as the Committee Against Torture and the HRC), is that the procedural safeguards in refugee status determination are generally assimilated into those against expulsion (*refoulement*) if there is a risk of harm.[540]

At the EU level, Article 18 of the CFR – enshrining the right to asylum – has been interpreted as involving both a right to *seek* and a right *to be granted asylum*, which has become legally binding primary law in the Union. Accordingly, the 2011 Recast Qualification Directive – by reasserting its compliance with the CFR and Article 18 in particular – establishes that Member States shall grant either refugee status or subsidiary protection to a third-country national or stateless person who qualifies as a refugee or as a person eligible for subsidiary protection, respectively. Furthermore, with the entry into force of the Lisbon Treaty, the right to asylum embodied in Article 18 of the CFR has become a 'subjective and enforceable right of individuals under the Union's legal order',[541] directly applicable within domestic legal systems without further incorporation and transposition.

The elaboration of an adequate system of access to asylum procedures in line with international standards of refugee and human rights law becomes even more compelling in light of the trend to delocalise migration controls

[537] Da Lomba 2004, n 260 above, 10.
[538] See, *Jabari v Turkey*, above n 52, para 39; *D and Others v Turkey*, above n 289.
[539] See eg, *D and Others v Turkey*, above n 289; *TI v UK*, above n 53; *Hirsi v Italy*, above n 4.
[540] Cantor 2015, n 268 above, 104–05.
[541] Gil-Bazo 2008, n 334 above, 33.

and asylum models outside the Union far from the procedural and substantive protection standards guaranteed within the European borders. There is therefore a need to conduct further research on the contribution of international human rights bodies to the status of refugees beyond the principle of *non-refoulement*, in particular in relation to the right to asylum.

Chapter two also analysed the concept of 'safe third country' as EU Member States are not required to examine the substance of the protection claim, if a 'safe third country' exception applies. A State can expel an asylum seeker without an examination on the merits as long as it establishes that the third country will ensure effective protection, and provided the foreigner is treated – before removal – as if she were entitled to protection from *refoulement*. Doctrine and jurisprudence widely endorse the view that a refugee may be transferred to a third country only if the latter guarantees either 'comparable' or 'equivalent' protection to that granted in the sending State. It is argued here that the principle of *non-refoulement* is a necessary – but not in and of itself a sufficient – criterion to establish the safety of a third country. Whilst the presumption of safety should always be open to rebuttal, *de jure* and *de facto* compliance with international refugee and human rights law in the readmitting country is always required for a safe transfer of responsibility to take place.[542] Sending States, for instance, must assure, before removal, that readmitting countries offer effective protection from indirect *refoulement* by granting either permission to stay, or access to an examination procedure of asylum seekers' claims.[543]

Chapter two also examined the right to an effective remedy, which is guaranteed by international treaties relevant to asylum cases, such as the ICCPR, the CAT, and the ECHR. However, with the development of the Common European Asylum System, asylum procedures are also partly governed by Union law, including Article 47 of the CFR of the EU, which has given rise to copious case law. Of particular relevance are the 2005 Procedures Directive and the Recast Procedures Directive, which enshrine an explicit right to an effective remedy before a court or tribunal and provide that the guarantees they offer shall be claimed before the national courts of EU Member States.

With regard to human rights law, Article 2(3) of the ICCPR explicitly recognises the right to an effective remedy. From the case law of the HRC, it emerges that States shall always allow an individual to challenge an expulsion order, in particular if appeal proceedings are available under domestic law. Moreover, according to the Committee, States parties shall establish judicial and administrative mechanisms for addressing alleged breaches of rights, and guarantee full reconsideration of a protection claim. The lack of such remedies would imply a violation of the prohibition on torture (Article 7) because the applicants could be directly or indirectly removed to their country of origin, where they risk being subjected to ill-treatment.[544]

[542] Noll 2001, n 510 above, 161–82.
[543] Battjes 2006, n 247 above, 398.
[544] See, e.g., *Alzery v Sweden*, above n 32, para 11.8.

Whilst the CAT does not contain a specific provision on the right to an effective remedy, it can be implicitly derived from Article 3 on the prohibition of *refoulement*. The Committee Against Torture has indeed made clear that the right to an effective remedy underpins the entire Convention. Therefore, the requirements of effective, independent, and impartial administrative or judicial review must always be respected before expulsion or removal, when there is a plausible allegation that Article 3 issues arise.

The right to an effective remedy under Article 13 of the ECHR has been understood as requiring a right to challenge a decision of expulsion before an independent and impartial authority. Such an appeal must have automatic suspensive effect of the enforcement of the deportation, in order to prevent the execution of measures that are contrary to the Convention and whose effects are potentially irreversible.[545] Through the analysis of older and recent case law, this chapter also showed how the right to an effective remedy, as interpreted by the European courts, has so far largely contributed to filling the gap in international law stemming from the absence of clear-cut provisions on the right to access asylum procedures.

Article 13 of the ECHR requires independent and rigorous scrutiny of the applicant's claim that a real risk exists of treatment contrary to Article 3 in the readmitting country. The ECtHR has emphasised how the right to have a review of an unfavourable decision on refugee status or an expulsion order should not be hindered by national procedural rules, such as short notice or short time limits for lodging an appeal. The recognition of an effective remedy as a human right implies the right of every person to be defended, represented, and advised. It follows that time limits for bringing proceedings must not be too short, so that the asylum seeker may have sufficient time to appeal an expulsion measure before the order is enforced.

The sole Opinion of Judge de Albuquerque in the extraterritorial context of the *Hirsi* case would tell States that the enforcement of *non-refoulement* has two procedural consequences: the duty of the State to advise the individual in question about entitlement to obtain international protection, and the duty to provide access to individualised and fair asylum procedures and effective remedies. As such, access to the territory should be ensured. *Non-refoulement* and access to fair and effective procedures are 'so intertwined that one could say they are two sides of the same coin.'[546] For these procedural guarantees to be effective, they need to be realised onshore in respect of every asylum seeker, regardless of whether he or she is able to claim protection within the borders of the destination State, at a State border, or on the high seas after being rescued/intercepted by the authorities of a European State, NGOs, merchant vessels, or

[545] See, eg, *Gebremedhin v France*, above n 291, paras 66–67; *Garabayev v Russia*, above n 421; *Baysakov and Others v Ukraine*, above n 422, para 71; *Muminov v Russia*, above n 422, para 101.

[546] *Hirsi v Italy*, above n 4, Concurring Opinion 44.

even the authorities of third States carrying out maritime operations on behalf and/or with the support of European States.[547]

A few exceptions in the most recent jurisprudence of the ECtHR challenge the overall approach of the Court to date, potentially influencing future case law on the right to an effective remedy against expulsion orders. For example, the decision of the Fourth Section of the ECtHR to contest the removal of two asylum seekers from Hungary to Serbia, despite its inclusion in a list of safe third countries, is particularly relevant in light of the proposal for a Recast Asylum Procedures Regulation aimed at creating an EU common list of safe third countries.[548] With this case under discussion before the Grand Chamber, it can be questioned whether the previous decision will be confirmed, considering the restrictive approach the Court has adopted in recent migration-related cases. For instance, in *Khlaifia v Italy*, the Grand Chamber rejected a violation of Article 13 taken together with Article 4 of Protocol 4, thus overturning (unexpectedly, some would perhaps argue) the decision of the Chamber. In its assessment, the Court held that the situation of extreme difficulty confronting the Italian authorities at the relevant time due to a major migration crisis should also be taken into account.

Without creating improper overlapping, on 18 September 2017, the Grand Chamber Panel accepted the Hungarian government's request that the *Ilias and Ahmed* case be referred to the Grand Chamber, thus making the Chamber's intervention, which contests the schematic and arbitrary use of the safe third country notion, ongoing. Another key case pending before the Grand Chamber is *ND and NT v Spain* concerning the push back of migrants who tried to enter Spain via the Melilla border.[549] The EU and its Member States are indeed increasingly resorting to formal and informal bilateral agreements to remove asylum seekers and other unauthorised/undesirable aliens, especially in the context of counter-terrorism measures, as will be argued in Chapter four of this book. Therefore, it remains to be seen how *Ilias and Ahmed* and *ND and NT* will be decided, and whether and to what extent the new interpretation of the Court in *Khlaifia* – which disregards the mandatory nature of the procedural obligation to conduct personal interviews – will contribute to making the human rights of migrants increasingly dependent on the subjective discretion of police and border authorities, thus jeopardising the fundamental principles of effectiveness and legal certainty.[550]

[547] See on this point also, *Hirsi v Italy*, Concurring Opinion 45, above n 4; Parliamentary Assembly of the Council of Europe, 'Resolution 1821 (2011) on the Interception and Rescue at Sea of Asylum Seekers, Refugees, and Irregular Migrants', paras 9.3–9.6.

[548] *Ilias and Ahmed v Hungary*, above n 412.

[549] *ND and NT v Spain*, App nos 8675/15 and 8697/15 (3 October 2017).

[550] The effectiveness of a provision of the Convention is ensured by taking into account its object and purpose in good faith, in line with Art 31 of the VCLT, as discussed in Chapter 1 of this book. See, the Dissenting Opinion of Judge Serghides attached to the *Khlaifia v Italy* case, above n 433.

Agreements Linked to Readmission and Refugee Rights: Introduction to Chapters 3, 4, and 5

AGREEMENTS LINKED TO readmission are examined critically here to assess whether their implementation can hamper refugee access to protection, which is understood as the combination of the foundational principle of *non-refoulement* and two procedural entitlements: the right to access asylum procedures and the right to an effective remedy before removal – entitlements analysed in Chapter two. The main categories of *agreements linked to readmission* that have been identified as instruments of bilateral cooperation between European States and third countries include standard readmission agreements, diplomatic assurances – especially those contained within MoUs – and agreements for technical and police cooperation to preventively intercept undocumented migrants at sea.

Readmission agreements and agreements for technical and police cooperation can arguably be used to remove asylum seekers before their asylum procedures are initiated. In contrast, diplomatic assurances aim to create a legally sustainable method for the deportation of both individuals who have been excluded from refugee status under Article 1(f) of the Geneva Convention, and refugees who can be removed on national security grounds under Article 33(2) of the same Convention. A further point of divergence needs to be pointed out. Whereas standard readmission agreements and diplomatic assurances are designed to smooth the return process from the territory of a European State to a third country – namely, when the concerned individuals are clearly under the territorial jurisdiction of the sending State – agreements for technical and police cooperation lie at the margins of jurisdiction. Indeed, they might apply also to migrants and refugees intercepted and pushed-back (either directly or indirectly) before entering the territorial jurisdiction of a European State. The existence of different *loci* in which all these bilateral arrangements encounter the refugee explains the sequence of Chapters three, four, and five. Therefore, by systematising the three different classes of interstate arrangements in light of their underlying purpose and unifying theme, these chapters aim to bring coherence to the multidimensional and complex topic of readmission.

3

Readmission Agreements and Refugee Rights

I. INTRODUCTION

IN THE FRAMEWORK of bilateral cooperation on migration controls between European States and third countries, readmission agreements stand as key tools in the removal of unauthorised migrants and asylum seekers who ought to be undergoing asylum procedures elsewhere. Therefore, this chapter examines the intersection between migration control and core refugee rights by investigating whether the implementation of standard readmission agreements may hamper access to protection for asylum seekers subject to a transfer procedure.[1]

Readmission agreements are international accords 'which address procedures, on a reciprocal basis, for one State to return non-nationals in an irregular situation to their home State or a State through which they have transited.'[2] A preliminary question which permeates the ensuing analysis is whether general international law generates an obligation upon States to readmit their own and foreign nationals, and, if so, how this obligation relates to readmission agreements (Section II). Section III offers an overview of the technical content of standard readmission agreements in order both to increase knowledge about the substance of these instruments and to assess their relationship with the decision to remove irregular migrants and asylum seekers to countries of origin or transit. The accords concluded by Albania with Italy and the UK, respectively, are taken as units of analysis. They are, indeed, amongst the most sophisticated and detailed pieces of legislation within the quite varied category of standard interstate readmission agreements.

[1] As a preliminary note, this chapter leaves aside any investigation on Assisted Voluntary Return and Reintegration programmes launched by international organisations, such as UNHCR and IOM.

[2] IOM Glossary 2011. In the EU context, readmission agreements are defined as 'agreements between the EU and/or a Member State with a third country, on the basis of reciprocity, establishing rapid and effective procedures for the identification and safe and orderly return of persons who do not, or no longer, fulfil the conditions for entry to, presence in, or residence on the territories of the third country or one of the Member States of the European Union, and to facilitate the transit of such persons in a spirit of cooperation.' See European Migration Network (EMN), *Glossary*, http://emn.intrasoft-intl.com/Glossary/viewTerm.do?startingWith=R&id=223.

Since competence in the 'Area of Freedom, Security and Justice' remains shared and the EU and Member States continue to pursue their readmission procedures in a parallel manner, this study focuses on the bilateral arrangements of individual States (in particular EU Member States) with third countries, which constitute the bulk of the instruments in this field. Whilst Section IV describes the relationship between the readmission policies of the EU and individual Member States, Section V draws an overview of the EU Return Directive[3] and the Asylum Recast Procedures Directive,[4] which regulate, respectively, the transfer of unauthorised migrants and asylum seekers to 'safe third countries.'

As readmission agreements do not generally include separate provisions on refugees, a real risk exists of removing asylum seekers, as unauthorised migrants, to allegedly 'safe third countries.' This work will accordingly examine whether the mild reference to human rights in the body of the agreements is enough to guarantee the observance of the applicable safeguards. In this regard, the insertion of non-affection provisions is described as an instructive technique to resolve normative conflicts in practice (Section VI).

In the first comprehensive manuscript on EU readmission agreements, Coleman conducts a legal analysis of the EU readmission policy,[5] and as such, his book is taken as a key benchmark and point of comparison when assessing interstate arrangements. This chapter builds on the similarities between EU and interstate readmission agreements and expands then beyond EU-negotiated accords. Coleman concludes that a formal application of these treaties follows a decision of national law, in compliance with EU law, on the transfer of a protection-seeker either on 'safe third country' grounds or after the denial of/exclusion from, refugee status.[6] Thus, readmission agreements do not provide the legal basis for removing asylum seekers,[7] and are not 'safe third country' agreements.[8] Rather, they are administrative arrangements designed only to facilitate the execution of an expulsion decision, which must always be taken in consonance with international and European refugee obligations.[9]

[3] Council Directive 2008/115/EC on common standards and procedures in Member States for returning illegally staying third-country nationals (Return Directive).

[4] Directive 2013/32/EU of the European Parliament and of the Council of 26 June 2013 on common procedures for granting and withdrawing international protection (recast) (Recast Procedures Directive). Reference is also made to the previous Council Directive 2005/85/EC on minimum standards on procedures in Member States for granting and withdrawing refugee status (Procedures Directive).

[5] N Coleman, *European Readmission Policy: Third Country Interests and Refugee Rights* (Martinus Nijhoff, 2009).

[6] ibid, 314.

[7] This Chapter refers to the term 'legal basis' as used by Coleman to explain the relationship between readmission agreements and the removal decision. See Coleman 2009, n 5 above, 305, 315.

[8] An example of a bilateral 'safe third country' agreement is the *Agreement between the Government of Canada and the Government of the United States of America for cooperation in the examination of refugee status claims from nationals of third countries*, 5 December 2002, http://www.cic.gc.ca/english/department/laws-policy/safe-third.asp.

[9] ibid.

This chapter agrees with Coleman's conclusion that no issue of incompatibility with refugee and human rights law seems to stem from the *text* of readmission agreements[10] – purely administrative tools used to articulate the procedures for a smooth deportation of irregular migrants and rejected refugees. Nevertheless, it adds another piece to the readmission puzzle. Instances of unregulated practices of border removal, including situations of emergency and mass arrivals, and cases of informalisation of agreements linked to readmission, are brought into the analysis in order to observe whether the existence of a readmission agreement, in spite of saving clauses inscribed therein, may yet boost the employment of cursory identification and removal procedures in dissonance with human rights and refugee law (Section VII).

Section VIII explores the reasons that might drive two States concluding a readmission agreement to tie their hands with more stringent procedural human rights clauses requiring monitoring and compliance with refugee law standards. These interrogatives hint at the political costs of a drafting process aimed at supplementing the content of readmission agreements with procedural human rights clauses. Finally, after examining why the incorporation of procedural human rights clauses adding extra safeguards for removable refugees is to be hailed as an added value, Section IX outlines some ways forward for draft provisions within reformed readmission agreements.[11]

II. OBLIGATION UNDER INTERNATIONAL LAW TO READMIT PERSONS

A. Readmitting Own Nationals

The identification of the nationality of the person to be transferred is a *conditio sine qua non* for the implementation of any readmission order. However, such a process has proved to be highly controversial in the relationship between requesting and requested States.[12] A comprehensive analysis of readmission agreements implicates the primary duty to investigate on what basis the obligation to readmit a person is grounded. This Section addresses, therefore, the following question: does general international law create an obligation on States to readmit their own and foreign nationals? If so, how does this obligation relate to readmission agreements? Readmission can be defined as an 'act by a State accepting the re-entry of an individual (own national, third-country national

[10] While the focus of this chapter is interstate readmission agreements, Coleman's research regards EU readmission agreements. See Coleman 2009, n 5 above.

[11] Part of the analysis of this chapter has already been published in M Giuffré, 'Readmission Agreements and Refugee Rights: from a Critique to a Proposal' (2013) 32(3) *Refugee Survey Quarterly* 79.

[12] For a detailed analysis of the identity determination dilemmas in readmission procedures, see S Carrera, *Implementation of EU Readmission Agreements* (Springer, 2016) 13–21.

or stateless person)'.[13] However, for the purpose of this book, attention will be paid to the first two groups and, in particular, third-country nationals. Although asylum seekers cannot avail themselves of the protection of their home country, readmission agreements are nevertheless used to transfer the concerned persons to a 'safe third country' of transit.[14]

According to part of the doctrine, the obligation to readmit own nationals is traditionally derived from the right of every State to expel foreigners and the right of everyone to return to one's country.[15] The right to return has been enshrined in several international instruments. For instance, pursuant to Article 13(2) of the UDHR, 'Everyone has the right to leave any country, including his own, and to return to his country.'[16] Article 12(4) of the ICCPR provides that 'No one shall be arbitrarily deprived of the right to enter his own country' while Article 5(d)(ii) of the International Convention on the Elimination of All Forms of Racial Discrimination (ICERD) recognises 'The right of everyone … to equality before the law … in the enjoyment of the right to leave any country, including one's own, and to return to one's own country.'[17] Finally, pursuant to Article 3(2) of Protocol 4 of the ECHR, 'No one shall be deprived of the right to enter the territory of the State of which he is a national.'

In this view, State obligations to readmit nationals who are not allowed to remain in the territory of the host country exist towards individuals as beneficiaries of the right to return by virtue of the principle of nationality.[18] According to Weis:

> Nationality in the sense of international law is a technical term denoting the allocation of individuals, termed nationals, to a specific State – the State of nationality – as members of that State, a relationship which confers upon the State of nationality … rights and duties in relation to other States.[19]

However, the theory whereby the obligation to readmit depends on the individual right to return erroneously conflates the relationship between individuals and the State with the obligation owed by one State to another State. Accordingly, international obligations to readmit one's own nationals on one hand, and foreign nationals on the other, have to be distinguished from the right of any

[13] IOM Glossary 2011.

[14] The grounds on which an asylum seeker is transferred to a 'safe third country' are illustrated in Chapter 2 of this book.

[15] See K Hailbronner, 'Comments on the Right to Leave, Return and Remain' in V Gowlland-Debbas (ed), *The Problem of Refugees in the Light of Contemporary International Law Issues* (Martinus Nijhoff, 1996); K Hailbronner, 'Readmission Agreements and the Obligation of States under Public International Law to Readmit their Own and Foreign Nationals' (1997) 57 *Zeitschrift für ausländisches öffentliches Recht und Völkerrecht* 2–5; Coleman 2009, n 5 above, 28.

[16] UDHR, adopted 10 December 1948, UNGA Res 217A(III).

[17] ICERD, adopted 4 January 1969, entered into force 7 March 1966, 660 UNTS 195.

[18] See R Jennings and A Watts, *Oppenheim's International Law* (Longman, 1992) 857; Coleman 2009, n 5 above, 29.

[19] P Weis, *Nationality and Statelessness in International Law* (Kluwer, 1979) 59.

given individual to return. Such a juxtaposition, however, is now anachronistic as the existence of a customary duty to readmit third-country nationals seems to have been phased out by most recent practice. In Hailbronner's view, the duty to readmit would rest on the sovereign right of States to regulate access to and expulsion from their territory. Therefore, the refusal of a country to readmit its own nationals expelled from the territory of another State would entail a breach of the territorial sovereignty of the host State and jeopardise the right of that State to expel foreigners.[20] The obligation of a State to reaccept its nationals also lies within the principle of the responsibility of a State for the welfare of its nationals who have been expelled from the territory of the host country.[21]

Much of the doctrine considers the obligation of a State to readmit its own nationals as a norm of customary law because of the coexistence of *opinio juris* and consistent State practice.[22] However, as stated by the Legal Service of the EU Council of Ministers in 1995, there is no international obligation under customary law to readmit involuntary nationals. In this view,

> it is doubtful whether, in the absence of a specific agreement [to readmit] between the concerned States, a general principle of international law exists, whereby these States would be obliged to readmit their own nationals when the latter do not wish to return to their State of origin.[23]

The implication of such a statement is that no international law obligation exists for non-European countries to accept back involuntary own nationals, third-country nationals and stateless people unless a clear readmission agreement is in force between the parties to make readmission *de facto* enforceable in practice. Subsequent practice shows again how readmission of involuntary nationals has broadly taken place as long as a readmission agreement was in place, regardless of the unwillingness of deportees.

To facilitate and enforce the readmission of involuntary migrants, a majority of readmission agreements (eg, the accord between the EU and Georgia) explicitly state that transfer will take place regardless of the will of the person to be readmitted. Plender has also shown how globally, several constitutional regimes

[20] Hailbronner 1997, n 15 above, 8, 11–12.

[21] ibid, 7. I have engaged with the debate on the obligation to readmit in international law in M Giuffré, 'The Obligation to Readmit and the Relationship between Interstate and EU Readmission Agreements' in F Ippolito and S Trevisanut (eds), *Migration in Mare Nostrum: Mechanisms of International Cooperation* (CUP, 2015).

[22] See Hailbronner 1997, n 15 above; Coleman 2009, n 5 above, 32–33. Goodwin-Gill, less specifically, refers to the obligation to readmit nationals as 'firmly fixed within the *corpus* of general international law.' See GS Goodwin-Gill, *International Law and the Movement of Persons between States* (OUP, 1978) 137. Weis describes the obligation to readmit as 'universally recognized' and 'generally accepted.' Weis 1979, n 19 above, 47–48; D Martin, 'The Authority and Responsibility of States' in A Aleinikoff and V Chetail (eds), *Migration and International Legal Norms* (TMC Asser Press, 2003) 31–45; M Panizzon, 'Readmission Agreements of EU Member States: A Case for EU Subsidiarity or Dualism?' (2012) 31(4) *Refugee Survey Quarterly* 107.

[23] Council Legal Service Opinion, as cited in the Council Doc 6658/99, 4, http://data.consilium.europa.eu/doc/document/ST-6658-1999-INIT/en/pdf.

frame the right to enter one's country of origin as a fundamental human right. However, it remains contested whether the unwillingness of an individual to be expelled by the host State of destination translates into a 'right not to return', and the scope of the relationship between the sovereign duty to readmit and the right of individuals.

The right to leave – enshrined in several international instruments, such as Article 13(2) of the UDHR, Article 12(1) of the ICCPR, Article 5(d)(ii) of the ICERD, and Article 2(2) of Protocol No 4 to the ECHR – would be frustrated *prima facie* by the application of an international norm obliging States to readmit involuntary deportees.[24] Without pushing this argument further, it is, however, worth noting that the existence of norms regulating State sovereignty as well as access, residence, and expulsion of aliens seems to support the view that 'interstate obligations to readmit nationals exist also independently of an individual's willingness to return.'[25] The two norms operate indeed on two different levels and require a case-by-case analysis.

It seems that the obligation to readmit individuals unwilling to return derives from treaty law, as evidenced by the proliferation of readmission agreements negotiated to make removal effective and obtain the cooperation of the requested State. In 2014, less than 40 per cent of migrants who received an expulsion order left the EU. Since then, this rate has remained at 36–37% (with the exception of 45.8% in 2016).[26] For example, Italy repatriated 15,979 people (out of 25,300 of those receiving an expulsion order), mainly to those countries within which readmission agreements exist and function properly. As also stated by the Spokeswoman at UNHCR South Europe, without readmission agreements, the actual enforcement of removal becomes almost impossible.[27]

In the *van Duyn* case, the ECJ held that 'it is a principle of international law … that a State is precluded from refusing its own nationals the right of entry or residence.'[28] As also affirmed by the UK in its submission to the Court, 'a national, however undesirable and potentially harmful his entry may be, cannot be refused admission into his own State. A State has a duty under international law to receive back its own nationals.'[29] While this was perhaps true in the past, most recent State practices point to a different direction. Home States tend to expeditiously cooperate in the readmission of their own nationals – by issuing, for instance, any necessary papers within a reasonable time – but often only when a readmission agreement or readmission clauses within other types of

[24] G Noll, 'The Non-Admission and Return of Protection Seekers in Germany' (1997) 9(3) *IJRL* 415, fn 7.

[25] Coleman 2009, n 5 above, 32.

[26] European Commission, "Managing migration in all its aspects: Commission note ahead of the June European Council 2018", Brussels, 7.

[27] As cited in V Polchi, 'Migranti, il rebus delle espulsioni: "Rimpatri impossibili senza accordi". Nella UE ogni stato ha le sue regole', *La Repubblica* (29 January 2016). See also, Carrera 2016, n 12 above, 14; A Algostino, 'L'esternalizzazione soft delle frontiere e il naufragio della Costituzione', *Costituzionalismo.it* (16 July 2017) 137, 143–46.

[28] *Yvonne Van Duyn v Home Office*, Case 41/74 [1974] ECR 1337, 1351.

[29] ibid, 1345–46.

cooperative arrangements are in place.[30] Therefore, we must ask to what extent the proliferation of treaty law in the field of removal of irregular migrants influences the customary status of the obligation to readmit. Does the fact that States tend to conclude the highest number of readmission agreements, deemed indispensable for executing expulsion, indicate that readmission is governed by these bilateral treaties rather than by a customary norm?

Treaties play an important role in determining the existence of customary international law because they help shed light on how States view certain rules of international law. In the *North Continental Shelf* case, the ICJ confirmed that treaties may codify pre-existing customary international law, but may also lay the foundation for the development of new customs based on the norms contained in those treaties.[31] Among the various ways in which treaties may interplay with customary law, the Court affirmed that the treaty negotiating process may crystallise an emerging customary rule. In this view, readmission agreements might be seen as confirming and putting into concrete terms the existence of the general international law obligation to readmit.[32] Indeed, codification of a norm in treaty law does give rise to questions over its customary status. A rule can continue to exist under both customary and treaty law as long as the two criteria of consistent State practice and *opinio juris* are fulfilled. At the same time, the presence of several bilateral agreements on the same subject might be regarded as evidence of a customary norm.[33]

It is thus imperative to assess whether the modalities in which readmission agreements are concluded prevent the existence of a customary norm because of the lack of an *opinio juris*. This risk arises when States tie the conclusion of agreements concerning the readmission of own nationals to the granting of benefits. While, in the past, EU Member States have not generally offered compensatory incentives to persuade third countries to sign an arrangement for the readmission of own nationals, Italy has been an interesting exception, as it tended to tie the conclusion of a readmission agreement with labour accords establishing yearly or seasonal immigration quotas.

Nowadays, however, the enhancement of the struggle against 'irregular' migration and the effort to curtail migratory flows has led EU countries to expand their arsenal of incentives (in particular development aid, and economic and technical support) to obtain the cooperation of third countries in accepting

[30] Hailbronner 1997, n 15 above, 45. See below, in this Section, for further details and recent examples.

[31] *North Sea Continental Shelf (Germany v Denmark)*, 20 February 1969, ICJ Rep 3. See also, I Brownlie, *Principles of Public International Law*, 4th edn (Clarendon Press, 1990) 13.

[32] Hailbronner 1997, n 15 above, 8, 14; M Schieffer, 'The Readmission of Third Country Nationals within Bilateral and Multilateral Frameworks' in M den Boer (ed), *The Implementation of Schengen, First the Widening, Now the Deepening* (European Institute of Public Administration, 1997) 100; Coleman 2009, n 5 above, 36.

[33] H Thirlway, 'The Law and Procedure of the International Court of Justice' (1990) 87 *British Yearbook of International Law* 86.

removals from Europe.[34] Informal readmission agreements concerning own nationals and third-country nationals are increasingly negotiated on the basis of conditionality. On 13 May 2015, the European Commission adopted the highly debated European Agenda on Migration, whose objective is to address the root causes of migration by 'mainstream[ing] migration issues into development cooperation.'[35] Through a 'more for more' approach – used as a way to increase EU and Member States' leverage – aid funds and most of the 'development' policies implementing the European Agenda are made conditional on swift removals to third countries.[36] It should be briefly noted here that these policies lack any appropriate monitoring mechanism to ensure that humanitarian and development objectives will be fulfilled.[37] A fine balance of incentives and pressure is always utilised to enhance third countries' cooperation on readmission.[38] This also entails assistance to third countries to strengthen their 'capacity to ensure functioning civil registries and fingerprint or biometrics digitalisation, as well as capacity building in migration management.'[39]

Moreover, requested States do not always reply promptly to readmission requests, and do not efficiently cooperate in the identification of the individual to be readmitted, and in the delivery of travel documents and *laissez-passers*.[40] A report issued by the UK Chief Inspector of Borders and Immigration underlined that there are some countries (eg, Iran) where removal to cannot be enforced either because of the difficult internal situation or because of the unwillingness on the part of the requested State to identify and issue travel documents to its own nationals.[41] Additional obstacles include the unwillingness of third countries to readmit their own citizens, especially if suspected of

[34] Commission (EC), 'Study on the Links between Legal and Illegal Migration' (Communication from the Commission to the Council, the European Parliament, the European Economic and Social Committee and the Committee of the Regions) COM(2004) 412 final 14, 4 June 2004.

[35] Communication from the Commission to the European Parliament, the Council, the European Economic and Social Committee and the Committee of the Regions a European Agenda on Migration (13 May 2015) COM/2015/0240 final, 8 (European Agenda on Migration 2015).

[36] ibid, 9.

[37] See generally, D Davitti and A La Chimia, 'A Lesser Evil? The European Agenda on Migration and the Use of Aid Funding for Migration Control' (2017) 10 *Irish Yearbook of International Law* 133.

[38] Council of the EU, 'Increasing the effectiveness of the EU system to return irregular migrants', 10170/15, Brussels, 22 June 2015, para 12.

[39] Communication from the Commission to the European Parliament, the European Council, the Council and the European Investment Bank on establishing a new Partnership Framework with third countries under the European Agenda on Migration (EU Migration Partnership Framework), https://ec.europa.eu/home-affairs/sites/homeaffairs/files/what-we-do/policies/european-agenda-migration/proposal-implementation-package/docs/20160607/communication_external_aspects_eam_towards_new_migration_ompact_en.pdf.

[40] JP Cassarino, 'Informalizing Readmission Agreements in the EU Neighbourhood' (2007) 42(2) *The International Spectator* 179, 187, 192; Carrera 2016, n 12 above, 14.

[41] Independent Chief Inspector of Borders and Immigration (2015) *An Inspection of Removals October 2014–March 2015* (London, December 2015) fn 18: https://assets.publishing.service.gov.uk/government/uploads/system/uploads/attachment_data/file/547681/ICIBI-report-on-Removals-_December_2015.pdf.

terrorism-related activities, and the unwillingness on the part of the individuals to cooperate with the enforcement of their removal.[42] Pakistan, for instance, unilaterally suspended the implementation of the readmission agreement with the EU – and denied the disembarkation of 70 persons on-board a joint flight organised by Frontex in November 2015 because some deportations were considered unjustified.[43] It also failed to reply within the given time limits,[44] rejected *prima facie* evidence of nationality, and refused both to accept people suspected of links with terrorism and to readmit nationals if their passport did not have biometric identifiers and the name of the person at issue was not inserted in its national biometric database.[45]

To sum up, some authors suggest that the existence of a customary norm on the obligation to readmit would be endangered if States agreed to negotiate it, as in the case of readmission agreements.[46] These accords are generally drafted using reciprocal language whereby contracting parties accept mutual and identical obligations. Nonetheless, the majority of treaties of last generation involve States with different economic backgrounds where requested States do not share the same interest in the readmission of migrants as compared to requesting States. In these circumstances and in the absence of explicit methods of compensation, the interest countries of origin may have in collaborating in the readmission of own nationals resides in the possibility of improving their political and economic relations with the country of destination and receiving financial support.[47]

Others argue, instead, that the fact that the conclusion of a readmission agreement increasingly implies a *quid pro quo* does not undermine *ipso facto* the customary status of the obligation to readmit. Two States can decide, indeed, to negotiate an agreement to set up clear and explicit procedures facilitating the actual transfer of unauthorised migrants.[48] Any incentive that requested States receive from requesting States in exchange for the conclusion of a readmission

[42] European Migration Network (EMN), 'Practical measures to reduce irregular migration' (October 2012), para 7.2.3: https://ec.europa.eu/home-affairs/sites/homeaffairs/files/what-we-do/networks/european_migration_network/reports/docs/emn-studies/irregular-migration/00a_emn_synthesis_report_irregular_migration_october_2012_en.pdf.

[43] See *Express Tribune*, 'Deportees and readmissions' (4 December 2015), https://tribune.com.pk/story/1003975/deportees-and-readmissions/.

[44] For example, as of May 2016, Greece has reported that 592 of its readmission requests to Pakistan have remained unanswered. See European Migration Network (EMN), 'Good practices in the return and reintegration of irregular migrants: Member states' entry bans policies and use of readmission agreements' between Member States and third countries' (Synthesis Report for the EMN Focussed Study 2014) para 3.1.3.3, https://ec.europa.eu/home-affairs/sites/homeaffairs/files/what-we-do/networks/european_migration_network/reports/docs/emn-studies/emn_study_reentry_bans_and_readmission_agreements_final_december_2014.pdf.

[45] This information comes from a set of interviews carried out by Carrera for his book *The Implementation of EU Readmission Agreements*. See Carrera 2016, n 12 above, 17.

[46] Hailbronner 1997, n 15 above, 48–49.

[47] See Nordic Joint Advisory Group 1999, Council doc 7707/99, 18. See also, Coleman 2009, n 5 above, 39; Davitti and La Chimia 2017, n 36 above.

[48] Coleman 2009, n 5 above, 40.

agreement may be read as a sort of compensation for the limitation of their sovereignty, due to the fact that the agreement lays down a set of precise procedures on time limits, swift issuance of travel documents, authorities involved, and administrative constraints establishing how readmission is to be implemented, including for the repatriation of people suspected of very serious crimes, such as terrorism.[49] Therefore, in principle, the granting of either explicit or implicit reciprocal benefits would not *per se* preclude States from having an *opinio juris* regarding their obligation to readmit own nationals.

The analysis above shows how the exact scope and operation of the 'duty' to readmit own nationals – and its existence – remains by and large contested both in law and practice. A number of arguments buttress the view that this norm has a customary value. However, what has notably changed over the last few years, in particular since 2015, is the increase of the spectrum of benefits and incentives granted to the third countries to expand readmission rates. Expulsion is clearly easier with those countries that have entered into a readmission agreement.[50] Moreover, the proliferation of informal agreements linked to readmission and the arsenal of benefits and incentives to persuade third countries to cooperate through the 'more for more' approach (particularly in the aftermath of the 2015–16 'humanitarian refugee crisis')[51] would point to a different direction. Readmission agreements are indeed increasingly used to overcome legal and practical obstacles between the two States concerned, and make such cooperation attractive for the government and the population of the requested State. Therefore, one could conclude that such views on the customary value of the duty to readmit own nationals – which clearly lack compactness and uniformity – might be ascribed to the ambiguity of international law itself, rather than to the single bilateral readmission agreements.

B. Readmitting Third-Country Nationals

Over the last two decades, compelling arguments have buttressed the view that readmitting own nationals is a customary norm – a conclusion which is now contested by the most recent practice of the proliferation of readmission agreements and the plethora of related incentives. However, it cannot be safely argued that there exists a norm of customary law requiring States to readmit foreign persons. Hailbronner has attempted to derive such a norm from the principle of neighbourliness, which would lead States to control unauthorised migratory

[49] ibid.

[50] For example, the Renewed Action Plan emphasises that promoting cooperation on readmission with third countries is an essential element to increase return rates. See Communication from the Commission to the European Parliament and the Council on a more effective return policy in the EU – A Renewed Action Plan, 2 March 2017, COM(2017) 200 final 14.

[51] E Guild and S Carrera, 'Rethinking asylum distribution in the EU: Shall we start with the facts?', *CEPS Commentary, CEPS, Brussels*, 17 June 2016.

flows in order to impede their transit across the territories of neighbouring countries.[52] Readmission, in this perspective, would be a sort of reparation for failing to prevent irregular migrants from crossing the border. Accordingly, readmission agreements would codify the penalisation of third States through which migrants have transited before reaching the destination country. Although the lack of both a well-established State practice and *opinio juris* testify to the absence of an obligation of general international law to readmit third-country nationals, Hailbronner suggests that a European customary norm in *status nascendi* might be inferred from the proliferation of readmission agreements concerning the removal of third-country nationals.[53]

However, several objections have been made to the application of the principle of neighbourliness to the control of migratory flows. In this regard, Lammers argues that:

> Neighbourship law in principle involves an obligation for a State to *abstain* from conduct – or to take such positive action as is necessary to convince private persons or entities in its territory to abstain from conduct .... It purports to enable neighbouring States to *coexist* by setting certain limits to the exercise and enjoyment of their territorial sovereignty and it does not in principle compel them to undertake positive action for the benefit of other States or to *improve* their mutual condition through cooperation.[54]

The present description of the concept of neighbourliness, based on 'harmonious reciprocal relations between States, consisting of corresponding obligations and rights', proves how this notion cannot be used to create a positive obligation on States to control borders since this would be an unbalanced allocation of responsibility.[55] Furthermore, the legal concept of neighbourliness is likely to be open to political and subjective interpretations. While, on the one hand, requesting States might interpret it as imposing upon transit countries the duty to readmit third-country nationals, on the other hand, transit countries could be damaged by the new migratory burdens, which cause a shrinking of national sovereignty.[56]

Therefore, the view that no customary rule requiring readmission of foreign persons exists is more convincing, as demonstrated by the fact that States usually agree to collaborate to fight irregular immigration – by readmitting third-country nationals – under the incentive of good political and economic relations, visa facilitations, financial and technical aid, and development assistance.[57] States' obligation to readmit does not apply, under general international law, to citizens

[52] See Art 74 of the UN Charter.

[53] Hailbronner 1997, n 15 above, 31–37.

[54] JG, Lammers, *Pollution of International Watercourses: A Search for Substantive Rules and Principles of Law* (Brill, 1984) 568.

[55] Coleman 2009, n 5 above, 45.

[56] ibid.

[57] See eg, P Cuttitta, 'Readmission and Forcibly Return in the Relations between Italy and North African Mediterranean Countries', *Paper Presented at the Ninth Mediterranean Research Meeting*

of third countries or stateless persons who have transited through the requested State or have been granted a stay permit.[58] In particular, governments can refuse to accept readmission of undocumented persons whose nationality can be difficult to establish. In these circumstances, readmission agreements can turn out to be very helpful, since they generally formalise the obligation of States to readmit both their own nationals and third-country nationals who are irregularly present in the territory of the other contracting party.[59] The decisive factor is the issue of transit, as well as the granting of a visa or other title of residence by the requested State.[60] All in all, while readmission of one's own nationals finds a legal basis in general international law – leaving open, however, the discussion on involuntary deportees – readmission of third-country nationals can be grounded only in treaty law.

A further issue points to the lack of specific obligations concerning refugees and stateless persons in the text of readmission agreements, with these categories of people often summarily subsumed under the same terms as 'third-country nationals.' However, under the 1951 Geneva Convention and the 1954 Convention relating to the Status of Stateless Persons,[61] a State must readmit recognised refugees and stateless persons to whom it has issued a travel document in keeping with Article 28 of these Conventions. Indeed, a State must readmit refugees and stateless persons if they have received (from the country in question) travel documents 'for the purpose of travelling outside their territory, unless compelling reasons of national security or public order otherwise require ...'[62]

(Florence and Montecatini Terme, 12–15 March 2008), organised by the Mediterranean Program of the Robert Schumann Centre for Advanced Studies at the European University Institute 7, 9–10; F Trauner and I Kruse, 'EC Visa Facilitation and Readmission Agreements: Implementing a New EU Security Approach in the Neighbourhood' (23 April 2008), *CEPS Working Document*, http://www.ceps.eu/book/ec-visa-facilitation-and-readmission-agreements-implementing-new-eu-security-approach-neighbour; Coleman 2009, n 5 above, 62.

[58] See, *inter alia*, Hailbronner 1997, n 15 above; F Pastore, 'L'Obbligo di Riammissione in Diritto Internazionale' (1998) 4 *Rivista di Diritto Internazionale* 973, 976; I Kruse, 'EU Readmission Policy and its Effects on Transit Countries: the Case of Albania' (2006) 8 *EJML* 2, 7.

[59] D Bouteillet Paquet, 'Passing the Buck: A Critical Analysis of the Readmission Policy Implemented by the European Union and its Member States' (2003) 5 *EJML* 361–62. 2.

[60] Hailbronner 1997, n 15 above, 27. As explained in the ILC Commentary on expulsion of aliens, readmission agreements are of interest in determining the State of destination for an expelled alien. Under Draft Art 22, 'Where the State of nationality or any other State that has the obligation to receive the alien under international law has not been identified and no other State is willing to accept the alien, that alien may be expelled to any State where he or she has a right of entry or stay or, where applicable, to *the State from where he or she has entered the expelling State*.' See ILC Commentary on expulsion of aliens, (2011) *Yearbook of the International Law Commission*, vol II, Part Two, 32.

[61] Convention relating to the Status of Stateless Persons, 360 UNTS 117, entered into force 6 June 1960.

[62] Art 28 of the 1951 Geneva Convention and the 1954 Convention relating to the Status of Stateless Persons (effective from 1960). For further discussion on this point, see Coleman 2009, n 5 above, 48–49.

III. READMISSION AGREEMENTS: AN OVERVIEW

Without impinging on the rights of those who are legitimately entitled to stay, readmission agreements aim to create a legal framework for removal. By providing for readmission without formalities, these bilateral arrangements allow border authorities to handle transfers of third-country nationals without the involvement of diplomatic channels.[63]

This book does not aim to describe the readmission legislation and deportation policies of the selected countries through a comparative enquiry of the national measures of removal. Rather, it purports to investigate, from an international law perspective, whether the implementation of bilateral readmission agreements – although designed to contrast unauthorised migration – might also hamper refugees' access to protection.

Today, readmission is a network composed of differing institutional instruments, ranging from development aid to visa facilitation, from technical cooperation for the externalisation of migration controls to labour exchanges. However, this chapter concentrates on *standard* readmission agreements, seen as a fundamental component of the numerous and various national policies of expulsion, removal, and repatriation of people who have an irregular status in the destination country, or who have sought to irregularly enter the territory of a State. The effectiveness of the whole system of expulsion/deportation rests upon efficient modalities of execution of removal decisions.[64] Since readmission of irregular migrants depends on a profitable cooperation between destination States and countries of origin or transit of migrants, it is imperative to shed light on bilateral agreements which facilitate the carrying out of all the procedures necessary for guaranteeing the readmission of own nationals and third-country nationals.

In 1994 and 1995, the Council of Justice and Home Affairs (JHA) of the EU adopted two recommendations concerning, respectively, a specimen bilateral readmission agreement between a Member State and a third country, and guiding principles to be followed in drafting protocols on the implementation of a readmission agreement.[65] More specifically, the purpose of the specimen

[63] Hailbronner 1997, n 15 above, 9.

[64] For a detailed overview of readmission procedures, see IOM, Manual on Readmission (2010): https://publications.iom.int/system/files/pdf/manual_on_readmission1_en.pdf. On the definition of 'effectiveness of cooperation, as including also human rights protection of readmitted migrants, and not only capacity to carry out swift removals, see JP Cassarino, *Readmission Policy in the European Union*, Study for the Directorate General for Internal Policies, Policy Department C: Citizens' Rights and Constitutional Affairs, Civil Liberties, Justice and Home Affairs (Bruxelles, European Parliament, 2010), 43–46 (Cassarino 2010b).

[65] See Recommendation concerning a specimen bilateral readmission agreement between a Member State of the European Union and a third country, adopted on 30 November and 1 December 1994, SN 10339/94. Any provisions on the rights of refugees and asylum seekers contained in a previous draft were abandoned in the finalised version of the text.

agreement was to help EU Member States standardise their readmission procedures with third countries. While no significant differences may be detected in the text of the readmission agreements separately concluded by EU Member States with third countries, a certain degree of variation in wording and substance is, however, inevitable, as their negotiation is significantly dependent on the political relations between the two relevant parties.

In sketching out the different sections of standard readmission agreements, this chapter takes as units of analysis the accords concluded by Albania with Italy and the UK, respectively. Albania constitutes a special case insofar as it was the first country in Europe to execute a readmission agreement with the European Community (now the EU). At the same time, this case study reveals the salience of interstate readmission strategies. Indeed, the negotiation process between the EU and Albania took so long that Italy lost interest in the EU's initiatives and decided to boost its own cooperation with Albania, thus realising that the activities taken at bilateral level had, *de facto*, significantly contributed to stemming massive irregular inflows from the Balkans.[66] Additionally, the accords concluded separately by Albania with Italy and the UK are among the most sophisticated and detailed pieces of legislation within the varied category of existing interstate readmission agreements.

A. Readmission of Nationals and Third-Country Nationals: The Case of Albania

Scrutiny of the text of readmission agreements is a stepping stone, not only for the acquisition of further knowledge on the technical and legal content of the treaties, but also to better understand their relationship with other sources of EU law as well as international and European refugee and human rights law. Moreover, the description of the technical content of readmission agreements will also be instructive for the debate on the opportunity to include human rights procedural clauses in the text of these bilateral accords as a further guarantee for the rights of refugees and asylum seekers. Notwithstanding the differences in the content of particular readmission agreements – which depend on the relationship between the two involved countries – this Section outlines the main aspects of standard readmission agreements, taking as units of analysis the accords concluded by Albania with Italy and the UK, respectively, and indicating differences in their wording only where relevant.

Besides a Preamble, the Italy–Albania readmission agreement is composed of five numbered and titled sections. Section I describes the readmission obligations of the two Contracting Parties; Section II lays down the readmission

[66] See FM Piddu, 'Le Missioni in Albania della Marina Militare' (1998) *Rivista Marittima* 49; J Chaloff, 'Lessons from the Italy-Albania Readmission Agreement', in C Mackenzie (ed) *Return and Readmission to Albania: The Experience of Selected EU Member States* (IOM, 2006) 112.

obligations of third-country nationals; Section III indicates the readmission procedure for Contracting Parties' citizens; Section IV regulates admission in transit for the purpose of transferring third-country nationals to another State; Section V contains general dispositions.

The structure of the agreement between Albania and the UK is slightly different, but the substance is almost the same.[67] The Preamble is followed by a first Article on definitions; Section I (so-called 'Part I') concerns the readmission of citizens and people with a right to abode; Section II deals with the readmission of third-country nationals; Section III defines transit operations; Section IV sets out general and final provisions. Additionally, both agreements have an Executive Protocol attached to the main text of the accords.

Both the Preambles generally point out the objective of the agreements, namely the strengthening of the bilateral cooperation between the two Contracting Parties – having regard to the need to abide by human rights as recognised by international instruments – in order to combat irregular immigration and facilitate the removal of persons whose residence or presence in the territory is unauthorised. The Italian accord also refers to the intent of both parties to regulate readmission on the basis of the principle of reciprocity and in a spirit of cooperation.

In both the readmission agreements, with Italy, and with the UK, Section I determines that the requested Contracting Party shall readmit without particular formalities any persons who do not meet, or who no longer meet the conditions for entry to or residence in the territory of the requesting State, provided that the individual is properly identified and it is proven or reasonably presumed that the individual is a citizen of the requested country.[68] The UK's readmission agreement includes also persons with a right of abode in the requested Contracting Party, and people who were citizens of the requested Party but have subsequently relinquished their citizenship without acquiring a new one. Moreover, the requesting State shall readmit, at the request of the requested Contracting Party, any person who formerly departed from its own territory if subsequent checks reveal that at the time of departure that person neither was a citizen of the requested Contracting Party, nor had a right of abode in said country.[69]

Section II of both agreements sets up the obligation to readmit, without unnecessary formalities, third-country nationals – persons who do not have the nationality of either of the Contracting Parties to the agreement – if they do not fulfil, or no longer fulfil, regulations of entry to or residence in the territory of

[67] In the UK–Albania Readmission Agreement, 'Sections' are named 'Parts.' However, we will continue to use the terms 'Sections' to render easier their joint reading with the Sections of the Readmission Agreement between Albania and Italy. https://www.gov.uk/government/publications/agreement-between-the-uk-and-albania-on-the-readmission-of-persons.

[68] Art 2(1) of the UK's Readmission Agreement and Art 1 of Italy's Readmission Agreement.

[69] The latter option applies only to the UK's readmission agreement. See Art 2(1)(2) of the UK's Readmission Agreement and Art 1(3) of Italy's Readmission Agreement.

the requesting State. Pursuant to the UK–Albania arrangement, the obligation to readmit is conditional upon *proof*: (i) that the unauthorised migrant holds, or held at the time of her unlawful entry into the territory of the requesting party, a visa or a valid residence permit issued by the requested State; (ii) that the irregular migrant meets the requirements of the requested State's national legislation for entry and residence of aliens.[70] Each Contracting Party shall also readmit to the territory of its State if it is *reasonably presumed* that the third-country national had entered or resided in the territory of the requested State.[71] The accord with the UK adds that, in cases in which both Contracting Parties have issued a visa or residence permit, responsibility shall reside with the State whose visa or residence permit expires last (Article 7(2)). The same exemptions from the obligation to readmit third-country nationals are envisaged by the two arrangements in a number of situations, including cases in which the third party national has been granted refugee status by the requesting party.[72]

B. Readmission Procedure

As far as the UK–Albania readmission agreement is concerned, Section I addresses some aspects of the readmission procedure of citizens and individuals with a right of abode, while Section II lays down the readmission procedure of third country nationals. Pursuant to Article 4, any request for readmission shall be made in writing to the competent authority of the requested State, and shall contain information as set out in Article 1 of the annexed protocol. In cases concerning readmission of both nationals and third-country nationals, the reply to the request for readmission will be given in writing within 15 working days.[73]

Article 3 of the agreement lists the means of evidence for establishing identity and citizenship of persons to be readmitted, provided that they are citizens or other persons with a right of abode in the requested Contracting Party. Entry or residence of the third party national in the territory of the requested State shall be *proven* by the application of border seals or other proper annotations in their travel documents by border authorities at entry or departure from the territory of the requested country (Article 9(1)). In contrast, entry or residence may be *reasonably presumed* on the basis, for example, of transport documents, proof of payment for hotel, medical service, as well as reliable statements of both *bona fide* witnesses and the third-country national in question (Article 9(2)).

[70] Art 7(1) of Section II of the UK's Readmission Agreement.

[71] Art 2 of Section II of Italy's Readmission Agreement requires, instead, that entry or residence in the territory of the requested State is proven.

[72] Art 8(2)(a), (b), (c), (g) of Section II of the UK's Readmission Agreement; Art 3(a), (c), (d), (e) of Section II of Italy's Readmission Agreement. The two selected countries also provide for different regimes of exceptions.

[73] See Arts 6(2) and 10(3).

Under Article 1 of Albania's agreement with Italy, citizenship may be ascertained through citizenship certificates or any other naturalisation documents, identity cards, passports, seaman's books, and children's travel documents in lieu of passports. The annexed protocol sets up all the procedures for the readmission of both nationals and third-country nationals by establishing the competent authorities and the timetable for replying to a readmission request in order to avoid overly lengthy bureaucratic mechanisms. For instance, both third-country nationals and individuals whose citizenship of one of the Contracting Parties is presumed may be immediately readmitted – through direct contact between the Border Police Offices of both countries – if apprehended while irregularly crossing the border of the requesting party.

However, third-country nationals should possess a valid stay permit issued by the requested State, or travel documents containing proper annotations by border authorities of the requested country.[74] If the unauthorised presence of third-country nationals is detected when they already are within the territory of the requesting State, readmission may be executed within eight days starting from the date of receipt of the readmission application, which will take place even in the absence of a formal reply to the readmission request.[75] For nationals whose citizenship is presumed, the time limit is seven days.[76] It should be observed that in the absence of a specific provision requiring the requested State to send an acknowledgement of receipt of the application, the fate of the readmitted migrant might be put at risk by a transfer executed on the basis of a request that has never been received.

C. Further Dispositions

Both Section III of the readmission agreement between Albania and the UK and Section IV of the agreement between Albania and Italy regulate the issue of transit for removal purposes.[77] Italy's accord explicitly lays down a safeguard for asylum seekers by establishing that transit may be refused if the readmitted person is at risk of being subjected, in the country of destination, to persecution for reasons of nationality, religion, or sexual orientation, as well as membership in a particular social and political group (Article 9).

Article 13 of the readmission agreements that Albania concluded with the UK and Italy, respectively, provides that any controversies surrounding the interpretation of the treaty shall be resolved through diplomatic channels. Every year,

[74] See para D(1) of the Annexed Protocol to the Italy–Albania Readmission Agreement.

[75] See para D(2) of the Annexed Protocol to the Italy–Albania Agreement. If detected migrants are nationals of the requested party, the reply to the readmission request must be given within 48 hours (para A(2) of the Annexed Protocol).

[76] See para B(3)) of the Annexed Protocol to the Italy–Albania Agreement.

[77] See Art 13 of the UK's Agreement and Art 7 of Italy's Agreement.

representatives of the two contracting parties meet in order to discuss problems concerning the implementation of the agreements, and to jointly formulate new proposals and amendments to ensure a smooth readmission procedure.[78]

Both texts of the readmission agreements contain a *non-affection* clause that regulates the relation of these instruments with other treaties – including human rights treaties – and international obligations. For instance, Article 11 of Italy's accord indicates that the agreement at issue does not affect the Contracting Parties' obligations on admission or readmission under any other international treaties, but it does not specifically refer to human rights and refugee law instruments.[79] In contrast, Article 21 of the UK Agreement refers to a number of international human rights and refugee law instruments Contracting Parties shall comply with when readmitting a person. Since both these conventions and readmission agreements are international treaties with no hierarchical relationship under international law, potential conflicts between a readmission agreement and any other treaty obligations binding the EU Member State or the third country in question would be solved in favour of the international instruments listed in the non-affection clause.[80]

IV. THE RELATIONSHIP BETWEEN INTERSTATE AND EU READMISSION AGREEMENTS

The EU's readmission policy constitutes the general framework placed above and beyond the broad cobweb of bilateral readmission agreements between EU Member States and third countries.[81] The interrelatedness between national and supranational readmission policies is corroborated by the fact that Member States continue to pursue their readmission procedures in parallel with the EU strategy, as envisaged by paragraph 7 of the Preamble of the Return Directive, which underlines 'the need for Community and bilateral readmission agreements with third countries to facilitate the return process.'

Readmission has therefore turned out to be an underlying component of the EU immigration and asylum policy, which has been progressively defined and consolidated after the entry into force of both the Amsterdam and the Lisbon Treaties. In addition, the *Stockholm Programme – an Open and Secure Europe Serving and Protecting the Citizens*, adopted in December 2009, portrays readmission agreements, at both bilateral and supranational level, as a building block in EU migration management. Article 79(3) of the TFEU expressly gives authority to the EU to stipulate agreements with third States for the readmission

[78] See Arts 14 and 15 of Italy's Agreement.

[79] See below for a more detailed analysis of non-affection clauses.

[80] Coleman 2009, n 5 above, 105.

[81] While the European Commission has received 21 mandates for negotiating readmission agreements, 17 arrangements are already in force.

of third-country nationals who do not, or who no longer, fulfil the conditions for entry, presence, or residence in one of the Member States.

The issue of division of competences has stirred up a heated debate over the years, and Member States have openly contested an alleged exclusive competence of the EU.[82] In this regard, after examining the different claims to exclusive and shared competence, Panizzon concludes that 'shared competence over readmission, and as a result, "agreements dualism", should, in principle, remain unencumbered.'[83] Although recognising the dual commitment of the EU and individual Member States in this area, Panizzon, however, suggests that shared competence may trigger a race to the bottom over human rights standards. In her view, the reasons why EU readmission agreements would be better tools in safeguarding the rights of the readmitted persons are twofold:[84] (i) in 2011 the EU Commission proposed that future directives negotiating readmission agreements would not cover third-country nationals;[85] (ii) according to the same proposal, EU arrangements will contain a safeguard clause requiring suspension of the treaty if the readmitting country does not respect human rights.[86]

Yet, this approach seems to be overcome by most recent State practice orientated to negotiate agreements also for the readmission of third-country nationals. Moreover, as long as the EU does not provide incentives (such as labour quotas) for source countries, States of transit for migrants will inevitably prefer concluding agreements with individual EU Member States. The Lisbon Treaty does not bestow upon the Union the exclusive power to negotiate readmission agreements. Indeed, Article 4(2)(j) of the TFEU incorporates 'Freedom, Security and Justice' – which clearly encompasses readmission – in the field of shared competence. Therefore, the relationship between the EU and Member States continues to be shared and grounded on the principle of 'sincere cooperation' enshrined in Article 4(3) of the Treaty on the EU (TEU).[87]

In case of the coexistence of previous state-negotiated arrangements, these continue to be in force and are used, but, by virtue of the 'safeguard clause', EU readmission agreements take precedence over State-negotiated ones in case of incompatibilities.[88] The JHA Council of May 1999 stated that a Member State

[82] On the division of competences between the EU and Member States, see, *inter alia*, P Craig and G De Burca, *EU Law: Text, Cases and Materials*, 6th edn (OUP, 2015) 74 ff.

[83] Panizzon 2012, n 22 above, 132.

[84] ibid.

[85] Commission, 'Evaluation of EU Readmission Agreements' (Communication) COM(2011) 76 final, 9, 23 February 2011: http://eur-lex.europa.eu/LexUriServ/LexUriServ.do?uri=COM:2011:0076:FIN:EN:PDF (EC Evaluation of EU Readmission Agreements).

[86] ibid, 12.

[87] For an analysis of the Area of Freedom, Security and Justice (AFSJ) after Lisbon and Stockholm, see T Kostakopoulou, 'An Open and Secure Europe? Fixity and Fissures in the Area of Freedom, Security and Justice after Lisbon and Stockholm' (2010) 19(2) *European Security* 151; D Acosta Arcarazo and CC Murphy (eds), *EU Security and Justice Law: After Lisbon and Stockholm* (Hart Publishing, 2014).

[88] It is often mistakenly assumed that the role of Member States is totally dismissed once the Commission and the Council independently decide to negotiate and conclude an EU readmission

must always notify the Council of its intention to negotiate a bilateral readmission arrangement, and can continue with the process only if the European Community has not already stipulated a treaty with the concerned third State or 'has not concluded a mandate for negotiating such an agreement.'[89] Exceptions include where Member States require more detailed arrangements to compensate an EU agreement or a negotiating mandate containing only general statements. However, 'Member States may no longer conclude agreements if they might be detrimental to existing Community agreements.'[90] To put it differently, they 'shall exercise their competence to the extent that the Union has not exercised its competence. The Member States shall again exercise their competence to the extent that the Union has decided to cease exercising its competence.'[91] Should a State contravene this obligation, the European Commission could bring an infringement procedure before the Court of Justice of the EU under Article 258 of the TFEU.

V. REMOVAL DECISIONS: THE *RETURN* AND THE *RECAST PROCEDURES* DIRECTIVES IN CONTEXT

Asylum seekers and beneficiaries of other forms of international protection are often subject to a removal order enforced through a readmission agreement. The primary question of this chapter is whether refugees' access to protection might be impaired by the implementation of standard readmission agreements. In order to address this issue, a preliminary sub-question needs to be answered first. It asks whether these bilateral accords stand as the legal basis for 'safe third country' removal decisions. In this regard, readmission by a third country follows the removal stage, which refers to the actual decision, under national law and EU law, to remove an irregular migrant or an asylum seeker against her will. In this chain, readmission agreements are administrative instruments acting as a bilateral conduit between the requesting and the requested States with a view to facilitating the transfer and readmission of persons who have

agreement, thereby overlooking the fact that the mandate of the Commission only consists in 'brokering the agreement.' As Kovanda put it in 2006, 'once an agreement is negotiated, the Community responsibility is over. Its day-to-day implementation, the actual decision about sending a person back and the actual operation it involves – all this is entirely within the competence of our Member States.' See *Euroasylum*, interview with K Kovanda, Special Representative for Readmission Policies, DG Relex (April 2006), as cited in JP Cassarino 2010b, n 64 above, 18.

[89] JHA Council, 'Conclusion on Readmission Agreements – Consequences of the Entry into Force of the Amsterdam Treaty', 27–28 May 1999 (JHA Council 1999), http://europa.eu/rapid/press-release_PRES-99-168_en.htm. For an appraisal of the EU readmission policy, see C Billet, 'EC Readmission Agreements: A Prime Instrument of the External Dimension of the EU's Fight against Irregular Immigration. An Assessment after Ten Years of Practice' (2010) 12 *EJML* 45.

[90] JHA Council 1999.

[91] Art 2(2) TFEU.

been found irregularly entering, being present in, or residing in the territory of the requesting State. They therefore address the horizontal relationship between two States involved in the readmission policy, and are put into action only once the removal decision process ends.

Before proceeding with the question on the relationship between agreements linked to readmission and the removal decision, attention has to be focused on Article 38 of the Recast Procedures Directive, which allows States to transfer asylum seekers to 'safe third countries' for the purpose of examining asylum claims. The connection between readmission agreements and 'safe third country' practices has raised various doubts and concerns in the international community. As discussed in Chapter two of this book, a burgeoning literature has addressed the shortcomings of 'safe third country' policies, in particular with respect to their connection with accelerated procedures for removing unauthorised migrants apprehended at the EU borders.

The 'safe third country' concept implies that access to an effective asylum procedure can be denied if individuals have transited through another 'safe third country' before reaching the State in which they are ultimately soliciting protection. On this view, refugees should request asylum in the first safe country they are able to reach. Since transfer of responsibility for asylum seekers to another 'safe' country does not find a legal basis in general international law, readmission agreements are commonly relied upon by the EU and its Member States to obtain the necessary cooperation for readmitting third-country nationals. They not only regulate the removal of irregular migrants but also that of rejected refugees and asylum seekers whose application was not examined on its merits on the basis of a 'safe third country' exception.

EU Member States may also decide to engage in the negotiation of readmission agreements or in other kinds of informal cooperation on migration control with countries that have a doubtful track record in human rights. Some of these countries are either amongst the largest 'producers' of refugees, or transit States with no adequate facilities to process applications and grant asylum.[92] Nevertheless, rebuttal of the safety of a country in individual circumstances is a protection imperative.[93]

As far as irregular migrants are concerned, the main EU instrument regulating the removal of unauthorised aliens is the Return Directive. It also recognises the need for EU and bilateral readmission agreements with third countries to facilitate the removal process,[94] and sets out common rules concerning removal, return, detention standards, safeguards for returnees, and re-entry bans for

[92] R Dunstan, 'Playing Human Pinball. The Amnesty International United Kingdom Section Report on UK Home Office "Safe Third Country" Practice' (1995) 7(4) *IJRL* 606, 611.

[93] See, eg, *MSS v Belgium and Greece*, App no 30696/09 (21 January 2011) para 253; *TI v UK*, App no 43844/98 (7 March 2000); G Noll, *Negotiating Asylum: The EU Acquis, Extraterritorial Protection and the Common Market of Deflection* (Martinus Nijhoff, 2000), 200.

[94] Preamble of the Return Directive, para 7.

people subjected to a removal decision.[95] The Return Directive has established a supranational framework of procedural safeguards and rights subject to the judicial scrutiny of the CJEU.[96] Irregular migrants subject to an expulsion procedure are entitled to challenge or seek review of a removal decision before a competent and impartial body, which has the power to suspend the enforcement of such an order. The Return Directive also provides for access to legal advice, representation and linguistic assistance. Removal can also be postponed if there is a risk of *refoulement* and taking into account 'the third's country national physical state and mental capacity [and] technical reasons, such as lack of transport capacity, or failure of the removal due to lack of identification.'[97]

The Recast Procedures Directive is the instrument used by EU Member States to determine the measures for granting or withdrawing refugee status and to ascertain whether asylum seekers can be removed to a 'safe third country' responsible for the examination of their asylum claims.[98] The legal status of asylum seekers is thus assessed during an initial phase following their arrival in the territory of one of the EU Member States.

Readmission agreements do not provide the legal basis for the removal of refused/excluded refugees. They are only used to enable the transfer to the country of origin or transit of all those people whose protection claims have been denied on the grounds set in the Procedures and Qualification Directives.[99] It should also be underlined that, formally, the 'safe third country' exceptions envisaged by the Procedures Directive and its Recast version have been rarely used by Member States. Indeed, the latter have usually had difficulties in obtaining the cooperation of the readmitting country and have tended to examine individual circumstances prior to expulsion.

Nevertheless, nothing prevents EU Member States from using readmission agreements to enforce 'safe third country' policies. In this respect, asylum seekers can be subject to readmission procedures as third-country nationals. If there is

[95] In the *El Dridi* case, the Court ruled that national legislation imposing a prison sentence solely on the grounds of refusal to obey an order to leave the territory within the time limit given is contrary to the Return Directive. State authorities should, rather, pursue their efforts to enforce the removal decision, which continues to produce its effects. See *Hassen El Dridi, alias Karim Soufi*, Case C-61/11 PPU, ECLI:EU:C:2011:268, para 58.

[96] See generally, S Peers, T Harvey, J Kenner and A Ward, *The EU Charter of Fundamental Rights: A Commentary* (Hart Publishing, 2014). See also, 'Proposal for a Directive of the European Parliament and of the Council on common standards and procedures in Member States for returning illegally staying third-country nationals (recast)', Brussels.

[97] Return Directive, Art 9.

[98] For an overview of the Recast Procedures Directive, see European Council on Refugees and Exiles (ECRE), *Comments from the European Council on Refugees and Exiles on the Amended Commission Proposal to Recast the Asylum Procedures Directive*, COM(2011) 319 final, September 2011; ILPA, *Comments on the Revised Commission Proposal of 1 June 2011 on Common Procedures for Granting and Withdrawing International Protection status (Recast)* COM(2011) 319 final, 5 December 2011.

[99] Council Directive 2004/83/EC of 29 April 2004 on minimum standards for the qualification and status of third-country nationals as refugees or as persons who otherwise need international protection, OJ L 304/12, 30 September 2004 (Qualification Directive).

proof that a person has already been recognised as a refugee in a third country, she should be transferred to that country by means of a readmission agreement. A similar reasoning pertains to asylum seekers who have transited through, or resided in, a 'safe third country.' Indeed, Article 33(2)(c) of the Recast Procedures Directive overtly requires that Member States consider an application for asylum inadmissible if a country which is not a Member State is considered to be a 'safe third country' for the applicant.[100] Whereas a protection claimant is rejected on substantive grounds, an EU Member State may request readmission to the country of origin as its own national, or to any other State as a third country national.

A further issue giving cause for concern appertains to the potential violation of refugee rights as a consequence of accelerated procedures of expulsion laid down in the major part of readmission agreements, including those selected for the present analysis. For instance, the Italy–Albania readmission agreement provides that both third country nationals and individuals whose citizenship of one of the Contracting Parties is presumed may be immediately readmitted if apprehended while irregularly crossing the border of the requesting party.[101] While the end of the unauthorised presence of third-country nationals apprehended when they are already within the territory of the requesting State can be executed within eight days,[102] for nationals whose citizenship is presumed, the time limit is, instead, seven days.[103] In both circumstances, readmission will take place even in the absence of a formal reply to the readmission request.[104]

If it holds true that Member States can decide to not apply all the procedural safeguards of the Return Directive to people apprehended in the external border region,[105] it should also be noted that swift mechanisms of expulsion should not be utilised, at least in theory, in all those cases in which intercepted persons claim to be at risk of *refoulement*.[106] Additionally, Article 43 of the Recast Procedures Directive requires that Member States shall provide for procedures, in accordance with the basic principles and guarantees of Chapter II, in order to decide at the border or in transit zones on asylum applications made at such locations.[107] Such guarantees include the right to remain pending the examination of an asylum application *at first instance* (Article 9).[108]

[100] Ex Art 25(2)(c) of the 2005 Procedures Directive.

[101] See paras D(1) and B(2) of the Annexed Protocol to the Agreement between Italy and Albania for the Readmission of People at the Frontier, Tirana, 18 November 1997. In this case, third-country nationals need to have documents certifying their transit through the requested State.

[102] ibid, para D(2).

[103] ibid, para B(3).

[104] ibid, paras D(2) and B(3).

[105] Return Directive, Art 2(2)(a). The procedural safeguards accorded to third-country nationals subjected to a return decision are listed in Chapter III (Arts 12–14) of the Return Directive.

[106] See Art 4(4)(b) of the Return Directive.

[107] Ex Art 35 of the 2005 Procedures Directive.

[108] Ex Art 7 of the 2005 Procedures Directive. Furthermore, pursuant to Art 3(1) of the Recast Dublin Regulation, 'Member States shall examine any application for international protection by a

From the above-mentioned provisions, it appears that, in principle, asylum seekers cannot be removed to a third country until their asylum application has been examined, and an unfavourable decision handed down. Therefore, removal should not give rise to concerns as long as the safety of the readmitting country is individually established and the safeguards developed by the case law of the CJEU and national and EU legislation – *in primis* the Return Directive and the Recast Procedures Directive – are scrupulously and fairly observed.[109] However, whilst an expulsion decision can be pronounced or enforced only once the protection claim has been rejected at first instance, Member States have always shown a certain reluctance to accept as a general rule that appeals can have suspensive effect on the expulsion order (either automatic or upon request).[110] Within this procedural gap – which the Recast Procedures Directive has not been able to fill – EU Member States have a certain margin of manoeuvre in deciding whether to remove asylum seekers who have not completed the appeal phase of their protection claims.

Scholarship has traditionally labelled bilateral readmission agreements as detrimental to refugee rights. Notwithstanding this, in line with Coleman's arguments, one must conclude that no issue of incompatibility with refugee and human rights law seems to stem from their *technical content*. Readmission agreements constitute purely administrative tools serving the purpose of smoothing the final stage of the removal procedure for irregular migrants and rejected refugees. These bilateral instruments do not define criteria for the legality of a person's presence in an EU Member State. This assessment is made by national authorities in compliance with domestic administrative law and with full respect of the procedural safeguards enshrined in international and EU law. Moreover, international law offers technical tools to resolve conflicts of treaties and attribute precedence to human rights instruments.

Nevertheless, readmission agreements can also be used, in practice, to smooth the removal of asylum seekers whose claims will be examined elsewhere,

third-country national or a stateless person who applies on the territory of any one of them, including at the border or in the transit zones.'

[109] In a number of cases, the CJEU has tried to balance the protection of human rights with the effort to ensure speed and effective removal of irregular migrants. See, eg, CJEU cases *El Dridi*, above n 94; *Z Zh v Staatssecretaris van Veiligheid en Justitie* and *Staatssecretaris van Veiligheid en Justitie v I O*, Case C-554/13 [2015] ECLI:EU:C:2015: 377; *Bashir Mohamed Ali Mahdi*, C-146/14 PPU ECLI:EU:C:2014:1320. For a comprehensive analysis, see S Peers, 'Jump before you're pushed: The CJEU rules on the voluntary departure of irregular migrants' (11 June 2015), http://eulawanalysis.blogspot.com/2015/06/jump-before-youre-pushed-cjeu-rules-on.html; S Peers, 'Irregular Migrants: Can Humane Treatment be Balanced against Efficient Removal?' (2015) 17(4) *EJML* 289. On the Return Directive, see also, I Majcher, 'The EU Returns Directive and the Use of Prisons for Detaining Migrants in Europe' (21 July 2014),http://eulawanalysis.blogspot.com/2014/07/the-eu-returns-directive-and-use-of.html.

[110] See A Baldaccini, 'The Return and Removal of Irregular Migrants under EU Law: An Analysis of the Return Directive' (2009) 11(1) *EJML* 1, 12. See Chapter 2 of this book for further discussion on the right to an effective remedy.

and asylum seekers waiting for the outcome of their appeal against denial of their protection claims at first instance. As Section VII will show, once we shift from law to the implementation of law, the relationship between readmission agreements and refugee rights turns out to be not as coherent and consistent as previously imagined. It is this key point that underpins this book's arguments and unique perspective.

VI. CONFLICTS OF TREATIES AND NON-AFFECTION CLAUSES: READMISSION AGREEMENTS *VERSUS* INTERNATIONAL HUMAN RIGHTS TREATIES

Readmission agreements are designed to regulate the transfer of persons only between the two Contracting Parties. In studying the relationship between readmission agreements and international human rights treaties, it is to be emphasised that States cannot contract out of their pre-existing obligations under international refugee and human rights law by concluding a subsequent agreement on the readmission of irregular migrants. Pursuant to the principle of *pacta sunt servanda*, enshrined in Article 26 of the VCLT, States must respect their agreements. Since Article 34 of the VCLT provides that 'a treaty does not create either obligations or rights for a third State without its consent', changes to multilateral refugee law instruments cannot be created by a new treaty binding only a few States of the international community. Therefore, the obligations of States derived from all international refugee and European human rights instruments remain unaltered, even after the conclusion of a bilateral readmission agreement. Moreover, Article 41 of the VCLT provides that

> two or more of the parties to a multilateral treaty may conclude an agreement to modify the treaty as between themselves alone if the [modification in question] is not prohibited by the treaty and does not affect the enjoyment by the other parties of their rights under the treaty or the performance of their obligations.

A correlated question is whether conflicts may arise between a readmission agreement and other international conventions concerning refugee and human rights protection. This treaty relationship would actually not be problematic if both the national decision on the legal status of the asylum seekers and the order to return those with no title to stay in the EU territory were taken in full compliance with European and international law standards. Moreover, bilateral readmission arrangements sometimes contain a *non-affection* clause requiring the Contracting Parties to comply with rights and duties under other refugee and human rights conventions. It is thus unlikely that requesting States will encounter a situation where they would have to choose between contrasting obligations when implementing a bilateral readmission agreement. The rationale is that Contracting Parties do not intend to affect their previous obligations under international refugee law when they agree to mutually control irregular migration.

However, firstly, not all readmission agreements contain non-affection clauses requiring States to comply with international human rights treaties. Secondly, despite the existence of non-affection clauses, the implementation of bilateral agreements of migration control – as we will better observe later in this book – may enhance the risk of direct and indirect *refoulement* and thus lead to violations of refugee rights as a consequence of asylum seekers' transfer to third countries without examination of their protection claims. If 'the effective execution' of the original treaty cannot be guaranteed, and these *inter se* arrangements impair the performance of *erga omnes* protection obligations under, for instance, the Geneva Convention, Article 41 VCLT would be breached.

The proliferation of treaties inevitably insinuates the possibility of normative conflicts and doubts as to the agreement to be applied when the same State is party to two or more treaty regimes with divergent purposes. Despite there being no generally accepted definition of what constitutes a conflict between treaties, it could be argued that a conflict in the strict sense exists when a State is not able to simultaneously comply with all the requirements of two norms.[111] Beyond Article 30 VCLT – which, however, sets the order of precedence only of successive treaties on the same subject-matter, and cannot therefore address all the problems concerning the priority of a particular treaty – all other applicable maxims hardly seem to provide a response to the resolution of normative conflicts.

For instance, whilst a certain rule, such as *lex prior*, may focus on earlier treaties, another equally valid rule may take into account the evolving intent of the parties within a dynamic legal system by prioritising the most recent treaty (*lex posterior derogat legi priori*). This rule is usually applicable when the parties have not expressed any indication as to the way in which conflicts should be resolved. Recent discourses have focused on the *lex specialis* doctrine, whereby the more narrowly precise treaty governing a specific subject-matter overrides a treaty regulating more general issue-areas.[112] While, at times, some of these diverging principles may be used concurrently (when, for instance, the subsequent treaty is also the more specific one), in many other cases the unclear relationship among these canons implies an inevitable conflict and uncertainty about the rule to be favoured.[113]

Any reader would realise that no single rule among those above mentioned could be applied satisfactorily to situations involving various partners, and the

[111] SA Sadat-Akhavi, *Methods of Resolving Conflicts between Treaties* (Martinus Nijhoff Publishers, 2003) 5; CJ Borgen, 'Resolving Treaty Conflicts' (2005) 37 *The George Washington International Law Review* 573, 575.

[112] See eg, M Koskenniemi, 'Study in the Function and the Scope of the *Lex Specialis* Rule and the Question of 'Self-Contained' Regimes', UN Doc ILC(LVI)/SG/FIL/ CRD.1 and Add.1., 4 and 7 May 2004; A Lindroos, 'Addressing Norm Conflicts in a Fragmented Legal System: The Doctrines of *Lex Specialis*' (2005) 74 *Nordic Journal of International Law* 27.

[113] Lindroos 2005, n 112 above, 41.

VCLT is *de facto* incapable of resolving serious conflicts between treaties.[114] Some authors have thus endorsed the flexible 'principle of political decision' whereby it is up to the State concerned (in particular decision-makers) to make a political decision regarding which commitment it prefers.[115] Since State practice remains *de facto* ambiguous and 'no particular principle or rule can be regarded as of absolute validity',[116] non-affection clauses are an instructive legal technique for resolving potential conflicts between treaties.

By intervening at the drafting stage, the incorporation of saving (non-affection) clauses might be helpful for establishing either the priority of the treaty in question or the priority of another treaty.[117] These clauses should, however, be only used when a first attempt to reconcile concurrent norms has failed, thus obliging States to give precedence to one of the two conflicting provisions.[118]

In order to avoid a general scheme of substantive hierarchisation of treaties, saving clauses could be used to indicate that a certain current treaty is *in casu* hierarchically superior or inferior to a previous one.[119] By increasing coherence in the international legal system, such a solution would offer greater certainty that either a specific agreement will be honoured, or mechanisms of legal recourse can be put in motion in case of infringement.[120] Considering treaties as agreements setting forth norms of expected behaviour, non-affection clauses would swell predictability of outcomes as to which treaty would be applicable in case of conflict.[121]

In point of fact, readmission agreements are not consistent in the use of non-affection clauses. According to Coleman, these clauses are not imperative and have a purely declaratory value insofar as they cement the applicability of international obligations and in the extent to which such obligations already bind Contracting Parties.[122] In sum, they do not create obligations for the two involved States, and may be considered, at most, as an additional safeguard to avoid the application of readmission agreements after deciding to expel an asylum seeker in breach of international law.

However, when a *proviso* on the precedence of human rights treaties is formulated in a more detailed fashion, not only does it generate more stringent and definite obligations than those derived by customary international law; it also distinctly articulates how the agreement at hand can be enforced in

[114] J Klabbers, *Treaty Conflicts and the European Union* (Cambridge University Press, 2009) 88–90.

[115] See M Zuleeg, 'Vertragskonkurrenz im Völkerrecht. Teil I: Verträge zwischen souver änen Staaten' (1977) 20 *German Yearbook of International Law* 246 ff, as cited in Klabbers 2009, n 113 above, 88.

[116] W Jenks, 'The Conflict of Law-Making Treaties' (1953) 30 *British Yearbook of International Law* 407.

[117] H Blix and JH Emerson (eds), *The Treaty Makers' Handbook* (Oceana, 1973) 210–22.

[118] Sadat-Akhavi 2003, n 111 above, 87.

[119] Borgen 2005, n 111 above, 638, 644.

[120] ibid, 644.

[121] ibid, 647.

[122] Coleman 2009, n 5 above, 306.

accordance with earlier human rights treaties. It should be emphasised again here that not all readmission agreements contain non-affection clauses, and that human rights violations are factual regardless of the presence of detailed provisions. The readmission agreement between the UK and Albania contains a sophisticated articulation of human rights instruments. Indeed, Article 21 prescribes that:

> The provisions of this Agreement *shall* not affect the Contracting Parties' rights and duties under:
>
> (a) other international agreements on extradition, transfer of convicted persons, mutual legal assistance in criminal matters and readmission or transit conveyance in cases of removal of persons generally;
> (b) *the Convention Relating to the Status of Refugees*, done at Geneva on 28 July 1951 as amended by the Protocol done at New York on 31 January 1967;
> (c) *any international agreement on human rights*;
> (d) *international agreements on asylum*, in particular the Convention determining the State responsible for examining applications for asylum lodged in one of the Member States of the European Communities, done at Dublin on 15 June 1990;
> (e) any other international agreement (emphasis added).

The mandatory character of this provision – confirmed by the use of the word 'shall' – seems to indicate that respect for *all* rights and principles proclaimed in the Geneva Convention and its 1967 Protocol, as well as in any other international agreement on human rights and asylum, constitutes an underlying component of the agreement itself.[123] An interpretation whereby all the norms of the above-mentioned instruments are incorporated by reference is mostly significant insofar as we consider that not *all* of the norms of the Geneva Convention and relevant human rights treaties amount to customary international law. Therefore, non-affection clauses may create obligations that are more onerous than those deriving from general international law.

Given that the international legal system is a web of interrelated agreements that affect each other, thoughtful drafting of saving clauses is more likely to foresee and avoid potential conflicts among treaties.[124] Because of the risk of asylum seekers being affected by the application of a readmission agreement, it would be apposite to insert specific references to the duty of States to comply with international refugee and human rights treaties without altering the scope and objective of the bilateral accords, which are clearly aimed at expediting the removal of irregular migrants to countries of origin or transit.

[123] According to D'Acquisto and D'Avanzo, generally 'shall' denotes 'must'; a mandatory intent even if the latter is used above all to establish requirements or conditions.' See G D'Acquisto and S D'avanzo, 'The Role of SHALL and SHOULD in Two International Treaties' (2009) 3(1) *Critical Approaches to Discourse Analysis across Disciplines* 36.

[124] Borgen 2005, n 111 above, 637.

As a matter of public international law, it is also particularly important to decode the value of references to human rights and democracy in the Preamble of any bilateral readmission agreement, to gauge whether they constitute mere assumptions on which the accord is predicated or rather the real objectives of the treaty. This interpretative exercise is particularly salient with regard to those agreements not containing saving clauses. In this respect, the role of the Preamble can be misleading since it is often used as a location where Contracting Parties declare their common values, especially in agreements of a political character.

The text of bilateral readmission agreements generally contains preambular references to human rights, but seldom to specific international human rights instruments.[125] Rather than the genuine objectives of the treaty, the impression is that they constitute a statement of shared values to the effect that the parties attach importance to human rights and democratic principles. A slightly more accurate example, but still restricted in its scope, is the 1997 Agreement between Italy and Albania on the readmission of people at their borders. While in the Preamble, the Parties bear on the respect of international conventions on human rights protection and in particular on the rights of migrant workers, in Article 3(d), the Parties exclude from the personal scope of the Agreement both nationals of third countries who have been recognised as refugees under the 1951 Geneva Convention, as amended by the 1967 Protocol, and stateless people pursuant to the 1954 New York Convention.

It is crucial to highlight that EU Member States remain bound by international refugee and European human rights obligations whenever they expel a person to a third country. Therefore, expulsions executed by means of readmission agreements do not automatically entail an increased risk of *refoulement*, provided the removal decisions are taken in consonance with the whole gamut of safeguards enshrined in the Recast Procedures Directive, as well as the legally binding international human rights instruments ratified by the EU Member States as a whole. In this regard, non-affection clauses intervene to ensure greater legal certainty and confer precedence on human rights and refugee law treaties. However, 'there [is] … no sufficient guarantee that the authorities would treat asylum applicants differently than any other illegal aliens, or any explicit commitment by the requested State to examine an asylum claim of a readmitted individual.'[126]

Moreover, as the next Section will discuss, informal practices of border control can at any time be performed by State authorities, thus dismantling the spectrum of guarantees and rights owed to asylum seekers under bilateral and multilateral international treaties.

[125] See, eg, the Preamble of the readmission agreement between Italy and Algeria; and the Preamble (Recital 4) of the UK–Albania Readmission Agreement.

[126] A Hurwitz, *The Collective Responsibility of States to Protect Refugees* (OUP, 2009) 71.

VII. INFORMAL BORDER PRACTICES: WHEN REFUGEES BECOME INVISIBLE

The European Commission and the Member States have always framed the effective implementation of a readmission policy on the basis of successful removal rates.[127] However, some of the main challenges include the lack of transparency and accountability,[128] the difficulty in the identification of the individual to be readmitted, the informalisation of cooperation paths with third countries,[129] and their impact on the rights of asylum seekers. The partiality of statistical data on removal numbers, asylum seekers involved and the fate of third-country nationals during and after the expulsion procedure, as well as the lack of transparency in the implementation of readmission agreements, prevent a comprehensive understanding of the actual use of these bilateral arrangements.[130]

Readmission agreements *per se* cannot be expected to eliminate problems linked to the transfer of individuals. Much will depend on the goodwill of requested States to cooperate, supply documents, reply to the application request, and assist third-country nationals readmitted into their territory, including asylum seekers who should be channelled into procedures of assessment of their protection claims. Moreover, the possibility of informal border removal operations and diverging State practices creating tensions with protection obligations cannot be excluded in absolute terms. In this respect, Coleman's conclusion is that more quantitative and qualitative studies would be required in relation to informal border practices. Although such a dual-pronged analysis mapping in detail formal and informal readmission practices would be beyond the scope of this chapter, a host of examples stretching from East to the South can be illustrative of the risks run by refugees casually knocking at European doors.[131]

Practices of informal removal of asylum seekers without examination of protection claims (in particular from Slovakia and Poland to Ukraine) were

[127] Carrera 2016, n 12 above, 7–11.

[128] On accountability – defined as 'a dual relationship (operationalised through norms and procedures) between the public and a body – see T Corthaut, B Demeyere, N Hachez and J Wouters, 'Operationalizing the Accountability of Informal International Lawmaking', in P Joost, RA Wessel, and J Wouters (eds), *Informal International Lawmaking* (Oxford University Press, 2012) 312.

[129] For a critical view on informalisation of bilateral agreements on migration management, see C Favilli, 'Quali modalita` di conclusion delgi accordi internazionali in materia di immigrazione?' (2005) lxxxviii *Rivista di Diritto Internazionale* 156; F De Vittor, 'Responsabilità degli Stati e dell'Unione Europea nella conclusione e nell'esecuzione di "accordi" per il controllo extraterritoriale della migrazione, (2018) 2(1) *Diritti Umani e Diritto Internazionale* 5–27; and A Spagnolo, 'Di intese segrete e alibi parlamentari: tra la decisione del TAR sull'Accordo col Niger e il Global Compact sulle migrazioni', *SIDIBlog*, 5 December 2018, http://www.sidiblog.org/2018/12/05/di-intese-segrete-e-alibi-parlamentari-tra-la-decisione-del-tar-sullaccordo-col-niger-e-il-global-compact-sulle-migrazioni/.

[130] For a thorough analysis of the implementation challenges and dynamics of readmission agreements, in particular those concluded by the EU, see Carrera 2016, n 12 above, 37–52.

[131] Description of some of these cases can be found in Giuffré 2013, n 11 above.

mainly due to a deficiency of the domestic asylum system and of the procedural guarantees toward refugees, rather than to the existence of specific provisions within the bilateral agreement with Ukraine expressly authorising the readmission of asylum seekers.[132]

Cursory readmission procedures have been provided by both the 1998 Exchange of Notes between Italy and Tunisia on the entry and stay of nationals of the two countries, and their 2009 bilateral accord on the readmission of third-country nationals without a stay permit.[133] On 26 October 2010, Italy implemented its readmission agreement with Egypt by removing 68 migrants claiming to be Palestinian refugees. They were sent back on a charter flight to Cairo without being given the possibility of lodging an asylum application. An Egyptian consular official was even present at Catania's airport to identify her own nationals.[134] The text of the 2007 agreement between Italy and Egypt does not provide for accelerated procedures of identification and readmission.[135] Moreover, it contains a non-affection clause requiring the two involved States to comply with international human rights treaties and the Geneva Convention (Article 11(1)). Therefore, swift practices of identification and removal resulted from an informal implementation of the agreement itself within the framework of patterns of border control in dissonance with well-established rules of international and European law. For instance, in 2011, 3,592 individuals were repatriated to Tunisia and 965 to Egypt in the name of the efficiency required by the implementation of the readmission agreements between Italy and the two relevant North-African countries.[136] Although the Schengen Border Code (SBC) and the Return Directive require notification of expulsion decisions, the majority of migrants were not notified about the removal order or the location

[132] See generally, HRW, *Ukraine on the Margins: Background Migration Trends in Ukraine*, Research Paper, New York, 29 November 2005, http://www.hrw.org/en/node/11521/section/4.

[133] *Exchange of Notes between Italy and Tunisia on the Readmission of Persons in Irregular Position*, Rome, 4 August 1998; Readmission Agreement between Italy and Tunisia, 28 January 2009.

[134] See details on the case, in F Vassallo Paleologo, *Eritrei – Respinti dall'Italia, Espulsi dalla Libia, Sequestrati in Egitto*, Meltingpot, 6 December 2010, http://www.meltingpot.org/articolo16080.html.

[135] *Cooperation Agreement in the field of readmission between Italy and Egypt*, Rome, 9 January 2007. Under Art 2(2), the time limits incumbent upon the requested party to reply to a readmission request range from 7 days (when nationality is ascertained) to 21 days (when nationality is presumed).

[136] See Fortress Europe, *Espulsi 3,592 tunisini, nei Cie tornerà la calma?* (1 November 2011), http://fortresseurope.blogspot.com/2011/11/espulsi-3592-tunisini-nei-cie-tornera.html; See HRW, *Egypt: Don't Deport Eritreans*, 15 November 2011, http://www.hrw.org/news/2011/11/15/egypt-don-t-deport-eritreans; Y Maccanico, *The EU's Self-Interested Response to Unrest in North Africa: The Meaning of Treaties and Readmission Agreements between Italy and North African States*, Statewatch, January 2012, 6, http://www.statewatch.org/analyses/no-165-eu-north-africa.pdf. For an overview on the state of irregular migration in Italy, see E Fornalé, 'The European Returns Policy and the Re-Shaping of the National: Reflections on the Role of Domestic Courts' (2012) 31(4) *Refugee Survey Quarterly* 144–46. See also, A Triandafyllidou, 'Irregular Migration in Europe: Myths and realities (Routledge, 2016).

to which they were being sent. In addition, they were not given any chance to challenge the transfer decision and to suspend execution of the expulsion.

The agreement signed on 5 April 2011 between Italy and Tunisia contains provisions to accelerate the readmission of unwanted migrants without formalities after their identification by a consular official, or after a cursory reconstruction of nationality.[137] The existence of good relations between requesting and requested States – enshrined in the negotiation of such an informal and unpublished readmission agreement – was considered sufficient to expel people, regardless of the unstable social, political, and economic situations in their home countries. Readmission agreements have thus been invoked by representatives of the Ministry of the Interiors to solicit Italian judges to validate accelerated measures of removal/expulsion in the absence of the traditional set of safeguards offered by the domestic system.[138]

In 2011, masses of undocumented migrants and refugees, following the upheavals in North Africa, landed in Italy in disarray. A large number of these individuals, especially Tunisians, were denied access to Eurodac (the EU asylum fingerprint identification database) and to the informative mechanisms offered by UNHCR.[139] They were confined for a long time in either overcrowded detention centres or onboard ships,[140] subjected to summary identification procedures by their consular officials, or rapidly expelled to their countries of origin outside of any standards envisaged by the EU Asylum Directives, the Return Directive, or bilateral readmission agreements.[141]

Three Tunisian nationals – who remained on ships moored in the Palermo harbour for a few days – lodged a complaint before the ECtHR,[142] which was discussed in Chapter two of this work. At the hearing before the Court, the Italian Government affirmed that the aim of the bilateral agreement between Italy and Tunisia was to facilitate the removal of irregular migrants through simplified procedures (on the basis of the mere identification by the Tunisian consular authorities) and that it constituted a legal basis for the holding of the applicants on the island of Lampedusa pending their prompt removal.[143] The Grand Chamber acknowledged the Chamber's argument that the standardised nature of the refusal-of-entry orders were merely based on the applicants'

[137] M Tazzioli, 'Cronologia degli Accordi Italia-Tunisia' *Storie Migranti*, December 2011, http://www.storiemigranti.org/spip.php?article1004.

[138] See F Vassallo Paleologo, 'Accordi di riammissione e diritto di polizia' *Il Lavoro Culturale*, 3 February 2012, http://www.lavoroculturale.org/asylum-1-accordi-di-riammissione-e-diritto-di-polizia/.

[139] See, eg, UNHCR, IOM and Save the Children Italy Press Release, *Le Organizzazioni Umanitarie chiedono di incontrare i migranti egiziani e tunisini che sbarcano sulle coste italiane*, 30 April 2013.

[140] Nearly 600 Tunisians have been detained on board two ships in the harbour of Palermo and Porto Empedocle. See Migrants at Sea, *Italy Continues Shipboard Detention of Hundreds of Tunisians*, 28 September 2011, http://migrantsatsea.wordpress.com/2011/09/28/italy-continues-shipboard-detention-of-hundreds-of-tunisians/? See also, the *Khlaifia* case before the ECtHR. *Khlaifia and Others v Italy*, App no 16483/12 (15 December 2016).

[141] Statement by an UNHCR official (personal communication, 1 September 2011).

[142] *Khlaifia v Italy*, above n 140.

[143] ibid, para 83.

nationality, with no reference to the personal situations of the applicants, due to the bilateral agreement of April 2011 in force between Tunisia and Italy.[144] However, it overturned the Chamber's conclusion that these elements were sufficient to consider the expulsion collective in nature, as the applicants were subjected to two identification procedures, including one carried out by Tunisian consular authorities. This finding made it unnecessary for the Court to address the question whether the agreement of April 2011 could be considered a 'readmission' agreement.[145] It further noted that the fact that the agreement had not been made public deprived the migrants of the possibility to foresee the consequences of its application.[146]

At least from 2010, the UK has been keen to enforce removals to Zimbabwe.[147] However, in 2018, the British government announced its intention to repatriate some 2,500 undocumented Zimbabweans following an (unpublished) accord apparently reached on 13 February 2018 in Harare, between one of Zimbabwe's Vice Presidents and the British Ambassador to Zimbabwe.[148] As a consequence, several Zimbabwean embassy officials started interviewing nationals at Home Office centres across the UK, thus accelerating the removal process following former President Mugabe's ouster. For example, a Zimbabwean woman with an ongoing asylum claim was subject to a 're-documentation interview' by Zimbabwean officials to establish her identity, issue travel documentation, and speed her removal procedures.[149] This would not only breach the principle of confidentiality, but would also expose asylum seekers to risk for their life and liberty. Under Article 30 of the Recast Asylum Procedures Directive, during the process of examining a claim, no information can be disclosed by the Member State to alleged actor(s) of persecution, and no information can be obtained from the alleged actor(s) of persecution.[150]

Other informal practices of identification and readmission have taken place on the basis of interstate agreements. For instance, Italian authorities have brought Gambian nationals before Gambian liaison officers before they were potentially

[144] ibid, para 213.

[145] ibid, paras 254–255.

[146] ibid, para 102.

[147] 'Enforced returns to Zimbabwe will resume, https://www.gov.uk/government/news/enforced-returns-to-zimbabwe-will-resume (14 October 2010).

[148] *UK Immigration Justice Watch Blog*, 'Is Mnangagwa's New Government paving the way for UK mass removals of failed Zimbabwean Asylum Claimants?' (14 February 2018), https://ukimmigrationjusticewatch.com/2018/02/14/is-mnangagwas-new-government-paving-the-way-for-uk-mass-removals-of-failed-zimbabwean-asylum-claimants/#more-5824.

[149] Frances Perraudin, 'Home Office held "illegal interview" with asylum seeker' (20 March 2019), *The Guardian*, https://www.theguardian.com/uk-news/2019/feb/12/i-can-hardly-sleep-the-zimbabweans-facing-deportation-from-uk.

[150] *UK Immigration Justice Watch Blog*, 'Effect of the "repatriation agreement" between the Zimbabwean and UK authorities: Breach of claimant's confidentiality or careless exposure to risk?' (24 December 2018): https://ukimmigrationjusticewatch.com/2018/12/24/effect-of-the-repatriation-agreement-between-the-zimbabwean-and-uk-authorities-breach-of-claimants-confidentially-or-careless-exposure-to-risk/. On the principle of confidentiality, see also Chapter 4 of this book.

able to apply for asylum. This entails the implicit presumption that nationals of those States with which Italy has signed readmission agreements are not in need of international protection and are therefore removable to their countries of origin.[151] Lacking parliamentary approval, the agreements negotiated with Niger and Sudan are also particularly problematical for the fundamental rights of migrants. The Italian government has presented the accord with Niger,[152] which has not been published yet, as the legal basis for the Italian mission in Niger[153] – an operation intended to curb the influx of migrants to Italy.[154]

The Italy–Sudan agreement aims instead to establish a framework of cooperation to accelerate the procedures for removal of their own citizens.[155] Under Article 9 of this Memorandum, the competent Sudanese authorities shall proceed

> without delay to interview people who have been repatriated, in order to ascertain their nationality ... and on the basis of the interview's outcome, without undertaking any further checks as to their identity, they issue a laissez-passer [document] as quickly as possible, thus enabling the Italian authorities to organize the repatriation.[156]

Externalisation of identification procedures to accelerate removal to the country of origin is also the purpose of Article 14, which provides that in situations of 'necessity and urgency' – quite an indefinite concept – the procedures to establish the identity of the persons to be repatriated *may be undertaken in Sudanese territory*' (emphasis added). While it is unclear what guarantees readmitted people (especially asylum seekers) will have in Sudan, it should also be observed that the EU Return Directive requires that readmission follows the adoption of a removal decision on the basis of identification procedures carried

[151] An operative agreement (*Memorandum d'intesa fra il Dipartimento della pubblica sicurezza italiano e il Ministero dell'interno del Gambia sul rafforzamento della cooperazione nel settore della gestione delle frontiere dell'immigrazione e della sicurezza*) was signed between Italy and Gambia on 6 June 2015 to speed up repatriation procedures. See Y Maccanico, 'The Italian Roadmap: Hotspots, readmission, asylum procedures and the reopening of detention centres', *Statewatch* (2015), http://www.statewatch.org/news/2015/dec/no-279-Italian-Road-Map-2015.pdf; ECRE, 'EU migration cooperation with third countries: More harm than good?' (15 September 2017), https://www.ecre.org/eu-migration-cooperation-with-third-countries-more-harm-than-good.

[152] *Accordo di cooperazione in materia di difesa tra il Governo della Repubblica Italiana e il Governo della Repubblica del Niger*, Rome, 26 September 2017.

[153] Ministero della Difesa, *Missione Bilaterale di Supporto nella Repubblica del Niger (MISIN)*, September 2018, https://www.difesa.it/OperazioniMilitari/op_intern_corso/Niger_missione_bilaterale_supporto/Pagine/default.aspx.

[154] *Il Fatto Quotidiano*, 'Migranti, Trenta: "Via a missione militare in Niger: un successo del governo". Ma a gennaio M5S votò contro, Lega si astenne' (20 September 2018), https://www.ilfattoquotidiano.it/2018/09/20/migranti-trenta-via-a-missione-militare-in-niger-un-successo-del-governo-ma-a-gennaio-m5s-voto-contro-lega-si-astenne/4638422/.

[155] *Memorandum d'intesa tra il Dipartimento della pubblica sicurezza del Ministero dell'interno italiano e la Polizia nazionale del Ministero dell'interno sudanese per la lotta alla criminalità, gestione delle frontiere e dei flussi migratori ed in materia di rimpatrio*, 3 August 2016.

[156] Translation provided by Statewatch. For the Italian text, see http://www.asgi.it/wp-content/uploads/2016/10/accordo-polizia-Italia-Sudan_rev.pdf.

out within the European territory.[157] On 24 August 2016, a group of Sudanese nationals, swiftly repatriated on the basis of these simplified readmission procedures without having the possibility to claim international protection, lodged a complaint before the ECtHR for violation of Article 4 of Protocol 4, and Article 3, Articles 13 and Article 14 of the ECHR (discrimination on the ground of their national origin).[158]

States are required to execute accelerated procedures in accordance with international and European human rights law, as well as refugee law. Otherwise, there exists a deficiency in the domestic system of admission and readmission; and this constitutes the starting point for any possible reform initiatives. Readmission agreements are not *per se* the cause of informal border practices, but they can be executed in a context of structural protection deficiency. The existence of a readmission agreement may therefore amplify the presumption of the requesting State that it will obtain the full cooperation of the requested country. Having established positive relations in many other areas related to readmission, the latter will be considered a reliable 'safe third country', regardless of the status of the removed person. This becomes particularly glaring when a self-proclaimed state of emergency 'imposes' agile, rapid, and informal removal practices in the face of mass arrivals of displaced people. Consequences for asylum seekers are predictable.

It should also be noted that readmission agreements generally establish that their implementation shall not affect the contracting parties' duties under other readmission or transit conveyance accords on the removal of persons.[159] Such a clause implies the risk of Contracting Parties not being obliged to apply the standard readmission treaty. They can use further formal or informal cooperation arrangements to expel unauthorised migrants and asylum seekers, such as MoUs, Exchange of Letters, as well as *ad hoc* Exchanges of Notes between diplomatic or consular authorities. These instruments do not generally contain the same safeguards as readmission agreements, and are also not subjected to public scrutiny and monitoring.[160]

[157] For comments on the text of the Italy–Sudan MoU, see Associazione per gli Studi Giuridici sull'Immigrazione (ASGI), *MOU between the Italian public security department and the Sudanese national police. A reading guide* (2016), http://www.statewatch.org/news/2016/nov/asgi-italy-sudan-mou.pdf. See also, the Report by the Human Rights and Migration Law Clinic of Turin, *MoU between Italy and Sudan: A legal analysis* (2017), https://www.asgi.it/wp-content/uploads/2017/10/Report-Memorandum-of-Understanding-Sudan-Italy-SL-Clinic-UniTO.pdf.

[158] *WA and Others v Italy*, App no 18787/17, Communicated to the Italian government on 24 November 2017 (pending).

[159] See eg, Art 21 of the Agreement between the UK and Albania on the Readmission of Persons, Tirana, 14 October 2003; Art 21 of the Agreement between the UK and Bulgaria on the readmission of Persons, Sofia, 21 February 2003; Art 11 of the Agreement between Italy and Albania on the readmission of people at the frontier, Tirana, 18 November 1997.

[160] For a critique on the use of informal arrangements to readmit undocumented migrants, see P Garcia Andrade, 'La Dimension Externe de la Politique Migratoire de l'UE: un Bilan au travers de ses Instruments' in M Dony (ed), *La Dimension Externe de l'Espace de Liberté, de Sécurité et de Justice au Lendemain de Lisbonne et de Stockholm: un Bilan à Mi-parcours* (Éditions de l'Université de Bruxelles, 2012).

A. Readmission of Asylum Seekers: The EU's Trend Toward Informalisation

As a response to the 2015–16 migratory flows, the EU and Member States have accelerated the negotiation of questionable readmission agreements and enhanced informal paths of cooperation with third countries, including refugee-producing States such as Mali, Afghanistan, Nigeria, Senegal, and Ethiopia.[161] As readmission agreements lack popularity among nationals of the third countries and migrants abroad, incentives, financial support and 'development' aid have been offered in exchange for accepting removals from Europe.[162] While not renouncing to the negotiation of formal readmission agreements,[163] the above-mentioned incentives are used to further enhance existing cooperation with a given country. Adopting bilateral arrangements on the management and readmission of migrants without following the procedures required by Article 218 TFEU – which include the democratic scrutiny of the European Parliament – enhances legal (un)certainty on the terms of the accords and impedes a proper democratic accountability and judicial oversight, thus heightening the risk of violations for apprehended migrants and refugees. As explained by Carrera, the informalisation of readmission procedures relies on a 'soft spot' approach (ie, finding the authority or actor in the third country who might be willing to cooperate) and avoids rule of law constraints, public debate and democratic scrutiny. Moreover, such a process of informalisation takes place also with regards to interstate readmission agreements.

Pauwelyn, Wouters, and Wessel argue that 'informality' might also have positive effects when the legitimacy of norms derives from 'thick stakeholder consensus' (resulting from the participation of governmental and non-governmental actors), replacing 'thin State consent', which is the traditional basis for international agreements.[164] In their view, even a non-binding instrument and informal patterns of cooperation can produce legal effects on the basis of the expectations parties may have in good faith. However, it is also true that presenting these arrangements as non-legal documents enhances legal uncertainty because of the lack of sufficient procedural guarantees designing interstate challenges. There is also a risk of individuals being deprived of the

[161] See Fourth Progress Report on the Partnership Framework with third countries under the European Agenda on Migration (13 June 2017) COM(2017) 350 final: https://eeas.europa.eu/sites/eeas/files/4th_progress_report_partnership_framework_with_third_countries_under_european_agenda_on_migration.pdf.

[162] See Davitti and La Chimia 2017, n 37 above.

[163] See, eg, the opening of negotiations for an EU Readmission agreement with both Tunisia (the Commission received the mandate in December 2014 and it entered into force on 12 October 2016) and Nigeria (the Commission received mandate in September 2016 and it entered into force on 26 October 2016).

[164] J Pauwelyn, R Wessel and J Wouters 'Informal International Lawmaking: An Assessment and Template to Keep It Both Effective and Accountable' in J Pauwelyn, R Wessel and J Wouters (eds), *Informal International Lawmaking* (OUP, 2012) 500.

possibility to enforce their rights before national and international/supranational courts.[165] Moreover, informalisation at the EU level also risks frustrating the coordination with the readmission agreements concluded by Member States at the bilateral level, as prevalence of EU readmission agreements over those negotiated by Member States, in case of incompatibilities, applies only with legally binding instruments.[166] The 2016 Council Conclusions on expulsion state that these legally non-binding arrangements can create the conditions for negotiating future formal readmission agreements. However, what their added value is in comparison to formal readmission agreements and how they can be compatible with each other is not clear.[167]

This plethora of informal non-binding EU working arrangements on readmission can be read in the context of the Action Plan agreed in November 2015 at the EU Valletta Summit, where the EU emphasised the priority to 'develop practical cooperation arrangements and bilateral dialogues on implementation of returns …'.[168] One of the first outcomes was the negotiation of the Joint Declaration on Ghana–EU Cooperation on Migration of 16 April 2016, which aimed to expand the speed and efficiency of removal procedures and the organisation of pilot identification missions in EU Member States.[169] The Council Conclusions 'on the expulsion of illegally staying third-country nationals', adopted in May 2016, underlines that these informal readmission agreements should pertain in particular to own nationals.[170] Moreover, Council Conclusions on 'External Aspects of migration' identify Pakistan, Bangladesh and Afghanistan as key countries of origin and transit with which cooperation on removal/readmission should be enhanced.[171]

A further emblematic example of informalisation of agreements linked to readmission is offered by the EU–Turkey deal, which took the form of a press 'statement' published on the website of the European Council on

[165] Carrera 2016, n 12 above, 47; R Wessel, Draft paper, '"Soft" International Agreements in EU External Relations', presented at the ECPR SGEU Conference, *Hard and Soft Law in the European Union* (Paris 13–15 June 2018) 21.

[166] A clause indicating the prevalence of EU readmission agreements in case of incompatibilities is included in all accords concluded by the EU, with the exception of those with Russia and Albania. See also, 2184th Council meeting Justice and Home Affairs, Doc 8654/99, Brussels, 27–28 May 1999, p 6. For an analysis of the interplay between EU and interstate readmission agreements, see F Casolari, 'L'interazione tra accordi internazionali dell'Unione europea ed accordi conclusi dagli Stati membri con Stati terzi per il contrasto dell'immigrazione e irregolare' (2018/1) *Diritto, Immigrazione e Cittadinanza* 1, 9–16, 27.

[167] See Carrera 2016, n 12 above, 47.

[168] See para 9 of the Valletta Summit Political Declaration, 11–12 November 2015, http://eeas.europa.eu/statements-eeas/2016/160416_04_en.htm.

[169] ibid, para 11.

[170] Council of the EU Conclusions on the expulsion of illegally staying third-country nationals. 8828/16, Brussels, 11 May 2016.

[171] Council of the EU Conclusions on the external aspects of migration. 9111/16, Brussels, 23 May 2016, para 8.

18 March 2016.[172] In March 2017, the General Court of the CJEU affirmed that it lacks jurisdiction to hear and determine the actions of annulment brought by three asylum seekers against the EU–Turkey deal.[173] In its Order, the General Court considered that this press release, with which the EU had communicated the new agreement, should be attributed only to the Heads of State or Government of the Member States of the EU, who met with the Turkish Prime Minister, and not to the European Council itself. In the absence of an act of a European institution, the Court considered it lacked competence to adjudicate on the case. On 12 September 2018, the Court of Justice (First Chamber) dismissed the appeal as manifestly inadmissible. It thus confirmed the General Court's main finding, according to which the EU–Turkey Statement does not relate to an act of the European Council nor of any other body, office or agency of the Union, and as a consequence, the actions fall outside the jurisdiction of the Court of Justice.[174]

In accordance with Article 218 TFEU, an international agreement in an area covered by the ordinary legislative procedure (and migration is such an area), the Council (not the European Council) shall adopt a decision on the negotiation of the agreement following recommendations by the Commission and shall then conclude the agreement after receiving the consent of the European Parliament. On the contrary, the EU–Turkey deal – like a number of other informal agreements linked to readmission – has seen only the involvement of the European Council, which is not part of the procedure set by Article 218 TFEU.

The EU–Turkey Statement raises at least two other responsibility-related questions. First, were Member States in a position to commit the EU to accession negotiations, visa facilitation, EU funds, readmission and resettlement if they were acting in their autonomous international law capacity? Secondly, who would be responsible for human rights breaches against migrants and asylum seekers trapped in this shared containment web between Turkey and the EU, which includes also readmission?

The questionable link between readmission and access to protection is exemplified in the approach proposed by the Council of the European Union in a Discussion Paper on Commission Communication 'Towards a reform of the Common European Asylum System and enhancing legal avenues to Europe'.[175]

[172] EU–Turkey Statement, 18 March 2016, at: http://www.consilium.europa.eu/en/press/press-releases/2016/03/18-eu-turkey-statement/. For an analysis of the Statement, see C Favilli, 'La cooperazione UE-Turchia per contenere il flusso dei migranti e richiedenti asilo: obiettivo riuscito?' in (2016) 10 *Diritti Umani e Diritto Internazionale* 405 ff; F Roman, 'L'accordo di cooperazione in ambito migratorio tra Unione Europea (UE) e Turchia' *SIDIBlog*, 21 March 2016, http://www.sidiblog.org/2016/03/21/laccordo-ue-turchia-le-criticita-di-un-accordo-a-tutti-i-costi/.

[173] *NF, NG and NM v European Council*, Joined Cases T-192/16, T-193/16 and T-257/16 ECLI:EU:T:2017:128.

[174] *NF, NG and NM v European Council*, Joined Cases C-208/17, C-209/17 and C-210/17 ECLI:EU:C:2018:705.

[175] Discussion paper on Commission Communication 'Towards a reform of the Common European Asylum System and enhancing legal avenues to Europe', Brussels, 12 April 2016 (OR. en) 7861/16.

While there is a proposal on opening additional legal avenues for people in need of international protection by creating an EU policy on resettlement, and increasing other legal entry options, such as private sponsorship, it is also explicitly stated that 'reinforced cooperation with key countries of origin on *readmission and return* is considered by the Commission as a *necessary complement to enhancing legal avenues*' (emphasis added).[176]

As discussed above, on 18 March 2016, Turkey and EU Heads of State or Government agreed on a set of principles providing the framework for cooperation in managing the refugee and migrant flows to Europe and Turkey. The joint Statement provides for a mechanism of systematic and 'rapid return of all migrants not in need of international protection crossing from Turkey to Greece and to take back all irregular migrants intercepted in Turkish waters.'

Migrants arriving in Greece are duly registered and their asylum applications processed in accordance with the Recast Procedures Directive. Those people whose applications have been declared unfounded or inadmissible are transferred to Turkey. Moreover, the bilateral agreement provides that for every Syrian being readmitted to Turkey from Greece, another Syrian will be resettled from Turkey to the EU, prioritising those migrants who have not previously entered or tried to enter the EU irregularly. Turkey is also committed to taking any necessary measures to prevent new irregular arrivals on Greek islands and cooperating with the EU to this end. In turn, EU Member States will accelerate the fulfilment of the visa liberalisation roadmap with a view to lifting the visa requirements for Turkish citizens and speeding up the disbursement of €3 billion to Turkey under the Facility for Refugees.

Readmission to Turkey and resettlement to the EU are two elements of the cooperation between Turkey and the EU, which has so far been based on the 2001 readmission agreement with Greece and the readmission agreement with the EU, which entered into force on 1 June 2016. Despite the fact that the EU–Turkey Statement explicitly refers to *non-refoulement* and the prohibition of collective expulsions, there is a high risk that speedy implementation of such readmission policy violates the rights of deportees. The agreement lacks, for example, any reference to the specific vulnerabilities of people landing on the Greek islands. Moreover, punishing a migrant who has illegally entered a European State to seek asylum and rewarding another Syrian who did not make such a perilous attempt would clearly be at odds with Article 31 of the 1951 Convention.[177]

As stated by Gil-Bazo, 'the practice of informal agreements raises particular issues in so far as it denies access to an asylum procedure in any of the countries

[176] ibid.

[177] Under Art 31 of the Refugee Convention: 'The Contracting States shall not impose penalties, on account of their illegal entry or presence, on refugees who, coming directly from a territory where their life or freedom was threatened in the sense of Art 1, enter or are present in their territory without authorisation, provided they present themselves without delay to the authorities and show good cause for their illegal entry or presence.'

involved and may result in refoulement.'[178] Considering the systemic deficiencies of the asylum system in Greece, including access to the procedure and adequate reception facilities,[179] the readmission policy between Greece and Turkey is an example of the devastating impacts that cooperation between a European State and a third country can have on access to protection. Indeed, under Article 33(2)(c) of the Recast Procedures Directive, an asylum application can be declared inadmissible if a third country is considered to be safe for the applicant. As readmission to Turkey is founded on the presumption of safety of this country, the risk exists that an asylum seeker is removed without prior individualised consideration of her protection claim on the ground that a safe third country will take such a responsibility. However, Turkey – which hosts the largest number of refugees worldwide – is not bound to treat asylum seekers in accordance with the Geneva Convention and does not comply with the safety criteria set out in Article 38 of the Recast Procedures Directive.[180] Since mid-January 2016, Turkish authorities have expelled hundreds of Syrian men, women, and children to Syria.[181] The presumption of safety of Turkey, cemented by the readmission arrangement with the EU, has also increased the number of documented push-backs of refugees to Turkey by Bulgarian and Greek police forces.[182] And as a 'deportation agency' hired by the EU, Turkey has removed people back to their countries of origin, such as Afghanistan and Yemen, where they would face extreme life-threatening dangers.[183]

As reported by several NGOs and International Organisations, Turkey has a dismal human rights track record, and migrants and asylum seekers are generally left with no legal representation and inadequate living resources.[184] In a number of cases, the ECtHR has also found Turkey responsible for inhuman and degrading treatment of migrants and detainees.[185] Over the first 30 days after the entry into force of the EU–Turkey readmission/resettlement scheme, migrant flows across the Aegean fell by about 80 per cent.[186]

[178] MT Gil-Bazo, The Safe Third Country Concept in International Agreements on Refugee Protection Assessing State Practice' (2015) 33(1) *Netherlands Quarterly of Human Rights* 42, 76.

[179] Systemic deficiencies have been recorded by the ECtHR in *MSS v Belgium and Greece* (above n 93) but also by the CJEU in *NS and ME*, Joined Cases C-411/10 and C-493/10, [2011] ECR I-13095.

[180] Those coming from non-European countries can indeed only obtain a status of 'conditional refugees', which is granted on a temporary basis under the Turkish Law on Foreigners and International Protection, which came into effect in 2014.

[181] See Amnesty International (AI), 'Turkey: Illegal mass returns of Syrian refugees expose fatal flaws in EU-Turkey deal' (1 April 2016), https://www.amnesty.org/en/press-releases/2016/04/turkey-illegal-mass-returns-of-syrian-refugees-expose-fatal-flaws-in-eu-turkey-deal/ (Amnesty International 2016); *Human Rights Watch* (*HRW*), 'Border Guards kill and injure asylum seekers' (10 May 2016), https://www.hrw.org/news/2016/05/10/turkey-border-guards-kill-and-injure-asylum-seekers.

[182] ibid.

[183] ibid.

[184] See Amnesty International 2016, n 180 above; Amnesty International, 'Turkey 2017/2018' (2018), https://www.amnesty.org/en/countries/europe-and-central-asia/turkey/report-turkey/.

[185] See, eg *Abdolkhani and Karimnia v Turkey*, App no 30471/08 (22 September 2009); and *SA v Turkey*, App no 74535/10 (15 December 2015).

[186] *Financial Times*, 'Turkey to boost legal protection for migrants, easing EU returns' (25 April 2016), https://www.ft.com/content/b60b3afe-0af9-11e6-b0f1-61f222853ff3. See also, European

By linking readmission of irregular migrants with resettlement, such a 'one to one' programme – which might be used also as a model for other States – is meant to create an incentive to a third country to readmit the highest number of migrants in order to enhance the resettlement commitment of the EU. If we then consider that Turkey has restricted entry visa requirements and has negotiated readmission agreements with several countries of origin – as indicated in the EU–Turkey Action Plan – it can be assumed that the EU is increasingly delegating to Turkey the policy of containment of migration flow, despite the risk of chain *refoulement* of people in need of protection.[187]

VIII. 'CARROTS' AND 'STICKS': PROTECTING HUMAN RIGHTS THROUGH READMISSION AGREEMENTS?

Whilst Section VI outlined non-affection clauses as a proper and elegant legal technique to reduce treaty conflicts, conferring primacy upon international human rights and refugee law instruments, Section VII has dragged us back to the reality of informal practices of border control where refugees become even more invisible, and even more vulnerable. It remains to be asked whether there is a need to create, beyond non-affection clauses, more precise procedural human rights clauses within the text of readmission agreements.

The incorporation of non-affection clauses and procedural human rights safeguards within existing or future readmission agreements would impose upon sending States the duty to fully and rigorously determine whether asylum seekers can be safely involved in the readmission process, and to ascertain, through a monitoring mechanism, whether the readmitting State in fact complies with agreed standards of refugee protection.

At this point, however, the reader would ask: first, why should requesting and requested States tie their hands by agreeing to more stringent procedural human rights clauses, requiring monitoring and compliance with refugee law standards? Second, what incentives might requesting States have in seeking the termination or suspension of a readmission agreement as a consequence of human rights violations? These questions hint at the political costs of a drafting process aimed at supplementing the content of readmission agreements with procedural human rights clauses. Regrettably, the answers given will be nothing but the outcome of a – sometimes unbalanced – trade-off where no 'right' solution can be smoothly offered, and which would serve to accommodate the diverging interests of two different and competing actors.

Commission, 'Implementing the EU-Turkey Agreement – Questions and Answers', http://europa.eu/rapid/press-release_MEMO-16-1494_en.htm.

[187] See ECRE, 'Time to Save the Right to Asylum – ECRE Memorandum to the European Council Meeting 17–18 March 2016' (March 2016), https://www.ecre.org/time-to-save-the-right-to-asylum-ecre-memorandum-to-the-european-council-meeting-17-18-march-2016/.

A. Requested States

Readmission amounts to a bilateral cooperation based on asymmetric costs and benefits where requesting and requested States clearly share different interests. Despite the fact that readmission agreements are in principle framed on grounds of reciprocity, they are *de facto* founded on *unbalanced reciprocities* mostly biased in favour of the sending States' interests.[188] It means that their mutual obligations cannot equally apply to both parties. Indeed, the implementation of these arrangements often has a different impact for the populations, the economy, the structural institutional and legal capacity of the two involved countries, in terms of enforcement of readmission decisions, reception of migrants, and compliance with human rights and refugee law, as required by non-affection clauses. To compensate for the unbalanced reciprocities underlying the cooperation on readmission and removal, the conclusion of readmission agreements is always motivated by expected benefits that are differently perceived by the two parties.[189] However, while incentives can be used to foster third countries' cooperation on readmission, they do not ensure sustainability of this cooperation in the long term. This is due to the 'asymmetrical impact of the effective implementation of the agreements', and the differing interests of the requesting and requested States in readmitting nationals and third-country nationals.

Far from being an end in itself, readmission agreements are generally used to enhance cooperation in other strategic areas, such as labour quotas, development aid, special trade concessions, visa facilitations or the lifting of visa requirements, financial assistance, police cooperation, border security, or the construction of reception capacity in readmitting countries that generally lack the administrative and legal background as well as the infrastructure to receive immigrants and assess protection claims.[190] For instance, the 2007 Italy–Egypt readmission agreement was accompanied by a bilateral debt-swap accord that was highly beneficial for Egypt, as well as by trade concessions and temporary entry quotas for Egyptian nationals into Italy. France also conditioned the implementation of the 2005 agreements on development, science, and environment upon the acceptance by Pakistan of a readmission agreement.[191]

A typical model of cooperation in readmission is that of Albania, which became in turn a recipient of Italian development aid and technical and military assistance. Italy and Albania signed on the same day (18 November 1997) a

[188] JP Cassarino, 'Dealing with Unbalanced Reciprocities: Cooperation on Readmission and Implications' in JP Cassarino (ed), *Unbalanced Reciprocities: Cooperation on Readmission in the Euro-Mediterranean Area* (Middle East Institute, 2010) (Cassarino 2010a), 4.

[189] ibid, 5.

[190] Coleman 2009, n 5 above, 68. In this regard, the Council of Europe suggests that transit countries should be assisted in organising access to fair asylum procedures. Parliamentary Assembly CoE, para 67.

[191] See Parliamentary Assembly CoE Report, para 81.

readmission agreement and a labour accord setting planned quotas for Albanian workers. Likewise, the 2006 readmission agreement between the UK and Algeria was signed in the context of tight negotiations, including such strategic issues as police cooperation, energy, and technical assistance in the war on terrorism.[192]

Migration salience, *geographic proximity*, and *incentives* have been emphasised as the three factors influencing the conclusion of standard readmission agreements.[193] However, the European Agenda on Migration (2015) makes clear that the EU Commission will revise its approach to readmission agreements, 'prioritising the main countries of origin of irregular migrants'.[194] This consideration compounds the above question on why should requested States accept binding themselves with non-affection clauses and more stringent procedural human rights clauses while performing readmission. In this respect, it could be argued that third countries tend to cooperate more efficiently when compensated. Therefore, the arsenal of expected benefits so far utilised to conclude readmission agreements might once again constitute the most powerful political and economic 'weapons' EU Member States have at their disposal to persuade third countries to accept the costs of readmission in compliance with human rights and refugee law standards.

B. Requesting States

After examining the *do ut des* component of readmission agreements from the readmitting country standpoint, another general question arises: what motivation might the requesting State have in endorsing the political and financial costs of more 'individual-centred' and 'human rights-oriented' treaties delineating extra reciprocal obligations for the States involved?

It should first be emphasised how the insistence on both wide-ranging priority clauses and procedural human rights clauses can prevent (or postpone) the conclusion of further agreements with countries that possess a dismal record on human rights and democracy. In this sense, they could have an 'anticipatory' effect by pushing the third country to respect human rights and observe certain procedural safeguards toward asylum seekers before ratification is deposited. Indeed, it has been argued how 'it is much easier to use the pending ratification of a treaty as a means of persuasion than to rely on the human rights clause after ratification …'.[195]

Despite acknowledging the understandable reluctance of a requesting State to accept the burden of a drafting process that would impose additional legal

[192] Cassarino 2010a, n 188 above, 6–7. See also, Coleman 2009, n 5 above, 62–63.
[193] Cassarino 2010a, n 188 above, 15.
[194] European Agenda on Migration 2015, p 10.
[195] E Riedel and M Will, 'Human Rights Clauses in External Agreements' in P Alston (ed), *The EU and Human Rights* (OUP, 1999) 741.

ties, human rights clauses and non-affection provisions permit governments and border authorities to be confronted with 'in law' well-defined obligations, mostly when transfer decisions are taken at the border and in transit zones. As signatories of refugee and human rights law conventions, requesting States should have an obvious interest in taking all necessary measures to avoid asylum seekers being excluded from accelerated removal procedures, and, if it happens, to ensure that fundamental rights are not infringed as a consequence of a misguided removal to an unsafe third country of transit. Beyond the crucial legal ground, the political costs the sending State could incur in case of *refoulement* to a place where the asylum seeker does not have access to a fair assessment of her protection claim (thus running the risk, for example, of being repatriated) would undoubtedly be higher than the costs deriving from monitoring the readmitting State.

In this regard, Article 10(3)(b) of the Recast Procedures Directive also requires that EU Member States ensure that determining authorities examining asylum applications have access to

> [p]recise and up-to-date information ... obtained from various sources, such as EASO and UNHCR and relevant international human rights organisations, as to the general situation prevailing in the countries of origin of applicants and, where necessary, in countries through which they have transited, and that such information is made available to the personnel responsible for examining applications and taking decisions.[196]

Thus, providing for a monitoring mechanism within the framework of a readmission agreement would give substance and contextual specificity to one of the rules of the Recast Procedures Directive, thereby confirming how the supervision of the viability of safe havens in third countries would have an overall beneficial impact on 'safe third country' policies. The cooperation of third countries is a pre-condition for the effective implementation of 'safe third country' exceptions, and readmission agreements are key tools to implicitly obtain such cooperation, despite that they do not usually mention asylum seekers and refugees in their text.[197]

From a mere State-sovereignty and migration-control perspective, the ability of a government to show that its removal policy is implemented effectively could bring about a lowering in the number of irregular arrivals. Indeed, a smooth transfer of unauthorised migrants and asylum seekers to 'safe third countries' might send the dissuasive signal to third-country nationals that obtaining permanent residence or access to asylum procedures in an EU Member State may not be that easy. At the same time, it is noteworthy that restrictive measures

[196] Compared with Art 8(2)(b) of the 2005 Procedures Directive, Art 10(3)(b) of the Recast Procedures Directive only adds a reference to information obtained from the European Asylum Support Office.

[197] Coleman 2009, n 5 above, 67.

of border control and pre-arrival interceptions have so far hardly deterred people from migrating and fleeing their countries, even at the cost of their own lives.

It should additionally be considered that making non-affection clauses and procedural human rights clauses essential elements of a readmission agreement would also be in line with Article 60(1) of the VCLT, which provides that 'a material breach of a bilateral treaty by one of the parties entitles the other to invoke the breach as a ground for terminating the treaty or suspending its operation in whole or in part.' However, it remains to be asked what interest EU Member States – which generally play the role of sending countries – may have in agreeing to suspend or terminate a treaty whose purpose is to alleviate migration pressure in their territories.

On the one hand, it can be contended that a suspension clause would turn out to be beneficial for the requested State, well aware that maintaining a situation of human rights violations in its own territory would lighten the readmission burden. On the other hand, suspending or terminating a readmission agreement *de jure* or *de facto* would strengthen the international image of the requesting State as a credible and reliable actor in the protection of human rights. It would, moreover, be the most workable alternative to obviating the damage sustained upon both removed individuals and sending State if an unsafe removal takes place, especially when the human rights situation in the readmitting country precipitously deteriorates. In these circumstances, not only would States discredit their international standing, but they would also run the risk of incurring international responsibility for the commission of an international wrongful act on grounds of *refoulement*.

To sum up, a handful of answers can be offered to address the question why States should accept the burden of drafting potential new readmission agreements. *In primis*, in an era of treaty congestion, the insertion of non-affection provisions stands as a potential bulwark against treaty conflict, and has a flywheel effect in increasing legal certainty for both governments involved in the removal process. Moreover, by making a clear manifesto of their human rights commitments within the text of readmission agreements, Contracting Parties would reinforce their image as credible players in the human rights arena, seriously committed to abiding by international obligations toward removed migrants and asylum seekers.

IX. LOOKING AHEAD: AIMS AND FUNCTIONS OF PROPOSED PROCEDURAL HUMAN RIGHTS CLAUSES IN READMISSION AGREEMENTS

The following questions are examined in this Section: beyond non-affection clauses, is there a need to create more precise procedural human rights clauses within the text of readmission agreements? Or would this constitute a superfluous reiteration by virtue of the fact that European States have already agreed to be bound by human rights law? Would these *provisions* impose obligations upon States beyond those already binding them under customary and treaty law?

The system of protection of refugee rights within the text of bilateral readmission agreements is quite rudimentary. This is essentially due to the fact that they do not decide upon the legal status of migrants and asylum seekers, and do not authorise the transfer decision. However, some of these instruments, such as the readmission agreement between the UK and Albania, contain a non-affection clause committing the parties to respect the rights of migrants in accordance with international refugee and human rights treaties.

The existence of preambular references to human rights in the text of readmission agreements is not always sufficient to reduce the risk of grave violations. Moreover, these general principles do not form part of the operative components of bilateral treaties that are essential for the achievement of the purpose and object of the agreement.[198] Generic mention of human rights generates only programmatic principles rather than specific obligations that could be invoked as conditions for the implementation of the treaty and for justifying its suspension in case of material breaches of the treaty itself. The author's concern here does not extend to those cases where a readmission request follows an expulsion decision regularly issued by a judicial or administrative authority, or those cases where border authorities remove a person with no grounds for staying in the territory of the requesting State after ascertaining that no claim for asylum has been expressed and no risk of *refoulement* exists. Rather, uneasiness attaches to readmission agreements in two particular circumstances: first, when asylum seekers are apprehended while attempting to irregularly cross the border, in transit zones, and in situations of emergency with massive arrivals of mixed influxes and lack of adequate monitoring by NGOs, international organisations, lawyers, and media; secondly, when access to asylum procedures is denied to those asylum seekers who have transited through a 'safe third country' before soliciting protection within the borders of an EU Member State. No guarantee exists, indeed, in the text of readmission agreements that the protection claims of the removed asylum seekers will be ensured in the readmitting country.

There is no doubt that major efforts are being made to restore the structural deficiencies of the asylum and migration management systems of EU Member States. In particular, refugees should always be allowed to claim asylum and have their application examined in the country of arrival within the EU. However, whereas the protection net does have some holes in practice, and refugees risk being subjected to removal procedures without due guarantees, specific *procedural human rights clauses* – intended as provisions setting out State duties toward removed migrants and asylum seekers – could be encompassed in the text of readmission agreements to avert, *ad residuum*, possible human rights

[198] Eibe R and Will M, 'Human Rights Clauses in External Agreements' in Alston P (ed), *The EU and Human Rights* (Oxford University Press, 1999) 724.

violations in the implementation of a readmission procedure. For the purpose of this chapter, attention is placed on asylum seekers in need of protection and subject to informal removals.

On the one hand, it can be argued strongly that embellishing readmission agreements with clauses framing in detail State obligations with regard to the rights of removed migrants and asylum seekers could operate as a 'window dressing'. It would indeed give the impression that agreements are comprehensive, well-drafted, and therefore potentially exempt from further scrutiny. On the other hand, these provisions could nonetheless be a tool in the hands of EU Member States to require third countries (and vice versa) to fulfil clear procedures ensuring compliance with international human rights and refugee law standards.

Proponents of standard readmission agreements argue that such agreements are harmless, highlighting their neutrality as one of the reasons. If these bilateral arrangements do not formally provide a legal basis for removal, and the national decision to transfer an asylum seeker to a 'safe third country' is mainly taken pursuant to the criteria set in the Recast Procedures Directive, it is also clearly undeniable that this Directive does not create obligations for the third, readmitting State. As Costello observes, the lack of communication between the two Contracting Parties may simply 'shift "disorder" from one arena to another.'[199]

It could also be contended that laying out, as a prerequisite for readmission, that third countries must respect human rights and ensure access to asylum procedures would be an incentive for readmitting States not to respect such standards in order to prevent 'unwanted removals'. The response to this argument will state the obvious: the fact that the requested party decides not to comply with human rights and refugee law standards in order to receive fewer migrants and asylum seekers should warn the requesting State that its potential partner is actually not that safe for deportees. Therefore, before negotiating an agreement, sending States should ensure that receiving countries have not only ratified, but have also correctly implemented relevant international instruments concerning refugee rights. A system of regular monitoring and reports related to both the human rights situation in readmitting countries and the legal guarantees their asylum legislation offers to refugees could be useful to complement the action of the requesting parties.

A. Proposal on Specific Procedural Human Rights Clauses

Enhancing the protection of asylum seekers requires a comprehensive approach involving, above all, an overhaul of the EU asylum regime and effective access

[199] C Costello, 'The Asylum Procedures Directive and the Proliferation of Safe Country Practices: Deterrence, Deflection and the Dismantling of International Protection?' (2005) 7(1) *European Journal of Migration Law* 35, 49.

to asylum procedures and effective remedies.[200] My contribution, however, is limited to scrutinising the role readmission agreements might play in this context, and proposing measures that States might agree upon in a bilateral framework. Therefore, some selective and concrete ways forward for draft provisions adding extra procedural safeguards for removable refugees are sketched out here as a platform for further discussion. Although these clauses derive from an examination of the agreements' text, they are in line with similar (though not identical) proposals made by the Parliamentary Assembly of the Council of Europe and the European Commission with regard to EU readmission agreements.[201]

Taking note of the 2011 Communication of the Commission on the evaluation of the EU readmission agreements, the Council has reasserted the importance of EU readmission agreements in order to tackle irregular immigration.[202] However, it did not make any explicit reference to the human rights provisions recommended by the Commission in February 2011.[203] Therefore, the policy debate continues to be open, as readmission agreements are a very sensitive and novel topic in EU affairs, and negotiations with certain partners can be difficult to conclude.[204] In particular, there is a need to make human rights part of the ordinary discourse and part of bilateral readmission practices of EU Member States with third countries, especially with regards to the involvement of asylum seekers and third-country nationals.

A great risk exists for individuals apprehended at the border (including airports) to be removed through fast-track procedures, as provided for in the text of several readmission agreements. A clause which clearly excludes individuals in need of protection from the personal scope of these bilateral instruments would be opportune, especially in chaotic situations of mass mixed influxes, or in the absence of monitoring by lawyers and NGOs, where the rights of newly arrived migrants can be easily prejudiced. Building on a recommendation of

[200] As explained in Chapter 1 of this book, on 12 June 2013, the European Parliament voted for the final adoption of the asylum package, and in May 2016, the Commission adopted the first and second package of proposals for CEAS reform. See, http://www.europarl.europa.eu/legislative-train/theme-towards-a-new-policy-on-migration/file-reform-of-the-common-european-asylum-system-(ceas).

[201] Parliamentary Assembly of the Council of Europe (CoE), *Report on Readmission Agreements: A Mechanism for Returning Irregular Migrants*, Doc 12168, 16 March 2010, para 7.3 (Parliamentary Assembly CoE Report); EC Evaluation of EU Readmission Agreements, n 85 above.

[202] See Council Conclusions defining the EU strategy on readmission, JHA Council Meeting Luxembourg, 9 and 10 June 2011.

[203] On the same line, also the paper presented by Presidency of the Council of the European Union entitled 'Operationalizing the Council Conclusions of 9–10 June 2011 defining the European Union Strategy on Readmission (doc. 5728/12 MIGR 11)', 7 March 2012.

[204] See European Policy Centre, 'EU Readmission Agreements: Towards a more strategic EU approach that respects human rights?', *Policy Dialogue*, 21 March 2012, p 2, http://www.epc.eu/prog_details.php?cat_id=6&pub_id=1435&prog_id=6.

the EU Commission regarding, however, EU readmission agreements,[205] the first proposed clause would appear as follows:

> '(1) Before the Requesting Contracting Party removes the individual apprehended at the border to the territory of the Requested Contracting Party, it shall ensure that accelerated readmission procedures are conditional on the information, collected by Border Authorities, that persons seeking protection are not involved.'

Readmission agreements are to be considered international treaties, setting reciprocal obligations between Contracting Parties. They are not, therefore, the suitable *loci* for EU Member States to grant an individual right to an effective remedy against an expulsion decision or a denial of asylum at first instance. The right to appeal the removal order with a suspensive effect must be established in national legislation in accordance with the ECHR and EU law, in particular the Charter of Fundamental Rights, the Return Directive, and the Recast Procedures Directive, as far as asylum seekers are concerned. Therefore, efforts should be directed toward: first, a more stringent monitoring of national police activities during frontier operations (to avoid asylum seekers being involved in cursory readmission procedures); and secondly, the prompt implementation by States of the Recast Procedures Directive whereby

> Member States shall allow applicants to remain in the territory until the time limit within which to exercise their right to an effective remedy has expired or, when this right has been exercised within the time limit, pending the outcome of the remedy.[206]

Having said that, European States have developed different procedural channels for assessing asylum applications: indeed, 'an asylum seeker may face admissibility procedures, border procedures, Dublin procedures, accelerated procedures, or even prioritised or otherwise fast-track procedures.'[207] In particular, 'accelerated procedures under EU law involve appeals subject to shorter time limits and which often have no (automatic) suspensive effect over removal decisions, thereby exposing asylum seekers to the risk of deportation before their appeal is decided.'[208]

[205] Pursuant to Recommendation 10 of the EU Commission, '[p]rovisions ... highlighting in general the importance for border guards to identify persons seeking international protection could be included in the Practical Handbook for Border Guards. A clause making the accelerated procedure conditional on such information might be also introduced in the text of the agreements.' See EC Evaluation of EU Readmission Agreements, n 85 above, 12. The right to be informed at border crossing points will be strengthened by the Recast Procedures Directive.

[206] Art 46(5) of the Recast Procedures Directive.

[207] For a detailed account of these practices, see Asylum Information Database (AIDA), 'Accelerated, prioritised and fast-track asylum procedures Legal frameworks and practice in Europe' *ECRE* (May 2017), https://www.ecre.org/wp-content/uploads/2017/05/AIDA-Brief_AcceleratedProcedures.pdf.

[208] ibid, 2.

With regard to third-country nationals more generally, Article 13(2) of the Return Directive provides that a competent judicial or administrative authority or a competent body *can* decide to temporarily suspend the enforcement of a removal decision, while Member States shall always postpone removal when it would violate the principle of *non-refoulement* (Article 9(1)(a)). No reference is, however, made to the suspension of the execution of removal and the deferral of the request for readmission in case of pending appeals against negative decisions on asylum at first instance.

Although both the Return Directive and the Recast Procedures Directive contain, to a different extent, rules on the suspensive effect of appeals,[209] there might be *de facto* attempts by States to informally transfer a person when an appeal is still pending, thereby 'undermining legal safeguards at both the procedural and substantive level.'[210] Indeed, the Recast Procedures Directive does not provide that appeals against unfavourable asylum decisions taken in accelerated procedures have full automatic suspensive effect.[211] This is at odds with the jurisprudence of the ECtHR on Article 13, which in several cases has recognised the importance of the suspensive effect of expulsion/deportation orders pending appeals.[212] The European Council on Refugees and Exiles (ECRE)'s analysis of the amended Article 46(6) is illustrative of the main obstacles regarding the access to an effective remedy under the Procedures Directive:

Essentially, in its examination of whether an appeal in those cases would have suspensive effect, the court or tribunal would begin examining the merits of the appeal, but would only later complete the examination and rule on the appeal itself. This process creates double scrutiny of the same material, burdening the already stretched judicial systems. Moreover, if the court or tribunal decides, on the basis of the preliminary assessment, that the asylum seeker need not remain in the territory, but after a full examination of the appeal concludes that the asylum seeker is nevertheless in need of international protection, the individual may have already been removed and subjected to irreversible harm. As a result, the appeal could be disadvantaged on the basis of a rapid, incomplete assessment of the case.[213]

States are not obliged to halt the readmission request and its enforcement until the entire application of the asylum seeker, including the appeal, has been

[209] See Art 46(5) of the Recast Procedures Directive and Arts 9 and 13(2) of the Return Directive.

[210] See Byrne, Noll and Vedsted-Hansen (eds), *New Asylum Countries? Migration Control and Refugee Protection in an Enlarged European Union* (Kluwer Law International, 2002), 12.

[211] See Art 46(6) in conjunction with Art 31(8) of the Recast Procedure Directive.

[212] See, eg, *Conka v Belgium*, App no 51564/99 (5 February 2002); *Olaechea Chuas v Spain*, App no 24668/03 (10 August 2006); *Gebremedhin v France*, App no 25389/05 (26 April 2007) para 66; *Muminov v Russia*, App no 42502/06 (11 December 2008) para 101; *Abdolkani and Karimnia v Turkey*, above n 184, para 108; *Baysakov and Others v Ukraine*, App no 54131/08 (18 February 2010) para 71; *IM v France*, App no 9152/09 (17 May 2011).

[213] ECRE, 'Comments from the European Council on Refugees and Exiles on the Amended Commission Proposal to Recast the Asylum Procedures Directive, COM (2011)' (September 2011) 37.

completed. As the Procedures Directive gives States full *discretion* to allow the asylum seeker to stay in the territory pending an appeal against an unfavourable decision taken in accelerated procedures, readmission agreements could contribute to ensuring legal certainty, complementing the safeguards of the Procedures Directive. They might thus be seen as the proper *loci* to reiterate the duty of border authorities to allow migrants and asylum seekers to await the outcome of their appeals before removing them to third countries.[214] This would be an additional, clear-cut, and residual safeguard in case where States decide to either formally or informally remove a person while a judicial review of an unfavourable decision at first instance is still pending.

The main purpose of readmission agreements is to speed up the process of removal of irregular migrants without formalities, and on the basis of *prima facie* valid pieces of evidence. To obviate any risk for involved asylum seekers, the second proposal – in line with the Parliamentary Assembly of the Council of Europe – would be the following:

> '(2) The Requesting Contracting Party shall stay the request for readmission and the enforcement of readmission until the Competent Authorities have ruled on the asylum seeker's application, including the appeal.'

Readmission agreements do not govern the treatment owed to asylum seekers, given the distinction between asylum procedures and readmission procedures. However, at times, the edges of these two spheres of action can blur, especially when asylum seekers are removed to a 'safe third country' before their admission procedures have been accomplished. Under Article 38 of the Recast Procedures Directive, EU Member States can transfer an asylum seeker to a so-called 'safe third country' if a number of conditions apply. While this work is critical on the use of 'safe third country' policies, arguing that asylum applications should be assessed instead within the European borders where the individual claims protection,[215] the possibility of being removed on such a ground is nevertheless part of the EU legal framework. So far, the Recast Procedures Directive only requires that the person seeking international protection is provided with a document informing the authorities of the readmitting country that her application has not been examined in its substance.[216] Under Article 38(4) of the Recast Procedures Directive, EU Member States are required to channel the asylum seeker into asylum procedures when the requested country refuses to let her '*enter* its territory.'[217]

[214] See Parliamentary Assembly CoE Report. The European Commission has recommended that EU readmission agreements should clearly state that they can 'be applied only to persons whose return/removal has not been suspended.' See Evaluation of EU Readmission Agreements, n 85 above, 12.

[215] The debate on the risks of the 'safe third country' notion has been broadly addressed in Chapter 2 of this work.

[216] See Art 38(3)(b) of the Recast Procedures Directive, replacing Art 27(3)(b) of the 2005 Procedures Directive.

[217] Ex Art 27(4) of the 2005 Procedures Directive.

However, the requesting State has no obligation to take charge again of the removed asylum seeker if it is ascertained that the requested State, despite permitting admission to its territory, has subsequently prevented the applicant from accessing asylum procedures. Therefore, removal should not be undertaken without the assurance – exchanged within the communication channels set up in the framework of a bilateral *treaty* – that the third country has *explicitly agreed* to readmit the individual concerned as an asylum seeker whose protection claim will be examined in its merits.

Beyond informing the authorities of the requested State that the asylum application of the deportee has not been examined in its substance – as provided by Article 38(3)(b) of the Recast Procedures Directive – States must ensure that the agreement to readmit non-nationals amounts to consenting to grant access to status determination procedures pursuant to the 1951 Geneva Convention. Silence or failing to respond to the informative note sent by the requesting State should not be considered as constituting the consent of the requested State both to readmit and provide protection.[218] Claiming such a high threshold would also be in line, *mutatis mutandis*, with Article 35 of the VCLT whereby

> [a]n obligation arises for a third State from a provision of a treaty if the parties to the treaty intend the provision to be the means of establishing the obligation and the third State expressly accepts that obligation in writing.[219]

Enhanced legal certainty on the rights of removed asylum seekers can thus be obtained if the requested country expressly consents in writing to the provision of international protection for the readmitted asylum seeker. 'Informal arrangements, in so far as they are incapable of guaranteeing *de jure* the fulfilment of obligations should be deemed inappropriate.'[220] For instance, in *MSS v Belgium and Greece*, the ECtHR was of the opinion that

> the diplomatic assurances given by Greece to the Belgian authorities did not amount to a sufficient guarantee. ... The agreement document is worded in stereotyped terms ... and merely referred to the applicable legislation, with no relevant information about the situation in practice.[221]

If access to asylum procedures is denied in the 'safe third country', a readmission agreement could be a suitable instrument for imposing upon the sending State the duty of *re*-admitting the applicant and granting her access to asylum

[218] According to the ICJ, silence is not sufficient to express consent. See, eg, *Kasikili v Sedudu Island (Botswana v Namibia)*, 13 December 1999, ICJ Rep 1045; and *Sovereignty over Pulau Ligitan and Pulau Sipadan (Indonesia v Malaysia)*, 23 October 2001, ICJ Rep 575.

[219] Although, during the preparatory works on Art 35, the rule of 'implied consent' was proposed, States unanimously voted that the obligation had to be accepted 'in writing.' See OR 1969 Plenary 60, paras 8, and 158, para 49.

[220] ibid, 35.

[221] *MSS v Belgium and Greece*, above n 93, para 354.

procedures.[222] While respecting the sovereignty of the third country, a monitoring system should be created to supervise the human rights situation in the readmitting State and certify whether removed asylum seekers have been effectively channelled into mechanisms of protection claims' determination.[223] While this would be quite a complex option, it is not clear what composition such a supervisory committee could have. Suggestions may include lawyers, diplomatic officers working at the embassies to NGOs and parliamentary delegations from international organisations.[224] As this would be a cumbersome and tiring process, especially for the individuals involved, removals of asylum seekers to allegedly 'safe third countries' should in principle be avoided. However, using this procedural safeguard as *extrema ratio* within the text of a readmission agreement, the third proposed clause can be formulated as follows:

> '(3) If the person who is the subject of readmission is an asylum seeker whose protection claim has not been examined on its merits before removal, the following conditions shall apply:
>
> a) The reply to the request for readmission provided by the Competent Authorities of the Requested Contracting Party shall contain a confirmation in writing that the individual concerned is an asylum seeker, and that the substance of his/her protection claim will be thoroughly examined.
>
> b) The Competent Authorities of the Requesting Contracting Party shall ensure that the Requested Contracting Party guarantees access to asylum procedures. If such an access is denied, the persons taken in charge shall be readmitted by the Requesting Contracting Party without formality and sent through the normal asylum channels. A monitoring Committee shall be created for this purpose.'

Finally, a 'suspension clause' with reciprocal effects could be activated where there are persistent human rights violations and risks for the readmitted persons in the third country concerned.[225] While the Italy–Albania readmission agreement does not have a suspension provision, Article 25(2)(3) of the UK agreement with Albania affirms in sweeping terms that each Contracting Party shall terminate or suspend the agreement by giving notification in writing to the other

[222] This would also be in consonance with Draft Art 29(2) of the ILC Codification on expulsion of aliens, whereby 'in no case may the earlier unlawful expulsion decision be used to prevent the alien from being readmitted.'

[223] For example, the EU Commission recommends the setting up of a 'post-return' monitoring mechanism in the readmitting countries with a view of gathering information about the human rights situation of persons (especially third-country nationals) after their readmission procedure is completed. See EC Evaluation of EU Readmission Agreements, 13–14. The Parliamentary Assembly CoE Report (para 6.13) also suggests the readmitting country should draw up an annual report with 'statistical data on the fate of asylum seekers (on issues such as detention, release, expulsion, access to asylum system etc)'.

[224] Parliamentary Assembly CoE Report, para 7.5.

[225] See Evaluation of EU Readmission Agreements, 12. Of the same opinion, also Panizzon 2012, n 22 above, 132; European Parliament, 'EU Readmission Agreements Facilitating the return of irregular migrants' (April 2015): http://www.europarl.europa.eu/RegData/etudes/BRIE/2015/554212/EPRS_BRI%282015%29554212_EN.pdf.

party *on important grounds*. Whether infringement of human rights in the readmitting country is to be conceived of as a possible pre-condition for treaty suspension is not clear, but such a possibility is not excluded. Therefore, in light of the foregoing, the fourth proposed clause, drafted in more specific terms, could be the following:

> '(4) Each Contracting Party may either suspend or terminate the Agreement on important grounds, which include the deterioration of human rights in the territory of the Requested Contracting Party.'

B. Non-affection Clauses and Procedural Human Rights Clauses: Added Value or Mere Reiteration of Internationally Recognised Standards?

EU Member States are embedded in a thick web of human rights norms binding them at universal and regional level. This might seemingly induce scholars and practitioners dealing with readmission agreements to regard any further insertion of non-affection clauses or further legal safeguards for asylum seekers as a superfluous duplication.

To address these arguments, it can first be pointed out that procedural human rights clauses and non-affection provisions create positive obligations upon both EU Member States and third countries towards individuals subjected to a removal decision, including asylum seekers. The imposition of such safeguards for readmitted asylum seekers upon the readmitting country could arguably be inducing EU Member States to further transfer their refugee responsibilities to a 'safe third country' well beyond their borders. However, this would overlook the fact that EU Member States are already entitled to declare an asylum application inadmissible upon a 'safe third country' exception by virtue of the Recast Procedures Directive.[226] For in doing so, they have to verify the human rights situation in the readmitting country and abide by a number of safeguards when removing an asylum seeker.[227] Therefore, an increase of transfers is not the most likely outcome of new procedural safeguards, especially if considering that individuals might eventually be readmitted by the sending State if the receiving country *de facto* denies access to asylum procedures.

Previously contracted refugee and human rights law obligations are a key benchmark for States cooperating in the readmission of asylum seekers. As such, States shall abide by them even when implementing a joint migration control arrangement, which somehow restricts the liberty of the individual concerned. Nonetheless, it is crucially important to highlight that both EU Member States and non-EU third countries are not always bound by the same human rights instruments, particularly with regard to the EU *acquis communautaire*.

[226] Art 33(2)(c) of the Recast Procedures Directive (ex Art 25(2)(c) of the 2005 Procedures Directive.
[227] Art 38 of the Recast Procedures Directive (Art 27 of the 2005 Procedures Directive).

As practice shows, third countries do not always offer the same legal safeguards granted by EU Member States. Moreover, the jurisdictional reach of EU supranational judges will be limited in cases involving violations of fundamental rights that are committed far away from the EU borders. In this view, readmission agreements should instead contain a clause whereby parties commit themselves to treat third-country nationals in compliance with relevant international human rights and refugee law. Whilst these clauses could be a replication for EU Member States (though not necessarily so), they might also constitute a fundamental benchmark for third countries, especially when they readmit asylum seekers who have only been transferred on a 'safe third country' ground. Nevertheless, readmission agreements should not be negotiated with countries that 'produce' the highest number of refugees, and have not ratified the key international human rights instruments.

Asylum seekers who are scheduled to be transferred pursuant to a 'safe third country' exception (therefore not on substantive grounds) remain 'presumptive' refugees. However, while *non-refoulement* obligations continue to apply to them, they are also treated as unauthorised residents with no right to freely circulate in the territory of the EU. Shifting in practice 'from the status of victim (the basis of humanitarian action) to that of illegal immigrant (the basis of police action)',[228] they are transferred, like fully-fledged irregular migrants, to a third-transit country under the terms of a readmission agreement. The proposed obligation for the requesting State both to ascertain that the readmitting country effectively ensures access to asylum procedures, and to take charge again of the asylum seeker in case of non-compliance by the requested country, offers an additional safeguard.

Elaboration (or reiteration) of State obligations regarding asylum seekers could be instructive for a host of other reasons. First, it increases legal certainty for both applicants and governments involved in the transfer of irregular migrants, and permits frontier authorities to be confronted with well-defined international obligations and enforcement procedures, mostly when removal decisions are taken at the border and in transit zones. Since transfer treaties always involve a limitation of rights, the agreement itself should be 'in law.'[229] A formal and transparent treaty is the necessary platform for two States that reciprocally decide to limit rights in compliance with the international standards they have accepted.

As a second motive, reiterating procedural human rights obligations is relevant mostly for those norms that do not have a customary status or that cannot expressly be derived from the text of international human rights and refugee

[228] M Agier, 'Forced Migration and Asylum: Stateless Citizens Today' in C Audebert and M Kamel Doraï (eds), *Migration in a Globalized World: New Research Issues and Prospects* (Amsterdam University Press, 2010) 186.

[229] T Clark and F Crépeau, 'Human Rights in Asylum Sharing and Other Human Transfer Agreements' (2004) 22(2) *Netherlands Quarterly of Human Rights* 232.

law treaties. For instance, access to asylum procedures does not amount to a widely accepted right under positive law,[230] and its normative content is partly construed by judges. If the 1951 Geneva Convention does not explicitly require States to guarantee fair access to refugee status determination procedures, it is also true that depriving asylum seekers of an individual examination of their personal condition would expose them to the risk of *refoulement*, thereby undermining the object and purpose of the Convention.[231] The jurisprudence of human rights bodies has thus recognised the existence of an implicit right to access fair and effective asylum procedures.[232] The content of readmission agreements and other transfer arrangements would therefore not only be in line with international human rights and refugee law, but also with the relevant corresponding standards developed by the case law of human rights bodies and courts.[233]

Human rights procedural clauses will not be a panacea because of the lingering flaws associated with any removal process, especially when asylum seekers are involved. Readmission agreements are flexible instruments giving a high level of discretion to governments in determining whether and how to implement removals. However, the fact that they do not reflect specific obligations on refugee rights runs the risk of either maintaining procedural national differences or lowering current protection levels below international human rights law standards. Non-affection provisions and procedural human rights clauses – setting uniform standards – might therefore be an added value.

X. READMISSION AGREEMENTS AND ACCESS TO PROTECTION: CONCLUDING REMARKS

This chapter carried out a broad examination of standard readmission agreements depicted as administrative instruments creating a legal framework for removal. Whilst general international law seems to provide only for the legal basis for a State's obligation to readmit its own nationals (leaving open the issue of the involvement of involuntary deportees), treaty law, and more specifically, readmission agreements, are the instruments that establish an obligation to readmit third-country nationals. At the same time, this research shows how different factors can challenge the customary status of the obligation to readmit

[230] A different and wider regime of protection is offered by the EU CFR, which expressly confers a right to asylum (Art 18). See MT Gil-Bazo, 'The Charter of Fundamental Rights of the European Union and the Right to be Granted Asylum in the Union's Law' (2008) 27 *Refugee Survey Quarterly* 33.

[231] The correlation between the right to access asylum procedures and the principle of *non-refoulement* has been discussed in Chapter 2 of this book.

[232] For a thorough review of relevant literature and case law on the right to access asylum procedures before removal, see Chapter 2 of this book.

[233] Clark and Crépeau 2004, n 229 above, 239.

nationals. Despite these factors – such as 'practical and procedural obstacles to readmission imposed by requested States, the proliferation of readmission agreements reiterating the obligation to readmit own nationals, and the fact that readmission agreements are concluded on the basis of *quid pro quo*'[234] – some scholars affirm the customary value of this norm may be presumed to persist.[235] Lacking a body of ascertainable law in this area, the main conclusion is that ambiguity of international law (rather than of the single readmission agreements), does not allow a clear-cut and uniform response on the status of such a norm.

Placing interstate readmission agreements under the umbrella of the EU readmission policy, it is important to observe that the Lisbon Treaty does not bestow upon the Union the exclusive power of negotiating readmission agreements, since the 'Area of Freedom, Security and Justice' pertains to the field of shared competence grounded on the principle of 'sincere cooperation.'[236] A Member State can carry on with the negotiation of a bilateral readmission arrangement only if the EU has not already stipulated a treaty with the concerned third State or has not concluded a mandate for negotiating such an agreement. Exceptions include cases in which Member States require more detailed arrangements to complement an EU agreement or a negotiating mandate containing only general statements. Such coordination risks being frustrated by the proliferation of informal readmission agreements at both interstate and EU level.

Human rights concerns have been expressed in respect to the connection of interstate readmission agreements with both 'safe third country' practices and the usage of accelerated procedures for removing unauthorised migrants apprehended at the EU borders. Nonetheless, this chapter concurs with Coleman that the text of readmission agreements is not *per se* incompatible with refugee rights. The legal status of asylum seekers is indeed regulated during an initial phase following their arrival in the territory of one of the EU Member States. Bilateral readmission agreements hold only a subsidiary function aimed at enabling transfer to the country of origin or transit of all those people whose protection claims have already been rejected in accordance with the EU Recast Procedures and Qualification Directives.

However, in situations of informal border controls and massive arrivals of migrants and refugees where monitoring is generally lacking, the implementation of readmission agreements (especially informal agreements) may contribute to hampering the access of asylum seekers to protection. *Refoulement* can thus occur as a consequence of accelerated removal mechanisms jeopardising the right to access both asylum procedures and effective remedies. Moreover, there is a risk for asylum seekers who have transited through 'safe third countries' to be removed by means of a readmission agreement. This warrants the inclusion

[234] Coleman 2009, n 5 above, 33.
[235] ibid.
[236] See Art 4(3) of the TEU.

of saving clauses and reciprocal procedural obligations that add additional safeguards for refugees without altering the scope and objective of the accords, which are clearly aimed at expediting the removal of irregular migrants to countries of origin or transit. Thus, without any aim of providing an exhaustive response to the refugee rights-related problems arising from the implementation of formal or informal readmission agreements, some proposals of draft provisions are brought forward as a springboard for further debate amongst legal scholars and policy-makers.

Despite recognising the costs, especially for the requesting State, arising from a new drafting process that gives centrality to human rights, the alternative of incurring international responsibility for violating the *non-refoulement* obligation following the implementation of a readmission agreement would definitively be more troubling. On the whole, the development and improvement of non-affection clauses and itemised procedural human rights clauses within the text of bilateral readmission agreements should be positively considered if we want to see them acting as effective conditionality tools.

In view of a coherent and solid regime of readmission, foremost importance is attached to States' compliance with existing norms of international refugee and European human rights law as well as EU asylum procedures. Nonetheless, when States fail to act within such a well-established legal framework, the procedural safeguards of readmission agreements might offer a residual and complementary protection to removed asylum seekers. Beyond enhancing legal certainty for governments and frontier authorities, they would present the advantage of making fundamental rights part of ordinary business and bilateral cooperation, rather than principles merely subject to specialised human rights instruments,[237] thereby emphasising the implicit acceptance by both parties, during removal operations, of a 'human rights *acquis*.'

It cannot be ignored, however, that there is an inherent contradiction in concluding (or implementing) readmission agreements with States that 'produce' refugee flows. Criticism and judicial challenges will inevitably follow. As with Sisyphus, condemned for all eternity to roll a huge stone up a mountain only to have it roll back down to the bottom as soon as he reaches the summit, such a vicious and fruitless circle is destined to reproduce an absurd struggle where migrants and refugees end up being incessantly shipped across borders and entrapped by uncertain State interests.

[237] E Paasivirta, 'Human Rights, Diplomacy and Sanctions: Aspects to "Human Rights Clauses" in the External Agreements of the European Union' in Jarna Petman and Jan Klabbers (eds), *Nordic Cosmopolitanism: Essays in International Law for Martti Koskenniemi* (Brill Publishing, 2003) 157.

4

Negotiating Rights and Diplomatic Assurances under Memoranda of Understanding

I. INTRODUCTION

A FOREIGN NATIONAL may be considered irremovable by a host State for various administrative and practical reasons (eg lack of travel documents or of a means to remove the person to his/her country of origin). One significant category, however, comprises those persons who cannot be deported due to human rights concerns in the country to which they would be transferred. Nonetheless, such persons may in principle be deemed undeserving of refugee protection in the host State, or otherwise undesirable, including on the basis of alleged serious crimes committed prior to their arrival or due to public safety concerns arising from their conduct after arrival.

'Undesirable aliens' encompass individuals whose refugee status has been outright denied under Article 1(F) of the Convention relating to the Status of Refugees (Refugee Convention).[1] They may also include those falling under Article 33(2) of the Geneva Convention after a successful status determination procedure. Under Article 33(2), the benefits of *non-refoulement*

> may not, however, be claimed by a refugee whom there are reasonable grounds for regarding as a danger to the security of the country in which he is, or who, having been convicted by a final judgment of a particularly serious crime, constitutes a danger to the community of that country.

Failing to qualify either for refugee status or *non-refoulement* protection under the Geneva Convention, but sheltered from removal under international human rights law due to the risk of undergoing inhumane treatment in their country of origin, they end up trapped in a legal and 'status' limbo.

[1] Burgeoning literature has been produced on exclusion from refugee status. See, *inter alia*, S Singer, 'Terrorism and Article 1F(c) of the Refugee Convention: Exclusion from Refugee Status in the United Kingdom' (2014) 12 *Journal of International Criminal Justice* 1075; SS Juss, 'Complicity, Exclusion, and the "Unworthy" in Refugee Law' (2012) 31 *Refugee Survey Quarterly* 1; G Gilbert, 'Exclusion and Evidentiary Assessment' in G Noll (ed), *Proof, Evidentiary Assessment and Credibility in Asylum Procedures* (Martinus Nijhoff, 2005).

Diplomatic assurances are bilateral instruments designed to facilitate the transfer of such undesirable, but otherwise irremovable, persons suspected, or even convicted, of serious crime(s), or considered a threat to the security of the host country. They refer to an undertaking by the receiving State to the effect that the person concerned will be treated in accordance with conditions set by the sending State or, more generally, in keeping with its human rights obligations under international law.[2] Such assurances can take a variety of forms. In the context of the transfer of a person from one State to another, diplomatic assurances refer to 'an undertaking by the receiving State to the effect that the person concerned will be treated in accordance with conditions set by the sending State or, more generally, in keeping with its human rights obligations under international law'.[3] Assurances are usually issued *ad hoc* by the Embassy or the Ministry of Foreign Affairs of the requested State and addressed to the requesting country in charge of repatriating the individual. In extradition cases, judicial bodies may also provide additional guarantees. The UK approach, for example, is unique, as it has resulted in the negotiation of Memoranda of Understanding (MoUs) with third countries, producing standardised written accords that enumerate a long list of assurances on the fair and humane treatment to be afforded to the deportees. At the same time, they also '[allow] the government to seek more specific personal assurances depending on individual circumstances.'[4] MoUs stand, therefore, as framework agreements reflecting a mutual understanding on respect of human rights in every case of removal. *Individualised diplomatic assurances*, by contrast, are case-by-case accords negotiated either independently, in relation to a certain person to be removed, or under an MoU with regard to specific individuals after an emergency arises. In the following Sections, the terms 'assurances' and 'individualised assurances' are at times used interchangeably.

Although States have mainly relied on diplomatic assurances in the field of extradition of persons convicted (or suspected) of previous criminality,[5] their potential application is broader.[6] They may be utilised in the context of deportation/expulsion and 'extraordinary rendition' to undergo interrogation elsewhere.[7] Unlike extradition, which requires formal acts by two States,

[2] UNHCR, *Note on Diplomatic Assurances and International Refugee Protection* (Geneva, August 2006) 2.

[3] ibid, 2.

[4] Ninth Report of the Foreign Affairs Committee (House of Commons), 9 July 2008, para 65, http://www.publications.parliament.uk/pa/cm200708/cmselect/cmfaff/533/53306.htm (Ninth Report of the Foreign Affairs Committee).

[5] For a definition of 'extradition', see Art 1 of the European Convention on Extradition.

[6] Diplomatic assurances have been used, for example, to remove rejected asylum seekers and to transfer detainees from Guantanamo Bay. See E Hamdan, *The Principle of Non-refoulement under the ECHR and the UN Convention against Torture and Other Cruel, Inhuman or Degrading Treatment or Punishment* (Brill, 2016) 306.

[7] See Chapter 1 of this book for definitions of these terms. According to the ECtHR, the term 'extraordinary rendition' refers to 'an extra-judicial transfer of persons from one jurisdiction or

expulsion or deportation occur on the basis of unilateral decisions of the sending State, in principle consistently with international human rights and refugee law.[8] However, in many cases, 'asylum, immigration, and extradition removal proceedings overlap'.[9] For example, in a number of cases, persons whose extradition is requested by the country of origin are asylum seekers or individuals excluded from refugee status on the grounds of terrorist activity. If there is a real risk to their life in their countries of origin, they cannot be deported or surrendered under human rights law, and host States have to find other means to ensure protection and avoid acting with impunity.[10] In these circumstances, the existence of diplomatic assurances is seen as part of the factual evidence in determining the *non-refoulement* test.[11]

Over the past decade, several Western countries – *in primis* the US, Canada, the UK, Sweden, Austria, Germany, Italy, Spain, the Netherlands and Russia – relied on diplomatic assurances before sending a notable number of individuals whose presence was deemed unconducive to the public good of the host country, to undergo interrogation and trials abroad.[12] This creates an urgency to accommodate diplomatic assurances within the broader plastic body of a book aimed at painting as complete a picture as possible of the diverse typologies of written bilateral agreements linked to the readmission of unauthorised/undesirable migrants. In particular, the goal of this chapter is to investigate whether the implementation of diplomatic assurances – negotiated independently or within the framework of a MoU – may hamper refugees' access to protection: the combination of *non-refoulement* and the individual's right to access asylum procedures and effective remedies before removal. It will ask whether they are effective in practice in preventing torture and ill-treatment in the receiving country.

State to another, for the purposes of detention and interrogation outside the normal legal system, where there was a real risk of torture or cruel, inhuman or degrading treatment'. See *El-Masri v Former Republic of Macedonia*, App no 39630/69 (13 December 2012) para 221. To read extensively on counter-terrorism detention, see F de Londras, *Detention in the War on Terror: Can Human Rights Fight Back?* (Cambridge University Press, 2011).

[8] UNHCR, *Note on Diplomatic Assurances and International Refugee Protection* (2006) 2.

[9] M Jones, 'Lies, Damned Lies and Diplomatic Assurances: The Misuse of Diplomatic Assurances in Removal Proceedings' (2006) 8 *European Journal of Migration and Law* 9, 11.

[10] On the debate about devising a coherent response that respects both human rights and non-impunity under international law, see G Gilbert and AM Rusch, 'Jurisdictional Competence through Protection: To What Extent Can States Prosecute the Prior Crimes of Those to Whom They Have Extended Refuge?' (2014) 12 *Journal of International Criminal Justice* 1093.

[11] V Pergantis, 'Soft Law, Diplomatic Assurances and the Instrumentalisation of Normativity: Whither a Liberal Promise?' (2009) 56 *Netherlands International Law Review* 137, 148.

[12] For a survey of developments on the use of diplomatic assurances by European governments and domestic jurisprudence, see Amnesty International (AI), *Dangerous Deals: Assurances in Europe* (2010), 18. On the practice of the US and Canada, see eg A Deeks, 'Promises not to Torture: Diplomatic Assurances in US Courts' (American Society of International Law, 2008); J Cook (ed), 'State Department Legal Advisor Testifies regarding Diplomatic Assurance' (2008) 102 *AJIL* 882–84; A Constantinides, 'Transjudicial Dialogue and Consistency in Human Rights Jurisprudence: A Case Study on Diplomatic Assurances against Torture' in OK Fauchald and A Nollkaemper (eds), *The Practice of International and National Courts and the (De)Fragmentation of International Law* (Hart Publishing, 2012) 289–91.

A. Structure of the Chapter

Section II introduces the *Abu Qatada* saga as a key case study, which epitomises the endeavours of the UK to legitimise the removal of suspected terrorists to undergo interrogations and trials abroad. Abu Qatada was, indeed, the first person to challenge, before the ECtHR, a deportation order to Jordan issued on the basis of an MoU enumerating a series of guarantees for the fair and humane treatment of the deportee. Moreover, the criteria developed by the Court in the assessment of the reliability of diplomatic assurances have been taken as benchmarks also for the following case law. The content of the MoUs signed by the UK with Ethiopia, Jordan, Lebanon, Libya, and Morocco – taken as illustrative examples and units of analysis – is therefore examined.[13]

Section III engages in a doctrinal debate on the legal status of diplomatic assurances under international law. It first explores whether diplomatic assurances are considered treaties, political agreements, or something in between. Section III.E. investigates if and when diplomatic assurances – regardless of their legal status – can be deemed reliable instruments to eliminate the risk of torture and inhuman treatment. This entails an assessment of, firstly, whether the State giving the assurance can be expected to comply with the agreement; and secondly, how reliability can be strengthened. A review is then conducted of the criteria under which diplomatic assurances might be considered sufficiently reliable tools in the implementation of a safe transfer to a third country. These criteria, however, are not exhaustive, and constitute only a preliminary discussion, prior to any broader analysis on reliability. Section III.F. also sheds light on the nascent trend toward a 're-politicisation of human rights'[14] and questions the utility and appropriateness of a binary system of human rights protection, which devolves upon the sphere of politics what States have already reserved to the sphere of law.

Section IV is the core of this chapter. It asks if the implementation of diplomatic assurances – whether negotiated either independently or within the framework of MoUs – can undermine refugees' access to protection. It does so through the lens of international refugee and human rights law. It is here worth recalling that this book defines 'access to protection' as the combination of *non-refoulement* and access to asylum procedures and to effective remedies. As there is a dearth of jurisprudence from international human rights bodies involving

[13] Ninth Report of the Foreign Affairs Committee, para 65. See Memorandum of Understanding Concerning the Provision of Assurances in Respect of Persons Subject to Deportation, Ethiopia–UK, 12 December 2008 (Ethiopia–UK MOU); Memorandum of Understanding regulating the provision of undertakings in respect of specified persons prior to deportation, Jordan–UK, 10 August 2005 (Jordan–UK MOU); Memorandum of Understanding, Libya–UK, 18 October 2005 (Libya–UK MOU); Memorandum of Understanding Concerning the Provision of Assurances in Respect of Persons Subject to Deportation, Lebanon–UK, 23 December 2005 (Lebanon–UK MOU); Memorandum of Understanding Concerning Persons Subject to Deportation for Reasons of Involvement in Terrorism, Morocco–UK, 24 September 2011 (Morocco–UK MoU).

[14] Vedsted-Hansen, 'The European Convention on Human Rights, Counter-Terrorism, and Refugee Protection' (2010) 29(4) *Refugee Survey Quarterly* 45, https://academic.oup.com/rsq/article/29/4/189/1595538 – pdf p 60.

the enforcement of MoUs, cases on the use of single diplomatic assurances under migration law proceedings are the focus of analysis. However, examples are also drawn from the numerous cases of diplomatic assurances exchanged within the framework of extradition.

In carrying out such an analysis, this chapter will shed light on the constant tension between the claim for the inclusion of human rights in the removal process and the demand for enhanced State security and international cooperation in the suppression of crime. It is clear that an extensive review of the legal issues relevant to the links between exclusion (mainly on grounds of terrorism) and refugee rights is worthy of a book of its own. However, the present focus is on just one of the strategies that States are developing to combat the terrorist threat by removing suspected people back to their countries of origin. Indeed, this chapter places and enriches itself within a broader volume tackling diverse categories of agreements linked to readmission. Whilst diplomatic assurances are generally negotiated to facilitate the transfer of individuals considered a threat to the public safety of the host country, they have also been used to remove asylum seekers whose claims have been rejected or who have been excluded from refugee status on national security grounds. However, as Section V illustrates, States have also relied upon diplomatic assurances to deport those asylum seekers whose claims have not been assessed yet. This chapter exposes this anomaly in the system and critically discusses it, highlighting the potential risks stemming from the extension of the use of diplomatic assurances to people whose asylum applications have not yet been examined on their merits before removal.

Finally, Section VI summarises the main findings and engages in a general critique of diplomatic assurances after an assessment of the law (the content of the bilateral agreements at issue) and practice (the actual implementation of the agreements). It finds that decisions to transfer a person to an unsafe country, deny her access to effective remedies, refuse her asylum, or exclude her from refugee status and subsidiary protection are not taken on the basis of diplomatic assurances – whether formalised in MoUs or not. Nevertheless, their negotiation in individualised circumstances can influence, to a certain extent, these decisions, thereby hampering refugees' access to protection.

Part 1

II. DEPORTATION AT ALL COSTS? THE CASE OF THE UK AND DIPLOMATIC ASSURANCES

In the *Abu Qatada v UK* case, the ECtHR was asked, for the first time, to appraise the reliability of diplomatic assurances, negotiated under a standardised MoU, in the assessment of the risk to the applicant (a radical Muslim cleric who was recognised as a refugee) upon removal to Jordan.[15]

[15] *Othman (Abu Qatada) v UK*, App no 8139/09 (17 January 2012).

This judgment has spawned an intense debate amongst legal scholars, human rights practitioners, State officials, and civil society. What, for example, is the legal value of diplomatic assurances? Would diplomatic assurances eradicate the risk of *refoulement* to torture and ill-treatment? Would friendly bilateral relations be sufficient elements for a national or international court to consider assurances on fundamental rights reliable? What is the impact that the ECtHR's ruling might have on the future use of diplomatic assurances to remove people whose presence is deemed unconducive to the public good on national security grounds?

The UK government has been labelled as 'the most influential and aggressive promoter in Europe of the use of diplomatic assurances' to forcibly repatriate people considered threats to national security to countries where they would suffer human rights violations, including inhuman treatment and torture.[16] Terrorist crimes are generally very hard to prove, and evidence dealing with matters of public security contains classified information. The use of such evidence in criminal proceedings would necessarily imply their disclosure to the public, which is something States have difficulty doing. In this regard, what has raised more concerns from a human rights law perspective, is that the evidence used by the Special Immigration Appeals Commission (SIAC) and the Appeal Court is based on secret material that cannot be challenged and that is too sensitive to be considered in full by an open court for such national security reasons.[17] Thus, migrants suspected of terrorism – who are excluded by the scope of Article 1(f) of the Geneva Convention, but who cannot be removed, under international human rights law, because of the peril of *refoulement* – risk being detained for indefinite periods of time without any formal charge, as the security-sensitive evidence incriminating them cannot be disclosed.[18] Since lesser measures, such as surveillance and control orders do not remove the threat of terrorism, the UK, flanked by many other governments, casts deportation as the only solution.

The UK have thus increasingly started to rely on diplomatic assurances in order to allow British courts to authorise smooth deportation of unwanted foreigners in compliance with international human rights standards. MoUs were perceived as a suitable instrument to create a stable and standardised formal basis for deportation. It was thus presumed that, by obtaining international legitimacy, the UK's deportation with assurances policy would have been less exposed to the attacks of human rights circles, which have always been reproachful of any stratagems designed to displace the risk abroad through cooperation with third countries. While attempts to deport under this policy have been incessantly litigated over the last decade (with small successes from the Home Office

[16] Amnesty International 2010, n 12 above, 28.

[17] R Braswell, 'Protection against Torture in Western Security Frameworks: The Erosion of Non-*refoulement* in the UK–Libya MOU' (October 2006) *RSC Working Paper no 35*.

[18] See Anti-Terrorism Crime & Security Act 2001, Part 4, Section 23.

point of view), there are currently no live deportation with assurances (DWA) cases.[19] In 2017, almost 12 years after this policy started, only 11 people have been deported and one administratively removed under the aegis of an MoU with diplomatic assurances. Therefore, as anticipated by the Newton Committee, this policy might be more useful as a deterrent against the settling of alleged terrorists in the UK rather than an effective tool enabling deportations.[20] However, recent changes to citizenship deprivation laws and increasing travel from Europe to Syria and Iraq to fight with terrorists might swell the number of deportations.[21]

Even if international human rights law does not prohibit *per se* deportation on national security grounds, the UK Privy Council Review Committee in 2004 held that

> Seeking to deport terrorist suspects does not seem to us to be a satisfactory response, given the risk of exporting terrorism. If people in the UK are contributing to the terrorist effort here or abroad, they should be dealt with here. While deporting such people might free up British Police, intelligence, security and prison service resources, it would not necessarily reduce the threat to British interests abroad, or make the world a safer place more generally. Indeed, there is a risk that the suspects might even return without the authorities being aware of it.[22]

Placing these bilateral accords within an international human rights legal framework, this chapter will explore whether deportation policies aimed at preserving national security have been or could be executed at the expense of the rights of asylum seekers whose refugee status has been rejected, excluded from protection on national security grounds, or removed before examination of asylum claims.

A. Outlining the Content of the UK's MoUs

It is for that reason that the MoUs agreed so far by the UK with Ethiopia, Jordan, Lebanon, Libya, and Morocco deserve particular attention. Although the content of these MoUs differs slightly from case to case, a cluster of common traits can still be identified. Whilst sometimes they reiterate international human rights

[19] See D Anderson and C Walker, *Deportation with Assurances* (July 2017) 26–28, https://assets.publishing.service.gov.uk/government/uploads/system/uploads/attachment_data/file/630809/59541_Cm_9462_Accessible.pdf. On 18 April 2016, judges at the Special Immigration Appeals Commission (SIAC) in London halted the deportation of six Algerian terrorism suspects. See A Maniar, 'A Significant Blow to Deportation with Assurances', https://onesmallwindow.wordpress.com/2016/05/06/a-significant-blow-to-deportation-with-assurances/.

[20] UK Privy Counsellor Review Committee, 'Anti-Terrorism, Crime and Security Act 2001 Review Report', December 2003, HC 100.

[21] D Walker, 'International and Comparative Law and Practice' in Anderson and Walker 2017, n 19 above, 53.

[22] UK Privy Counsellor Review Committee, 'Anti-Terrorism Crime and Security Act 2001 Review Report' (December 2003), para 54.

commitments, at other times they are more detailed, providing for specific post-removal monitoring through prompt and regular visits from the representative of an independent body, who will conduct private interviews with the readmitted person.[23] Agreements concerning further details of the monitoring have also been added to the MoUs.

Although MoUs contain diverse typologies of assurances, States still have ample discretion in their implementation and acceptance. The arrangements will apply to citizens of the requested country[24] – or in the case of Libya and Lebanon, to stateless persons and any third-country nationals the receiving State is prepared to admit[25] – following a written request made under the terms of the agreement. Thus, despite lacking an obligation to honour the assurances, it will be for the receiving State to decide whether to give further assurances, if appropriate in an individual case, as a response to the requests made under the Memorandum by the sending country.[26] This means that it is possible to shift from MoUs to bespoke assurances to push the protection of the person in question to a higher level of commitment. Whether States decide to negotiate tailored or 'one-size-fits-all' solutions will depend on the whole set of circumstances concerning the removal of a specific individual to a certain receiving country.[27]

Moreover, MoUs provide for retrial for those convicted *in absentia*. Only the agreement with Libya explicitly contains an assurance that the receiving State will not impose the death penalty 'if its laws allow', and requires Libyan authorities to use 'all the powers available to them' to ensure that, if the death penalty is imposed, it would not be carried out.[28] With regard to Jordan, on 10 August 2005, the UK Chargé d'Affaires in Amman and the Jordanian Ministry of the Interior signed a side letter on the death penalty, due to the fact that, 'for constitutional reasons', Jordan was unable to make a formal declaration in the MOU itself. The side letter recorded that, if someone deported under the agreement was sentenced to death, 'the British Government would consider asking the Jordanian Government to commute the sentence,'[29] and the Jordanian Government would commit itself to not carry out the death penalty.[30]

Another point to notice in the description of the content of MoUs is that they do not use the terms 'torture' or 'inhuman and degrading treatment' explicitly.[31] Rather, deported persons are entitled to 'adequate accommodation,

[23] UK–Jordan MoU, Application and Scope, para 4.

[24] UK–Jordan MoU, Application and Scope, paras 1–2.

[25] UK–Libya MoU, Application and Scope, para 1; UK–Lebanon MoU, Application and Scope, para 1.

[26] UK–Libya MoU, Application and Scope, para 5; UK–Jordan MoU, Application and Scope, para 6; UK–Lebanon MoU, Application and Scope, para 5.

[27] See Anderson and Walker 2017, n 19 above, 49

[28] UK–Libya MoU, Assurances, para 2.

[29] See *Abu Qatada v SSHD*, [2007] UKSIAC 15/2005, para 352.

[30] See *Abu Qatada v UK*, above n 15, para 23.

[31] Justice, 'Home Office Review of Counter-Terrorism and Security Powers', *Written Submissions* (August 2010) 44.

nourishment, and medical treatment, and [to] be treated in a humane and proper manner, in accordance with internationally accepted standards.'[32] Additional safeguards include that the deportee: will be entitled to prompt consultation with a lawyer; will be informed of the reasons for the arrest and of any charge against her; and will receive regular visits from a representative of the monitoring body. The individual must be brought without undue delay before a civilian judge for the determination of the lawfulness of her detention and will receive a fair and public hearing before an independent and impartial civilian court. She will be allowed adequate time and facilities to prepare her defence, and to call and examine witnesses. The deportee will be allowed to defend herself in person or through legal assistance, and to freely observe her religion. Every judgment will be then pronounced publicly. However, in specified circumstances, the press and public may be excluded.[33]

Part 2

III. LEGAL STATUS OF DIPLOMATIC ASSURANCES: AN OPEN-ENDED DOCTRINAL DEBATE

The main purpose of diplomatic assurances is to provide guarantees against torture and ill-treatment. Scholarship and human rights circles have so far mostly associated the weaknesses of diplomatic assurances in removing the risk of human rights violations for the deportee with their alleged non-legally-binding character. However, by engaging in the scholarly debate on the status of diplomatic assurances under international law, Part 2 of this chapter concludes that the 'binding or not binding' question is not, in fact, the determining element in grasping the impact these bilateral agreements have on refugee rights.

At times, assurances are embodied within documents called 'MoUs', which can be either treaties or soft law instruments. However, this classification does not depend on their registration with the UN Secretariat as a treaty under Article 102 of the UN Charter.[34] Whilst failure of registration does not affect the legal status of an agreement, it may hamper the possibility of using it before

[32] See the UK–Libya and the UK–Lebanon MoUs, and the UK–Etiophia MoU, Assurances, para 1; the UK–Jordan MoU, Understanding, para 1. See SIAC, *DD and AS v SSHD*, 27 April 2007, SC/42 and 50/2005 (*DD and AS v SSHD*) para 218.

[33] All these safeguards are inscribed in the UK–Lebanon MoU, Assurances, paras 2–6; the UK–Libya MoU, Assurances, paras 4–9; and the UK–Jordan MoU, Undertakings, paras 2–8. In addition, the agreement with Jordan provides that access to consular posts of the sending State will not be limited (para 5).

[34] For instance, several bilateral treaties concluded by either the US or the UN are called MoUs (Iraq–UN 1996, 1926 UNTS 9 (No 32851); Korea–US MoU on communication security equipment 1993, 1751 UNTS 217 (No 30579).

a dispute settlement body.[35] It has been argued that the title of a bilateral agreement as a Memorandum is not indicative of its legal status; rather it is only one indicator to determine – together with the language of the agreement, its object and purpose, and the preparatory works – the *intention* of the parties.[36]

In this debate, attempting to define what is meant by informal and non-legally binding agreements can be helpful. Saurugger and Terpan define 'soft law' as:

> Those norms situated in-between hard law and non-legal norms .... Hard law corresponds to the situation where hard obligation (a binding norm) and hard enforcement (judicial control or at least some kind of control including the possibility of legal sanctions) are connected. Non-legal norms follow from those cases where no legal obligation and no enforcement mechanism can be identified .... In-between these two opposite types of norms lie different forms of soft law: either a legal obligation is not associated with a hard enforcement mechanism or a non-binding norm is combined with some kind of enforcement mechanism.[37]

According to Pauwelyn, Wessel and Wouters, informal law-making is characterised by three elements:[38] the output, the process, and the actors involved – that respectively give rise to diverse degrees of informalisation/formalisation.[39] In terms of outputs, international cooperation can lead to the adoption of instruments other than treaties, such as statements, declarations, guidelines (which might still have legal and normative effects),[40] and in the area of readmission, MoUs, administrative arrangements, exchanges of letters, etc.[41] With regard to the process, international cooperation might be informal when it takes place 'in a loosely organised network or forum'.[42] Informality of actors refers instead to the exclusion of traditional diplomatic actors (eg heads of State or government, foreign ministers, embassies) in the negotiation process.[43]

Despite the enduring debate on the normative status of diplomatic assurances, no clear and uniform answer has yet been elaborated.[44] Therefore, this

[35] T Worster, 'Between a Treaty and Not: A Case Study of the Legal Value of Diplomatic Assurances in Expulsion Cases' (2012) 21(2) *Minnesota Journal of International Law* 253, 286–87.

[36] A Aust, *Modern Treaty Law and Practice* (Cambridge University Press 2000) 20.

[37] S Saurugger and F Terpan, 'Studying Resistance to EU Norms in Foreign and Security Policy', *European Foreign Affairs Review*, Special Issue (2015) 1, 5.

[38] The authors refer to 'law-making' to indicate any 'norm-setting or public policy-making by public authorities.

[39] J Pauwelyn, R Wessel and J Wouters (eds), *Informal International Lawmaking* (OUP, 2012).

[40] According to Pauwelyn, the output of informal international lawmaking 'must be normative in that it steers behaviour or determines the freedom of actors.' J Pauwelyn, 'Informal International Lawmaking: Framing the Concept and Research Questions' in Pauwelyn, Wessels and Wouters 2012, 16.

[41] ibid, 15–16.

[42] ibid, 17.

[43] ibid, 17. The theme of informalisation has been addressed also in Chapter 3, in particular with regard to the recent trend of the EU toward informalisation of readmission agreements.

[44] For a general overview of the debate, see L Skoglund, 'Diplomatic Assurances against Torture – An Effective Strategy? A Review of Jurisprudence and Examination of the Arguments' (2008) 77 *Nordic Journal of International Law* 319; Worster 2012, n 35 above.

work will not take a definitive stance on the legal value of diplomatic assurances. However, the main arguments on either side are herein illustrated for the purpose of scrutinising whether their normative quality plays any role in refugees' access to protection and in the humane treatment of the deportee.

A. Diplomatic Assurances as Treaties?

Under Article 2(1)(a) of the Vienna Convention on the Law of Treaties (VCLT), treaties may be defined as 'international agreement[s] concluded between States in written form and governed by international law, whether embodied in a single instrument or in two or more related instruments and whatever its particular designation.' As legally binding instruments – where the parties communicate to each other the promise of certain behaviour – they are *enforceable* through the legal system adopting them. States and individuals can, therefore, lodge complaints concerning transgressions of the agreement itself. Contrarily, if diplomatic assurances are conceived as non-treaties, the sending State may not rely on the UN dispute settlement process in case of breaches of the agreement.

An increasing number of governments resort to diplomatic assurances not to torture, and to administer fair treatment of deportees as a pre-condition for the removal of unwanted foreigners. This raises two interrelated questions: first, whether diplomatic assurances are mere political commitments to act toward certain agreed ends, without any legally binding effect; second, whether such a reliance on bilateral assurances can defy fundamental rights, *in primis* the prohibition of torture, as enshrined within international human rights treaties.

The first issue merits closer examination. With regard to the second point, it is here sufficient to argue – as in Chapter three – that changes to multilateral refugee and human rights law instruments cannot be caused by a new treaty binding only a few States within the international community. Indeed, pursuant to Article 34 of the VCLT, 'a treaty does not create either obligations or rights for a third State without its consent.' Therefore, the *erga omnes* obligations found in all international refugee and human rights instruments that are applicable to States – for example the obligation not to 'expel, return ("refouler") or extradite a person to another State where there are substantial grounds for believing that he would be in danger of being subjected to torture'[45] – remain unaltered after the exchange of bilateral diplomatic assurances on security-related deportation (either in the form of MoUs or not, regardless of their legal status). Under Article 41 of the VCLT,

> two or more of the parties to a multilateral treaty may conclude an agreement to modify the treaty as between themselves alone if the [modification in question] is

[45] Art 3 of the CAT. On the duty of States to respect *non-refoulement* as an *erga omnes* obligation, see AM Salinas de Frías, 'States' Obligations under International Refugee Law and Counter-Terrorism Responses' in AM Salinas de Frías, K Samuel and N White (eds), *Counter-Terrorism: International Law and Practice* (OUP, 2012) 130–32.

> not prohibited by the treaty and does not affect the enjoyment by the other parties of their rights under the treaty or the performance of their obligations.

The VCLT recognises that various international agreements exist that do not fall within the scope of the Convention.[46] Yet, it does not make any explicit reference to the status of diplomatic assurances under international law. Therefore, the scholarly debate is still open in respect of the legally binding nature of such arrangements.[47] Klabbers believes that the very idea that some agreements are not binding is essentially impracticable, as it does not explain what other purposes an international agreement can have.[48] Thus, even if the intention of the States involved is solely to create commitments, 'gentlemen agreements' aim to produce a normative effect intending to influence future behaviour.[49] Klabbers criticises that, according to some scholars, the parties to a gentlemen agreement desire 'to become bound in a normative order other than law, the orders most often mentioned being "politics" and "morality".'[50] Similarly, Noll perceives as 'quite meaningless' the existence of non-binding agreements that do not play any role in altering the risk assessment undertaken by the sending State.[51] The cardinal factor is whether the risk of torture and ill-treatment is in fact eliminated by the mutual understanding of the parties with regard to the removed individual.

Some suggest that when diplomatic assurances contain an undertaking intended to create new legal obligations beyond mere restatements of pre-existing obligations in international law (for example, the establishment of a monitoring mechanism), a new agreement has been reached.[52] It is this new undertaking that might constitute a key element in overcoming a risk of ill-treatment.[53]

[46] Art 3 of the VCLT.

[47] Aust poses the same question with regard to MoUs more generally. See Aust 2000, n 36 above. See also, VU Degan, *Sources of International Law* (Martinus Nijhoff Publishers, 1997) 358–62.

[48] J Klabbers, *Developments in International Law: The Concept of Treaty in International Law* (Kluwer, 1996) 4, 6.

[49] This shorthand term encompasses all those arrangements generally known as non-legally binding agreements, soft law instruments, political agreements, international understandings, etc. Their denomination is, however, of little importance.

[50] Klabbers 1996, n 48 above, 19.

[51] G Noll, 'Diplomatic Assurances and the Silence of Human Rights Law' (2006) 7 *Melbourne Journal of International Law* 10.

[52] Worster 2012, n 35 above, 285. It is also to be noted that, in the case of *erga omnes* human rights obligations, the need to restate them is unclear considering that States cannot excuse themselves from compliance.

[53] As long as diplomatic assurances are *ad hoc* guarantees documented in writing, such as through an exchange of notes, they might satisfy the treaty requirements under Art 2(1) of the VCLT. In this case, they would be governed by the Vienna Convention treaty rules. While the ILC does not explicitly provide for non-legally binding agreements, their existence is not excluded. It states that 'although the term "treaty" in one sense connotes only the single formal instrument, there also exist international agreements, such as the exchange of notes, which are not a single formal instrument, and yet are certainly agreements to which the law of treaties applies. Similarly, many single instruments of daily use, such as an 'agreed minute, or a 'memorandum of understanding", could not appropriately be called formal instruments, but they are undoubtedly international agreements subject to the law of treaties'. See International Law Commission, VCLT with Commentaries, *Yearbook of the ILC 1966*, vol II, 187, Art 2(2).

In criticising the Austian distinction between the legally binding and non-legally binding nature of international agreements, Klabbers observes that

> in the former case, [States] become intentionally legally bound; in the latter, they become so bound without having intended as much, by virtue of good faith, estoppel, or reliance. But if that is the case, what can be said to justify the distinction?[54]

B. Diplomatic Assurances as Binding Unilateral Statements?

Diplomatic assurances can also be conceived of as legal obligations insofar as they might amount to *binding unilateral statements*.[55] As formulated by the International Court of Justice (ICJ) in the *Nuclear Test Case*:

> It is well recognized that declarations made by way of unilateral acts, concerning legal or factual situations, may have the effect of creating legal obligations. Declarations of this kind may be, and often are, very specific ... An undertaking of this kind, if given publicly, and with intent to be bound, even though not made within the context of international negotiations, is binding ...[56]

According to the ICJ, the intention of the parties to be bound must be obtained by interpretation of the act. Likewise, the ECtHR has acknowledged that every time a State entertains diplomatic communication by taking a commitment in good faith and limiting its freedom of action, it expresses an intention to follow the statement and to be bound.[57] Only after the intent to be bound is uttered, does the obligation become legal:

> when it is the intention of the State making the declaration that it should become bound according to its terms, the intention confers on the declaration the character of a legal undertaking, the State being thenceforth legally required to follow a course of conduct consistent with the declaration.[58]

In the *Einhorn v France* case, the ECtHR defined diplomatic assurances as treaties despite conceding that they could alternatively amount to binding unilateral statements, in other words, 'a unilateral international undertaking requiring the United States to fulfil the obligations it had entered into, failing which its international responsibility would be engaged ....'[59] However, in the *Einhorn* case, extradition was sought by the US, which, consequently, had all the interest in complying with the given assurances. What is different is a case of expulsion and

[54] Klabbers 1996, n 48 above, 111.

[55] Worster 2012, n 35 above, 340–44.

[56] *Nuclear Test Case (Australia v France)*, 20 December 1974, ICJ Rep 253, para 43 (*Nuclear Test Case*).

[57] See *Ahmad, Awat, Ahsan and Mustafa (Abu Hamza) v UK*, App nos 24027/07, 11949/08, and 36742/08, Partial Decision as to Admissibility (6 July 2010) para 105.

[58] *Nuclear Test Case*, n 56 above, para 43.

[59] *Einhorn v France*, App no 71555/01, Final Decision as to Admissibility (16 October 2001) para 30.

removal ordered for the purpose of deporting an asylum seeker whose refugee status has yet to be determined, or whose status has already been refused or revoked. The receiving State simply replies to a request by the sending country without having any primary interest in readmitting the individual at issue and gives, to this end, specific assurances that she will be treated fairly.

C. Diplomatic Assurances as Non-legally Binding Agreements?

The legal status of diplomatic assurances is inconclusive: that said, States do intentionally commit themselves at different levels. The presumption of a lack of legal boundaries constitutes, at times, the main reason for States entering into more informal accords – generally negotiated and signed by diplomats – without parliamentary scrutiny and implementation in national legislation. The elements explaining the gradual proliferation of informal patterns of cooperation on readmission are invisibility and confidentiality, higher flexibility in changing circumstances thanks to the ease in amending their text, adaptability to short-term security concerns, the desire to avoid a lengthy ratification process (in particular in time of crisis), and the limited costs of defection as disputes can be resolved during negotiations.[60]

Although the doctrine continues to be divided, one view is that diplomatic assurances are international commitments – political promises meant to be kept – but not necessarily legally binding.[61] Indeed, it is absolutely possible that non-legally binding instruments may nonetheless bring about legal consequences.[62] Whilst a diplomatic assurance is not legally binding, it may evoke legal consequences as a matter of fairness and estoppel. It means that although the leverage added by the assurance is mainly political, if an agreement is made in good faith States are estopped from reneging upon their original commitment.[63] However, even if, by virtue of the doctrine of estoppel, a State should abstain from acting to the detriment of an agreement that has been concluded in good faith, it

[60] JP Cassarino, 'Informalizing Readmission Agreements in the EU Neighbourhood' (2007) 42(2) *The International Spectator* 179, 189–190. See also, C Lipson, 'Why are Some International Agreements Informal?' (1991) 45(4) *International Organization* 495, 501; Aust 2000, n 36 above, 39–40. According to Aust, the fact that the agreement is easy to modify and does not require implementation in domestic legislation leads governments to have a certain lack of care in drafting an MoU.

[61] See, eg, UN High Commissioner for Human Rights Louise Arbour, 'Statement on Human Rights Day: On Terrorists and Torturers', 7 December 2005, http://www.unhchr.ch/huricane/huricane.nsf/0/3B9B202D5A6DCDBCC12570D00034CF83?opendocument. According to M Nowak, former Special Rapporteur on Torture, diplomatic assurances 'carry no legal effect and no accountability if breached; and the person whom the assurances aim to protect has no recourse if the assurances are violated.' See Special Rapporteur on Torture, Report submitted in accordance with General Assembly Resolution 59/182, UN Doc A/60/316, 30 August 2005, para 51; Skoglund 2008, n 44 above, 336.

[62] Aust 2000, n 36 above, 46.

[63] ibid, 46.

is also true that the *pacta sunt servanda* rule applies only to treaties. Indeed, Article 2(1)(a) of the VCLT only applies to international agreements 'governed by international law', which thus excludes instruments not intended to create mutually binding obligations.

D. What is the Legal Value of the UK's MoUs?

Shifting attention to formalised assurances, the Vienna Convention Official Record reports that the UK delegation considered that Memoranda 'were not international agreements subject to the law of treaties because the parties had not intended to create legal rights and obligations, or a legal relationship, between themselves.'[64] The heated debate that animated the delegates to the Vienna Conference on the introduction of the 'intent' element as part of the treaty definition ended with the exclusion of intent from the VCLT. However, two points can be noted: first, labelling an agreement as an MoU does not automatically exclude it from the sphere of treaties as long as it creates rights and obligations; secondly, some authors suggest that the kind of intent to take into consideration when assessing the normative status of an agreement would be the 'objective intent', *consensus ad idem*, as stated in the text of the accord. Such an 'objective intent' differs from the 'subjective intent' of the parties, which is an aspect of the 'agreement' element with the designation traced by Article 2(1) and extremely difficult to prove.[65]

A State cannot rely on the fact that an MoU or an *Aide Memoire* was signed by an administrative officer (for example the Head of the Police) to deem it not legally binding. Indeed, under Article 46 of the VCLT, 'a State may not invoke the fact that its consent to be bound by a treaty has been expressed in violation of a provision of its internal law regarding competence to conclude treaties as invalidating its consent'. The only exception is given by a 'manifest' infringement of a 'rule of its internal law of fundamental importance'. Article 46 clarifies that 'a violation is manifest if it would be objectively evident to any State conducting itself in the matter in accordance with normal practice and in good faith.' Article 46 is therefore used to ensure stability and predictability of the obligations of an international agreement.[66] Whilst a State is free to decide if it wishes to enter into a treaty or not, it cannot use sovereignty as an excuse once it has objectively concluded an agreement.[67] Indeed, 'if a State concludes an

[64] United Nations Conference on the Law of Treaties, Vienna, Austria Second Session 9 April–22 May 1969, 228 para 35, A/CONF.39/C.1/SR.87.

[65] For a detailed discussion on the intent element, see Worster 2012, n 35 above, 273–75. See also, K Widdows, 'What is an Agreement in International Law?' (1979) 50(1) *British Yearbook of International Law* 117, 121.

[66] See *Legal Status of Eastern Greenland (Denmark v Norwey)*, 5 April 1933, PCIJ Ser A/B no 53. See also, Institute of International Law and Justice, 'Note on the invalidity of treaties under Article 46'.

[67] Worster 2012, n 35 above, 301.

agreement that is expressly legally binding, then the State could never succeed in arguing that it did not intend for that result. The document speaks for itself.'[68]

In Worster's words, an international accord could be, in its substance, either a treaty or not, regardless of its title as an MoU.[69] As States are entitled to exercise or not exercise their treaty-making powers, if they decide to enter into binding agreements, they generally do so through clear and explicit language. As we will see below, according to some, the diplomatic assurances negotiated under the MoUs in question are considered legally binding, while for others they are not.

On the one hand, Worster believes that phrasings such as '[the deportee] *will* be brought promptly before a judge',[70] 'will be informed promptly of any charge against him',[71] and 'will receive a fair and public hearing'[72] cannot be interpreted as mere political arrangements, but rather as assertions of State obligations under international law with application in the single case of removal.[73] For example, the MoU between the UK and Jordan states that 'it is understood that the authorities of the UK and Jordan will comply with their human rights obligations under international law regarding a person returned under this arrangement.'[74] Similarly, under the MoUs with Libya and Lebanon, the two parties 'will comply with their human rights obligations.'[75] According to Worster, these agreements use mandatory language by referring to assurances as 'conditions',[76] or stating that they 'will apply to such a person ....'[77] In his view, the monitoring mechanisms created under the MoUs with Lebanon, Libya, and Ethiopia create a new agreement – and an obligation additional to those already binding those States under international human rights law.[78]

On the other hand, the British government has clearly affirmed that MoUs are used as a means for the State – in the exercise of its free treaty-making power – to preserve a high degree of autonomy under a non-legally binding bilateral arrangement.[79] Although the intention of the British government is a particularly important element, its statements are only indicative of the normative quality of the assurances. Indeed, attention should be paid to the language of the agreements. In this regard, someone could argue that the text of the MoUs signed by the UK with Ethiopia, Jordan, Lebanon, Libya, and Morocco – through the

[68] ibid, 304.
[69] ibid.
[70] Jordan–UK MoU, Understanding 2.
[71] ibid, Understanding 3.
[72] ibid, Understanding 7.
[73] Worster 2012, n 35 above, 330.
[74] UK–Jordan MoU.
[75] UK–Lebanon and UK–Libya MoUs.
[76] UK–Jordan MoU.
[77] UK–Lebanon and UK–Libya MoUs.
[78] Worster 2012, n 35 above, 279–80.
[79] See, on this point, K Jones, 'Deportation with Assurances: Addressing Key Criticism' (2008) 57 *ICLQ* 188. In *Abu Qatada*, above n 15, the ECtHR held that 'whatever the status of the MoU in Jordanian law, the assurances have been given by officials who are capable of binding the Jordanian State.' (para 201).

use of terms such as 'will', 'arrangement', or 'understanding' – confirms the willingness of the parties not to be legally bound. This terminology, beyond the explicit statements of the State, would denote the lack of a clear recognition of the intention of States to enter into a legally binding agreement and to be held accountable for any breach of the accord. States have generally embraced the ICJ finding in the *Qatar v Bahrain* case that terminology cannot alone be sufficient to determine the normative status of an agreement as a treaty or not.[80] However, the fact that the parties explicitly relied on a diplomatic terminology that expresses intention not to be legally bound cannot be ignored.[81]

Despite the new cluster of diplomatic assurances, SIAC and the Court of Appeal continued to hold that Abu Qatada would face 'a flagrant denial of justice' if deported to Jordan.[82] To overcome the objections of the British courts, the Home Secretary decided to conclude a new 'mutual legal assistance agreement' with Jordan, which entered into force in July 2013.[83] This Treaty comprises a number of fair trial guarantees for deportees and a stringent ban on the use of torture-obtained evidence. Thus, on 7 July 2013, Abu Qatada finally agreed to be sent back to Jordan following a formal approval of the Treaty by Jordan's King Abdullah.

In light of the foregoing, the doctrine continues to be divided. Whilst for some, the UK's MoUs with Ethiopia, Lebanon, Libya, Jordan, and Morocco are legally binding, others believe that they cannot automatically be regarded as treaties on the grounds of being instruments embodying an agreement.[84] Nevertheless, this chapter only aims to map out these different positions to show how the question on the legal value of diplomatic assurances remains unsettled, and no uniform answer exists. Despite the fact that the UK's MoUs refer to the duty of States to comply with human rights under international law, there is room to question why States need to duplicate their human rights commitments within the frame of a diplomatic accord, which does not contain all those mechanisms of enforcement and monitoring provided by international human rights treaties – especially with regard to bodies for individual complaints.

E. Is 'To Bind or Not to Bind?' the Right Question?

Despite the heated debate on the legal status of assurances, *in practice*, States consider this appraisal an important, but not decisive, element in the assessment of risk for the deportee. *De facto*, since governments can also keep faith

[80] See *Maritime Delimitation and Territorial Quest (Quatar v Bahrain)*, 1 July 1994, ICJ Rep 112.
[81] ibid, para 195.
[82] See *Othman (Abu Qatada) v SSHD*, SC/15/2005, 12 November 2012, para 66, 73.
[83] Treaty on Mutual Legal Assistance in Criminal Matters between the United Kingdom of Great Britain and Northern Ireland and the Hashemite Kingdom of Jordan, London, 24 March 2013, entry into force 1 July 2013.
[84] Jones 2008, n 79 above, 188.

with their international political commitments in order to avoid undesirable consequences, such as disruption of their bilateral relations and (possibly) their international image, they argue that the risk of torture or inhuman treatment is not necessarily reduced or eliminated by means of a legally binding diplomatic assurance. To be effective, addressees of non-legally binding agreements 'will need to be convinced to follow their normative guidelines, more so than with legally binding norms whose effectiveness can be presumed to be backed-up by some form of sanctions or compliance pull.'[85] While an analysis of theories of international relations would be beyond the scope of this work, it is worth noting that a neoliberal institutionalist such as Keohane, in considering the long-term reputational consequences of non-compliance, has observed that 'for reasons of reputation, as well as fear of retaliation and concerns about the effects of precedents, egoistic governments may follow the rules and principles of international regimes even when myopic self-interest counsels them not to.'[86]

This notion (of reputation) is highly subjective, for it is shaped by State actors' perceptions. Moreover, the search for (good) reputation and the possible fear of retaliation do not make State actors automatically compliant with their commitments/obligations, or even law-abiding. The conclusion of an MoU shows that the signatories are convinced about the legitimacy of their reciprocal commitments without necessarily respecting them; reputation only constitutes one motive for explaining State actors' compliance (if any).

Legal scholarship remains highly divided on the normative quality of diplomatic assurances, and the different stances seem difficult to reconcile through a minimum common denominator. Likewise, the judiciary does not provide a uniform answer. Thus, in determining the status of these highly disputed arrangements in international law, a case-by-case approach should be adopted by giving greater weight to the *intentions* of the parties as inferred from both the phrasing of the agreement, and the positions taken by the two governments during the negotiation process.

However, intentions (taken in the broadest sense) may not be equally shared by the parties involved and are not necessarily fully expressed in diplomatic assurances. While the phrasing of the accord is of importance in determining its meaning and purpose, the context and the way in which the signed agreement will be treated politically and in official rhetoric are also essential to understanding its legal and political consequences.

That said, the key question for the purpose of assessing the impact of diplomatic assurances on refugee rights is not whether they are *binding*, but whether they are *reliable*,[87] or, in other words, whether they are meant to be kept. If

[85] Pauwelyn 2012, n 39 above, 31.

[86] RO Keohane, *After Hegemony: Cooperation and Discord in the World Political Economy* (Princeton University Press, 1984) 106.

[87] It is here worth clarifying that the two concepts are not unconnected. As we will see below, a legally binding assurance can also add value to the reliability of assurances.

this is the case, even a political commitment might affect the assessment of the risk for the removed.[88] In this respect, what counts most in the assessment of reliability is the human rights track record of the receiving country and its extraneousness to practices of torture and violent interrogation.

(i) Strengthening Reliability: What Incentives and Threats?

The question of whether an individual (for the purpose of this chapter an asylum seeker, or a person either excluded from refugee status or whose status has been rejected or revoked) has a real and personalised risk of being subject to ill-treatment upon removal requires a determination of whether or not such assurances are reliable. This entails an assessment, from a State perspective, of: first, whether the government giving the assurance can be expected to comply with the agreement; and secondly, how reliability may be strengthened. If the prospects of compliance are overly remote, any removal would be unlawful as the risk for the deportee cannot be eliminated.

Nonetheless, international human rights treaties' supervisory bodies have generally been more cautious in endorsing the reliability of assurances in the eradication of the risk for the deportee. The *Agiza v Sweden* case,[89] for example, demonstrates how the Committee Against Torture did not consider the discourse on trust compelling. Indeed, despite the fact that Sweden ensured Egypt's compliance with the bilateral commitments by holding that 'failure to honour the guarantees would impact strongly on other similar European cases in the future',[90] allegations of torture started to circulate quite soon after the deportation.

Governments generally assume that compliance depends less upon the legal status of the agreement and more on the incentives the two involved States might have to keep their promises. Although it is often maintained that a State that flouts binding international human rights obligations cannot be trusted to respect a non-legally binding promise in a specific case, the same reasoning can also be applied – in their view – with regard to legally binding assurances. Since assurances have been supplied at the highest level of government, and lack of compliance is likely to do serious damage to diplomatic relations and international reputation, the effects of infringement would be more detrimental than those deriving from flouting a multilateral obligation owed to several States at once. The more individualised assurances are, the more incentives a State has to comply with the exchanged guarantees. However, if negotiated during the asylum determination process, individualised assurances can undermine the principle of confidentiality, which is an essential requirement of fair asylum procedures.[91]

[88] Skoglund 2008, n 44 above, 337.

[89] *Agiza v Sweden*, Comm no 233/2003 (20 May 2005) UN Doc CAT/C/34/D/233/2003.

[90] ibid, para 4.24.

[91] For a broader discussion on the principle of confidentiality and asylum procedures, see below in this chapter.

It has been argued how 'the *de facto* function of a diplomatic assurance is to elevate the circumstances of a single person to a case of "diplomatic significance" or "personal trust" between senior State officials.'[92] By means of a bilateral agreement – more than through a multilateral arrangement where States seldom rely on State complaint mechanisms – the sending State should be more inclined to monitor whether the other party follows through on the accord.

According to the representative of the British government in the *Abu Qatada* case before SIAC,

> States look not only to the legal status of international documents when deciding their behaviour but to the whole political context.... This MoU, while imposing less than a legal obligation, was made with respect to one State only, with an exceptionally strong political commitment on the part of both governments.[93]

The same approach has been adopted at the level of the national judiciary also by SIAC:

> The answer here is precisely that [the assurance] is bilateral, and is the result of a long-standing and friendly relationship in which there are incentives on both sides to comply once the agreement was signed. The failure of those who regard these arrangements as unenforceable ... is a failure to see them in their specific political and diplomatic context, a context which will vary from country to country.[94]

This approach seems to assume that, regardless of the informal format of Memoranda, the receiving country would be more committed to respecting standards mutually agreed on a bilateral level than at the multilateral level because of the 'serious bilateral consequences if things went wrong.'[95] Beside the immediate interest of a State in readmitting a national, a government might also decide to regulate, in agreement with another country, the treatment of a deportee for the sake of enhancing its international standing. Indeed, the long-term costs for defaulting States would include attracting negative publicity, worsening their reputation, and diminishing credibility as actors able to keep faith with their commitments.[96]

The decision to sign the agreement is detached from actual compliance with the accord itself. Compliance may also depend on different political calculations concerning possible benefits or sanctions in other related areas, such as trade or development aid. In the majority of security-related deportations, the receiving State has a minor interest in negotiating an assurance, which is the outcome of a request made by the sending State with a view to conferring legitimacy to the removal of a person deemed not conducive to the public good.

[92] N Larsaeus, 'The Use of Diplomatic Assurances in the Prevention of Prohibited Treatment' (October 2006) *RSC Working Paper no 32*, 8.

[93] *Oman Othman v SSHD*, SC/15/2005, 26 February 2017, para 296.

[94] *BB v SSHD*, 5 December 2006, SC/ 39/2005, para 508.

[95] Jones, 2008, n 79 above, 187.

[96] Skoglund 2008, n 44 above, 355. See also, Jones 2008, n 79 above, 188.

As a consequence, the receiving State needs particular motivations to meet the demands of the sending State. The lack of incentives was probably the reason for failed diplomatic assurances between the British government and Egypt in 1999 concerning the deportation of Mr Youssef.[97]

Generally speaking, assessing the reliability of diplomatic assurances is perhaps relatively easier when they are intended to prevent receiving States from sentencing to death a certain person.[98] In these circumstances, the authorities of the sending State can seemingly better monitor whether the deportee is effectively channelled into a formal process that envisages capital punishment as the sanctioning solution. However, supervising compliance with assurances against torture or other inhuman and degrading treatment turns out to be very complicated, as it requires constant vigilance by competent and independent personnel in relation to abuses committed by security forces in detention centres.[99]

For instance, the British SIAC, though accepting that Libyan authorities had entered the MoU with the UK in good faith, did not find diplomatic assurances reliable in the specific case of two individuals ordered to be deported to Libya on security grounds. Given that Libyan authorities had in the past unexpectedly changed course, there was a real risk that their position could vary again after the delivery of the assurances.[100]

(ii) Monitoring Mechanisms

A viable manner of supervising whether diplomatic assurances are respected seems to be through the creation of independent monitoring bodies. Taking again the UK as the object of analysis, it has identified local or national organisations to conduct post-removal monitoring visits, such as the Ethiopian National Human Rights Commission, the Institute for Human Rights of the Beirut Bar Association, *Organisation Marocaine des Droits Humains* (OMDH), or the Adaleh Centre for Human Rights appointed by the Jordanian government to monitor the treatment of individuals repatriated on the basis of the Memorandum agreed with the UK. However, a host of shortcomings exist in practice, in particular in relation to the difficulty in permanently funding and maintaining these bodies, the presence of officers and cameras on prison visits, and the

[97] *Youssef v The Home Office*, Queen's Bench Division, 30 July 2004, [2004] EWHC 1884 (*Youssef v The Home Office*).

[98] Reliability of diplomatic assurances in cases involving the death penalty cannot, however, be taken for granted. For example, in the *Venezia* judgment, the Italian Constitutional Court held that the formula 'sufficient assurances' is not constitutionally admissible, since cases regarding the death penalty and, therefore, the right to life, require an 'absolute guarantee' that the capital punishment will not be executed. See *Judgment no 223, Venezia v Ministero di Grazia e Giustizia*, Italian Constitutional Court, 27 June 1996, para 5.

[99] Report of the independent Expert on the Protection of Human Rights and Fundamental Freedoms while Countering Terrorism to the UN Commission on Human Rights, UN Doc E/CN.4/2006/94, 16 February 2006, para 56.

[100] *DD and AS v SSHD*, above n 32, paras 334–371.

risk for local monitoring committees working with foreign authorities to see contracts with their own government or international NGOs jeopardised.[101]

The monitoring body can also authorise medical examinations. Since the MoU with Libya does not specify who the members of the committee should be, the UK asked the Gaddafi International Foundation for Charity to take on these functions. But the fact that the son of the then Head of State, Colonel Gaddafi, was the leader of the organisation inescapably called into question its independence from the government. It is hard to imagine, indeed, that torture would have been denounced by it, and, even if this were the case, that legal redress would have been provided to the victims of such treatment.[102]

Similarly, in the *Arar* case – concerning a Canadian national suspected of terrorism and rendered by the US to Syria – the Canadian consul visiting the captive, once confronted with diverging information on the detention conditions, preferred to believe the Head of the Syrian Intelligence Service rather than Mr Arar. As Canada had an interest in the outcome of Mr Arar's interrogation, he was not considered a reliable source of information, thus diminishing the protection owed to a national and his fundamental rights.[103] Therefore, the Commission of Inquiry, called to decide about Mr Arar's removal to Syria, found that the applicant had been tortured despite assurances, and concluded that this finding is a concrete example proving that assurances from regimes which practise torture against detainees are of no value and cannot be accepted as reliable sources for a safe transfer.[104]

Many other reasons can contribute to rendering the supervisory system ineffective. Because of the fear of retributive torture, the captive might be unable to admit to having undergone torture or violent interrogation methods when he or she receives visits from diplomats and members of the monitoring committee. Many detainees have expressed similar frustrations. For instance, after two weeks of interrogation and torture, Mr Arar started receiving diplomatic visits, which took place in the presence of a Colonel, an interpreter, and three other Syrian officials. Although those visits were his lifeline, Mr Arar found them unbearably frustrating, since he was unable to denounce torture for the fear of being beaten again.[105]

Additionally, if the deportee is an alleged terrorist, an enemy of, or a threat to, the sending country, diplomats might have no interest in genuine disclosure

[101] See the analysis made by the UK Independent Reviewer of Terrorism Legislation in, A David and W Clive, *Deportation with Assurances*, July 2017, 18–20.

[102] An analysis of the Libyan monitoring framework is traced in the SIAC case *DD and AS v SSHD*, above n 32.

[103] Noll 2006, n 51 above.

[104] Commission of Inquiry into the actions of Canadian Officials in relation to Mr Arar's removal to Syria, *Report of the Events relating to Maher Arar – Factual Background* (Minister of Public Works and Government Services 2006) (Report of the Events relating to Maher Arar).

[105] M Arar, 'Statement' in R Meeropol (ed), *America's Disappeared: Secret Imprisonment, Detainees, and the War on Terror* (Seven Stories Press, 2004) 68–69.

of the truth through an investigation of the reasons behind the accusations of torture. First, the two governments may share the common interest of acquiring intelligence information. Second, admission of ill-treatment would confirm previous criticisms on the risks of deportation, and would potentially endanger good relations with the partner in other areas, such as in control and prevention of irregular migration.[106] Third, it is not difficult to imagine that the readmitting State might decide to withdraw cooperation on counter-terrorism matters in the event that a breach was discovered.[107] Fourth, any finding of violation of the assurances would result in the embarrassing acknowledgement that an unlawful removal in breach of the international obligation against torture has been carried out, thus tarnishing the international image of the two involved States and undermining their bilateral relationship. Indeed, the receiving State would not have any interest in denouncing lack of compliance, and thereby depicting itself as an unreliable actor.[108] Such a silencing effect by the diplomats and the captives acts as a sort of virus on any assurances: such a virus makes them unreliable instruments as long as they are negotiated with notoriously unsafe countries.

(iii) Enforcement Mechanisms

Since diplomatic assurances are mainly grounded in an *ex ante* trust in a foreign country, a careful assessment of their role in eliminating the risk of *refoulement* should be carried out. To my knowledge, each time an individual has been removed within the framework of a bilateral exchange of diplomatic assurances on national security grounds, she has been excluded from the effective control of the judiciary, because of the inability of the sending State to exercise jurisdiction to act upon a finding of transgression.[109] A victim of torture is generally entitled to seek civil, criminal, and international legal remedies against both the sending and readmitting country. Successful civil or criminal actions can also give rise to compensatory or punitive redress, which has a more symbolic value, as compared to the irremediable physical and mental damage suffered by the torture victim.[110] For example, in a number of cases where European States were involved in the unlawful rendition of suspected terrorists to the US – where wrongful treatment had predictably occurred – the ECtHR found violations of Article 3. However, payments of modest compensation took place years after the events.[111]

[106] Noll 2006, n 51 above, 122–23.

[107] Justice 2010, 50.

[108] E Schmid, 'The End of the Road on Diplomatic Assurances: The Removal of Suspected Terrorists under International Law' (2011) 8(1) *Essex Human Rights Review* 229.

[109] Noll 2006, n 51 above.

[110] JG Johnston, 'The Risk of Torture as a Basis for Refusing Extradition and the Use of Diplomatic Assurances to Protect against Torture after 9/11' (2011) 11 *International Criminal Law Review* 1, 46.

[111] See, eg, *El-Masri v FYRM*, above n 7; *Al-Nashiri v Poland*, App no 28761/11 (16 February 2015); *Husayn (Abu Zubaydah) v Poland*, App no 7511/13 (16 February 2015); and *Nasr Ghali v Italy*, App no 44883/09 (23 February 2016).

The question, therefore, is: what guarantees, if any, are available as a consequence of violations of diplomatic assurances?[112]

Traditional political responses in the event of infringement of assurances include diplomatic protest as well as the threat of economic and political sanctions. When the removal of a person to the country of origin is likely to provoke irremediable violations of her fundamental rights, insufficient reliance can be made on discretionary principles of estoppel and good faith, which might be detrimental to legal certainty.

Those supporting diplomatic assurances as non-legally binding agreements would argue that, if a transgression occurs, conflicts might be solved only through diplomatic processes.[113] From an inter-state perspective, where no countermeasures can be invoked if a violation of a non-legally binding treaty occurs, other unfriendly actions can be undertaken by the parties to an international agreement, such as diplomatic protest, retorsion, or the refusal to render any more prisoners.[114]

It should also be highlighted that no special forum exists – under a bilateral political agreement – to pursue an action alleging violations of diplomatic assurances. In addition, domestic courts have been quite reluctant to attribute a legal personality to foreign States in domestic legal proceedings. Since individuals are not a party to the agreement and no mechanism of individual complaints exists, diplomatic assurances do not guarantee an individual standing to allege a breach of the accord. The MoUs agreed by the UK do not contain any provision for adjudication, enforcement, or sanction for breach of any kind. However, there is no need for the agreement to contain provisions on enforcement or adjudication, because if, in the opinion of one of the contracting parties, there is a violation, enforcement measures can be taken under the law of international State responsibility, including proportionate and non-forcible countermeasures. As stated in the *Commentary to the ILC Draft Articles on the Expulsion of Aliens* (2014):

> (1) It is undisputed that an expulsion in violation of a rule of international law entails the international responsibility of the expelling State for an internationally wrongful act....
>
> (2) The fundamental principle of full reparation by the State of the injury caused by an internationally wrongful act is stated in article 31 of the articles on State responsibility, while article 34 sets out the various forms of reparation, namely restitution (article 35), compensation (article 36) and satisfaction (article 37).[115]

[112] Jones 2006, n 9 above, 28.

[113] Aust 2000, n 36 above, 45.

[114] Retorsion is an 'unfriendly' conduct that is not inconsistent with any international law obligations. See Oppenheim and Roxburgh, *International Law: A Treatise*, Vol 1, 3rd edn (The Lawbook Exchange Ltd, 2005) 43.

[115] Draft articles on the expulsion of aliens, with commentaries 2014, http://legal.un.org/ilc/texts/instruments/english/commentaries/9_12_2014.pdf. Adopted by the International Law Commission at its sixty-sixth session, in 2014, and submitted to the General Assembly as a part of the Commission's report covering the work of that session (A/69/10), 49.

While either State may withdraw from the aforementioned UK MoUs by giving six months' notice, the terms of the agreements will continue to apply to any person deported under the arrangements. No provision regulates the consequences in cases of breach of this requirement, or where a detainee is discovered to be a victim of torture. *Mutatis mutandis*, an interesting case on potential remedies in case of breach of assurances is offered by the MoU between the US and the UK armed forces allowing for the removal of prisoners on request, in accordance with Article 45 of the Fourth Geneva Convention. The case of *Yunus Rahmatullah* shows how the retransfer to the sending country in case of ill-treatment is not in fact guaranteed.[116] The applicant was passed on to US authorities by the British Army, and then transferred to Bagram in Afghanistan. Following allegations of mistreatment in Afghanistan, the UK sought his transfer sending a letter to the US authorities, who ignored this request. Given that it was impossible, in the present case, to persuade a close ally to comply with the MoU and its legal obligations under international humanitarian law, one cannot expect that other countries with less shared history of cooperation and friendly relations could impose remedies on one another.[117] Moreover, since there is little prospect of detainees gaining redress from the domestic legal systems of the receiving countries, 'one would think that this lack of any provision for enforcement went directly to the question of the reliability of assurances.'[118]

However, international bodies stand as the most suitable arenas for seeking legal redress against perpetrators of serious human rights violations. In particular, universal and regional human rights bodies are the most appropriate venues through which States and individuals may seek to adjudicate breaches of fundamental rights, even if they derive from breaches of diplomatic assurances. It should be noted that UN human rights treaty-monitoring bodies, such as the Committee Against Torture or the HRC, can accept individual complaints for violations of the prohibition of torture, through failure of the receiving State to enforce diplomatic assurances, only if the receiving State has itself accepted the jurisdiction of the Committee.

In the process of finding out breaches of assurances and providing the individual with effective remedies, two elements need to be borne in mind. First, the sending State is understandably very reluctant to publicly admit that an accord to prevent the future risk of ill-treatment resulted – despite assurances – in the actual commission of that same mistreatment at the hand of a State clearly

[116] *Secretary of State for Foreign and Commonwealth Affairs and Another v Yunus Rahmatullah*, 31 October 2012, [2012] UKSC 48. Subsequent civil actions include, *Belhaj v Straw and Others*, 17 January 2017, [2017] UKSC 3; *Rahmatullah (Respondent) v Ministry of Defence and Another (Appellants)*, 17 January 2017, [2017] UKSC 1 and [2017] UKSC 3.

[117] See on this case, Anderson and Walker 2017, n 19 above, 81.

[118] E Metcalf, 'The False Promise of Assurances against Torture' (2009) 6(1) *Justice Journal* 63.

described as reliable and safe by virtue of the strong political relations linking the two governments.

Second, in its prognostic assessment of the risk, the sending State should be persuaded in good faith that there is *no danger* of proscribed treatment upon removal. Accordingly, the role of an international human rights body – such as the ECtHR – would be limited to ascertaining that the sending State has lived up to the obligation of *non-refoulement* in good faith by receiving a number of safeguards from the readmitting country. *Non-refoulement* – as implicitly enshrined, for example, in Article 3 of the ECHR – is a duty of prevention, and not one of result. The obligation is exhausted when the Court is satisfied that a State made its best efforts to reconstruct what might happen sometime in the future, rather than when that State has achieved a specific result. The appraisal of the risk is, indeed, a speculative exercise where the Court is asked to examine the foreseeable consequences of sending the applicant to the receiving country, bearing in mind all available information.[119] Therefore, regardless of the legal status of the assurances, it would be meaningless if a deportee, tortured upon removal, were to lodge a new complaint before the same Court that had previously given the green light to deportation following the satisfactory *ex ante* assessment of the risk made by the sending State.

(iv) When Assurances are Reliable and When They are Not: An Easy Distinction?

In light of the foregoing, this Sub-section asks under what circumstances diplomatic assurances can be considered sufficiently reliable instruments to eliminate the risk of torture or other inhuman treatment. As we will better observe in Part 3 of this chapter, international human rights bodies have generally rejected *ipso facto* assurances as reliable bases for safe transfer. In the *Ben Khemais v Italy* case, for example, the ECtHR held that the fact the complainant had not suffered immediate ill-treatment upon his removal to Tunisia, as assured by the authorities of this State, would not amount to a reliable prediction of the fate of that person in the future.[120]

The implicit importance of the Court's reasoning lies in the consideration that a long-term assessment of the safety of the receiving country for the individual must also be done in light of the general human rights situation in the receiving country. Although a court or any other supervisory body should consider the existence of stable relations between the two involved States, and gauge the personalised risk existing at the material time of the expulsion, these bodies cannot ignore the potentially irremediable consequences for the deportee

[119] See, eg, *Saadi v Italy*, App no 37201/06 (29 January 2008) para 130. See also, *Yearbook of the ILC 2001*, Vol II, Part 2, 'Commentary to Article 14', paras 14, 145. See also, A Marchesi, *Obblighi di condotta e obblighi di risultato* (Giuffrè, 2003).

[120] *Ben Khemais v Italy*, App no 246/07 (24 February 2009) para 64.

if torture is practised once the spotlights are off in a particular case and the visits from diplomats monitoring the detainee become more infrequent.

The criteria crafted by the ECtHR – which cannot be considered exhaustive – include: (i) whether the terms of the assurances have been disclosed to the Court; (ii) whether they are specific or rather general and vague; (iii) whether the agent giving the assurances is able to bind the receiving State and, additionally, its local authorities; (iv) whether the assurances concern treatment that is legal or illegal in the readmitting State; (v) whether the two States have strong and durable relations; (vi) whether the readmitting State has traditionally respected previous assurances of a similar sort; (vii) whether monitoring mechanisms exist to supervise compliance; (viii) whether an effective system of protection against torture is in force in the receiving country, in terms of investigation, prosecution of torture-related crimes, and cooperation with international monitoring bodies; (ix) whether the applicant has previously been ill-treated; and (x) whether the reliability of assurances has already been examined by national courts of the sending State.[121]

These criteria are important for at least two main reasons: first, they have informed the ensuing case law of the Court on deportation with assurances; second, they point to the salience of State *practice* in assessing the safety of a State in cases of security-related deportation. States have tried to strengthen the reliability of diplomatic assurances by delegating monitoring responsibilities to an independent and authoritative third party, composed not necessarily of diplomats, but ideally of members of NGOs and human rights organisations. Such oversight would play a crucial role in the assessment of the risks for the individual in question. It has been argued that contacts with detainees should take place over time and be carried out by individuals with the necessary expertise. As the HRC suggests, a video recording of all interrogations can also be kept.[122] A monitoring body could exercise external pressure on the sending State not to conceal any information about human rights transgressions. It can also stand as a deterrent for the receiving country by means, for example, of publication of monitoring reports of violations and the institutionalisation of automatic enforcement mechanisms and avenues of legal redress when illegal practices are detected. The receiving State should also demonstrate its engagement in political and legal reforms that can increase confidence that it will comply with the promises taken. Moreover, a certain degree of verification of its criminal justice and penal processes (including independent legal and medical access in general and not just for 'deportation with assurances' purposes) should be guaranteed.[123] However, even if diplomats phrase assurances in very specific terms, with monitoring mechanisms coupled with a system of public reports of abuses, these cannot be considered reliable in those contexts where torture is common practice.

[121] *Abu Qatada v UK*, above n 15, para 189.
[122] HRC, *General Comment no 20*, 10 March 1992.
[123] Anderson and Walker 2017, n 19 above, 82.

While most literature has delved into the legal status of diplomatic assurances, this issue does not seem to be decisive in determining whether the risk faced by the individual in the readmitting country is in fact removed and whether refugees' access to protection may be hampered. As governments tend to violate human rights obligations taken on at a multilateral level, States are prone to justifying diplomatic assurances against ill-treatment on the basis of the reliability of their partners, regardless of both their human rights track record and the legally binding nature of the undertakings.

F. Diplomatic Assurances: Toward a 'Repoliticisation' of Rights?

Although the UN human rights committees and the ECtHR have acknowledged the reliability of diplomatic assurances when mechanisms of control are in place, it is not an automatic equation that more accountable and enforceable security-driven agreements will eliminate *per se* the risk of ill-treatment within the borders of a country that makes of torture a systematic practice – a practice that, *inter alia*, is often justified in the name of cooperation with Western governments in countering terrorism. Through the analysis of international human rights case law, the following Sections will show how *refoulement* occurred even when diplomatic assurances had been given.

The fact that the sending and receiving governments do not want their international reputations and diplomatic relationships damaged by lack of adherence to the accord still provides no guarantee against the perpetration of a wrongful act. Therefore, despite the existence of a friendly diplomatic relationship, a State partner with a dismal long-standing attitude to human rights obligations which have been undertaken at a multilateral level should be considered unreliable.

With regards to the legal status of assurances, the use of the term 'diplomatic' does not *ipso facto* exclude their legally binding nature. Attention should be drawn to the intention of the parties, the actual object of the agreements, and the organs that have negotiated them, in order to ensure that they are able to bind the State in accordance with Article 46 of the VCLT. A case-by-case approach would, therefore, be fitting.[124]

The existence of legally binding agreements does not prevent commission of the wrongful act, but does have an impact on the *ex post* enforcement mechanisms in case of human rights abuses. Enforcement is an element that courts (and possibly States) *should* take into consideration in the *ex ante* assessment of the risk of torture. It indicates to what extent the two States would be able to commit themselves, by being willingly subjected to mechanisms to determine their responsibility in case of departure from the assurances. In this sense, it could also have a deterrent effect.

[124] See A Gianelli, 'Obbligo di *non-refoulement* e assicurazioni diplomatiche' in *Studi in onore di Vincenzo Starace*, vol I (Editoriale Scientifica, Napoli, 2008) 368.

However, *in practice*, States do not deem the legal status of diplomatic assurances – which is related to the existence of enforcement procedures – particularly relevant to the assessment of their reliability. Indeed, political motivations and friendly diplomatic relations play a *de facto* greater role in the decision of States to cooperate in safe removal of detainees. *Ex post* enforcement is perceived as an essential component of an effective system of human rights protection, but it pursues the purpose of supplying the individual with the instruments to seek and obtain justice only *after* a violation of her rights has occurred. The combination of all these elements explains why the normative quality of diplomatic assurances is not deemed by political and judicial authorities a decisive asset to the assessment of the impact assurances have on refugee rights.

These considerations also raise two further issues, which cannot be answered in the course of this chapter: why States need to frame their human rights commitments within bilateral political agreements, which replicate standards that have already been enshrined within international human rights treaties; and whether the proliferation of bilateral instruments precluding torture in a specific case undermine the object and purpose of multilateral human rights treaties aimed at granting protection against torture in a *general* manner.[125] It should be observed that the use of diplomatic assurances against torture might contribute to diluting internationally recognised standards: it makes an individual's exposure to abuses upon deportation, if not necessarily more likely, at least more acceptable.

A legally binding assurance can legitimately restate pre-existing obligations, but may also apply them specifically to the case of removal of a person under the bilateral agreement. Indeed, 'an obligation might be doubly owed, due to having been made obligatory by two different sources.'[126] However, this does not clarify the added value of repeating in generic form commitments which States have already entered into in human rights treaties.[127]

Diplomatic assurances are generally sought when the sending country bears a reasonable suspicion that the receiving State is abusive. The two detrimental, but still inevitable, consequences are: on the one hand, the implicit recognition of the existence and perpetuation of systematic violations of torture in the readmitting country; and, on the other hand, the creation of a two-tier system that differentiates between the individual shielded by the assurances and all other detainees who continue to be subjected to inhuman and degrading treatment or torture.

Moreover, Article 41(2) of the International Law Commission (ILC) *Articles on State Responsibility* (ILC Articles) provides that 'no State shall recognize as lawful a situation created by a serious breach within the meaning of article 40,

[125] For a discussion on the relationship between diplomatic assurances and the multilateral framework of human rights protection, see Schmid 2011, n 108 above, 230–34.

[126] Worster 2012, n 35 above, 276.

[127] The SIAC, for example, explained in these terms Algeria's failure to agree an MoU with the UK. See *Y v SSHD*, 24 August 2006, SC/36/2005, para 256.

nor render aid or assistance in maintaining that situation.' Pursuant to Article 40, a breach of a norm, such as the prohibition of torture, 'is serious if it involves a gross or systematic failure by the responsible State to fulfil the obligation.' Article 41(2) not only refers to the formal recognition of an unlawful situation, but also prohibits acts that would imply such recognition.[128] Article 41(2) 'extends beyond the commission of the serious breach itself to the maintenance of the situation created by that breach, and it applies whether or not the breach itself is a continuing one.'[129] As to the elements of 'aid or assistance', it is implicit that the State has 'knowledge of the circumstances of the internationally wrongful act', as provided for in Article 16 of the ILC Articles.[130]

For the purpose of this chapter, the typical scenario is one of bilateral cooperation for the removal of suspected terrorists to a country with questionable and violent techniques of interrogation in order to extract information that can be helpful to both the sending and receiving State. The issue of State responsibility under general international law will not be discussed here; however, it can be noted that, if it is proved that the sending country transfers unwanted aliens to a third country with knowledge of the circumstances of the internationally wrongful act (*in casu*, the use of torture), it might be engaging in violation of Article 41 by aiding and abetting the responsible State in maintaining that situation.

Although diplomatic assurances (either in the form of an MoU or as individualised assurances) have often been considered by national authorities to be trustworthy tools for removing the risk of mistreatment for the deportee, academics, human rights organisations, and international human rights bodies have repeatedly questioned their reliability. Goodwin-Gill, for example, indicates at least four reasons why diplomatic assurances lack efficacy: (i) they are based on trust; (ii) post-removal monitoring mechanisms are insufficient to prevent mistreatment, on account of the fact that torture is secretly administered and the detainees have no interest in occasionally reporting abuses that could cause reprisals; (iii) non-state actors can be the potential perpetrators of torture; and (iv) it is unlikely that States will be held accountable in case of violations.[131]

According to Theo Van Boven, the former UN Special Rapporteur on Torture, even when there is not a consistent pattern of gross and flagrant human

[128] ILC Draft articles on Responsibility of States for Internationally Wrongful Acts, with commentaries 2001: Commentary to Article 41, p 114, http://legal.un.org/ilc/texts/instruments/english/commentaries/9_6_2001.pdf.

[129] ibid, 115.

[130] ibid, 115. Pursuant to Art 16, 'A State which aids or assists another State in the commission of an internationally wrongful act by the latter is internationally responsible for doing so if: (*a*) that State does so with knowledge of the circumstances of the internationally wrongful act ....' Art 16 will be discussed more in detail in Chapter 5 of this book.

[131] GS Goodwin-Gill, 'Diplomatic Assurances and Deportation', Presented at JUSTICE/Sweet & Maxwell Conference on Counter-terrorism and Human Rights, 28 June 2005, p 2, as cited in Braswell 2006, n 17 above, 15.

rights violations in the receiving country, the potential risk of torture or other forms of inhuman treatment in the individual case is sufficient to exclude *a priori* the usage of diplomatic assurances.[132] Post-removal monitoring mechanisms have so far proven ineffective both in relieving individuals from the risk of torture, and as an instrument of accountability.[133] They neither have a statutory mandate allowing unimpeded and unannounced visits, nor possess that authority or influence to ensure that an independent investigation of the allegations of torture is carried out.[134] The existence of such a fragile backdrop for human rights protection in security-related transfers 'leads us to question whether security and migration control constitute legitimate enough interests to undermine the application of the principles of legal certainty, transparency, and democratic control to State action abroad.'[135]

In extradition proceedings, negotiation on the treatment of the person in question is carried out by the criminal justice systems of the two countries involved. Instead, in deportations with assurances on security grounds, dialogue is between political authorities. Such deference to bilateral diplomacy might end up being particularly dangerous when the fundamental rights of vulnerable individuals are at stake. Diplomatic assurances are predominantly negotiated with countries where torture is widespread and routine and where, consequently, the damage for the applicant would be irremediable if torture occurred *in concreto*. Moreover, if the protection of the rights of the deportees can be ensured by the pre-existent set of human rights treaties concluded at universal and regional level, one must question the utility and appropriateness of a binary system of human rights protection, which devolves upon the sphere of politics what States have already afforded to the sphere of law.[136]

The emerging anomaly is a progressive 'repoliticisation of human rights by way of moving their protection and shifting power from the legal or judicial sphere to that of diplomacy and transnational security networking.'[137] An individual identified as an 'object of "diplomatic significance" and "personal trust"

[132] Special Rapporteur of the UN Commission on Human Rights on Torture and other cruel, inhuman, or degrading treatment or punishment, *Report Submitted pursuant to General Assembly Resolution 58/164*, UN Doc A/59/324, 1 September 2004, paras 34, 37–39 (Special Rapporteur on Torture 2004).

[133] See Special Rapporteur on Torture, *Report submitted in accordance with General Assembly Resolution 59/182*, UN Doc A/60/316, 30 August 2005, para 46.

[134] Amnesty International 2010, n 12 above, 12.

[135] Garcia Andrade poses this question in the framework of migration controls at sea. See P Garcia Andrade, 'Extraterritorial Strategies to Tackle Irregular Immigration by Sea: A Spanish Perspective' in V Mitsilegas and B Ryan (eds), *Extraterritorial Immigration Controls* (Brill, 2010) 344.

[136] On this difference, see Klabbers 1996, n 48 above, 19. It is also to be noted that, in barring removal to a non-convention State when there is a real risk of torture, inhuman and degrading treatment, the Court adopts the same approach in cases of both expulsion and extradition. See, *Lopez Elorza v Spain*, App no 30614/15 (9 April 2018) para 103; *Harkins and Edwards*, App nos 9146/07 and 32650/07 (9 July 2012) para 120; and *Babar Ahmad and Others v the United Kingdom*, App nos. 24027/07, 11949/08, 36742/08, 66911/09 and 67354/09 (24 September 2012) para 168.

[137] Vedsted-Hansen 2010, n 14 above, 60.

between senior State officials', while possibly more protected, would also run the risk of being placed at the mercy of the fluctuating exigencies of foreign relations.[138] Although this does not sound like the most comforting scenario, it is also true that, in many cases, the activism of the judiciary has countered the choices made by the executive branch, who are generally more concerned over securing and controlling migration at the expense of the human rights of foreigners. Indeed, terrorism can drive the ECtHR to grant States a wider margin of appreciation in case of 'war or other public emergency threatening the life of the nation';[139] State security concerns cannot, however, defer judicial review and trump fundamental human rights obligations.[140]

As Vedsted-Hansen observes, although assurances can be perceived as an attempt to translate human rights protection into an essentially political issue, they should be subjected to the judicial control of independent bodies.[141] Nevertheless, the fact that they can be disobeyed – as several cases have demonstrated – reveals how 'the dilemmatic relationship between law and policy persists, and the shifting of power to the executive and security sphere invites for continued legal and academic attention.'[142]

Part 3

IV. ACCESS TO PROTECTION: THE RELATIONSHIP BETWEEN REFUGEE RIGHTS AND DIPLOMATIC ASSURANCES

Before delving into the interwoven relationship between diplomatic assurances and refugee rights, the reader might benefit from a brief summary of the main points made so far. Part 2 of this chapter pointed out how doctrine continues to be divided on the legal status of diplomatic assurances. This status can be an element in assessing the existence of enforcement mechanisms and the extent to which a State would commit itself by agreeing to be subjected to mechanisms of determination of responsibility in case of an infringement of the assurances. However, *in practice*, the legal status of assurances is not deemed a primary asset by the sending State in its prognostic assessment of the risk. States tend, indeed, to have a greater reliance on friendly political relations and the relocation of the deportee into the sphere of 'high diplomacy.'

This chapter takes as its unit of analysis diplomatic assurances formalised within MoUs – written bilateral agreements that lay out mutual understandings on the treatment of the deportees in a general fashion. Ample latitude is then given to States in deciding the modalities of enforcement of the assurances

[138] Larsaeus 2006, n 92 above, 2

[139] See Art 15(1) of the ECHR.

[140] See, eg, Vedsted-Hansen 2010, n 14 above, 61.

[141] ibid, 60.

[142] ibid, 62

negotiated under the general framework of an MoU. However, because of the dearth of jurisprudence on MoUs, cases on the use of single diplomatic assurances must be included in the analysis.

International courts have repeatedly highlighted how diplomatic assurances alone are insufficient,[143] and how the relevant government should conduct an independent risk-analysis to assess whether, at the practical level, the specific assurances delivered in an individual case alter the risk assessment. The next Subsections combine both the study of law and its implementation by relying on NGOs and International Organisations' reports as well as on the case law of international human rights bodies. They examine whether the use of diplomatic assurances, in principle and in practice, can hamper refugees' access to protection, that is to say, non-*refoulement*, as well as access to fair asylum procedures, and effective remedies before removal.

A. Diplomatic Assurances and Access to Asylum Procedures and Effective Remedies

Diplomatic assurances assume relevance for supervisory bodies, including refugee status determination commissions, national courts, or international human rights bodies invested with the task of determining whether a particular asylum seeker is entitled to protection, and whether assurances eliminate the risk of prohibited treatments faced by an individual scheduled to be deported to her country of origin.[144] Although diplomatic assurances do not affect the right to access asylum procedures, they can impact eligibility to asylum. In principle they cannot be sought from the country of origin or the country of former habitual residence (in the case of stateless asylum seekers) of an asylum seeker whose application is in course of examination. However, assurances might be given unilaterally by the country of origin or former habitual residence when it has knowledge or suspicion that a national or a certain individual has sought asylum in another State. Additionally, a person may apply for asylum after the request for diplomatic assurances has been submitted to facilitate deportation of a person whose presence is considered unconducive to the public good.

What is important to stress is that, in all of these different scenarios, the principle of confidentiality and the right to privacy categorically bar the host State from sharing information with the applicant's home country pending determination of the asylum claim, in order to avoid having her or her family members exposed to a risk of persecution, and to prevent such information being used

[143] See, *Ben Khemais v Italy*, above n 120, para 57; *Toumi v Italy*, App no 25716/09 (5 April 2011) para 51.

[144] See, eg, Committee against Torture, *General Comment no 1 on Art 3 of the Convention*, UN Doc A/53744, Annex IX, 52 (1998) para 7.

for purposes contrary to human rights law. Pursuant to Article 12 of the UDHR and Article 17 of the ICCPR, 'no one shall be subjected to arbitrary interference with his privacy, family, home, or correspondence. Everyone has the right to the protection of the law against such interference or attacks.'[145] Likewise, Article 8 of the ECHR provides that 'Everyone has the right to respect for his private and family life, his home, and his correspondence' and restrictions are allowed only in accordance with the law. As the HRC explains in its *General Comment 16 on Article 17*,

> the principle of confidentiality requires that effective measures have to be taken by States to ensure that information concerning a person's private life does not reach the hands of persons who are not authorized by law to receive, process, and use it.[146]

At the EU level, the principle of confidentiality is explicitly recognised by Article 30 of the Recast Procedures Directive whereby:

> For the purposes of examining individual cases, Member States shall not: (a) disclose information regarding individual applications for international protection, or the fact that an application has been made, to the alleged actor(s) of persecution or serious harm; (b) obtain any information from the alleged actor(s) of persecution or serious harm in a manner that would result in such actor(s) being directly informed of the fact that an application has been made by the applicant in question ....[147]

Likewise, Article 45(2)(b) of the Recast Procedures Directive[148] requires Member States to ensure that, in considering withdrawing the international protection status of a third country national in accordance with Article 14 and 19 of the Recast Qualification Directive, they adhere to the same procedural guarantees on confidentiality.

In line with the above-mentioned provisions, the UNHCR 'Note on Procedural Standards for refugee status determination under the UNHCR's Mandate' points out that every official who provides services to asylum seekers is 'under a duty to ensure the confidentiality of information received from or about asylum seekers and refugees.'[149] The fact that the applicants have made such a request should also be taken into consideration.[150] Moreover, disclosure of information without the consent of the individual concerned shall be subject to the

[145] Under Art 16 of the UN Convention on the Rights of the Child, 'Every child has the right to privacy. The law should protect the child's private, family and home life.' Convention on the Rights of the Child 1577 UNTS 3, entry into force 2 September 1990.

[146] See, HRC, *General Comment 16 on Art 17 of the ICCPR*, UN doc HRI/GEN/1/Rev.1, 23 (1988) para 10.

[147] Art 30 of the Recast Procedures Directive replaces Art 22 of the 2005 Procedures Directive.

[148] Art 45(2)(b) of the Recast Procedures Directive replaces Art 38(1)(d) of the 2005 Procedures Directive.

[149] UNHCR, *Note on Procedural Standards for Refugee Status Determination under the UNHCR's Mandate*, 20 November 2003, 2-1 (UNHCR Note on Procedural Standards).

[150] UNHCR, 'Asylum Processes (Fair and Efficient Asylum Procedures', *Global Consultations on International Protection*, EC/GC/01/12, 31 May 2001, para 50 (m).

approval of a Protection Staff member, and, in appropriate cases, the UNHCR Department of International Protection (DIP).[151] Asylum seekers must always be informed of their right to confidentiality and should also be assured that the UNHCR would not contact or share information with the country of origin about their condition or refugee status, unless they have expressly authorised the host country's authorities to do so.[152]

Therefore, a status determination authority must not provide the State of origin or other entities within the State with any information that a certain individual is seeking protection or has already obtained asylum, even if the situation in the home country has changed. Such an obligation is valid also in those cases in which a person has been denied asylum.[153] States must abide by the confidentiality rule not only during the assessment of protection needs, but also during the examination of exclusion grounds. In this phase, it might be possible to share data about a particular asylum seeker for the sake of gathering intelligence information on an individual's suspected terrorist activities. Although the exclusion procedure is not the core of this study, it is important to remember that 'even in such situations, the existence of the asylum application should still remain confidential.'[154]

States cannot avail themselves of diplomatic assurances in denying access to asylum procedures but can only rely on them as part of the factual elements necessary for assessing the risk for the asylum seeker and how well-founded her fear of persecution may be if she is repatriated to her home country. Therefore, diplomatic assurances cannot give rise to a declaration of inadmissibility of an asylum claim or to restrictions of essential procedural safeguards, but can only be used to determine the eligibility criteria for the recognition of an individual as a refugee or as a person in need of complementary protection.[155] If exchanged during the phase of assessment of her claim, assurances can involve violation of confidentiality and thus undermine the credibility of the entire process.[156]

The fact that the host country has received diplomatic assurances cannot constitute a basis for rejecting an asylum application – which should always be examined in its substance – but might require, according to the circumstances, a prioritisation of the treatment of such claims.[157] For example, applications concerning people suspected of terrorism or giving rise to possible considerations of exclusion under Article 1(f) of the Geneva Convention should not be

[151] UNHCR Note on Procedural Standards, n 149 above, 2-1.

[152] ibid. See also, UNHCR, *Guidance Note on Extradition and International Refugee Protection* (April 2008) 24.

[153] See, UNHCR Submission, *Inquiry into Asylum and Protection Visas for Consular Officials and the Deportation, Search and Discovery of Vivian Solon* (2005) para 9 (UNHCR Inquiry into Asylum and Protection Visas).

[154] UNHCR, *Background Note on the Application of the Exclusion Clauses: Article IF of the 1951 Convention Relating to the Status of Refugees* (4 September 2003) 540.

[155] UNHCR Note on Diplomatic Assurances, n 2 above, paras 41–42.

[156] UNHCR Inquiry into Asylum and Protection Visas, n 153 above, para 12.

[157] UNHCR Note on Diplomatic Assurances, n 2 above, para 46.

considered manifestly unfounded, but should rather be assessed on a priority basis by specialised exclusion units with designated Eligibility Officers operating within the institution in charge of asylum determination.[158]

As the UNHCR emphasises, diplomatic assurances cannot only be limited to eradicating a specific threat – such as the risk of torture – but must 'effectively eliminate *all* reasonably possible manifestations of persecution in the individual case' (emphasis added).[159] The institution responsible for asylum determination must ascertain, in other words, that the person in question would not be exposed to any other particular form of persecution beyond torture, for example, disproportionate punishment or discrimination. In conducting such an evaluation, the decision-making authority must also verify that the entity issuing the assurance has effective control over the actions of those State or non-State actors the risk of persecution emanates from.[160] An effective system of monitoring of the internal situation of the country at issue is, therefore, an essential requisite, although such a solution does not automatically provide the individual with mechanisms of enforcement against possible post-removal violations of the assurances.

Moreover, the evaluation of diplomatic assurances as a reliable criterion for eliminating the risk of persecution in the home country, and, therefore, denying asylum, shall be made in accordance also with international human rights law, which provides wider protection, especially when the applicant falls within one of the exclusion clauses of the Geneva Convention.[161] For instance, the ECtHR, the HRC, and the Committee Against Torture have acknowledged the right of a person, prior to her removal, to have legal recourse to an independent reviewing body to challenge the transfer, and gauge the reliability of assurances obtained in response to allegations of torture.[162] Seeking diplomatic assurances during the asylum determination process can contribute to a violation of the procedural safeguards of asylum mechanisms, such as the principle of confidentiality,[163] thus affecting the final outcome of the proceedings.[164] Although a detailed analysis of the procedural and substantive aspects of asylum determination is not at issue here, it is worth noting that diplomatic assurances have been

[158] ibid. See also, UNHCR Note on the Application of the Exclusion Clauses, n 154 above, para 101.

[159] UNHCR Note on Diplomatic Assurances, n 2 above, para 51.

[160] ibid, paras 51–52.

[161] The exclusion provisions of the Geneva Convention are listed in Art 1(d)(e)(f).

[162] See *Agiza*, above n 89, para 13.7.

[163] In a number of cases, assurances against torture were sought prior to completion of asylum procedures. See, eg, *Sihali v SSHD*, 26 March 2010, SC/38/2005, para 28, where diplomatic assurances were deemed an integral part of the immigration decision to refuse asylum. A detailed review of domestic cases has been provided in M Giuffré, 'An Appraisal of Diplomatic Assurances One Year after *Othman (Abu Qatada) v United Kingdom* (2012)' (2013) 2(2) *International Human Rights Law Review* 266. See also, HRW, *Commentary on State Replies CDDH Questionnaire on Diplomatic Assurances* (March 2006),http://www.hrw.org/sites/default/files/related_material/eu0306_diplo.pdf.

[164] As explained by the UNHCR, the basis of the right to confidentiality is the right to privacy enshrined in Art 12 of the UDHR and Art 17 of the ICCPR. See UNHCR Inquiry into asylum and protection visas, n 153 above.

progressively entering into the evidentiary assessment process. In some cases, the fact that the authorities of the country of origin were informed that their own nationals had (unsuccessfully) applied for asylum exposed the deportees to the risk of persecution.[165] As the UNHCR recognises, even if 'in exceptional circumstances, contact with the country of origin may be justified on national security grounds … the existence of the asylum application should not be disclosed.'[166]

In a number of other cases, the HRC and the Committee Against Torture have found that by seeking diplomatic assurances on the treatment of the applicants while their asylum proceedings were still under way, the authorities of the respondent State breached the principle of confidentiality whereby no information can be given to the government of the country of origin – the source of fear for the applicant.[167] In the *Agiza* and *Alzery* cases, for instance, the enforcement of the removal procedures was thus so swift that no possibility of challenging exclusion and expulsion arose for the two asylum seekers.

Since Article 3 of the Convention Against Torture implies the right to an effective, independent, and impartial review of the decision to expel or remove,[168] the Committee Against Torture held that there was an express breach of Article 22, highlighting that all remedies (against the exclusion from refugee status and the expulsion decision) should have been exhausted before removal. Likewise, the HRC has interpreted the right to an effective remedy under Article 2(3) of the ICCPR as requiring States parties to provide administrative and judicial review of deportation orders to avoid violations of the principle of *non-refoulement* enshrined in Article 7 of the ICCPR.[169]

Despite the fact that in cases of extradition, the requesting State is likely to be the home country of the individual in question, and is privy to the person's whereabouts, confidentiality should still be respected when commencing asylum proceedings. And despite the fact that information related to extradition may have a bearing on the eligibility of the person to asylum, the decision on asylum and the decision on the extradition request should always be conducted in parallel and constitute two separate procedures.

In *Khaydarov v Russia*, for example, the ECtHR held that, if the order to extradite the applicant to Tajikistan was to be enforced, there would be a violation of Article 3 of the Convention.[170] Whether diplomatic assurances were one of the major elements the Russian deciding authority relied upon to determine

[165] For more information on the 'Dutch-Congolese case', see the following websites: http://www.pilates.ekoregion.biz.pl/?pilates=Rita_Verdonk; and http://www.expatica.com/nl/news/local_news/netherlands-passed-asylum-details-to-congo-26049.html.

[166] UNHCR, *Guidelines on International Protection: Application of the Exclusion Clauses: Article 1F of the 1951 Convention relating to the Status of Refugees* (2003) 501.

[167] For a recollection of facts, see the two cases before the HRC and the Committee Against Torture: *Alzery v Sweden*, Comm no 1416/2005 (3 November 2006) UN Doc CCPR/C/88/D/1416/2005; *Agiza v Sweden*, above n 89.

[168] *Agiza v Sweden*, above n 89, para 13.8.

[169] ibid, para 11.8.

[170] *Khaydarov v Russia*, App no 21055/09 (20 May 2010) para 164.

the refusal of the asylum request of Mr Khaydarov is a matter of speculation. But what is certain is that diplomatic assurances were sought during his asylum determination process, thus violating basic rules of fairness requiring that no information on the applicant is shared with the country of origin. The outcome of the extradition proceedings was affected accordingly.

Asylum seekers whose refugee status (or subsidiary protection) has been refused or who have been excluded from international protection on national security grounds are entitled to an effective remedy, meaning the right both to appeal a negative decision within a reasonable time, and to remain in the territory awaiting the outcome of the appeal.[171] In addition, independent judicial scrutiny of diplomatic assurances at national and international level may prevent an unlawful removal to torture.

In the great majority of cases concerning deportation with assurances, the ECtHR has recorded no breach of Article 13, owing to the fact that the decision to expel an individual after rejection of her asylum claim, or the application of an exclusion order, had been reviewed by a domestic court of appeal. Therefore, the exchange of diplomatic assurances should not impair the right to an effective remedy as long as a person (including an asylum seeker who has either been rejected or excluded from refugee status/subsidiary protection) has been allowed to both challenge the expulsion decision and to remain in the territory awaiting the outcome of the appeal.[172]

In those few cases where the ECtHR found violations of Article 13, responsibility was not attributed to the existence of diplomatic assurances *per se*, since deportees were always entitled to challenge their expulsion decision. Breaches of rights were instead caused by lack of automatic suspensive effect of the appeal to set aside an expulsion order that could produce potentially irreversible effects for the removed individual.[173] For instance, an extreme, urgent procedure in lieu of rigorous and effective scrutiny of the claim can reduce the rights of the defence and the examination of the complaint to a minimum.[174]

B. Diplomatic Assurances and *Non-refoulement*

In order to avoid *refoulement*, asylum seekers are entitled to not be expelled pending a final determination of their status. The standard of scrutiny is slightly different depending on the instrument. For example, according to the Committee

[171] UNHCR Executive Committee, Conclusion no 8, *Determination of Refugee Status*, CCVIII, 1977, paras 6–7 (UNHCR Conclusion no 8).

[172] UNHCR Conclusion no 8, paras 6–7.

[173] See, eg, *Chahal v UK*, App no 22414/93 (25 October 1996/15 November 1996) paras 153–154; *Soldatenko v Ukraine*, App no 2440/07 (23 October 2008) paras 82–83; *Muminov v Russia*, App no 42502/06 (11 December 2008) paras 102, 105; *Abdulazhon Isakov v Russia*, App no 14049/08 (8 July 2010) paras 136, 138–139.

[174] See, eg, *MSS v Belgium and Greece*, App no 30696/09 (21 January 2011) paras 386–389.

against Torture, the complainant must prove that 'there are substantial grounds for believing that he [or she] *would be in danger* of being subjected to torture.'[175] The HRC and the ECtHR affirm, by contrast, that a person cannot be deported to a country where she might face a *real risk* of being subject to torture or cruel, inhuman and degrading treatment.[176] 'Substantial grounds' must exist that demonstrate that the risk of torture is a necessary and foreseeable consequence of the individual's removal.[177]

The applicant is not required to substantiate 'beyond any reasonable doubt' that she would suffer ill-treatment. If, in this context, diplomatic assurances have been provided, they could be relied upon only as factual elements for conducting such a determination on the safety of the receiving country in the individual case. If assurances cannot mitigate the risk of persecution and ill-treatment, the host State cannot remove the individual, in accordance with the duty of *non-refoulement*.

However, under Article 33(2) of the Geneva Convention, a person may be transferred to her country of origin if an individualised finding is made that she constitutes a present or future serious threat to the security of, or to the community of, the host State as a consequence of her conviction of a crime of a particularly grave nature.[178] In any case, *refoulement* must be necessary and proportionate, and must represent the last possible resort when the risk for the host country far outweighs the risk of harm for the deportee.[179] Moreover, the decision to apply Article 33(2) shall always be taken on the basis of a set of procedural safeguards, such as the right to be heard and to appeal, as well as the right to be granted sufficient time to seek admission to another State, thus avoiding being sent back to the same country where persecution is feared.[180]

The protection afforded by human rights law is undoubtedly broader than that provided by refugee law since *non-refoulement* applies to any person whose life and liberty can be threatened in the receiving country, for reasons beyond the five grounds of persecution set out in the Geneva Convention. Diplomatic assurances may thus be accepted only if they offset the risk to the deportee,

[175] Art 3 of the CAT.

[176] HRC, *General Comment no 20*, para 9.

[177] HRC, *ARJ v Australia*, Comm no 692/1996 (28 July 1997) UN Doc CCPR/C/60/D/692/1996, para 6.9; *GT v Australia*, Comm no 706/1996 (4 November 1997) UN Doc CCPR/C/61/D/706/1996, paras 8.1 and 8.2. See also, ECtHR, *Soering v UK*, App no 14038/88 (7 July 1989) para 88; *Chahal v UK*, above n 173, para 74.

[178] Sir E Lauterpacht and D Bethlehem, 'The Scope and Content of the Principle of *Non-refoulement*: Opinion' in E Feller, V Türk and F Nicholson (eds) *Refugee Protection in International Law: UNHCR's Global Consultations on International Protection* (Cambridge University Press, 2003) paras 164–166.

[179] UNHCR Note on Diplomatic Assurances, n 2 above, para 13; see also, UNHCR, *Factum of the Intervenor, UNHCR, Suresh v the Minister of Citizenship and Immigration; the Attorney General of Canada*, SCC No 27790) (UNHCR Suresh Factum) in (2002) 14(1) *IJRL* 141, paras 74–84.

[180] Arts 33(2) and 33(3) list a set of safeguards. See also, UNHCR Note on Diplomatic Assurances, n 2 above, para 14.

and if the sending State, in all good faith, assumes that the element of trust suffices to consider assurances as reliable instruments. In order to be effective, the authorities of the receiving country must be in the position to ensure *de facto* compliance with the assurance itself. For example, this criterion cannot be satisfied if State authorities are not able to supervise the activity of the security forces of a prison where the deportee is kept in custody, and to ensure compliance with the given assurance.[181]

Diplomatic assurances are not explicitly mentioned in international human rights treaties. Nonetheless, States regularly use them to demonstrate compliance with *non-refoulement* obligations, and as a consequence, relevant human rights treaty-monitoring bodies consider assurances in the pre-removal risk assessment. No formal regulation of deportation with assurances exists, and various international human rights organisations, as well as the Council of Europe and the Committee Against Torture, have opposed any proposals for the creation of guidelines pointing to best practice or setting minimum standards for the use of assurances.[182] Likewise, the criteria crafted by the ECtHR to assess the reliability of a readmitting State can only be considered preliminary benchmarks.[183]

Indeed, international human rights bodies' case law shows that they have often found assurances inadequate in reducing personalised risk to an adequate level (ie, where there is no real risk or 'substantial grounds' to fear proscribed treatment), especially where no effective monitoring mechanism is in place, when the assurances are indeterminate or inaccurate, or when their substance is supported only by the ratification of the main international human rights instruments by the receiving country. In practice, the decisive issue is not whether assurances have been given, but whether and to what extent they effectively reduce or eliminate the risk to the individual at the material time of removal.[184] On the other hand, notably, diplomatic assurances have not been banned as a tool for enhancing overall protection by either eliminating the risk of torture altogether or reducing it below the necessary threshold to avoid *refoulement*.

[181] See *Chahal v the UK*, above n 173, para 105.

[182] See, eg, Amnesty International, *Reject rather than Regulate: Call on Council of Europe Member States not to establish minimum standards for the use of diplomatic assurances in transfers to risk of torture and other ill-treatment* (2 December 2005), https://www.amnesty.org/en/documents/ior61/025/2005/en/. See also Human Rights Watch, *No Guidelines on Empty 'No Torture' Promises: Council of Europe Rejects Minimum Standards for Diplomatic Assurances* (3 Apr 2006). With regard to the Committee aginst Torture's proposal, see, UNCAT, *Thirty-Second Session, Summary of the Record of the First Part (Public) of the 617th Meeting* (2 August 2004) UN Doc CAT/C/SR.617, para 29.

[183] See below for discussion on this point.

[184] See *Chahal v UK*, above n 173, para 105; *Saadi v Italy*, above n 119, para 148; *Agiza v Sweden*, above n 89, para 13.4; and *Kislov v Russia*. Here extradition to Belarus was not considered in breach of Article 3, thus making irrelevant whether there was no reference to the prohibition of torture in the assurances. *Kislov v Russia*, App n 3598/10 (9 July 2019) para 79.

Although MoUs and individualised diplomatic assurances do not provide the legal basis for the removal of a person to her country of origin, they are often used as a *conditio sine qua non* to removal. And, in numerous cases, national and (mostly) international courts have found that, despite assurances, a violation of the principle of *non-refoulement* occurred or would occur upon removal to a third country. While the present review revolves around the case law of international human rights bodies, some key domestic decisions regarding transfer by means of MoUs are also relevant.

In the *Youssef v The Home Office* case,[185] assurances were sought because of 'evidence that detainees were routinely tortured by the Egyptian Security Service.'[186] However, the British request for an assurance concerning prison visits was declined by the Egyptian government 'on the ground that they would constitute interference in the scope of the Egyptian judicial system and an infringement of national sovereignty.'[187] In contrast, in *DD and AS v Secretary of State for the Home Department*,[188] assurances were given by Libyan authorities. Nevertheless, SIAC blocked the removal of two individuals from the UK to Libya by stating that the risk that they would be ill-treated was not 'well-nigh unthinkable' considering the weak monitoring mechanism.[189] Moreover, SIAC saw as flawed the argument that Libya would honour the assurances in the interests of preserving amicable political relations.

State authorities have sometimes considered assurances unnecessary when the risk of torture was not systematic and widespread. On this ground, for instance, the Audiencia Nacional in Spain agreed the extradition of Mr Ali Aarrass to Morocco. However, the HRC found a breach of Article 7 of the ICCPR as Spain had failed to properly assess the credibility of the risk.[190] In its Sixth Periodic Report on the UK, it also argued that diplomatic assurances are not *per se* able in practice to eliminate the risk of violation of Article 7, especially if the practice of torture and degrading treatment is systematic, however stringent any follow-up procedures may be.[191]

Viewed overall, the Committee Against Torture and HRC have since adopted a case-by-case approach in assessing the reliability of diplomatic assurances. By emphasising in *Alzery* and *Agiza* that the relevant bilateral agreements were not sufficient to reduce the risk of torture upon removal,[192] room was still left for the

[185] *Youssef v Home Office*, above n 97.
[186] ibid, para 6.
[187] ibid, para 14.
[188] *DD and AS v SSHD*, above n 32.
[189] ibid, paras 371, 428.
[190] *Ali Aarrass v Spain*, Comm no 2008/2010 (30 September 2014) UN Doc CCPR/C/111/D/2008/2010. See also, *Ali Aarass v Morocco*, Comm no 477/2011 (25 June 2015) UN Doc CAT/C/52/D/477/2011.
[191] HRC, *Consideration of reports submitted by State parties under Article 40 of the Covenant, Sixth Periodic Report, UK* (CCPR/C/GBR/CO/6, Geneva, 30 July 2008) para 12.
[192] ibid; *Alzery v Sweden*, above n 167, paras 11.3–11.5.

view that assurances might be acceptable if differently modelled via supervision and enforcement mechanisms, and if crafted in a detailed and clear fashion.[193] For example, in *Abichou v Germany*, the Committee Against Torture upheld the respondent State's argument that greater weight may be given to diplomatic assurances in connection with cases of extradition for ordinary crimes, such as drug trafficking, rather than deportation of suspected terrorists.[194] Conversely, it has considered as unreliable those diplomatic assurances that do not 'detail with sufficient specificity the monitoring undertaken and the steps taken to ensure that it both was, in fact and in the complainant's perception, objective, impartial and sufficiently trustworthy.'[195] The Committee Against Torture has not excluded altogether the use of diplomatic assurances, but has set out strict requirements for their effective use by sending States, such as accepting assurances only with regard to States that do not systematically breach the CAT.[196] For example, it has not given particular weight to those non-specific assurances reiterating States' obligations under other international human rights treaties.[197] Furthermore, it has placed particular importance on the existence of follow-up mechanisms in those cases in which the applicant had previously been subject to torture in the requesting State.[198]

Likewise, in a number of cases, the HRC found that the applicants' extradition amounted, *inter alia*, to a violation of Article 7 of the ICCPR, particularly when diplomatic assurances contained *no concrete mechanism for their enforcement*. The Committee reiterated that 'at the very minimum, the assurances procured should contain such a *monitoring* mechanism and be safeguarded by arrangements made outside the text of the assurances themselves, which would provide for their effective implementation' (emphasis added).[199] The existence of assurances is just one of the elements relevant to the overall determination of the risk. Where public reports have widely described the inhuman treatment meted out to detainees, especially those held for political and security reasons, a real risk of torture could be envisaged.[200]

[193] *Agiza*, above n 89, para 13.4. See eg, *Attia v Sweden*, Comm no 199/2002 (17 November 2003) UN Doc CAT/C/31/D/199/2002, paras 4.12–4.13.

[194] *Abichou v Germany*, Comm no 430/210 (21 May 2013) UN Doc CAT/C/50/D/430/2010, paras 2.1, 6.5–6.6.

[195] *Pelit v Azerbaijan*, Comm no 281/2005 (5 June 2007) UN Doc CAT/C38/D/281/2005, para 11. For similar reasoning, see *Toirjon Abdussamatov and 28 other complainants v Kazakhstan*, Comm no 444/2010 (1 June 2012) UN Doc CAT/ C/48/D/444/2010, para 13.10.

[196] *Concluding Observations on Canada*, UN doc CAT/C/CR/34/CAN, 7 July 2005, para 5(e); *Concluding Observations on the US*, UN Doc CAT/C/USA/CO/2, 25 July 2006, para 21; *Concluding Observations on the Russian Federation*, CAT/C/RUSS/CO/4, 6 February 2007, para 16.

[197] *Kalinichenko v Morocco*, Comm no 428/2010 (25 November 2011) CAT/C/47/D/428/2010, paras 6.3 and 15.6.

[198] See *Boily v Canada*, Comm no 327/2007 (14 November 2011) CAT/C/47/D/327/2007, para 14.4.

[199] *Zhakhongir Maksudov and Adil Rakhimov, Yakub Tashbaev and Rasuldzhon Pirmatov v Kyrgyzstan*, Comms nos 1461,1462,1476 and 1477/2006 (31 July 2008) UN Doc CCPR/C/93/D/, para 12.5.

[200] See also *Valetov v Kazakhstan*, Comm no 2104/2011 (17 March 2014) UN Doc CCPR/ C/110/D/2104/2011, para 14.6.

(i) Diplomatic Assurances and Non-refoulement *in the ECtHR's Case Law*

The ECtHR has always attached the greatest importance to the human rights record of the receiving country in order to assess the safety of removals, especially when carried out in the framework of national security decisions against persons with respect to whom there are suspicions of prior criminality. In a host of cases, the Court has accepted the use of assurances provided by the Prosecutor of the receiving State, as failure to comply with them would seriously undermine the credibility of the country.[201]

The ECtHR had reviewed various cases involving diplomatic assurances against torture and ill-treatment prior to 2008.[202] However, in the well-known *Saadi v Italy* case, it sought to lay out some general criteria for gauging the reliability of diplomatic assurances, case by case. On the specific facts, it pointed out that the individual 'real risk' of ill-treatment for the deportee could not be obliterated by a generic note, which only observed that Tunisian laws respected the rights of prisoners, and that Tunisia had acceded to the relevant international treaties and conventions.[203] It also insisted on the importance of looking beyond the subjective affirmation of the receiving State by also examining its actions and human rights track record in practice, especially when 'reliable sources have reported practices resorted to or tolerated by the authorities which are manifestly contrary to the principles of the Convention.'[204]

In its subsequent jurisprudence, the Court was frequently not persuaded that diplomatic assurances could guarantee effective protection against violations of Article 3 when there was a lack of a system of torture prevention, and a dismal human rights situation with endemic or persistent use of torture in the readmitting country, regardless of the formal ratification of human rights instruments.[205] The Court is not absolved indeed from the obligation to examine

[201] See, eg, *Chentiev and Ibragimov v Slovakia*, App no 65916/10 (21 February 2012) para 33.

[202] See, eg, *Shamayev and Others v Georgia and Russia*, App no 36378/02 (12 April 2005) para 153; *Burga Ortiz v Germany*, App no 1101/04 (16 October 2006) paras 9–10; *Sanchez Munte v Germany*, App no 43346/05 (16 October 2006) paras 7–8. See also, *Mamatkulov v Turkey*, App nos 46827/99 and 46951/99 (4 February 2005) paras 295, 303, 322, and Dissenting Opinion, para 10.

[203] *Saadi v Italy*, above n 119, paras 147–148.

[204] ibid. See also *Rakhimov v Russia*, App no 50552/13 (15 December 2014); *Nizamov and Others v Russia*, App nos 22636/13, 24034/13, 24334/13 and 24528/13 (7 May 2014) para 43; *Klein v Russia*, App no 24268/08 (1 April 2010) para 57. See also, *Hirsi Jamaa and Others v Italy*, App no 27765/09 (23 February 2012) para 128.

[205] See eg, *Mukhitdinov v Russia*, App no 20999/14 (19 October 2015) para 49; *Khalikov v Russia*, App no 66373/13 (6 July 2015) para 53; *Rustamov v Russia*, App no 11209/10 (3 July 2012) para 131; *Nizomkhon Dzhurayev v Russia*, App no 31890/11 (3 October 2013) para 132; *Baysakov and Others v Ukraine*, App no 54131/08 (18 February 2010) paras 51–52; *Yuldashev v Russia*, App no 1248/09 (8 July 2010), para 85; *Sultanov v Russia*, App no 15303/09 (4 November 2010) para 73; *Gaforov v Russia*, App no 25404/09 (21 October 2010) paras 132, 138; *Khaydarov v Russia*, App no 21055/09 (20 May 2010) paras 105, 111, 115; *Soldatenko v Ukraine*, App no 2440/07 (23 October 2008) para 73; *Ismailov v Russia*, App no 2947/06 (24 April 2008) para 127.

whether 'assurances provided in their *practical application*, a sufficient guarantee that the applicant would be protected'.[206]

The ECtHR's case-by-case approach has not changed, even after the much-debated judgment in *Abu Qatada v UK*.[207] Indeed, the Court has often focused attention on the extent of monitoring and contact between the detainee and diplomatic authorities or the foreign lawyer.[208] The fact that the authorities of the receiving country might previously have mistreated the applicant has been a further element weighed in the balance while assessing the reliability of diplomatic assurances.[209]

A crucial requirement for effectively implementing diplomatic assurances is the capacity of the receiving State to exercise effective control over the individual's ultimate whereabouts. Considering that torture is often secretly or even unofficially administered, and given the difficulty of obtaining information in such circumstances, extradition and deportation have sometimes been halted when national or international bodies doubted that the assurances of the receiving State, despite its good faith, could practically be enforced.[210] These are all elements to weigh in the balance when assessing the capacity of diplomatic assurances to avert the risk of *refoulement*.

A key issue therefore, is whether the government issuing the assurances is able to control the territory and any public officials operating within its territory. Only if the responsible entity has the power to enforce the agreements, and can be trusted in this role, can the assurances be used to assess the likelihood of a State's compliance with its human rights obligations.[211] The diverse elements considered by the Court in determining the suitability of an assurance also demonstrate how the ratification of human rights instruments by the receiving State, or relevant domestic law, does not *ipso facto* establish that it is safe for the individual in question. Indeed, to the extent that there is any presumption of safety of the receiving State, this must be rebuttable.[212]

[206] *Saadi*, above n 119, paras 147–148. The Court also referred to *Chahal v UK*, above n 173, para 105.

[207] See eg, *Nabid Abdullayev v Russia*, App no 8474/14 (14 March 2016), para 66; *Mamazhonov v Russia*, App no 17239/13 (23 March 2015) para 134; *Zarmayev v Belgium*, App no 35/10 (27 Feb 2014) para 92; *Izomkhon Dzhurayev and Others v Russia*, App no 1890/11 (3 October 2013) para 111; *Labsi v Slovakia*, App 33809/08 (15 May 2012) para 119; *Othman (Abu Qatada) v UK*, above n 15, para 187; *Ben Khemais v Italy*, above n 120, para 57. In many other cases, the Court asserts its competence in reviewing assurances. See, eg, *Trabelsi v Belgium*, App no 140/10 (4 September 2014) paras 138–139, 151; *Ryabikin v Russia*, App no 8320/04 (19 June 2008) para 119; *Abdulazhon Isakov v Russia*, App no 14049/08 (8 July 2010) para 111; *Muminov v Russia*, App no 42502/06 (11 December 2008) para 97.

[208] See, eg, *Ben Khemais v Italy*, above n 120, para 85; *Labsi v Slovakia*, ibid, paras 130–131. Reference to the lack of enforcement mechanisms as an element of inadequacy of diplomatic assurances was pointed out by the Committee Against Torture in *Agiza*, above n 89, para 13.4.

[209] See, eg, *Koktysh v Ukraine*, App no 43707/07 (10 December 2009) para 16.

[210] *Shamayev*, above n 202, paras 344–345; *Chahal v UK*, above n 173, para 105; *Soering v UK*, para 97. See also *The Government of the Russian Federation v Akhmed Zakaev*, Bow Street Magistrates' Court, Decision of Hon. T Workman, 13 November 2003 (case concerning extradition to Russia).

[211] See, eg, *Baysakov v Ukraine*, above n 205, para 51.

[212] *MSS v Belgium and Greece*, above n 172, para 353.

Following *Saadi*, the ECtHR has ruled on a vast number of cases concerning individuals (generally alleged terrorists and suspects of criminal conspiracy linked to fundamentalist Islamist groups) facing deportation, or who had already been transferred under the auspices of diplomatic assurances. In the majority of cases, it determined that removal of the applicants did or would violate Article 3.[213] In some other cases, the ECtHR has instead upheld the reliability of those assurances considered sufficiently specific, clear and unequivocal.[214] In *Ouabour v Belgium*, the Court lamented the lack of diplomatic efforts to obtain assurances from the receiving country that the applicant would not be exposed to inhuman and degrading treatment after his extradition.[215] A crucial obstacle frequently identified by the Court has been the provision of general and vague explanations by the government of the requesting State,[216] as well as the existence of the same formulaic assurances within a standardised document indicating the data of each single applicant (who had not yet been deported),[217] and with no evidence of the existence of enforcement and monitoring mechanisms by which individuals could lodge complaints against ill-treatment.[218]

Unsurprisingly, the Court has been slow to endorse any assurance from a State with a dismal human rights record of monitoring and protecting detainees against torture and mistreatment, especially when sources have reported unlawful practices resorted to or tolerated by the authorities of that State.[219]

[213] See eg, *UN v Russia*, App no 14348/15 (26 July 2016) para 39; *Nabid Abdullayev v Russia*, App no 8474/14 (14 March 2016) para 66; *Mamazhonov v Russia*, above n 207, para 134; *Zarmayev*, above n 207, para 92; *Izomkhon Dzhurayev*, above n 207, para 111; *Labsi v Slovakia*, above n 207, para 119; *Othman (Abu Qatada) v UK*, above n 15, para 187; *Ben Khemais v Italy*, above n 120, paras 61–65; *Toumi v Italy*, App no 25716/09 (5 April 2011) para 85; *Trabelsi v Italy*, above n 207, para 52; *Sellem v Italy*, App no 12584/08 (5 March 2009) paras 43–44; *Abdelhedi v Italy*, App no 2638/07 (24 March 2009) paras 50–51; *Ben Salah v Italy*, App no 38128/06 (24 March 2009) paras 39–40; *Bouyahia v Italy*, App no 46792/06 (24 March 2009) paras 42–43; *CBZ v Italy*, App no 44006/06 (24 March 2009) paras 43–44; *Darraji v Italy*, App no 11549/05 (24 March 2009) paras 66–67; *O v Italy*, App no 37257/06 (24 March 2009) paras 44–45; *Soltana v Italy*, App no 37336/06 (24 March 2009) paras 46–47; *Hamraoui v Italy*, App no 16201/07 (24 March 2009) paras 45–46. See also, *Gasayev v Spain*, App no 48514/06 (17 February 2009) 8. Also in *Bakoyev v Russia*, the ECtHR held the applicant's extradition to Uzbekistan – which had provided diplomatic assurances on the fair treatment of the transferee – on the finding that it would not give rise to a violation of Art 3 of the Convention. See *Bakoyev v Russia* App no 30225/11 (5 February 2013) paras 120–121.

[214] See, eg, *Makhmudzhan Ergashev v Russia*, App no 49747/11 (16 October 2012) paras 15, 17, 75; and *Rrapo v Albania*, App no 58555/10 (25 September 2012) para 19; *Harkins and Edward v the UK*, App nos 9146/07 and 32650/07 (17 January 2012) para 85.

[215] *Ouabour v Belgium*, App no 26417/10 (2 June 2015) para 77.

[216] See, eg, *Trabelsi v Belgium*, above n 207 § 135.

[217] See *Sellem*, above n 213, para 18; *Cherif*, above n 213, para 26; *Abdelhedi*, above n 213, para 17; *Ben Salah*, above n 213, para 14; *Bouyahia*, above n 213, para 16; *CBZ*, above n 213, para 17; *Darraji*, above n 213, para 35; *Soltana*, above n 213, para 205; *Hamraoui*, above n 213, para 15; *Ben Khemais v Italy*, above n 120, para 27. See also, A Izumo, 'Diplomatic Assurances against Torture and Ill-treatment: European Court of Human Rights Jurisprudence' (2008) 42 *Columbia Human Rights Law Review* 233.

[218] *Akram Karimov v Russia*, App no 62892/12 (28 May 2014) para 133. See also *Abdulkhakov v Russia*, App no 14743/11 (2 October 2012), para 150.

[219] Violations of Art 3 of the Convention have been found, for example, in the following cases: *Koktysh*, above n 209, para 64; *Klein v Russia*, above n 204, para 57; *Mamadaliyev v Russia*, App no 5614/13 (24 July 2014) paras 66–72; *Kadirzhanov and Mamashev v Russia*, Apps nos 42351/13

Lack of expertise by the diplomatic staff visiting the detainee, required for effective follow-up, has also been a concern. This includes the absence of 'any practical mechanisms setting out, for instance, a procedure by which the applicant could lodge complaints with them or for their unfettered access to detention facilities.'[220]

The salience of individualised and detailed assurances was clearly emphasised in the long-expected 2012 *Abu Qatada v UK* judgment, which represented a first opportunity for the Strasbourg judges to consider the UK's practice of negotiating MoUs to allow removing suspect terrorists to their countries of origin.[221] As we read in the judgment,

> it is not for [the] Court to rule upon the propriety of seeking assurances, or to assess the long-term consequences of doing so; its only task is to examine whether the assurances obtained in a particular case are *sufficient to remove any real risk* of ill-treatment (emphasis added).[222]

The Court thus concluded that deportation with assurances would not be in violation of Article 3 of the Convention. Yet, on the facts of that case, removal would result in a breach of Article 6 because of the real risk that evidence obtained through torture would be admitted at Abu Qatada's retrial in Jordan, thus amounting to a 'flagrant denial of justice.'

Specifically, while admitting that torture in Jordan remained 'widespread and routine',[223] the ECtHR considered that diplomatic assurances negotiated in the framework of the 2005 MoU were specific and comprehensive enough – in the context of the strong political relations between the UK and Jordan – to remove any real risk of ill-treatment of Abu Qatada.[224] Yet this analysis is

and 47823/13 (17 July 2014) paras 98–100; *Akram Karimov*, above n 268, para 133–134; *Gayratbek Saliyev v Russia*, App no 39093/13 (17 April 2014), paras 67–68; *Ismailov*, above n 205, paras 88–89; *Izomkhon Dzhurayev*, above n 207, paras 133–135; *Sidikovy v Russia*, App 73455/11 (20 June 2013) para 150; *MG v Bulgaria*, App no 59297/12 (25 March 2014). By contrast, in the *Ahmad v UK* case regarding extradition to the US, the Court argued that it 'has even more rarely found that there would be a violation of Art 3 if an applicant were to be removed to a State which had a long history of respect of democracy, human rights and the rule of law.' *Ahmad v UK*, App no 24027/07 (12 April 2012) para 179. See also *Boumediene v Bosnia and Herzegovina*, App no 38703/06 (18 December 2008); *Al-Moayad v Germany*, App no 35865/03 (20 February 2007). None of these individuals lodged an asylum application, with the exception of the applicant in *MG v Bulgaria*. On the *Ahmad* case, see N Mavronicola and F Messineo, 'Relatively Absolute? The Undermining of Art 3 ECHR in *Ahmad v UK*' (2013) 76(3) *Modern Law Review* 589.

[220] *Turgunov v Russia*, App no 15590/14 (14 March 2016) paras 54–59; *Tadzhibayev v Russia*, App no 17724/14 (2 May 2016) paras 46–47; *Khamrakulov v Russia*, App no 68894/13 (15 September 2015) paras 69–70; *Gayratbek Saliyev*, ibid, para 66. See also *Izomkhon Dzhurayev*, above n 207, para 133; *Kadirzhanov and Mamashev*, ibid, para 96.

[221] For an extensive coverage of the UK law and practice on terrorism, see C Walker, *Terrorism and the Law* (OUP, 2011).

[222] *Abu Qatada v UK*, above n 15, para 185.

[223] ibid, para 191.

[224] ibid, para 194. On the policy of deportation with assurances in the UK, see also C Walker, 'Deportation with Assurances: UK Experience and Angst', *Lawfare* (November 2013), https://www.lawfareblog.com/clive-walker-deportation-assurances-uk-experience-and-angst.

open to criticism as a departure, potentially quite dangerous, from the Court's previous case law on Article 3, examined earlier. Perhaps in the light of States' concern regarding counter-terrorism measures, and their common endeavour to speed removal of potential threats from European territory, the Court observed that the extent to which States fail to comply with international human rights obligations against torture is, at most, only one factor to be weighed up in the assessment of diplomatic assurances' reliability. States should not refrain from seeking assurances from countries that systematically violate human rights; otherwise 'it would be paradoxical if the very fact of having to seek assurances meant one could not rely on them.'[225]

Yet it remains (at the least) unclear how, in *Abu Qatada*, the ECtHR – which unconditionally accepted that Jordanian government was 'incapable of properly investigating allegations of torture and excluding torture evidence'[226] – was able to be assured that a suspected terrorist would *not* be mistreated to extract a confession. While the applicant always challenged the reliability of diplomatic assurances negotiated under the MoU, he ultimately did agree to leave the UK for Jordan following the entry into force of a formal 'mutual legal assistance agreement'.[227] This treaty comprised a number of fair trial guarantees for deportees and a stringent ban on the use of torture-obtained evidence.[228] Nevertheless, despite the existence of a wide range of safeguards (an MoU, bespoke assurances, and a mutual legal assistance treaty), Jordanian judges later ruled that the confession by his co-defendant *was admissible*, even though it did not constitute sufficient grounds for conviction.[229] This not only appears to breach Article 6 of the ECHR, but also the 2013 UK–Jordan mutual legal assistance treaty itself.[230]

Overall, the approach of the ECtHR in *Abu Qatada* thus resembles that of a tightrope walker: a court nimbly – but not always convincingly – seeking to balance, on one hand, the protection of human rights (within and beyond a State's borders) with, on the other, State concern to avert potential terrorism by displacing not only the perceived threat but also the responsibility for guaranteeing the human rights of those who might constitute that threat.

[225] *Abu Qatada v UK*, above n 15, para 193. See also, *Chahal*, above n 173, Joint Partly Dissenting Opinion, para 1.

[226] *Abu Qatada v UK*, above n 15, para 285.

[227] See Statement by Abu Qatada's lawyer, E Fitzgerald QC, cited in R Booth and S Malik, 'Abu Qatada arrives in Jordan after eight-year deportation battle', *The Guardian* (7 July 2013), https://www.theguardian.com/world/2013/jul/07/abu-qatada-jordan-deportation-battle. See also, A Travis 2013.

[228] Art 27 of the Treaty places the onus on the prosecution to prove beyond any doubt that the statement has been obtained out of free will and choice and has not been acquired through torture or ill-treatment.

[229] A Su, 'Isis beheadings of journalists are against Islam, says Abu Qatada', *The Guardian* (7 September 2014), http://www.theguardian.com/world/2014/sep/07/isis-beheadings-islam-abu-qatada.

[230] Art 7(3) of the 2013 UK–Jordan Treaty, n 83 above.

V. DIPLOMATIC ASSURANCES ON *ASYLUM SEEKERS'* REMOVABLE TO 'SAFE THIRD COUNTRIES'?

Section IV above is the core of this chapter and it provides the answer to the main research question. It showed how no individual should, in principle, encounter a violation of her right to access fair asylum procedures and effective remedies, and a breach of her right to *non-refoulement*, if basic procedural rules are respected. The principle of confidentiality, embodied in soft and hard law instruments, prevents the host State from sharing information (through, for example, diplomatic assurances) with the applicant's home country pending a determination of the asylum claim. Moreover, as long as a rejected or excluded asylum seeker is entitled to challenge the decision on her status as well as the expulsion order – thus questioning the reliability of assurances – no violation of the right to an effective remedy and to *non-refoulement* would take place.

Nevertheless, Section IV also revealed how the negotiation of diplomatic assurances can *de facto* hamper refugees' access to protection. In shifting from the study of the agreements *per se* to their actual implementation, a string of cases show that seeking diplomatic assurances during the asylum determination phase contributes to defying the procedural safeguards of asylum mechanisms, such as the principle of confidentiality, thus affecting the final outcome of the proceedings and the fairness of the entire process. In some circumstances, asylum seekers have been rejected or excluded from refugee status/subsidiary protection after requesting diplomatic assurances from the home country. Deprived of their right to access administrative and judicial review of their exclusion/rejection decision and of the deportation order, they incurred violations of the right to an effective remedy. Finally, substantive international human rights case law, especially from the ECtHR, testifies to the risk of *refoulement* for people removed, generally on national security grounds, to countries of origin on the basis of diplomatic assurances against torture and ill-treatment.

The above-examined decisions primarily concern people whose protection claims had been rejected or who were transferred on security grounds after exclusion from refugee status/subsidiary protection. However, in a few cases, the ECtHR has assessed diplomatic assurances as one of the elements for eradicating the risk of ill-treatment of asylum seekers *before* asylum procedures were completed. It is important to note that removal then is not to the country of origin but to a 'safe third country' of transit. This Section intends to separately outline and examine this dangerous and unexplored anomaly in the system of protection, thereby questioning consequences for refugee rights. Generally, the Court reserves particular attention for the plight of asylum seekers as they belong to a particular vulnerable group.[231] Thus, whilst assessing the opportunity of removal with assurances, it underlines how much regard should be had

[231] *MSS v Belgium and Greece*, above n 172, para 251.

'to the fact that the measure is applicable not to those who have committed criminal offences but to aliens who, often fearing for their lives, have fled their own country.'[232]

The ECtHR heretofore has rejected the use of diplomatic assurances for refugees and asylum seekers, but it has to a certain extent endorsed them with regard to people whose protection claims had been denied or who were subjected to exclusion. Only time will tell whether the Court's attitude toward asylum seekers will not be contaminated by the approach adopted with regard to people who, for different reasons, are not entitled to refugee protection. By now, it is worth observing how the ECtHR in few cases – which, therefore, do not amount to a trend *in status nascendi* – seems to have led contracting parties to negotiate assurances rather than taking responsibility for asylum seekers who are about to be removed or have already been removed.[233] In the *Hirsi v Italy* judgment, for example, Judge Pinto de Albuquerque proposed 'to provide the applicants with practical and effective access to an asylum procedure in Italy.'[234] By contrast, in its final recommendations, the Court unexpectedly urged the respondent State to take 'all possible steps to obtain assurances from the Libyan authorities that the applicants will not be subjected to treatment incompatible with article 3 of the Convention or arbitrarily repatriated.'[235]

In the *MSS v Belgium and Greece* case, the Court affirmed that diplomatic assurances by Greece did not amount to a sufficient guarantee because they were worded in stereotypical terms and did not address the specific situation of the asylum seeker in question.[236] However, the Court appears to foreshadow that accepting fully detailed and individualised assurances would by all means be plausible if they were able to counteract any risk of ill-treatment. Without outlawing diplomatic assurances *per se*, the ECtHR proposes a case-by-case approach, with a special focus on the human rights situation of the readmitting country. Even countries where torture and ill-treatment of detainees is known to be widespread and systematic have been considered safe, if adequate assurances are given. Moreover, as international human rights bodies and national courts have substantively recognised, in many cases, *refoulement* occurred as a consequence of expulsion of suspected terrorists under the auspices of assurances.[237]

In the *Saadi v Italy* case, the ECtHR rejected the UK's argument that, in the case of a threat to national security, stronger evidence has to be adduced to prove that the applicant would be at risk of torture or ill-treatment in the receiving country. Under this view, the individual is not required to prove that a 'real

[232] *Amuur v France*, App no 19776/92 (25 June 1996) para 43.

[233] V Moreno-Lax, '*Hirsi Jamaa and Others v Italy* or the Strasbourg Court versus Extraterritorial Migration Control?' (2012) 12(3) *HumanRLR* 592–3.

[234] *Hirsi v Italy*, n 204 above, Concurring Opinion 82.

[235] *Hirsi v Italy*, n 204 above, para 211.

[236] *MSS v Belgium and Greece*, above n 172, para 354.

[237] See, eg, the *Arar* case. Commission of Inquiry into the actions of Canadian Officials in relation to Mr Arar's removal to Syria, *Report of the Events relating to Maher Arar*.

risk' exists, but rather that such a risk is 'more likely than not.'[238] Accordingly, the threshold for determining the safety and reliability of the readmitting country giving assurances is seemingly lower when dealing with people expelled on national security grounds, regardless of whether they are the object of an exclusion provision. Are we ready to exclude the possibility that this threshold could one day not also be applied to asylum seekers transferred to a 'safe third country' or repatriated after diplomatic assurances have been used in their asylum proceedings? That would certainly amount to a procedural race to the bottom, as one could argue. States seem nevertheless eager and well-equipped to run such a race.

VI. ACCESS TO PROTECTION, DIPLOMATIC ASSURANCES, AND MoUs: A CONCLUDING CRITIQUE

The key findings can be summarised as follows. First, even if national and international courts consider assurances legally permissible and able in principle to reduce the risk of *refoulement*, they are not always effective in practice in preventing torture.[239] As a result, national courts and, primarily, international human rights bodies have frequently held that *refoulement* took place or would take place upon removal. Second, if the exchange of assurances does not *per se* constitute a hurdle to asylum seekers' access to asylum procedures, it might affect the fairness of the proceedings and alter the outcome of the decision-making process. Indeed, most of the reviewed cases on the use of diplomatic assurances show how they are being implemented to speed up the process at the expense of pre-removal individual guarantees, such as the right to fair asylum procedures and effective remedies against rejection/exclusion and the decision of expulsion.

As explained above, both the UN Committees and the ECtHR generally accept the suitability of assurances. However, they reject assurances as a reliable basis *ipso facto* for a safe transfer and instead take into account a number of factors, such as the authority issuing the assurance, its capacity to control a certain situation, and the general human rights conditions in the receiving country.

The UN Committee Against Torture and the HRC have often found assurances inadequate in reducing the risk of torture upon removal because of the

[238] *Saadi v Italy*, above n 119, para 122. For a critique of the balancing test between individual protection and national security, see, *inter alia*, P De Sena, 'Lotta al terrorismo e tutela dei diritti umani: conclusioni' (*The Fight against International Terrorism and the Protection of Human Rights: Concluding Remarks*) in P Gargiulo and MC Vitucci (eds), *La tutela dei diritti umani nella lotta e nella guerra contro il terrorismo* (Giuffré, 2009) 159–67; A Saccucci, 'Divieto di Tortura ed Esigenze di Sicurezza nel Contesto della War on Terror: Verso una Flessione "al Ribasso" degli Obblighi Internazionali?' (2009) 1 *Diritti Umani e Diritto Internazionale* 5–31; A Tancredi, 'Assicurazioni Diplomatiche e Divieto "Assoluto" di *Refoulement* alla Luce di Alcune Recenti Pronunzie della Corte Europea dei Diritti Umani' (2010) 4(1) *Diritti Umani e Diritto Internazionale* 41–64.

[239] Johnston 2011, n 110 above, 48.

way in which they were formulated.[240] Such reasoning seems to concede that UN human rights treaty-monitoring bodies would accept assurances if differently modelled through supervision and enforcement mechanisms, and if crafted in a detailed and clear fashion.[241] Moreover, greater weight appears to be placed on diplomatic assurances provided in connection with cases of extradition for ordinary crimes, such as drug trafficking, rather than deportation of suspected terrorists.[242]

According to the ECtHR, the fact that a person has not suffered immediate ill-treatment upon removal is not a reliable prediction of their fate in the future.[243] The importance of this approach is in its emphasis that an assessment of the safety of the receiving country for the individual must be done in the long run, and in light of the general human rights situation in that place. Although a court or other supervisory bodies should consider the subsistence of stable relations between the two States involved, and gauge the personalised risk existing at the material time of the expulsion, these bodies cannot neglect the possibly irremediable consequences for the deportee if torture is nonetheless practised *after* conviction in a fair trial, or once the 'spotlights are off' a particular case, and monitoring visits become more rare.

Indeed, whilst assurances concerning the death penalty can be more easily supervised, it has been suggested that diplomatic assurances on humane treatment might suffice only in three cases: (i) where the assuring State does not exhibit patterns of torture toward prisoners and suspect terrorists; (ii) where 'a previous systemic pattern of torture has been brought under control'; and (iii) when 'although isolated, non-systemic acts continued, there [i]s independent monitoring by a body with a track record of effectiveness, and criminal sanctions against transgressors.'[244]

More specifically, the criteria crafted by the ECtHR (discussed above)[245] are only the starting point of any discussion on reliability. If satisfied, they might create a presumption of sufficiency, but in no way whatsoever can they be considered exhaustive. States have indeed tried to strengthen the reliability of diplomatic assurances in a number of ways, including by delegating monitoring responsibilities to an independent and authoritative third party, which may be composed not necessarily of diplomats, but preferably of members of NGOs and human rights organisations. Contacts with detainees should take place over

240 See, eg, *Alzery*, above n 167, paras 11.3–11.5; *Agiza*, above n 89, para 13.4.

241 See, eg, *Attia*, above n 193, paras 4.12–4.13.

242 *Abichou*, above n 194, paras 2.1, 6.5, 6.6.

243 See eg, *Ben Khemais v Italy*, above n 120, para 64.

244 These are the criteria developed by the applicant in his submission in the *Abu Qatada v UK* case before the ECtHR. See *Abu Qatada v UK*, above n 15, para 168. For a recent account on criteria to assess the reliability of diplomatic assurances, see S Maini, 'Does International Law Permit Deportation with Assurances?', *International Law Square* (January 2016), https://ilsquare.wordpress.com/2016/01/30/does-international-law-permit-deportation-with-assurances/.

245 *Abu Qatada v UK*, above n 15, para 189.

time and be carried out by individuals with the necessary expertise. As the HRC suggests, a video recording of all interrogations can also be kept.[246] A monitoring body may be able to exercise external pressure on the sending State not to conceal any information about human rights transgressions of the receiving State. It can also deter mistreatment in the receiving country by means, for example, of publishing reports of alleged violations and promoting legal intervention and redress when illegal practices are detected.[247] On the other hand, independent organisations, such as the International Committee of the Red Cross, Human Rights Watch or Amnesty International, are not always willing to take on the monitoring function. Moreover, even if diplomats phrase assurances in very specific terms, coupling the activation of monitoring mechanisms with a system of public reports of abuses, they still might not be reliable in contexts where torture is pervasive, especially in cases regarding suspected terrorists.

States do not make expulsion decisions solely on the basis of diplomatic assurances (either in the form of MoUs or bespoke assurances). Nevertheless, assurances are one of the main elements – and, at times, quite dangerously, one of the most important ones – weighed in the balance when considering the expulsion of a person convicted or suspected of serious crimes. In contrast, in the case law of international human rights bodies, diplomatic assurances are generally upheld as one factor amongst many in the assessment of the risk, rather than trusted at face value.[248]

However, even if assurances are considered legally permissible and able in principle to reduce the risk of *refoulement*, they are not always effective in practice in preventing torture and ill-treatment because of the way in which torture is secretly administered and the difficulty of obtaining information by the captive.[249] As a result, national courts and, primarily, international human rights bodies have frequently held that *refoulement* took place or would take place upon removal. This *ex ante* crisis of guarantees assumes even more salience when considered *ex post facto*, as no enforcement mechanisms to protect deported individuals from the *breach* of a diplomatic assurance are envisaged. Therefore, negotiation of assurances must be case-specific and consider the entire human rights situation in the readmitting country, including its torture track record, in order to verify whether assurances are sufficient to protect from such a risk. For example, it is not enough that the promisor has ratified international human rights instruments to consider it safe; its compliance with

[246] HRC, *General Comment no 20* (10 March 1992).

[247] In case of an alleged human rights violation, enforcement measures can be taken under the law of international State responsibility, including proportionate and non-forcible countermeasures. Reparation is also possible under Art 31 of the ILC Articles on State responsibility.

[248] For example, while deciding on the reliability of assurances, the ECtHR attaches considerable importance also to 'information and evidence obtained subsequent to the applicants' extradition.' See *Shamayev*, above n 202, para 345.

[249] JG Johnston, 'The Risk of Torture as a Basis for Refusing Extradition and the Use of Diplomatic Assurances to Protect against Torture after 9/11' (2011) 11(1) *International Criminal Law Review* 48.

human rights *in concreto* must be gauged. As the analysis of the case law of human rights bodies has shown, the sending State incurs responsibility for violation of *non-refoulement* (a duty of prevention, not a duty of result) if it has reasonable grounds to foresee that a violation of human rights will occur in the receiving State and, despite this, removes the individual.

A dangerous employment of assurances may occur in at least five circumstances:

(i) when the assessment of the risk excessively relies on the assurances given by the readmitting government, which may be the primary source of the feared mistreatment, without bringing into the picture the general human rights situation and the pervasiveness of torture in the receiving country;
(ii) when the receiving country has a history of failing both to comply with assurances and to investigate the allegations of prohibited treatment against other detainees;
(iii) when the assurances are negotiated during the examination of the asylum claim, thus violating the principle of confidentiality and the right of an asylum seeker to access and enjoy fair asylum procedures;
(iv) when the existence of diplomatic assurances accelerates the rejection of the protection claim and the enforcement of the removal procedures, thus preventing the individual from both challenging the decisions and having access to an effective remedy; and
(v) when an efficient system of monitoring is lacking, and the government issuing the assurances is not able to enforce the agreement because of the lack of control of the territory or the security forces of the prison where the individual in question is detained.

Even with new, sophisticated monitoring procedures, there will always be limits in detecting torture and eliminating the personal risk for the deportee. A number of contradictions are inherent in the process of seeking assurances given that 'even as the sending State seeks protection for one, so it acquiesces in the torture of others.'[250] Moreover, it remains unanswered why States need to frame their human rights commitments within bilateral political agreements – despite being subject to judicial control – which replicate human rights standards that have already been enshrined within international human rights treaties creating clear, binding obligations and mechanisms of individual complaints.

[250] I have discussed elsewhere the reasons why extradition treaties are better suited to dealing with the removal of suspected or convicted criminals. See M Giuffré, 'Deportation with Assurances: Human Rights and the Case of People Suspected or Convicted of Serious Crimes' (2017) 15(1) *Journal of International Criminal Justice* 75. GS Goodwin-Gill and R Husain, 'Diplomatic Assurances and Deportation', unpublished conference paper, *JUSTICE/Sweet & Maxwell Conference on Counter-terrorism and Human Rights* (28 June 2005), cited in N Larsaeus, 'The Use of Diplomatic Assurances in the Prevention of Prohibited Treatment' (*RSC Working Paper no 32*, October 2006, at 3). See also G Noll, 'Diplomatic Assurances and the Silence of Human Rights Law' (2006) 7 *Melbourne Journal of International Law* 104.

Beyond the progressive politicisation of rights, diplomatic assurances – as bilateral political arrangements – would duplicate transfer procedures, which can be better codified within bilateral extradition *treaties* aimed at facilitating the transfer of a suspected or convicted criminal to another country by ensuring greater legal certainty.[251] Generally speaking, executives have sought diplomatic assurances – both in the context of extradition (with a view to future legal process) and of deportation (which may or may not entail such a prospect) – and national courts have in the main upheld their use in cases where there is alleged prior criminality. However, given that the safety of removal is a matter of fact, it may be highly problematic, from a human rights law perspective, to entertain the possibility of transferring a person, with the assurance she will not be ill-treated, to a country where torture is notoriously practised. *In GS v Bulgaria*, in 2019, the Court has halted removal of an applicant to Iran holding that 'assurances against torture by a State in which it is *endemic or persistent* should as a rule be approached with caution.'[252] Going beyond the concept of mere 'caution', I conclude States should categorically refrain from relying on diplomatic assurances – whether framed or not within standardised MoUs or extradition treaties – with countries that persist in the usage of torture and inhuman and degrading treatment.

Finally, devolving upon diplomats and political acts the protection of fundamental rights in security-related deportations would also defend the maintenance of a regime of exceptionalism for people suspected of serious criminality and who cannot be removed to their country of origin. Yet, although the primary and most suitable option should thus be prosecution in the host country, there is often notable difficulty in pursuing this route because of the difficulty in collecting evidence, lack of witnesses, and limited ability of the police to carry out investigations far from the place where the crime has been committed.[253] In this context, diplomatic assurances become a convenient political tool for governments and intelligence services to transfer abroad undesirable foreigners, despite the fact that the deportees have not been convicted of any crime, and that one of the bars to removal contained in the extradition treaties would apply. Indeed, the recent proliferation of diplomatic assurances and security-related deportations symbolises the new tendency of governments to consider foreigners a threat to public safety,[254] thus strengthening the 'link' between migrants/refugees and terrorism, and conflating the logic of individual protection with the logic of security.

[251] The responsibility for infringement of the guarantees provided by diplomatic assurances can only be raised at a political, rather than judicial level. See N Canestrini, *Estradizione verso l'estero e diritti fondamentali: una analisi critica* (September 2016), http://www.canestrinilex.com/risorse/estradizione-verso-lestero-e-diritti-fondamentali-una-analisi-critica/#ixzz4NAeuQY4a. See also, Giuffré 2017, n 250 above.

[252] *GS v Bulgaria*, App no 36538/17 (19 April 2019) para 93.

[253] See S Singer, '"Undesirable and Unreturnable" in the United Kingdom' (2017) 36 (1) *Refugee Survey Quarterly* 9, 27.

[254] E Brouwer, 'Immigration, Asylum and Terrorism: A Changing Dynamic Legal and Practical Developments in the EU Response to the Terrorist Attacks of 11.09' (2003) 4 *EJML* 399.

5

Pre-Arrival Maritime Interception, Push-Backs and Agreements for Technical and Police Cooperation

I. INTRODUCTION

IN THE CONTEXT of the pro-active management of European frontiers, diverse bilateral strategies have been devised to keep migrants and refugees away from the EU's territory, or to rapidly remove them. These strategies have been attempted through various types of agreements linked to readmission between European States and third countries of origin or provenance of migrants. While both standard readmission agreements and diplomatic assurances are being used to remove foreigners who have already crossed the EU borders, agreements for technical and police cooperation are being negotiated to set up joint patrols for the pre-emptive containment of unwanted arrivals in Europe.

Drawing a line of demarcation between pre-arrival and post-arrival removals, this chapter focuses on readmission performed before individuals enter into the territory of a European State, bearing in mind that during interdiction and diversion manoeuvres outside of the territorial jurisdiction of the European destination country, the phases of arrival (or non-admission) and removal overlap. The arrangements used for preventing access to Europe may be deemed an underlying component of the progressive externalisation of migration controls – either in the territorial waters of a third country or on the high seas,[1] with the expectation of diluting State responsibilities by letting refugees 'fall into a gaping crack in the human rights system.'[2] Since refugees often travel in mixed flows, crossing the sea by boat together with other migrants, restrictive external migration controls can also end up affecting the rights of people genuinely in need of protection.[3]

[1] Art 86 of the UN Convention on the Law of the Sea (UNCLOS) defines negatively 'high seas' as 'all parts of the sea that are not included in the exclusive economic zone, in the territorial sea or in the internal waters of a State, or in the archipelagic waters of an archipelagic State.' UNCLOS, adopted 10 December 1982, entered into force 16 November 1994, 1833 UNTS 3.

[2] J Dench and F Crépeau, 'Interdiction at the Expense of Human Rights: A Long-term Containment Strategy' (2003) 21(4) *Refuge – Canada's Periodical on Refugees* 1, 3.

[3] See BS Chimni, 'Aid, Relief, and Containment: The First Asylum Country and Beyond' (2003) 40 *International Migration* 75, 76.

According to available records, in May 2009, Italy embarked on a forcible and indiscriminate removal policy, deflecting hundreds of people towards North Africa before they could enter the territorial waters of any European State. The Italy–Libya push-back campaign is, therefore, a key case study to explore: (i) whether bilateral agreements for technical and police cooperation provide the legal framework for the diversion of intercepted refugees to countries of embarkation; and (ii) whether pre-arrival interceptions and push-backs can hamper refugees' access to protection in Europe.

It is worth noting that any enquiry into State practice is fraught with an unavoidable degree of uncertainty due to the inaccessibility of relevant information. For instance, in the case of interdictions on the high seas resulting in the hand-back of migrants and refugees to the country of embarkation, ambiguity and uncertainty are caused by the lack of transparency and the absence of monitoring mechanisms such as media, NGOs, and international organisations.[4] In order to compensate for such vagueness, this chapter has chosen to focus on the arrangements between Italy and Libya to better grasp the main functions of agreements for technical and police cooperation, whose content can vary from country to country.

The 2009 push-back campaign is, arguably, one of the most controversial policies ever adopted by a European government to directly combat irregular immigration by sea, and opened the way to the ongoing 'pull-back practice', which became systematic in 2017 thanks to revived cooperation between Italy and Libya. In February 2012, the ECtHR delivered a landmark judgment in the *Hirsi v Italy* case by holding that Italy had extraterritorial human rights obligations with regard to 24 refugees from Somalia and Eritrea handed over to Libyan authorities after being intercepted by Italian warships.[5] Italy exercised 'effective control and authority' over intercepted migrants, thus creating a 'jurisdictional link' between the State and the individuals concerned.

As a consequence of the events of 2011,[6] the bilateral agreements between Italy and Libya have been suspended. Despite the death of Colonel Gaddafi, this study remains relevant for the following reasons. First, there is still a need to establish whether or not there is a legal framework underpinning the 2009 push-back campaign. Second, southern European States continue to face influxes of seaborne migrants and refugees from North Africa, and need guidance about clear-cut extraterritorial human rights obligations, and the possible types of responsibility they could incur. Third, Italy and Libya are re-establishing

[4] B Miltner, 'Human Security and Protection from *Refoulement* in the Maritime Context', in A Edward and C Ferstman (eds), *Human Security and Non-Citizens: Law, Policy and International Affairs* (CUP, 2010) 195, 215.

[5] *Hirsi Jamaa and others v Italy*, App no 27765/09 (23 February 2012).

[6] Reference is here made to both the indiscriminate lethal force used by the Gaddafi government to retain power, and the Italian involvement in the humanitarian intervention against the Libyan government.

cooperation within the field of migration control. This has led, for example, to the adoption of a new practice of pull-backs carried out by Libyan authorities with the technical, political and economic support of Italy, in particular through coordination of the rescue services. Fourth, sea routes constantly change and, in their attempts to reach Europe, people continue to opt for increasingly perilous and difficult journeys. Accordingly, new bilateral agreements might be negotiated. Therefore, the legal analysis of the Italy–Libya case is pertinent for other situations where refugees are found in extraterritorial settings by European States or third countries performing exit border controls in cooperation with European States.

To address what has been defined as a 'humanitarian refugee crisis' (2015–16),[7] the EU has opted for a strategy based on the full externalisation of migration and border controls aimed at eradicating (unauthorised) access to Europe, mostly through dedicated financial and technical support to third countries of origin or transit.[8] The so-called EU–Turkey deal to halt the flow of irregular migrants to Greece (as discussed in Chapter three), the EU–Libya cooperation at maritime and land borders, talks on extraterritorial processing camps in neighbouring States, information campaigns in third countries on the 'risks' of irregular migration, and the 2017 Italy–Libya Memorandum of Understanding (MoU) – reviving the 2008 Berlusconi–Gaddafi Treaty of Friendship – to train, equip and fund the Libyan Coastguard (partly through EU resources) are but a few examples of an outright containment scheme designed to completely outsource controls and thwart departures. The focus is no longer on preventing arrivals, impeding access to determination procedures, or deflecting flows to other destinations, but on forestalling exits. These are no ordinary measures of *non-entrée*. Instead, they are a targeted means of frustrating the exercise of the right to leave – nullifying the refugee's flight.

Given that migrants are consequently trapped in conflict-ravaged and/or unstable States and exposed to risks of ill-treatment, persecution and exploitation, the question arises over how far these newly fashionable policies can reasonably be pursued. These new forms of 'contactless control', practised on demand by partner countries, far outside the geographical European space, present novel problems of compliance with international human rights standards and determination of responsibility for non-compliance. Whilst offshore controls have been in existence in various guises for some time, the strategy

[7] E Guild and S Carrera, 'Rethinking asylum distribution in the EU: Shall we start with the facts?', *CEPS Commentary* (CEPS, Brussels, 17 June 2016).

[8] Sections on contactless controls and State responsibility, throughout this chapter, are partly taken from M Giuffré and V Moreno-Lax, 'The Raise of Consensual Containment: From "Contactless Control" to "Contactless Responsibility" for Migratory Flows' in S Juss (eds), *The Research Handbook on International Refugee Law* (Edward Elgar Publishing, 2019); and M Giuffré, 'From Turkey to Libya: The EU Migration Partnership from Bad to Worse' (2017) *Eurojus*, http://rivista.eurojus.it/from-turkey-to-libya-the-eu-migration-partnership-from-bad-to-worse/.

launched by the EU in 2016 represents a powerful shift in asylum and migration policy and practice. By transferring the coercive management of exiles to third countries, it aims to eliminate any physical contact, direct or indirect, between refugees and the authorities of potential destination States. The ultimate goal is to sever any jurisdictional link with European countries, in an attempt to elude any concomitant responsibility.

In revealing the hidden objective of these new measures, this chapter will first investigate whether the implementation of transferred means of migration control may hamper refugee rights. It will then question whether these practices of 'contactless control' do indeed insulate EU countries from accountability for violations suffered by migrants and refugees in third countries, or rather whether they engage the international responsibility of European States for breaches of human rights obligations, such as the principle of *non-refoulement*, and the rights of access to asylum procedures and to an effective remedy.

A. Structure of the Chapter

Sections II and III provide an initial overview of State practice and the content of the agreements for technical and police cooperation. This background analysis offers a thorough portrayal of the plethora of bilateral arrangements between Italy and Libya, including the more recent accords through which Italy delegates push-back to its Libyan partner. Although the content of these accords and the practice of push-backs have sparked the interest of scholars and human rights practitioners, the subject has often been laden with confusion from both a terminological and substantive point of view – largely due to the fact that some agreements have not been published. However, only when the main terms of the accords at issue are clarified, including their purpose and the rules of engagement they set up, can the more complex issues be examined, such as: the legal basis underpinning the push-back campaign in 2009; whether access to protection is hampered by the implementation of these accords; the engagement of European States' jurisdiction and potential responsibility in cases of both direct push-backs and contactless control over migrants at sea. Section III also discusses the issues related to a thorough assessment of safety of the third readmitting country.

Through the scrutiny of the diverse motivations advanced by Italy to justify diversion operations at sea, Section IV investigates whether either the 2007 and 2009 Protocols or the 2008 Partnership Treaty (individually taken) stand alone as the legal basis for push-backs. It then illustrates the shift toward the more recent pull-back practice on the basis of which Italy, with the support of the EU, increasingly delegates to Libya rescue, interception, and disembarkation of boat migrants, thus preventing access to protection in Europe. Section V shows how the legal analysis of the Italy–Libya case is pertinent for other situations in which States within or outside Europe (*in primis* the US and Australia) entrust or used to entrust third countries of provenance of migrants and refugees with the duty of patrolling both their territorial and international waters to deter unauthorised immigration. Sections V.A and V.B offer a brief assessment of the EU response to migration by sea and provide an overview of the main tasks of Frontex and the European Border Coast Guard Agency.

Section VI examines search and rescue duties and due diligence obligations which apply to anyone found in distress at sea. It also illustrates how refugees' access to protection – understood here as the combination of *non-refoulement* and access to asylum procedures and effective remedies – is undermined by the enforcement of maritime pre-arrival interception and rescue, resulting in removal to an unsafe country.

Section VII investigates whether European States could be held indirectly accountable, under Article 16 of the International Law Commission Articles on State Responsibility (ASR),[9] for an internationally wrongful act committed by a third country by means of its 'aiding and assisting' the third country in illicit operations. By depicting the main elements of the Italy–Libya cooperation, a possible reading of the State responsibility riddle in the case of violations of the principle of *non-refoulement* is offered. As a free-standing part, Section VII aims to examine whether State responsibility under general international law can be triggered in the case of joint operations of migration control. This issue emerges as a novelty if compared with previous chapters, which confined themselves to assessing whether States comply with primary obligations under international human rights and refugee law treaties by ensuring access to protection to refugees and asylum seekers.

One of the main problems in pronouncing on the responsibility of European States in cases of joint migration controls has been the lack of information about the relevant accords and their implementation. For example, whereas the engagement rules within the bilateral agreements normally entrust Libya with the enforcement of maritime patrols, the actual execution of the accords may give rise to more complex operational scenarios, where Italian authorities are also implicated to varying degrees (eg, through technical, economic and political support, but also coordination of rescue operations). In this regard, Section VII explores the issue of 'contactless' jurisdiction and independent responsibility of European States, *in primis* Italy, to shed light on the latest cases of migrant push-backs by proxy. Even in the absence of written agreements entrusting Libyans with the rescue of migrants at sea, recent pull-backs by Libyans and communication between competent State authorities reveal a clear collaboration between the Italian Maritime Rescue Coordination Centre (MRCC) and the Libyan Coastguard engaged in the patrolling of the Mediterranean.

[9] ILC, 'Articles on the Responsibility of States for Internationally Wrongful Acts' (2001), UNGA A/56/10, corrected by A/56/49 vol I/Corr.4.

II. THE CHANGING READMISSION PARADIGM: FROM PUSH-BACKS TO PUSH-BACKS BY PROXY (PULL-BACKS)

According to available records, between 6 May and 6 November 2009, 834 persons were driven back to Libya and 23 to Algeria through the autonomous intervention of Italian vessels deployed in the course of nine different maritime operations run by Italian forces.[10] If history repeats itself, the relationship between Italy and Libya on migration control is no exception. Indeed, ahead of the EU Council summit, on 3 February 2017, the Italian Prime Minister and the Head of the National Reconciliation Government of the Libya State signed an 'MoU on cooperation in the development sector, to combat illegal immigration, human trafficking and contraband and on reinforcing the border security'.[11] The 2017 MoU also revives the full array of old agreements on migration control, which had seemingly been suspended during the Arab Spring and the escalation of the Libyan civil war.

The establishment of links with the UN-recognised government in post-Gaddafi Libya has taken time and it is only recently that the EU, both independently and through Italy, has resumed relations with its Southern neighbour. The renewed interest in Libya stemmed from the fact that, since the sealing off of the Aegean border after the EU–Turkey deal in March 2016, the Central Mediterranean route in 2017 again saw the highest volume of maritime traffic in terms of unauthorised arrivals.[12]

In January 2017, a European Commission Communication for the Southern Mediterranean set out the goals to both step up the training programme of the Libyan Coastguard to autonomously conduct search and rescue (including disembarkation) in Libyan waters and strengthen Libya's Southern border (in the Sahara Desert) to hinder irregular movements through Libya and into Europe.[13] The EU also started a programme to train Libyan Coastguard officers in the rescue and interdiction of migrant boats.[14] The training and assistance

[10] UNHCR, *Submission in the Case of Hirsi*, March 2010, para 2.1.3, http://www.unhcr.org/refworld/pdfid/4b97778d2.pdf. See also CPT, *Report to the Italian Government on the visit to Italy carried out by the European Committee for the Prevention of Torture and Inhuman or Degrading Treatment or Punishment (CPT) from 27 to 31 July 2009*, 28 April 2010, http://www.cpt.coe.int/documents/ita/2010-inf-14-eng.pdf (CPT Report). While these operations were generally conducted by the Coast Guard and the Revenue Police, the Italian Navy intervened only twice. The push-back issue has already been introduced in Chapter 2.

[11] To read more on the content of the Italy–Libya MoU, see Giuffré 2017, n 8 above.

[12] EUNAVFOR MED Op Sophia – Six-Monthly Report 1 January–31 October 2016, Council doc. 14978/16 (EU RESTRICTED), 30 November 2016, 4–5, http://statewatch.org/news/2016/dec/eu-council-eunavformed-jan-oct-2016-report-restricted.pdf.

[13] Joint Communication to the European Parliament, the European Council and the Council, Migration on the Central Mediterranean route: 'Managing flows, saving lives', JOIN(2017) 4 final, 25 January 2017.

[14] European Council, 'EUNAVFOR MED Operation Sophia: mandate extended by one year, two new tasks added' (20 June 2016), https://www.consilium.europa.eu/en/press/press-releases/2016/06/20/fac-eunavfor-med-sophia/.

offered by the EU, and Italy in particular, should enable Libya to autonomously conduct rescue and 'pull-back' operations of all migrants and refugees setting sail from Libyan shores toward Europe as part of mixed operations to control borders and 'rescue lives' at sea.

On a number of occasions, a clear operative involvement of Italian authorities can be recorded, particularly in the location of migrant boats and in the facilitation of the diversion of migrants to Libya.[15] For instance, in May 2018, an application was lodged to the ECtHR concerning events that unfolded on the morning of 6 November 2017. On the basis of a communication sent by the MRCC in Rome, both the Libyan Coast Guard and a rescue ship of the German NGO 'SeaWatch' were simultaneously sent to assist a migrant dinghy in distress. The uncoordinated and confrontational rescue process ended with 20 people drowning at sea, 59 persons being brought by SeaWatch to Italy, and 47 others being pulled-back by Libyan authorities.[16]

A. Assessment of Safety

Bilateral cooperation on readmission primarily purports to confront the 'humanitarian crisis' deepened by the flight of thousands seeking better living conditions in Europe. It is important to emphasise here that neither the denial of entry of a vessel into territorial waters, nor the refusal to allow disembarkation, amounts *per se* to a breach of the principle of *non-refoulement*. For such a violation to occur it is necessary that interdiction results in the physical removal/diversion of intercepted refugees to territories (either countries of origin or transit) where their life and liberty would be threatened.[17] The evaluation of a third country's safety is, therefore, a *conditio sine qua non* for European States to avoid responsibility both under human rights treaties and general international law. Especially in those instances where migrants and refugees are preventively interdicted on the high seas or in the territorial waters of a third country, 'the less one may rely on the *ex post* control by [EU] courts and tribunals (which is the very idea of outsourcing), the more we need to engage in an *ex ante* control [of the safety of the State].'[18]

[15] See Amnesty International, *Libya's Dark Web of Collusion: Abuses Against Europe-bound Refugees and Migrants*, 11 December 2017, https://www.amnesty.org/en/documents/mde19/7561/2017/en/. See P Biondi, 'Italy Strikes Back Gain: A Push-Back Firsthand Account', *Border Criminologies*, 15 December 2017, https://www.law.ox.ac.uk/research-subject-groups/centre-criminology/centreborder-criminologies/blog/2017/12/italy-strikes.

[16] S Kirchgaessner and L Tondo, 'Italy's deal with Libya to "pull back" migrants faces legal challenge', *The Guardian* (8 May 2018), https://www.theguardian.com/world/2018/may/08/italy-deal-with-libya-pull-back-migrants-faces-legal-challenge-human-rights-violations.

[17] GS Goodwin-Gill and J McAdam, *The Refugee in International Law*, 3rd edn (OUP, 2007) 277–78.

[18] G Noll, 'Law and the Logic of Outsourcing: Offshore Processing and Diplomatic Assurances' *Refugee Protection in International Law, Contemporary Challenges Workshop*, (Oxford, 24 April 2006) 1.

At the same time, regardless of whether a country is considered generally safe because of the presence of adequate asylum procedures and judicial oversight, every individual should be entitled to rebut the presumption of safety of that State for him or herself in the particular case.[19] Even when States are faced with mounting pressure from mass flows of migrants and refugees by sea, their discretion in determining how to react is not absolute and a duty exists for contracting governments, not only under refugee and human rights law, but also under the law of the sea on search and rescue and, more particularly, under the UN Convention on the Law of the Sea (UNCLOS), to cooperate to assist ships' masters in delivering persons rescued at sea to a 'place of safety'[20] – meaning, in general terms, a location where basic human needs are met and where 'rescue operations are considered to terminate.'[21]

In the case of the 2009 push-backs, as with the push-backs by proxy in 2017, the Italian government has *de facto* considered Libya a reliable partner in migration control and rescue at sea. If abuses escalated further in early 2011, the Gaddafi regime's treatment of migrants had been known to undermine human rights for a long time.[22] The situation of migrants and refugees in Libya has dramatically worsened since Gaddafi was ousted, and even more so since 2015. People rescued in the Mediterranean report horrible conditions, including involvement of migrants in the slave trade.[23] They claim they would rather die at sea than go back to Libya.[24] Therefore even if the Libyan coastguard were well trained in search and rescue, the refugees on the boat would panic as soon as they realised their diversion to Libya. These situations can be very dangerous if we consider that more than 4000 deaths at sea in 2016 were caused through panic situations during rescue operations.[25]

In the failed State of Libya with no stable government in place, the situation on the ground is so chaotic that no clear-cut rules and consistent practices can be identified. Although Libya acceded to the SAR Convention, for a long time it

[19] T Spijkerboer, 'Stretching the Limits. European Maritime Border Control Policies and International Law' in MC Foblets (ed), *The External Dimension of the Immigration & Asylum Policy of the EU* (Bruylant, 2009).

[20] See amendments to both the International Convention on Maritime Search and Rescue (SAR) and the International Convention for the Safety of Life at Sea (SOLAS) (adopted May 2004, entered into force 1 July 2006). Amendment to ch V of SOLAS and to chs III and IV of the SAR. Resolutions MSC 155 (78) and MSC 153 (78), 20 May 2004.

[21] IMO Resolution 167 (78), Annex 34, Guidelines on the Treatment of Persons Rescued at Sea (adopted 20 May 2004) para 6.12.

[22] See Amnesty International Report 2017, above n 15.

[23] L Gouliamaki, 'Migrant slavery in Libya: Nigerians tell of being used as slaves', *BBC News*, 2 January 2018, https://www.bbc.com/news/world-africa-42492687.

[24] J Caye, 'Report of Libyan Coast Guards attacking migrants raises concerns – via ECRE', *Forumasile*, 11 November 2016, https://forumasile.org/2016/11/11/report-of-libyan-coast-guards-attacking-migrants-raises-concerns-via-ecre/.

[25] SeaWatch, 'Reply to the statement of the Commander of the European operation Sophia on the training of Libya's so called "coastguard"', 6 November 2016, https://sea-watch.org/en/a-safepassage-is-the-only-way-to-cut-migrants-deaths/.

has not provided the required notification regarding the limits of its search and rescue (SAR) region; nor has it designated a responsible rescue coordination centre, which is an essential requirement for international registration of the SAR zone. A rescue coordination centre must operate 24/7, its staff must speak English, and it should be endowed with both ambulance vehicles and relevant communication means. The lack of a proper coordination centre could be why the International Maritime Organization (IMO) declined, in December 2017, the Libyan request to have a SAR region, thus *de facto* entrusting the Italian MRCC with the full coordination of rescue missions on the high seas.[26] Between 2017 and 2018, Libya has frequently reportedly endangered rescue missions in the Mediterranean, in particular those conducted by lifeboats sent by the MRCC in Rome.[27] Only in June 2018 was the establishment of a Libyan SAR Region confirmed by the IMO.

III. OVERVIEW OF THE FIRST WAVE OF BILATERAL AGREEMENTS LINKED TO READMISSION BETWEEN ITALY AND LIBYA

States avail themselves of bilateral agreements for technical and police cooperation to combat irregular immigration and trans-border crimes, such as terrorism, illegal traffic of drugs, trafficking of human beings, and organised crime. For the purpose of this work, this wording is used to indicate arrangements between two States, Italy and Libya, which aim to establish a common action against unauthorised immigration by means of a programme of joint patrols or delegated patrols resulting in rescue/naval interdiction and deflection of intercepted people to their ports of departure.

Trying to analyse all the informal bilateral agreements, on the basis of which Libyan authorities both authorised Italian vessels to cross Libyan territorial waters and accepted readmission of intercepted migrants in each single operation, is a painstaking process. Moreover, the content of some of these instruments remains unpublished and detailed information is often missing.

On 13 December 2000, Italy and Libya initiated their bilateral cooperation on irregular migration.[28] A Memorandum was signed in January 2006

[26] See M Monroy, 'A seahorse for the Mediterranean: Border surveillance for Libyan search and rescue zone', https://digit.site36.net/2018/01/03/border-surveillance-technology-for-new-libyan-search-and-rescue-zone/.

[27] See, eg, the following incidents involving the rescue vessels Bourbon Argos, Sea-Eye, and Iuventa. Information can be retrieved, respectively, at: P Kingseley and C Stephen, 'Libyan navy admits confrontation with charity's rescue boat', *The Guardian*, 28 August 2016, https://www.theguardian.com/world/2016/aug/28/libyan-navy-admits-confrontation-charity-rescue-boat-msf; Statewatch, 'Deadly incident on the Mediterranean Sea: Rescue organisation accuses Libyan coast guard', 28 December 2016, http://www.statewatch.org/news/2016/dec/med-libya-rescues.htm.

[28] The Agreement in question concerned collaboration in the fight against terrorism, organised crime, illegal trafficking of drugs, and irregular immigration, on the basis of which the two countries exchanged information on irregular immigration and ensured reciprocal assistance to combat this

concerning the common engagement in the fight against irregular immigration, culminating in a Protocol[29] and an Additional Operating and Technical Protocol on cooperation in the fight against irregular immigration (Protocol and Additional Protocol), signed on 29 December 2007.[30] The 2007 accords assume great prominence because, for the first time, Italy and Libya concluded arrangements to ensure practical operability of the commitments made in the 2000 Agreement, which was limited to generically recommending that the parties exchange information and provide mutual assistance and cooperation.

A Treaty on Friendship, Partnership, and Cooperation (Partnership Treaty) was concluded in Tripoli on 30 August 2008.[31] This Partnership Treaty was followed by the negotiation of an Executive Protocol to the 2007 agreements, signed on 4 February 2009, which still remains unpublished.[32] The 2008 Partnership Treaty reshaped the system of legal sources by incorporating in Article 19 the commitments previously adopted by the parties – especially the 2000 Agreement and the 2007 Protocols – to intensifying bilateral cooperation in the fight against terrorism, organised crime, trafficking of drugs, and irregular immigration. For the purpose of this chapter, the arrangements under scrutiny are the 2007 and 2009 technical Protocols, as well as the 2008 Partnership Treaty.[33]

The content of the 2007 arrangements (Protocol and Additional Protocol) – which should be jointly examined – was disclosed only in 2009. Pursuant to Article 1(1) of the Additional Protocol, the parties agreed to establish joint missions whereby Libya committed to patrolling both its coastline and international waters while Italy agreed to supply its Southern-Mediterranean partner with six vessels on a temporary basis. Also, under Article 5 of the Protocol, Italy availed itself of the EU budget for the construction of a system to control Libyan territorial and maritime frontiers to combat the phenomenon of unauthorised

phenomenon. See *Accordo tra la Repubblica Italiana e la Gran Giamahiria Araba Libica Popolare Socialista per la Collaborazione nella Lotta al Terrorismo, alla Criminalità Organizzata, al Traffico Illegale di Stupefacenti e Sostanze Psicotrope e All'Immigrazione Clandestina* (Rome, 13 December 2000). Another agreement was reached in July 2003 intended to define the modalities of cooperation between respective police authorities for the purpose of preventing unauthorised flows from Africa, but its content has not been published.

[29] *Protocollo tra la Repubblica Italiana e la Gran Giamahiria Araba Libica Popolare Socialista* (Tripoli, 29 December 2007) (Protocol).

[30] *Protocollo Aggiuntivo Tecnico-Operativo al Protocollo di Cooperazone tra la Repubblica Italiana e la Gran Giamahiria Araba Libica Popolare Socialista, per fronteggiare il fenomeno dell'immigrazione Clandestina* (Tripoli, 29 December 2007) (Additional Protocol).

[31] *Trattato di Amicizia, Partenariato, e Cooperazione* (Bengazi, 30 August 2008) ratified by Italy with Law no 2009/7 (Partnership Treaty).

[32] *Protocollo Aggiuntivo Tecnico-Operativo concernente l'aggiunta di un articolo al Protocollo firmato a Tripoli il 29/12/2007 tra la Repubblica Italiana e la Gran Giamahiria Araba Libica Popolare Socialista, per fronteggiare il fenomeno dell'immigrazione clandestina* (Tripoli, 4 February 2009) (Executive Protocol).

[33] For further information on the content of the agreements, including translation in Italian, refer to M Giuffré, 'State Responsibility Beyond Borders: What Legal Basis for Italy's Push-Backs to Libya?' (2013) 24(4) *IJRL* 692.

migration to Europe. For the first 90 days operations were to be conducted by a mixed crew, as a training period, after which the Italian personnel on board were to be progressively reduced (Article 1(4)).[34] A Joint Operations Command – under the responsibility of a representative appointed by Libya, and a vice-commandant appointed by Italy, with advisory tasks – was created with the purpose of arranging daily enforcement patrols.

Libyan authorities were, thus, totally entrusted with the command and responsibility for any initiative taken during operational missions.[35] Under Article 2 of the 2007 Protocol, Italian officials were employed on board vessels only to conduct training activities, to give technical assistance, and for maintenance of the vessels.

Neither the Protocols concluded in December 2007 nor the 2009 Executive Protocol expressly prescribed rules for the interception and deflection to Libya of seaborne migrants halted by Italian authorities in international waters or closer to the Italian territory.[36] Therefore, the legality of both the naval interdiction and bilateral readmission programmes will be mainly discussed in relation to their modalities of execution.

IV. IN SEARCH OF A LEGAL FOUNDATION FOR PUSH-BACKS TO LIBYA

The diverse legal bases put forward by the Italian government to justify its cooperation with Libya also show that Italy ought to know about the treatment of migrants and refugees in Libya. Sovereign discretion cannot warrant displacement of fundamental rights, first and foremost the principle of *non-refoulement*. European States have a duty to know, before removal, how migrants and refugees will be treated in the readmitting countries. They should abide by international refugee and human rights law, whether they are engaged in the implementation of search and rescue operations, anti-smuggling activities, or the performance of migration controls in tandem with another country.

Gaining knowledge of the rules of engagement and the subdivision of responsibilities under the agreements enables an assessment of both the different legal competences of the two States, and the degree of assistance provided

[34] The Italian government decided to put a stop to the presence of Italian personnel aboard Libyan vessels after an incident occurred on 12 September 2010. On this date, one of the vessels supplied by Italy to Libya and run by a mixed crew fired at a Sicilian trawler. See *Repubblica*, 'I libici mitragliano un peschereccio. Finanzieri italiani sulla nave di Tripoli' (13 September 2010), http://www.repubblica.it/cronaca/2010/09/13/news/i_libici_mitragliano_un_peschereccio_finanzieri_italiani_sulla_nave_di_tripoli-7043116/.

[35] See Art 1(5) of the 2007 Additional Protocol.

[36] See A Terrasi, 'I Respingimenti in Mare di Migranti alla Luce della Convenzione Europea dei Diritti Umani', (2009) 3 *Diritti Umani e Diritto Internazionale* 591; see also, generally, S Trevisanut, 'Immigrazione Clandestina via Mare e Cooperazione fra Italia e Libia dal Punto di Vista del Diritto del Mare' (2009) 3 *Diritti Umani e Diritto Internazionale* 609.

by Italy to Libya. It also contributes to better assessing which State would have primary responsibility in the case of human rights violations, and to what extent the other State could be indirectly complicit in the commission of an international wrongful act. Moreover, the analysis of an emblematic case study, such as the Italy–Libya cooperation, contributes to showing how *de-territorialised* State action can undercut the rights of refugees intercepted before entering the territorial jurisdiction of the European intercepting/delegating country. Finally, a comparison will be drawn between old practices of push-back and the new strategies of pull-back, designed to delegate even more to a third country the patrolling of the external maritime borders of Europe.

A purposive interpretation of some critical provisions of the 2007–09 bilateral accords for technical and police cooperation and the 2017 MoU – an interpretation that does not overstretch the literal reading of the text – reveals how removal to/retention on Libyan soil is the inevitable and foreseeable outcome of a cooperation policy that expressly pursues the goal of preventing and combating unauthorised arrivals to Europe by patrolling international waters and the Libyan coast.[37] The interception of ships and their diversion to a third country, or the act of handing migrants over to the authorities of a third State are not powers expressly prescribed in the 2009 Executive Protocol, in the 2007 agreements for technical and police cooperation, or in the most recent accords. Thus, the question as to whence this enforcement jurisdiction can be inferred remains open, and as such deserves further discussion.[38]

Nevertheless, a *bona fide* interpretation of a number of provisions implicitly entails recognition of the underlying purpose of these accords, namely, the restriction of unauthorised arrivals of migrants in Europe through a programme of technical and police cooperation with Libya.[39] This goal is also corroborated by the numerous statements of representatives of the Italian and Libyan governments.[40] With the EU Migration Partnership Framework, launched in 2016, the EU has even more explicitly supported Italy's collaboration with Libya, to the point of contributing also to part of the expenses for the patrolling of maritime borders. In the framework of the intensive technical, logistical and financial support crafted by these bilateral instruments of migration control,

[37] The removal/readmission-related purpose of the push-back policy has been confirmed by the CPT, *Report to the Italian Government on the visit to Italy carried out by the European Committee for the Prevention of Torture and Inhuman or Degrading Treatment or Punishment (CPT) from 27 to 31 July 2009*, 28 April 2010, http://www.cpt.coe.int/documents/ita/2010-inf-14-eng.pdf (CPT Report 2010) 11. See also, paras 1(1) and (3) of the Preamble to the 2007 Additional Protocol. For a broader discussion on treaty interpretation based on the 'ordinary meaning' of the text and its 'object and purpose', refer to Chapter 1 of this book.

[38] See, on this point, Section IV.C.

[39] The joint commitment to the struggle against illegal immigration is reiterated in the preambles of the 2007 Protocols and in Art 19 of the 2008 Partnership Treaty.

[40] See, *Hirsi v Italy*, above n 5, para 181. See also, the Statement by the Italian Ambassador to Libya, Trupiano, 5, http://www.camera.it/470?stenog=/_dati/leg16/lavori/stenbic/30/2009/1013&pagina=s020.

Libya undertook to readmit migrants and refugees intercepted by either Italian or Libyan authorities after transiting through Libya on their way to Europe.

However, it is likely that further instruments, which are not readily available, have played a role in shaping the push-back and pull-back campaigns: for instance, *ad hoc* notes exchanged by competent border authorities, or other informal accords, where consent is given by fax or telephone, on the basis of which Italian vessels were authorised to enter Libyan territorial waters, and Libya assented to the readmission of third-country nationals.[41] As far as the push-backs of 6 May 2009 are concerned, the Italian Ministry of the Interior declared that the authorisation by the Libyan government for the readmission of migrants was issued during the night, after long negotiations.[42] While this *ad hoc* consent between the States concerned constitutes the legal basis for the exercise of enforcement jurisdiction consisting in the transfer of migrants from one vessel to another with a view to readmission, the 2007 and 2009 technical Protocols, as well as the 2008 Partnership Treaty, taken as a whole, constitute the legal and political framework within which the 2009 push-backs were performed. Likewise, the plethora of accords negotiated by Italy and Libya under the aegis of the EU in 2017 constitutes the economic, technical, political, and logistical framework of support within which collaboration on push-backs by proxy could take place.

In its official response to the Council of Europe Committee on the Prevention of Torture (CPT) during its July 2009 mission to Italy, the Italian government put forward diverse and incongruous legal justifications for its push-back policy.[43] The main explanations advanced by the Italian government to validate push-backs were: SAR measures; migration control activities in pursuance of the Protocol on the Smuggling of Migrants;[44] and police operations carried out by Italy on behalf of Libya to push-back to the country of departure those who had irregularly evaded border controls. These arguments are analysed in one of my previous articles,[45] which underlines the existence of two different legal frames authorising, on the one hand, interception or rescue operations on the high seas, and, on the other hand, the removal of migrants and refugees to the country of embarkation. Without repeating the main passages, the next Section will summarise the primary findings.

[41] *Mutatis mutandis*, see *Medvedyev v France*, App no 3394/03 (29 March 2010) 97.

[42] See Meltingpot, 'Migranti riaccompagnati in Libia' (7 May 2009), http://www.meltingpot.org/articolo14467.html.

[43] Response of the Italian Government to the CPT Report, app I (Response Italian Government), https://rm.coe.int/16806ce533.

[44] Protocol against the Smuggling of Migrants by Land, Sea and Air, Supplementing the United Nations Convention against Transnational Organized Crime (adopted 15 November 2000, entered into force 28 January 2004) (Protocol against Smuggling).

[45] M Giuffré, 'State Responsibility beyond Borders: What Legal Basis for Italy's Push-backs to Libya?' (2012) 24(4) *International Journal of Refugee Law* 692.

A. Italy–Libya Push-Backs and 'International Cooperation Principles'

Although interdiction and deflection activities by Italian authorities went beyond the literal meaning of the Italy–Libya agreements, and the actual scope of Italy's maritime operations could not be foreseen, I believe the text of the bilateral Protocols is (perhaps purposely) somewhat vague. As a consequence, an ample margin of discretion for intervention is left to Italian authorities. At the same time, the push-back practice – involving a consistent sequence of acts and pronouncements – would have been impossible without the broader framework of interactions between Italy and Libya created by the 2007 and 2009 bilateral agreements for technical and police cooperation, and also by the 2008 Partnership Treaty.

The systematic character of Italy's push-back operations and the lack of protest by Libya should not be overlooked. Moreover, whereas the readmission of own nationals is by and large accepted as a customary obligation in international law,[46] readmission of third-country nationals is only possible on the basis of an agreement between two States. As a final avenue, by invoking generic 'international cooperation principles', the Italian government has justified redirection of intercepted ships as a response to Libya's request. Indeed, migrants and refugees in their attempt to reach Europe had infringed Libyan migration law by irregularly fleeing the country after eluding local border controls.[47] Due to the absence of a precise legal framework and a standardised readmission procedure, the agreements for technical and police cooperation concluded between Italy and Libya in 2007 and 2009 seem to embody these 'international cooperation principles'. However, it is possible that a more direct expression of these principles is contained in other classified and informal accords, on the basis of which Libya assented to the readmission of undocumented migrants in *ad hoc* notes during the course of the 2009 maritime interceptions.[48]

Article 2(1) of the 2007 Additional Protocol would explain Italy's participation in those activities of control of external maritime borders. It provides that the Joint Operations Command may request the intervention of Italian units, ordinarily deployed in the Italian island of Lampedusa, for conducting '*anti-immigration* activities', the *telos* of all agreements linked to readmission between Italy and Libya. Although nothing in the text specifies what exactly these 'anti-immigration activities' are, it is possible to infer that push-backs amount to a

[46] See, Chapter 3 of this book for an examination of the customary status of the obligation to readmit own nationals and third-country nationals, and the doubts concerning readmission of involuntary nationals.

[47] Response Italian Government, n 43 above, para c.

[48] For example, in *United States v Gonzalez*, a conversation by telephone was considered to be an 'arrangement' between governments. See Judge Kravitch, *United States v Gonzalez*, 776 F.2nd (11 Circuit, 1985) 936 as cited in Papastavridis, 'European Court of Human Rights: Medvedyev et al v France' (2010) 59 (3) *International Comparative Law Quarterly* 875 fn 55 (Papastavridis 2010a).

practice denoting the consensus of both parties to the Italian enforcement of police actions on behalf of Libya.

Push-backs would be, in other words, a procedure falling 'within specific agreements, aimed at "returning to requesting States those migrants, being intercepted in international waters, who had escaped the controls of the relevant authorities" of the countries from which shores they departed.'[49] This interpretation would also be consistent with the Preambles to the 2007 Protocol and the 2009 Executive Agreement, whereby Italy and Libya commit to intensifying their cooperation to combat unauthorised immigration.

In addition, the 2007 Protocols include provisions dealing with the common commitment to the restraint of irregular immigration to Europe through joint patrols in the Libyan territorial waters and in international waters under Libyan command and responsibility.[50] Coping with unauthorised immigration also subsumes the possibility of both sighting and halting any crafts with '*clandestine*' passengers on board, as Article 2(1)(d) of the 2007 Additional Protocol sets forth. Article 2 of the 2009 Executive Agreement provides, instead, that 'the two countries undertake to repatriate clandestine immigrants [from their territory] and to conclude agreements with the countries of origin in order to limit clandestine immigration.'[51]

Since freedom of navigation reigns on the high seas, vessels are subject – save in exceptional cases – to the exclusive jurisdiction of their flag State (Article 92(1)). Naval interdiction on the high seas is grounded in international agreements between two or more States aimed at exercising the right of visit to combat criminal activities not listed in Article 110 UNCLOS and performed by vessels without nationality or not sailing the flag of a State party to the agreement.[52] In particular, Article 110 requires that, '[e]xcept where acts of interference derive from powers conferred by treaty', States may exercise a 'right of visit' with regard to ships of uncertain nationality and flagless ships to verify the vessel's right to fly its flag. If, after document inspection, suspicion remains, the interdicting vessel 'may proceed to a further examination on board the ship, which must be carried out with all possible consideration.'

As stated above, the Italian government has also adduced the implementation of the Palermo Protocol on Smuggling of Migrants as one of the legal bases for push-backs. The Palermo Protocol entrusts States to stop and search vessels without nationality or flying a flag of convenience ensuring safety/humane

[49] Response Italian Government, n 43 above.

[50] Art 2 of the Protocol and Art 1 of the Additional Protocol.

[51] Translation supplied by the ECtHR in *Hirsi*, above n 5, para 19. See also, Tondini 2010, n 175 below, 4.

[52] See S Trevisanut, 'The Principle of *Non-Refoulement* at Sea' (2008) 12 *Max Planck UNYB* 205, 240. On the right of visit, see also E Papastavridis, 'The Right of Visit on the High Seas in a Theoretical Perspective: *Mare Liberum* versus *Mare Clausum* Revisited (2011) 24(1) *Leiden Journal of International Law* 45–69.

treatment of persons on board, and taking due account of security of the vessel, its cargo, and legal and commercial interests of interested States.[53] Under Article 8(7) of the Protocol,

> a State Party that has reasonable grounds to suspect that a vessel is engaged in the smuggling of migrants by sea and is without nationality or may be assimilated to a vessel without nationality may board and search the vessel. If evidence confirming the suspicion is found, that State Party shall take appropriate measures in accordance with relevant domestic and international law.

While the Protocol allows a State party to request the assistance of other States parties in suppressing the use of a vessel without nationality that is suspected of engaging in the smuggling of migrants by sea,[54] it does not expressly prohibit coastal States from granting permission to receive intercepted migrants either. Moreover, the text of the Protocol only envisages the repatriation of migrants to countries of origin or permanent residence (Article 18(1)), not necessarily to countries of transit, such as Libya. Article 18(8) provides that its implementation shall not affect the obligations entered into under any other applicable bilateral or multilateral treaty, or any other applicable operational arrangement regulating, in whole or in part, the removal of unauthorised persons. Moreover, a saving clause plainly requires States conducting enforcement operations at sea to respect humanitarian law, human rights, and refugee law, in conformity with the principles of *non-refoulement* and non-discrimination (Article 9). The obligation to comply with these fundamental international rules imposes upon the intercepting State both the responsibility to act in the full observance of the principles in question, and the duty to ascertain whether these norms are respected *de jure* and *de facto* in the third cooperating country in order to prevent the commission of an international wrongful act.

In addressing the distinction between treaties and other international accords, the ICJ has clearly sustained that 'where … the law prescribes no particular form, parties are free to choose what form they please provided their intention clearly results from it.'[55] On this view, it can be argued that the diplomatic note of 7 June 2002 between France and Cambodia – on the basis of which a Cambodian vessel was intercepted by French authorities – amounts to a binding agreement as it 'enumerates commitments … and thus create rights and obligations in international law.'[56]

[53] See Arts 8 and 9 of the Protocol against Smuggling.

[54] Art 8(1) of the Protocol against Smuggling.

[55] See *Temple of Preah Vihear case (Cambodia v Thailand), Preliminary Objections*, 26 May 1961, ICJ Rep 17, 31. *The Aegean Continental Shelf Case (Greece v Turkey)*, 19 December 1978, ICJ Rep 3, 38–44.

[56] See *Maritime Delimitation and Territorial Quest (Quatar v Bahrain)*, 1 July 1994, ICJ Rep 112, para 25. See also J Klabbers, *Developments in International Law: The Concept of Treaty in International Law* (Kluwer, 1996) 215; Papastavridis 2010a, n 48 above, 867, 874.

The right of visit on the high seas should not be conflated with the assertion of enforcement jurisdiction, which instead depends on the prior establishment of legislative jurisdiction and would enable the intercepting State to bring the vessel to the port of the boarding State, arrest and try the offenders, confiscate the vessels, etc.[57] While 'legislative jurisdiction' concerns the power to prescribe rules, enforcement jurisdiction concerns 'the power to take executive action in pursuance of the making of decisions or rules.'[58]

Redirection to a third country after interception either on the high seas or in the territorial waters of a coastal State is practically and legally possible only with the consent of the coastal State itself on the basis of either formal or informal accords.[59] This is true in particular when the readmitting State is different from the flag State of the intercepting vessel. In this case, diversions are executed on account of an accord between the State toward which the ship is redirected and the flag State of the interdicting vessel, which might perform, for instance, police actions on behalf of the former country.

On the high seas, enforcement jurisdiction can only be exercised with the consent of the flag State, which can be granted either by a pre-existing bilateral or multilateral treaty or by an *ad hoc* accord. In the context of control of irregular migration by sea, Italian authorities were potentially entitled, in keeping with Article 110(1) of the UNCLOS, to exercise a right of visit of intercepted flagless boats, even outside any specific bilateral or multilateral agreement. However, the legal framework authorising deflection of migrants and refugees is still not clarified, as uncertainty exists over whether a further power of seizure can be inferred from the right of visit. Neither general international law nor the UNCLOS explicitly confers other rights upon the intercepting State and any further assertion of jurisdiction.[60] It should be noted that the right to visit an intercepted vessel 'does not *ipso facto* entail the full extension of the jurisdictional power of the boarding States.'[61] If the vessel (regardless of whether it is loaded with migrants or not) is brought to a port for further investigation, the exercise of jurisdiction would be limited to inquiring as to the nationality of the vessel and intentions of the persons on-board.[62] Therefore,

> [s]uch actions as seizing the ship and apprehending the persons on board; ordering the ship to modify its course towards a destination outside the territorial waters or the contiguous zone; escorting the vessel or steaming nearby until the ship is heading

[57] E Papastavridis, 'Enforcement Jurisdiction in the Mediterranean Sea: Illicit Activities and the Rule of Law on the High Seas' (2010) 25(4) *The International Journal of Marine and Coastal Law* 569, 577 (Papastavridis 2010c).

[58] I Brownlie, *Principles of Public International Law*, 7th edn (OUP, 2008) 297.

[59] Trevisanut 2009, n 36 above, 614.

[60] MH Nordquist, *United Nations Convention on the Law of the Sea, A Commentary*, Vol III (Martinus Nijhoff, 1985) 127.

[61] Papastavridis 2010c, n 57 above, 583.

[62] ibid, 584.

> on such course; conducting the ship or the persons on board to a third country or handing them over to the authorities of a third State, do not readily follow from the terms of the [law of the sea] treaties.[63]

As every law enforcement operation at sea must be reasonable and must meet the principles of necessity and proportionality,[64] it cannot be taken for granted that powers of detention or removal to the country of departure are implicitly encompassed in this provision. Therefore, even if it is accepted that interception of migrants and refugees in international waters fell within Article 110(1) with regard to vessels without nationality, the initial aim of a maritime operation might shift to something different – for example, in the context of the 2009 Italy–Libya push-backs, from a SAR operation to a measure of border control and *vice versa*.[65]

The 2007 Protocols for the first time established maritime joint patrols, with six vessels temporarily rendered to Libya. Then, through the Bengasi Partnership Treaty in 2008, the two Contracting Parties renewed their common commitment in several fields of action, including the fight against unauthorised immigration. This led to the adoption of the 2009 Executive Protocol, which defines the organisation of the joint patrolling missions conducted by vessels operated by a mixed crew. The Executive Protocol, by supplying Libyans with six vessels on a permanent basis (replacing the Italian flag with a Libyan one), significantly shifted their control of unauthorised migration to Europe in a more pro-active direction. Although Italy had repeatedly solicited Libya's participation in joint patrols, Libya had always refrained from taking part in the operations. Indeed, until May 2009, Libya remained resistant to the idea of letting a military boat flying the Italian flag across Libyan territorial waters to drive migrants back to the North African coast.[66] The provision of vessels on a permanent basis and the operational definition of technical cooperation envisaged by the 2009 Executive Protocol changed the context of their collaboration, thus paving the way for the push-back practice (and, in 2017, for the push-back by proxy strategy).

The salience of the Italy–Libya agreements can be condensed into two principal points. First, the technical Protocols encapsulate those 'international cooperation principles' that aim to curtail irregular migration to Europe. Whether removal to the country of departure is deemed a police action of

[63] V Moreno-Lax, 'Seeking Asylum in the Mediterranean: Against a Fragmentary Reading of EU Member States' Obligations Accruing at Sea' (2011) 23(2) *International Journal of Refugee Law* 174–220 (Moreno-Lax 2011a) 188.

[64] See *The Arctic Sunrise Arbitration, Netherlands v Russia*, Award on the Merits, PCA Case No 2014-02, ICGJ 511 (PCA 2015), 14 August 2015, Permanent Court of Arbitration [PCA], para 326. See also, Guyana v Suriname, Award, ICGJ 370 (PCA 2007), 17 September 2007, Permanent Court of Arbitration [PCA], para 445.

[65] The possible change in the purpose of a maritime operation was also endorsed by S Trevisanut, '*Non-refoulement* at Sea' (*Governing Migration by Sea: a Legal Perspective Workshop*, Oxford, 17–18 November 2011).

[66] ibid.

Italy on behalf of Libya, or an autonomous Libyan initiative taken with Italy's support and assistance (as in the 2009 cases) or a practice entirely carried out by Libya with minimal physical intervention by Italian authorities (as in the 2017 cases discussed in the next Section) does not alter the ultimate goal of this plethora of bilateral arrangements. Secondly, such a vast range of accords encompasses the arsenal of incentives utilised by Italy to persuade Libya to more proactively cooperate in both curbing irregular migration, and in accepting the readmission of third-country nationals rescued/intercepted in their desperate flight to Europe. As such, the aggregation of all these accords constitutes the legal and political framework within which Italy–Libya cooperation on migration control (including the push-back and pull-back policy) was put into action.

B. Italy's Comprehensive Support to Libya and the Shift from Push-Backs to Push-Backs by Proxy ('Pull-Backs')

The reasons for a transit country, such as Libya, to accept the burden of thousands of readmitted migrants and refugees must be examined in order to uncover parallels between past and current practices of migration control at sea. The previous Sub-section shows that Italy and Libya do not have the same interest in the readmission of migrants who are not Libya's nationals, but foreign nationals passing through its territory on their way to Europe. Moreover, Libya does not have legal institutional capacity or adequate facilities to manage the massive presence of irregular migrants and refugees. Therefore, if it is willing to invest resources in patrolling its territorial and maritime borders, this was motivated by expected benefits. Technical cooperation and assistance in terms of training, consulting, exchange of intelligence information and supply of vessels and equipment are the most common incentives used by Italy to induce Libya to cooperate on prevention of unauthorised immigration under the 2007 and 2009 technical Protocols and, more recently, the 2017 MoUs signed with both the UN-backed government of Al-Sarraj and General Haftar.

The 2008 Partnership Treaty marks the first most significant step toward diplomatic normalisation and the creation of a favourable climate between these two countries, coupled with EU initiatives, such as the more recent EU Migration Partnership Framework, EUBAM and EUNAVFOR Med missions.[67] By cooperating with Italy and the EU in the fight against irregular migration, international terrorism, and the smuggling and trafficking of human beings, not only did Libya obtain political, economic, and technical benefits (eg, the lifting of the European trade embargo and the construction of a gas pipeline to Italy)

[67] For an overview of the Partnership Treaty, see N Ronzitti, 'The Treaty on Friendship, Partnership, and Cooperation between Italy and Libya: New Prospects for Cooperation in the Mediterranean' (Institute of International Affairs, 2009), http://www.iai.it/pdf/DocIAI/iai0909.pdf.

but it also had a chance to improve its international standing.[68] It has therefore been argued that 'it is this whole bilateral cooperative framework which secures a minimum operability in the cooperation on readmission more than the "reciprocal" obligations contained in a standard readmission agreement.'[69] Since the 2007–09 accords for technical and police cooperation and the 2017 MoUs do not constitute standard readmission agreements and are quite vague in defining the scope of migration control activities and push-back procedures, the parties rely on having a wider margin of manoeuvre to respond to short-term security concerns and new situations fraught with uncertainties.[70]

As asserted by the Italian government, in its observations in the *Hirsi* case,[71] and iterated by a former Italian Minister of the Interior on several official occasions, the Protocols signed in 2007 and 2009 with Libya, as well as the 2008 Partnership Treaty, may constitute both the legal foundation for push-back missions, and crucial tools in the fight against 'clandestine' immigration.[72] Accordingly, the Italian vessels deployed in international waters, together with the vessels donated to Libya, were part of a wider surveillance and 'border control system aimed to strike migratory flows at the root.'[73] The accords signed with several Libyan authorities and militias in 2017, including for the provision of vessels and the training course for officers for coastal security are also part of this long-term cooperative strategy.

Although, in the complex contingencies of patrol operations, States authorise/coordinate interception/rescue/removals through telephone and/or unpublished and informal exchanges of notes, they generally prefer to secure operability of bilateral cooperation tools on highly sensitive issues, such as readmission (quite unpopular in countries of origin or transit of migrants) through flexible but still written (even if unpublished) documents.[74] These accords ensure, at least, more

[68] See JP Cassarino, 'Informalizing Readmission Agreements in the EU Neighborhood' (2007) 42 *The International Spectator* 183; E Paoletti, 'Relations among Unequals? Readmission between Italy and Libya' in JP Cassarino (ed), *Unbalanced Reciprocities: Cooperation on Readmission in the Euro-Mediterranean Area* (Middle East Institute, 2010) 70 (Cassarino 2010a).

[69] JP Cassarino, 'Dealing with Unbalanced Reciprocities: Cooperation on Readmission and Implications', in Cassarino 2010a, n 68 above, 8.

[70] ibid. For an analysis of the evolution of Italy–Libya cooperation and the different types of agreements, see I Gjergji, *Sulla governance delle migrazioni. Sociologia dell'underworld del comando globale* (Franco Angeli, 2016), 114–22.

[71] See Italian Government Submissions in *Hirsi v Italy*, above n 5, para 65.

[72] R Maroni, Minister of the Interior, 'Resoconto. Sommario and Stenografico' 5 (Oral information at Senato della Repubblica, XVI Legislatura, 25 May 2009), http://www.senato.it/service/PDF/PDFServer/BGT/00424000.pdf. See also, *Adnkronos*, 'Immigrati, Maroni: "L'accordo con la Libia funziona. Avanti con i respingimenti." Bruxelles: chiarimenti da Italia e Malta' (31 August 2009), http://www.adnkronos.com/IGN/News/Politica/?id=3.0.3718416369.

[73] See M Nesticò, 'Immigrazione: Consegnate a Libia tre Motovedette GDF – D'Arrigo, Equipaggi Libici Addestrati da GDF' (Associazione Finanzieri Cittadini e Solidarietà, 17 May 2009), http://www.ficiesse.it/home-page/3065/immigrazione_-consegnate-a-libia-tre-motovedette-gdf---d_arrigo_-equipaggilibici-addestrati-da-gdf.

[74] Cassarino 2010a, n 68 above, 8.

credibility and predictability in terms of compliance with the commitments of, and responsiveness to, the expectations of the parties on a more regular basis. As Nolte pointedly observed, 'treaties are not just dry parchments. They are instruments providing stability to their parties and to fulfil the purposes which they embody.'[75]

The foregoing analysis demonstrates that Libya's cooperation on patrolling sea and land borders, and readmission of undocumented third-country nationals intercepted by Italian authorities, builds on a solid platform of costs–benefits analysis that started in early 2000 and continues today in different forms, resulting in push-backs by proxy (pull-backs) carried out directly by Libyan authorities. Although the only possible conclusion is that push-backs and push-backs by proxy do not find in treaties a clear legal basis, it can be argued that the wide-ranging series of written accords concluded between Italy and Libya, as well as those unpublished notes exchanged between national authorities in the course of patrol and rescue operations, constitute the multifaceted legal and political scaffold supporting the practice of interdiction, deflection and/or pull-back of undocumented migrants and refugees to the port of embarkation. Considering the high costs of readmission for Libya – in social, political, and economic terms – it is plausible that, beyond unilateral acquiescence, *ad hoc* consent is necessary for each and every maritime operation resulting in the actual disembarkation and readmission of third-country nationals. Authorisation on a case-by-case basis is, in contrast, not required in those situations in which search and rescue as well as disembarkation are outright delegated to a third country.

V. NOT AN ISOLATED CASE: OUTLINING FURTHER AGREEMENTS FOR TECHNICAL AND POLICE COOPERATION

Deflections to Libya – country of embarkation but not of origin of undocumented migrants heading to Europe – find a first precedent in the Italian interdictions at sea in response to the massive influx of migrants from Albania in 1997. Also, operations were authorised by a set of agreements concluded between the two countries.[76]

The cases briefly reviewed in this Section demonstrate that the analysis of the Italy–Libya case is pertinent for other situations in which countries within or outside Europe entrust or used to entrust third countries of provenance of migrants and refugees with the patrolling of both their territorial waters and

[75] ILC, *Report on the Work of its Sixtieth Session, Treaties over time in particular: Subsequent Agreements and Practice*, A/63/10, Annex A (2008) 365, http://untreaty.un.org/ilc/reports/2008/2008report.htm.

[76] While on 25 March 1997, an agreement was signed in the form of an Exchange of Letters, on 2 April 1997, the two States signed a Protocol encompassing all the technical enforcement measures Italy could adopt to hold back the masses of irregular migrants arriving by sea. Finally, in November 1997, a readmission agreement was signed that entered into force on 1 August 1998.

international waters in order to prevent unauthorised inflows to Europe. In the late 1990s, arrivals of migrants from North Africa 'threatening' to transgress the European border ceased as a consequence of the enhanced bilateral cooperation in the field of readmission and police cooperation between European States and Southern Mediterranean countries,[77] such as Tunisia,[78] Morocco,[79] Algeria,[80] and more recently Egypt and Libya.[81]

Spain, in its endeavour to contain irregular migration by sea set up joint patrols authorised by a host of bilateral agreements with several African countries, including Morocco in 2003, Senegal and Mauritania in 2006, Cape Verde in 2007, Gambia, Guinea Bissau, and Guinea Conakry in 2008.[82] These documents would constitute the legal basis for joint sea patrols between the Spanish Guardia Civil and African security forces aiming to decrease the number of arrivals of migrants and refugees from African countries of origin or transit.[83]

Because of the lack of public access to the text of these arrangements, it is not possible to inquire as to their exact content, the degree of involvement of Spanish authorities in the enforcement of maritime operations, and the legal safeguards applied by Spain to the passengers of detected vessels.[84] All in all, however, the rationale of the accords negotiated by Italy and Spain with African countries points to conditioning the transfer of technical equipment, vessels, funding, and the organisation of training courses to a more decisive engagement of countries of origin or transit in the prevention of irregular migration flows to Europe.

Without any claim of exhaustiveness, it is also worth observing that both the US and Australia have been particularly involved in interdiction and extraterritorial processing policies. The US has mainly targeted irregular boat arrivals from Haiti and Cuba. As provided by a bilateral agreement signed by the US and Haiti in September 1981, after intercepting and searching vessels suspected of transporting irregular migrants from Haiti, people transferred aboard US Coast

[77] See A Di Pascale, 'Migration Control at Sea: The Italian Case' in B Ryan and V Mitsilegas (eds), *Extraterritorial Immigration Control: Legal Challenges* (Martinus Nijhoff, 2010) 296.

[78] On 6 August 1998, an agreement was signed in the form of an Exchange of Letters concerning the entry and readmission of people in an irregular position. Another agreement on police cooperation was concluded on 13 December 2003.

[79] Readmission agreement signed on 27 July 1998.

[80] Agreement on the movement of persons signed on 24 February 2000.

[81] The details of the Agreements between Italy and Libya have already been provided in Section III. With regard to Egypt, while an Agreement on police cooperation was concluded on 18 June 2000, a Readmission Agreement was signed only on 9 January 2007.

[82] For an analysis of all these agreements, see P Garcia-Andrade, 'Extraterritorial Strategies to Tackle Irregular Immigration by Sea: a Spanish Perspective' in Ryan and Mitsilegas 2010, n 77 above, 311 ff; J Rijpma *Frontex: Successful Blame Shifting of the Member States?* (2010) *Elcano Newsletter*.

[83] See, for instance, the reply of Frontex to the NGO ILPA (Immigration Law Practitioners' Association).

[84] ibid, 321.

Guard cutters were subjected to a summary screening, and very few persons were provided with a full asylum hearing and taken to the US to pursue their claims.[85] With the exception of those Cubans intercepted by US authorities and transferred to Guantanamo Bay for extraterritorial processing after showing credible and genuine claims for protection to on-board adjudicators, all other arrivals were transferred to Cuba.[86]

As far as Australia is concerned, in September 2001, in the aftermath of the *Tampa* incident,[87] the Australian government launched the 'Pacific Solution'.[88] If the attempts to tow or escort these boats back to Indonesia failed, asylum seekers were transferred to Manus Island or Nauru for extraterritorial processing of their protection claims.[89] In September 2013, Australia inaugurated 'Operation Sovereign Borders'.[90] While the details of this operation have not been publicly disclosed, media reports indicate that intercepted people were transferred to lifeboats stocked with food, water and medical supplies, which were then towed back to the edge of, or into, Indonesia's territorial waters.[91] As of October 2018,

[85] Migrants Interdiction Agreement (23 September 1981) US–Haiti, 33 UST 3559, 3560. For an overview of the practice of interdiction on the high seas and extraterritorial processing at Guantanamo Bay, see D Ghezelbash, 'Shifting Sands and Refugee Boats: The Transfer of Migration Control Policies between the United States and Australia', in JP Gauci, M Giuffré and L Tsourdi, *Forced Migration(s): Critical Perspectives on Refugee Law* (Martinus Nijhoff Publishers, 2014). See also A Dastyari and E Libbey, 'Immigration Detention in Guantanamo Bay' (2012) 6(2) *Shima: The International Journal of Research into Island Cultures* 49. See also B Frelick, 'US Refugee Policy in the Caribbean: No Bridge Over Troubled Waters' (1996) 20(2) *Fletcher Forum of World Affairs* 67; SH Legomsky, 'The USA and the Caribbean Interdiction Program' (2006) 18(3)–(4) *International Journal of Refugee Law (IJRL)* 677, 679.

[86] ibid 72. Interdiction and extraterritorial processing on Guantanamo Bay continue to this day. See D Ghezelbash, *Refuge Lost: Asylum Law in an Interdependent World* (CUP, 2018) 74–77.

[87] For an analysis of the incident, see CMJ Bostock, 'The International Legal Obligations owed to the Asylum Seekers on the MV Tampa' (2002) 14(2)–(3) *IJRL* 279; M Crock and D Ghezelbash, 'Do Loose Lips Bring Ships? The Role of Policy, Politics and Human Rights in Managing Unauthorized Boat Arrivals' (2010) 19 *Griffith Law Review* 238.

[88] For an analysis of the Pacific Solution, see, *inter alia*, S Kneebone, 'The Pacific Plan: The Provision of "Effective Protection"?' (2006) 18 *International Journal of Refugee Law* 696.

[89] See Migration Amendment (Excision from Migration Zone) Act 2001 (Cth), amending s 5(1) of Migration Act 1958 (Cth). See M Crock, 'In the Wake of *The Tampa*: Conflicting Visions of International Refugee Law in the Management of Refugee Flows' (2003) 12(1) *Pacific Rim Law & Policy Journal* 49.

[90] On the recent Australian plan to 'tow back boats to Indonesia, see M O'Sullivan, '"Push backs" of Boats to Indonesia', Castan Center for Human Rights Law, 18 July 2013, http://castancentre.com/2013/07/18/push-backs-of-boats-to-indonesia/. On extraterritorial controls in Australia, see, *inter alia*, AL Hirsch, 'The Borders Beyond the Border: Australia's Extraterritorial Migration Controls' (2017) 36(3) *Refugee Survey Quarterly* 48; NF Tan, 'State responsibility and migration control: Australia's international deterrence model' in T Gammeltoft-Hansen and J Vedsted-Hansen (eds), *Human rights and the dark side of globalisation: Transnational law enforcement and migration control* (Routledge, 2017); A Hirsch, 'The Extra-Territorialisation of Migration Control and the Right to Seek Asylum', *RightNow* (2018), http://rightnow.org.au/opinion-3/the-extra-territorialisation-of-migration-control-and-the-right-to-seek-asylum/.

[91] See B Doherty and H Davidson, 'Orange Lifeboats Used to Return Asylum Seekers to Be Replaced by "Fishing Boats"', *The Guardian* (4 March 2015), https://www.theguardian.com/australia-news/2015/mar/05/orange-lifeboats-used-to-return-asylum-seekers-to-be-replaced-by-fishing-boats.

Australia had interdicted and removed over 800 people as part of 'Operation Sovereign Borders'.[92]

In May 2011, a bilateral agreement was negotiated with Malaysia with the aim to deter asylum seekers from travelling by boat to Australia.[93] Under the terms of the arrangement, up to 800 asylum seekers, arriving in Australia by boat, would be removed to Malaysia where they would 'go to the back of the [asylum] queue.'[94] In return, Australia would commit to accepting the resettlement of 4000 UNHCR-recognised refugees from Malaysia over four years. Quite quickly however, the Australian High Court struck down the agreement on the ground that Malaysia did not provide sufficient safeguards regarding asylum seekers transferred from Australia.[95]

A. Introducing Frontex

The Lisbon Treaty regards the development of a 'common immigration policy' and the gradual introduction of an 'Integrated Border Management[96] as major political objectives.[97] According to the Council, Integrated Border Management encompasses, *inter alia*, border control, detection and investigation of cross-border crimes, migration control measures in third countries, cooperation with neighbouring countries, inter-agency cooperation for border management and coordination of the activities of Member States and the EU in the above-mentioned areas.[98]

Operational cooperation between the Member States, including cooperation under the aegis of Frontex is one of the main components of this strategy.[99]

[92] J Kelly and G Chambers, 'Operation Sovereign Borders block 33 boats', *The Australian* (24 October 2018), https://www.theaustralian.com.au/national-affairs/immigration/operation-sovereign-borders-block-33boats/news-story/71e6c8a3b7bf0e758da705c9e17df894.

[93] Arrangement between the Government of Australia and the Government of Malaysia on Transfer and Resettlement (25 July 2011) (Australia–Malaysia Arrangement).

[94] See Q&A, 'Gillard Reaches Asylum Agreement with Malaysia' (7 May 2011), http://www.abc.net.au/news/stories/2011/05/07/3210503.htm?site=qanda.

[95] *Plaintiff M70/2011 v Minister for Immigration and Citizenship and Another; Plaintiff M106 (by his litigation guardian, Plaintiff M70/2011) v Minister for Immigration and Citizenship and Another*, [2011] HCA 32, 31 August 2011. For an analysis of the case, J McAdam and T Wood, 'Australian Asylum Policy All at Sea: An Analysis of *Plaintiff M70/2011 v Minister for Immigration and Citizenship* and the Australia–Malaysia Arrangement' (2012) 61 *International and Comparative Law Quarterly* 274; S Lowes, 'The Legality of Extraterritorial Processing of Asylum Claims: The Judgment of the High Court of Australia in the "Malaysian Solution" Case' (2012) 12 *Human Rights Law Review* 168; M Foster, 'The Implications of the Failed "Malaysian Solution": The Australian High Court and Refugee Responsibility Sharing at International Law' (2012) 13 *Michigan Journal of International Law* 395.

[96] The Integrated Border Management concept was first established by the European Commission on the basis of the Laeken Conclusions of Dec 2001. See, 'Towards integrated management of the external borders of the EU member states', COM(2002) 233 final, 7 May 2002. See also Presidency Conclusions, Laeken 14–15 Dec 2001, Council Doc SN 300/1/01 REV 1, para 42.

[97] See Arts 77(1)(c) and 79(1) of the TFEU.

[98] EU Finnish Presidency, Council Conclusions of 4–5 December 2006, Press Release 15801/06, 27.

[99] Council Regulation (EC) No 2007/2004 of 26 October 2004 establishing the European Agency for the Management of Operational Cooperation at the External Borders of the Member States

As a response to the annulment by the ECJ of the 2010/252/EU Council Decision,[100] in April 2013, the European Commission presented a proposal for a Regulation establishing rules for the surveillance of the external sea borders in the context of operational cooperation coordinated by Frontex.[101] However, the Meijers Committee, in May 2013, issued a report pointing to the flaws of the new proposal,[102] and in May 2014 the Council eventually adopted Regulation (EU) No 656/2014.[103] This Regulation – which is based on the IMO Guidelines – replaces the 2010 Council Decision and aims to ensure the efficient monitoring of the crossing of external borders including through border surveillance, while contributing to ensuring the protection and saving of lives. According to the new Regulation, the responsible third-State Rescue Coordination Centre (RCC) can designate a place of safety. Moreover, Recital 1 of the Regulation states that:

> Border surveillance is not limited to the detection of attempts at unauthorised border crossings but equally extends to steps such as intercepting vessels suspected of trying to gain entry to the Union without submitting to border checks, as well as arrangements intended to address situations such as search and rescue that may arise during a border surveillance operation at sea and arrangements intended to bring such an operation to a successful conclusion.

of the European Union, [2004] OJ L349/1 (Frontex Regulation), as amended by Regulation (EU) no 1168/2011 of the European Parliament and of the Council of 25 October 2011. See also, Regulation (EC) No 863/2007 of the European Parliament and of the Council of 11 July 2007, establishing a mechanism for the creation of Rapid Border Intervention Teams and amending Council Regulation (EC) No 2007/2004 as regards that mechanism and regulating the tasks and powers of guest officers, [2007] OJ L199/30 (RABIT Regulation).

[100] See *Parliament v Council*, Case C-355/10, ECLI:EU:C:2012:516.

[101] Proposal for a Regulation of the European Parliament and of the Council 'establishing rules for the surveillance of the external sea borders in the context of operational cooperation coordinated by Frontex' (COM(2013) 197 final), 12 April 2013. This Section will not provide a detailed examination of Frontex as burgeoning literature has already been produced on this EU Agency. See, *inter alia*, E Papastavridis, '"Fortress Europe" and FRONTEX: Within or Without International Law?' (2010) 79(1) *Nordic Journal of International Law* 75 (Papastavridis 2010b); A Liguori and N Ricciutti, 'Frontex ed il rispetto dei diritti umani nelle operazioni congiunte alle frontiere esterne dell'Unione Europea' (2012) 6(3) *Diritti Umani e Diritto Internazionale* 539; J Rijpma, 'Hybrid Agencification in the Area of Freedom, Security and Justice and its Inherent Tensions: the Case of Frontex', in M Busuioc, M Groenleer and J Trondal (eds), *The Agency Phenomenon in the European Union: Emergence, Institutionalisation and Everyday Decision-making* (Manchester University Press, 2012); R Mungianu, *Frontex and Non-Refoulement: The International Responsibility of the EU* (CUP, 2016); V Moreno-Lax, *Accessing Asylum in Europe* (OUP, 2017); M Fink, *Frontex and Human Rights: Responsibility in 'Multi-Actor Situations' under the ECHR and EU Public Liability Law* (OUP, 2018).

[102] To read the Meijers Committee Note, refer to 'Note on the Proposal for a Regulation establishing rules for the surveillance of the external sea borders in the context of operational cooperation coordinated by Frontex (COM(2013) 197 final), 23 May 2013, http://www.statewatch.org/news/2013/may/meijers-committee-note-surveillance-external-sea-borders.pdf.

[103] Regulation (EU) No 656/2014 establishing rules for the surveillance of the external sea borders in the context of operational cooperation coordinated by the European Agency for the Management of Operational Cooperation at the External Borders of the member states of the EU (FRONTEX).

The Regulation – which, however, only applies in the context of Frontex operations – provides that States shall comply with the principle of *non-refoulement* and shall observe their obligation to render assistance to any vessel or person in distress at sea.[104] More specifically, Article 10 requires that a person intercepted or rescued in the territorial sea or the contiguous zone shall be disembarked in the coastal Member State.[105] If, instead, interception occurs on the high seas, disembarkation may take place in the third country from which the vessel is assumed to have departed, or, if that is not possible, in the host Member State.[106]

Regulation 656/2014 is complemented by Regulation 2016/1624 as part of the integrated border management system.[107] Building on the foundations of Frontex, on 6 October 2016, the EU officially launched the European Border and Coast Guard Agency (EBCG) designed to monitor the EU's external borders and work together with Member States to quickly identify and address any potential security threats to the EU's external borders.[108] The EBCG Agency, elaborated in Regulation 2016/1624, will continue to be referred to as Frontex. It has 'shared responsibility' with EU Member States in the implementation of European integrated border management.[109] In case of lack of compliance and if urgent action is needed, the Agency has a right to intervene (ie, send EBCG teams) to address 'migration pressures'.

The Regulation also provides the new Frontex with competence over search and rescue of persons in distress at sea,[110] and encompasses SAR operations 'in situations which may arise during border surveillance operations at sea' within the concept of European integrated border management.[111] As a last note, joint border operations always require the decision of the Member State in question to request assistance by the new Frontex. The Regulation envisages a new complaint mechanism in cases of alleged rights violations, and confers on the EBCG the power to conduct joint removal missions and to be involved in national removal operations, also in cooperation with third countries.[112]

[104] Art 9 para 1 Frontex Reg.

[105] Art 10(a).

[106] Art 10(b).

[107] Regulation (EU) No 2016/1624 on the European Border and Coast Guard of 16 September 2016, [2016] OJ L 251/1, 16.9.2016 (EBCG Reg).

[108] European Commission, 'Securing Europe's external borders: Launch of the European Border and Coast Guard Agency', http://europa.eu/rapid/press-release_IP-16-3281_en.htm.

[109] See Arts 4 and 5 of the EBCG Reg.

[110] Art 14(3) of the EBCG Reg. See D Ghezelbash, V Moreno-Lax, N Klein, B Opeskin, 'Securitization of search and rescue at sea: the response to boat migration in the Mediterranean and offshore Australia' (2018) 67(2) *ICLQ* 315, 323–27.

[111] Art 4 of the EBCG Regulation.

[112] For an in-depth analysis of the new EBCG Agency, see S Carrera, S Blockmans, JP Cassarino, D Gros and E Guild, 'The European Border and Coast Guard: Addressing Migration and Asylum Challenges in the Mediterranean?' (CEPS Task Force Report) 30 July 2017.

The various *Hera* and *Nautilus* maritime operations constitute some of the joint missions that have been performed at the external borders of the EU Member States. Without going into the details of these missions, it is worth observing that *Hera* was first launched, on 17 July 2006, at the request of Spain engaged with the management of irregular migrant flows to the Canary Islands. Additionally, Frontex authorities attempted to prevent the departure of boats loaded with migrants heading to Europe by intercepting them directly in the territorial waters of the countries of embarkation and carrying them back to ports of departure – namely Senegal, Mauritania, and Cape Verde – with no screening of their protection claims.[113] With regard to the *Nautilus* operation, its main goal was 'to strengthen the control of the Central Mediterranean maritime border … and also to support Maltese authorities in interviews with the immigrants' who mostly came from Eritrea, Somalia, Ethiopia, and Nigeria.[114] First established in June 2007,[115] Nautilus 2008 followed the reach of an agreement between participating Member States whereby migrants rescued in the Libyan SAR Area would be removed to Libya, or to the closest safe port if readmission to Libya was not possible.[116] Lacking Libya's consent, intercepted migrants were all disembarked on Italian and Maltese soil.[117]

In the aftermath of the Arab Spring, the EU started both to earmark considerable sums of humanitarian aid for North African countries and to support the transfer of foreign nationals from Libya to their countries of origin.[118] Border control and surveillance policies were also reinforced through the mobilisation of Frontex. For example, on 20 February 2011, after a request from Italy, the EU Agency deployed the Joint Operation EPN *Hermes* aimed at 'assisting Italy in controlling vessels carrying immigrants and refugees'[119] and at 'detecting and preventing illegitimate border crossings to the Pelagic Islands, Sicily, and the Italian mainland.'[120] Frontex officials also carried out the pre-screening of intercepted migrants, interviewed migrants on travel routes, and gathered information on arrival numbers for the purpose of developing risk analyses.

[113] *BBC News*, 'Stemming the immigration wave', 10 September 2006, http://news.bbc.co.uk/2/hi/europe/5331896.stm.

[114] Frontex Press Release, 'Joint Operation Nautilus 2007 – the end of the first phase', 6 August 2007.

[115] To read more on Nautilus 2006 and Nautilus 2007, refer to the European Commission, SEC (2008) 150 final; for Nautilus 2008 and Nautilus 2009, see Frontex General Report 2008 and Frontex General Report 2009.

[116] Frontex Press Release, 'Go ahead for Nautilus 2008', 7 May 2008.

[117] Frontex Press Release, 'HERA 2008 and Nautilus 2008 Statistics', 17 February 2009.

[118] See Commission Press Release, 'The European Commission's humanitarian response to the crisis in Libya' MEMO/11/143, Brussels, 4 March 2011; Commission factsheet, 'Humanitarian aid and civil protection: Libya crisis', 25 October 2011, http://ec.europa.eu/echo/news/2011/20110823_02_en.htm.

[119] EU Commissioner Malmström, Statement announcing the launch of the Frontex operation 'HERMES' in Italy as of 20 February 2011, MEMO/11/98, Brussels, 20 February 2011.

[120] Frontex Press Release, 'HERMES 2011 running', 21 February 2011, 2.

Started in February 2011, the *Hermes* mission was then extended on several occasions,[121] and ran until the end of August 2012.[122] In the effort primarily to thwart unauthorised entries by strengthening Europe's border control response capability in the Central Mediterranean, Frontex, and the EU more broadly, have been criticised for not doing enough to prevent deaths at sea.[123] Although Regulation 2016/1624 reinforces Frontex and expands its level of autonomy, the main function of search, rescue and disembarkation remains in the hands of the Member States, and it does not have a more proactive role in protecting rights.[124]

B. The 'Humanitarian Refugee Crisis' and EU Response to Migration by Sea

Operation *Mare Nostrum* – an Italian military and humanitarian mission whose aim was to control migration flows by strengthening surveillance and SAR activities – was replaced, in November 2014, by Frontex Operation *Triton.*[125] While *Mare Nostrum* rescued thousands of lives in international waters, *Triton* – whose primary focus was border management – only operated within 30 miles off the Italian coast, with the risk that an increasing number of migrants and refugees could die during their passage to Europe.[126] As long anticipated, the number of victims in the Mediterranean has been rising dramatically following the end of the operation *Mare Nostrum.* In the first two months of 2015, the number of people arriving by sea was almost twice that in the same period of the previous year. Against this critical backdrop, the Italian government decided to informally propose to the EU new strategies to cope with such a huge humanitarian crisis.

[121] Frontex, 'Hermes Operation Extended', http://www.frontex.europa.eu/news/hermes-operation-extended-OWmwti.

[122] For an analysis of the Hermes operation, see S Carrera, L den Hertog and J Parkin, 'EU Migration Policy in the wake of the Arab Spring. What prospects for EU-Southern Mediterranean Relations?' *MEDPRO Technical Report no 15*, August 2012, pp 4–5.

[123] *Human Rights Watch*, 'EU: Put Rights at Heart of Migration Policy', 20 June 2011 http://www.hrw.org/news/2011/06/20/eu-put-rights-heart-migration-policy. See also, Parliamentary Assembly of the Council of Europe Report 'Lives lost in the Mediterranean Sea: Who is responsible?', Committee on Migration, Refugees and Displaced Persons, Rapporteur T Strik. See also J Shenker, 'Aircraft carrier left us to die, say migrants', *The Guardian*, 8 May 2011, http://www.guardian.co.uk/world/2011/may/08/nato-ship-libyan-migrants.

[124] For an analysis of Regulation (EU) No 2016/1624, see F Esteve i García, 'The Search and Rescue Tasks Coordinated by the European Border and Coast Guard Agency (Frontex) Regarding the Surveillance of External Maritime Borders', in (2017) 5 *Paix et sécurité internationales: revue maroco-espagnole de droit international et relations internationales* 93–116. For an exhaustive examination of Frontex responsibility and human rights, see Fink 2018, n 101 above.

[125] See Council Conclusions on 'Taking action to better manage migratory flows', Justice and Home Affairs Council meeting Luxembourg (10 October 2014), http://www.consilium.europa.eu/uedocs/cms_data/docs/pressdata/en/jha/145053.pdf.

[126] See Frontex, 'Frontex launches call for participation of the EU Member States in Joint Operation Triton', http://frontex.europa.eu/news/frontex-launches-call-for-participation-of-the-eu-member-states-in-joint-operation-triton-b9nupQ.

The underlying idea was 'to make all possible efforts to *prevent the departure of migrants* from the southern shores of the Mediterranean' (emphasis added)[127] through the 'direct involvement of reliable third countries in the maritime surveillance and rescue and search activity.'[128]

Whereas the only way to truly save migrants' lives is to address the situation at its roots and find durable solutions which eradicate poverty and conflicts in migrants' countries of origin, it is certain that people will continue to put their lives at risk as long as there is war and hardship in our neighbourhood near and far.[129] Nevertheless, following the Council conclusions of June 2018, the Commission has been exploring the possibility of 'Regional Disembarkation Platforms' (RDPs) in third countries. These externalised platforms would serve the purpose of outsourcing SAR services and shifting border management operations in the Mediterranean to third countries outside Europe.[130] It is here crucial to pinpoint the dangerousness of policies aiming to hold people back within territories where their life and liberty can be put at risk, either at the hands of human traffickers and government authorities in States of transit or at the hands of their original persecutors upon removal to their home countries.

Therefore, in line with their international human rights obligations, European States should refrain from the temptation to curtail migration flows by preventing refugees' passage through bilateral and multilateral cooperation instruments aimed at intercepting migrants before they are able to leave their countries of origin or transit. Such a practice would indeed *prima facie* frustrate Article 13(2) of the UDHR, Article 12(1) of the ICCPR, Article 5(d)(ii) of the ICERD,[131] and Article 2(2) of Protocol No 4 of the ECHR, which provide for the right to leave any country. The possibility of creating humanitarian channels and visa for refugees escaping international and internal armed conflicts, thus *a priori* avoiding dangerous journeys by sea, continues to be neglected by European Ministers as a concrete and safe solution to the 'crisis'.

From January 2014 to 20 May 2018, 15,438 people are reported to have lost their lives in the Mediterranean. At the informal Summit held at La Valletta

[127] See Statewatch, 'Italy's Non-Paper on Possible Involvement of Third Countries in Maritime Surveillance and Search and Rescue' (13 March 2015) para 6, http://www.statewatch.org/news/2015/mar/italian%20med.pdf.

[128] ibid.

[129] European Commission Statement, 19 April 2015, https://europa.eu/rapid/press-release_STATEMENT-15-4800_en.htm.

[130] F Maiani, '"Regional Disembarkation Platforms" and "Controlled Centres": Lifting the Drawbridge, Reaching Out Across the Mediterranean, or Going Nowhere?' (2018), http://eumigrationlawblog.eu/regional-disembarkation-platforms-and-controlled-centres-lifting-the-drawbridge-reaching-out-across-the-mediterranean-or-going-nowhere/; S Carrera and K Lannoo, 'We're in this boat together: Time for a Migration Union', CEPS Policy Insights No 2018/09, June 2018.

[131] While the right to life is not broadly analysed in this work, it is nonetheless important to stress the human rights implications of policies aimed at preventing departure and thus stemming migratory flows to Europe.

on 3 February 2017, the European Council agreed a Declaration (the Malta Declaration) concerning the external aspects of migration and the Central-Mediterranean route. It states that the EU primary goal is to train and equip the Libyan coastguard in order to bolster its capacity to stop people smugglers, increase search and rescue operations, and prevent departure of unseaworthy boats headed toward Europe.

To address the 'humanitarian refugee crisis', the EU has thus opted for an emerging strategy based on further externalisation of migration controls.[132] Quite questionably, the EU and Member States have made financial and political support, as well as cooperation on development, conditional on third countries' effective implementation of exit controls. As held by the European Council, the new EU Migration Partnership Framework (MPF) is based on 'effective incentives and adequate conditionality' [but] 'cooperation on readmission and return will be a key test of the partnership between the EU and [its] partners'.[133]

Beyond the EU–Turkey readmission programme,[134] questionable readmission agreements and enhanced cooperation on removals have also been proposed with refugee-producing countries, such as Mali, Afghanistan, Nigeria, Senegal, and Ethiopia with the objective of offering financial support in exchange for accepting readmissions from Europe. The EU and Member States also plan to expand their schemes of cooperation on management of migration to other countries, such as Egypt, Tunisia, and Sudan. The EU MPF also sets out the goals to both step up the training programme of the Libyan coastguard to autonomously conduct search and rescue (including disembarkation) and strengthen Libya's southern border to hinder migratory flows to Libya and from there into Europe.

The EU's direct involvement in these initiatives is also facilitated by the EU Border Assistance Mission to Libya (EUBAM),[135] which furnishes assistance related to 'border management' as well as targeted 'advice and capacity-building in the area of … migration [and] border security'.[136] The Common Security and Defence Policy EUNAVFOR MED *Sophia* mission has directly delivered training to the Libyan Coastguard since October 2016.[137] On 27 March 2019, the EU

[132] See, eg, the establishment of the EU Migration Partnership Framework (MPF), discussed in Chapter 3 of this book. To read more on this issue, see Giuffré 2017, n 8 above. See also, C Bauloz, 'The EU Migration Partnership Framework: An External Solution to the Crisis?' *EUmigration lawblog.eu*, 31 January 2017, http://eumigrationlawblog.eu/the-eu-migration-partnership-framework-an-external-solution-to-the-crisis/.

[133] Council of the EU, 'External aspects of migration – Monitoring results, 10822/16, 4 July 2016, http://data.consilium.europa.eu/doc/document/ST-10822-2016-INIT/en/pdf.

[134] See Chapter 3 of this book for an analysis of the 2016 EU–Turkey Statement.

[135] EU Border Assistance Mission in Libya (EUBAM), https://eeas.europa.eu/csdp-missions-operations/eubam-libya_en.

[136] 'EUBAM Libya: mission extended, budget approved', EC Press Release, 4 August 2016, http://www.consilium.europa.eu/en/press/press-releases/2016/08/04-eubam-libya-mission-extended/.

[137] 'Operation SOPHIA: package 2 of the Libyan Navy Coast Guard and Libyan Navy training launched today', EEAS Press Release, 30 January 2017, https://eeas.europa.eu/headquarters/head

Political and Security Committee approved its extension for six months with a temporary suspension of the use of naval units as Member States were not able to reach an agreement on disembarking rescued people at ports other than Italian ones.[138] So, the Italian–Libyan cooperation should be inscribed within this wider, EU-backed framework, ultimately underpinned by the EU MPF and the Global Approach to Migration.[139]

This Section was instrumental to a broader understanding of the EU response to unauthorised arrivals by sea, land, and air, beyond the specificity of the Italian context. To conclude this first Part of the chapter – which rests on, as far as possible, precise illustration of facts and empirical material – the next Sections will critically assess Italy's cooperation on migration management with African countries (from push-backs to push-backs by proxy) against the backdrop of refugee rights analysed in Chapter two. State duties at sea under human rights law and law of the sea will also be expounded. This is to show the continued relevance of the legal analysis carried out throughout this chapter with regard to the role of bilateral agreements for technical and police cooperation in hampering refugees' access to protection, and the potential international responsibility of States engaged in extraterritorial migration controls.

VI. STATE DUTIES AT SEA

Section IV presented the whole spectrum of bilateral agreements for technical and police cooperation used by Libya to perform interception and readmission activities, regardless of Italian officials' presence on-board the interdicting crafts placed under Libyan command. Moreover, it showed how these bilateral accords, implemented beyond territorial frontiers, represent a key component of the legal and political framework within which the removal of refugees to the country of embarkation is made possible after interception either by European States or their proxies.

International responsibility for human rights violations may arise every time States exercise jurisdiction.[140] Such responsibility is closely related to the existence of a State's obligation, and is intended to verify whether a certain State is liable for the violation of the obligation in point. Mindful of the vastness of obligations incumbent upon States under both the law of the sea and international human rights law, focus is placed here on responsibility triggered by violations of the fundamental principle of *non-refoulement*, which is closely correlated to

quarters-homepage/19518/operation-sophia-package-2-libyan-navy-coast-guard-and-libyan-navy-training-launched-today_en. See also UNSC Res 2312 (2016), extending UNSC Res 2240 (2015).

[138] ANSA, 'Operation Sophia extended, but without naval support' (27 March 2019).

[139] Global Approach to Migration and Mobility, COM(2011) 743 final, 18 November 2011.

[140] M Milanovic, 'From Compromise to Principle: Clarifying the Concept of State Jurisdiction in Human Rights Treaties' (2008) 8 *Human Rights Law Review* 411, 417.

the lack of access to asylum procedures and effective remedies for individuals intercepted at sea. Before delving into human rights obligations in a maritime context, the next Sub-section will offer an overview of search and rescue obligations which apply to anyone (not only migrants and refugees) found in distress at sea.

A. Search and Rescue

'Search and rescue' obligations require States to disembark rescued people to a 'place of safety', broadly defined as 'a place where the rescue operations are considered to have been completed.'[141] A 'place of safety', however, 'is not necessarily the closest one to the place where people were rescued.'[142] Pursuant to Article 98(1) of the UNCLOS,

> every State shall require the master of a ship flying its flag, in so far as he can do so without serious danger to the ship, the crew, or the passengers ... to render assistance to any person found at sea in danger of being lost [and] to proceed with all possible speed to the rescue of persons in distress, if informed of their need of assistance.

Similarly, the SOLAS Convention provides that

> [t]he master of a ship at sea which is in a position to be able to provide assistance, on receiving a signal from any source that persons are in distress at sea, is bound to proceed with all speed to their assistance ....[143]

No delimitation *ratione personae* is made, and 'any person' in distress at sea can benefit from the SAR duties falling upon States.[144] As Article 98(1) of the UNCLOS requires implementing legislation to acquire the force of law,[145] the obligation of the flag State is predominantly an obligation of conduct, and not an obligation of result (ie, not an obligation to ensure that all people in distress will be saved).[146] Additionally, the flag State has a due diligence duty to monitor whether the master of a vessel flying its flag properly discharges its duties under the UNCLOS and SOLAS Conventions.[147]

[141] The SAR Convention sets the duty to disembark the shipwrecked in a 'safe place.' See also, the IMO Resolution MCS 167/78 of 20 May 2004 and the amendments to the SAR and SOLAS Conventions.

[142] See Response Italian Government, para c.

[143] SOLAS, chapter V, reg 33(1).

[144] SAR Annex, chapters 2 and 3, para 2.1.10.

[145] See Papastavridis, 'Rescuing "Boat People" in the Mediterranean Sea: The Responsibility of States under the Law of the Sea', *EJIL Talk*, 31 May 2011, https://www.ejiltalk.org/rescuing-boat-people-in-the-mediterranean-sea-the-responsibility-of-states-under-the-law-of-the-sea/.

[146] On the distinction between obligations of conduct and obligations of result, see, R Ago, Special Rapporteur (1967) II-1 *Yearbook of the International Law Commission* 4, 20.

[147] Arts 98(1), UNCLOS and SOLAS, Chapter V, Regulation 33. While the flag State would be directly responsible for any omission of public vessels to discharge this duty of rescue, it would not be directly responsible for the actions of a master of a private vessel who does not comply with this

While the coastal State exercises full sovereign authority over territorial seas (up to 12 nautical miles from the baseline), an exception is provided in the right of innocent passage (continuous and expeditious) of surface vessels (Article 17 UNCLOS) and the right of safe haven/safe harbour for vessels/aircrafts in distress. Innocent 'passage includes stopping and anchoring, but only in so far as the same are incidental to ordinary navigation or are rendered necessary by *force majeure* or distress or for the purpose of rendering assistance to persons, ships or aircraft in danger or distress' (Article 18). Therefore, vessels flying the flag of a State other than the coastal State can enter the territorial waters or the SAR zone of the coastal State to offer humanitarian rescue and contribute to disembark people in a place of safety.[148] Nevertheless, in breach of international law, NGOs (and occasionally also the Italian Coastguard) operating at sea to save lives have been unlawfully attacked by Libyan authorities both in their territorial waters and on the high seas.[149] Moreover, vessels transporting hundreds of traumatised migrants rescued at sea have been denied access to ports for several days, despite the fact they were in a situation of distress.

The State holding primary responsibility for the delivery of the intercepted migrants to a 'place of safety' is the State responsible for the SAR region where assistance is rendered.[150] It should ensure coordination and cooperation among parties to the SAR and SOLAS Conventions so as to alleviate the burden imposed on ship-masters. This is a due diligence obligation to guarantee disembarkation in a place of safety and not an absolute duty (ie, an obligation of result) for the SAR responsible State to ensure disembarkation in its ports. However, the above-mentioned treaties do not require a State to accept rescued persons. A non-legally binding instrument such as the 2009 Circular adopted by the IMO's Facilitation Committee has indicated that the State responsible for the SAR region is the most likely location for accepting rescued migrants and refugees.[151] While a clear default obligation of disembarkation in the SAR

obligation. Nevertheless, the flag State may incur international responsibility for not acting with due diligence. For a discussion on due diligence, as well as obligations of conduct and obligations of result, see *Request for an Advisory Opinion Submitted by the Sub-Regional Fisheries Commission (SRFC) (Request for Advisory Opinion Submitted to the Tribunal)*, Advisory Opinion of 2 April 2015, ITLOS Rep 2015, 4. See also, D Guilfoyle and E Papastavridis, 'Mapping Disembarkation Options: Towards Strengthening Cooperation in Managing Irregular Movements by Sea', UNHCR *Background Paper* (2014), 12, https://www.refworld.org/pdfid/5346438f4.pdf.

[148] Under Regulation 33, Annex, SOLAS, 'The Government responsible for search and rescue region in which assistance is rendered shall ensure that survivors are disembarked and delivered to a place of safety as soon as reasonably practicable.'

[149] For an analysis of NGOs rescue activity at sea, see E Papastavridis, 'Recent *Non-Entrée* Policies in the Central Mediterranean and their Legality: A New Form of *Refoulement*?' (2018) 12(3) *Diritti Umani e Diritto Internazionale* 493–510.

[150] SAR Annex, para 3.1.9 and SOLAS, chapter V, reg 33 (1-1). On the latest amendments to the SAR Convention and its application in the Mediterranean, see S Trevisanut, 'Search and Rescue Operations in the Mediterranean: Factor of Cooperation or Conflict?' (2010) 25 *International Journal of Maritime & Coastal Law* 526–35.

[151] IMO, 'Principles relating to Administrative Procedures for Disembarking Persons Rescued at Sea', IMO Doc FAL.3/Circ.194 (22 January 2009) para 2.3 ('IMO Principles').

responsible State is lacking under the SAR and SOLAS Conventions, it could be argued that such default rule of disembarkation does exist for Italy with regard to the European Border and Coast Guard Agency (Frontex) coordinated maritime operations[152] for which Italy is the host Member State. Therefore, Italy must ultimately accept disembarkation in its territory as the host Member State in the context of *Joint Operation Themis* (operational since 1 February 2018).[153] Additionally, Italy is designated as the State of disembarkation in all interdiction and SAR activities conducted in the context of EUNAVFOR MED Operation Sophia, off the coast of Libya.[154]

Broadly speaking, under maritime law, only the flag State has jurisdiction over a vessel on the high seas but in the case of boat refugees, the flag State could be the very State from which they are fleeing. Although disembarkation in the next port of call is not a rule of customary law,[155] some scholars, and the UNHCR, maintain that the obligation on the coastal State to accept disembarkation may implicitly be inferred from the maritime conventions.[156]

The absence of a clear-cut definition of a 'place of safety' might not *per se* be damaging, since it would allow for a case-by-case approach which takes into account the particular circumstances of each rescue situation and the different categories of stowaways.[157] In this regard, the 'Guidelines on the treatment of persons rescued at sea', from the Maritime Safety Committee of the IMO, emphasise how 'the need to avoid disembarkation in territories where the lives and freedoms of those alleging a well-founded fear of persecution would be threatened is a consideration in the case of asylum-seekers and refugees recovered at sea.'[158] However, these Guidelines still fall short of a duty of disembarkation in any particular place, and a number of examples show how coastal States keep on bouncing responsibilities for disembarkation. In some circumstances, such uncertainty has led to episodes of non-rescue, delays, or the sinking of overloaded boats with the consequent death of the passengers on board.[159]

[152] See Papastavridis 2018, n 149 above.

[153] See Art 10(1) of Regulation (EU) No 656/2014.

[154] See E Papastavridis, 'EUNAVFOR Operation Sophia and the International Law of the Sea' (2016) 2 *Maritime Safety and Security Law Journal* 57 ff.

[155] RA Barnes, 'Refugee Law at Sea' (2004) 53 *ICLQ* 47, 63.

[156] UNHCR, *Problems Related to the Rescue of Asylum Seekers in Distress at Sea*, UN doc EC/SCP/18, 26 August 1981, paras 19–21. Similarly, a circular of the IMO Facilitation Committee recommends that '[i]f disembarkation from the rescuing ship cannot be arranged swiftly elsewhere, the Government responsible for the SAR area should accept the disembarkation of the persons rescued … into a place of safety under its control …' See Circular FAL.35/Circ.194, 'Principles relating to administrative procedures for disembarking persons rescued at sea' (14 January 2009).

[157] V Moreno-Lax 2011a, n 63 above, 198.

[158] IMO, *Guidelines on the treatment of persons rescued at sea*, Resolution MSC 167(78), 20 May 2004, para 6.17, subsequently endorsed by the UN General Assembly in UN doc A/RES/61/222, 16 March 2007.

[159] On 3 October 2013, a boat carrying migrants and refugees to Italy sank off the Italian island of Lampedusa. While 155 people were rescued, the death toll reached 339. See also the *MV Salamis* incident on 4 August 2013. Further information can be retrieved in: JP Gauci and P Mallia, 'Access to Protection: A Human Right' (National Report – Malta, December 2013) 36.

While some authors suggest that the State coordinating the search and rescue has a residual obligation to allow disembarkation if no other place is found, the issue remains contentious.[160]

It is undeniable that the different bodies of law suggest contrasting ways to deal with the problem of irregular migration at sea. However, despite these ambiguities in the existing law, the humanitarian needs of migrants and refugees at sea should stimulate prompt practical responses.[161] For example, if rescue units or other suitable ships can temporarily be used to discharge initial succours in cases of distress, survivors must in the end be disembarked in a 'place of safety', which may only be on dry land.[162] As stated by the ECtHR – which broadly relied on reports of international human rights organisations – Libya could not be considered a 'place of safety' because of the well-documented inadequacy of its response to flows of migrants and asylum seekers.[163] Moreover, as provided by the IMO Guidelines, a vessel cannot be conceived of as a final 'place of safety.' The fact that a State is legally bound to disembark a person rescued at sea in a safe haven implicates the duty to collect thorough information on the conditions of reception and treatment of rescued migrants and refugees in the receiving country.

In accordance with the UNHCR's proposed definition, 'interception' embraces all those extraterritorial activities carried out by a State to keep undocumented migrants, including refugees, away from its territory, thus preventing entry by land, sea, or air.[164] At face value, 'rescue' and 'interception'

[160] S Trevisanut, 'Is There a Right to be Rescued at Sea? A Constructive View' (June 2014) *Questions of International Law* 1, 7 (Trevisanut 2014b).

[161] N Klein, 'A Case for Harmonizing Laws on Maritime Interceptions of Irregular Migrants' (2014) 63 *International and Comparative Law Quarterly* 787, 804. See also M Di Filippo, 'Irregular Migration and Safeguard of Life at Sea: International Rules and Recent Developments in The Mediterranean Sea' in A del Vecchio (ed), *International Law of the Sea: Current Trends and Controversial Issues* (Eleven International Publishing, 2014) 9–20.

[162] Resolution MSC.167(78), 20 May 2004, n 158 above, paras 6.13–6.14. Indeed, 'an assisting ship should not be considered a place of safety based solely on the fact that the survivors are no longer in immediate danger once aboard the ship. An assisting ship may not have appropriate facilities and equipment to sustain additional persons on board without endangering its own safety or to properly care for the survivors. Even if the ship is capable of safely accommodating the survivors and may serve as a temporary place of safety, it should be relieved of this responsibility as soon as alternative arrangements can be made' (para 6.13). Moreover, 'A place of safety may be on land, or it may be aboard a rescue unit or other suitable vessel or facility at sea that can serve as a place of safety until the survivors are disembarked to their next destination' (para 6.14).

[163] *Hirsi v Italy*, above n 5, paras 123–126.

[164] UNHCR Executive Committee, *Interception of Asylum Seekers and Refugees: The International Framework and Recommendations for a Comprehensive Approach*, UN Doc EC/50/SC/CPR.17, 9 June 2000. Interception may encompass interdiction of boats ('active' or 'physical' interception) as well as 'passive' measures, such as implementation of restrictive visa requirements, carrier sanctions, and the establishment of airlines liaison officers in countries of origin or transit of immigrants to identify those possessing false or inadequate documentation and to prevent their departure to the destination country. On practices deterring asylum seekers, see B Gorlick, 'Refugee Protection in Troubled Times: Reflections on Institutional and Legal Developments at the

appear to be profoundly different, but examination indicates both their similarities and ambiguities in practice. As a general rule, when vessels respond to persons in distress at sea, they are not necessarily engaged in interception. 'Rescue' can, indeed, be described as 'an operation to retrieve persons in distress, provide for their initial medical or other immediate needs, and deliver them to a place of safety.'[165] However, problems arise when, for example, a State coastguard encounters an unseaworthy boat allegedly transporting undocumented migrants.[166] Pull-backs carried out by Libyan authorities in 2017–18 have also been justified as search and rescue activities resulting in disembarkation in the coastal State.

It is important to note that the classification of push-backs and push-backs by proxy as either rescue measures or external maritime border control operations is immaterial for the purpose of establishing State responsibility under general international law and human rights law; in both cases what counts is whether human rights obligations have been violated as a consequence of the above-mentioned practices.[167] Nevertheless, this categorisation matters for the purpose of EU law. Indeed, assuming that 'search and rescue' missions do not fall under the Schengen Border Code (SBC), States generally prefer to deem their activities on the high seas to be 'rescue' missions rather than 'interceptions'.[168]

That said, Article 3(b) of the SBC sets forth that it is to be applied without prejudice to 'the rights of refugees and persons requesting international protection to EU Member State authorities, in particular as regards *non-refoulement*', while Article 5(4)(c) allows for derogation from normal entry criteria on account of humanitarian grounds or because of international obligations. Since the *ratione loci* of the Code exceeds the perimeter of EU Member States,[169]

Crossroads', in N Steiner, M Gibney, and G Loescher (eds), *Problems of Protection: the UNHCR, Refugees, and Human Rights* (Routledge, 2003) 86.

[165] SAR Annex, para 3.1.9; and SOLAS, chapter V, reg 33 (1-1).

[166] Miltner 2010, n 4 above, 220.

[167] See, eg, *Hirsi v Italy*, above n 5, para 81.

[168] Pursuant to Art 1, the SBC aims to establish rules governing the border control of persons crossing the external borders of the Member States of the European Union. As stated in recital 6 of the Code, border control is intended to 'help to combat illegal immigration and trafficking in human beings and to prevent any threat to the Member States' internal security, public policy, public health and international relations.'

[169] Schengen Border Code, paras 2.1.3 and 2.2.1, Annex VI. While at sea, controls can be performed 'in the territory of a third country' (SBC, para 3.1.1, Annex VI), checks can be carried out also 'in [railway] stations in a third country where persons board the train' (SBC, para 1.2.2, Annex VI). For an analysis of the extraterritorial scope of the SBC, refer to Chapter 2 of this book. See also M den Heijer, 'Europe beyond its Borders: Refugee and Human Rights Protection in Extraterritorial Immigration Control' in Ryan and Mitsilegas 2010, n 77 above, 176–80 (den Heijer 2010a); V Moreno-Lax, '(Extraterritorial) Entry Controls and (Extraterritorial) Non-refoulement' in P De Bruycker, D Vanheule, MC Foblets, J Wouters and M Maes (eds), *The External Dimension(s) of EU Asylum and Immigration Policy* (Bruylant, 2011) 444–47.

> both interdiction and search and rescue measures undertaken by EU Member States anywhere at sea with the purpose of border control, or in the course of a maritime surveillance operation, shall be considered as coming within the remit of the Schengen Border Code and subject to its provision on *non-refoulement*.[170]

According to the EU Commission tasked to elaborate on the material scope of application of the SBC, 2009 push-backs to Libya amounted to border surveillance operations falling within the purview of the SBC by virtue of Article 12, whereby border surveillance measures are aimed to prevent unauthorised border crossings.[171]

Therefore, by rejecting a fragmentary approach to maritime obligations, States should prioritise a systemic interpretation of their duties at sea, thus making their border control measures consistent with international human rights and refugee standards.[172] This means that the different bodies of law operating at sea (human rights law, refugee law, law of the sea, and search and rescue) should be harmonised taking into account the diverging policy interests that are at stake.[173] Indeed, as some argue,

> [States] cannot circumvent refugee law and human rights requirements by declaring border control measures – that is, the interception, turning back, redirecting, etc. of refugee boats – to be rescue measures. In the case of both rescue at sea and border control measures *vis à vis* migrants who are not in distress at sea, the following procedures are required: transfer of the protection seekers and migrants to a safe place on EU territory; conduct of proceedings in order to examine the asylum application; legal review of the decision.[174]

'Search and rescue' has often been adduced as the legal basis for both interception of shipwrecked flagless boats and the deflection of interdicted people to ports of embarkation.[175] Nevertheless, even portraying the 2009 Italy–Libya push-backs as 'rescue activities' only, it cannot be denied that – as a State party to the SAR and SOLAS Conventions – Italy failed to comply with its obligation to cooperate to assist ship masters in delivering persons rescued at sea to a 'place of safety.' A rescue operation can only be considered to be fully accomplished when survivors finally disembark on safe, dry land, and not when they are initially rescued. The same considerations also apply in those cases in which Italy cooperates with Libya in the location of migrants' boats, or is engaged in

[170] V Moreno-Lax 2011a, n 63 above, 211.

[171] Letter from ex-Commissioner Barrot to the President of the LIBE Committee of 15 July 2009. See *Hirsi v Italy*, above n 5, para 34. See also B Nascimbene, 'Il Respingimento degli Immigrati e i Rapporti tra l'Italia e l'Unione Europea' (Istituto Affari Internazionali, 2009) 1, 4.

[172] Moreno-Lax 2011a, n 63 above, 220.

[173] Klein 2014, n 161 above, 789.

[174] A Fischer-Lescano, T Lohr and T Tohidipur, 'Border Controls at Sea: Requirements under International Human Rights and Refugee Law' (2009) 21 *IJRL* 256, 291.

[175] See, eg, the analysis conducted by M Tondini, 'Fishers of Men? The Interception of Migrants in the Mediterranean Sea and their Forced Return to Libya' (Inex Paper, 2010).

long-distance support of Libyan pull-backs by means of technical, economic, and logistical assistance, or even coordination of rescue operations.

Under Article 98 of the UNCLOS,

> every State shall … promote the establishment, operation and maintenance of an adequate and effective search and rescue service regarding safety … and, where circumstances so require, by way of *mutual regional arrangements co-operate with neighbouring States* for this purpose.

Therefore, while cooperation on search and rescue with third countries would in principle be possible, the delegating State (*in casu* Italy) should ensure that human rights of migrants and refugees are respected in the country of disembarkation in order to avoid incurring responsibility for violations of the duty to *non-refoulement* and breaches of their law of the sea obligations.

(i) Duty to Rescue and Right to be Rescued?

The duty to protect (for example, the duty to rescue those in distress on the high seas) might be considered to derive from the principle of 'effectiveness'.[176] The concept of due diligence – from which the positive effect of human rights is inferred[177] – requires thus States to be proactive for preventive and protective purposes.[178]

No consensus exists in scholarship on the existence of a right to be rescued under the law of the sea.[179] The main objective of the law of the sea and search and rescue rules under the UNCLOS and the relevant IMO instruments (SOLAS and SAR Conventions) is indeed the allocation of competences, and not the protection of human rights of individuals. Therefore, the duty to render assistance can be considered, as some argue, the operational obligation stemming from the application of the human right to life at sea.[180] While the existence of such an individual right under the law of the sea and other maritime conventions can be easily dismissed, it could instead be argued that the right to be rescued is part of the normative contours of the right to life under specific circumstances.[181]

[176] VP Tzevelekos and EK Proukaki, 'Migrants at Sea: A Duty of Plural States to Protect (Extraterritorially)?' (2017) 86(4) *Nordic Journal of International Law* 427.

[177] D Shelton, 'Positive and Negative Obligations' in D Shelton, A Goult (eds), *The Oxford Handbook of International Human Rights Law* (OUP, 2013) 562–83.

[178] See, eg, *Osman v UK*, App no 23452/94 (28 October 1998) before the ECtHR; and *Velásquez-Rodriguez v Honduras (Judgment)*, Series C no 4, 29 July 1988, para 172 before the IACtHR; J Coppens, 'The Law of the Sea and Human Rights in the *Hirsi Jamaa and Others v. Italy* Judgment of the European Court of Human Rights' in Y Haeck, E Brems (eds), *Human Rights and Civil Liberties in the 21st Century* (Springer, 2014) 186.

[179] See eg, Trevisanut 2014b, n 160 above, 5–8; E Papastavridis, 'Is There a Right to Be Rescued at Sea? A Sceptical View', (June 2014) 4 *Questions of International Law* 17–32.

[180] Trevisanut 2014b, n 160 above, 8.

[181] Papastavridis 2014, n 179 above, 19.

Tzevelekos and Proukaki suggest that the right to be rescued and the corresponding duty to rescue derive from the notion of positive obligations under international human rights law. In this view, the law of the sea offers the tools to reach the goals of human rights law,[182] but does not afford any legal avenue for the judicial redress of wrongs for the people in question. Such redress can indeed be provided, at an international level, only under the relevant human rights treaties. As already emphasised in the previous Section, law of the sea and human rights law do complement and reinforce each other and must be read as part of a comprehensive approach to State obligations toward migrants encountered at sea.[183] As Article 311(2) of the UNCLOS reads:

> This Convention shall not alter the rights and obligations of States Parties which arise from other agreements compatible with this Convention and which do not affect the enjoyment by other States Parties of their rights or the performance of their obligations under this Convention.

Therefore, whilst UNCLOS does not contain human rights provisions, it does not explicitly exclude the application of human rights in certain contexts. In most cases, human rights obligations require States to do what they are already allowed to do under the law of the sea, 'turning the right to exercise jurisdiction into a duty to take measures to protect, ensure and fulfil human rights.'[184] According to the ECtHR, States should not only refrain from human rights violations, but also take steps to safeguard the lives of those within their jurisdiction,[185] in particular if the authorities in question knew or ought to have known at the time of the existence of a real and immediate risk to the life of an individual, and they failed to take measures, within the scope of their powers, that might have been expected to eliminate that risk.[186] The issue of whether SAR operations can be considered to involve the jurisdiction of the intervening State under human rights law is still debated. While it is doubtless that the jurisdiction of the flag State is engaged where people in distress are under the control of a rescuing State vessel, the same conclusion cannot be smoothly reached with regard to rescue operations carried out by private vessels.[187] In the *Hirsi* case, the ECtHR specified that Italy's responsibility was engaged from the moment people in distress were taken on board Italian warships.[188]

[182] Tzevelekos and Proukaki 2017, n 176 above, 4.

[183] For instance, Butler and Ratcovich argue that '[t]he duty to rescue everyone in distress at sea can … be seen as a natural corollary of the right to life.' G Butler and M Ratcovich, 'Operation Sophia in Uncharted Waters: European and International Law Challenges for the EU Naval Mission in the Mediterranean Sea' (2016) 85(3) *Nordic Journal of International Law* 235, 253.

[184] I Papanicolopulu, 'Human Rights and the Law of the Sea' in DJ Attard, M Fitzmaurice and NA Martinez Gutierrez (eds), *The IMLI Manual on International Maritime Law: The Law of the Sea* (OUP, 2014) 531.

[185] See, eg, *LCB v UK*, App no 23413/94 (9 June 1998) para 36.

[186] *Osman v UK*, above n 178, para 116.

[187] Papastravidis 2014, n 179 above, 27.

[188] *Hirsi v Italy*, above n 5, paras 76–78.

This would also be in line with Article 92 of the UNCLOS on the exclusive jurisdiction of the flag State.

In the *Xhavara* case, the ECtHR recognised that the jurisdiction of Italian authorities derived from both the existence of a bilateral agreement with Albania and the collision with the Albanian vessel transporting migrants.[189] Reasoning by analogy, it can be argued that jurisdiction under the ECHR is engaged also in cases where rescue operations are performed on the basis of a SAR agreement, and when there is a contact between the rescuers and the persons in distress. However, this conclusion would be more complicated in those instances in which rescued people are not taken on-board, or there is no involvement in a SAR operation. A coastal State has a duty to provide assistance if people in distress are within its SAR region, which is considered a non-jurisdictional area, namely a zone where States only have obligations, not rights.[190] More specifically, the coastal State holds here limited jurisdiction, which is solely functional to the performance of SAR services. Such *de jure* jurisdiction can be inferred from the obligation to 'promote the establishment, operation and maintenance of an adequate and effective search and rescue service' and to cooperate with other States to this end, as required by Article 98(2) of the UNCLOS. Loss of lives at sea can thus entail a violation of the State's due diligence obligation to provide *adequate and effective* SAR services in its SAR region.[191]

A breach of the right to life can also arise, in particular if the relevant authorities had knowledge of the peril. However, it would be difficult to establish a jurisdictional link between the coastal State and the endangered person if no distress call had been launched, and the State had no knowledge of the boat in distress. The negligence of the State could be nevertheless invoked by other States on the basis of the law of the sea treaties or by individuals contesting violations of the right to life, as recognised by the ECtHR in *Beru v Turkey*[192] and *Kemaloglu v Turkey*.[193] Having said that, the question remains whether the jurisdiction of the coastal State can be presumed in its SAR zone with regard to the application of human rights law.

According to Papastavridis, vessels in distress entering the SAR zone of a certain coastal State do not fall *ipso facto* under the jurisdiction of that State. As SAR regions are not maritime zones – but only functional zones, in accordance with Article 98(2) UNCLOS – States do not exercise sovereignty or sovereign rights. Therefore, it cannot be held that even if coastal States do not exercise *de jure* control over a vessel in distress, they may have *de facto* control over any vessels

[189] *Xhavara v Italy and Albania*, App no 39473/98, Admissibility Decision (11 January 2001).

[190] See Art 2(1) and Annex, Art 2(1)(7) of SAR Convention.

[191] C Pitea, 'Diritto alla Vita', in L Pineschi (ed), *La Tutela Internazionale dei Diritti Umani: Norme, Garanzie e Prassi* (Giuffré, 2006) 314, 318.

[192] *Berü v Turkey*, App no 47304 /07 (11 January 2011).

[193] *İlbeyi Kemaloğlu and Meriye Kemaloğlu v Turkey*, App no 19986/06 (10 July 2012). See also Trevisanut 2014b, n 160 above, 14.

entering their SAR zone. A certain level of effective control is needed, such as at least awareness of the location of the craft or the perilous situation.[194]

In line with Papastavridis, Trevisanut's argument is that a State *receiving a distress call* from a boat on the high seas has the duty to intervene even if the boat is outside its territorial or SAR waters. Such an obligation would derive indeed from a factual relationship that she defines as 'exclusive long distance *de facto* control'.[195] This coastal State may not be the one that is primarily responsible for the SAR zone where the vessel in distress is positioned. However, a jurisdictional link for the purpose of the right to life is created between the vessel and persons who have requested assistance, on one hand, and the recipient State, on the other hand, as soon as it acknowledges the distress call and acquires knowledge of the location and situation of distress. Once jurisdiction is established, a right to be rescued at sea, as a corollary to the right to life, will follow.[196] If then the State is unable to intervene due to geographical distance, it has still an obligation to take any measures to ensure protection of those in need by activating relevant SAR services.[197] In other words, the existence of a link between a State and a certain factual situation creates the law, in accordance with the principle *ex facto jus oritur*.[198]

The acknowledgement of such '*de facto* control' also finds support in other emergency cases (although not taking place at sea) in which the ECtHR recognises a positive obligation to provide emergency services 'where it has been brought to the notice of the authorities that the life or health of an individual is at risk on account of injuries sustained as a result of an incident.'[199] In the context of SAR operations, this principle means that as soon as an endangered person, or a third party who notices the distress situation, sends a distress call (even from a location on the high seas outside the SAR zone of the recipient State), a jurisdictional link is created between the endangered person and State authorities receiving the call, thus creating an obligation for them to activate emergency services (either directly or indirectly, if geographical distance does not allow them to intervene in due time).[200]

Additionally, all States who are in chain involved with a migrant not only have an obligation to refrain from directly causing wrong, but they also have

[194] Papastravidis 2014, n 179 above, 27.
[195] Trevisanut 2014b, n 160 above, 12–13.
[196] Papastavridis 2014, n 179 above, 28–29.
[197] Trevisanut 2014b, n 160 above, 13.
[198] According to Di Stefano, 'Le principe de l'effectivité est le trait d'union entre le droit et le fait'. G Di Stefano, *L'ordre internationale entre légalité et effectivité. Le titre juridique dans le contentieux territorial* (Pedone, 2002) 257. *Contra*, see the sceptical approach by FC Matsumoto, *L'effectivité en droit international* (Bruylant, 2014).
[199] *Furdik v Slovakia* (Admissibility decision) App no 42994/05 (2 December 2008). On the knowledge element in the context of positive obligations, see V Stoyanova, 'Causation between State Omission and Harm within the Framework of Positive Obligations under the European Convention on Human Rights' (2018) 18(2) *Human Rights Law Review* 309, 315.
[200] Trevisanut 2014b, n 160 above, 9, 13.

some responsibility to proactively offer the migrant in question some protection (according to their own capabilities). A duty to prevent or protect is triggered as soon as the State knows or foresees (or is reasonably expected to know or foresee) the existence of a threat/risk. Therefore, for instance, the flag State of a merchant vessel that spots a boat in distress and refuses to provide assistance would be responsible in two ways first, if it directly instructs the master of the private vessel not to render assistance – in this case the master could be deemed a '*de facto* organ' of the State in keeping with Article 8 of the ASR; secondly, for infringement of its positive obligations under the right to life, which prescribes both a duty to prevent and a duty to punish.[201] As the master of a merchant vessel should always record any reasons for failure to render assistance, the flag State has a positive obligation under Article 2 of the ECHR to take measures to both prevent the loss of lives and investigate any deaths potentially caused by both State agents and individuals.[202]

States might also engage concurrent liability for failure to protect.[203] Therefore, following a case-by-case approach, a State who hands over a migrant (either directly or indirectly) to a third country where her life and liberty can be threatened, in breach of the principle of *non-refoulement*, can be considered responsible just like the receiving State – ie, the latter for committing the actual wrongful act (a negative obligation), the former for failure to prevent the violation (even if extra-territorially), in accordance with the positive dimension of the same right. This also shows how migration management requires active cooperation between States as duty-bearers toward migrants and refugees on the move.[204]

[201] For a detailed account of relevant case law, see M Milanovic (ed), *Extraterritorial Application of Human Rights Treaties: Law, Principles, and Policy* (OUP, 2011); M Gondek, *The Reach of Human Rights in a Globalized World:* Extraterritorial Application of Human Rights Treaties (Intersentia, 2009); M Sheinin, 'Extraterritorial effect of the ICCPR', in F Coomans and MT Kamminga (eds), *Extraterritorial application for Human Rights Treaties* (Intersentia, 2004) 73.

[202] It is common bad practice, however, for commercial shipping not to inform flag State authorities when they identify the situations of danger at sea. For case law on the positive obligation under Art 2 of the ECHR, see, *inter alia*, *Gongadze v Ukraine*, App no 34056/02 (8 November 2005); and *Dink v Turkey*, App no 2668/07 (14 September 2010).

[203] On 'failure to protect' life as a ground for violation of Art 2 of the ECHR, see *Gongadze v Ukraine* and *Dink v Turkey*, n 202 above.

[204] On the duty to co-operate, see Art 7 Protocol against the Smuggling of Migrants by Land, Sea and Air Supplementing the United Nations Convention against Transnational Organized Crime, above n 44. The Preamble to the Geneva Convention affirms that 'considering that the grant of asylum may place unduly heavy burdens on certain countries … a satisfactory solution … cannot … be achieved without international co-operation.' See also UNSC Res 2240, above n 137, in which the Security Council '[e]xpress[es] … strong support to the States in the region affected by the smuggling of migrants and human trafficking, and emphasiz[es] the need to step up coordination of efforts in order to strengthen an effective multidimensional response to these common challenges in the spirit of international solidarity and shared responsibility …' (Preamble). According to the Security Council, that task 'requires a coordinated, multidimensional approach with States of origin, of transit, and of destination.'

As the ECtHR held in *Hirsi*, 'treaties must be interpreted in good faith ... and in accordance with the principle of effectiveness'.[205] Such a principle, which refers to the existence of factual links between the individual and the State (for example, geographical proximity) triggers the positive and (extraterritorial) duty to protect people in danger as long as the State of destination is aware of the situation (or could be reasonably expected to know) and is in a position to save lives.[206]

B. Hampering Access to Protection through Pre-arrival Interceptions

In some circumstances, national jurisprudence has adopted a restrictive interpretation of the *ratione loci* of the principle of *non-refoulement*. For example, in a case concerning the push-back of Haitians who attempted to flee their country and seek protection in the US, the US Supreme Court refused the extraterritorial relevance of *non-refoulement*, as codified in Article 33(1) of the Geneva Convention.[207] Nevertheless, the *Sale* case has been harshly criticised by the Inter-American Commission on Human Rights, which held that 'that Article 33 had no geographical limitations.'[208] Likewise, in the *Prague Airport* case, the English Court of Appeal concluded that *Sale* was 'wrongly decided' as it shall be 'impermissible to return refugees from the high seas to their country of origin.'[209]

Placing our attention on international human rights bodies, it is possible to observe that the jurisprudence of the HRC,[210] the Committee Against Torture,[211]

[205] *Hirsi v Italy*, above n 5, para 179.

[206] Tzevelekos and Proukaki 2017, n 179 above, 8.

[207] See the US Supreme Court, *Sale, Acting Commissioner, Immigration & Naturalization Service v Haitian Centres Council* 509 US 155; 113 S Ct 2549 (1993).

[208] Inter-American Commission on Human Rights, *The Haitian Centre for Human Rights et al v US*, Case 10.675, Report no 51/96, para 157. Among scholars, see eg, GS Goodwin-Gill, 'The Haitian *Refoulement* Case: A Comment' (1994) 6 *IJRL* 103; SH Legomsky, 'The USA and the Caribbean Interdiction Program' (2006) 18 *IJRL* 679; JY Carlier, 'Droit d'asile et des Réfugiés: de la Protection aux Droits' (2007) 332 *Recueil des Cours de l'Académie de Droit International* 107.

[209] *R (European Roma Rights Centre) and Others v Immigration Officer at Prague Airport*, 22 May 2003, [2003] EWCA Civ 666, paras 34–35.

[210] The HRC recognises the applicability of the *non-refoulemen*t obligation under the relevant Covenant where individuals are either within or outside the territory of a State party, as long as they are under the control of the State itself. See, eg, HRC General Comment no 31, 'The nature of the general legal obligation imposed on States parties' UN Doc CCPR/C/21/Rev.1/Add. 13, 26 May 2004, para 12); 'Concluding Observations on the United States of America' UN Doc CCPR/C/USA/CO/3Rev.1, 18 December 2006, para 16); *Mohammad Munaf v Romania*, Comm no 1539/2006 (21 August 2009) UN Doc CCPR/C/96/D/1539/2006, para 14.2; General Comment no 2, 'The prohibition of torture and cruel treatment or punishment (Art 7)' UN Doc HRI/HEN/1/rev.1, 28 July 1994, para 9; *Kindler v Canada*, Comm no 470/1991 (11 November 1993) UN Doc CCPR/C/48/D/470/1991, para 13.2.

[211] On the extraterritorial applicability of the Convention to any territory 'under the *de facto* effective control of the State party', see 'Conclusions and Recommendations on the United States of

and the ECtHR[212] – as examined in Chapter two – have increasingly confirmed the extraterritorial applicability of the relevant treaties when States deal with individuals who risk being subjected to torture or degrading treatment if handed over to the authorities of their countries of origin or transit. The ECtHR has also clearly emphasised States' duty to prevent *refoulement* from occurring, wherever jurisdiction is exercised.[213] While the applicability of the principle of *non-refoulement* in cases of expulsion and extradition has been recognised on several occasions, the applicability of this principle to people intercepted on the high seas during offshore migration operations has been less conclusive – at least this was so until the 2012 *Hirsi* decision.[214] In that judgment, the ECtHR held that there had been an extraterritorial violation of Article 3 of the ECHR on account of the fact that the applicants were exposed to the risk of ill-treatment in Libya, and to the risk of repatriation to Somalia and Eritrea.[215] According to the Court, Italy had exercised a 'continuous and exclusive *de jure* and *de facto* control' over the migrants found at sea,[216] thus upholding the same jurisdiction threshold applied in *Medvedyev*, where, however, the intercepted vessel was simply escorted from the international waters to France.

The Court's reasoning is not exhaustive on this point and the *Hirsi* case gives room to contend that also *minimal control* would be sufficient to engage the jurisdiction of the State exercising migration controls beyond borders.[217] Thus shifting emphasis from State action *per se* to the *consequences* of that action, physical contact does not amount to an essential requisite to engage jurisdiction. On this view, jurisdiction (and potentially responsibility) under international human rights law can also be engaged in those operations of looser-control at sea where State action falls short of arresting or detaining

America', 1–19 May 2006, CAT/C/USA/C/2, para 15; *JHA v Spain*, Comm 323/2007 (21 November 2008) UN Doc CAT/C/41/D/323/2007; see also General Comment 2 'Implementation of Article 2 by States parties', 24 January 2008, CAT/C/GC/2, para 6; *Sonko v Spain*, Comm 368/2008 (20 February 2012) UN Doc CAT/C/47/D/368/2008, para 10.3.

212 See, eg, *Medvedyev v France*, above n 41; *Xhavara v Italy*, above n 189; *Women on Waves v Portugal*, App no 31276/05 (3 February 2009); *Hirsi v Italy*, above n 5; *Al Jedda v UK*, App no 27021/08 (7 July 2011); *Al-Skeini v UK*, App no 55721/07 (7 July 2011); *Al-Saadoon v UK*, App no 61498/08 (2 March 2010).

213 See, eg, *Hirsi v Italy*, above n 5; *Xhavara v Italy*, above n 189, 5; *WM v Denmark*, App no 17392/90 (14 October 1992).

214 For commentary on the *Hirsi v Italy* case and the application of *non-refoulement* on the high seas, see M Giuffré, 'Watered-Down Rights on the High Seas: *Hirsi Jamaa and Others v Italy*' (2012) 61(3) *International and Comparative Law Quarterly* 728; Moreno-Lax V, '*Hirsi Jamaa and Others v Italy* or the Strasbourg Court versus Extraterritorial Migration Control?' (2012) 12(3) *Human Rights Law Review* 574; M den Heijer, 'Reflections on *Refoulement* and Collective Expulsion in the *Hirsi* Case' (2013) 25(2) *IJRL* 695.

215 For an analysis of the extraterritorial applicability of the principle of *non-refoulement* and the *Hirsi v Italy* case, see Chapter 2 of this book.

216 *Hirsi v Italy*, above n 5, para 81.

217 ibid, para 79.

the individuals concerned.[218] Physical contact or boarding of the vessel are not needed to engage *de facto* jurisdiction, as demonstrated in the *ND and NT* case.[219]

Likewise, the *Women on Waves* case is an example of engagement of jurisdiction despite the fact that the Portuguese Navy vessel did not have any physical contact with the Dutch vessel navigating outside the territorial waters of Portugal.[220] In the *Xhavara* case, collision between an Italian warship and the Albanian boat involved in migrant smuggling was sufficient to bring those people under Italian jurisdiction.[221] Actions such as forcing a boat to change its route by either closing access to ports, screaming, or steaming nearby until it is heading out of the territorial waters or the contiguous zone, as well as conducting or escorting the ship to a third country, can amount to 'effective control'. If preventing entry to territorial waters does not automatically amount to *refoulement*, violations of this principle arise if – as a consequence of these actions or omissions – the persons concerned are transferred to the frontiers of a territory where their life and liberty can be seriously threatened. Therefore, interdicting authorities shall always determine whether a specific third State is 'safe, accessible, and reachable for the boat in question.'[222]

The *Hirsi* ruling also confirms States' obligation to inform refugees about their rights, ensure access to asylum procedures and effective remedies, and assess the safety of the third country. Although the Geneva Convention does not expressly bind States to grant access to asylum procedures, such an obligation can be implicitly derived from the principle of *non-refoulement* (Article 33(1)) whose content and scope need to be shaped in good faith through the joint reading of international refugee and human rights law instruments, interpreted on the basis of their ordinary meaning in light of their object and purpose.[223] Therefore, not only should refugees be entitled to substantiate their protection claims before competent authorities onshore in order to dispel any risk of ill-treatment upon removal but, if intercepted on the high seas, they should also be disembarked in a safe place and receive access to fair and effective asylum procedures.[224] This would be in line with a harmonised approach to State

[218] R Bank, 'Refugees at Sea; Introduction to Article 11 of the 1951 Convention' in A Zimmermann (ed), *The 1951 Convention Relating to the Status of Refugees and its 1967 Protocol: A Commentary* (OUP, 2011), 841.

[219] *ND and NT v Spain*, App nos 8675/15 and 8697/15 (3 October 2017) para 54.

[220] *Women on Waves v Portugal*, above n 212, para 43.

[221] *Xhavara v Italy and Albania*, above n 189, para 1.

[222] Bank 2011, n 218 above, 849.

[223] See, in particular, Arts 3 and 13 of the ECHR, Art 3 of the CAT, and Art 7 of the ICCPR, which have been examined in Chapter 2 of this book. On the interplay between refugee law and human rights law, see T Clark and F Crépeau, 'Mainstreaming Refugee Rights. The 1951 Refugee Convention and International Human Rights Law' (1999) 17(4) *Netherlands Quarterly of Human Rights* 389. The EXCOM Conclusion no 95 (LIV) on International Protection (10 October 2003) underlines the 'complementary nature of international refugee and human rights law.'

[224] For an analysis of the extraterritorial applicability of the right to access asylum procedures, see Chapter 3 of this book.

obligations toward migrants and refugees at sea. International courts have also emphasised the need to ensure considerations of humanity in the interpretation and application of the law of the sea.[225] Saving human lives can be understood to include not only prevention of loss of lives at sea, but also protection from persecution and other human rights violations as a consequence of disembarkation in an unsafe country. As saving human lives is a common theme of the law of the sea, this legal regime should be read together with other areas of law, such as search and rescue, human rights law, and refugee law, even in the face of contrasting policy imperatives.[226] It can thus be argued that States have 'a positive protection obligation, not immediately absolute in the sense of the prohibition of torture, but a positive due diligence obligation to save lives';[227] in other words 'an obligation to deploy adequate means to exercise best possible efforts, to do the utmost to obtain this result.'[228]

This chapter's main conclusion is that the implementation of bilateral agreements on technical and police cooperation can hamper refugees' access to protection – that is to say *non-refoulement* as well as access to asylum procedures and effective remedies. Indeed, as explained in Chapter two, the enforcement of *non-refoulement*, under international refugee and human rights law, has two procedural consequences: the duty of the State to advise the individual in question about her entitlement to obtain international protection, and the duty to provide access to fair asylum procedures and effective remedies.[229]

The jurisprudence of the ECtHR, more than other international bodies, has interpreted the prohibition of *refoulement* as requiring access to an effective and rigorous examination of protection claims,[230] even in extraterritorial contexts. To give an example, in *Hirsi v Italy*, for the first time, the Court recognises the

[225] See, eg, *Corfu Channel (UK v Albania) (Merits)*, 9 April 1949, ICJ Gen List n 1; *M/V Saiga (No 2) (Saint Vincent and the Grenadines v Guinea) (Admissibility and Merits)*, 1 July 1999, List of Cases no 2, para 155.

[226] Klein 2014, n 161 above, 813–14.

[227] GS Goodwin-Gill, 'Refugees and Migrants at Sea: Duties of Care and Protection in the Mediterranean and the Need for International Action', Notes for a Presentation, Jean Monnet Centre of Excellence on Migrants' Rights in the Mediterranean University of Naples 'L'Orientale' (11 May 2015). While people are not at the centre of the law of the sea, it can nonetheless significantly contribute to the protection of people in maritime contexts. For an extended analysis, see I Papanicolopulu, *International Law and the Protection of People at Sea* (OUP, 2018).

[228] *Responsibilities and obligations of States sponsoring persons and entities with respect to activities in the Area, Advisory Opinion*, International Tribunal for the Law of the Sea, Seabed Disputes Chamber, 1 February 2011, ITLOS Rep 2011, para 110.

[229] For the view that *non-refoulement* entails an obligation to ensure access to an effective remedy that is available in law and in practice, see W Kälin, M Caroni and L Heim, 'Article 33 para 1 (Prohibition of Expulsion and Return (Refoulement)' in Zimmermann 2011, n 218 above, 1395. See eg, *Agiza v Sweden*, Comm no 233/2003 (20 May 2005) UN Doc CAT/C/34/D/233/2003, para 13.8; *Jabari v Turkey*, App no 40035/98 (1 July 2000) para 50. For further case law, refer to Chapter 2 of this book.

[230] For instance, in the *Amuur v France* decision, the ECtHR asserted that effective access to asylum procedures must be ensured also to asylum seekers retained in the international zone of an airport. See *Amuur v France*, App no 19776/92 (25 June 1996) para 43.

duty of the intercepting State to guarantee access to asylum procedures when refugees are intercepted on the high seas.

Preventing people from lodging their protection claims would both heighten the risk of *refoulement* and indirectly lead to a violation of Article 3 of the European Convention.[231] Along the same lines, the Court found that the summary expulsion of interdicted refugees without access to an individualised status determination procedure and without a thorough and rigorous assessment of their requests, before the removal measure was enforced, amounted to a violation of Articles 3 and 13 of the Convention and Article 4 of Protocol 4.[232]

To sum up, since States must also fulfil these procedural guarantees (*non-refoulement*, access to asylum procedures, and effective remedies) in respect of migrants and refugees found at sea,[233] intercepting/rescuing migrants and refugees before they are able to enter the territorial jurisdiction of a European State, and pushing them back (whether directly or by proxy) to an unsafe third country undercuts the individual right to seek asylum and receive protection from *refoulement*.

VII. PUSH-BACKS AND PUSH-BACKS BY PROXY: STATE RESPONSIBILITY IN EXTRATERRITORIAL (AND EXTERNALISED) IMMIGRATION CONTROLS

A. Jurisdiction and Responsibility

This chapter could have stopped at Section VI, which sought to answer the key research question this work intends to tackle, namely whether the implementation of bilateral agreements for technical and police cooperation at sea may hamper refugees' access to protection. However, due to the sensitivity and complexity of the issue of extraterritorial migration controls, the following sections pursue the analysis further by exploring the debate on State Responsibility under general international law in situations of bilateral cooperation against irregular migration. As discussed in the previous Section, the implementation of agreements for technical and police cooperation beyond borders may *de facto* restraint the enjoyment of essential refugee rights. However, it cannot automatically be inferred that European States which cooperate with third countries in patrolling external maritime borders are internationally responsible under human rights law if intercepted migrants and refugees are removed to countries where their life is irremediably endangered.

[231] *Hirsi v Italy*, above n 5, paras 185, 201–205.

[232] ibid, paras 205–207. On the extraterritorial applicability of the right to an effective remedy under the ECHR, see Chapter 2 of this book.

[233] *Hirsi v Italy*, Concurring Opinion 44–45, above n 5. See also, the Parliamentary Assembly of the Council of Europe, 'Resolution 1821 (2011) on the Interception and Rescue at Sea of Asylum Seekers, Refugees, and Irregular Migrants', paras 9.3–9.6.

A prerequisite to engaging responsibility under human rights law is that States exercise jurisdiction over persons removed to unsafe ports of departure as a consequence of joint patrols carried out either on the high seas or in the coastal waters of the country of embarkation.[234] But let us assume that either it is difficult to establish whether or not a State exercises jurisdiction, or it can be shown that it did not exercise such effective control as demanded by human rights law to establish jurisdiction. At this point, reference to the ASR would enable identification of an internationally accountable actor, even if indirectly, whenever States engage in human rights violations with regard to people that do not fall under their effective control and authority.

The study of State Responsibility is not intended here to be comprehensive, but is limited to an overview of the kinds of liability a European State might incur in contexts of cooperative migration control. However, I then move more specifically into the subject of indirect responsibility under Article 16 of the ASR to investigate Italy's possible complicity with Libya for violation of the principle of *non-refoulement* while performing activities of migration control at sea. It would, moreover, exceed the scope of this chapter to proceed with a comprehensive analysis of concepts such as jurisdiction, attribution, the different conditions for asserting responsibility, and its legal consequences. Nevertheless, a number of specifications are needed.

In general international law, 'jurisdiction' points to the authority of the State to regulate the conduct of natural and legal persons by means of its domestic law.[235] Such authority, which is grounded in, and delimited by international law, includes both the power to prescribe and the power to enforce legal rules.[236] As discussed in Chapter two, 'jurisdiction' in human rights treaties is mainly understood as *factual power* that a State exercises over persons or territory.[237] Every time a State exercises this power – meaning effective control and authority over a territory or a person – it must protect and ensure the rights of the

[234] This point has already been examined in Chapter 2 of this book. See, as an example, the *Hirsi v Italy* case, above n 5.

[235] See Chapter 2 of this book for a broader discussion on 'jurisdiction.'

[236] On the issue of jurisdiction in international law, see C Staker, 'Jurisdiction' in Malcolm Evans (ed), *International Law* (OUP, 2018) chapter 10. See also M Shaw, *International Law* (CUP, 2008) 645.

[237] Milanovic 2011, n 201 above, 53. On a different view, Papanicolopulu argues that a State should not be completely relieved from its obligations under human rights law even if it does not exercise control over territory that is subject to its jurisdiction, for instance when territory is controlled by armed groups or is occupied by a foreign state. An example is the *Ilascu* case, where the ECtHR recognised the existence of (limited) positive obligations also for Moldova. I Papanicolopulu, 'A Response to Milanovic on Extraterritorial Application of Human Treaties: The significance of international Law Concepts of Jurisdiction' *EJIL Talk* (4 December 2011), https://www.ejiltalk.org/a-response-to-milanovic-on-extraterritorial-application-of-human-treaties-the-significance-of-international-law-concepts-of-jurisdiction/#more-4171. See also *Ilascu v Moldova and Russia*, App no 48787/99 (8 July 2004).

people concerned.[238] Moreover, doctrine,[239] as well as the jurisprudence of the International Court of Justice (ICJ)[240] and international human rights bodies, have been interpreting 'jurisdiction' as operating extraterritorially.[241]

Being a prerequisite for the human rights obligation to apply, jurisdiction is a condition for engaging potential State responsibility.[242] However, the two concepts should not be equated. Whilst 'State jurisdiction', in human rights law, is 'a question of a State's control over the victims of [human rights] violations … or, more generally, control over the territory in which they are located',[243] 'responsibility' is triggered by the breach of the obligation the State has to secure human rights to people within its jurisdiction. Jurisdiction in international law delimits municipal legal systems of States,[244] and is an emanation of one State's sovereignty; that is, the claim both to regulate its own public order, and exercise

[238] See, eg, *Delia Saldias de Lopez v Uruguay*, Comm no 52/1979 (29 July 1981) UN Doc CCPR/C/OP/1, para 12.1. On the application of the concept of 'functional jurisdiction' to activities taking place beyond territorial frontiers, see Gammeltoft-Hansen 2011, n 289 below, 124.

[239] See, eg, GS Goodwin-Gill, 'The Extraterritorial Reach of Human Rights Obligations: A Brief Perspective on the Link to Jurisdiction' in L Boisson de Chazournes and MC Kohen (eds), *International Law and the Quest for its Implementation/Le Droit International et la Quête de sa Mise en Oeuvre: Liber Amicorum Vera Gowlland-Debbas* (Brill, 2010) 293; Milanovic 2011, n 201 above; S Besson, 'The Extraterritoriality of the European Convention on Human Rights: Why Human Rights Depend on Jurisdiction and What Jurisdiction Amounts to' (2012) 25(4) *Leiden Journal of International Law* 857; S Kim, '*Non-Refoulement* and Extraterritorial jurisdiction: State Sovereignty and Migration Controls at Sea in the European Context' (2017) 30(1) *Leiden Journal of International Law* 49.

[240] Relevant are the two judgments of the ICJ in the *Wall Advisory Opinion* and in the *Congo-Uganda* case where the Court held that State responsibility under human rights law may be engaged by States carrying out a military occupation of a foreign territory. See *Legal Consequences of the Construction of a Wall in the Occupied Palestinian Territory* (Advisory Opinion), 9 July 2004, ICJ Rep 136, paras 109–111; see also *Armed Activities on the Territory of Congo (Democratic Republic of Congo v Uganda)*, 19 December 2005, ICJ Rep 168, paras 216, 220. In the absence of a general rule imposing the respect of human rights obligations only within State territory, the ILC has affirmed that acts or omissions attributable to a State can engage its international responsibility, 'regardless of whether they have been perpetrated in national or foreign territory.' See 'Report of the ILC on the work of its twenty-seventh session', *Yearbook of the ILC 1975*, vol II, 84.

[241] See, eg, the HRC's oft-quoted case *Lopez-Burgos v Uruguay*, above n 238, paras 12.1–12.2. On a general note, the ECtHR has considered a decisive element for determining State jurisdiction (and, therefore, the application of the relevant treaty) whether a certain person falls within the effective control and authority of a contracting State, regardless of whether it is exercising public powers or not. See, eg, *Loizidou v Turkey*, App no 15318/89, Preliminary Objections (23 March 1995) paras 62–64; *Cyprus v Turkey*, App no 25781/94, Judgment – Just satisfaction (10 May 2001) paras 76, 80; *Ilascu v Moldova and Russia*, above n 237, para 384; *Ocalan v Turkey*, App no 46221/99 (12 May 2005) para 91; *Issa v Turkey*, App no 31821/96 (16 November 2004) paras 68–71; *Pad and Others v Turkey*, App no 60167/00 (28 June 2007) paras 53–55; *Al-Saadoon v UK*, above n 212, para 81; *Al-Skeini v UK*, above n 212, para 149; *Hirsi v Italy*, above n 5, para 81. See also, *WM v Denmark* (above n 213) concerning extraterritorial *non-refoulement* from an embassy in the territory of a non-Contracting Party to the ECHR.

[242] O De Schutter (ed), *International Human Rights Law: Cases, Materials, Commentary* (CUP, 2010) 124.

[243] Milanovic 2008, n 140 above, 446.

[244] ibid 447.

power *vis-à-vis* other States.[245] Unlike the human rights context – where jurisdiction is 'a question of fact, of actual authority and control'[246] – in general international law, this power relies on legal entitlements or competences.[247]

The rules of State responsibility concern 'the general conditions under international law for the State to be considered responsible for wrongful actions or omissions, and the legal consequences which flow therefrom.'[248] In Ago's words, 'it is one thing to define a rule and the content of the obligation it imposes, and another to determine whether that obligation has been violated and what should be the consequences of the violation.'[249] Therefore, it would be important to verify what kind of responsibility could be established, under general international law, when States commit an international wrongful act while carrying out external migration controls autonomously or in conjunction with another actor.

On a general note, States are responsible for any conduct of their organs whether they 'exercise legislative, executive, judicial, or any other functions.'[250] As outlined by Article 2 of the ILC Codification, the requirements for determining an international wrongful act are twofold: first, the conduct at issue must be attributable to the State; second, the conduct must consist of the infringement of an international legal obligation in force at that time for that State.

As interception and removal measures can assume various forms, identifying the exact scope of both States' obligations toward refugees in the context of controls at sea, and concurrent responsibilities in case of infringement of these obligations, could be complicated. In particular, the following Sub-sections concentrate on the police cooperation set up by the bilateral technical Protocols concluded between Italy and Libya in 2007 and 2009 (resulting in the 2009 push-backs); and on the pull-backs started in 2017 in the Central Mediterranean.

The patterns of State cooperation connected to readmission of unwanted migrants, who often travel along with refugees, are multifarious. European countries may train the border guards of a third State; supply them with patrol boats; exchange police and immigration officers; participate with their own

[245] ibid, 420; Brownlie 2008, n 58 above, 297.

[246] See *Al-Skeini v UK*, above n 212, paras 132–133 ff. See also Milanovic 2008, n 140 above, 447.

[247] F Berman, 'Jurisdiction: The State' in P Capps, MD Evans and S Konstadinidis (eds), *Asserting Jurisdiction* (Hart Publishing, 2003) xix.

[248] J Crawford, *The International Law Commission's Articles on State Responsibility: Introduction, Text and Commentaries* (CUP, 2002) 74.

[249] R Ago, 'Second Report on State responsibility, by Special Rapporteur – the origin of international responsibility', Extract from the *Yearbook of the ILC 1970*, vol II, doc A/8010/Rev.l, 178, para 7(c). The dichotomy between primary and secondary rules of international law is not defended as correct by part of the literature. Linderfalk, for instance, criticises the assumption that State responsibility can be described as separate from the ordinary rules of international law. See U Linderfalk, 'State Responsibility and the Primary-Secondary Rules Terminology – The Role of Language for an Understanding of the International Legal System' (2009) 78 *Nordic Journal of International Law* 53, 72.

[250] Art 4(1) of the ASR. Additionally, under Art 5, States may engage responsibility even for '[t]he conduct of a person or entity which is not an organ of the State under article 4 but which is empowered by the law of that State to exercise elements of the governmental authority …'

officials in mixed crews; coordinate rescue operations; send coordinates for the location of boats in distress; intercept boat migrants by means of their own vessels and hand them over to the authorities of the country of embarkation; or delegate such functions directly to the third State itself.

Since in joint migration controls, European States can attract either direct or indirect responsibility if they disregard refugee or human rights law, responsibility should be tackled on an *ad hoc* basis following rules on attribution of State conduct. For the purpose of this work, the conduct that should be attributable to a European State to establish the international wrongful act, and therefore its international responsibility, would be the removal of intercepted refugees 'to territories where their lives and freedoms would be threatened.'[251] State practice, since the adoption of the 1951 Geneva Convention, has provided persuasive evidence that the principle of *non-refoulement* has achieved the status of customary international law.[252] As a matter of human rights law, the principle of *non-refoulement* is a corollary of the prohibition on torture, cruel, inhuman and degrading treatment or punishments, as enshrined in several international instruments,[253] such as the ICCPR and the CAT, ratified by both Italy and Libya.[254]

B. Independent Responsibility and Attribution of State Conduct to Another State

Relying on the empirical material deployed in Sections II and III, this Sub-section sketches out two kinds of responsibility that a European State may incur where it is involved in a common action against irregular migration together with a third country. First, in the case of joint border controls – even when patrols have been moved to the territorial waters of a non-EU third country – States can be found independently responsible. In these circumstances, Article 47 of the ASR requires the conduct of State organs to be attributable to the two States and to entail a breach of their international obligations, *in casu* the principle of *non-refoulement*.[255]

[251] Goodwin-Gill and McAdam 2007, n 17 above, 277.

[252] See Chapter 2 of this book for further details. For an opposite view, see JC Hathaway, *The Rights of Refugees under International Law* (CUP, 2005) 363–70.

[253] In this vein, the *jus cogens* value of *non-refoulement* can be derived by the absolute prohibition on torture. Under Art 41(2) of the ILC Codification, 'No State shall recognize as lawful a situation created by a serious breach within the meaning of article 40, nor render aid or assistance in maintaining that situation.' Art 40(1) refers to the international responsibility 'entailed by a serious breach by a State of an obligation arising under a peremptory norm of general international law.'

[254] See, Chapter 2 of this book for an analysis of *non-refoulement* under human rights law.

[255] Under Art 47 of the ASR: 'Where several States are responsible for the same internationally wrongful act, the responsibility of each State may be invoked in relation to that act.' See also Arts 2 and 4. Pursuant to Art 2 of the ASR: 'There is an internationally wrongful act of a State when conduct consisting of an action or omission: (*a*) is attributable to the State under international law; and (*b*) constitutes a breach of an international obligation of the State.' See also Art 4 of the ASR. For further analysis, refer to Crawford 2002, n 248 above, 145–46.

A second possible scenario exists where responsibility is assigned to a European State for the actions of the border guards of a third country. In this case, foreign border authorities should be conceived of as subsidiary organs of the EU country and executors of its immigration policies. Pursuant to Article 6 of the ASR,

> the conduct of an organ placed at the disposal of a State by another State shall be considered an act of the former State under international law if the organ is acting in the exercise of elements of the governmental authority of the State at whose disposal it is placed.

Acting on instructions is not sufficient to attribute the conduct of a State organ to another State and it is necessary that the organs of the third country 'act in conjunction with the machinery of that [EU] State and under its exclusive direction and control, rather than on instructions from the sending State.'[256] It is likely that Italy would not be assigned separate responsibility for conduct attributable to it when interception is conducted by vessels under Libyan command in either Libyan territorial waters or on the high seas. In these circumstances, Libya would be fully competent to decide upon matters related to navigation, patrolling, and interception. By contrast, on 6 May and 30 August 2009, refugees intercepted on the high seas were transferred to Italian vessels, shipped to Libya, and handed over to Libyan authorities.

Independent responsibility might also be invoked *ex hypothesi* by a situation in which Libyan ships enter Italian territorial waters to rescue or interdict boat migrants and refugees and drive them back to North Africa's shores. Indeed, the coastal State – which holds primary responsibility both for addressing any protection claim and for transporting rescued migrants in a reasonable time to a 'place of safety'[257] – by authorising the third country to intervene, exercises its sovereign authority. Since, under Article 33(1) of the UNCLOS, a State retains jurisdiction over immigration matters in its contiguous zone, Italy would remain primarily responsible if it authorised Libya to intercept migrants, including refugees, in this area.

The application of Article 6 of the ASR should also be excluded in the case of Italy's push-backs and Libya's pull-backs. Indeed, in both circumstances, Libya operates within its own command on-board vessels supplied by the Italian government. Therefore, the argument that African border guards receive training, funding, technical equipment, and assistance cannot be utilised to consider

[256] Crawford 2002, n 248 above, ibid, 103.

[257] Pursuant to Art 2(1) of the UNCLOS, the sovereignty of a coastal State extends to the territorial sea. See, generally, Trevisanut 2008, n 52 above; E Turco Bulgherini, 'Acque Territoriali e Sicurezza Marittima' (2010) 3 *Online Gnosis Rivista Italiana di Intelligence* 30, http://gnosis.aisi.gov.it/Gnosis/Rivista24.nsf/servnavig/57. See also, UNHCR Executive Committee, 'Conclusion on Protection Safeguards in Interception Measures', UN doc no 97 (LIV) – 2003, 10 October 2003, para (a)(i), http://www.unhcr.org/496323740.html.

African border authorities as subsidiary organs of the Italian government.[258] It remains, thus, to be seen which alternative avenues can satisfactorily be pursued through the institution of State responsibility.

C. Indirect Responsibility for Aiding and Assisting Another State

A State could be held indirectly accountable for an internationally wrongful act committed by another State by means of its 'aiding and assisting' the third country itself in performing an illicit operation through supportive political statements, the provision of infrastructures, technical utilities, or financial support. Under Article 16 of the ILC Codification,

> a State which aids or assists another State in the commission of an internationally wrongful act by the latter is internationally responsible for doing so if: (a) that State does so with knowledge of the circumstances of the internationally wrongful act; and (b) the act would be internationally wrongful if committed by that State.

As indicated in the chapeau to Article 16, wrongful conduct refers to violations of international obligations by the assisted State, the 'latter', 'which distinguishes the situation of aid or assistance from that of co-perpetrators or co-participants in an internationally wrongful act.'[259] Therefore, Article 16 'establishes a distinct wrong of complicity, independent of the wrong committed by the perpetrating State,[260] which remains primarily responsible, while the assisting State has a purely supporting role.[261]

To give an example, a State may be liable for violation of the principle of non-*refoulement* where it knowingly assists another State to divert refugees to a place where their life or liberty might be threatened.[262] Even if the first State does not itself carry out the unlawful conduct, but supplies equipment with knowledge of the intentions of the assisted State, a strong enough link exists to establish complicity. Therefore, this Sub-section, slightly departing from the context of the 2009 push-backs, explores whether Article 16 of the ASR could be used to delimit State responsibility within the framework of the general cooperation between Italy and Libya established by the technical Protocols on migration control.

Italian jurisdiction was engaged, under human rights law, for sending refugees intercepted on the high sea (on 6 May and 30 August 2009) back to Libyan ports on its own vessels, in violation of the fundamental rights of individuals

[258] See den Heijer 2010a, n 169 above, 192–93.

[259] Crawford 2002, n 248 above, 148.

[260] ibid. Instead, for the issue of joint responsibility of several States for the same injury, see Art 47 of the ASR.

[261] ibid.

[262] M Foster, 'Protection Elsewhere: The Legal Implications of Requiring Refugees to Seek Protection in Another State' (2007) 28 *Michigan Journal of International Law* 223, 263.

placed under its control. With regard to the push-backs of 6 May, the ECtHR found that Italy had jurisdiction and therefore responsibility for violations of the fundamental rights of removed persons. Diverse operational missions can, however, be performed. For instance, on the remaining occasions in 2009, migrants and refugees were interdicted by Italian authorities and transferred to Libyan vessels in charge of carrying them back to Tripoli. In many other cases, which obtained less public attention, Libyan authorities instead performed interceptions directly in their territorial waters or on the high seas, without the intervention of Italian warships.

Major attention rests on the modalities of collaboration and assistance deriving from the terms of the bilateral technical Protocols and the Partnership Treaty. For instance, under the terms of the 2007 and 2009 technical Protocols, Libya was autonomously committed to sea patrols, which may result in the diversion of migrants and refugees to the country of embarkation under the full command of Libyan authorities. Article 16 of ILC Codification does not tackle attribution or questions of joint and several liabilities, since the abetting State does not itself commit the internationally wrongful act but assists another State, which performs the illicit conduct. Thus, as Crawford explains, 'by assisting another State to commit an internationally wrongful act, a State should not necessarily be held to indemnify the victim for all the consequences of the act, but only for those which … flow from its own conduct.'[263]

Although, according to the text of the 2007 and 2009 technical Protocols, only Libyan authorities on board the military vessels were entrusted with the responsibility and the legal authority for the operational missions at sea, Italy has substantively supported its partner by providing funding, training, consultancy, as well as surveillance equipment. Therefore, the question is whether a certain threshold is reached to establish that Italy was aware that its assistance could be used to perform wrongful conduct.

Regrettably, there is little jurisprudence of help in defining the contours of 'aiding and assisting' responsibility.[264] This leaves ample room for interpretation. According to the ICJ, for example, it is not necessary that the assistance provided by the aiding State be essential to the commission of the international wrongful act, but it must at least have 'contributed significantly to that act.'[265] In addition, the violation constituting the internationally wrongful conduct must involve the infringement of a norm that would amount to wrongful conduct in both States.[266]

[263] Crawford 2002, n 248 above, 151.

[264] Although Art 16 of the ASR is not strictly relevant for the *Genocide Convention Case*, the ICJ takes the opportunity to make some observations on the concept of 'aid or assistance'. See *Application of the Convention on the Prevention and Punishment of the Crime of Genocide (Bosnia and Herzegovina v Serbia and Montenegro)*, 26 February 2007, ICJ Rep 43, paras 420–424.

[265] Crawford 2002, n 248 above, 149.

[266] ibid.

A fairly wide category of actions can be encompassed within the reach of Article 16, such as training, economic assistance, the provision of confidential information,[267] as well as political or legal aid, even in the form of treaties employed to facilitate the performance of the illicit act.[268] As the scope *ratione materiae* of Article 16 is so vast, the mental element has been interpreted very restrictively.[269] If on the one hand, it can be presumed that a State is aware of the circumstances making the conduct of the assisted State internationally wrongful, it is also true that configuring such responsibility is not an easy task. Indeed, the threshold for establishing indirect responsibility is very high, and the process of proving that aid or assistance has been intentionally given 'with a view to facilitate the commission of the wrongful act' would be cumbersome.

The mental element requirement still remains a hotly debated issue because of the problems of representing a State as an entity able to formulate conscious decisions.[270] Moreover, in order to avoid responsibility, a State could intentionally avoid making public pronouncements stating its will.[271] Taking into account the difficulty in determining the state of mind of a State, such a strict mental requirement would also lead to the exclusion of those cases where States commit international wrongful acts not from a desire to violate human rights, but because they implicitly accept the risk that breaches of fundamental rights may occur while pursuing different and less harmful objectives.[272] Rather than focusing on the mental reasons driving State action, greater attention should be drawn on the assessment of whether the assisting State was aware that its assistance would be put to wrongful use.

Conversely, the ILC is very keen to emphasise that a high threshold must be met, otherwise international responsibility could be triggered anytime a State engages in bilateral cooperation with a third country.[273] It has, thus, stressed that the 'eventual possibility' that a wrongful act could derive from a State's assistance is not sufficient to establish the link between the facilitating act and the wrongful conduct.[274] Rather, it is to be proved that an accomplice State aided

[267] J Crawford, 'Second Report on State Responsibility' *Yearbook of the ILC 1999*, vol II (part I) 50, fn 349.

[268] B Graefrath, 'Complicity in the Law of International State Responsibility' (1996) 29 *Revue Belge de droit International* 370, 374. On the scope of 'aid and assistance', see HP Aust, *Complicity and the Law of State Responsibility* (CUP, 2011) 192–230.

[269] G Nolte and HP Aust, 'Equivocal Helpers-Complicit States, Mixed Messages and International Law' (2009) 58 *ICLQ* 1, 10.

[270] M den Heijer, *Europe and Extraterritorial Asylum* (Hart, 2012) 97.

[271] On the difficulty of inferring intention, and therefore complicity, from public statements, see Graefrath 1996, n 268 above, 375–76.

[272] K Nahapetian, 'Confronting State Complicity in International Law' (2002) 7 *UCLA Journal of International Law* 99, 126–27.

[273] Nolte and Aust 2009, n 269 above, 14.

[274] 'Report of the ILC on the work of its thirtieth session', *Yearbook of the ILC 1978*, vol II (Part II) 49–50, para 18.

another country by accepting, with knowledge of the facts, the serious risk that wrongful acts would be committed.[275]

(i) Italy's Responsibility for 'Aiding and Assisting' Libya? The Push-Backs Case

In light of the above, what remains to be explored is whether, by assisting Libya in patrolling its territorial and international waters to intercept and remove migrants and refugees to a territory where their life could be irremediably endangered, Italy acted with full knowledge of the circumstances in which its aid or assistance would be used. Providing assistance that facilitates only occasional wrongdoings should not be sufficient to raise the threshold of State responsibility to a level falling within Article 16 of the ASR.[276]

The case of Italy–Libya cooperation in migration control in 2009 raises a host of perplexities and questions in this regard. As discussed in Chapter two, 834 persons were pushed-back to the port of departure, within the framework of a well-organised policy, over the course of nine separate operations, during which migrants and refugees were handed over to the Libyan authorities after their interception on the high seas by Italian warships. Push-backs, frequently repeated over six months between 6 May and 6 November 2009, were carried out in a systematic fashion with the approval of both governments. On several other occasions, after the entry into force of the 2009 Executive Protocol, Libyan officials interdicted irregular migrants and refugees heading to Europe, in their territorial waters or on the high seas, without the intervention of Italian vessels. Unfortunately, keeping track of the number of people halted and removed to Libya before they could encounter the authorities of a European State is practically impossible.

Despite the transfer of the maritime operations to Libyan authorities, and the attempt to keep the details of 'anti-immigration activities' classified, a great deal of information on the treatment of migrants in Libya, and the form of its cooperation with Italy, is in the public domain. As explained in Section II, Italian officials were always on board the vessels used to ship migrants and refugees back to Libya, or to transfer passengers to Libyan crafts. They thus had full knowledge of the circumstances, and were fully aware that intercepted refugees were terrified of being returned to Libyan guardianship.[277] In this respect, there is room to presume not only that Italy was conscious of the 'eventual possibility'

[275] ibid. See also, *Genocide Convention Case*, above n 264, para 432.

[276] den Heijer 2012, n 270 above, 101.

[277] As Excerpts of an interview of a Lieutenant of the Italian Revenue Police involved in the maritime operations can be drawn from F Viviano, 'Noi Finanzieri Ostaggi di Tripoli Su Quelle Navi Non Vogliamo Salire', *Repubblica* (15 September 2010), http://www.repubblica.it/cronaca/2010/09/15/news/finanziere_mazara-7088107/.

of the harmful use of its aid but, more decisively, that it knew its aid would be put to wrongful use. Because of the lack of a clear-cut definition of 'aiding and assisting', the concept of 'complicity' is very controversial and is not a settled area of international law, in particular with regard to the different forms of complicity (ie, whether omission is also included), the nexus element (ie, whether active participation or mere contribution is required), and the subjective element of intent.[278]

The Italian overarching intent to outsource its responsibilities for migrants and refugees, by supporting Libya in its role of watchdog of Europe's gateways for the containment of irregular migration by sea, has been corroborated by the numerous public and official statements from both the Italian and Libyan governments.[279] It has also been confirmed by factual data and by the conclusion of bilateral agreements establishing a detailed framework for mutual cooperation.

For example, over the last decade, Italy has assisted Libya on a regular basis with the provision of funding, vessels, satellite devices, technical equipment for patrolling land and maritime borders, night-vision devices, binoculars, all-terrain vehicles (ATV), life boats, and sacks for the transportation of corpses.[280] It has also provided training for border officials, confidential information, consultancy, money for the construction of reception centres[281] and for charter flights both to deport irregular migrants from Libya to source countries,[282] and to transfer police officers stationed at Libyan diplomatic and consular offices to work on migration issues. Additionally, the 2009 Protocol explicitly requires Italy to assist Libya in boosting migrants' repatriation. Thus, Italy should also have known the risks migrants and refugees would be exposed to, even if the command and direction of the operations was entirely under Libya's authority.

In order to infer that the assistance provided by Italy to Libya falls under the scope of Article 16, it should be demonstrated that aid and assistance were intentionally given 'with a view to facilitate the commission of the wrongful act' by Libya, and that the accomplice State accepted, with full 'knowledge' of the facts, the serious danger that a wrongful act would be carried out.[283] Such conduct would include the violation of the customary principle of

[278] See M den Heijer, 'Europe beyond its borders', in Ryan and Mtsilegas 2010, n 77 above, 169; see also Aust 2011, n 268 above, 197, 219.

[279] See, eg, the communication published on the website of the Minister of the Interior, 'Contrasto immigrazione, Maroni: intesa firmata in Libia', http://www.governo.it/Notizie/Ministeri/dettaglio.asp?d=41871.

[280] See P Cuttitta, 'Readmission in the Relations between Italy and North African Mediterranean Countries' in Cassarino 2010a, n 68 above, 49.

[281] See Paoletti 2010, n 68 above, 59.

[282] See European Commission Report, 'Technical Mission to Libya on Illegal Migration' (27 November–6 December 2004) doc 7753/05, 59–61, http://www.statewatch.org/news/2005/may/eu-report-libya-ill-imm.pdf.

[283] For a comprehensive analysis of the subjective element, refer to Aust 2011, n 268 above, 230–49.

non-refoulement, which also enjoys a peremptory status as a corollary to the prohibition of torture.

Is it possible to assume that Italy knew or could reasonably expect – at that material time – that a real risk existed of migrants and refugees being removed to the territory of a country where they could suffer torture, or other inhuman and degrading treatment? Has Italy pushed back migrants with the intent to put their life at risk in Libya? If so, it could potentially be held accountable for assisting Libya in violating the principle of *non-refoulement*.[284] To establish complicity it should be proved that Italian authorities, in full knowledge of the facts, exposed intercepted refugees to inhuman and degrading treatment by removing them to Libya, which, *inter alia*, did not offer any guarantees against repatriation to Somalia and Eritrea.[285]

As confirmed by the ECtHR in the *Hirsi* judgment, Italy not only 'could not ignore' the treatment reserved by Libya to migrants and refugees, but it also had an obligation to proactively find out the real situation of migrants and refugees before proceeding with their expulsion.[286] Numerous reports by international organisations and NGOs depicted the grievous treatment of irregular immigrants in Libya at the material time in which push-backs took place.[287] According to the ECtHR, 'it was for the national authorities, faced with a situation in which human rights were being systematically violated … to find out about the treatment to which the applicants would be exposed after their return.'[288] This positive obligation to acquire knowledge before carrying out a certain action in tandem with a third State might also influence the way in which complicity can be established. Immediately after the first push-back operation, several human rights organisations raised concerns about such practice by both urging the Italian government to stop collective expulsions, and by highlighting the appalling conditions in which migrants and refugees were compelled to live once in Libya.[289]

[284] On violations of Art 16 of the ASR as a consequence of *refoulement*, see Nolte and Aust 2009, n 269 above, 17.

[285] ibid, para 137. On the existence of the 'knowledge' requirement in the Italy–Libya cooperation, see also T Gammeltoft-Hansen, 'The Externalisation of European Migration Control and the Reach of International Refugee Law' in E Guild and P Minderhoud (eds), *The First Decade of EU Migration and Asylum Law* (Martinus Nijhoff, 2011) 295. Moreover, in 2004, the European Commission, after a technical mission to Libya, had collected and published statistics on removals.

[286] *Hirsi v Italy*, above n 5, para 133. The Court refers here to *Chahal v UK*, App no 22414/93 (25 October 1996/15 November 1996) paras 104–105; *Jabari v Turkey*, above n 229, paras 40 and 41; and *MSS v Belgium and Greece*, App no 30696/09 (21 January 2011) para 359.

[287] See *Hirsi v Italy*, above n 5, paras 123–126.

[288] ibid, para 133.

[289] See L Holmstrom (ed), *Conclusions and Recommendations of the UN Committee Against Torture: Eleventh to Twenty-second Sessions (1993–1999)* (Martinus Nijhoff, 2000) 133, section C, para 5; UNHCR, 'Follow-up from UNHCR on Italy's Push-backs' (Briefing Notes, 12 May 2009), http://www.unhcr.org/4a0966936.html; Amnesty International, 'Dichiarazione della Sezione Italiana di Amnesty International dopo i Nuovi Respingimenti di Migranti verso la Libia' (11 May 2009), http://www.amnesty.it/flex/cm/pages/ServeBLOB.php/L/IT/IDPagina/2007; *Human Rights Watch*,

In the circumstance of pre-border controls jointly carried out by Italy and Libya or by Libya alone in 2009, complicity could be considered established only if the conditions posed by Article 16 of the ASR are fully met. They are summarised as follows: first, however complicated the process of detecting what the intention of a State is, the mental element of the Italian government should reach a threshold sufficient to trigger its indirect responsibility. As required by paragraph (a) of Article 16, to be internationally responsible, an aiding State should have acted 'with knowledge of the circumstances of the internationally wrongful act.' Not only does Italy's intention to remove migrants and refugees to an unsafe country emerge from the pronouncements and practice of the Italian government,[290] but Italy was also able to base its safety appraisal upon an enormous variety of available information concerning the human rights situation in Libya. However, it can be more complicated to prove the existence of the mental element (ie, the intent to push-back in order to put refugees' lives at risk).

Second, an unequivocal link should be established between the facilitating act and the subsequent wrongful conduct. Paragraph (b) of Article 16 requires that 'the act would be internationally wrongful if committed by [the assisting] State.' Although the provision of training, technical equipment, and funding does not amount *per se* to an unlawful practice, Italy's indirect responsibility could, nonetheless, be inferred if it were proved that its assistance in refugees' removal to Libya occurred with full knowledge of the systematic human rights violations that migrants and asylum seekers would suffer in the recipient country. Libya is not a party to the 1951 Geneva Convention or to the ECHR, but is subject to the ICCPR and the CAT. Therefore, as far as the duty of *non-refoulement* is concerned, as accruing from the ICCPR – alongside customary international law/*jus cogens*, as the case may be – the second condition for the establishment of complicity for provision of aid and assistance should be fulfilled.

(ii) Italy's Responsibility for 'Aiding and Assisting' Libya? The Case of Push-Backs by Proxy

This Sub-section asks whether there is an autonomous basis in the law of international responsibility for holding European States accountable for complicity in human rights violations occurring in Libya even in those circumstances in which they do not directly exercise physical control over intercepted/rescued migrants. As discussed in previous Sections, the threshold for determining indirect responsibility, in particular with regard to the mental element, is significantly high.[291]

'Italy/Libya: Migrants Describe Forced Returns, Abuse: EU Should Press Italy to Halt Illegal Forced Returns to Libya' (21 September 2009), http://www.hrw.org/news/2009/09/17/italylibya-migrants-describe-forced-returns-abuse.

[290] See, eg, the Statement of the Ministry of the Interior, R Maroni.

[291] On complicity in cases of externalised migration controls, see Giuffré, 'State Responsibility beyond Borders: What Legal Basis for Italy's Push-Back to Libya?' (2012) 24 *IJRL* 692. This Sub-section is mainly taken from the following chapter: Giuffrè and Moreno-Lax 2019, n 8 above.

Therefore, in order to avoid responsibility, a State could intentionally refrain from making public pronouncements stating its will.[292] Moreover, the proposition that the threshold should not be deemed met, unless 'the relevant State, by the aid or assistance given, *intends* to facilitate the wrongful conduct',[293] would raise the bar so much as to render recourse to Article 16 ASR very difficult (emphasis added). However, if we shift attention to the more recent practice of push-backs by proxy, the fact that the funds, training, and other capacity-building activities delivered by European States to Libya are for the *explicit* purpose of 'significantly reduc[ing] migratory flows', 'combat[ing] *transit*', and 'preventing departures' means that these activities appear, on the one hand, to meet this threshold (emphasis added).[294] On the other hand, it is unlikely that Italy supported Libya with the *specific intention* to facilitate the commission of torture or other similar crimes in the readmitting country. Indeed, according to the ILC ASR Commentary,

> a State is not responsible for aid or assistance under Article 16 unless the relevant State organ intended, by the aid or assistance given, to facilitate the occurrence of the wrongful conduct and the internationally wrongful conduct is actually committed by the aided or assisted State.[295]

In any event, such a stringent approach on the mental element was expressly discussed in draft versions of Article 16 ASR, but failed to make its way into the final text.[296] So, in the absence of specific wording to that effect, following accepted rules of interpretation, it is posited that 'knowledge of' should not be confounded with 'intent to' within the ASR complicity framework. This does not amount to triggering international responsibility any time a State engages in bilateral cooperation with a third country.[297] The 'eventual possibility' that a wrongful act could derive from a State's assistance is not sufficient to establish the link between the facilitating act and the wrongful conduct.[298] Rather, in line with the ICJ's pronouncements in the *Genocide Convention Case*, it is to be proven that an accomplice State aided another country by accepting, with *knowledge* of the facts, the *serious risk* that wrongful acts would be perpetrated (emphasis added).[299] The Court ruled that

[292] On the difficulty of inferring intention, and therefore complicity, from public statements, see Graefrath 1996, n 268 above, 375–76.

[293] Draft articles on Responsibility of States for Internationally Wrongful Acts, with commentaries, *Yearbook of the ILC 2001*, vol II, Part II, 66, para 5 (ILC ASR Commentary).

[294] Malta Declaration by the members of the European Council on the external aspects of migration: addressing the Central Mediterranean route, paras 3, 5, 6(j).

[295] ILC ASR Commentary, n 293 above, 66, para 5.

[296] Draft Art 25 referred to the intent element of the aiding State as 'in order to enable', while Draft Art 27 spoke of 'for the commission of'. But none of the formulas were retained in the end.

[297] Nolte and Aust 2009, n 269 above, 14.

[298] 'Report of the ILC on the work of its thirtieth session', *Yearbook of the ILC 1978*, Vol II (Part II) 49–50, para 18.

[299] See *Genocide Convention Case*, above n 264, paras 432 and 420–424.

> there [was] no doubt that the conduct of an organ or a person furnishing aid or assistance to a perpetrator of the crime of genocide [could] not be treated as complicity in genocide unless at the least that organ or person *acted knowingly*, that is to say, in particular, was *aware of the specific intent* (*dolus specialis*) of the principal perpetrator (emphasis added).[300]

In the instances of the Italy–Libya MoU in 2017, the wealth of reliable sources available on the prevailing situation in this country, coupled with the specific demands placed on Libya to stop irregular migration, could be said to reach the benchmark of required knowledge. The issue is to ascertain whether the assisting (European) State(s) were/are aware that their assistance may, foreseeably, be used to perform wrongful conduct, but it is not necessary that the aid provided be specifically directed towards, or be essential to, the commission of the violation, provided that it 'contributed significantly to [it]'.[301] So, while it is not for the complicit State to assume *any* chance of the harmful use of its aid,[302] the plausible likelihood that the aid will be wrongfully utilised will activate Article 16 ASR. In our case, the fact that retention (or 'accommodation') of those concerned in Libya in sub-standard conditions is being presented as a life-saving mechanism sparing the dangers of maritime journeys is no excuse, where the dangerous situation which they (will) remain exposed to on dry land is 'well-known and easy to verify on the basis of multiple sources'.[303] In line with the Genocide case, it could be argued that Italy 'acted knowingly, that is to say, in particular, was aware of the specific intent (dolus specialis) of [Libya] the principal perpetrator.'[304] However, it cannot be neglected that the EU has also expressly condemned the human rights abuses taking place in Libya, thus sending an indication of the lack of specific intent on the part of the EU and its Member States to facilitate the commission of such crimes.[305]

The second condition foreseen in Article 16(b) ASR requires a commonality of obligations between both cooperating parties for complicity to be established, which may be problematic in certain respects. The point is to prevent the assisting State from 'do[ing] by another State what it cannot do by itself' without infringing international law.[306] Libya is not a party to the 1951 Geneva

[300] ibid, para 412.

[301] ILC ASR Commentary, n 293 above, 66, para 5. See also J Crawford, *The International Law Commission's Articles on State Responsibility: Introduction, Text and Commentaries* (CUP, 2002) 149.

[302] ibid, para. 4.

[303] *Hirsi v Italy*, above n 5, para 131.

[304] *Genocide Convention Case*, above n 264.

[305] Joint Statement on the Migrant Situation in Libya, issued by the African Union – EuropeanV Union Summit of 29 – 30 November 2017, http://www.consilium.europa.eu/media/31871/33437-prlibya20statement20283020nov2010. pdf, On lack of complicity by Italy, see A Skordas, 'A "blind spot" in the migration debate? International responsibility of the EU and its Member States for cooperating with the Libyan coastguard and militias', *EUMigrationLAwBlog.eu* (30 January 2018), http://eumigrationlawblog.eu/a-blind-spot-in-the-migration-debate-international-responsibility-of-the-eu-and-its-member-states-for-cooperating-with-the-libyan-coastguard-and-militias/.

[306] ILC ASR Commentary, n 293 above, 66, para 6.

Convention or to the ECHR. But, as Italy, it is subject to the ICCPR and the CAT.[307] Therefore, as discussed in the previous Sub-section, as far as duties of *non-refoulement* are concerned, the second condition for the establishment of complicity for provision of aid and assistance should be fulfilled.

D. Contactless Controls, Containment of Migratory Flows, and Independent Responsibility

European States may incur independent/principal responsibility for their own acts that are constitutive of a breach of international obligations. The general rule under international law (codified in Article 47 ASR) is that 'each State is separately responsible for the conduct attributable to it and that responsibility is not diminished or reduced by the fact that one or more other States are also responsible for the same act'.[308]

Adopting an approach similar to that taken in the cases of *Ilascu* or *Catan* with regard to the sponsorship by Russia of the violations perpetrated by the local authorities of the separatist regime of Transnistria,[309] it is advanced that European countries remain accountable for their support to third countries of transit, such as Libya, in their actions of 'consensual containment'. The funding, training, and equipping dispensed under bilateral arrangements, expressly conditioned on the Mediterranean partner's 'managing' migratory flows and impeding exit for transit towards Europe, can be said to constitute a form of 'decisive influence' akin to that at play in *Ilascu* and *Catan*.[310] Moreover, the number of 'strategic priorities' which stem from the long list of agreements and MoU between Italy and Libya can be considered – using the words of the ECtHR – as 'the formulation of essential policy'.[311]

In *Ilascu*, the Court argued that – both before and after 5 May 1998 (when the ECHR came into force with regard to Russia), in the security zone controlled by the Russian peacekeeping forces – the Moldavian Republic of Transdniestria (the MRTegime, set up in 1991–1992) survived by virtue of the military, economic, financial and political support supplied by Russia.[312] Given that the applicants fell under the jurisdiction of the Russian Federation for the purposes of Article 1 of the Convention, a continuous and uninterrupted link of responsibility on the part of Russia for the applicants' fate could be established. It was

[307] Libya is also party to the 1969 Convention Governing the Specific Aspects of Refugee Problems in Africa – which commits Libya to guaranteeing protection to people undergoing persecution and fleeing from dangerous geographical zones. Also, several agreements had been concluded between Italy and Libya that commit them to act in compliance with the UN Charter and the Universal Declaration of Human Rights (UDHR).

[308] ILC ASR Commentary, n 293 above, 104, para 1.

[309] *Ilascu v Moldova and Russia*, above n 237; *Catan v Moldova and Russia*, Apps no 43370/04, 8252/05 and 18454/06 (19 October 2012).

[310] *Catan*, ibid, para 111; *Ilascu*, n 237 above, para 392.

[311] *Jaloud v the Netherlands*, App no 47708/08 (20 November 2014) para 63.

[312] *Ilascu v Russia and Moldovia*, above n 237, para 392.

therefore of little consequence that since 5 May 1998 the agents of the Russian Federation had not taken part directly in the actions complained of in the application. According to the Court, Russia not only made no attempt to put an end to the violations against the applicants, but it also did not take any measures to *prevent* such infringements of the Convention.[313]

While the influence exercised by European States falls short of military occupation or direct control, it is nonetheless decisive enough to determine the course of events to the extent that, without such massive support, the third country would not stop migrants on their way to the EU (to the EU's advantage). For example, the Libyan coastguard performed 19,452 pull-backs in 2017 on Italy's behalf.[314] Beyond the Libya case, the EU–Turkey deal, discussed in Chapter three, is a *sine qua non* for the sustained reduction of irregular maritime traffic through the Aegean border, without which we would predictably see a rise in flows through that route, like prior to March 2016. It is the continued support and commitment to the EU–Turkey deal by the EU Member States and Turkey that enables the significant reduction of arrivals witnessed in Greece through the Eastern Mediterranean from March 2016 onward, as per the Commission's own evaluation.[315] This 'decisive influence' would constitute, it is posited, a form of indirect but nonetheless effective control that amounts to 'jurisdiction' under Article 1 ECHR, thus triggering the responsibility of European States under the Convention in case of human rights violations.

The issue of jurisdiction and exercise of border controls outside the territory of the destination State is addressed in *Kebe and Others v Ukraine*.[316] The case concerns three individuals from Ethiopia and Eritrea who covertly boarded a commercial vessel flying the flag of the Republic of Malta with the intention to seek asylum abroad. On 24 February 2012, sometime before the vessel anchored in the port of Mykolayiv, in Ukraine, the head of the Border Control Service in the Southern Region of Ukraine was informed that there were two nationals of Eritrea and a national of Ethiopia on-board the vessel and that they might require international protection.[317]

On 25 February 2012, Ukrainian border guards boarded the Maltese vessel – in agreement with the captain – and met with the applicants. The Court decided to strike the case out of the list insofar as it concerned the second and the third applicants, as one died after lodging the application and the other voluntarily returned to his home country. It is here only worth noting that the border guards arguably tried to discourage the first applicant from applying for international

[313] ibid, paras 392–394.

[314] For updated figures on the number of rescued/intercepted migrants and bodies retrieved at sea, see https://www.iom.int/sites/default/files/situation_reports/file/IOM-Libya-Maritime-Update-Libyan-25Oct-28Nov.pdf.

[315] Fifth report on the Progress made in the implementation of the EU–Turkey Statement, 2 March 2017, COM(2017) 204.

[316] *Kebe and Others v Ukraine*, App no 12552/1 (12 April 2017) paras 75–77.

[317] ibid, paras 17–20.

protection in Ukraine. When carrying out border checks, Ukrainian border guards gave him no information about asylum procedures, and also told him that they could not accept asylum applications under domestic law, and that there was no impediment to removing him to any other country, including that of his origin, before an appeal was determined. As the risk of being brought back to a country where he arguably faced treatment contrary to Article 3 of the Convention was real, imminent and foreseeable, the Court found a violation of the right to an effective remedy in conjunction with Article 3.[318]

Ukraine therefore exercised jurisdiction under Article 1 of the Convention over the applicant from the moment the border authorities met him on-board a Maltese vessel, to the extent that the matter concerned his possible admission to Ukraine and the exercise of related rights and freedoms set forth in the Convention. In denying him leave of entry, Ukraine exercised, through State agents, its sovereign powers to control the entry of aliens into its territory, despite the fact that this occurred on-board a vessel flying a flag of another State.

Likewise, in *ND and NT v Spain*, the Court of Strasbourg confirms that if border guards prevent an individual from entering the State's territory, there is still an obligation upon the State to ensure access to asylum procedures and protection from collective push-backs.[319] Therefore, even if the border crossing had been placed at the Spanish frontier or on Moroccan territory, the applicants – who were trying to cross into Ceuta and Melilla – would still have fallen under Spain's jurisdiction as they were under the continuous and exclusive control of Spanish authorities.[320] As in *Amuur v France* – where the Court held that States cannot deny access to asylum in the international zones of airports[321] – the *ND and NT* case shows that States cannot instrumentally move their borders to address a particular situation.[322]

[318] ibid, paras 104–108.

[319] *ND and NT v Spain*, above n 219. For a note on the case, see A Pijnenburg, 'Is *ND and NT v Spain* the new *Hirsi*?' *EJIL Talk* (17 October 2017), https://www.ejiltalk.org/is-n-d-and-n-t-v-spain-the-new-hirsi/.

[320] ibid, para 51. An amendment to the Spanish Aliens Act, adopted in March 2015, provided the possibility of 'rejection at the border' for persons intercepted at the border between Morocco and the enclaves of Ceuta and Melilla, to avoid their irregular entry in Spain. While condemned by the ECtHR, Spain has restated that it would not revise its legislation, and appealed the decision before the Grand Chamber of the Court. See *ND and NT v Spain* (above n 219), 6 April 2018, Third party intervention: the AIRE Centre, Amnesty International, DCR, ECRE and ICJ, https://www.asylumlawdatabase.eu/en/content/nd-and-nt-v-spain-application-nos-867515-and-869715-third-party-intervention-aire-centre.

[321] *Amuur v France*, above n 230. Mutatis mutandis, the Court of Strasbourg has recognized the duty of States to apply the Convention, in particular the safeguard of Article 5, also in other cases concerning retention of foreign nationals in transit zones of airports. See, eg, *Riad e Idiab v Belgium*, App nos 29787/03 and 29810/03 (24 Apr 2008); *Nolan and K. c. Russia*, App no 2512/04 (12 February 2009); *Z.A. c. Russia ZA and others v Russia*, App nos 61411/15, 61420/15, 61427/15, 3028/16 (28 March 2017); *Shamsa v Poland*, App nos 45355/99 and 45357/99 (27 November 2003)

[322] *ND and NT v Spain*, above n 219, para 53. Nevertheless, it has been reported that in August 2018, Spain collectively expelled a group of 116 persons to Morocco within 24 hours, relying on a

What is more, 'it is not open to a Contracting State to enter into an agreement with another State which conflicts with its obligations under the Convention'.[323] And '[t]his principle carries all the more force [when] the absolute and fundamental nature of the right not to be subject to ... grave and irreversible harm [is at stake]' – as is the case in Libya and Turkey.[324] But not only acts of (active/passive) wrongdoing are covered; also the 'power to prevent' the abuse in question may lead to responsibility being engaged in case of an omission to act.[325] Against a background of decisive influence, being in a position to avoid the possibility of ill-treatment from materialising is relevant under Article 1 ECHR.[326] In these circumstances, the Convention provisions apply 'to a State *wherever* it may be acting or *may be able to act* in ways appropriate to meeting the obligations in question' (emphasis added).[327] The duty to prevent is activated 'the instant the State learns of, or should normally have learned of, the existence of a serious risk' of a violation.[328]

Knowingly entering into an agreement with unsafe countries, such as Libya and Turkey (as discussed in Chapter three) where risks of (direct and indirect) *refoulement*, in both its material and procedural facets, are blatant and reliably documented, with the result of heightening the possibility of an Article 3 ECHR violation instead of diminishing or avoiding it, should be adjudged to trigger the action of the ECHR.[329] The eventual violation that may result from the combination of support delivered by European countries, on one hand, and direct action in contravention of the relevant standards by the third countries, on the other hand, will be *jointly* attributable to the third countries and the European State for their independent contributions to a single harmful outcome. This would be in line with the *Corfu Channel Case*, where the damage caused to British vessels ensued from the concurrent effect of a third State laying underwater mines (possibly Yugoslavia) and the omission of Albania, which failed to

1992 bilateral readmission agreement. See Spanish Commission of Aid to Refugees (CEAR), 'CEAR muestra su preocupación tras la expulsión "acelerada" de las 116 personas migrantes que llegaron ayer a Ceuta', 23 August 2018, https://bit.ly/2o2SgQf.

[323] *Al-Saadoon v UK*, above n 212, para 138.

[324] ibid.

[325] For this same approach, see The Hague Court of Appeal, *Mustafic-Mujic v The Netherlands*, [2011] LJN: BR 5386; and *Nuhanovic v The Netherlands*, [2011] LJN: BR 5388 (both confirmed by the Supreme Court, in *The Netherlands v Nuhanovic* and *The Netherlands v Mustafic-Mujic*, [2014] 53 ILM 512). For analysis, see Dannenbaum, 'Killings in Srebrenica, Effective Control, and the Power to Prevent Unlawful Conduct' (2012) 61 *ICLQ* 713, pointing out at 723 how the ICJ allows for such an interpretation in the *Genocide Convention Case*, above n 264, para 401.

[326] Brownlie speaks of 'the power to take executive action' in Brownlie 2008, n 58 above, 299.

[327] *Mutatis mutandis*, *Genocide Convention Case*, above n 264, 183.

[328] ibid, para 431. The rule has been endorsed by the ICJ on several occasions. Besides the *Genocide Convention Case*, above n 264, see also *Order on the Request for the Indication of Provisional Measures, Case Concerning the Application of the International Convention on the Elimination of All Forms of Racial Discrimination (Georgia v Russia)*, 15 October 2008, ICJ Gen List no 140.

[329] *Hirsi*, above n 5, para 131; *MSS v Belgium and Greece*, above n 286, paras 366–367.

warn about their presence and ended up being reponsible for the entirety of the composite wrongdoing.[330]

Several instances of cooperation between Italy and Libya have been recorded since 2017. Emblematic is the *SeaWatch* case, which was submitted to the ECtHR in May 2018.[331] The dangerous coordination between the two State authorities led to the death of a number of migrants at sea and the unsafe removal of some of the boat passengers to Libya on 6 November 2017. When interceptions and pull-backs were not carried out directly by Libyan authorities off African shores, Italy intervened by undertaking overall SAR control and delegating push-backs to Libya. Although Italy's involvement in the coordination of rescue operations in the Central Mediterranean has been explicitly encompassed in the MoU signed on 2 February 2017 with the Libyan Government of National Accord, such a practice has been known for long time, thus making Italy 'the only country that provides SAR to the area sitting next to territorial waters of Libya',[332] and coordinatesLibyan coastguard's operational response in Central Mediterranean. Practice shows that the Italian MRCC not only sends instructions to all vessels on the high sea that might potentially intervene in rescue operations, thereby producing 'effects outside [Italian] territory',[333] but it also intervenes directly by stationing its military and naval assets in Libya to both offer logistical support and coordination of the joint activities of the Libyan Coastguard and Navy and fight 'illegal migration'.[334] Therefore, Italy might be

[330] *Corfu Channel (UK v Albania) (Merits)*, 9 April 1949, ICJ Gen List no 1, 17–18 and 22–23. See also A Nollkamper, 'Introduction', in A Nollkaemper and I Plakokefalos (eds), *Principles of Shared Responsibility in International Law: An Appraisal of the State of the Art* (CUP, 2014) 13; and M den Heijer, 'Issues of Shared Responsibility before the European Court of Human Rights' *SHARES Research Paper 06* (2012) ACIL 2012-04, 18–19.

[331] *SS and Others v Italy*, App no 21660/18 (pending). To read more on the facts of this case, see, https://www.theguardian.com/world/2018/may/08/italy-deal-with-libya-pull-back-migrants-faces-legal-challenge-human-rights-violations.

[332] CILD, *Guidance on Rescue Operations in the Mediterranean*, https://cild.eu/wp-content/uploads/2017/07/KYR-Protection-and-Maritime-Safety_EN.pdf; see also *Human Rights Watch*, 'UE: delegare i soccorsi alla Libia significa mettere vite a repentaglio' (19 June 2017), https://www.hrw.org/it/news/2017/06/19/305148.

[333] *Drozd and Janousek v France and Spain*, App no 12747/87 (26 June 1992) para 91; *Al-Skeini v UK*, above n 212, para 133. On Italy's responsibility, see, *inter alia*, JP Gauci, 'Back to Old Tricks? Italian Responsibility for returning People to Libya?' *EJIL Talk* (June 2017), https://www.ejiltalk.org/back-to-old-tricks-italian-responsibility-for-returning-people-to-libya/#comments.

[334] The Italian mission in support of the Libyan Coastguard was approved by the Italian Parliament (Chamber of Deputies, 28 July 2017 and launched on 2 August 2017), http://www.camera.it/leg17/1132?shadow_primapagina=7161; See also, https://www.difesa.it/OperazioniMilitari/op_intern_corso/Libia_Missione_bilaterale_di_supporto_e_assistenza/Pagine/missione.aspx. See A Cammilli, 'La marina militare coordina la guardia costiera libica?', *Internazionale*, 28 March 2018, https://www.internazionale.it/bloc-notes/annalisa-camilli/2018/03/28/marina-militare-italiana-guardia-costiera-libica. On 25 July 2017, the Council of the European Union extended EUNAVFOR MED's mandate, while also amending its mandate to set up a monitoring mechanism of trainees belonging to the Libyan Coastguard. See, 'EUNAVFOR MED Operation Sophia: mandate extended until 31 December 2018'. Council of the European Union. July 2017, https://www.consilium.europa.eu/en/press/press-releases/2017/07/25/eunavformed-sophia-mandate-extended/

considered to exercise 'effective control and decisive influence' over Libyan SAR and interception operations.[335]

VIII. CONCLUDING REMARKS

Push-backs to Libya were conducted between May and November 2009 without serious consideration of both the risk of *refoulement* and the lack of effective asylum legislation in the readmitting country. Such a practice evolved in 2017 into an even more established policy of push-back by proxy through which Italy delegates to Libya the rescue/interception of migrants and refugees at sea with a view to their prompt diversion to the ports of departure. Whereas Section VII.C.(i) explores the possibility to invoke Italy's indirect liability for 'aiding and assisting' Libya, Section VII.D argues that independent responsibility under international law could potentially be invoked, especially in those cases where Italy executed interception and accompaniment operations using its own vessels, or when it exercised 'decisive influence' on Libya – via logistical assistance, coordination and instructions to facilitate push-backs by proxy. Externalisation of migration controls on the part of European States may generally entail a hazardous shift of responsibility to third countries, which are often mischaracterised as 'safe' without in fact offering asylum seekers safeguards comparable to those available within the EU.

This chapter primarily sought to demonstrate that, although 'readmission' of intercepted migrants does not readily follow from the text of bilateral agreements for technical and police cooperation or other accords on coordination of rescue operations at sea, these instruments are used to entrust a non-European third country with the command and responsibility of patrol, rescue, and removal operations, which are generally carried out in international waters or in the coastal waters of the third country itself. Since their purpose is to avoid arrivals by pushing back (either directly or indirectly) unauthorised/unwanted migrants back to the ports of departure, these activities of maritime border

In the *Chiragov v Armenia* case, the ECtHR held that 'the "NKR" and its administration survives by virtue of the military, political, financial and other support given to it by Armenia which, consequently, exercises effective control over Nagorno-Karabakh and the surrounding territories, including the district of Lachin. The matters complained of therefore come within the jurisdiction of Armenia for the purposes of Article 1 of the Convention.' See *Chigarov and Others v Armenia*, App no 13216/05 (16 June 2015) paras 176 and 186.

The level of 'high degree of integration' between the authorities of the two States has also been confirmed by the judge of Catania adjudicating on a case concerning the rescue ship *Open Arms* of the NGO Proactiva. The judge clearly affirms that the interventions of Libyan vessels occur 'under the aegis of the Italian navy' to whom coordination of SAR missions is essentially entrusted. See *Decreto di convalida e di sequestro preventivo*, Tribunale di Catania, Sezione del Giudice per le indagini preliminari, 27 March 2018. See, F De Vittor, 'Soccorso in mare e favoreggiamento dell'immigrazione irregolare: sequestro e dissequestro della nave Open Arms', (2018) 2 *Diritti Umani e Diritto Internazionale* 443–452.

[335] On this point, see *Catan v Moldova and Russia*, above n 309, para 122.

control tend to prevent *ab initio* European States from exercising jurisdiction. However, jurisdiction has been established by the ECtHR in push-back cases on the high seas – because of *de jure* and *de facto* control exercised by Italy – and a number of arguments have been put forward in the previous Section to expound why Italian jurisdiction would be engaged also in cases of push-back by proxy. Italy indeed continues to exercise 'decisive influence and effective control' over both Libyan SAR and interception operations.

The 2009 push-backs of migrants and refugees do not have a clear legal basis, as can be seen in the incongruous arguments provided by the Italian government. Nonetheless, their content is vague enough to open the way to some kind of collaboration between Italy and Libya in what they call 'anti-immigration activity', or 'fight against illegal immigration'. This study has two main findings. First, it proves that the wide-ranging series of accords between Italy and Libya – including the 2007 and 2009 agreements for technical and police cooperation, the 2008 Partnership Treaty, and the 2017 accords and MoU – constitute the multifaceted legal and political scaffold supporting the practice of interdiction and deflection of undocumented migrants and refugees to their ports of embarkation. Second, the actual implementation of these arrangements can hamper refugees' access to protection – the overarching concept which includes *non-refoulement* and access to asylum procedures and effective remedies in the European State that the intercepted refugee strove to reach.

Bearing in mind that due diligence and the customary principle of safety of life at sea should always be respected, in both the push-back and pull-back cases, migrants and refugees interdicted/rescued either by Italian authorities or by Libyan vessels under Italian coordination were not granted the right to access onshore asylum procedures, or to challenge the refusal of entry, but were taken on-board in international waters in order to be removed directly to Libya, where well-founded reasons existed to presume that their life and liberty would be threatened.[336] The wide availability of reliable information describing the miserable human rights situation of migrants and refugees in the readmitting country, corroborates the view that Italy ought to know the conditions of migrants and refugees in Libya. When migration controls are entirely shifted to a third country, no chance exists for a European State to monitor the fate of intercepted migrants and refugees. Therefore, this chapter shows how international human rights law complements State obligations under the law of the sea by '[importing] an additional legal meaning to the term "place of safety" for the disembarkation of rescued migrants.'[337]

[336] Although States have the sovereign right to decide the forms of entry and stay in their territory, it is nevertheless important that stringent checks at the border and interception measures do not obstruct the identification of those with genuine international protection claims. See V Türk and F Nicholson, 'Refugee Protection in International Law: An Overall Perspective' in E Feller, F Nicholson, and V Türk (eds), *UNHCR Refugee Protection in International Law* (CUP, 2003).

[337] E Papastavridis, 'Rescuing Migrants at Sea: The Responsibility of States under International Law' (Academy of Athens, 27 September 2011) 38, http://papers.ssrn.com/sol3/papers.cfm?abstract_

International human rights bodies have made it clear that extraterritorial jurisdiction does not rely on competence and legal entitlements only, but on factual authority and control also,[338] even in cases where bilateral agreements tend to blur jurisdiction and responsibility by displacing the theatre of action beyond territorial frontiers. Considering that very complex operational situations may be put into motion, a case-by-case approach is the most suitable strategy to determine the degree of involvement of a European State in the performance of external migration controls. Core norms under the law of the sea, search and rescue conventions, international refugee and human rights law shall be applicable in every offshore operational context, regardless of whether third countries rescue, patrol, and divert intercepted migrants and refugees autonomously, or in conjunction with a European State.

id=1934352. To read more on the interplay between human rights law and law of the sea, see E Papastavridis, 'European Convention on Human Rights and the Law of the Sea: The Court of Strasbourg in Unchartered Waters?' in M Fitzmaurice and P Merkouris (eds), *The Interpretation and Application of the European Convention of Human Rights* (Martinus Nijhoff, 2013).

[338] Milanovic 2008, n 140 above, 428.

6

Conclusion

I. ON THE INTERTWINEMENT OF AGREEMENTS LINKED TO READMISSION AND REFUGEE RIGHTS

A CENTRAL CONCERN of this work has been to examine whether the implementation of *agreements linked to readmission* may hamper refugees' access to protection in Europe. These agreements include a plethora of bilateral accords concluded by European States with third countries both for smoothing the removal of irregular migrants with no right to remain in the territory, and for preventing arrivals by outsourcing or off-shoring migration controls. These final pages will therefore draw together all the main findings and suggestions proposed.

The central contention of this work is that States increasingly tend to connect asylum with the fight against irregular immigration, thus often myopically adopting asylum measures driven by strict border-control considerations. Therefore, as knots on a thread, readmission agreements, diplomatic assurances, and agreements for technical and police cooperation have been analysed in sequence both to shed light on their main features, and to investigate whether their implementation can undermine refugees' access to protection. 'Protection' is hitherto understood as the combination of the right to *non-refoulement* – a foundational principle of refugee law – and two correlated procedural entitlements, namely, the right to access asylum procedures and the right to an effective remedy, before removal.

In reconstructing the meaning of core refugee rights, Chapter two explored, through the lens of international human rights and refugee law, the content and scope of the relevant protection standards binding European States each time that they deal with refugees' admission and readmission. Reference was also made to EU law, especially the Charter of Fundamental Rights, which, since the entry into force of the Lisbon Treaty lies at the heart of the Union human rights paradigm. Because of the vastness of the issue concerning the obligations of States under international and European law in the frame of immigration controls, the emphasis of Chapter two drew on the right to *non-refoulement*, and the right to access asylum procedures and effective remedies before removal. These rights are described as overarching terms whose full meaning can be better shaped through the use of different international refugee and human rights instruments, which require a European State to comply with a number of obligations every time it decides to remove an asylum seeker apprehended either within the country or at its borders. However, Chapter two also contributes to the discussion on the extraterritorial applicability of *non-refoulement*, showing how this principle can be invoked outside the territorial jurisdiction of the destination State, including in those more recent cases of 'contactless' migration controls at sea where interception and rescue operations are conducted by third countries with the massive support of European States. Moreover, Chapter two describes the right to an effective remedy as an entitlement requiring independent and rigorous scrutiny of the applicant's claim that a real risk exists of serious harm in the readmitting country. In order to be effective, access to the territory should thus be ensured, whether asylum seekers are apprehended at the borders, or intercepted/rescued beyond borders. Therefore, the lack in international law of an express right to asylum is compensated for by the evolution of the European case law on effective remedy, which reveals the interrelatedness of *non-refoulement* and the right to access fair and effective procedures before formal or informal readmission takes place.

With regard to the question on the relationship between agreements linked to readmission and the removal decision, this work concludes that none of the three selected categories of bilateral arrangements (standard readmission agreements, diplomatic assurances on the fair and humane treatment of the deportee, and agreements for technical and police cooperation) constitutes *per se* the legal basis for the transfer of irregular migrants and asylum seekers to third countries. Decisions to remove an individual, refuse asylum, or exclude her from protection are not taken by States by means of one of the selected agreements linked to readmission. However, they all facilitate the enforcement of the removal orders and, to a greater or lesser extent, influence the choice of the host State, or intended host State, to transfer unauthorised/unwanted foreigners to the authorities of a third country, thus hampering, in certain circumstances, refugees' access to protection; that is to say the combination of the right to *non-refoulement* and the right to access asylum procedures and effective remedies.

The quick answer to the question on the compatibility of the *text* of agreements linked to readmission with refugee rights is that no noteworthy issue of inconsistency seems to rise. Readmission agreements constitute purely administrative tools serving the purpose of smoothing the final stage of the removal procedure for irregular migrants, rejected refugees, and asylum seekers whose claims will be examined elsewhere. They do not define criteria for the legality of a person's presence in the host State, as this assessment is made by national authorities in compliance with domestic administrative law and the procedural safeguards enshrined in international (and EU) law. Similarly, diplomatic assurances for the fair and humane treatment of the deportee tend to be very detailed, especially when formalised within written standardised MoUs. Finally, 'readmission' of intercepted migrants and refugees does not readily follow from the text of bilateral agreements for technical and police cooperation, which aim to combat irregular migration to Europe through a system of cooperation and joint patrols with the country of embarkation.

The seeming compatibility of the text of agreements linked to readmission with refugee rights is inherent to their personal scope of application. Indeed, these instruments are specifically designed to tackle only the removal of *irregular migrants*. However, mixed flows are a reality. Asylum seekers can be deported by means of a readmission agreement on a 'safe third country' ground, or can travel on-board the same boat along with other undocumented migrants intercepted at sea. In practice, the lives of these two vulnerable categories of foreigners are so intertwined that any analysis limited to assessing the compatibility with refugee rights of the *text* of agreements linked to readmission – without considering how their *actual implementation* also involves people seeking asylum – would be an insufficient and short-sighted one.

Therefore, with regard to the central question on the impact on refugee rights of agreements linked to readmission, three key points need to be highlighted here. First, the fact that readmission agreements do not offer the legal basis for removal decisions is not, in my view, the end of the story. Indeed, in situations of informal border controls and/or emergency, the existence of a *readmission agreement* may boost the use of swift and accelerated identification and removal procedures with the risk of transferring asylum seekers, as unauthorised migrants, to allegedly 'safe third countries'. Second, the actual negotiation of *diplomatic assurances* in concrete situations might not only violate the principle of confidentiality of asylum applications, but it can also influence removal decisions to countries where there is a risk of torture and inhuman and degrading treatment. Access to protection could therefore be hampered, in particular if assurances are exchanged with regard to asylum seekers sent to 'safe third countries' before an examination of their asylum claims is completed. Third, push-backs and push-backs by proxy through the implementation of bilateral *agreements for technical and police cooperation* aiming to intercept and divert migrants and refugees back to 'unsafe' countries of embarkation – before they are able to enter the territorial jurisdiction of a European State – *de facto* undermine refugees' access to protection.

From the foregoing, it emerges that the enforcement of bilateral agreements linked to readmission can jeopardise the right to *non-refoulement*, the right to access asylum procedures, and the right to an effective remedy before removal. This result is not, however, uniform but assumes various degrees of intensity according to the right under consideration, the agreement at hand, as well as the time and place of application of the agreement itself – that is to say the point at which the State encounters the refugee. Therefore, examining all these accords as part of the overarching 'agreements linked to readmission' concept not only gives us the possibility of unveiling their similarities and their common purpose – namely, facilitating the removal and readmission of unauthorised/unwanted foreigners to countries of origin and transit – but also, the opportunity to disclose their divergences and their altered paths. At the same time, getting to the end of this work, I also note that there is more communality between these three categories of agreements than expected, in particular with regard to the importance they place on *bilateral* relations. Such commonality includes the incentives the two involved parties have to persuade the partner State to negotiate and/or to comply with the commitments taken; the modality of negotiation/conclusion of the accords, which even more frequently denies parliamentary scrutiny and public accountability; and finally, the detrimental effects they might have on refugees' access to protection. Having stated that, such an impact is mutable, and as a consequence, the follow up to the analysis varies from accord to accord.

II. THE WAY FORWARD

This book does not seek to question the States' entitlement to both exercise their sovereignty and control their borders, even by means of bilateral cooperation with third countries. I rather contend that European States must always guarantee the rights of asylum seekers falling under their jurisdiction, whether they are found within their borders, at the border, or outside their borders. The contours of these rights, in their territorial and extraterritorial dimension, are explored in Chapter two (*non-refoulement* and access to asylum procedures and effective remedies). As a consequence, States should not cooperate on migration control with entities that do not abide by the law. The ECtHR emphasised this concept in *Al-Saadoon v UK* by holding that 'it is not open to a Contracting State to enter into an agreement with another State which conflicts with its obligations under the Convention.'[1]

In relation to the way forward in the removal/readmission process, and considering the different traits of the selected agreements, a number of recommendations that may help States ensure better protection of the rights of refugees subjected to a formal or informal removal decision have been put forward. First, diplomatic assurances – whether framed within MoUs or not – are not reliable when issued by governments that practice torture, have previously infringed similar undertakings, or notoriously fail to investigate the allegations of prohibited treatment against other detainees.

Second, where European States engage in the negotiation of arrangements on extraterritorial migration control with third countries, they shall ensure that sufficient guarantees toward refugees are in place. This might imply the insertion, within the text of so-called agreements for technical and police cooperation, of specific clauses designed both to exclude asylum seekers from the personal scope of application of the accords and to ensure that they can express the reasons for their fear of being removed. Such an addition might be

[1] *Al-Saadoon and Mufdhi v United Kingdom*, App no 61498/08 (30 June 2009) para 138.

insufficient where practices at variance with fundamental rights are still put in place. Moreover, *mutatis mutandis* and echoing *Al-Saadoon*, bilateral agreements designed to stem migratory flows by sea should not be negotiated with countries that produce the largest numbers of refugees, or with transit countries that are notoriously known for the poor treatment meted out to migrants and refugees on their territory.

Third, as readmission agreements do not generally include separate provisions on refugees, I consider an added value the insertion of both non-affection clauses and procedural human rights clauses creating extra safeguards for asylum seekers running the risk of being removed as unauthorised migrants, to allegedly 'safe third countries.' To this end, this work makes a number of concrete proposals of draft provisions as a platform for further discussion among legal scholars and policy-makers.

There is an inherent contradiction in concluding (or implementing) readmission agreements both with States producing refugee flows, and with unsafe countries of transit. Chapter three criticises removals of asylum seekers to so-called 'safe third countries'. However, as these policies continue to be part of both the EU and State legal framework, the insertion of non-affection clauses and itemised procedural human rights clauses within the text of future bilateral readmission agreements should be positively considered if we want to see them more as effective conditionality tools. Despite the costs deriving from a drafting process that gives centrality to human rights, I argue that the alternative of incurring international responsibility for violating the *non-refoulement* obligation following the implementation of a readmission agreement would definitively be more troubling. Beyond enhancing legal certainty for governments and frontier authorities, non-affection clauses and human rights procedural safeguards would, moreover, present the advantage of making fundamental rights part of ordinary business and bilateral cooperation, rather than principles merely subject to specialised human rights instruments, thereby emphasising the implicit acceptance by both parties, during removal operations, of a 'human rights *acquis*'.

Chapter four involves diplomatic assurances within the broad category of agreements linked to readmission. The bombing attacks in September 2001 and July 2005 constituted a turning point in the strategic approach of the US, the UK, and their allies more generally, to national security, by reinforcing cooperation with countries of origin of 'dangerous radicals'. However, I am of the view that balancing arguments weighing up national security and the rights of foreigners should not be used to excuse derogations from fundamental human rights, such as *non-refoulement* to torture and inhuman treatment.[2] Moreover,

[2] On this point, see GS Goodwin-Gill, 'Current Challenges in Refugee Law' in JP Gauci, M Giuffré and L Tsourdi, *Forced Migration(s): Critical Perspectives on Refugee Law* (Martinus Nijhoff Publishers, 2014) 19.

as earlier explained, I question the reliability of diplomatic assurances issued by governments that practise torture against detainees, even if the deportee has been elevated to a case of high diplomatic significance. In a context in which the removal of suspected terrorists to unsafe countries has become highly a politicised issue, likely to be subjected to electoral interests myopically pandering to the xenophobic or panic-stricken reactions of public opinion, restating the salience of human rights as justiciable obligations becomes all the more urgent.

Chapter four also discusses a worrisome dimension of the 'deportation with assurances' scheme, namely that States see as pointless requesting assurances against torture from countries that do not publicly practise it. In the vicious circle created by security-related memoranda, torture becomes, therefore, the prerequisite for keeping out certain countries from the arena of cooperation on the safe removal of third country nationals, but at the same time, and paradoxically, the *conditio sine qua non* for this cooperation. Just as Prometheus's liver is eaten by a giant eagle all day and becomes whole again during the night in an endless cycle, the dynamic of diplomatic assurances plus torture appears hard to break through.

Chapter five collects and analyses both instances of State practice and the agreements for technical and police cooperation, taking Italy and Libya push-back and push-back by proxy policies as an emblematic case study. Such a review is not only of value in itself, but it also can serve as a point of reference in similar cases for courts and tribunals, as well as legal practitioners and policy-makers, even outside the European geographical context. Bilateral agreements to set up joint offshore migration patrols or remote cooperation aimed at shifting rescue/interception (and therefore diversion) to third countries have become increasingly attractive because of the presumption that States can be divested of their refugee and human rights law obligations by moving beyond their territorial frontiers. However, in light of the current drive toward reinvigoration of these cooperation agreements, this work aims to enhance European States' awareness that they cannot be divested of both their previously-contracted human rights obligations and their international responsibility (either direct or indirect) every time they offshore, or outsource, migration controls to the authorities of a third State. This applies even when such a shift occurs on the basis of long distance 'influence' on the third country (through technical, logistical, economic support), which is so decisive to constitute *de facto* control.

Considering the role that law can play in promoting refugee rights, the suggestions developed throughout this work can foster continuous progress in refugee protection and improve the understanding of readmission agreements, diplomatic assurances, and agreements for technical and police cooperation, used to remove unwanted/unauthorised aliens. I am confident the analysis developed in this work with regard to a number of case studies can be extended to the same categories of agreements negotiated by destination States, within and outside Europe, with other third countries of origin or transit.

This work also showed that lack of transparency is problematic both at the supranational and national level. Chapter three revealed how informalisation of EU agreements linked to readmission – negotiated outside the procedural framework provided by Article 218 of the TFEU – enhances legal uncertainty because of the lack of sufficient procedural guarantees, thereby depriving individuals of the possibility to enforce their rights.[3] Likewise, interstate agreements concerning the readmission of migrants, deportation of undesirable aliens, and technical and police cooperation on migration control have often not been made public or have not followed the parliamentary scrutiny for approval. The lack of control on the terms of the accords impedes a proper democratic accountability and judicial oversight. This fosters a system where the legislator is by-passed in favour of the executive,[4] the operability of the agreements is subject to the health of diplomatic relations, and responsibilities and procedural safeguards are diluted, with a heightened risk of violations for apprehended migrants and refugees. While formal requests for access to international agreements have been made to the Ministries of the Interior and Foreign Affairs, some of them have been rejected.[5] Of relevance to this work are, for instance, the acts concerning the implementation of the 2017 MoU between Italy and Libya.[6] However, access to these documents has been denied on the vague ground that their leaking could jeopardise the relations between the two involved countries.[7] In the case of the cooperation agreement between Italy and Niger, in contrast, the Italian Administrative Tribunal ordered the Ministry of Foreign Affairs – which had previously refused to disclose the content of the act – to publish the accord.[8] Access to these bilateral agreements concerning migration control, international relations, and cooperation with third countries would be in compliance with, *inter alia*, the principle of equality, impartiality, and efficiency in the use of public resources. Moreover, for international agreements to produce legal effects they should be made public in order to place them under democratic control at a time in which crucial international relations issues –

[3] Key is the EU–Turkey deal and the ensuing annulment cases before the CJEU where the Court itself considered to lack competence to adjudicate the case. P, Joined Cases C-208/17, C-209/17, and C-210/17, ECLI:EU:C:2018:705. See Chapter 3 for further details. See also Wessel 2018, n 6 below, 21; S Carrera, *Implementation of EU Readmission Agreements: Identity, Determination, Dilemmas and the Blurring of Rights* (Springer Open, 2016) 47.

[4] R Wessel, Draft paper, '"Soft" International Agreements in EU External Relations', presented at the ECPR SGEU Conference, *Hard and Soft Law in the European Union* (Paris, 13–15 June 2018) 22. See also P Garcia Andrade, 'The Role of the European Parliament in the Adoption of Non-Legally Binding Agreements with Third Countries' in J Santos Vara and SR Sánchez-Tabernero (eds), *The Democratization of EU International Relations Through EU Law* (Routledge, 2018) 121.

[5] See, eg, the appeals brought by ASGI lawyers against first instance rejection by the Italian Ministries of the Interior and Foreign Affairs. These requests have been made under the Freedom of Information Act (FOIA), Legislative Decree no 97 (2016).

[6] See Chapter 5 of this book for further details on this MoU.

[7] Appeal before the Italian *Conseil d'Etat (Consiglio di Stato)* is still pending.

[8] Judgment no 5606/2018, Administrative Tribunal of Lazio, 28 September 2018, https://www.asgi.it/wp-content/uploads/2018/11/sentenza-16-novembre-niger-foia.pdf.

which have an impact on the fundamental rights of individuals – are increasingly dealt with by administrative decisions, which supplant the traditional legislative and political *iter*.[9]

Continuing to dig deeper into this topic, and as a next step, I identify four strands of enquiry on issues that remain unresolved in this book, or continue to be unsettled in international law. First, the right to asylum, meaning a right to be granted asylum, remains a highly contested issue in international law, demanding new and more enlightened research, which is able to navigate the complexities of different legal regimes, national and international courts' rulings, and State practice, to go beyond narrowly constructed notions of protection. Second, scholars should continue exploring the concrete meaning of the 'effective control' element as a facet of the concept of jurisdiction. Such a study would help lawyers, judges, and State authorities to clearly establish whether, beyond any coercive conducts imposed on a person through the use of direct force, jurisdiction under human rights law can be engaged also when less intrusive measures entailing migratory containment by means of operations of contactless control are in place. As discussed in Chapter five, the recent containment policies carried out by European States are no longer designed only to prevent arrivals, impede access to determination procedures, or deflect flows to other destinations, but rather to forestall migrants' exit, in cooperation with third countries of origin or transit, thereby nullifying the right to leave – a core right which requires further analysis.

Third, scholarship should more thoroughly address the issue of the legal status of diplomatic assurances to better comprehend why States need to frame their human rights commitments within bilateral political agreements that replicate standards that have already been enshrined within international human rights treaties; and whether such a reliance on bilateral *diplomatic* assurances can defy the protection of fundamental rights, *in primis* the prohibition of torture, included within international human rights *treaties*. Also remaining unclear is the compatibility between formal and informal bilateral agreements linked to readmission, such as those negotiated by the EU or its Member States with third countries to expedite the removal of unauthorised migrants and asylum seekers.

A fourth strand of enquiry could be directed to developing the debate on the different kinds of responsibility arising from joint operations of migration control involving States as well as international organisations to stem migratory flows and impede access in Europe. I refer in particular to the study of joint responsibility under Article 47 of ILC Articles, whereby several States can be held directly responsible for the commission of the same wrongful act. Moreover, in June 2018, the European Council proposed the setting up of 'regional

[9] ASGI, '[Tribunale Amministrativo Regionale] Lazio: l'accordo internazionale tra Italia e Niger deve essere reso pubblico' (28 November 2018), https://www.asgi.it/asilo-e-protezione-internazionale/tar-lazio-accordo-niger/.

disembarkation arrangements' (under the aegis of the IMO and UNHCR) to 'eliminate the incentive [of migrants] to embark on perilous journeys', externalise SAR services, and shift the management of border controls to third countries on the other side of the Mediterranean. Considering that these pre-emptive strategies – as well as push-backs and push-backs by proxy analysed in Chapter five – are aimed at halting migrants' departure and impeding them from reaching Europe, further studies might be directed to understand how the actual implementation of these new arrangements would comply with the right to leave and the principle of *non-refoulement*, and thus ensure access to international protection outside Europe.

To conclude, this book aims to develop the concept of *readmission* as a broad notion encompassing diverse cooperative arrangements of migration control. It reveals the baleful impact readmission policies at times may have on refugees' access to protection, in particular the right to *non-refoulement*, as well as the right to access asylum procedures and effective remedies before removal. Despite the fact that asylum is an intensely political topic and one that States tend to address through draconian measures, this work demonstrates how 'international human rights law and refugee law in fact "exercise control" over State action both within or beyond borders.' It also pulls together areas of law and policy that are generally considered neatly distinct, and therefore unrelated also in a temporal sense. Removal and readmission have indeed been studied *vis-à-vis* refugees' access to protection, in search of a link that at face value appears overly remote. However, a fully-fledged analysis, intertwining legal and practical issues, reveals how in certain operative scenarios, especially in situations of extraterritorial migration controls, admission and readmission tend to overlap and answers are more convoluted than expected. It is this complexity that invites continued scholarly and legal attention.

Bibliography

Acharya UD, 'War on Terror or Terrors Wars: The Problem in Defining Terrorism' (2009) 37(4) *Denver Journal of International Law and Policy* 653

Acosta Arcarazo D and Murphy CC (eds), *EU Security and Justice Law: After Lisbon and Stockholm* (Hart Publishing, 2014)

AdnKronos, 'Immigrati, Maroni: "L'accordo con la Libia funziona. Avanti con i respingimenti". Bruxelles: chiarimenti da Italia e Malta' (31 August 2009)

Agier M, 'Forced Migration and Asylum: Stateless Citizens Today' in Audebert C and Kamel Doraï M (eds), *Migration in a Globalized World: New Research Issues and Prospects* (Amsterdam University Press, 2010)

AIDA, 'Accelerated, prioritised and fast-track asylum procedures. Legal frameworks and practice in Europe', *ECRE* (May 2017), https://www.ecre.org/wp-content/uploads/2017/05/AIDA-Brief_AcceleratedProcedures.pdf

Algostino A, 'L'esternalizzazione soft delle frontiere e il naufragio della Costituzione', *Costituzionalismo.it* (2017)

Amnesty International, 'Turkey 2017/2018' (2018), https://www.amnesty.org/en/countries/europe-and-central-asia/turkey/report-turkey/

——, *Libya's Dark Web of Collusion: Abuses Against Europe-bound Refugees and Migrants*, 11 December 2017, https://www.amnesty.org/en/documents/mde19/7561/2017/en/

——, 'Turkey: Illegal mass returns of Syrian refugees expose fatal flaws in EU–Turkey deal' (1 April 2016), https://www.amnesty.org/en/press-releases/2016/04/turkey-illegal-mass-returns-of-syrian-refugees-expose-fatal-flaws-in-eu-turkey-deal/

——, 'L'accordo Italia – Libia in materia di immigrazione mette a rischio i diritti umani' (18 June 2012), http://www.amnesty.it/accordo-italia-libia-in-materia-di-immigrazione-mette-a-rischio-i-diritti-umani

——, 'Dichiarazione della Sezione Italiana di Amnesty International dopo i Nuovi Respingimenti di Migranti verso la Libia' (11 May 2009), http://www.amnesty.it/flex/cm/pages/ServeBLOB.php/L/IT/IDPagina/2007

——, 'Dangerous Deals: Diplomatic Assurances in Europe' (2010)

——, 'Reject rather than Regulate: Call on Council of Europe member states not to establish minimum standards for the use of diplomatic assurances in transfers to risk of torture and other ill-treatment' (2 December 2005), http://www.amnesty.org/en/library/info/IOR61/025/2005

——, 'UK: Asylum – New Figures show dramatic rise in Wrong Decisions' (2004)

Anderson D and Walker C, *Deportation with Assurances* (July 2017), https://assets.publishing.service.gov.uk/government/uploads/system/uploads/attachment_data/file/630809/59541_Cm_9462_Accessible.pdf

Arar M, 'Statement' in Meeropol R (ed), *America's Disappeared: Secret Imprisonment, Detainees, and the War on Terror* (Seven Stories Press, 2004)

ASGI, *MOU between the Italian public security department and the Sudanese national police. A reading guide* (2016), http://www.statewatch.org/news/2016/nov/asgi-italy-sudan-mou.pdf

Aust A, *Modern Treaty Law and Practice* (Cambridge University Press, 2000)

Aust HP, *Complicity and the Law of State Responsibility* (Cambridge University Press, 2011)

Baldaccini A, 'The Return and Removal of Irregular Migrants under EU Law: An Analysis of the Return Directive' (2009) 11(1) *European Journal Immigration and Law* 1

Bank R, 'Refugees at Sea; Introduction to Art. 11 of the 1951 Convention' in Zimmermann A (ed), *The 1951 Convention Relating to the Status of Refugees and its 1967 Protocol – A Commentary* (Oxford University Press, 2011)

Barnes R, 'Refugee Law at Sea', (2004) 53(1) *International Comparative Law Quarterly* 47

Bartolini G, 'Osservazioni in Margine alla "Direttiva Procedure" 2005/85/EC' in Benvenuti P (ed), *Flussi Migratori e Fruizione dei Diritti Fondamentali* (Il Sirente, 2008)

Battjes H, *European Asylum and International Law* (Martinus Niijhoff, 2006)

Bauloz C, 'The EU Migration Partnership Framework: An External Solution to the Crisis?' *EUmigrationlawblog.eu*, 31 January 2017, http://eumigrationlawblog.eu/the-eu-migration-partnership-framework-an-external-solution-to-the-crisis/

Bauloz C, Ineli-Ciger M, Singer S, Stoyanova V, *Seeking Asylum in the European Union: Selected Protection Issues Raised by the Second Phase of the Common European Asylum System* (Brill, 2016)

BBC News, 'Mediterranean migrants: Hundreds feared dead after boat capsizes' (19 April 2015, http://www.bbc.co.uk/news/world-europe-32371348

Beale J, 'The Jurisdiction of a Sovereign State' (1923) 36 *Harvard law Review* 241

Berman F, 'Jurisdiction: The State' in Capps P, Evans MD and Konstadinidis S (eds), *Asserting Jurisdiction* (Hart Publishing, 2003)

Bernhardt R, 'Evolutive Treaty Interpretation, Especially of the European Convention on Human Rights' (1999) 42 *German Yearbook of International Law* 11

Besson S, 'The Extraterritoriality of the European Convention on Human Rights: Why Human Rights Depend on Jurisdiction and What Jurisdiction Amounts to' (2012) 25(4) *Leiden Journal of International Law* 857

Betts A, 'The Global Compact on Refugees: Towards a Theory of Change?' (2018) 30(4) *International Journal of Refugee Law* 623

Beyani C, 'The Role of Human Rights Bodies in Protecting Refugees' in Bayefsky A (ed), *Human Rights, Internally Displaced Persons and Migrant Workers* (Martinus Nijhoff, 2006)

Billet C, 'EC Readmission Agreements: A Prime Instrument of the External Dimension of the EU's Fight against Irregular Immigration. An Assessment after Ten Years of Practice' (2010) 12 *European Journal of Migration and Law* 45

Biondi P, 'Italy Strikes Back Gain: A Push-Back Firsthand Account', *Border Criminologies*, 15 December 2017, https://www.law.ox.ac.uk/research-subject-groups/centre-criminology/centreborder-criminologies/blog/2017/12/italy-strikes

Blix H and Emerson JH (eds), *The Treaty Makers' Handbook* (Oceana, 1973)

Boeles P, 'Effective Legal Remedies for Asylum Seekers according to the Convention of Geneva of 1951' (1996) 43 *Netherlands International Law Review* 291

Booth J and Malik S, 'Abu Qatada arrives in Jordan after eight-year deportation battle', *The Guardian* (7 July 2013)

Borchelt G, 'The Safe Third Country Practice in the European Union: A Misguided Approach to Asylum Law and a Violation of International Human Rights Standards' (2001–2002) 33 *Columbia Human Rights Law Review* 473

Borelli S, 'Estradizione, espulsione e tutela dei diritti fondamentali' in Pineschi Laura (ed), *La tutela internazionale dei diritti umani* (Giuffré, 2006)

Borgen CJ, 'Resolving Treaty Conflicts' (2005) 37(3) *The George Washington International Law Review* 573

Bossuyt M, 'The Court of Strasbourg Acting as an Asylum Court' (2012) 8(2) *European Constitutional Law Review* 203

Bostock CMJ, 'The International Legal Obligations owed to the Asylum Seekers on the MV Tampa' (2002) 14(2)–(3) *International Journal of Refugee Law* 279

Brandl U, 'Distribution of Asylum Seekers in Europe?: Dublin II Regulation Determining the Responsibility for Examining an Asylum Application' in Urbano De Sousa CD and De Bruycker P (eds), *The Emergence of a European Asylum Policy/L'émergence d'une politique européenne d'asile* (Bruylant, 2004)

Braswell R, 'Protection against Torture in Western Security Frameworks: The Erosion of Non-*refoulement* in the UK-Libya MOU' Refugee Study Centre Working Paper vol 35, October 2006, http://www.rsc.ox.ac.uk/publications/working-papers-folder_contents/RSCworkingpaper35.pdf

Brouwer E, 'Effective Remedies in Immigration and Asylum Law Procedures: A Matter of General Principles of EU Law' in Toner H, Guild E and Baldaccini A (eds), *Whose Freedom, Security And Justice?: EU Immigration and Asylum Law and Policy* (Hart Publishing, 2007)

——, 'Immigration, Asylum and Terrorism: A Changing Dynamic Legal and Practical Developments in the EU Response to the Terrorist Attacks of 11.09' (2002) 4(4) *European Journal of Migration and Law* 399

Brownlie I, *Principles of Public International Law*, 7th edn (Oxford University Press, 2008)

Bruin R and Wouters K, 'Terrorism and the Non-derogability of *Non-refoulement*' (2003) 15(1) *International Journal of Refugee Law* 5

Butler G and Ratcovich M, 'Operation Sophia in Uncharted Waters: European and International Law Challenges for the EU Naval Mission in the Mediterranean Sea' (2016) 85(3) *Nordic Journal of International Law* 235

Buxbaum HL, 'Territory, Territoriality, and the Resolution of Jurisdictional Conflict' (2009) 57(3) *American Journal of Comparative Law* 631

Byrne R, Noll G and Vedsted-Hansen J, 'Understanding Refugee Law in an Enlarged European Union' (2004) 15(2) *European Journal of International Law* 355

——, 'Western European Asylum Policies for Export: The Transfer of Protection and Deflection Formulas to Central Europe and the Baltics' in Byrne R, Noll G and Vedsted-Hansen J (eds), *New Asylum Countries? Migration Control and Refugee Protection in Enlarged European Union* (Kluwer Law International, 2002)

Byrne R and Shacknove A, 'The "Safe Third Country" Notion in European Asylum Law' (1996) 9 *Harvard Human Rights Journal* 185

Caflish L, 'Attribution, responsibility and Jurisdiction in International Human Rights Law' (2017) *Anuario Colombiano de Derecho Internacional (ACDI)*

Cammilli A, 'La marina militare coordina la guardia costiera libica?', *Internazionale*, 28 March 2018, https://www.internazionale.it/bloc-notes/annalisa-camilli/2018/03/28/marina-militare-italiana-guardia-costiera-libica

Canestrini N, *Estradizione verso l'estero e diritti fondamentali: una analisi critica* (September 2016), http://www.canestrinilex.com/risorse/estradizione-verso-lestero-e-diritti-fondamentali-una-analisi-critica/#ixzz4NAeuQY4a

Cantor D, 'Reframing Relationships: Revisiting the Procedural Standards for Refugee Status Determination in Light of Recent Human Rights Treaty Body Jurisprudence' (2015) 34(1) *Refugee Survey Quarterly* 79

Carletti C and Borraccetti M, 'Il Global Compact sulla migrazione tra scenari internazionali e realtà europea' (2018) 2 *Freedom, Security and Justice: European Legal Studies* 7

Carlier JY, 'Droit d'asile et des Réfugiés: de la Protection Aux Droits' (2007) 332 *Recueil des Cours de l'Académie de Droit International* 9

Carrera S, *Implementation of EU Readmission Agreements* (Springer, 2016)

Carrera S and Lannoo K, 'We're in this boat together: Time for a Migration Union' CEPS Policy Insights No 2018/09, June 2018

Carrera S, Blockmans S, Cassarino JP, Gros D, and Guild E, 'The European Border and Coast Guard: Addressing Migration and Asylum Challenges in the Mediterranean?' (CEPS Task Force Report) 30 July 2017

Carrera S, den Hertog L and Parkin J, 'EU Migration Policy in the wake of the Arab Spring. What prospects for EU-Southern Mediterranean Relations?' (August 2012) MEDPRO Technical Report No 15 http://storage.globalcitizen.net/data/topic/knowledge/uploads/20130606157357056 81_Carrera,%20Sergio%20et%20al.%20(2012).EU%20Migration%20Policy%20in%20the%20Wake%20of%20the%20Arab%20Spring.pdf

Casolari F, 'L'interazione tra accordi internazionali dell'Unione europea ed accordi conclusi dagli Stati membri con Stati terzi per il contrasto dell'immigrazione e irregolare' (2018) 1 *Diritto, Immigrazione e Cittadinanza* 1

Cassarino JP, 'Return Migration and Development: The Significance of Migration Cycles' in A Triandafyllidou (ed), *Routledge Handbook of Immigration and Refugee Studies* (Routledge, 2016) 220

——, 'Dealing with Unbalanced Reciprocities: Cooperation on Readmission and Implications' in Cassarino JP (ed), *Unbalanced Reciprocities: Cooperation on Readmission in the Euro-Mediterranean Area* (Middle East Institute, 2010)

——, *Readmission Policy in the European Union*. Directorate General for Internal Policies, Policy Department C: Citizens' Rights and Constitutional Affairs, Civil Liberties, Justice and Home Affairs (Brussels, European Parliament, 2010)

——, 'Informalizing Readmission Agreements in the EU Neighborhood' (2007) 42(2) *The International Spectator* 179

Cavaioli FJ, 'Patterns of Italian Immigration to the United States' (2008) 13 *The Catholic Social Science Review* 213

Caye J, 'Report of Libyan Coast Guards attacking migrants raises concerns – via ECRE', *Forumasile*, 11 November 2016, https://forumasile.org/2016/11/11/report-of-libyan-coast-guards-attacking-migrants-raises-concerns-via-ecre/

Celletti A, 'Interview with Franco Frattini', Italian Foreign Minister (Rome, 20 March 2011), http://www.esteri.it/MAE/IT/Sala_Stampa/ArchivioNotizie/Interviste/2011/03/20110320_intfr.htm?LANG=IT

Chaloff J, 'Lessons from the Italy–Albania Readmission Agreement' in Mackenzie C (ed), *Return and Readmission to Albania: The Experience of Selected EU Member States* (August 2006), http://www.albania.iom.int/en/E-Library/Books/EC%20research.pdf

——, 'From Labour Emigration to Labour Recruitment: The Case of Italy' in *Migration for Employment: Bilateral Agreements at a Crossroads* (OECD, 2004)

Chetail V, 'Are Refugee Rights Human Rights? An Unorthodox Questioning on the Relations between Refugee Law and Human Rights Law' in R Rubio Marin (ed), *Human Rights and Immigration. Collected Courses of the Academy of European Law* (Oxford University Press, 2014) 19

——, 'Looking Beyond the Rhetoric of the Refugee Crisis: The Failed Reform of the Common European Asylum System' (2016) 5 *European Journal of Human Rights* 584

Chetail V, De Bruycker P, Maiani F, *Reforming the Common European Asylum System: The New European Refugee Law* (Brill, 2016)

Chimni BS, 'Aid, Relief, and Containment: The First Asylum Country and Beyond' (2003) 40 *International Migration* 75

CILD, *Guidance on Rescue Operations in the Mediterranean* (2017), https://cild.eu/wp-content/uploads/2017/07/KYR-Protection-and-Maritime-Safety_EN.pdf

Clapham A, 'The Changing Character of Human Rights', *European Lecture delivered at Nissan Lecture Theatre St. Antony's College*, Oxford, 12 November 2015

Clark T and Crépeau F, 'Human Rights in Asylum Sharing and Other Human Transfer Agreements' (2004) 22(2) *Netherlands Quarterly of Human Rights* 232

——, 'Mainstreaming Refugee Rights. The 1951 Refugee Convention and International Human Rights Law' (1999) 17(4) *Netherlands Quarterly of Human Rights* 379

Clayton G, '"The right to have rights": The European convention on human rights and the procedural rights of asylum seekers' in Abass A and Ippolito F (eds), *Regional approaches to the protection of asylum seekers: An international legal perspective* (Ashgate, 2014)

Coleman N, *European Readmission Policy: Third Country Interests and Refugee Rights* (Martinus Nijhoff, 2009)

Colombo A and Sciortino G, 'Italian immigration: The Origins, Nature and Evolution of Italy's Migratory Systems' (2004) 9(1) *Journal of Modern Italian Studies* 49

Condorelli L and De Sena P, 'The Relevance of the Obligations Flowing from the UN Covenant on Civil and Political Rights to US Courts Dealing with Guantanamo Detainees' (2004) 2(1) *Journal of International Criminal Justice* 107

Constantinides A, 'Transjudicial Dialogue and Consistency in Human Rights Jurisprudence: a Case Study on Diplomatic Assurances against Torture' in Fauchald OK and Nollkaemper A (eds), *The Practice of International and National Courts and the (De-)Fragmentation of International Law* (Hart Publishing, 2012)

Coppens J, 'The Law of the Sea and Human Rights in the *Hirsi Jamaa and Others v. Italy* Judgment of the European Court of Human Rights' in Haeck Y, Brems E (eds), *Human Rights and Civil Liberties in the 21st Century* (Springer, 2014)

Cornelisse G, 'Territory, Procedures and Rights: Border Procedures in European Asylum Law' (2016) 35(1) *Refugee Survey Quarterly* 74

Corthaut T, Demeyere B, Hachez N and Wouters J, 'Operationalizing the Accountability of Informal International Lawmaking' in Joost P, Wessel RA, and Wouters J (eds), *Informal International Lawmaking* (Oxford University Press, 2012) 312

Costello C, *The Human Rights of Migrants and Refugees in European Law* (OUP, 2016)

——, 'The asylum procedures directive and the proliferation of safe country practices: deterrence, deflection and the dismantling of international protection' (2005) 7(1) *European Journal of Migration and Law* 35

——, 'Courting Access to Asylum in Europe: Recent Supranational Jurisprudence Explored' (2012) 12(2) *Human Rights Law Review* 307

——, 'The Asylum Procedures Directive and the Proliferation of Safe Country Practices: Deterrence, Deflection and the Dismantling of International Protection?' (2005) 7(1) *European Journal of Migration and Law* 35

Craig P and De Burca G, *EU Law: Text, Cases and Materials*, 6th edn (Oxford University Press, 2015)

Crawford J, *The International Law Commission's Articles on State Responsibility: Introduction, Text and Commentaries* (Cambridge University Press, 2002)

——, 'Second Report on State Responsibility', *Yearbook of the ILC 1999* vol II (part I)

Crawford J and Koskenniemi M (eds), *The Cambridge Companion to International Law* (CUP, 2012)

Crock M, 'In the Wake of Tampa: Conflicting Visions of International Refugee Law in the Management of Refugee Flows' (2003) 12(1) *Pacific Rim Law & Policy Journal* 49

Crock M and Daniel G, 'Do Loose Lips Bring Ships? The Role of Policy, Politics and Human Rights in Managing Unauthorised Boat Arrivals' (2010) 19(2) *Griffith Law Review* 238

Crowther S, 'The SIAC, Deportation, and European Law' (2010) 6(1) *Cambridge Student Law Review* 227

Cusumano E and Gombeer K, 'In deep waters: The legal, humanitarian and political implications of closing Italian ports to migrant rescuers' (2018) *Mediterranean Politics*

Cuttitta P, 'Readmission in the Relations between Italy and North African Mediterranean Countries' in Cassarino JP 2010a

——, 'Readmission and Forcibly Return in the Relations between Italy and North African Mediterranean Countries' (12–15 March 2008) Ninth Mediterranean Research Meeting, Florence, Montecatini Terme, 8, http://www.altrodiritto.unifi.it/frontier/storia/cuttitta.pdf

D'Acquisto G and D'Avanzo S, 'The Role of SHALL and SHOULD in Two International Treaties' (2009) 3(1) *Critical Approaches to Discourse Analysis across Disciplines* 36

D'Aspremont J, 'Softness in International Law: A Self-Serving Quest for New Legal Materials' (2008) 19(5) *European Journal of International Law* 1075

Da Costa K, *The Extraterritorial Application of Selected Human Rights Treaties* (Brill, 2012)

Da Lomba S, *The Right to Seek Refugee Status in the European Union* (Intersentia, 2004)

Dannenbaum T, 'Killings in Srebrenica, Effective Control, and the Power to Prevent Unlawful Conduct' (2012) 61 *ICLQ* 713

Dastyari A, United States, Migrant Interdiction and the Detention of Refugees in Guantánamo Bay (Cambridge University Press, 2015)

Dastyari A and Libbey E, 'Immigration Detention in Guantanamo Bay' (2012) 6(2) *Shima: The International Journal of Research into Island Cultures* 49

Davitti D and La Chimia A, 'A Lesser Evil? The European Agenda on Migration and the Use of Aid Funding for Migration Control' (2017) 10 *Irish Yearbook of International Law* 133

Davy U, 'Article 32: Expulsion' in Zimmermann A (ed), *The 1951 Convention Relating to the Status of Refugees and its 1967 Protocol: A Commentary* (Oxford University Press, 2011)

de Búrca G, 'After the EU Charter of Fundamental Rights: The Court of Justice as a Human Rights Adjudicator?' (2013) 20(2) *Maastricht Journal of European and Comparative Law* 168
De Koker C, 'Hassan v United Kingdom: The Interaction of Human Rights Law and International Humanitarian Law with regard to the Deprivation of Liberty in Armed Conflicts' (2015) 31(81) *Utrecht Journal of International and European Law* 90
De Londras F, *Detention in the War on Terror: Can Human Rights Fight Back?* (Cambridge University Press, 2011)
De Schutter O (ed), *International Human Rights Law: Cases, Materials, Commentary* (Cambridge University Press 2010)
——, 'Globalization and Jurisdiction: Lessons from the European Convention on Human Rights' (2006) 6 *Baltic Yearbook of International Law* 185
De Sena P, 'The Notion of "Contracting Parties' Jurisdiction" under Article 1 of the ECHR: Some Marginal Remarks on Nigro's Paper' (2011) 19 *Italian Yearbook of International Law* 75
——, 'Lotta al terrorismo e tutela dei diritti umani: conclusioni' in Gargiulo P and Vitucci MC (eds), *La tutela dei diritti umani nella lotta e nella guerra contro il terrorismo* (Giuffré, 2009)
——, *La nozione di Giurisdizione Statale nei Trattati sui Diritti dell'Uomo* (Giappichelli, 2002)
De Vattel E, *The Law of Nations* (Carnegie Institute, 1916 [1758])
F De Vittor, 'Responsabilità degli Stati e dell'Unione Europea nella conclusione e nell'esecuzione di "accordi" per il controllo extraterritoriale della migrazione' (2018) 2(1) *Diritti Umani e Diritto Internazionale* 5
F De Vittor, 'Soccorso in mare e favoreggiamento dell'immigrazione irregolare: sequestro e dissequestro della nave Open Arms', (2018) 2 *Diritti Umani e Diritto Internazionale* 443
De Weck F, *Non-Refoulement under the European Convention on Human Rights and the UN Convention Against Torture: The Assessment of Individual Complaints* (Brill, 2014)
De Wolf AH and Watson J, 'Navigating the Boundaries of Prevention: The Role of OPCAT in Deportations with Diplomatic Assurances' (2009) 27(4) *Netherlands Quarterly of Human Rights* 525
Del Guercio A, *La protezione dei richiedenti asilo nel diritto internazionale ed europeo* (Editoriale Scientifica, 2016)
Delicato V, 'I traffici di migranti nel Mediterraneo e gli accordi internazionali per la cooperazione di polizia' (2009) *Gli Stranieri* 458
Den Heijer M, 'Reflections on *Refoulement* and Collective Expulsion in the Hirsi Case' (2013) 25(2) *International Journal of Refugee Law* 265
——, *Europe and Extraterritorial Asylum* (Hart, 2012)
——, 'Europe Beyond its Borders: Refugee and Human Rights Protection in Extraterritorial Immigration Control' in Ryan B and Mitsilegas V (eds), *Extraterritorial Immigration Control: Legal Challenges* (Martinus Nijhoff 2010)
——, 'Whose Rights and Which Rights? The Continuing Story of Non-Refoulement under the European Convention on Human Rights' (2008) 19(3) *European Journal of Migration and Law* 277
Dench J and Crépeau F, 'Interdiction at the Expense of Human Rights: A Long-term Containment Strategy' (2003) 21(4) *Refuge* 1
Deeks A, *Promises not to Torture: Diplomatic Assurances in US Courts* (American Society of International Law, 2008)
Degan VU, *Sources of International Law* (Martinus Nijhoff, 1997)
Didier B, 'Criminalization of "Migrants": The Side Effect of the Will to Control the Frontiers and the Sovereign Illusion' in Bogusz B, Cholewinski R, Cygan A and Szyszczak E (eds), *Irregular Migration and Human Rights: Theoretical, European, and International Perspectives* (Martinus Nijoff, 2004)
Di Filippo M, 'The Reform of the Dublin System and the First (Half) Move of the Commission', *SIDIBlog* (2016), http://www.sidiblog.org/2016/05/12/the-reform-of-the-dublin-system-and-the-first-half-move-of-the-commission/

——, 'Irregular Migration and Safeguard of Life at Sea: International Rules and Recent Developments in The Mediterranean Sea' in del Vecchio A (ed), *International Law of the Sea: Current Trends and Controversial Issues* (Eleven International Publishing, 2014)

Di Pascale A, 'Migration Control at Sea: The Italian Case' in Ryan B and Mitsilegas V (eds), *Extraterritorial Immigration Controls: Legal Challenges* (Martinus Nijhoff, 2010)

Di Stefano G, *L'ordre internationale entre légalité et effectivité. Le titre juridique dans le contentieux territorial* (Pedone, 2002) 257

Doherty B and Davidson H, 'Orange Lifeboats Used to Return Asylum Seekers to Be Replaced by "Fishing Boats"', *The Guardian* (4 March 2015), https://www.theguardian.com/australia-news/2015/mar/05/orange-lifeboats-used-to-return-asylum-seekers-to-be-replaced-by-fishing-boats

Douglas Scott S, 'The Relationship between the EU and the ECHR Five Years on from the Treaty of Lisbon' in de Vries S, Bernitz U, and Weatherill S (eds), *The EU Charter of Fundamental Rights as a Binding Instrument: Five Years Old and Growing* (Hart Publishing, 2015)

Droege C, 'Elective Affinities? Human Rights and Humanitarian Law' (2008) 90 No 871 *International Review of the Red Cross* 501

Duffy A, 'Expulsion to Face Torture? *Non Refoulement* in International Law' (2008) 20(3) *International Journal of Refugee Law* 373

Dunstan R, 'Playing Human Pinball, The Amnesty International United Kingdom Section Report on UK Home Office *"Safe Third Country"* Practice' (1995) 7(4) *International Journal of Refugee Law* 611

Durieux JF, 'Of War, Flows, Laws and Flaws: A Reply to Hugo Storey' (2012) 31(3) *Refugee Survey Quarterly* 161

——, 'Protection Where? Or When?' (2009) 21 *International Journal of Refugee Law* 75

ECRE, *EU migration cooperation with third countries: More harm than good?* (15 September 2017), https://www.ecre.org/eu-migration-cooperation-with-third-countries-more-harm-than-good/

——, 'Time to Save the Right to Asylum – ECRE Memorandum to the European Council Meeting 17–18 March 2016' (March 2016), https://www.ecre.org/time-to-save-the-right-to-asylum-ecre-memorandum-to-the-european-council-meeting-17-18-march-2016/

——, 'Obstacle course in the EU leads to unfair treatment of asylum seekers', *ECRE Weekly Bullettin* (6 September 2013)

——, 'Safe Third Countries: Myths and Realities' (1995)

——, 'Comments from the European Council on Refugees and Exiles on the Amended Commission Proposal to Recast the Asylum Procedures Directive, COM (2011)' (September 2011)

Edwards A, 'Human Security and the Rights of Refugees: Transcending Territorial and Disciplinary Borders' (2009) 30(3) *Michigan Journal of International Law* 763

——, 'Tampering with Refugee Protection: The Case of Australia' (2003) 15(2) *International Journal of Refugee Law* 192

Eibe R and Will M, 'Human Rights Clauses in External Agreements' in Alston P (ed), *The EU and Human Rights* (Oxford University Press, 1999)

Elberling B, 'Article 16. Access to Courts' in Zimmermann (ed), *The 1951 Convention Relating to the Status of Refugees and its 1967 Protocol: A Commentary* (Oxford University Press, 2011)

Esteve García F, 'The Search and Rescue Tasks Coordinated by the European Border and Coast Guard Agency (Frontex) Regarding the Surveillance of External Maritime Borders' (2017) 5 *Paix et sécurité internationales: revue maroco-espagnole de droit international et relations internationales* 93

EUObserver, 'Internal EU report exposes Libya turmoil', 20 February 2017, https://euobserver.com/migration/136973

European Commission Report, 'Technical Mission to Libya on Illegal Migration' doc 7753/05 (27 November–6 December 2004) 59, http://www.statewatch.org/news/2005/may/eu-report-libya-ill-imm.pdf

European Commission, 'Managing migration in all its aspects: Commission note ahead of the June European Council 2018', Brussels

European Parliament, 'EU Readmission Agreements Facilitating the return of irregular migrants' (April 2015), http://www.europarl.europa.eu/RegData/etudes/BRIE/2015/554212/EPRS_BRI%282015%29554212_EN.pdf

European Policy Centre, 'EU Readmission Agreements: towards a more strategic EU approach that respects human rights?', Policy Dialogue, 21 March 2012, http://www.kbs-frb.be/uploadedfiles/kbs-frb/files/verslag/epc_readmissionagreements_210312.pdf

Express Tribune, 'Deportees and readmissions' (4 December 2015), https://tribune.com.pk/story/1003975/deportees-and-readmissions/

Farmer A, 'Non-Refoulement and *Jus Cogens*: Limiting Anti-Terror Measures that Threaten Refugee Protection' (2008) 32 *Expresso*, http://works.bepress.com/alice_farmer/1

Favilli C, 'La cooperazione UE-Turchia per contenere il flusso dei migranti e richiedenti asilo: obiettivo riuscito?' (2016) 10 *Diritti Umani e Diritto Internazionale* 405

——, 'Quali modalita` di conclusion delgi accordi internazionali in materia di immigrazione?' (2005) *Rivista di Diritto Internazionale* 156

Financial Times, 'Turkey to boost legal protection for migrants, easing EU returns' (25 April 2016), https://www.ft.com/content/b60b3afe-0af9-11e6-b0f1-61f222853ff3

Fink M, *Frontex and Human Rights: Responsibility in 'Multi-Actor Situations' under the ECHR and EU Public Liability Law* (OUP, 2018)

Fischer-Lescano A and Lohr T, *Border Control at Sea: Requirements under International Human Rights and Refugee Law* (European Centre for Constitutional and Human Rights, 2007)

Focarelli C, *International Law as a Social Construct* (OUP, 2013)

Foerster RF, *From Labour Emigration to Labour Recruitment: the Case of Italy* (Harvard University Press, 1919)

Forcese C, 'The Capacity to Protect: Diplomatic Protection of Dual Nationals in the "War on Terror"' (2006) 17(2) *European Journal of International Law* 369

Fornalé E, 'The European Returns Policy and the Re-Shaping of the National: Reflections on the Role of Domestic Courts' (2012) 31(4) *Refugee Survey Quarterly* 134

Fortress Europe, 'Espulsi 3,592 tunisini, nei Cie tornerà la calma?' (1 November 2011), http://fortresseurope.blogspot.com/2011/11/espulsi-3592-tunisini-nei-cie-tornera.html

Foster M, 'The Implications of the Failed "Malaysian Solution": The Australian High Court and Refugee Responsibility Sharing at International Law' (2012) 13 *Melbourne Journal of International Law* 395

——, 'Protection Elsewhere: The Legal Implications of Requiring Refugees to Seek Protection in another State' (2007) 28 *Michigan Journal of International Law* 223

——, *International Refugee Law and Socio-Economic Rights: Refuge from Deprivation* (CUP, 2007)

Francis A, 'Bringing Protection Home: Healing the Schism between International Obligations and National Safeguards Created by Extraterritorial Processing' (2008) 20 *IJRL* 273

Frelick B, 'US Refugee Policy in the Caribbean: No Bridge over Troubled Waters' (1996) 20(2) *Fletcher Forum of World Affairs* 67

Fullerton M, 'A Tale of Two Decades: War Refugees and Asylum Policies in the European Union' (2011) 10 *Washington University Global Studies Law Review* 81

——, 'The International and National Protection of Refugees' in Hannum H (ed), *Guide to International Human Rights Practice*, 4th edn (Transnational Publishers, 2004)

Gammeltoft-Hansen T, Guild E, Moreno-Lax V, Panizzon M, and Roele I, 'What is a Compact? Migrants' Rights and State Responsibilities Regarding the Design of the UN Global Compact for Safe, Orderly and Regular Migration', *Raoul Wallenberg Institute of Human Rights and Humanitarian Law* (October 2017)

——, *Access to Asylum: International Refugee Law and the Globalization of Migration Control* (Cambridge University Press, 2011)

——, 'The Externalisation of European Migration Control and the Reach of International Refugee Law' in Guild E and Minderhoud P (eds), *The First Decade of EU Migration and Asylum Law* (Martinus Nijhoff, 2011)

Garcia Andrade P, 'The Role of the European Parliament in the Adoption of Non-Legally Binding Agreements with Third Countries' in Santos Vara J and Sánchez-Tabernero SR (eds), *The Democratization of EU International Relations Through EU Law* (Routledge, 2018)

——, 'La Dimension Externe de la Politique Migratoire de l'UE: un Bilan au travers de ses Instruments' in Dony M (ed), *La Dimension Externe de l'Espace de Liberté, de Sécurité et de Justice au Lendemain de Lisbonne et de Stockholm: unBbilan à Mi-parcours* (Éditions de l'Université de Bruxelles, 2012)

——, 'Spanish Perspective on Irregular Immigration by Sea' in Ryan B and Mitsilegas V(eds), *Extraterritorial Immigration Controls: Legal Challenges* (Martinus Nijhoff, 2010)

Gauci JP, 'Back to Old Tricks? Italian Responsibility for returning People to Libya?' *EJIL Talk* (June 2017), https://www.ejiltalk.org/back-to-old-tricks-italian-responsibility-for-returning-people-to-libya/#comments

Gauci JP and Mallia P, 'Access to Protection: A Human Right' (National Report – Malta, December 2013)

Gavouneli M, *Functional Jurisdiction in the Law of the Sea* (Martinus Nijhoff, 2007)

Ghezelbash D, *Refuge Lost: Asylum Law in an Interdependent World* (Cambridge University Press, 2018)

——, 'Shifting Sands and Refugee Boats: The Transfer of Migration Control Policies between the United States and Australia' in Gauci JP, Giuffré M and Tsourdi L, *Forced Migration(s): Critical Perspectives on Refugee Law* (Martinus Nijhoff Publishers, 2014)

Ghezelbash D, Moreno-Lax V, Klein N, Opeskin B, 'Securitization of search and rescue at sea: the response to boat migration in the Mediterranean and offshore Australia' (2018) 67 *International and Comparative Law Quarterly* 315

Gianelli A, 'Obbligo di *non-refoulement* e assicurazioni diplomatiche' in *Studi in onore di Vincenzo Starace*, vol I (Napoli, 2008)

Gibney MJ and Hansen RA, *Immigration and Asylum: from 1900 to the Present* (Abc-Clio, 2005)

Gil AR, 'Collective expulsions in times of migratory crisis: Comments on the *Khlaifia* case of the ECHR' in *EU Immigration and Asylum Law and Policy* (11 February 2016), http://eumigrationlawblog.eu/collective-expulsions-in-times-of-migratory-crisis-comments-on-the-khlaifia-case-of-the-echr/

Gil Bazo MT, 'Asylum as a General Principle of International Law' (2015) 27(1) *International Journal of Refugee Law* 3

——, 'The Safe Third Country Concept in International Agreements on Refugee Protection Assessing State Practice' (2015) 33(1) *Netherlands Quarterly of Human Rights* 42

——, 'Article 40 1951 convention. Territorial Application Clause' in Zimmermann A (ed), *The 1951 Convention Relating to the Status of Refugees and its 1967 Protocol: A Commentary* (Oxford University Press, 2011) 1567

——, 'The Charter of Fundamental Rights of the European Union and the Right to be Granted Asylum in the Union's Law' (2008) 27(3) *Refugee Survey Quarterly* 33

——, 'Refugee Status and Subsidiary Protection under EC Law: The Qualification Directive and the Right to be Granted Asylum' in Toner H, Guild E and Baldaccini A (eds), *Whose Freedom, Security and Justice? EU Immigration and Asylum Law and Policy* (Hart, 2007)

——, 'The Practice of Mediterranean States in the Context of the European Union's Justice and Home Affairs External Dimension. The Safe Third Country Concept Revisited' (2006) 18(3)–(4) *International Journal of Refugee Law* 571

Gilbert G, 'Exclusion and Evidentiary Assessment' in G Noll (ed), *Proof, Evidentiary Assessment and Credibility in Asylum Procedures* (Martinus Nijhoff, 2005)

——, 'Is Europe Living Up to Its Obligations to Refugees?' (2004) 15(5) *European Journal of International Law* 963

Gilbert G and Rusch AM, 'Jurisdictional Competence through Protection: To What Extent Can States Prosecute the Prior Crimes of Those to Whom They Have Extended Refuge?' (2014) 12 *Journal of International Criminal Justice* 1093

Giuffré M, 'From Turkey to Libya: The EU Migration Partnership from Bad to Worse' (2017) *Eurojus*, http://rivista.eurojus.it/from-turkey-to-libya-the-eu-migration-partnership-from-bad-to-worse/

——, 'Access to Asylum at Sea? *Non-refoulement* and a Comprehensive Approach to Extraterritorial Human Rights Obligations' in Moreno-Lax V and Papastavridis E (eds), *Boat Refugees' and Migrants at Sea: A Comprehensive Approach Integrating Maritime Security with Human Rights* (Brill, 2017)

——, 'Deportation with Assurances: Human Rights and the Case of People Suspected or Convicted of Serious Crimes (2017) 15(1) *Journal of International Criminal Justice* 75

——, 'The Obligation to Readmit and the Relationship between Interstate and EU Readmission Agreements' in F Ippolito and S Trevisanut (eds), *Migration in* Mare Nostrum: *Mechanisms of International Cooperation* (Cambridge University Press, 2015)

——, 'Access to Protection: Negotiating Rights and Diplomatic Assurances under Memoranda of Understanding' in Gauci JP, Giuffré M and Tsourdi L, *Forced Migration(s): Critical Perspectives on Refugee Law* (Martinus Nijhoff Publishers, 2014)

——, 'Standard Readmission Agreements and Refugee Rights: from a Critique to a Proposal' (2013) 32(3) *Refugee Survey Quarterly* 79

——, 'An Appraisal of Diplomatic Assurances One Year after *Othman (Abu Qatada) v United Kingdom* (2012)' (2013) 2(2) *International Human Rights Law Review* 266

——, 'State Responsibility beyond Borders: What Legal Basis for Italy's Push-backs to Libya?' (2012) 24(4) *International Journal of Refugee Law* 692

——, 'Watered-Down Rights on the High Seas: *Hirsi Jamaa and Others v Italy*' (2012) 61(3) *International and Comparative Law Quarterly* 728

Giuffré M and Moreno-Lax V, 'The Rise of Consensual Containment: From "Contactless Control" to "Contactless Responsibility" for Migratory Flows' in Juss S (ed), *The Research Handbook on International Refugee Law* (Edward Elgar Publishing, 2019)

Gjergji I, *Sulla governance delle migrazioni. Sociologia dell'underworld del comando globale* (Franco Angeli, 2016)

Gondek M, *The Reach of Human Rights in a Globalized World: Extraterritorial Application of Human Rights Treaties* (Intersentia, 2009)

——, 'Extraterritorial Application of the European Convention on Human Rights: Territorial Focus in the Age of Globalization' (2005) 52(3) *Netherlands International Law Review* 349

Goodwin-Gill GS, 'Legal and practical issues raised by the movement of people across the Mediterranean' (2016) *Forced Migration Review* 83

——, 'Refugees and Migrants at Sea: Duties of Care and Protection in the Mediterranean and the Need for International Action', Notes for a Presentation Jean Monnet Centre of Excellence on Migrants' Rights in the Mediterranean University of Naples 'L'Orientale' (2015)

——, 'Current Challenges in Refugee Law' in Gauci JP, Giuffré M and Tsourdi L, *Forced Migration(s): Critical Perspectives on Refugee Law* (Martinus Nijhoff Publishers, 2014)

——, 'The Right to Seek Asylum: Interception at Sea and the Principle of Non-refoulement' (2011) 23(3) *International Journal of Refugee Law* 443

——, 'The Extraterritorial Reach of Human Rights Obligations: A Brief Perspective on the Link to Jurisdiction' in de Chazournes LB and Kohen MC (eds), *International Law and the Quest for its Implementation/Le Droit International et la Quête de sa Mise en Oeuvre: Liber Amicorum Vera Gowlland-Debbas* (Brill, 2010)

——, 'Diplomatic Assurances and Deportation' (JUSTICE/Sweet & Maxwell Conference on Counter-terrorism and Human Rights, 28 June 2005)

——, 'Article 31 of the 1951 Convention relating to the Status of refugees: Non-Penalization, Detention, and Protection' in Feller E, Turk V and Niccholson F (eds), *Refugee Protection in International Law: UNHCR's Global Consultations on Internatinal Protection* (UNHCR, 2003)

——, 'The Haitian *Refoulement* Case: A Comment' (1994) 6 *International Journal of Refugee Law* 103

——, 'The Language of Protection' (1989) 1(1) *International Journal of Refugee Law* 6
——, '*Non-refoulement* and the New Asylum Seekers' (1986) 26 *Virginia Journal of International Law* 897
——, *International Law and the Movement of Persons between States* (Oxford University Press, 1978)
Goodwin-Gill GS and McAdam J, *The Refugee in International Law*, 3rd edn (Oxford University Press, 2007)
Gorlick B, 'Refugee Protection in Troubled Times: Reflections on Institutional and Legal Developments at the Crossroads' in Steiner MN, Gibney M, and Loescher G (eds), *Problems of Protection: the UNHCR, Refugees, and Human Rights* (Routledge, 2003)
Gouliamaki L, 'Migrant slavery in Libya: Nigerians tell of being used as slaves', *BBC News*, 2 January 2018, https://www.bbc.com/news/world-africa-42492687
Graefrath B, 'Complicity in the Law of International State Responsibility' (1996) 29 *Revue Belge de Droit International* 371
Grahl-Madsen A, *The Status of Refugees in International Law* Vol 2 (AW Sijthoff, 1972)
Grotius H, *De iure belli ac pacis, libri duo* [1625] (translated by AC Campbell) (Batoche Books, 2001)
Guild E, 'Asymmetrical Sovereignty and the Refugee: Diplomatic Assurances and the Failure of Due Process. *Agiza v Sweden* and *Alzery v Sweden*' in Simeon J (ed), *Critical Issues inInternational Refugee Law. Strategies toward Interpretative Harmony* (Cambridge University Press, 2010)
——, *Security and Migration in the 21st Century* (Polity Press, 2009)
——, 'International Terrorism and EU Immigration, Asylum, and Borders Policy: the Unexpected Victims of 11 September 2001' in Carr F and Massey A (eds), *Public Policy And the New European Agendas* (Edward Elgar Publishing, 2006)
——, 'Who is an Irregular Migrant?' in Bogusz B, Cholewinski R, Cygan A and Szyszczak E (eds), *Irregular Migration and Human Rights: Theoretical, European and International Perspectives* (Martinus Nijhoff, 2004)
Guild E and Bigo D, 'Policing at a Distance: Schengen Visa Policies' in Didier Bigo and Elspeth Guild (eds), *Controlling Frontiers* (Ashgate, 2005)
Guild E and Carrera S, 'Rethinking asylum distribution in the EU: Shall we start with the facts?', *CEPS Commentary, CEPS, Brussels*, 17 June 2016
Guilfoyle D, *Shipping Interdiction and the Law of the Sea* (Cambridge University Press, 2012)
Guilfoyle D and Papastavridis E, 'Mapping Disembarkation Options: Towards Strengthening Cooperation in Managing Irregular Movements by Sea', UNHCR *Background Paper* (2014), https://www.refworld.org/pdfid/5346438f4.pdf
Hailbronner K, 'Comments on the Right to Leave, Return and Remain' in Gowlland-Debbas V (ed), *The Problem of Refugees in the Light of Contemporary International Law Issues* (Martinus Nijhoff Publishers, 1996)
——, 'Readmission Agreements and the Obligation of States under Public International Law to Readmit their Own and Foreign Nationals' (1997) 57 *Zeitschrift für ausländisches öffentliches Recht und Völkerrecht* 1
——, 'The Concept of "Safe Third Country" and Expeditious Asylum Procedures: A Western European Perspective' (1993) 5(1) *International Journal of Refugee Law* 31
——, 'Non-refoulement and "Humanitarian" Refugees: Customary International Law or Wishful Legal Thinking?' in Martin D (ed), *The New Asylum Seekers: Refugee Law in the 1980s* (Martinus Nijhoff, 1988)
Hailbronner K and Thym D (ed), *EU Immigration and Asylum Law: A Commentary*, 2nd edn (CH Beck, 2016)
Hamdan E, *The principle of non-refoulement under the ECHR and the UN Convention against Torture and Other Cruel, Inhuman or Degrading Treatment or Punishment* (Brill, 2016)
Hampson FJ, 'Using International Human Rights Machinery to Enforce the International Law of Armed Conflicts' (1992) *31 Revue de Droit Militaire et de Droit de la Guerre* 119

Harvey C, *Seeking Asylum in the UK, Problems and Prospects* (Butterworths, 2000)
Hathaway JC, *The Rights of Refugees under International Law* (Cambridge University Press, 2005)
——, *The Law of Refugee Status* (Butterworths, 1991)
Hathaway JC and Harvey CJ, 'Framing Refugee Protection in the New World Disorder' (2001) 34(2) *Cornell Journal of International Law* 257
Hathaway JC and Gammeltoft-Hansen T, 'Non-Refoulement in a World of Cooperative Deterrence' (2014) 53(2) *Columbia Journal of Transnational Law* 235
Hatton TJ, 'Seeking Asylum in Europe' (2004) 19 (38) *Economic Policy* 5
Hawkins KR, 'The Promises of Torturers: Diplomatic Assurances and the Legality of "Rendition"' (2006) 20 *George Town Immigration Law Journal* 213
Henkin L, 'That "S" Word: Sovereignty and Globalization, and Human Rights, Et Cetera' (The Robert L. Levine Distinguished Lecture Series) (1999) 68(4) *Fordham Law Review* 1
Hirsch AL, 'The Extra-Territorialisation of Migration Control and the Right to Seek Asylum', *RightNow* (2018), http://rightnow.org.au/opinion-3/the-extra-territorialisation-of-migration-control-and-the-right-to-seek-asylum
——, 'The Borders Beyond the Border: Australia's Extraterritorial Migration Controls' (2017) 36(3) *Refugee Survey Quarterly* 48
Hooper J, 'Awkward photo? There may be more to come as Colonel Gaddafi visits Rome', *The Guardian* (11 June 2009), http://www.guardian.co.uk/world/2009/jun/10/gaddafivisit-italy-berlusconi
Hruschka C, 'Strengthening effective remedies for asylum seekers in the Dublin procedure: from *Abdullahi* to Ghezelbash and *Karim*', *EDAL* (23 June 2016), http://www.asylumlawdatabase.eu/en/journal/strengthening-effective-remedies-asylum-seekers-dublin-procedure-abdullahi-ghezelbash-and
Human Rights and Migration Law Clinic of Turin, *MoU between Italy and Sudan: A legal analysis* (2017), https://www.asgi.it/wp-content/uploads/2017/10/Report-Memorandum-of-Understanding-Sudan-Italy-SL-Clinic-UniTO.pdf
Human Rights Watch, *Ue: delegare i soccorsi alla Libia significa mettere vite a repentaglio* (19 June 2017), https://www.hrw.org/it/news/2017/06/19/305148
——, 'Border Guards kill and injure asylum seekers' (10 May 2016), https://www.hrw.org/news/2016/05/10/turkey-border-guards-kill-and-injure-asylum-seekers
——, 'Egypt: Don't Deport Eritreans' (15 November 2011), http://www.hrw.org/news/2011/11/15/egypt-don-t-deport-eritreans
——, 'EU: Put Rights at Heart of Migration Policy' (20 June 2011), http://www.hrw.org/news/2011/06/20/eu-put-rights-heart-migration-policy
——, 'Italy/Libya: Migrants Describe Forced Returns, Abuse: EU Should Press Italy to Halt Illegal Forced Returns to Libya' (21 September 2009) http://www.hrw.org/news/2009/09/17/italylibya-migrants-describe-forced-returns-abuse
——, 'No Guidelines on Empty "No Torture" Promises: Council of Europe Rejects Minimum Standards for Diplomatic Assurances' (3 April 2006), http://www.hrw.org/news/2006/04/02/no-guidelines-empty-no-torture-promises
——, 'Still at Risk, Diplomatic Assurances, No Safeguard against Torture' (April 2005) Vol 17 No 4(d), http://www.hrw.org/sites/default/files/reports/eca0405.pdfHRW 2005b
——, 'Ukraine on the Margins: Background Migration Trends in Ukraine' (Research Paper New York, 29 November 2005), http://www.hrw.org/en/node/11521/section/4
Hungarian Helsinki Committee, 'Serbia As a Safe Third Country: A Wrong Presumption', September 2011, http://www.unhcr.org/refworld/docid/4e815dec2.html
Hurwitz A, *The Collective Responsibility of States to Protect Refugees* (Oxford University Press, 2009)
ILPA, 'Comments on the Revised Commission Proposal of 1 June 2011 on Common Procedures for Granting and Withdrawing International Protection status (Recast) COM(2011)' (5 December 2011)

InfoMigrants, 'Austria, Italy propose processing refugees on ships' (17 September 2018), https://www.infomigrants.net/en/post/12031/austria-italy-propose-processing-refugees-on-ships

International Organization for Migration, 'Migrants risking lives in the Mediterranean topped 45,000 in 2013' (28 January 2014), https://www.iom.int/news/migrants-risking-lives-mediterranean-topped-45000-2013-iom

Ippolito F and Velluti S, 'The Recast Process of the EU Asylum System: A Balancing Act between Efficiency and Fairness' (2011) 30(3) *Refugee Survey Quarterly* 24

Izumo A, 'Diplomatic Assurances against Torture and Ill Treatment: European Court of Human Rights Jurisprudence' (2008) 42(1) *Columbia Human Rights Law Review* 233

Jenks W, 'The Conflict of Law-Making Treaties' (1953) 30 *British Yearbook of International Law* 401

Jennings R and Watts Sir A (eds), *Oppenheim's International Law* (Longman, 1992)

Kälin W, Caroni M and Heim L, 'Article 33 para 1 (Prohibition of Expulsion and Return (Refoulement)' in Zimmermann A (ed), *The 1951 Convention relating to the Status of Refugees and its 1967 Protocol: A Commentary* (Oxford University Press, 2011)

Kate J and Newland K, 'Family Unity and Refugee Protection' in Feller E, Nicholson F, and Turk V (eds), *UNHCR Refugee Protection in International Law* (Cambridge University Press, 2003)

Jehl D and Johnston D, 'Rule Change Lets CIA Freely Send Suspects Abroad to Jails', *New York Times* (6 March 2005)

Jones K, 'Deportation with Assurances: Addressing Key Criticism' (2008) 57(1) *International and Comparative Law Quarterly* 183

Jones M, 'Lies, Damned Lies and Diplomatic Assurances: The Misuse of Diplomatic Assurances in Removal Proceedings' (2006) 8(1) *European Journal of Migration Law* 9

Johnston JG, 'The Risk of Torture as a Basis for Refusing Extradition and the Use of Diplomatic Assurances to Protect against Torture after 9/11' (2011) 11(1) *International Criminal Law Review* 1

Juss SS, 'Problematizing the Protection of "War Refugees": A Rejoinder to Hugo Storey and Jean-François Durieux' (2013) 32(1) *Refugee Survey Quarterly* 122

——, 'Complicity, Exclusion, and the "Unworthy" in Refugee Law' (2012) 31(3) *Refugee Survey Quarterly* 1

JUSTICE, 'Home Office Review of Counter-Terrorism and Security Powers' *Written Submissions* (August 2010)

Kelly J and Chambers G, 'Operation Sovereign Borders block 33 boats', *The Australian* (24 October 2018), https://www.theaustralian.com.au/national-affairs/immigration/operation-sovereign-borders-block-33boats/news-story/71e6c8a3b7bf0e758da705c9e17df894

Keohane RO, *After Hegemony: Cooperation and Discord in the World Political Economy* (Princeton University Press, 1984)

Kim S, 'Non-Refoulement and Extraterritorial jurisdiction: State Sovereignty and Migration Controls at Sea in the European Context' (2017) 30(1) *Leiden journal of International Law* 49

Kingseley P and Stephen C, 'Libyan navy admits confrontation with charity's rescue boat', *The Guardian*, 28 August 2016, https://www.theguardian.com/world/2016/aug/28/libyan-navy-admits-confrontation-charity-rescue-boat-msf

Kirchgaessner S and Tondo L, 'Italy's deal with Libya to "pull back" migrants faces legal challenge', *The Guardian* (8 May 2018), https://www.theguardian.com/world/2018/may/08/italy-deal-with-libya-pull-back-migrants-faces-legal-challenge-human-rights-violations

Kjaergaard E, 'The Concept of "Safe Third Country" in Contemporary European Refugee Law' (1994) 6 *International Journal of Refugee Law* 649

Klabbers J, *Treaty Conflicts and the European Union* (Cambridge University Press, 2009)

——, *Developments in International Law: The Concept of Treaty in International Law* (Kluwer, 1996)

Klein N, 'A Case for Harmonizing Laws on Maritime Interceptions of Irregular Migrants' (2014) 63 *ICLQ* 787

Kneebone S, 'The Pacific Plan: The Provision of 'Effective Protection'?' (2006) 18 *International Journal of Refugee Law* 696

Koh HH, 'Reflections on *Refoulement* and Haitian Centres Council' (1994) 35(1) *Harvard International Law Journal* 1

Koskenniemi M, 'Study in the Function and the Scope of the *Lex Specialis* Rule and the Question of 'Self-Contained' Regimes', UN Doc ILC(LVI)/SG/FIL/ CRD.1 and Add.1. (4 and 7 May 2004)

Kosta V, Skoutaris N, and Tzevelekos V (eds), *The EU Accession to the ECHR* (Hart Publishing, 2014)

Kostakopoulou T, 'An Open and Secure Europe? Fixity and Fissures in the Area of Freedom, Security and Justice after Lisbon and Stockholm' (2010) 19(2) *European Security* 151

Kruse I, 'EU Readmission Policy and its Effects on Transit Countries: The Case of Albania' (2006) 8(2) *European Journal of Migration and Law* 115

Kurt S, 'Somali Migrant Separated from Pregnant Wife during Rescue', *Times of Malta* (22 July 2010), http://www.timesofmalta.com/articles/view/20100722/local/somali-migrant-separated-from-pregnant-wife-during-rescue

Lambert H, 'The Next Frontier: Expanding Protection in Europe for Victims of Armed Conflict and Indiscriminate Violence' (2013) 25(2) *International Journal of Refugee Law* 207 (advance access 5 June 2013)

——, '"Safe Third Country" in the European Union: An Evolving Concept in International Law and Implications for the UK' (2012) 26(4) *Journal of Immigration, Asylum and Nationality Law* 318

——, 'The European Convention on Human Rights and the Protection of Refugees: Limits and Opportunities' (2005) 24(2) *Refugee Survey Quarterly* 39

——, 'Protection against Refoulement from Europe: Human Rights Law Comes to the Rescue' (1999) 48 *International Comparative Law Quarterly* 515

Larsaeus N, 'The Use of Diplomatic Assurances in the Prevention of Prohibited Treatment' (2006) *Refugee Study Centre Working Paper No 32*

Lauterpacht Sir E and Bethlehem D, 'The Scope and Content of the Principle of *Non-refoulement*: Opinion' in Feller E, Türk V and Nicholson F (eds), *Refugee Protection in International Law: UNHCR's Global Consultations on International Protection* (Cambridge University Press, 2003)

Lawson R, 'Life after Bankovic – On the Extraterritorial Application of the European Convention on Human Rights' in Coomans F and Kamminga M (eds), *Extraterritorial Application of Human Rights Treaties* (Intersentia, 2004)

Legomsky SH, 'The USA and the Caribbean Interdiction Program' (2006) 18(3)–(4) *International Journal of Refugee Law* 677

——, 'Secondary Refugee Movements and the Return of Asylum Seekers to Third Countries: The Meaning of Effective Protection' (2003) 15(4) *International Journal of Refugee Law* 567

Lenaerts K, 'Exploring the Limits of the EU Charter of Fundamental Rights' (2012) 8(3) *European Constitutional Law Review* 375

Liguori A and Ricciutti N, 'Frontex ed il rispetto dei diritti umani nelle operazioni congiunte alle frontiere esterne dell'Unione europea' (2012) 6(3) *Diritti Umani e Diritto Internazionale* 539

Linderfalk U, 'State responsibility and the primary–secondary rules terminology' (2009) 78(1) *Nordic Journal of International Law* 53

——, *On the Interpretation of Treaties: The Modern International Law as Expressed in the 1969 Vienna Convention on the Law of Treaties* (Springer, 2007)

Lindroos A, 'Addressing Norm Conflicts in a Fragmented Legal System: The Doctrines of *Lex Specialis*' (2005) 74(1) *Nordic Journal of International Law* 27

Lock T, 'End of an Epic? The Draft Accession Agreement on the EU's Accession to the ECHR' (2012) 31(1) *Yearbook of European Law* 162

Lowe V and Staker C, 'Jurisdiction' in Evans M (ed), *International Law* (Oxford University Press, 2010)

Lowes S, 'The Legality of Extraterritorial Processing of Asylum Claims: The Judgment of the High Court of Australia in the "Malaysian Solution" Case' (2012) 12(1) *Human Rights Law Review* 168

Lucassen L, Lucassen J, de Jong R, and van de Water M, 'Cross-cultural migration in Western Europe 1901–2000: A preliminary estimate', *IISH Research Paper 52*

Maccanico Y, 'The Italian Roadmap: Hotspots, readmission, asylum procedures and the reopening of detention centres', *Statewatch* (2015), http://www.statewatch.org/news/2015/dec/no-279-Italian-Road-Map-2015.pdf

——, 'The EU's Self-Interested Response to Unrest in North Africa: The Meaning of Treaties and Readmission Agreements between Italy and North African States' (*Statewatch* January 2012), http://www.statewatch.org/analyses/no-165-eu-north-africa.pdf

Maiani F, '"Regional Disembarkation Platforms" and "Controlled Centres": Lifting the Drawbridge, Reaching out Across The Mediterranean, or Going Nowhere?' (2018), http://eumigrationlawblog.eu/regional-disembarkation-platforms-and-controlled-centres-lifting-the-drawbridge-reaching-out-across-the-mediterranean-or-going-nowhere/

Maini S, 'Does International Law Permit Deportation with Assurances?', *International Law Square* (January 2016), https://ilsquare.wordpress.com/2016/01/30/does-international-law-permit-deportation-with-assurances/

Mallory C, 'European Court of Human Rights *Al-Skeini and Others v United Kingdom* (App no 55721/07) Judgment of 7 July 2011' (2012) 61(1) *ICLQ* 301

Mandal R, 'Protection Mechanisms Outside of the 1951 Convention ("Complementary Protection")', *UNHCR Legal and Protection Policy Research Series* (PPLA/2005/02, June 2005)

Maniar A, 'A Significant Blow to Deportation with Assurances', https://onesmallwindow.wordpress.com/2016/05/06/a-significant-blow-to-deportation-with-assurances/

Mann FA, 'Another Agreement Between States under National Law?' (1974) 68(3) *American Journal of International Law* 490

——, 'The Doctrine of Jurisdiction in International Law' (1964) 111 *Recueil des Cours* 1

Marchesi A, *Obblighi di condotta e obblighi di risultato* (Giuffré, 2003)

Mariniello T, (forthcoming 2019) 'Prolonged Emergency and Derogation of Human Rights: Why the European Court Should Raise its Immunity System' (2019) *German Law Journal*

Martin DA, Aleinkoff TA, Motomura H and Fullerton M, *Forced Migration: Law and Policy*, 2nd edn (West, 2013)

Martin D, 'The Authority and Responsibility of States' in Aleinikoff A and Chetail V (eds), *Migration and International Legal Norms* (TMC Asser Press, 2003)

Matonti A, 'Garanzie procedurali derivanti dall'art. 4 del Protocollo n. 4 CEDU: il caso *Khlaifia*' (2017) 11(2) *Diritti Umani e Diritto Internazionale* 523

Matsumoto FC, *L'effectivité en droit international* (Bruylant, 2014)

Mauro MR, 'Detention and Expulsion of Migrants: the *Khlaifia v Italy* case' (2015) XXV *The Italian Yearbook of International Law* 85

Mavronicola N and Messineo F, 'Relatively Absolute? The Undermining of Art 3 ECHR in *Ahmad v UK*' (2013) 76(3) *Modern Law Review* 589

McAdam J, 'The Enduring Relevance of the 1951 Refugee Convention' (2017) 29(1) *IJRL* 1

——, *Complementary Protection in International Refugee Law* (Oxford University Press, 2007)

McAdam J and Wood T, 'Australian Asylum Policy All at Sea: An Analysis of *Plaintiff M70/2011 v Minister for Immigration and Citizenship* and the Australia-Malaysia Arrangement' (2012) 61(1) *International Comparative Law Quarterly* 274

McLachlan C, 'The Principle of Systemic Integration and Article 31(3)(c) of the Vienna Convention' (2005) 54(2) *International Comparative Law Quarterly* 279

Meijers H, 'Refugees in Western Europe, "Schengen" Affects the Entire Refugee Law' (1990) 2(3) *International Journal of Refugee Law* 428

Meloni A, 'The Development of a Common Visa Policy under the Treaty of Amsterdam' (2005) 42(5) *Common Market Law Review* 1357

Meltingpot, 'Migranti riaccompagnati in Libia' (7 May 2009), http://www.meltingpot.org/articolo14467.html

Meron T, 'Extraterritoriality of Human Rights Treaties' (1995) 89(1) *American Journal of International Law* 78

Metcalf E, 'The False Promise of Assurances against Torture' (2009) 6(1) *Justice Journal* 63

Migrantes Online, 'Più di 50mila immigrati sbarcati da gennaio a oggi' (13 July 2011), http://www.migrantesonline.it/siti_migrantes/migrantes_online/00005082_Piu_di_50mila_immigrati_sbarcati_da_gennaio_a_oggi_.html

Migrants at Sea, 'Italy Continues Shipboard Detention of Hundreds of Tunisians' (28 September 2011) http://migrantsatsea.wordpress.com/2011/09/28/italy-continues-shipboard-detention-of-hundreds-of-tunisians/?

——, 'Memorandum of Understanding between Italy and Libyan NTC' (20 June 2011), http://migrantsatsea.wordpress.com/2011/06/20/memorandum-of-understandingbetween-italy-and-libyan-nct/

——, 'France and Italy Agree to Joint Naval Patrols Along Tunisian Coast to Block Migrant Departures' (8 April 2011), http://migrantsatsea.wordpress.com/2011/04/08/franceand-italy-agree-to-joint-naval-patrols-along-tunisian-coast-to-block-migrant-departures/

——, 'Libyan Rebel Leader Jalil Promises to Respect Immigration Agreements Between Libya and Italy' (29 March 2011), http://migrantsatsea.wordpress.com/2011/03/29/libyanrebel-leader-jalil-promises-to-respect-immigration-agreements-between-libya-and-italy/

Migration Watch UK, 'The Lisbon European Reform Treaty Impact on Asylum and Immigration Policy' (14 March 2008), http://www.migrationwatchuk.org/briefingPaper/document/82

Milanovic M, *The Extraterritorial Application of Human Rights Treaties* (Oxford University Press, 2011)

——, 'From Compromise to Principle: Clarifying the Concept of State Jurisdiction in Human Rights Treaties' (2008) 8(3) *Human Rights Law Review* 411

Mills A, 'Rethinking Jurisdiction in International Law' (2014) 84(1) *British Yearbook of International Law* 187

Miltner B, 'Human Security and Protection from Refoulement in the Maritime Context' in Edward A and Ferstman C (eds), *Human Security and Non-Citizens: Law, Policy and International Affairs* (Cambridge University Press, 2010) 195

——, 'Irregular Maritime Obligations: Refugee Protection in Rescue and Interception' (2006–2007) 30 *Fordham International Law Journal* 75

Mole N and Meredith C, *Asylum and the European Convention of Human Rights* (Council of Europe Publishing, 2010)

M Monroy, 'A seahorse for the Mediterranean: Border surveillance for Libyan search and rescue zone', https://digit.site36.net/2018/01/03/border-surveillance-technology-for-new-libyan-search-and-rescue-zone/

Monzoni P, 'Il Traffico di Migranti per Mare verso l'Italia: Sviluppi Recenti (2004-2008'(*CESPI Working Paper 43/2008*)

Moreno-Lax V, *Accessing Asylum in Europe. Extraterritorial Border Controls and Refugee Rights under EU Law* (OUP, 2017)

——, 'The "Safe Third Country" Notion Revisited: An Appraisal in light of General International Rules on the Law of Treaties, in Goodwin-Gill GS (ed) *International Migrations, 2010 Centre for Studies and Research in International Law and International Relations of The Hague Academy of International Law* (Martinus Nijhoff, 2013)

——, '*Hirsi Jamaa and Others v Italy* or the Strasbourg Court versus Extraterritorial Migration Control?' (2012) 12(3) *Human Rights Law Review* 574

——, 'Dismantling the Dublin System: *MSS v Belgium and Greece*' (2012) 14(1) *European Journal of Migration and Law* 1

——, 'Carrier Sanctions' in Peers S, Guild E, Acosta D, Groenendijk K and Moreno-Lax V (eds) *EU Immigration and Asylum Law*, 2nd edn Vol 2. (Martinus Nijhoff Publishers, 2012)

——, 'Seeking Asylum in the Mediterranean: Against a Fragmentary Reading of EU Member States' Obligations Accruing at Sea' (2011) 23(2) *International Journal of Refugee Law* 174

——, '(Extraterritorial) Entry Controls and (Extraterritorial) Non-refoulement' in De Bruycker P, Vanheule D, Foblets MC, Wouters J and Maes M (eds), *The External Dimension(s)of EU Asylum and Immigration Policy* (Bruylant, 2011)

——, 'Must EU Borders have Doors for Refugees? On the Compatibility of Schengen Visas and Carriers' Sanctions with EU Member States' Obligations to Provide International Protection to Refugees' (2008) 10 *European Journal of Migration Law* 315

Moreno-Lax V and Garlick M, 'Qualification: Refugee Status and Subsidiary Protection', in Peers et al, *EU Immigration and Asylum Law*, Vol 3, 2nd edn (Brill, 2015)

Moreno-Lax V and Costello C, 'The extraterritorial application of the EU Charter of Fundamental Rights: from territoriality to facticity, the effectiveness model' in Peers et al. (eds), *The EU Charter of Fundamental Rights* (Hart, 2014)

Morgades-Gil S, 'The Right to Benefit from an Effective Remedy against Decisions Implying the Return of Asylum-seekers to European *Safe* Countries' (2017) 19(3) *European Journal of Migration and Law* 255

Mungianu R, *Frontex and Non-Refoulement: The International Responsibility of the EU* (CUP, 2016)

Murray D, 'Abu Qatada's victory proves how low we have been laid', *The Spectator* (13 November 2012) http://blogs.spectator.co.uk/douglas-murray/2012/11/abu-qatadas-victory-proves-how-low-we-have-been-laid/

Nahapetian K, 'Confronting State Complicity in International Law' (2002) 7 *UCLA Journal of International Law* 99

Nascimbene B, 'Il Respingimento degli Immigrati e i Rapporti tra Italia e Unione Europea' *Affari Internazionali* (16 September 2009), http://www.affarinternazionali.it/articolo.asp?ID=1244

Nesticò M, 'Immigrazione: Consegnate a Libia tre Motovedette GDF – D'Arrigo, Equipaggi Libici Addestrati da GDF' (Associazione Finanzieri Cittadini e Solidarietà, 17 May 2009), http://www.ficiesse.it/home-page/3065/immigrazione_-consegnate-a-libia-tre-motovedette-gdf---d_arrigo_-equipaggilibici-addestrati-da-gdf

Nethery A, Rafferty-Brown B, and Taylor S, 'Exporting Detention: Australia-funded Immigration Detention in Indonesia' (2013) 26(1) *Journal of Refugee Studies* 88

Nielsen N, 'Italy's "floating hotspot" idea to sink in legal waters', *EUObserver* (2 June 2016), https://euobserver.com/migration/133659

Nigro R, 'Giurisdizione e Obblighi Positivi degli Stati Parti della Convenzione Europea dei Diritti dell'Uomo: il Caso *Ilascu*' (2005) *Rivista di Diritto Internazionale* 413

Noll G, 'Article 31 1951 Convention' in Zimmermann A (ed), *The 1951 Convention Relating to the Status of Refugees and its 1967 Protocol: A Commentary* (Oxford University Press, 2011)

——, 'Diplomatic Assurances and the Silence of Human Rights Law' (2006) 7 *Melbourne Journal of International Law* 104

——, 'Law and the Logic of Outsourcing: Offshore Processing and Diplomatic Assurances' (*Refugee Protection in International Law, Contemporary Challenges* workshop, Oxford, 24 April 2006)

——, 'Visions of the Exceptional: Legal and Theoretical Issues Raised by Transit Processing Centres and Protection Zones' (2003) 5 *European Journal of Migration law* 303

——, 'Formalism v. Empiricism: Some Reflections on the Dublin Convention on the Occasion of Recent European Case Law' (2001) 70 *Nordic Journal of International Law* 161

——, *Negotiating Asylum: The EU Acquis, Extraterritorial Protection and the Common Market of Deflection* (Martinus Nijhoff, 2000)

——, 'The *Non-Admission and Return* of Protection *Seekers* in Germany' (1997) 9(3) *International Journal of Refugee Law* 415

Nollkamper, 'Introduction' in Nollkaemper and Plakokefalos (eds), *Principles of Shared Responsibility in International Law* (CUP, 2014)

Nolte G (eds), *Treaties and Subsequent Practice* (OUP, 2013)

Nolte G and Aust HP, 'Equivocal Helpers-Complicit States, Mixed Messages and International Law' (2009) 58 *International & Comparative Law Quarterly* 1
Nordquist M, *United Nations Convention on the Law of the Sea, A Commentary*, Vol III (Martinus Nijhoff, 1985)
Nowak M, *UN Covenant on Civil and Political Rights. CCPR Commentary*, 2nd edn (Kehl, NP Engel Publisher, 2005)
Nowak M and McArthur E, *The United Nation Convention Against Torture: A Commentary* (Oxford University Press Oxford, 2008)
O'Boyle (2004), 'The European Convention on Human Rights and Extraterritorial Jurisdiction: A Comment on "Life after Bankovic"' in F Coomans and M Kamminga (eds), *Extraterritorial Application of Human Rights Treaties* (Intersentia, 2004)
O'Nions H, *Asylum – A Right Denied. A Critical Analysis of European Asylum Policy* (Ashgate, 2014)
O' Sullivan M, 'Push backs' of Boats to Indonesia' (Castan Center for Human Rights Law, 18 July 2013)
Oppenheim LFL and Roxburgh RF, *International Law: A Treatise*, Volume 1, 3rd edn (The Lawbook Exchange Ltd, 2005)
Paasivirta E, 'Human Rights, Diplomacy and Sanctions: Aspects to "Human Rights Clauses" in the External Agreements of the European Union' in Petman J and Klabbers J (eds), *Nordic Cosmopolitanism: Essays in International Law for Martti Koskenniemi* (Brill Publishing, 2003)
Panizzon M, 'Readmission Agreements of EU Member States: A Case for EU Subsidiarity or Dualism?' (2012) 31(4) *Refugee Survey Quarterly* 101
Paoletti E, 'Relations among Unequals? Readmission between Italy and Libya' in Cassarino JP (ed), *Unbalanced Reciprocities: Cooperation on Readmission in the Euro-Mediterranean Area* (Institute of International Affairs, 2010)
Papanicolopulu I, *International Law and the Protection of People at Sea* (OUP, 2018)
——, 'Human Rights and the Law of the Sea' in Attard DJ, Fitzmaurice M, Martínez Gutiérrez NA (eds), *The IMLI Manual on International Maritime Law: Volume I: The Law of the Sea* (OUP, 2014)
——, 'A Response to Milanovic on Extraterritorial Application of Human Treaties: The significance of international Law Concepts of Jurisdiction' *EJIL Talk* (4 December 2011), https://www.ejiltalk.org/a-response-to-milanovic-on-extraterritorial-application-of-human-treaties-the-significance-of-international-law-concepts-of-jurisdiction/#more-4171
Papastavridis E, 'Recent *Non-Entrée* Policies in the Central Mediterranean and Their Legality: A New Form of *Refoulement*?' (2018) 12 *Diritti Umani e Diritto Internazionale* 493
——, 'The Aquarius Incident and the Law of the Sea: Is Italy in Violation of the Relevant Rules?' *EJIL Talk* (27 June 2018)
——, 'EUNAVFOR *Operation Sophia* and the International Law of the Sea' (2016) 2 *Maritime and Security Law Journal* 57
——, 'Is There a Right to Be Rescued at Sea? A Sceptical View' (June 2014) 4 *Questions of International Law* 17
——, 'European Convention on Human Rights and the Law of the Sea: The Court of Strasbourg in Unchartered Waters?' in Fitzmaurice M and Merkouris P (eds), *The interpretation and application of the European Convention of Human Rights* (Martinus Nijhoff, 2013)
——, 'Rescuing Migrants at Sea: The Responsibility of States under International Law' (Academy of Athens, 27 September 2011), http://papers.ssrn.com/sol3/papers.cfm?abstract_id=1934352
——, 'European Court of Human Rights: *Medvedyev et al v France*' (2010) 59(3) *International & Comparative Law Quarterly* 867
——, '"Fortress Europe" and FRONTEX: Within or Without International Law?' (2010) 79(1) *Nordic Journal of International Law* 75
——, 'Enforcement Jurisdiction in the Mediterranean Sea: Illicit Activities and the Rule of Law on the High Seas' (2010) 25(4) *International Journal of Marine and Coastal Law* 569
Paquet DB, 'Passing the Buck: A Critical Analysis of the Readmission Policy Implemented by the European Union and its Member States' (2003) 5(3) *European Journal of Migration and Law* 359

Parliamentary Assembly of the Council of Europe, 'Lives lost in the Mediterranean Sea: Who is responsible?', Committee on Migration, Refugees and Displaced Persons, Rapporteur Ms Tineke Strik (26 March 2012)

——, 'Resolution 1821 (2011) on the Interception and Rescue at Sea of Asylum Seekers, Refugees, and Irregular Migrants' (21 June 2011)

——, 'Report on Readmission Agreements: A Mechanism for Returning Irregular Migrants' Doc 12168 (16 March 2010)

Pastore F, 'L'Obbligo di Riammissione in Diritto Internazionale' (1998) 4 *Rivista di Diritto Internazionale* 973

Pauwelyn J, 'Informal International Lawmaking: Framing the Concept and Research Questions' in Pauwelyn J, Wessel R and Wouters J, *Informal International Lawmaking* (OUP, 2014)

Pauwelyn J, Wessel RA and Wouters J, *Informal International Lawmaking* (OUP, 2014)

——, 'Informal International Lawmaking: An Assessment and Template to Keep It Both Effective and Accountable' in Pauwelyn J, Wessel R and Wouters J, *Informal International Lawmaking* (OUP, 2014)

Paz M, 'Asylum and Terrorism: The Death of Human Rights Law' (2016–2017) 102 *Iowa Law Review Bulletin* 41

Peers S, 'Irregular Migrants: Can Humane Treatment be Balanced against Efficient Removal?' (2015) 17(4) *EJML* 289

——, 'The CJEU and the EU's Accession to the ECHR: A Clear and Present Danger to Human Rights Protection', *EU Law Analysis*, 18 December 2014

——, Harvey T, Kenner J and Ward A, *The EU Charter of Fundamental Rights: A Commentary* (Hart Publishing, 2014)

——, 'Immigration, Asylum and the EU Charter of Fundamental Rights' in Guild E and Minderhoud P (eds), *The First Decade of EU Migration and Asylum Law* (Brill, 2012) 437

——, 'UK and Irish Opt-outs from EU Justice and Home Affairs (JHA) Law', Statewatch Analysis No 4, EU Lisbon Treaty (*Statewatch*, 26 June 2009), http://www.statewatch.org/news/2009/jun/uk-ireland-analysis-no-4-lisbon-opt-outs.pdf

——, *EU Justice and Home Affairs Law*, 2nd edn (Oxford University Press, 2006)

——, 'Readmission Agreements and EC External Migration Law' Statewatch Analysis No 17 (*Statewatch*, 2003), http://www.statewatch.org/analyses/no-17-readmission.pdf

Peers S and Rogers N, *EU Immigration and Asylum Law* (Martinus Nijhoff Publishers, 2006)

Peers S, Guild E and Tomkin J (eds), *EU Immigration and Asylum Law (Text and Commentary): Volume 1: Visas and Border Controls* (Brill, 2014)

Pergantis V, 'Soft Law, Diplomatic Assurances and the Instrumentalisation of Normativity: Wither a Liberal Promise?' (2009) 56(2) *Netherlands International Law Review* 137

Perraudin F, "Home Office held Illegal interview" with asylum seeker' (20 March 2019), *The Guardian*, https://www.theguardian.com/uk-news/2019/feb/12/i-can-hardly-sleep-the-zimbabweans-facing-deportation-from-uk

Perugini N and Gordon N, *The Human Right to Dominate* (OUP, 2015)

Piddu FM, 'Le Missioni in Albania della Marina Militare' (1998) *Rivista Marittima* 49

Pijnenburg A, 'Is *ND and NT v Spain* the new *Hirsi*?' *EJIL Talk* (17 October 2017) at https://www.ejiltalk.org/is-n-d-and-n-t-v-spain-the-new-hirsi/

Pitea C, 'Diritto alla Vita', in L Pineschi (ed), *La Tutela Internazionale dei Diritti Umani: Norme, Garanzie e Prassi* (Giuffre', 2006)

Pobjoy JM, *The child in international refugee law* (Cambridge University Press, 2017)

Polchi V, 'Migranti, il rebus delle espulsioni: "Rimpatri impossibili senza accordi". Nella UE ogni stato ha le sue regole', *La Repubblica* (29 January 2016)

Prechal A, 'The Court of Justice and Effective Judicial Protection: What Has the Charter Changed?' in Paulussen C, Takacs T, Lazic V and van Rompuy B (eds), *Fundamental Rights in International and European Law* (Springer, 2015)

Rai News, 'Migranti, la nave Sea Watch entrata in acque italiane per il maltempo', http://www.rainews24.rai.it/it/canale-tv.php?id=13231

Raible L, 'Title to Territory and Jurisdiction in International Human Rights Law: Three Models for a Fraught Relationship' (2018) 31(2) *Leiden Journal of International Law* 315

Reneman M, *EU Asylum Procedures and the Right to an Effective Remedy* (Hart Publishing, 2014)

——, 'Access to an Effective Remedy before a Court or Tribunal in Asylum Cases' in Guild E and Minderhoud P (eds), *The First Decade of EU Migration and Asylum Law* (Martinus Nijhoff, 2011) 401

Repubblica, 'I libici mitragliano un pescherreccio. Finanzieri italiani sulla nave di Tripoli' (13 September 2010), http://www.repubblica.it/cronaca/2010/09/13/news/i_libici_mitragliano_un_peschereccio_finanzieri_italiani_sulla_nave_di_tripoli-7043116/

Ress R, 'Problems of Extraterritorial Human Rights Violations. The Jurisdiction of the European Court of Human Rights' (2002) 12 *Italian Yearbook of International Law* 51

REUTERS, 'Austria, Italy propose holding migrants on ships for days' (14 September), https://www.reuters.com/article/us-europe-migrants-austria-italy/austria-italy-propose-holding-migrants-on-ships-for-days-idUSKCN1LU2C7

Riedel E and Will M, 'Human Right Clauses in External Agreements' in Alston P (ed), *The EU and Human Rights* (Oxford University Press, 1999)

Rijpma, J, 'Hybrid Agencification in the Area of Freedom, Security and Justice and its Inherent Tensions: The Case of Frontex' in Busuioc M, Groenleer M and Trondal J (eds), *The Agency Phenomenon in the European Union: Emergence, Institutionalisation and Everyday Decision-making* (Manchester University Press, 2012)

——, *Frontex: Successful Blame Shifting of the Member States?* (2010) *Elcano Newsletter*

Robinson N, *Convention relating to the Status of Refugees: Its History, Contents and Interpretation. A Commentary* (Institute of Jewish Affairs, 1953)

Roßkopf R, 'Dublin III Beyond *M.S.S. and N.S*: Amending the Recast Proposal for the Dublin II Regulation No 343/2003' (2012) 50(2) *AWR Bulletin* 60

Roman E, *Cooperation on Readmission in the Mediterranean Area and its Human Rights Implications*, PhD Thesis (2017)

Roman E, 'L'accordo di cooperazione in ambito migratorio tra Unione Europea (UE) e Turchia' *SIDIBlog*, 21 March 2016, http://www.sidiblog.org/2016/03/21/laccordo-ue-turchia-le-criticita-di-un-accordo-a-tutti-i-costi/

Ronzitti N, 'The Treaty on Friendship, Partnership, and Cooperation between Italy and Libya: New Prospects for Cooperation in the Mediterranean' (Institute of International Affairs, 2009), http://www.iai.it/pdf/DocIAI/iai0909.pdf

Rooney JM, 'The Relationship between Jurisdiction and Attribution after *Jaloud v the Netherlands*' (2015) 62(3) *Netherlands International Law Review* 407

Roxstrom E, Gibney M and Einarsen T, 'The Nato Bombing Case (*Bankovic et al v Belgium et al*), and the Limits of Erstern Human Rights protection' (2005) 23 *Boston University International Law Journal* 56

Ryngaert C, *Jurisdiction in International Law* (OUP, 2015)

Saccucci A, 'Divieto di tortura ed esigenze di sicurezza nel contesto della *war on terror*: verso una flessione "al ribasso" degli obblighi internazionali?' (2009) 1 *Diritti Umani e Diritto Internazionale* 5

Sadat-Akhavi SA, *Methods of Resolving Conflicts between Treaties* (Martinus Nijhoff, 2003)

Salinas de Frías AM, 'States' Obligations under International Refugee Law and Counte-Terrorism Responses' in Salinas de Frías AM, Samuel K and White N (eds), *Counter-Terrorism: International Law and Practice* (Oxford University Press, 2012)

Saurugger S and Terpan F, 'Studying Resistance to EU Norms in Foreign and Security Policy', (2015) 20(2) *European Foreign Affairs Review* 1

Schabas W, *Non-refoulement, Human Rights and International Cooperation in Counter-terrorism* (Liechtenstein, 2006)

Schachter O, 'The Twilight Existence of Non-Binding International Agreements' (1997) 71(2) *American Journal of International Law* 296

Scheinin M, 'Impact on the Law of Treaties' in Kamminga MT and Scheinin M (eds), *The Impact of Human Rights Law on General International Law* (Oxford University Press, 2009)

Schieffer M, 'The Readmission of Third Country Nationals within Bilateral and Multilateral Frameworks' in Den Boer M (ed), *The Implementation of Schengen, First the Widening, Now the Deepening* (European Institute of Public Administration, 1997)

Schmid A, *Links between Terrorism and Migration: An Exploration* (The International Centre for Counter-Terrorism, 2016), http://dx.doi.org/10.19165/2016.1.04

Schmid E, 'The End of the Road on Diplomatic Assurances: The Removal of Suspected Terrorists under International Law' (2011) 8(1) *Essex Human Rights Review* 297

Schneider J, 'Comment to Hirsi (part II): Another Side to the Judgment' (Strasbourg Observers, 5 March 2012), http://strasbourgobservers.com/2012/03/02/hirsi-part-ii-another-side-to-the-judgment/

Schultz J, 'The Internal Protection Alternative in Refugee Law: Treaty Basis and Scope of Application under the 1951 Convention Relating to the Status of Refugees and Its 1967 Protocol' (Brill, 2018)

——, 'The European Court of Human Rights and Internal Relocation: An Unduly Harsh Standard?' in Gauci JP, Giuffré M and Tsourdi L, *Forced Migration(s): Critical Perspectives on Refugee Law* (Martinus Nijhoff Publishers, 2014)

Scovazzi T, 'Tortura e formalismi giuridici di basso profilo' (2006) *Rivista di Diritto Internazionale* 905

Sharpe M, *The Regional Law of Refugee Protection in Africa* (OUP, 2018)

Shaw M, *International Law* (Cambridge University Press 2008)

Sheinin M, 'Extraterritorial effect of the ICCPR' in Coomans F and Kamminga MT (eds), *Extraterritorial application for Human Rights Treaties* (Intersentia, 2004) 73

Shelton D, 'Positive and Negative Obligations' in Shelton D, Goult A (eds), *The Oxford Handbook of International Human Rights Law* (Oxford University Press, 2013) 562

Shenker J, 'Aircraft carrier left us to die, say migrants', *The Guardian* (8 May 2011) http://www.guardian.co.uk/world/2011/may/08/nato-ship-libyan-migrants

Simma B and Alston P, 'The Sources of Human Rights Law: Customs, Jus Cogens, and General Principles' (1992) 12 *Australian Yearbook of International Law* 102

Simpson JH, *The Refugee Problem* (OUP, 1939)

Singer S, '"Undesirable and Unreturnable" in the United Kingdom' (2017) 36(1) *Refugee Survey Quarterly* 9

——, 'Terrorism and Article 1F(c) of the Refugee Convention: Exclusion from Refugee Status in the United Kingdom' (2014) 12 *Journal of International Criminal Justice* 1075

Skoglund L, 'Diplomatic Assurances against Torture – An Effective Strategy? A Review of Jurisprudence and Examination of the Arguments' (2008) 77(4) *Nordic Journal of International Law* 319

Skordas A, 'A "blind spot" in the migration debate? International responsibility of the EU and its Member States for cooperating with the Libyan coastguard and militias', *EUMigrationLAwBlog.eu* (2018), http://eumigrationlawblog.eu/a-blind-spot-in-the-migration-debate-international-responsibility-of-the-eu-and-its-member-states-for-cooperating-with-the-libyan-coastguard-and-militias/

——, 'Human Rights and Effective Migration Policies: An Uneasy Co-existence. The *Conka* Judgment of the European Court of Human Rights' in Urbano de Sousa CD and de Bruycker P, *The Emergence of a European Asylum Policy* (Bruylant, 2004)

Sky News, 'Abu Qatada Stays as Theresa May Loses Appeal', http://news.sky.com/story/1070407/abu-qatada-stays-as-theresa-may-loses-appeal

Sorel JM, 'Some Questions About the Definition of Terrorism and the Fight Against Its Financing' (2003) 14(2) *European Journal of International Law* 365

Spagnolo A, 'Di intese segrete e alibi parlamentari: tra la decisione del TAR sull'Accordo col Niger e il Global Compact sulle migrazioni', *SIDIBlog*, 5 December 2018, http://www.sidiblog.org/2018/12/05/di-intese-segrete-e-alibi-parlamentari-tra-la-decisione-del-tar-sullaccordo-col-niger-e-il-global-compact-sulle-migrazioni/

Spanish Commission of Aid to Refugees (CEAR), 'CEAR muestra su preocupación tras la expulsión "acelerada" de las 116 personas migrantes que llegaron ayer a Ceuta', 23 August 2018, https://bit.ly/2o2SgQf

Spijkerboer T, 'Stretching the Limits. European Maritime Border Control Policies and International Law' in Foblets MC et al (eds), *The External Dimension of the Immigration & Asylum Policy of the EU* (Bruylant, 2011)

——, 'Subsidiarity and "Arguability": the European Court of Human Rights' Case Law on Judicial Review in Asylum Cases' (2009) 21(1) *International Journal of Refugee Law* 1

——, 'The Human Costs of Border Control' (2007) 9 *European Journal of Migration Law* 137

——, 'Higher Judicial Remedies' in Geoffrey Care and Hugo Storey (eds), *Asylum Law: First International Judicial Conference on Asylum Law* (International Association of Refugee Law Judges, 1995) 217

Staker C, 'Jurisdiction' in Evans M (ed), *International Law* (Oxford University Press, 2018)

Statewatch, 'Deadly incident on the Mediterranean Sea: Rescue organisation accuses Libyan coast guard', 28 December 2016, http://www.statewatch.org/news/2016/dec/med-libya-rescues.htm

Stoyanova V, 'Causation between State Omission and Harm within the Framework of Positive Obligations under the European Convention on Human Rights' (2018) 18(2) *Human Rights Law Review* 309

——, 'How Exceptional Must "Very Exceptional" Be? Non-Refoulement, Socio-Economic Deprivation, and *Paposhvili v Belgium*' (2017) 29(4) *International Journal of Refugee Law* 580

Straub T, 'The Criminal Refugee: The Treatment of Asylum Seekers with a Criminal Background in International and Domestic Law' (2012) 24(4) *International Journal of Refugee Law* 892

Stevens D, 'What do We Mean by Protection?' (2013) 20(1) *International Journal on Minority and Group Rights* 233

Suntinger W, 'The Principle of *Non-Refoulement*: Looking rather to Geneva than to Strasbourg?' (1995) 49 *Austrian Journal of Public and International Law* 203

Tan NF, 'State responsibility and migration control: Australia's international deterrence model' in Gammeltoft-Hansen T and Vedsted-Hansen J (eds), *Human rights and the dark side of globalisation: Transnational law enforcement and migration control* (Routledge, 2017)

Tancredi A, 'Assicurazioni diplomatiche e divieto "assoluto" di *refoulement* alla luce di alcune recenti pronunzie della Corte europea dei diritti umani' (2010) 4 *Diritti Umani e Diritto Internazionale* 41

Tazzioli M, 'Cronologia degli Accordi Italia-Tunisia' (*Storie Migranti*, December 2011), http://www.storiemigranti.org/spip.php?article1004

Terrasi A, 'I Respingimenti in Mare di Migranti alla Luce della Convenzione Europea dei Diritti Umani' (2009) 3 *Diritti Umani e Diritto Internazionale* 591

The Guardian, 'Abu Qatada: Theresa May loses latest attempt to deport Islamist cleric' (27 March 2013) http://www.guardian.co.uk/world/2013/mar/27/abu-qatada-theresa-may-loses

The Sun, 'Home Secretary slams Qatada decision as "unacceptable"' (7 February 2012) http://www.thesun.co.uk/sol/homepage/news/4114354/Home-Secretary-slams-Qatada-decision-as-unacceptable.html

Thirlway H, 'The Law and Procedure of the International Court of Justice' (1990) 61 *British Yearbook of International Law* 1

Tomasi di Lampedusa G, *The Leopard* (1958)

Tondini M, 'Fishers of Men? The Interception of Migrants in the Mediterranean Sea and their Forced Return to Libya', Inex Paper (2010)

Toner H, Guild E and Baldaccini A (eds) *Whose Freedom, Security And Justice? EU Immigration and Asylum Law and Policy* (Hart, 2007)

Trauner F and Kruse I, 'EC Visa Facilitation and Readmission Agreements: Implementing a New EU Security Approach in the Neighbourhood' *CEPS Working Document* (23 April 2008) http://www.ceps.eu/book/ec-visa-facilitation-and-readmission-agreements-implementing-new-eu-security-approach-neighbour

Travis A, 'Abu Qatada "will voluntarily go back to Jordan when new treaty is ratified"', *The Guardian* (10 May 2013), http://www.guardian.co.uk/world/2013/may/10/abu-qatada-jordan-treaty-ratified

Trechsel S, *Human Rights in Criminal Proceedings* (Oxford University Press, 2005)

Trevisanut S, 'The Principle of *Non-Refoulement* And the De-Territorialization of Border Control at Sea' (2014) 27(3) *Leiden Journal of International Law* 661

——, 'Is There a Right to be Rescued at Sea? A Constructive View' (2014) *Questions of International Law* 3

——, *Immigrazione irregolare via mare diritto internazionale e diritto dell'Unione europea* (Jovene, 2012)

——, '*Non refoulement* at Sea' (*Governing Migration by Sea: A Legal Perspective* Workshop, Oxford, 17–18 November 2011)

——, 'Search and Rescue Operations in the Mediterranean: Factor of Cooperation or Conflict?' (2010) 25 *International Journal of Marine and Coastal Law* 523

——, 'Immigrazione Clandestina Via Mare e Cooperazione fra Italia e Libia dal Punto di Vista del Diritto del Mare' (2009) 3 *Diritti Umani e Diritto Internazionale* 609

——, 'The Principle of *Non-Refoulement* at Sea' (2008) 12 *Max Planck Yearbook of United Nations* 218

Triandafyllidou A, *Irregular Migration in Europe: Myths and realities* (Routledge, 2016)

Tsourdi E, 'What Role for the Court of Justice of the EU in the Development of a European Asylum Policy? The Case of Loss and Denial of International Protection in the EU' (2012) 2(3) *Tijdschrift voor Bestuurswetenschappen en Publiekrecht* 212

Turco Bulgherini E, 'Acque Territoriali e Sicurezza Marittima' (2010) 3 *Online Gnosis Rivista Italiana di Intelligence*, http://gnosis.aisi.gov.it/Gnosis/Rivista24.nsf/servnavig/57

Türk V and Garlick M, 'From Burdens and Responsibilities to Opportunities: The Comprehensive Refugee Response Framework and a Global Compact on Refugees' (2016) 28(4) *International Journal of Refugee Law* 656

Türk V and Nicholson F, 'Refugee Protection in International Law: An Overall Perspective' in Feller E, Nicholson F, and Türk V (eds), *UNHCR Refugee Protection in International Law* (Cambridge University Press, 2003)

Tzevelekos VP, 'Reconstructing the Effective Control Criterion in Extraterritorial Human Rights Breaches: Direct Attribution of Wrongfulness, Due Diligence, and Concurrent Responsibility' (2014) 36 *Michigan Journal of International Law* 129

Tzevelekos VP and Proukaki EK, 'Migrants at Sea: A Duty of Plural States to Protect (Extraterritorially)?' (2017) 86(4) *Nordic Journal of International Law* 427

UN Committee Against Torture and Holmstrom L (ed), *Conclusions and Recommendations of the UN Committee Against Torture: Eleventh to Twenty-second Sessions (1993–1999)* (Martinus Nijhoff, 2000)

UNHCR, 'Desperate Journeys: Refugees and migrants arriving in Europe and Europe's borders (January–August 2018)' (December 2018), https://data2.unhcr.org/en/documents/download/65373#_ga=2.138122995.253764426.1550604132-1861362090.1547930043

——, 'Global Trends 2017' (2018), www.unhcr.org/statistics/unhcrstats/5b27be547/unhcr-global-trends-2017.html

——, 'Global Compact on Refugees' (2018), https://www.unhcr.org/towards-a-global-compact-on-refugees.html

—— ExCom, Conclusion, 'Determination of Refugee Status' (1977), http://www.refworld.org/docid/3ae68c6e4.html

—— ExCom, Conclusion, 'Protection of Asylum seekers in Situations of Large-Scale Influx' (1981), http://www.unhcr.org/3ae68c6e10.html

——, 'Problems Related to the Rescue of Asylum Seekers in Distress at Sea' (26 August 1981)

——, 'Handbook on Procedures and Criteria for Determining Refugee Status under the 1951 Convention and the 1967 Protocol relating to the Status of Refugees' (1992), http://www1.umn.edu/humanrts/instree/refugeehandbook.pdf

——, '*Gene McNary, Commissioner, Immigration and Naturalization Service, et al. (Petitioners) v. Haitian Centers Council, Inc., et al.* (Respondents). Brief Amicus Curiae of the Office of the High Commissioner for Refugees in Support of Respondents' (October 1992), http://www.refworld.org/docid/3f336bbc4.html

—— (ed), *Commentary on the Refugee Convention* (UNHCR 1963, republished 1997)

—— ExCom, 'Interception of Asylum Seekers and Refugees: The International Framework and Recommendations for a Comprehensive Approach' (9 June 2000)

——, 'Global Consultations in Budapest Conclusions' (4 September 2001) http://www.unhcr.org/3b83b7314.html

——, 'Factum of the Intervenor, UNHCR, *Suresh v the Minister of Citizenship and Immigration; the Attorney General of Canada*, SCC No 27790)' (2002) 19(1) *International Journal of Refugee Law*

——, 'Background Note on the Application of the Exclusion Clauses: Article IF of the 1951 Convention Relating to the Status of Refugees' (4 September 2003), http://www.refworld.org/docid/3f5857d24.html

—— ExCom, 'Conclusion on Protection Safeguards in Interception Measures' (10 October 2003), http://www.unhcr.org/496323740.html

——, 'Guidelines on International Protection: Application of the Exclusion Clauses: Article 1F of the 1951 Convention relating to the Status of Refugees' (2003)

——, 'Note on Procedural Standards for Refugee Status Determination under the UNHCR's Mandate' (20 November 2003), www.refworld.org/pdfid/42d66dd84.pdf

—— Submission, 'Inquiry into Asylum and Protection Visas for Consular Officials and the Deportation, Search and Discovery of Vivian Solon' (2005)

——, 'Note on Diplomatic Assurances and International Refugee Protection' (Geneva, August 2006), www.refworld.org/pdfid/44dc81164.pdf

——, 'Advisory Opinion on the Extraterritorial Application of Non-Refoulement Obligations under the 1951 Convention relating to the Status of Refugees and its 1967 Protocol' (26 January 2007), http://www.refworld.org/docid/45f17a1a4.html

—— Position on the Situation of Asylum in Ukraine in the Context of Return of Asylum seekers (October 2007), http://www.unhcr.org/refworld/docid/472f43162.html

——, 'Guidance Note on Extradition and International Refugee Protection' (April 2008), www.refworld.org/docid/481ec7d92.html

——, 'Follow-up from UNHCR on Italy's Push-backs' (Briefing Notes, 12 May 2009) http://www.unhcr.org/4a0966936.html

——, 'Submission in the Case of Hirsi' (March 2010), http://www.unhcr.org/refworld/pdfid/4b97778d2.pdf

——, 'Refugee Protection and Mixed Migration' (2011), http://www.unhcr.org/pages/4a16aac66.html

——, Letter for a case before ECtHR: *Ghafori v Hungary* App no 40773/11 (30 August 2011)

——, A Year of Crises: Global Trends 2011 (2012), http://www.unhcr.org/4fd6f87f9.html

——, 'Asylum and Trends in 2012: Levels and Trends in Industrialized Countries' (21 March 2013) http://www.unhcr.org/5149b81e9.html

——, 'Global Trends 2017', www.unhcr.org/statistics/unhcrstats/5b27be547/unhcr-global-trends-2017.html

UNHCR, IOM and Save the Children Italy Press Release, 'Le Organizzazioni Umanitarie chiedono di incontare i migranti egiziani e tunisini che sbarcano sulle coste italiane' (30 April 2013)

Van Dijk P, Van Hoof F, Van Rijn A, Zwaak L, *Theory and Practice of the European Convention on Human Rights* (Intersentia, 2006)

Vassallo Paleologo F, 'Accordi di riammissione e diritto di polizia' (*Il lavoro culturale*, 3 February 2012), http://www.lavoroculturale.org/asylum-1-accordi-di-riammissione-e-diritto-di-polizia/

——, 'Eritrei – Respinti dall'Italia, Espulsi dalla Libia, Sequestrati in Egitto' (*Meltingpot*, 6 December 2010), http://www.meltingpot.org/articolo16080.html

Vedsted-Hansen J, 'The asylum procedures and the assessment of asylum requests' in Chetail and Bauloz (eds) *Research Handbook on International Law and Migration* (Edward Elgar Publishing, 2016) 439

——, 'Asylum Procedures Directive 2013/32/EU' in Hailbronner K and Thym D (eds), *EU Immigration and Asylum Law* 1285

——, 'The European Convention on Human Rights, Counter-Terrorism, and Refugee Protection' (2010) 29(4) *Refugee Survey Quarterly* 45

——, 'Non-admission Policies and the Right to Protection: Refugees' Choice versus State's Exclusion' in Nicholson F and Twomey PM (eds), *Refugee Rights and Realities – Evolving International Concepts and Regimes* (Cambridge University Press, 1999)

——, 'Europe's Response to the Arrival of Asylum Seekers: Refugee Protection and Immigration Control' (*UNHCR Working Paper no 6*, 1999)

Venturi D, 'The Grand Chamber's ruling in *Khlaifia and Others v Italy*: one step forward, one step back?' in *Strasbourg Observers* (10 January 2017), https://strasbourgobservers.com/2017/01/10/the-grand-chambers-ruling-in-khlaifia-and-others-v-italy-one-step-forward-one-step-back/

Venzke I, *How Interpretation Makes International Law: on Semantic Changes and Normative Twists* (Oxford University Press, 2012)

Verdirame G, 'Human Rights in Wartime: A Framework for Analysis' (2008) 6 *European Human Rights Law Review* 689

Verdussen M (ed), *L'Europe de la subsidiarité* (Bruylant, 2000)

Vicini G, 'The Dublin Regulation between Strasbourg and Luxembourg: reshaping non-refoulement in the name of mutual trust?' (2015) 8(2) *European Journal of Legal Studies* 50

Vierdag EW, 'The Country of First Asylum: Some European Aspects' in Martin D (ed), *The New Asylum Seekers: Refugee Law in the 1980s* (Martinus Nijhoff, 1988)

Villiger ME, *Commentary on the 1969 Vienna Convention on the Law of Treaties* (Martinus Nijhoff, 2009)

Viviano F, 'Noi Finanzieri Ostaggi di Tripoli Su Quelle Navi Non Vogliamo Salire' *Repubblica* (15 September 2010), http://www.repubblica.it/cronaca/2010/09/15/news/finanziere_mazara-7088107/

Vollmer B, 'Country Report UK: Undocumented Migration Counting the Uncountable. Data and Trends across Europe' (*Clandestino Project*, July 2009), http://clandestino.eliamep.gr/wp-content/uploads/2009/11/clandestino_report_united-kingdom_final_2.pdf

Waidlich S, 'First Instance Asylum Proceedings in Europe: Do Bona Fide Refugees Find Protection?' (2000) 14 *Georgetown Immigration Law Journal* 643

Walker C, 'Deportation with Assurances: UK Experience and Angst', *Lawfare* (November 2013), https://www.lawfareblog.com/clive-walker-deportation-assurances-uk-experience-and-angst

Walker D, 'International and Comparative Law and Practice' in D Anderson and C Walker, *Deportation with Assurances* (July 2017)

Weinzierl R and Lisson U, *Border Management and Human Rights* (German Institute for Human Rights 2007)

Weis P, *The Refugee Convention, 1951: The Travaux Préparatoires Analysed with a Commentary by the Late Dr Paul Weis* (Cambridge University Press, 1995)

——, *Nationality and Statelessness in International Law* (Brill, 1979)

——, 'The present state of International Law on Territorial Asylum' (1974) 31 *Schweizerisiches Jahrbuch fur Internationales Recht*

Wessel R, Draft paper, '"Soft" International Agreements in EU External Relations', presented at the ECPR SGEU Conference, *Hard and Soft Law in the European Union* (Paris 13–15 June 2018)

Widdows K, 'What is an Agreement in International Law?' (1979) 50(1) *British Yearbook of International Law* 117

Wilde R, 'Triggering State Obligations Extraterritorially: The Spatial test in Certain Human Rights Treaties' (2008) 40 *Israel Law Review* 142

Worster T, 'Between a Treaty and Not: A Case Study of the Legal Value of Diplomatic Assurances in Expulsion Cases' (2012) 21(2) *Minnesota Journal of International Law* 253

Wouters K, *International Legal Standards for the Protection from Refoulement: a Legal Analysis of the Prohibitions on Refoulement Contained in the Refugee Convention, the European Convention on Human Rights, the International Covenant on Civil and Political Rights and the Convention against Torture* (Intersentia, 2009)

Wouters K and Den Heijer M, 'The Marine I Case: A Comment' (2010) 22(1) *International Journal of Refugee Law* 1

Zimmermann A and Mahler C, 'Article 1A, para 2' in Zimmermann A (ed), *The 1951 Convention Relating to the Status of Refugees and its 1967 Protocol: A Commentary* (Oxford University Press, 2011)

Zuleeg M, 'Vertragskonkurrenz im Völkerrecht. Teil I: Verträge zwischen souveränen Staaten' (1977) 20 *German Yearbook of International Law* 246

Zwaan K (ed), *The Procedures Directive. Central Themes, Problem Issues, and Implementation in Selected Member States* (Wolf Legal Publishers, 2008)

Index